The Open University

A206
The Enlightenment

Studies, I

Edited by Michael Bartholomew, Denise Hall and Antony Lentin

First published in 1992 by

The Open University

Walton Hall

Milton Keynes

United Kingdom

MK7 6AA

ISBN 0 7492 1110 5

Edited, designed and typeset by The Open University.

This book forms part of an Open University course A206 *The Enlightenment*.

Printed and bound in Great Britain by William Clowes Limited, Beccles and London.

Contents

General Introduction

by Michael Bartholomew and Antony Lentin

1 The Enlightenment

> We saw that the *Encyclopédie* could be undertaken only in a philosophical century; that this century is here. (Diderot, article *Encyclopedia*, 1755, in *Encyclopédie* (*Texts*, I, p.9)

> ... our century received the complimentary title of the 'century of philosophy' from all sides, and ... we have already pre-selected its epitaph: Enlightenment! (Catherine the Great, 1786, quoted in Black, 1990, p.261)

> If it is now asked whether we at present live in an *enlightened* age, the answer is: No, but we do live in an age of *enlightenment*. (Kant, 'What is Enlightenment?', 1784, in *Texts*, II, p.308)

> The *divine right* of husbands, like the divine right of kings, may, it is to be hoped, in this enlightened age, be contested without danger. (Mary Wollstonecraft, *A Vindication of the Rights of Woman*, 1792, in Wollstonecraft, 1982, p.xvii)

This course presents some two dozen eighteenth-century texts – using that term to include music, paintings and buildings, as well as printed pages. The texts, which were produced during the second half of the eighteenth century, include an opera, an oratorio, a novel, a play, a so-called 'philosophical tale', poems, political documents, historical writing, and extracts from works on art, architecture, aesthetics, travel, medicine, penal reform, education and women's rights. They were chosen, first, because the Course Team felt them to be attractive, interesting and worthwhile in their own right – each text has its own intrinsic pleasures and challenges – but also because, taken together, they should give you a vivid sense of the European movement known as the Enlightenment.

'The Enlightenment' is the name given to a movement which 'lit up' intellectual, political, scientific and artistic life in eighteenth-century Europe. In every language, the word used to describe the movement has the connotation of light. In French, the eighteenth century is often known as *le siècle des lumières* – the century of lights. In German, the term for 'Enlightenment' is *Aufklärung*, derived from descriptions of weather, and carrying the sense of cloudy skies clearing up to reveal the sun. In Russian *prosveshchenie* and in Italian *illuminismo* likewise derive from the same metaphor. With one exception, the terms were coined during the eighteenth century itself, indicating that a new movement, which needed to be named, was recognized at the time. The movement was not invented by later historians. (The exception is the English term 'Enlightenment', which came into use only in the early nineteenth century.) Every manifestation of the movement is marked by the symbol of light: it appears, time and again, in philosophy, architecture, medicine, music, penal reform – in every area of intellectual life. Enlightenment thinkers aimed to bring light, clarity, order and reason to regions where formerly, in their view, there had been mystery, superstition, blind authority and darkness.

The European character of the movement is important and we have sought to represent it with texts from France, Germany, Russia, Austria, Italy, Scotland and England. (One text was written in England, in English, by an author, Equiano, who originated in West Africa.) However, while all of the texts were produced in a particular national context, their authors were none the less conscious of living in the same European cultural environment.[1] As the opening quotations from Diderot, Catherine the Great, Kant and Wollstonecraft suggest, European intellectuals believed themselves to be living in a distinct century, with its own precise and peculiar intellectual characteristics: 'the century of philosophy' and 'Enlightenment' or (as it is often called by historians, the 'Age of Reason'). And by calling themselves and each other 'philosophers' (or more usually the French word *philosophes*) they meant, not philosophers in the twentieth-century academic sense, but rather men and women intellectually and morally committed to a particular set of common assumptions and aspirations which they sought to see prevail in their own time. In the great French *Encyclopédie*, a monumental collective work absolutely central to the movement, Diderot stressed that the purpose of its contributors was nothing less than to bring about a 'revolution which will take place in the minds of men' (*Texts*, I, p.7).

We can draw out of the Enlightenment a common array of attitudes, and these will be set out presently; but it is important to point out, almost before we start, that our texts do not arrange themselves into a neat pattern, with each text plainly exhibiting a standardized range of Enlightenment characteristics. Any such neatness is sabotaged by individual quirks and idiosyncrasies, and in some cases perhaps by quite fundamental divergences. You may conclude that, in some cases, the divergences are so fundamental that the texts do not belong in the Enlightenment mainstream at all. Take the following list of characteristics, then, as a preliminary rough guide, not as a definitive catalogue.

2   The critique of despotism and arbitrary power

As the quotation from Mary Wollstonecraft suggests, Enlightenment thinkers rejected any notion that monarchs ruled by Divine Right. The *philosophes* criticized, often at serious personal cost, the cruel exercise of state or military power. But, however advanced they were in their political thinking, it is important to grasp that none of them favoured the introduction of political systems that we would recognize as democratic. While opposed to harsh and arbitrary despotisms, they did not envisage the participation in politics of most of the population. A map of assumptions and alignments drawn from nineteenth- or twentieth-century politics will be of little use in guiding you through the perhaps less familiar territory of eighteenth-century social and political attitudes.

It will emerge from the texts that most of the writers and creative artists had in mind an educated audience of like-minded people. They

---

[1]   In a powerful sense, this environment extended to North America, where Enlightenment ideas circulated among the intelligentsia, just as they did in Europe. However, to cover the American dimension of the movement is beyond the scope of this course.

wrote for, and were read by, members of the nobility and the professional classes, lawyers, physicians, clergymen. They did not have, nor did they intend to have, a mass readership. At best, the fruits of Enlightenment were intended to be of practical benefit to the people at large, but only eventually and indirectly, and only after they had been savoured and appreciated by the educated classes. They were not to be seized by the illiterate masses, who were often regarded with suspicion and even contempt. In Gibbon's uncompromising view, they were 'incapable of knowledge or reflection' (*Texts*, I, p.249). 'Instinctively', Catherine declared at the time of the French Revolution, 'I feel the greatest contempt for popular movements of all kinds' (Lentin, 1973, p.80). The *philosophes* wished to share and to spread their ideas – that was the whole purpose of the *Encyclopédie* – but across, and not too far down, the social scale. Even Dr Johnson, that most compassionate of men and principled opponent of slavery, shared a fundamental assumption of the age that 'in every society one class of men will be more ignorant than another and the poor commonly more ignorant than the rich' (Johnson set text, p.573). He did not for one moment believe that this basic social and cultural abyss could or should be bridged, save by a few rare and fortunate individuals.

Conversely, part of the attraction of Enlightenment culture was undoubtedly that a familiarity with the writings of the *philosophes*, attendance at concerts and galleries, membership of academies and clubs, gave social *cachet* to non-nobles aspiring to gentility. We know, for example, that most of the readers of the *Encyclopédie* in France came from this class. Likewise in Prussia and Russia, the path to professional advancement in the army, civil service or in society generally, led through the enlightenment-oriented schools patronized by Frederick and Catherine. 'Sociologically speaking', as has been well said, 'the Enlightenment was an elite addressing elites' (Dunthorne, 1991, p.18); and it has indeed been argued that one result of this was to widen the gap between elite culture and popular culture.

In continental Europe, the British constitution, with its checks and balances supposedly harmonizing the powers of monarch, lords, commons and judiciary, was much admired. It was not, and was not thought to be, democratic. What observers and admirers like Voltaire perceived in Britain, was a combination of settled and accountable government, domestic peace and growing prosperity, with an independent system of justice and redress against oppression, the rule of law in society, a marked level of religious toleration and of intellectual and political freedom. But there was no single form of government which was held out as the 'enlightened' blue-print. The *philosophes* regarded justice, tolerance and freedom to discuss and publish whatever one wished as the hallmarks of an 'enlightened' society; and the rulers of the absolutist states of Prussia, Russia and Austria strove or professed to rule by them. There was a school of thought, indeed, also supported by Voltaire, which held that progress could be more effectively brought about in states governed by 'enlightened' absolute rulers through direct intervention and control of the economy and social welfare and the patronage of education and culture, than in states where large numbers of citizens had a voice in deciding policy.

3   Enlightenment knowledge

For Enlightenment thinkers, the key to knowledge was 'Reason': the uninhibited pursuit of clear, logical, independent thought. 'Have courage to use your own understanding' was 'the motto of enlightenment' according to the Prussian philosopher Kant, who defined enlightenment as 'man's emergence from his self-incurred immaturity' (*Texts* II, p.305), that is, from his unquestioning submission to received wisdom. Scientific knowledge was held in supreme veneration. It overrode any claim to knowledge based on authority – divine or secular – or intuition, or mystic insight. If something was held to be true, it had to be scientifically true: that is to say, it had to be the outcome of dispassionate rational investigation. Any proposition, any statement, was either true or not true. If it was not true, it was a lie, a mistake or a fable, and had to be exposed as such. If it was unknowable by existing methods of empirical enquiry, then that too needed to be pointed out. The materials from which knowledge was constructed were sense data, which were to be systematically ordered by reason. This view of knowledge as something achievable only by the application of scientific method may appear less abstract if it is contrasted with other potential forms of knowledge.

Christians, for instance, traditionally claimed that certain precious and indispensable truths cannot be verified empirically: they are attainable only by God's having directly revealed them in scripture, whose absolute authority should be protected and, if necessary, enforced, by the church. With a few very notable exceptions, Enlightenment thinkers would have none of this. On principle they were sceptical of the Christian (or any other religious claim) to revelation, though they sometimes agreed that conventional religion had its uses in reconciling the masses to their lot and making them obedient. 'Philosophy for the magistrates', wrote Voltaire – in English –, 'damned stuff for the people' (i.e. 'rational thought for the rulers, the rubbish of conventional religion for the masses'). Other enlightenment thinkers, however, regarded such a cynical view as a sin against the light: the term 'truth', as revealed by reason, should be proclaimed, not dissembled –'The truth', declares the heroine of Mozart's opera *The Magic Flute*, 'even if it were a crime' *Texts*, II, p.761).

Another potential form of knowledge with which Enlightenment thinkers had little patience is that based on personal, mystical or artistic insight. Living, as we do, in a world that still lies in the shadow of the Romantics, we may be well-disposed to the Romantic claim that Artists are possessed of some sort of special insight or unique genius, which drives them to express truths that are otherwise unattainable. In the words of Shelley, writing in 1821: 'Poetry is indeed something divine. It is at once the centre and circumference of knowledge; it is that which comprehends all science, and that to which all science must be referred' (Clark, 1954, p.293). Shelley was reacting here against the Enlightenment, which would have claimed almost the exact opposite: it would have argued that poetry and art generally should be referred to objectively valid rules or 'laws', analogous to the laws of science. Sir Joshua Reynolds, painter and President of the Royal Academy, argued that artistry, far from being a mysterious, innate quality, was rather a trained ability to follow demonstrable rules of 'taste', in order to produce beautiful things.

How did scientific method achieve this high status during the eighteenth century? First, it was building on the triumphs of the 'Scientific Revolution' begun by Copernicus in the mid-sixteenth century, carried through in the next century by Galileo, Harvey, Descartes, and culminating in the work of Isaac Newton, who died in 1727. Taken as a whole, this work, which was institutionalized in the scientific academies which flourished in many European states, exhibited the universe as a perfectly intelligible system, whose structure and operations could be discerned by the scientific enquirer. Much had already been understood, and that which hadn't, it was widely believed, would yield to the steady advance of the scientist. The name of Newton is seldom far away in enlightenment texts. By showing that the heavens and the earth are governed by a single set of laws, which can be formulated clearly in the language of mathematics, he became a hero of the Enlightenment.

Secondly, scientific knowledge was preferred because it was considered immune from the vicious and often bloody disputes that had regularly disfigured politics and religion. The Reformation and Counter-Reformation were thought to have led to the civil wars in France, the Netherlands, England, Scotland and Ireland, and to the Thirty Years' War (1618–48). Thousands of lives had been lost, and apparently irreconcilable social divisions had been opened up in the territories across which the armies had raged. How much better if attention were directed at the establishment of non-doctrinaire, non-partisan, verifiable scientific knowledge by such bodies as the Royal Society of London and its continental and Scottish counterparts. Only one of the texts on this course, Lind's *Treatise of the Scurvy*, is a scientific enquiry, strictly defined. But you will find an enthusiasm for science and the application of scientific method in text after text. This enthusiasm stemmed from a widespread belief that scientific method would lead to the discovery of 'Nature and Nature's laws' in the broadest possible sense: that there existed 'natural laws' governing human as well as physical phenomena, and that the understanding of such laws would in turn bring improvements in every area of human activity, from medicine and midwifery to penal reform, education and social organization.

Confidence in the scientific method thus led to a confidence in the future. The *philosophes* thought that, by and large, things had got better, and that, as society became more enlightened, they would get better still. The historian, Gibbon, for example, while lamenting the decline and fall of the Roman Empire, concluded that the development of modern science and technology encourages 'the pleasing conclusion that every age of the world has increased, and still increases, the real wealth, the happiness, the knowledge, and perhaps the virtue, of the human race' (*Texts*, I, p.303).

4   The critique of Christianity

Few Enlightenment thinkers were Christians. Some, like the authors of the *Encyclopédie*, or the philosopher Hume, produced texts which hint strongly at scepticism or unbelief. Others, like Voltaire and Gibbon, wrote texts full of satire and irony to express their criticisms of Christianity, its churches and its practices. Voltaire tirelessly denounced religious fanaticism as '*l'infâme*' (the infamous thing). But this is not to say that they were atheists. A distinction, which will become clearer as the course develops, has to be made between, on one hand, belief in the Christian Revelation, and belief in the existence of God.

The position of many of the writers you will encounter is that, either frankly or covertly, they rejected as incredible orthodox Christian doctrines concerning the ways in which God is supposed to have revealed himself and his purposes through history, through the incarnation of his son and, through miracles, as these are reported in the Bible, and through the life (and further miracles) of the church. It was common among eighteenth-century intellectuals to believe none of this, yet to retain a belief that the universe is the handiwork of a good and wise god. The position is known as *Deism*. It fitted in well with an admiration of Newton's description of the universe, for God could be pictured as a remote deity who, aeons ago, wound up the universe and left it to run, regulated only by scientific laws which intelligent humans could discern. Deism, science, the stature of Newton, and the metaphor of light, reach a perfect conjunction in Pope's famous epitaph for the great Sir Isaac:

Nature, and Nature's Laws lay hid in Night.
God said, *Let Newton be!* and All was *Light*. (Butt, 1963, p.808)

And, as Norman Hampson (1968, p.77) wittily puts it: ' "If God said, Let Newton be!" Sir Isaac returned the compliment'.

There were, as you will discover, notable exceptions to the anti-Christian, or coolly sceptical temper of the Enlightenment. Haydn, for example, wrote an *oratorio*, a musical form which sets sections of the Bible to music. And Dr Johnson was a devout Anglican who, far from criticizing belief, wrote prayers which movingly express his Christian faith, (see Johnson set text, pp.775–80). But there was a general mistrust of what was scathingly called 'Enthusiasm' – that is to say, fervour, excessive and ostentatious piety, or claims to be inspired. Johnson shared this mistrust and defined 'enthusiasm' in his famous *Dictionary* as 'A vain belief of private revelation; a vain confidence of divine favour or communication'. The phrase 'He was no Enthusiast', when carved on a memorial tablet in a church recording the life of a worthy citizen, was intended to bestow approbation. None the less, while religion was no longer *central* to the personal outlook of the ruling elites, it continued to play an important part in the lives of the majority of people across Europe. Frederick and Catherine privately shared the scepticism of the *philosophes*, but they made sure that the religious susceptibilities of their subjects were not offended. Voltaire had a church built for his workers at his estate at Ferney.

Christianity itself was by no means a monolithic body of belief and practice. Western European Christianity had been fractured by the Reformation of the sixteenth century, and the Eastern Orthodox church had diverged from Roman Catholicism centuries before. By the mid-eighteenth century, when our period opens, the countries of Europe, each of which was predominantly Christian in belief, had churches whose interpretation of doctrine, and whose powers of enforcing orthodoxy, varied widely. In France, the Roman Catholic church wielded important independent powers. It exerted control over publication, censorship and the spread of scientific ideas. It proscribed, for example, inoculation against smallpox. Calvinism and Lutheranism had in Prussia left a tradition of obedience to the civil authorities, which Frederick found useful. Catholicism was the dominant faith in southern Germany and the Habsburg dominions: nothing was more bitterly resented in Austria than Joseph II's attempts to exclude papal authority and to grant official toleration to Protestants and Jews. In Russia, the Orthodox faith was a social bond to which Catherine paid public respect at the same time as she read the *Encyclopédie* and encouraged its free-thinking authors. In England, the Anglican Church had been established by the end of the sixteenth century and although it thereby had constitutional status, dissent and disbelief were tolerated. In Scotland, a Calvinist, Presbyterian church was established after the Reformation, and dissenters and disbelievers were harassed more energetically than in England. The unbelieving Scot, David Hume, for example, was barred from a university post because of his views, but he ran little danger of actually being locked up because of them. (Although if he had been from the lower orders, rather than from the well-to-do intelligentsia, his infidelity might have incurred greater social penalties.)

A non-sectarian movement which united believers of all faiths in the eighteenth century was Freemasonry, which spread from Britain in various forms across the continent. It added a further international element of mutual recognition and common standards. Freemasonry preached the existence of a Supreme Being or Great Architect of the Universe, and the natural (though not the social) equality of man. It enjoyed social conviviality and practised charity and philanthropy. Masonic themes appear in Mozart's opera *The Magic Flute*, and may be detected in Haydn's *Creation* and in Lessing's *Nathan The Wise*.

5 The veneration of the Ancients

Perhaps the most puzzling characteristic of the Enlightenment is its veneration for the Greeks and Romans. You will find Dr Johnson writing imitations of Roman verse; you will find Robert Adam promoting classical models as the ideal for the British grand country house; you will find Hume giving classical names to the disputants in his philosophical dialogues. A grounding in the classics formed part of the basic education of the elite in much of Europe, so that, as Johnson said, 'classical quotation is the *parole* of literary men all over the world' (Boswell, 1951 vol.ii, p.386). Why, though, did they not try to purge it from their culture, if they indeed intended to make a new world? Why should such a predominantly forward-looking movement habitually keep looking over its shoulder, back to classical Athens and (more especially) to Rome, as it strode ahead?

The answer will emerge as you work through the texts. Classical themes provided a common frame of reference within which ideas and actions were projected. Both Frederick and Catherine defended their absolute rule in terms of reference to classical antiquity that would have made sense to their readers, whether they agreed or not with the monarchs' claims that their rule was really 'republican' in spirit. Furthermore, the vast and universally respected heritage from antiquity was usefully ambiguous. The most radical of eighteenth-century ideas could be, either decently or protectively, clothed in classical garb, and thereby at least given a hearing. Moreover, the pagan, civic, classical world appealed strongly to those who disliked the continuing grip of a Christian culture that was, in their eyes, a relic from the Dark Ages. This view is perfectly symbolized by Gibbon's recollection of the moment when he decided to write his *Decline and Fall of the Roman Empire*. It was, he recalled:

> ... at Rome on 15 October 1764, as I sat musing amidst the ruins of the Capitol while the bare-footed friars were singing vespers in the Temple of Jupiter, that the idea of writing the decline and fall of the city first started to my mind. (Gibbon, 1891, p.151)

The presence of ascetic, grubby-footed Christian monks, in the ruins of the heart of a once great civilization, offended his classical sensibilities. Gibbon's contrasting image illuminates the attraction, aesthetic and ideological, of the pagan world in the eighteenth century.

6 *The Enlightenment tone*

The writers of the Enlightenment aimed to write clearly, succinctly and entertainingly. They had a message to convey, and it seemed to them that the most persuasive way of putting it over was to write stylishly and attractively, particularly since they were addressing an audience like themselves, of well-informed generalists, rather than specialists. 'True men of letters', wrote Voltaire, 'acquire the ability to venture into these different fields, even if they cannot cultivate them all' (*Texts*, I, p.11). For their purpose was didactic: to spread the knowledge which Enlightenment brought, and the message that Enlightenment brought knowledge and progress.

There was a reaction against the open expression of violent emotion in favour of a more restrained and disciplined approach. This owed something to classical influences and much to the urbanity of late seventeenth- and early eighteenth-century French and English culture. Voltaire, looking back at the cultural achievements of the age of Louis XIV, described that age as 'the most enlightened that has ever been' (Voltaire, n.d., p.1). English literature of the same period was often described as 'augustan', that is comparable in its 'correctness' and perfection to the classic works of the age of the Roman emperor Augustus. According to one modern critic, a 'tendency to avoid profound emotions is an integral portion of the eighteenth-century attempt to achieve the greatest possible pleasure by living in harmony with the laws of nature. Harmony is based upon the geometry of balance, and balance will be upset by profound emotion' (W.C. Shrader, quoted in Black, 1990, p.245). Mastery of form was often accompanied by a certain lightness of touch, and in particular, an ironic touch, which characterizes many of the texts.

Irony is a way of presenting matters without apparently exhibiting the writer's deepest emotion or intention. The reader, too, commonly feels no compulsion (though he or she is tempted) formally to assent to, or dissent from, what is being ironically presented by the writer. Reader and writer are complicit in a subversive, but unspecific act. In his *Dictionary*, Dr Johnson defined irony as 'a mode of speech in which the meaning is contrary to the words'. Thus, Gibbon's attitude to the barbarians and the place of religion in the Roman empire is often described as one of 'ironic' detachment. The ironic mode of much eighteenth-century writing is so common, yet somewhat inaccessible, at first, to the modern reader, that an example here might be useful. Gibbon, as you will see, saw the rise of Christianity – a religion for which he felt some distaste – as one of the chief symptoms of the downfall of the Roman empire. Here, he is describing the early Christians' claims to be able miraculously to raise the dead, and a challenge to that claim by 'a noble Grecian':

> ... it seems difficult to account for the scepticism of those philosophers who still rejected and derided the doctrine of the resurrection. A noble Grecian had rested on this important ground the whole controversy, and promised Theophilus, bishop of Antioch, that, if he could be gratified with the sight of a single person who had been actually raised from the dead, he would immediately embrace the Christian religion. It is somewhat remarkable that the prelate of the first eastern church, however anxious for the conversion of his friend, thought proper to decline this fair and reasonable challenge. (Gibbon, 1963, p.161)

Now, formally, Gibbon stands detached from the matters outlined in this passage: he does not explicitly give the reader his judgement on whether the dead were raised. Nor does he – even though the reader knows by now that Gibbon was hostile to Christianity – use emotional or intemperate language. The tone of the passage is cool and detached, and its impact derives from the ironic effect of innocuous phrases like 'it seems difficult to account for' or 'it is somewhat remarkable that'. If Gibbon has, by the time they reach this passage, coaxed readers on to his side, they will be led to share his mocking view of the early church without his ever having had to emerge from the winding pathways of irony and openly to declare his position, and without the readers' having formally to acknowledge their own, anti-Christian response. Boswell observed that Gibbon 'should have warned us of our danger, before we entered his garden of flowery eloquence, by advertising: "spring-guns and man traps set here" '.

Irony is often puzzling. We do not quite know how seriously to take the writer: is he or she intending quite the opposite of what he or she writes? Frederick, for example, burdened with the responsibilities of war and administration, called the palace from where he governed Prussia with unremitting care 'Sans-Souci' (free from care), and designed it in the lighthearted classical style known as 'rococo'. Or does the ironic tone indicate perhaps indecision – the writer's mind hasn't been made up? Or might it be a dry way of presenting something comically or satirically? Let us go back to Pope's famous epitaph on Newton for a moment:

Nature, and Nature's Laws lay hid in Night.
God said, *Let Newton be!* and All was *Light*.

Might even this be read ironically? Could it be that Pope was hinting that, great as Sir Isaac undoubtedly was, his admirers might have crossed the boundary between admiration and adulation?

Irony is a habitual mode in eighteenth-century writers and, baffling though it sometimes is, it has great pleasures in store for readers. Irony merges with the wit, humour and poise that characterize the period. Here is Gibbon again with a typically fine-balanced sentence which sums up the character of the Emperor Gordian:

> Twenty-two acknowledged concubines, and a library of sixty-two thousand volumes, attested the variety of his inclinations; and from the productions which he left behind him, it appears that the former as well as the latter were designed for use rather than for ostentation. (Gibbon, 1963, p.84)

Finally, in these comments on 'tone', the absence of relentless soul-baring, personal, tragic intensity needs comment. Mozart's music is as profound as anything ever composed, yet it emerges from an ordered structure, characterized by balance, decorum and control. Furthermore, you will find in *The Magic Flute* passages of sublime music, alternating with comic song and something akin to pantomime. In Haydn's *Creation*, a work whose subject could scarcely be grander, an entertaining lightness of manner marks even the most serious passages. And Voltaire's *Candide*, which relates a sequence of the most appalling misfortunes, is *funny*.

7 *Genres*

'Genre' is a term normally associated with the arts, and particularly with painting (where the genres of 'landscape', 'portrait' etc. are used in classification). But the term can usefully be extended to open up a consideration of the sorts or types or kinds (which is what *genre* literally means) of texts covered in this course. You will find texts operating within genres that are now virtually obsolete. The medical researcher, James Lind, cast his researches into the form of an exhaustive *treatise*. Hume, wrote his major philosophical work on religion in the form of a *dialogue*, a form which he borrowed from the Roman, Cicero (who, in turn, had borrowed it from the Greek, Plato). Voltaire, in *Candide*, developed a new genre which is part philosophical argument and part black comedy (to use a modern term). Lessing's play *Nathan the Wise* is concerned to combine naturalistic depiction of character with a weight of philosophical ideas. Mary Wollstonecraft's *Vindication of the Rights of Woman* is part philosophy, part psychology and part feminist manifesto. Laclos's fictional exposé of aristocratic French society, *Dangerous Acquaintances*, takes the form of an epistolary novel, or novel in letters. (Letter-writing itself was a genre, which even now retains some of its polite conventions: do we really mean '*Dear Sir or Madam*', '*Yours faithfully*'?.)

In poetry the typical eighteenth-century genre is the public, the rhetorical, not the private and confessional. In painting, a hierarchy of genres was observed. Today we are ready to accept that *any* object, person or scene can be, in principle, the subject matter for great painting: not so in the eighteenth-century academies, where still-life, for example, could not normally aspire to greatness. Each genre of painting had its own rules and its own conventions which were not to be mixed or confused. The same held true for architecture, literature and music. It was, however, perfectly possible for a writer to be adept in different genres: thus Johnson, as well as compiling his *Dictionary*, wrote dramatic verse, a poem on London modelled on the Roman satirist Juvenal, and biographies of the English poets; Mozart wrote both comic operas and a requiem mass. As for Voltaire, Gibbon described him as 'the most extraordinary man of the age, a poet, a historian, a philosopher, who has filled thirty quartos, of prose and verse, with his various productions, often excellent and always entertaining' (Gibbon, 1891, vol.i, p.100). Excellent and entertaining for the eighteenth-century reader, let us add, *each in its different genre*. Johnson poked fun at some of the stricter rules of drama, when defending Shakespeare from the criticisms of Voltaire; but no-one, least of all Johnson, doubted that, in every genre, rules there were and must be.

8   Nobility and patronage

It is significant, in this period of royal or aristocratic patronage, that few writers, artists or musicians were of noble birth, and that many were dependent on noble patrons or contacts in high places: Haydn spent thirty years in the service of the Princes of Esterhazy, living in the servants' quarters, before coming to London to give public concerts in the 1790s. Mozart scraped along on commissions – for example, the piano concerto which he wrote and performed for the coronation of the Habsburg emperor Leopold II in 1790, and his opera, *La Clemenza di Tito*, composed in honour of the same ruler. There were different kinds of patronage. Patronage might come from a monarch or aristocrat, as was the case with Robert Adam, or from a well-to-do commoner. But it might also come from an institution or academy, like the English Royal Academy, of which Reynolds became president; or the Royal Society of London, at whose request Captain Cook carried out scientific observations during his voyage to the Pacific in 1768. Most of the authors of our texts were emerging from, or had already succeeded in emancipating themselves from patronage, whether because, as in Gibbon's case, they had private means (though he had to retire to Switzerland in order to live within his means), or, as with Johnson, out of pride (though he also received a royal pension). Haydn bridged both systems: the expenses of the first performances of the *Creation* were defrayed by Prince Schwarzenberg, but Haydn also supplemented the gratuities he received from his aristocratic patrons by publishing and selling the score to subscribers in a manner that anticipated nineteenth-century practice.

9   Europe and the Enlightenment

The Enlightenment was a cosmopolitan movement, which transcended international politics and even wars. At its basis was a common culture, largely derived from wide acquaintance with the classics and an espousal of classical values. The geographical centre of the movement in the mid-eighteenth century was Paris: French language and culture were dominant in educated society across Europe. Even Johnson, who detested the ideas of both Voltaire and Rousseau, was well-versed in, and impressed by, Voltaire's works, particularly *Candide*. Hume was another admirer of *Candide*. So were Frederick and Catherine, both German born, but fluent French speakers who habitually spoke and wrote in French. Frederick dismissed German language and literature as unfit for polite society. Gibbon published his first book in French and hesitated as to whether to write the *Decline and Fall* in English or French.

Intellectuals travelled widely during the period. Boswell moved between Edinburgh, London, France – visiting Voltaire at Ferney, near the Swiss border – and Prussia – observing Frederick at Sans-Souci. Voltaire himself spent three years there as Frederick's guest. Gibbon and Hume spent time in France, as did the penal reformer, Howard, who also visited Russia. Haydn moved from what is now Hungary to London and wrote his *Creation* for both Viennese and London audiences. Diderot interviewed Catherine at St Petersburg. Boswell and Johnson made a celebrated journey to the Hebrides. Some went beyond Europe altogether, notably Captain Cook, who circumnavigated the globe. Olaudah

Equiano, by remarkable contrast, moved *into* European culture from a life which started in West Africa, where he was captured by slavers.

The Enlightenment, then, was cosmopolitan and well travelled. Inevitably though, it took on distinctive tinges within particular national contexts. Although Boswell, for example, could easily move between Edinburgh and London and find congenial intellectual company in both, Edinburgh life had characteristics which distinguished it from London – and from Paris, Milan, Berlin or St Petersburg.

Paris itself was no haven of toleration. The permission granted for the publication of the *Encyclopédie* was revoked in 1759, when the *Parlement* of Paris was informed by the Attorney General that its aims were 'to propagate materialism, to destroy religion, to inspire a spirit of independence and to nourish the corruption of morals'. Voltaire, himself the embodiment of the Enlightenment, spent much of his life in self-imposed exile in order to avoid the kind of persecution by church and state that dogged his fellow *philosophes*, Diderot and Rousseau.

The Enlightenment (or *Aufklärung*) in Germany was far less anti-religious and anti-clerical than in France, aiming at greater understanding and clarification of religious truths, not the undermining of Christian belief or depriving the churches of their privileges. Kant approved of enlightenment as self-emancipation through the use of reason, but he was content to see this subordinated to the concept of civil obligation: 'Argue as much as you like and about whatever you like, but obey!' (*Texts*, II, p.309).

In Austria the Habsburg emperor Joseph II was a dynamic ruler whose modernizing zeal extended to such *minutiae* as a prohibition on corsets and criticisms of Mozart's work – 'Too many notes, Herr Mozart'. But as a practising, though reformist Catholic, who closed down the monasteries in Austria, he abominated the free thinking of the *philosophes*.

10 Change 1750–1800

The texts in this course are arranged thematically, not chronologically. Thus, Part B, for example, links four texts which reflect the diverse influence of classical antiquity; the three texts in Part D share a common interest in religion (or, in Mozart's case, freemasonry), and so on. This thematic approach should help to draw together the features that unite texts originating in different countries and in different genres. However, this arrangement of the texts inescapably blunts the sense of the change which took place during the half-century covered by the course. And the changes were momentous. They were at their most momentous with the French Revolution of 1789. The course does not deal with the Revolution directly, but you will detect its rumblings in some of the documents of Catherine the Great, and many of the later texts on the course, notably in Mary Wollstonecraft's writings.

In a few of the texts, you will also detect the distant rumblings of the Industrial Revolution. By 1800, Britain had irreversibly embarked on its industrial transformation, and parts of mainland Europe were not far behind. The writers of the *Encyclopédie* (as you will see in TV1) were keen to publicize innovations in French industry and technology. The Scottish Enlightenment, to take another example, comes out of the 'improving' state of mind which was transforming Lowland agriculture, industry and commerce. Captain Cook's voyages, and Equiano's slavery were connected intimately with Europe's commercial expansion. Explicit references, within the texts, to the worlds of industry and commerce are rare, but the Industrial Revolution was stirring, none the less.

Less obviously momentous than either the French Revolution or the Industrial Revolution, but perhaps more important for an understanding of changes within the Enlightenment, are shifts in the sensibility, or frame of mind, or states of feeling, registered in our texts, especially those grouped together in Part E. The shift is from Reason to Feeling. The pivotal figure here is Rousseau, who started out as a friend and associate of the *philosophes*, but quickly moved to a rejection of their urban, rational, sociable outlook, in favour of the cultivation of solitariness, wildness and the primitive. Rousseau is the extreme example, but it is important to bear in mind that the course contains, at one end, Dr Johnson, the complete Londoner, writing polished, learned imitations of Roman poets, and at the other, Burns, seldom comfortable for long in Edinburgh society and writing a new verse that embodied the language of unlettered Ayrshire agricultural labourers.

To explore further, in this introduction, the changes during the period would be to spoil one of the pleasures and challenges of the texts. All that needs to be said at this stage is that it will be useful, as you read the texts, to locate them within the decade of their origination and to ponder the ragged, contradictory sequence of changes that mark a text as mid, or late eighteenth-century.

The aim of this introduction has been to give you rough bearings, before you move to the real business of the course – the examination of the texts, with the help of the individual 'studies' that follow in these two volumes. A danger of this introduction is that it might have codified the Enlightenment before you ever encounter it. To counteract this tendency to make the movement look as if it's neatly parcelled, the first sequence of texts has been deliberately chosen with a view to opening up questions of the viability and utility of our generalizations. The first sequence, therefore, brings into prominence the *variety* of the Enlightenment.

11   *References*

Black, J. (1990) *Eighteenth-Century Europe*, Macmillan, London.

Boswell, J. (1951) *The Life of Samuel Johnson*, Everyman, Dent, London.

Butt, J. (ed.) (1963) *The Poems of Alexander Pope*, Methuen, London.

Clark, D. (ed.) (1954) *Shelley's Prose*, University of New Mexico Press, Albuquerque.

Dunthorne, H. (1991) *The Enlightenment*, New Appreciations in History, 24, published by The Historical Association, London.

Gibbon, E. (1891) *Memoirs of Edward Gibbon*, edited by H. Morley, Routledge, London.

Gibbon, E. (1963) *The Decline and Fall of the Roman Empire*, Penguin, Harmondsworth. (First published 1776–88.)

Hampson, N. (1968) *The Enlightenment*, Penguin, Harmondsworth.

Lentin, A. (1973) *Russia in the Eighteenth Century*, Heinemann Educational Books, London.

Voltaire, (n.d.) *Le Siècle de Louis XIV*, Garnier, Paris.

Wollstonecraft, M. (1982) *A VIndication of the RIghts of Woman*, Penguin, Harmondsworth.

Part A
Varieties of Enlightenment

Contents

Study Timetable

The table below sets out the teaching materials you will need to have to hand for each unit of *Studies*, Part A. You may also use the table as a guide to help you work out your own study timetable. More detailed information about the relevant teaching materials, as well as an explanation of how they fit into the study, can be found on the first page of each individual study.

Encylopédie *(Study weeks 0–1)*

Studies/Texts	Radio	TV	AC	Set books
Studies I	R1	TV1	–	–
Texts I	–	–	–	–

Frederick the Great and Catherine the Great *(Study weeks 2–3)*

Studies/Texts	Radio	TV	AC	Set books
Studies I	R2	TV2	–	–
Texts I	–	–	–	–

Beccaria, Howard and Penal Reform *(Study week 4)*

Studies/Texts	Radio	TV	AC	Set books
Studies I		TV3	AC1632 (blue)	–
Texts I	–	–	–	–

Johnson and Boswell *(Study weeks 5–6)*

Studies/Texts	Radio	TV	AC	Set books
Studies I	R1	TV4	AC 1633 (green)	
Texts I	–	–		*Samuel Johnson*

Music in the Enlightenment and Haydn's *The Creation* *(Study weeks 7–8)*

Studies/Texts	Radio	TV	AC	Set books
Studies I	–	–	AC 1628 (red)	–
Texts I	–	–	AC 1626 (red)	–
–	–	–	AC 1627 (red)	–

Introduction

*Prepared for the Course Team by
Simon Eliot*

Introduction

Unlike the other parts of this course, 'Varieties of Enlightenment' is not organized around a specific set of ideas such as 'Reactions to Classical Antiquity' or 'Religion and Humanity'. Instead, this part has a more general purpose: to illustrate the diversity of content, of form, and of geographical origin of those cultural activities which together went to make up the Enlightenment.

As the General Introduction to the course has already pointed out, most works of the Enlightenment exhibit certain characteristic features such as a belief in the virtues of political liberty (though not democracy), a stress on the supremacy of scientific and empirical knowledge (this was particularly re-inforced by the *philosophes*' almost totally uncritical admiration of Newton and Newtonianism), a tendency to regard Christianity critically, and the veneration of the ancient Greek and Roman cultures. However, not all the works we are to study on this course have all these characteristics in equal measure, and some don't exhibit certain of the characteristics at all. Yet we still regard them in some sense as being products of the Enlightenment, and not just because they were produced during the time of the Enlightenment. Perhaps one of the ways of thinking about the Enlightenment is to imagine that its four main features (celebration of liberty, of science, of classical cultures, suspicion of Christianity) together made up a 'theme' on which all the actual works of the Enlightenment played variations: some were very close to this theme in the sense that they contained all the main features and gave them roughly equal prominence (for example the *Encyclopédie*), whilst others were more remote variations in that they contained only one or two characteristics, or combined them with other features that don't *seem* part of the Enlightenment at all (for example Catherine's autocracy, Johnson's self-tormenting Christianity).

A variety of content

We begin with the *Encyclopédie* because in some ways this could be thought of as a quintessentially Enlightenment text. Most of the contributors to it, in article after article (some of which you will be studying in the first two weeks), displayed all four of the main characteristics. The veneration of the classical cultures, for instance, can be found in *Philosophe* (anonymous), and in *Epicureanism* (Diderot); the celebration of science in *Experimental* (d'Alembert) and in *Inoculation* (Tronchin); a critical attitude to

Christianity in *Priests* (d'Holbach) and in *Consecrated Bread* (Diderot); and the promotion of political liberty in *Political Authority* (Diderot) and *Natural Equality* (de Jaucourt).

The second variation on the theme of Enlightenment can be found in our study of Frederick and Catherine. It's a more remote variation than the *Encyclopédie*, of course, because neither ruler displayed all four major characteristics in either attitude or action. Political liberty was substantially circumscribed in Prussia and even more so in Catherine's Russia. Frederick was himself sceptical about Christianity, but practical politics inclined him to tolerate it and even find it useful. The wars fought by Frederick to maintain and increase Prussian security and power were not motivated by enlightened thinking but by something much more ancient and compelling: the realities of statecraft. Nevertheless, both Frederick and Catherine thought of themselves, and were in turn regarded by many of their contemporaries, as 'enlightened' rulers and their attempts, genuine or hypocritical according to your view, to put enlightened ideas into practice, offer a fascinating variation on the theme of the Enlightenment.

Beccaria's work reminds us yet again of the practical orientation of much of Enlightenment thinking. His intention was to provide a theoretical basis for major judicial and penal reforms. He calls for the application of rational – almost scientific – thought to the subject, and proposes a scheme in which a system overdependent on extreme forms of retribution is replaced by a rational application of moderate measures aimed more at deterring and reforming criminals than at punishing them. Beccaria's views on the origin of crime are also characteristically those of the Enlightenment: he sees much crime as having social and economic causes such as poverty and ignorance rather than being the product of sin. Although Beccaria is rarely explicitly critical of Christianity, this stress on environmental rather than moral factors has the effect of moving our attention away from religious and towards secular explanations of human behaviour.

John Howard's investigations into prison conditions are another example of Enlightenment pragmatism. However, even this most practical enquiry into the issues of health and the nature of suffering in overcrowded and insanitary English prisons of the mid-eighteenth century is informed by the tone of a *philosophe*. Howard investigates prisons systematically, observing them personally and recording his observations, just like a scientist. He sees the overcrowding and mixing of prisoners not just as a way in which physical disease spreads but, like Beccaria, as a way moral disease spreads as well. His proposals for reform are both practical and symbolic: in wishing to admit the free circulation of air and light into the prisons, he wants literally to 'enlighten' them. Whether or not the new prisons that were built in the mid and late eighteenth century actually succeeded in putting Beccaria's and Howard's ideas into action, they certainly took up another characteristic feature of the Enlightenment, for many were constructed using the language of classical architecture to express the authority of the society that built them.

Samuel Johnson shared many of Beccaria's and Howard's views on penal reform (he wrote essays against the excessive use of capital punishment and on the folly of imprisoning debtors; see the Oxford *Johnson*, pp. 211–15, 283–90). He resembled the Encyclopedists in his drive to apply rational systematizing principles to the accumulation of knowledge (not only in his *Dictionary*; he also worked on the cataloguing of a great book collection, the Harleian, and on a new edition of Shakespeare). He shared their admiration for Greek and Latin culture: apart from imitating some of the forms of Latin poetry in English, Johnson also wrote a number of his own poems in Latin. Johnson's Christianity, however, set him apart. He was a passionate believer in, and promoter of, Christian values. All Johnson's Enlightenment characteristics were thus tinged in a way that makes him and his works decidedly different from all those you will study earlier in this Part. If the *Encyclopédie* can be regarded as being near the centre of the Enlightenment, Johnson's writings can be thought of as being on the periphery (as perhaps Rousseau's can, though for completely different reasons). Some critics do not regard Johnson as an Enlightenment figure at all. We have included him as a particularly striking variation on the theme, but you will need to make up your own mind about where he and his works stand.

Haydn shared Christianity with Johnson, but little else. Johnson's Christianity was coloured by his own pessimism: it was frequently dark, guilty and anxious. Haydn's, on the other hand, judging by *The Creation*, was optimistic and confident. The libretto emphasizes God as a creator of order and system (Parts I and II) and places human relationships at the very centre of this new order (Part III). To ensure that this mood is not compromised, the libretto ends the story before the Fall of Adam and Eve, thus neatly circumventing the Biblical event which would most threaten the work's optimism. The *philosophes'* characteristic suspicion of Christianity seems, by the time of *The Creation*, to be almost irrelevant, for Haydn's God, as literally the creator of light, is a deity in tune with the Enlightenment.

A variety of forms (genres)

But it was not just the characteristics of the *content* that were diverse; the *forms* these cultural activities took were also many and various. The systematizing rationality of Enlightened thinkers might well find its most immediate expression in works of reference such as the *Encyclopédie* or Johnson's *Dictionary*, but it could also take a more specific and immediately applicable form such as an investigatory essay into the nature of crime and punishment with an intention of reforming the penal system (as in Beccaria's *Dei Delitti e della Pene*) or of an empirical survey of actual social conditions (as in Howard's *An Enquiry into the Present State of the Prisons*).

The extent to which Enlightenment thinking was regarded not as an end in itself but as a guide to action can be judged by studying Frederick the Great of Prussia and Catherine the Great of Russia. In a whole host of forms (published essays, manifestos such as Catherine's *Nakaz*, confidential memoranda, private letters and letters designed for a wider audience), Frederick and Catherine explored the social, political and legal implications of the Enlightenment. How far they succeeded in introducing Enlightened thinking into their respective countries, and what their intentions were in doing so, are matters you will have to decide for yourselves. The fact that they made the attempt at all is evidence of the strong tendency for Enlightenment thinking to take practical forms or at least have some consequence in the real world. You will return to this important Enlightenment idea when you read Voltaire's *Candide* in Part C and discover with what contempt Voltaire regards thinkers like Pangloss, whose theories are neither derived from close observation nor lead to useful action.

Samuel Johnson, like Voltaire, Diderot and so many other writers of the period, could put his hand to many literary forms. His poem 'The Vanity of Human Wishes', although its Christian argument is far from typical Enlightenment thinking, is characteristically enlightened in its reference back to classical origins, being an imitation of a satire by Juvenal. Boswell's *Journal of a Tour to the Hebrides* is an example of another favourite form of the eighteenth century, the travelogue, which is not only an account of a real journey but also a journey through ideas or character (Radishchev's *A Journey from St Petersburg to Moscow*, to which Catherine the Great objected so strongly, was another example of this form).

Although 'Enlightenment' is not a term that is normally used to characterize a style or period of music, musical form was itself not uninfluenced by Enlightenment thinking, as you will see in our study of Haydn's *Creation*. The bringing of light out of darkness and order out of chaos are themes fundamental to the Biblical myth of creation, but they also chime well with the desire of the *philosophes* and others in the eighteenth century to dispel ignorance and establish a rational order among things. This drive is evident not only in the libretto of *The Creation*, but also in the musical devices used by Haydn to represent the process of the creation of the world: the music moves from the negative and uncertain (e.g. soft music in the minor key) to the positive and secure (e.g. loud music in the major key).

A variety of countries

Not only did works of the Enlightenment display diversity in terms of content and form, but also they came from a wide range of countries and cultures. We begin this Part most appropriately in France, which many contemporaries would have regarded (rightly or wrongly) as the heart of the Enlightenment. We then turn eastwards to look at the way the thinking of the French *philosophes* influenced the rulers of Prussia and Russia. A study of Beccaria's work on penal theory allows us to look at the way the Enlightenment affected thinking among the educated classes in the multiplicity of small states that made up Italy in the eighteenth century. Howard's work on the condition of English prisons introduces us to one of the ways in which Enlightenment thinking manifested itself in Great Britain; the work on Samuel Johnson reveals a very different form of English Enlightenment. Boswell's and Johnson's accounts of their journey through Scotland allows us to glimpse, albeit briefly and indirectly, the distinctly different nature of the Scottish Enlightenment. The centrality of the Christian religion in Johnson's work then re-directs us back across the Channel, this time to Austria, to see how religion might be handled by a pious but fundamentally more optimistic figure of the Enlightenment, Haydn.

In imitating many eighteenth-century travellers by going on this form of Grand Tour, we shall be able to appreciate what a pervasive influence the Enlightenment had. It affected most European countries to some degree or other, influencing, for instance, architecture in countries as diverse as Scotland and Spain, or social reform in such contrasting nations as England and Russia. Unlike travellers on a Grand Tour, however, we haven't the leisure to take things slowly so, for most of the countries we visit in the course we have included a brief historical survey to give you some idea of the background against which a particular national variation on the theme of the Enlightenment was being played out.

The Encyclopédie

Prepared For the Course Team by
Michael Bartholomew, Stephanie Clennell
and Linda Walsh

Contents

Encylopédie *(Study weeks 0–1)*

Studies/Texts	Radio	TV	AC	Set books
Studies, I	R1	TV1	–	–
Texts, I	–	–	–	–

For your work on the *Encyclopédie*, you will need this volume of *Studies*, and *Texts, I.* The first television and radio programmes are closely integrated with the study (you should refer to the relevant Broadcast notes associated with these programmes). TV1 'The *Encyclopédie*' is particularly important, for it gives you a sense of the physical presence and the significance of the volumes of the *Encyclopédie*, and a commentary on some of the wonderful plates. At the back of this volume of *Studies*, you will find a brief historical outline of France during the eighteenth century. You will need to familiarize yourself with it at some point during your work on the *Encyclopédie*. You can either read it straightaway, or plunge first into the study itself, picking up the historical background as and when you need it.

The Encyclopédie

ENCYCLOPEDIE,

O U.

DICTIONNAIRE RAISONNÉ

DES SCIENCES,

DES ARTS ET DES MÉTIERS,

PAR UNE SOCIÉTÉ DE GENS DE LETTRES.

Mis en ordre & publié par M. *DIDEROT*, de l'Académie Royale des Sciences & des Belles-Lettres de Pruffe ; & quant à la PARTIE MATHÉMATIQUE, par M. *D'ALEMBERT*, de l'Académie Royale des Sciences de Paris, de celle de Pruffe, & de la Société Royale de Londres.

Tantùm feries junƈturaque pollet,
Tantùm de medio fumptis accedit honoris ! HORAT.

TOME PREMIER.

A PARIS,

Chez
BRIASSON, *rue Saint Jacques, à la Science.*
DAVID l'aîné, *rue Saint Jacques, à la Plume d'or.*
LE BRETON, Imprimeur ordinaire du Roy, *rue de la Harpe.*
DURAND, *rue Saint Jacques, à Saint Landry, & au Griffon.*

M. DCC. LI.

AVEC APPROBATION ET PRIVILEGE DU ROY.

Figure 1
Title page of the
Encyclopédie. *'Encyclopedia,*
or an analytical dictionary of
the sciences, arts and trades,
by a society of men of letters.'
(University of Durham)

1 Introduction

If the spirit of the Enlightenment had to be represented by a single work, that work would be the seventeen volumes of text, and the eleven volumes of plates, of the *Encyclopédie*, published in France between 1751 and 1772. This vast encyclopedia was not a repository of safe, uncontentious information. On the contrary, it was polemical, tendentious, and sometimes scandalous. Its thousands of entries combined to promote a programme for the rational, scientific reconstruction of knowledge and of society. The man who launched the undertaking, Denis Diderot, summed up the bold programme:

> All things must be examined, debated, investigated without exception and without regard for anyone's feelings ... We must ride roughshod over all ancient puerilities, overturn the barriers that reason never erected, give back to the arts and sciences the liberty that is so precious to them. (Diderot, 1755)

Diderot was part of a remarkable intellectual movement which emerged in mid eighteenth-century France, and which was centred on Paris. The members of this loose, informal movement have become known as the *philosophes*. '*Philosophe*' translates as 'philosopher.' In this study, we shall retain the French word, for, in the context of the French Enlightenment, it signifies a range of interests much wider than what we would today recognize as philosophy. The *philosophes* were interested in politics, law, science, medicine, technology, religion, the arts, and public affairs generally. The *Encyclopédie* is the embodiment of their ideas.

2 *The* philosophes

There are strong family resemblances in the work of the *philosophes*, but they were not a monolithic group, all subscribing to a tightly-formulated manifesto. Moreover, their work stretched across three generations, with the earliest exploring the legacy of seventeenth-century thinkers like Descartes, Locke and Newton, and the last stretching forward to the French Revolution of 1789.

Although the *philosophes*, as you will see, were critical of many aspects of French society, they were not, nor did they feel themselves to be, solitary and misunderstood exiles in an intellectual wilderness. Far from being a wilderness, France since the time of Louis XIV, who reigned from 1643 to 1715, had been the acknowledged European leader in matters of taste and culture, as well as of social graces and manners. So much was this so that the educated classes in Germany and Russia often conversed and wrote in French. And further, under Louis XIV, France had been far ahead of other countries in the organization of the arts and sciences. Prestigious academies, designed to promote the study of language, science and art, had all been established.

The *philosophes* came from a variety of social backgrounds. Some were noblemen: Montesquieu, for instance, was a baron. Others were well-to-do. Voltaire, for example, was the son of a successful Parisian lawyer. Diderot's father was a fairly prosperous bourgeois master cutler. Others were from humbler backgrounds. D'Alembert, another prime mover of the *Encyclopédie*, was the illegitimate son of a nobleman, and was brought up by the wife of a Parisian glazier. Rousseau, who started as an associate of the *philosophes*, was the son of a watchmaker. The work that the *philosophes* undertook depended, to some extent, simply on how much they needed money. Writers like d'Alembert, Diderot and Rousseau, who were striving to earn a living by their writing, would turn their hands to all sorts of commissions – to translating, to popular writing, to transcribing music. Some writers sought patronage from the court, from noblemen, from the academies.

With some notable exceptions, the *philosophes* made little money from their writing. Publishers paid writers as little as they could. There was no system of royalties, and no strict copyright laws. So even if a book became very popular, author and publisher could rarely do much about pirated editions, especially if they were published abroad.

All writers, rich and poor alike, had to beware of censorship. By 1741 the royal government was employing 76 censors – 10 for jurisprudence, 10 for medicine, 10 for theology, 8 for mathematics, 2 for surgery, 1 for prints and the remaining 35 for literature, history and related subjects. By 1789 there were 178 censors. Technically, no book could be published without its first being submitted to the censors, whose task was to ensure that not one word was contrary to morality, public order or religion. When a book was passed, it received royal permission to be sold and circulated. If however, Royal permission was withheld, the book might sometimes be published by a system of 'tacit approval' – an informal and technically illegal assurance that a book might be published without fear of prosecution. The practice of 'tacit approval' was perfected when a liberal-minded administrator, Malesherbes, was appointed as Director of Publications in 1750, a post which put him in charge of the royal censors. Several of Voltaire's more significant works appeared under 'tacit approval'. But the royal censors were not the only watchdogs; the clergy and the *parlements* (law-courts) also insisted on their rights to protect society from subversive literature. On several occasions they persuaded the government into taking repressive action. Rousseau's *Émile*, for example, was published under 'tacit approval', but this approval was withdrawn after outcries from the Sorbonne (the Paris University theology faculty), the Archbishop of Paris and the *Parlement* of Paris (see the Rousseau study, in *Studies,* II). The situation could be additionally complicated if any book smacked of Jansenism; this would probably win the approval of the *parlements*, but equally, would win the hostility of the clergy at the Sorbonne or in the episcopate. (The brief study of France in the eighteenth century, at the back of this volume will give you the outlines of Jansenism, the Church, *parlements* and the administrative structure of the country.)

There were ways round the censorship. Books were published with foreign places of publication printed on their title pages, implying, falsely, that they had been published outside France. Some actually *were* published abroad. It was difficult for the authorities to censor foreign material. The structure and form of the book might be another way to avoid the censors. Satire was used, in a number of ingenious ways. A good example is Montesquieu's *Persian letters*, which he published, anonymously, in Holland in 1721. To satirize French society, he used the device of a supposed Persian visitor to Europe: Montesquieu's own critical views could thereby be made to come from the mouth of an exotic visitor.

Sometimes, censorship could have the opposite effect from what was intended. There were occasions when condemnation served simply to advertise a book. Anyone able to afford the consequent inflation in its price could usually manage to find a copy. Yet if this looks like a game, it was not much fun for any authors or publishers who found themselves in the Bastille, and even less pleasant for the obscure men and women who suffered cruelly at the hands of the law for circulating books 'contrary to morals and religion'. In October 1768, for example, for selling works by Voltaire and the atheist *philosophe* d'Holbach, two men and one woman were sentenced to three consecutive days in the *carcan* (an iron collar attaching the prisoner to a post on public display) after which the men were sent to be oarsmen on the Mediterranean galleys (for nine years and five years respectively) and the woman was to be imprisoned for five years.

One of the commonest devices used by the *philosophes* to evade censorship, and yet to attack authority and tradition, was irony. They said one thing, but meant another. You will find plenty of examples of this clever, elusive, effective mode when you read the text.

You will also find plenty of examples of another ingenious mode. *Philosophes* commonly advanced their radical ideas by presenting them as the views of ancient Greek or Roman authorities. Thus, you will find the most advanced views contained in entries nominally covering Greek philosophical systems like Epicureanism or Pyrrhonism.

Why were the censors worried? The answer will emerge if we list the concerns of the *philosophes*. The list will show that while some of their activities posed no threat to the régime, the spirit of critical enquiry and the hatred of injustice that ran through their work gave no comfort whatsoever to church and state authorities.

First, and to the obvious annoyance – and sometimes fury – of the Catholic Church, the *philosophes* tended to be anti-clerical. They had no time for the church and its works. Voltaire, chief among *philosophes*, produced the slogan '*Ecrasez l'infâme!*' ('Crush the infamous thing!'), the 'thing' being the oppressive authority of the church. *Philosophes* campaigned vigorously on behalf of victims of religious persecution. Most of the *philosophes* were themselves 'deists'. That is to say, they acknowledged that reason indicates the likely existence of a God, but they denied that this God has given a 'revelation' of himself and his purposes to humans through scripture, the life of Christ, miracles, and the church. A few *philosophes* went further, and denied the existence of God altogether, but whether atheist or deist, *philosophes* regarded orthodox religion as irrational, superstitious, and oppressive. (Deism is discussed more fully in the introduction to Part D, in *Studies*, II.)

Secondly, *philosophes* tended to regard knowledge based on experience as the best form of knowledge (as opposed to knowledge derived simply from authority, or from intuition or faith). They favoured explanations that ruled out the operation of immaterial agencies, be they 'the soul', or God. They recommended 'materialist' explanations of phenomena – explanations that derived from the conviction that the universe is composed simply and wholly of particles of matter, endlessly redistributing themselves, according to fixed scientific laws. The *philosophes* believed that science, which had received a tremendous boost from the work of their hero, Sir Isaac Newton, at the beginning of the century, would be a force for enlightenment and progress. In many ways, the *philosophes* regarded scientific knowledge as the supreme sort of knowledge: truths established by observation and experiment were secure. This confidence in the methods of science led to the belief that scientific methods could, and should, be applied not just to enterprises like astronomy and physics, but to medicine, the economy, the analysis of the human mind, to law, to the study of society and to practical technological enterprises. Above all, they were confident that the universe, including human beings, is explicable: it is not inherently mysterious, but susceptible to methodical, rational investigation.

Thirdly, *philosophes* were enthusiasts for technological and medical progress. They saw scientists, inventors and doctors as the curers of society's ills. The *Encyclopédie* has many articles on industrial machinery and processes, and on disease and surgery. TV1 'The *Encyclopédie*' concentrates on this aspect of the volumes. The *philosophes* were not idle dreamers. They were enthusiasts for the scheme projected by the English philosopher Bacon in the seventeenth century for 'the relief of man's estate'. In practice, though, the *philosophes* were often unable to bridge the large gap between scientific and philosophical theory on the one hand, and commercial and industrial application on the other. And, as you will see, the gap between medical theory and the actual cure of disease was sometimes unbridgeable.

Fourthly, the *philosophes* were interested in legal and constitutional reform. They tended to be critical of the French absolutist régime and to be full of admiration for the British constitution with its entrenched liberties. However, to many *philosophes*, traditional monarchy – the predominant form of government in Europe – seemed to be capable of satisfactory reform. The *philosophes* were united, though, in their opposition to arbitrary and capricious power. They sharply differentiated 'despotism' from absolute power that was subject to the 'fundamental laws' of the state, or to the principles of 'natural law'.

Fifthly, the *philosophes* championed reason, liberty and tolerance. Sometimes they spoke of equality, but it was of a theoretical sort: they were not democrats. They had no plans for the wholesale, egalitarian political reconstruction of society. As d'Alembert wrote to Frederick the Great, 'I think that the form of government is immaterial, provided that the government is just, that all the citizens have an equal right to its protection, that they are equally subject to the laws and equally punished if they break them' (2 August 1770 in Lentin, 1985, pp. 10–11).

Justice and liberty were the *philosophes*' watchwords, but rarely political equality. In the words of d'Holbach: 'never let us exclaim against inequality, which was always necessary, and is the indispensable condition of our happiness' (d'Holbach, 1773). Censors may have been reassured by such sentiments, and they had no quarrel, in principle, with the advance of science and technology. But the mockery of religion, and attacks on the exercise of state power needed constant surveillance.

3　The origins and design of the Encyclopédie

In 1745 or thereabouts, a French publisher named Le Breton formed the scheme of issuing a French translation of the popular British *Cyclopaedia or Universal Dictionary of Arts and Sciences* (1728) of the Scot, Ephraim Chambers. This was the first big general encyclopedia in English and is the ancestor of today's *Chambers' Encyclopaedia*. Le Breton obtained royal permission (called a *privilège*), and he engaged the *abbé*[1] Jean-Paul de Gua de Malves, member of the *Académie des Sciences* and professor of philosophy at the Collège de France, to direct the enterprise, with Jean d'Alembert (already well-known as a mathematician) to oversee the scientific and technical articles. A year later he invited Denis Diderot (then a relatively obscure writer, who had however recently translated an English medical dictionary) to supervise the translation. De Malves proved unreliable and soon dropped out. Thereupon, Le Breton appointed Diderot as editor or director, with d'Alembert as associate director.

The project very quickly changed its character from a mere translation to an original work. It soon extended far beyond Chambers's *Cyclopaedia*. It purveyed not only information, but original ideas, views and theories. It had been launched at an important moment in France's history, when critics of the absolutist régime set up by Louis XIV and continued under the then reigning monarch Louis XV, had begun to acquire solidarity and to feel themselves allies and brothers-in-arms in a great cause.

The *philosophes* were constantly in trouble with the authorities, and because of the state censorship, had to be careful, in the *Encyclopédie's* articles, to disguise their more radical opinions. For all that we must not think of the *Encyclopédie* as an 'underground' enterprise. It was launched with royal approval; and though it soon lost this approval and twice at least was officially suppressed, it always had strong supporters at court and was felt to be an important asset to France, both from a financial and a prestige point of view. The Académie Française, the very citadel of 'establishment', was in fact taken over by *philosophes* and *encyclopédistes* in the 1770s, and d'Alembert became its 'perpetual secretary'.

The *Encyclopédie* is arranged alphabetically, but in addition, as in any encylopedia, some system of dividing up the various branches of knowledge was required. A highly elaborate diagram was printed, aiming to show how knowledge is acquired and stored (see Fig. 2). The system produces some peculiarities: 'History', for example, becomes a sub-branch of 'Memory', and biography is excluded. Shakespeare appears only in the entry on 'Stratford'. But the system does succeed in making the questions of the acquisition and classification of knowledge – principally 'knowledge of Nature' and 'knowledge of Man' – central. At the same time, and here the *philosophes'* hostility to religion reveals itself, it pushes all theological questions out to the margins. In medieval classifications of knowledge, theology is at the centre: in the *Encyclopédie*, it is at the margin. (For a discussion of the strategy of the *philosophes*, see Darnton, 1984.)

D'Alembert, in a polemical foreword to Volume 3, says that he and his co-editor have deliberately included, not the genealogies of great families, but the genealogies of sciences, and have given prominence not to conquerors who have ravaged and laid waste the earth, but to immortal geniuses who have given it enlightenment. Diderot, in his important article *Encyclopedia*, which you will shortly be reading, describes the *Encyclopédie* as intended to survive a revolution – to be a work from which, should some cataclysm overtake the world, all human knowledge could be reconstructed. And he says that any work of this type needs to be produced by a group of private individuals, 'a society of men of letters and artisans'.

---

[1] *Abbés* were men who were nominally in holy orders, but who often had scarcely any attachment to the Church.

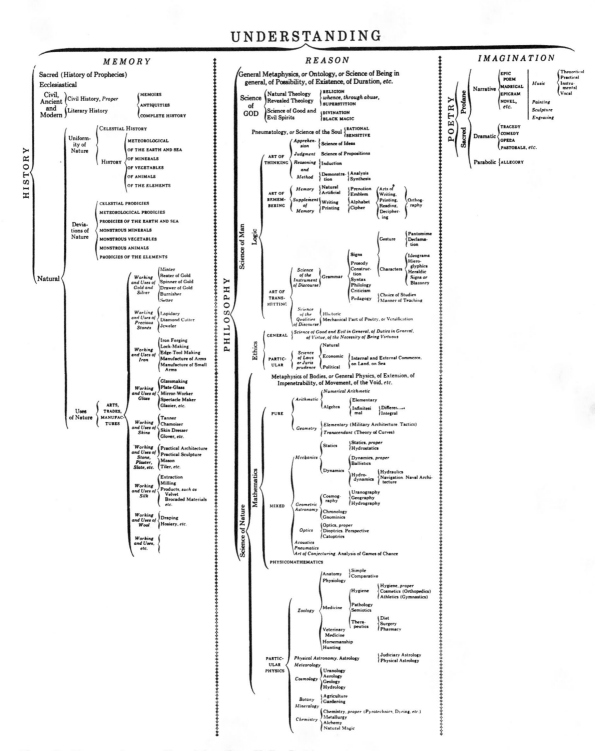

Figure 2   *Diagram of system of knowledge. (Roger-Viollet, Paris)*

4 *The publishing of the* Encyclopédie

Like many books in the eighteenth century, the *Encyclopédie* was financed by subscription. The enterprise was advertised, and subscribers then committed themselves, in advance, to buy the volumes as they were issued from the press.

Volume 1 of the *Encyclopédie* was published, after various hazards, in 1751 with an important *Preliminary Discourse* by d'Alembert. There were attacks on it from the Jesuits in their journal *Memoirs of Trévoux*, accusing it of 'dangerous' ideas and also, as an alternative charge, of plagiarism; and before long there were also attacks from the Jesuits' religious adversaries the Jansenists, alleging a 'conspiracy of so-called great minds' against religion and good order. This was no more than the *encyclopédistes* had expected; but at the end of 1751 a violent scandal broke out with indirect but serious consequences for the *Encyclopédie*. The Sorbonne had granted a higher degree to a certain *abbé* named de Prades who was a collaborator on the *Encyclopédie*; but then they had belatedly discovered that his thesis was full of 'blasphemous, heretical, erroneous and materialist views', views very close to those of d'Alembert in his *Preliminary Discourse*. A furious controversy ensued; the thesis was condemned by the Sorbonne, the *abbé* fled to Berlin, and the rumour was put about that the whole thing was a plot of the *encyclopédistes*, and that Diderot and d'Alembert had written most of the thesis themselves. The upshot was that in February 1752 the king issued an edict forbidding further publication of the *Encyclopédie* (of which Volume 2 had appeared during the scandal), and ordering the editors to hand over the manuscript material still in their possession. The situation looked black. But by great good fortune the minister in charge of censorship, or Director of Publications, Lamoignon de Malesherbes, was a man of great intelligence and liberal views and also possessed of powerful connections, since his father was the Chancellor of France. He had been opposed to the suppression, and through his influence (and that of the king's mistress, Mme de Pompadour, who hated the Jesuits and was therefore well disposed towards their enemies) the editors were encouraged to disregard the ban. Thus, the work was enabled once more to go ahead, though no longer with full royal approval, but with 'tacit approval'.

Meanwhile d'Alembert had acted with much offended dignity, announcing his own withdrawal from the great work until it and its authors and editors were treated with the respect due to them, and claiming (in a private letter to a friend) that 'there should be given us enlightened and reasonable censors, and not brute beasts in fur, sold out to our enemies'. It was not till July that he was persuaded after many entreaties to withdraw his resignation.

It was inevitable that the celebrated and notorious Voltaire would be drawn into the enterprise. For Volume 5, published in 1755, he contributed a number of articles – though in view of his now very bad relations with the government it was thought wisest to restrict him, at any rate to begin with, to apparently harmless topics such as *Elegance*, and *Taste*. He had been in correspondence with Diderot and d'Alembert for some years before this, but Diderot had refused a flattering invitation to meet him and the two were not close friends; Voltaire thought d'Alembert much the better writer of the two, whilst Diderot said of Voltaire that 'there will always be at least a dozen people in France who will be head and shoulders above him without needing to stand on tiptoe. In everything he does he comes second'. Nevertheless, the two recognized each other's indispensability to the *philosophes*' cause. Voltaire's relations with d'Alembert were warmer, and during 1756 d'Alembert paid a visit to him at his home near Geneva. It was a famous occasion, the conversation of the two celebrities becoming the object of much local interest; and as a result of it, d'Alembert published an article in Volume 7 (1757) on the subject of 'Geneva', in which he described the Genevan pastors as being more or less deists and rationalists on the lines of the French *philosophes*. Voltaire's influence was very strong in the article, and it seems that to some extent he had gulled d'Alembert. At all events the pastors themselves were not at all pleased. Indeed, they were angry, and issued a formal rebuttal which was circulated throughout Europe. The affair came at a bad moment for the *Encyclopédie*, for in the same year (1757) there had been an attempt to assassinate Louis XV. The would-be-assassin, named Damiens, was executed with unspeakable cruelties on 28 March 1757, and it was suggested that his mind had been unsettled by liberal opinions. (The cruelty of executions is one of the subjects of TV3 'Humanity and the Scaffold'.) In the atmosphere of repression which followed this, the king's council once more placed a ban on the *Encyclopédie* and tried to force the publishers to reimburse subscribers. The Pope, Clement XIII, issued a condemnation of the work. At this point, d'Alembert, already aggrieved and discontented, resigned once more, this time finally; and Voltaire withdrew at about the same period (subsequently using one or two of his contributions in his own *Philosophical Dictionary* of 1764). Diderot was thus left alone, although he was perhaps not altogether discontented to be left without rivals. Friends, including Catherine the Great, urged him to move the enterprise out of Paris, but he refused, and doggedly worked on behind locked doors. To Voltaire, who wrote advising him to give up altogether, he replied (19 February 1758): 'What is to be done? That which is proper to men of courage: to scorn our enemies, to attack them, and to profit, as we have already done, from the idiocy of our censors'. His publishers supported him, retaining the money they were supposed to return to subscribers, as part payment for the volumes of plates. In the event, the government in its extraordinary fashion, managed to combine the strictest possible public veto on the *Encyclopédie* with a sort of private wink of tolerance. It meant that the subsequent volumes, though printed in Paris, had to bear a Swiss imprint. It was forbidden to purchase the work in Paris, subscribers having to have it sent to addresses in the provinces.

There were many more dramas and vicissitudes in the history of the *Encyclopédie*, which was not completed until 1772, but this will have given you a general notion of them.

The *Encyclopédie* was a huge commercial and technical enterprise, comparable in scale to the greatest enterprises of French capitalism at the end of the eighteenth century (Proust, 1962; Darnton, 1979). As a commercial undertaking it was highly successful and the publishers made an estimated profit of more than two million livres from the various editions (£87,500 at 1780s prices). The original intention, announced in the 1751 Prospectus, of producing 1,625 copies of 8 folio volumes of text and 2 of plates at 280 livres, increased to a total of 4,255 copies of 17 volumes of text and 11 volumes of plates at 980 livres. There were reprints abroad of the folio edition in the 1770s and after that, cheaper quarto and octavo editions were produced. An estimated number of 25,000 copies (of all editions) was produced before 1789.

It was less profitable for the contributors, not all of whom were even paid for their articles. There were hundreds of contributors (of the 71,818 articles), some of whom were very well known, some obscure, and some who have still not been identified. They came from diverse backgrounds. Some were professional men of letters such as Diderot, d'Alembert and Voltaire: there were *abbés*, medical men, civil servants, manufacturers, army officers (many of them noble), members of the nobility and lawyers. All in all, the contributors were 'a cross-section of the professional and upper classes of France in the period 1745–65' (Lough, 1971, p.56).

It is more difficult to identify the subscribers, mainly because of incomplete records. The subscription lists have not survived. Certainly subscribers had to be fairly well off, as the price was so high. Some of them did not live long enough to receive the complete set of volumes. What is known comes from sources which do not give a comprehensive picture. There is, for example, the information produced in a law suit brought by a disgruntled subscriber, Luneau de Boisjarmain, against the publishers. The publishers claimed that three-quarters of the subscriptions were taken out by booksellers in the provinces and abroad. They estimated that about half of the subscribers were outside France, which is perhaps surprising in itself. In a famous study Daniel Mornet analysed the catalogues of 500 private libraries existing in 1750–80 and found 82 with copies of the *Encyclopédie*. The owners' backgrounds were similar to those of the contributors', that is '... reasonably prosperous people drawn from the middle and upper ranks of pre-revolutionary society' (Proust, 1962, p.60).

Many contributors and subscribers belonged to the 'establishment'. The *Encyclopédie* did create a stir by its controversial and didactic articles, but the bulk of it was a genuine encyclopedia, giving detailed and up-to-date information on a very wide range of subjects. The volumes satisfied a real demand for knowledge, on subjects as far apart as chemistry and cookery.

The eleven volumes of plates were one of the most important elements in the *Encyclopédie's* systematic display of information. Probably the plates caused more work and trouble for Diderot as editor than anything else in the work (see his reference to this in his *Salon of 1765* in *Texts*, II). They took nearly a quarter of a century to produce – there were in the end 2,885 in the eleven volumes, and producing them, according to Voltaire, provided work for over a thousand papermakers, printers, binders and engravers. But it had been agreed from the first that the plates were going to be essential in giving technical and scientific information. And so they are (see Fig. 3). They are beautifully produced and show in detail such things as agricultural methods, scientific and medical apparatus, manufacturing processes, surgery, anatomy and much else. Indeed, some of them provide the only detailed record we have about some practical activities in eighteenth-century France. You will see something of the plates, and get a feel of the whole impressive sequence of the volumes, in TV1 'The *Encyclopédie*'.

Figure 3
Bookbinding. (From Diderot, 1771)

It is clear that the *Encyclopédie* was known to a much wider public than that of the actual subscribers to the first edition both in France and abroad. The growing demand for it is shown by the number of cheaper editions which followed the expensive first edition. The press at the time played a large part in spreading knowledge about it, as did the critical discussions published in hostile journals, which quoted extensively from *Encyclopédie* articles. Grimm, one of the *philosophes* and a close friend of Diderot, regularly compiled a sort of cultural newsletter, the *Correspondance Littéraire*, which gave detailed information to a very select clientèle of royal and noble subscribers abroad. Catherine the Great was one of these. In March 1767, she wrote to a correspondent:

> Enough of the *Encyclopédie*! I cannot put that book aside! It is an inexhaustible source of excellent things, though there are some major inaccuracies here and there. But that is hardly surprising, for the authors have encountered every kind of opposition and unpleasantness; and they have certainly shown great courage and an invincible desire to serve and instruct those who persecuted them and yelled at them: *'No enlightenment! – we do not wish to learn anything'*. (*Texts*, I, p.69)

5   The text

From an encyclopedia which runs to 28 volumes, comprising nearly 72,000 articles and nearly 3,000 plates, it is plain that we can present you with only a handful of entries. In our selection, we have tried to represent both the major writers and the major themes of the work.

Figure 4
The folio edition of the
Encyclopédie. *(Photo*
courtesy of the Curators of the
Bodleian Library)

We have also tried to establish a pattern of exercises which will help you develop skill in analysing eighteenth-century texts. In turn, each of twenty or so extracts from the *Encyclopédie* will be introduced. You will then be given a couple of questions to ask of the extracts themselves, which are printed in *Texts*, I. Your job will be to read them in the light of these questions. Some of the entries are straightforward, some are baffling, many are amusing: in each case you should be able to bring back information, from the extract itself, which bears plainly on the questions we have posed. When you have worked on a particular section of the text, you should come back to the 'discussion' in this study. Resist the temptation to flit directly from 'exercise' to 'discussion'. The heart of the course is the series of texts, and by the end of your first fortnight of study, if you've addressed the *Encyclopédie* extracts systematically, you'll have grasped, in outline, the character of the Enlightenment. Equally, you will have become more fluent in the use of *direct textual evidence* to support your analyses.

We open with a group of entries which explore the conception of the *Encyclopédie* itself, and the role of the *philosophe*. Then we move on to a set of entries which discuss issues in Government and Society, and which show something of the *philosophes'* concerns for liberty and justice. Our third section, on Morality and Religion, exhibits the *philosophes* at their iconoclastic best. Our fourth section, which is coupled closely with TV1, and which introduces some of the superb plates, will open up to you the *philosophes'* enthusiasm for science, medicine and technology. The final, fifth section, on music, will be referred to when you reach the study on Haydn.

5.1   *The purpose of encyclopedias and the role of the* philosophes

We begin with three articles from the *Encyclopédie* which give the views of some *philosophes* about the work itself and their own role.

5.1.1   *Encyclopedia* by Diderot

Denis Diderot (1713–84) was the most profoundly original mind among the *philosophes.* He was a provincial, born in Langres, where his father was a master cutler, went to a Jesuit school and even thought of becoming a priest. He went to Paris to study law, but instead of completing his legal studies, as his father wished, he lived as a hack writer mainly by translating. When he proposed to marry Anne-Toinette Champion, a poor but respectable girl, his father objected and had him imprisoned in a monastery: Diderot escaped and married secretly, but the marriage was not a success, as the two had very little in common, except that they were both devoted to their daughter. Diderot was in trouble as soon as he began to publish his own works; *Pensées Philosophiques* (*Philosophical Thoughts*) (1746), which was condemned to be burned, and *Les Bijoux Indiscrets* (*Jewels of Indiscretion*) (1748), a pornographic novel. 'He is a young man who plays the wit and prides himself on his impiety; very dangerous; speaks of the holy mysteries with scorn', wrote a police inspector of the book trade in a report (Darnton, 1984, pp.181–2). The trouble became serious when he was arrested and imprisoned in the Château de Vincennes, for having issued his *Lettre sur les Aveugles* (*Letter on the Blind*); serious for the *Encyclopédie* too, as Diderot was already the editor (see Fig. 5).

After that, he was careful about what he published, and some of his greatest works did not appear until after his death. He devoted himself to the *Encyclopédie* for the next fifteen years, working heroically, refusing to be deterred even when it was banned, yet finding time for other writing too, of many kinds: speculative essays, plays, essays on his theory of the drama, short stories and novels – picaresque like *Jacques le Fataliste* (*Jacques the Fatalist,* dramatic like *La Religieuse* (*The Nun*), an indictment of forced vocations and convent life (the film of this was banned in France in 1966) – and perhaps his greatest work *Le Neveu de Rameau* (*Rameau's Nephew*). He wrote plans for the reform of education in Russia for Catherine the Great; and as you will see, he became a brilliant art critic. Later in the course, you'll be looking at his reviews of art exhibitions. Diderot's 5,000 articles for the *Encyclopédie* show the breadth of his knowledge and interests: they have a very personal stamp, showing him sometimes soberly describing an industrial process, sometimes poking fun at authority, and sometimes making wild imaginative leaps.

Diderot's article *Encyclopedia* appeared in Volume 5 in 1755. It is, according to A.M. Wilson (1972), Diderot's biographer, 'probably the most important single article in the whole seventeen volumes.'

The article is very long, too long to give you all of it, but we think that the extracts will give you a good idea of its flavour and some of its main points.

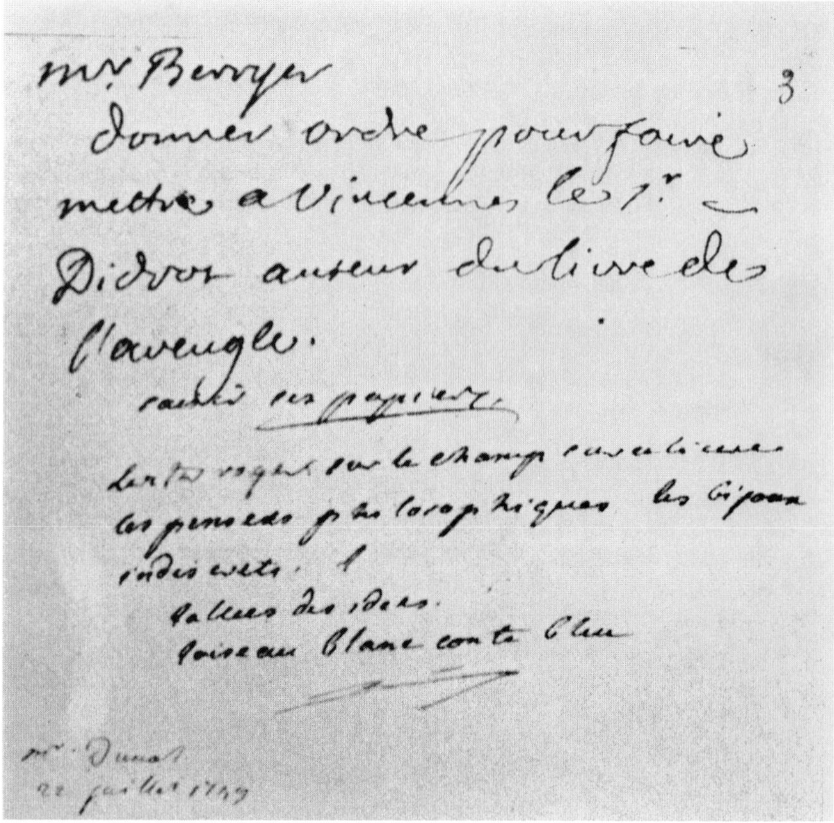
mr Berryer
donner ordre pour faire
mettre a Vincennes le Sr —
Didrot auteur du livre des
l'aveugle.
saisir ses papiers

Figure 5
Order for the arrest of Diderot. The order reads: "This is a warrant for the arrest and imprisonment in Vincennes of Diderot, author of the book on the blind, and for the seizure of his papers." (Bibliothèque Nationale, Paris)

EXERCISE Would you read the article now, with these questions in mind:

1. What were the aims of the *Encyclopédie*?
2. What methods of working were essential to the success of the work?
3. Why were the principal faculties of man taken as the general headings under which subjects were classified?
4. What does Diderot mean by a 'philosophical century'?

DISCUSSION

1. The main aim is to present existing knowledge in a structured way, and to hand it on, because knowledge will make people 'more virtuous and happier'. Like d'Alembert, Diderot was convinced that reason and knowledge would lead to progress. Knowledge, therefore, is for posterity just as much as for the present.
2. Team work is essential. The work needs both men of letters, who understand the links between fields of knowledge and also artisans who are specialists in technology and science. The work also needs the dedication of people who can work together for the general interest of humanity. Moreover, Diderot implies, they should be free to do the work in their own way.

3   'Why not give man the same place in our work as he has in the universe?' Diderot asks. Could anything '... give us a better starting point for the infinite number of connecting links ...' The *Encyclopédie* is collecting together human knowledge. There is no consideration here of a view of the universe as a divine creation.

4   A 'philosophical century'. Diderot means an age in which '... philosophy ... is beginning to shake off the yoke of authority and tradition and to follow the laws of reason ...' (remember that Diderot is using the term 'philosophy' to signify a very broad range of interests). Diderot is convinced that 'everything must be brought to light, boldly, without exceptions and unsparingly.' He is giving a pretty clear idea of what he understands by 'enlightenment'.

5.1.2   *Philosophe* (Anonymous)

There is some mystery about the origins of this article. It is unsigned and has often been attributed to Diderot, but it has been found that it is a modified version of an essay originally published in 1743 in a collection of essays (*Nouvelles Libertés de Penser*, Amsterdam 1743). It was Diderot's literary executor, Naigeon, who first attributed the article to Dumarsais, who had indeed written some 150 articles for the *Encyclopédie*, on grammar, which was his particular field, and on education and other subjects. Opinions differ still on the authorship of the article, but it remains a very clear statement of the main characteristics of an ideal *philosophe*.

EXERCISE   Would you read the article now and, as you read, pick out statements which describe the main characteristics that a *philosophe* ought to exhibit.

DISCUSSION   Here are some examples – though you may well choose different statements which seem to you to make a better summing-up.

A *philosophe* uses *reason* – '... the *philosophe*, even in his passions, acts only after reflecting.'

His approach is *empirical* – 'The *philosophe* bases his principles on an infinite number of particular observations.'

He makes a *balanced assessment* of *truth*, not committing himself beyond the evidence – '... he limits himself to being able to distinguish it [truth] when he can perceive it ... he can suspend judgement.'

He is committed to *society* – '... reason requires him to know, study and work to acquire sociable qualities.'

He *enjoys life* – 'He is a civilized man who wants to give pleasure and make himself useful.'

He has *humanity* – 'He is ... concerned with the bad or good fortunes of his neighbour.'

He has *integrity* – 'The more reason you find in a man the more integrity you find'. 'He is filled with the idea of the good of civil society.'

He is against unbalanced emotion – '... where fanaticism and superstition dominate, passion and anger dominate.'

Or you might choose the summing-up in the last paragraph: 'The true *philosophe* then is a civilized man who acts in all things according to reason, and who combines a spirit of reflection with social manners and qualities'.

5.1.3 *Men of Letters* by Voltaire
Voltaire wrote few entries for the *Encyclopédie*, but in *Men of Letters* he set out his own ideal of the *philosophe*.

EXERCISE   Read the article, and consider the following questions:

1   What characterizes the 'man of letters'?

2   What might lie behind Voltaire's final paragraph?

DISCUSSION   1   He is 'more independent of mind than other men'. He ranges widely, venturing into all sorts of topics: he can 'pass from the thorns of mathematics to the flowers of poetry'. He is the scourge of ignorance and superstition: 'astrologers' predictions, the divinings of magicians, all types of witchcraft, false prodigies, false marvels, and superstitious customs', all yield to his rational criticism.

2   Maybe the difficulties that beset the *philosophes* when they tried to publish their views lie behind Voltaire's wry comment that the happiest men of letters publish nothing at all. Overall, is there perhaps a tension in the article between, on one hand, his insistence that men of letters are socially useful and that they fare well under the endowments of Louis XIV, and, on the other hand, his hint, in this final paragraph that the profession of author sometimes brings humiliation?

5.2 *Government and society*
We have grouped together here a number of entries which discuss human nature, civil rights and politics.

5.2.1 *Political Authority* by Diderot
Diderot was writing at a time when the French, Catholic monarch exercised more or less unlimited power. Recall also that the *philosophes* tended to look enviously across the Channel, where the checks and balances of the British Constitution supposedly guaranteed the liberty of the subject and the limitation of royal prerogative.

EXERCISE   Read Diderot's entry now, seeking answers to the following questions. Make sure that your answers are well-supported by textual evidence.

1   What, according to Diderot, are the ultimate sources of acceptable political authority – what permits one person legitimately to rule over another?

2   Given that Diderot was likely to be critical of the French monarchy, how does he frame his criticisms? Do you detect glimmers of *irony* here? Is Diderot saying one thing and meaning another?

DISCUSSION   1   'Nature', according to Diderot, does not sanction the exercise of political power. He looks higher, to God, for legitimation. God permits, 'for the common good and the maintenance of society, that men establish among themselves an order of subordination'. But Diderot's chief point is that this order is only provisional. It is the result of a *contract* between the governed and the governor, a contract that can be revoked if ever the governor, or 'prince' fails to keep his side of the bargain: 'it is not the state that belongs to the prince, it is the prince who belongs to the state'. The people's 'consent' is crucial; it is only when this has been given that a tyrant ceases to be a tyrant and becomes a legitimate 'prince'.

2   There is nothing openly defiant or insubordinate in Diderot's article. That much is plain. This is no rousing democratic manifesto. But maybe Diderot is ridiculing both the legitimacy and the pomp of the French court. He says, for example, that 'only slaves whose minds are as limited as their hearts are debased' could possibly believe that the French royal family rules by some other principle than the nation's consent. Reasonable people, Diderot argues, know that 'if by the greatest of misfortunes the entire reigning family happened to die out, including the most remote descendants; then the sceptre and the crown would return to the nation.' Now, does Diderot *really* believe that the extinction of the French royal family would be a great misfortune? It's a matter of tone. It's far too early in the course to expect you to be able confidently to judge exactly what is intended by writers who habitually drop into an ironic mode of writing. But you should be detecting the possibility that something's going on beneath the surface of the text. In this case, what's going on is a skilful, subtle advocacy of a theory of political authority which denies the 'divine right of kings' and which asserts an alternative, contract theory of government. And the style of advocacy is such that a censor who was charged with the job of defending his divinely-ordained monarch from subversive criticism, could find no plainly insubordinate passages.

You may have found yourself frustrated by this exercise. There is nothing worse than failing to see a joke. In order to share a joke – to see when a writer has his tongue in his cheek – you need a familiarity with the writer's culture. And during these early weeks of the course you will still be finding your feet. It is not at all easy to read texts, in search of ironic sub-texts that run beneath them, but by the end of the course, it will be second nature to you, and you will regularly be savouring the many different forms of irony used by writers during the period.

The huge, multi-volume *Encyclopédie* was, in an obvious sense, as different as it could possibly be from an inflammatory political pamphlet, yet, in entries like this, you can see something of the critical spirit which, later, led both Revolutionaries and Monarchists to regard the *philosophes* as the fathers of the French Revolution.

5.2.2   *Natural Equality* by de Jaucourt

De Jaucourt (1704–80) came from a family of *noblesse d' épée*. He studied at Cambridge, Geneva and Leyden, in Holland, where he qualified as a doctor of medicine. He was one of the most prolific contributors to the *Encyclopédie*. In this entry, one of the fundamental principles of the *philosophes* – that 'human nature is the same in all men' – is enunciated.

EXERCISE   Read the article and find out what it is, according to de Jaucourt, that makes people equal.

DISCUSSION   It is *nature* – 'the constitution of human nature' – that makes people equal. This may sound somewhat commonplace, but the grounding in Nature of important concepts is an important feature of eighteenth-century discourse. You will learn much more about the many and various uses of the words 'Nature' and 'Natural' as the course develops. Here, what is important is to note that de Jaucourt holds that the moral and political principle of equality is underwritten by Nature – by the ways things are, or rather, *were*, before the 'state of nature' was modified by 'society'. Straight from the hand of Nature, each person is constituted to be 'born, grow, live and die in the same way'. This universal natural constitution, says de Jaucourt, makes people equal.

EXERCISE   What follows from this natural equality? How should material goods be distributed in society?

DISCUSSION   Everyone, no matter what their rank, deserves equally 'the duties of charity, of humanity, and of justice'. Notably, slavery is 'the violation of this principle.' But natural equality stops short of 'absolute' equality: the principle does not require that power and material wealth should be equally distributed.

EXERCISE   Does it look as if de Jaucourt is talking about humanity at large, or just males? Are women, in his view, naturally equal with men?

DISCUSSION   De Jaucourt does not say whether men and women are naturally equal. Is it possible to read the extract and interpret the word 'men' to signify 'men and women'? We can draw no conclusions. But the question needs to be opened. Light will be shed when you come to study the *Encyclopédie* entry on *Woman*.

De Jaucourt's entry is significant as a brief, ringing declaration of a liberal conception of equality, and its emergence in the France of the Old Régime is important. But we are still in the eighteenth, not the nineteenth century: it is inappropriate and anachronistic to expect programmes for political equality from the *philosophes*.

5.2.3   *The Slave Trade* by de Jaucourt

During the eighteenth century, the affluence of France and Britain, and especially the affluence of port cities like Bordeaux, Nantes, Bristol, Liverpool and Glasgow, depended heavily upon the slave trade which was integral to the economies of the West Indian and American colonies. The *philosophes* in France, and humanitarians like Dr Johnson in England, were stout in their opposition to slavery.

EXERCISE   Read the entry *The Slave Trade* from the *Encyclopédie*, and ponder the following question. Bring back textual support for your conclusions.

In discussions of slavery, moral and economic arguments were often entwined. Are they here? And if so, specify the relevant passages.

DISCUSSION   De Jaucourt is perfectly plain in declaring that slavery is a violation of 're-ligion, morality, natural laws, and all the rights of human nature'. (Note, incidentally, the use again here of 'nature' and 'natural law' as the grounds for a moral stance.) De Jaucourt delivers a comprehensive moral denunciation of slavery.

Yet he attends too, to the economic consequences of abolition, attempting to assure waverers that 'it is freedom, it is industry that are the real sources of abundance' – not slavery.

It is clear though, that if ever there is a clash between moral principle and economic imperative, moral principle should prevail.

5.2.4   *Woman (Natural Law)* by de Jaucourt, Desmahis *et al.*

The *Encyclopédie* entry on *Woman* is divided into several subsections written by different authors. *Woman (Anthropology)* discusses the role and image of women in past societies and emphasizes the ways in which they were associated with superstition and magic. *Woman (Jurisprudence)* looks at the legal status of women in the eighteenth century and in the past. *Women's Confinement* explores the medical aspects of childbirth, breast-feeding, post-natal infections and complications from haemorrhage, flatulence and afterpains to hysteria.

The sections we shall be looking at are *Woman (Natural Law)* by de Jaucourt and *Woman (Morality)* by Desmahis. These will provide insights into the way in which an enlightened encyclopedia comments on the legal and moral status of women in eighteenth-century France.

'Natural law' was a complex and commonly used concept in the eighteenth century. Its meaning was variable but it was almost always used to indicate a set of laws (or basis for justice) distinct from the actual, existing (i.e. positive or civil) laws of a country. It made an appeal to a higher authority (Nature, God or both) in order to set out the proper or equitable way of proceeding in particular human and civil affairs. Natural law, unlike the actual or existing laws of a particular country, was regarded as universal in that it applied to all men in all ages. Although it could be used to support a conservative cause, it was usually seen as a means of determining what is truly in accordance with the proper use of man's highest faculty, reason, and the only proper way of defining its dictates was through the widespread consultation of all rational beings. (Diderot's article *Natural Law*, in the *Encyclopédie*, expressed these views.) As we have already seen, in de Jaucourt's entry *The Slave Trade*, advocates of natural law approved only of those elements of civil or positive law which complied with the demands of natural law: de Jaucourt opposed 'the rights of humanity' to the 'civil laws of a gutter'. Natural law was closely allied with 'natural rights' and was used as a justification for questioning the justice of existing 'legal' practices such as the slave trade or, in the case of France the censorship laws and other autocratic practices. Thus, in the eighteenth century, natural law often carried strong reformist connotations.

The legal status of women in France varied between provinces and between classes. In general, however, the legal system prior to the Revolution (Old Law) recognized the jurisdiction of Church (canon) law on such church-related matters as marriage. Theological precedent dictated that a marriage should have only one head, i.e. the husband. Civil law upheld the view that the husband should be obeyed. A husband generally had total power over his wife's assets unless some of these were protected by a marriage contract. Such contracts thus assumed great importance among members of the nobility and bourgeoisie and might involve stipulations made by several members of the extended family. It was exceptionally rare for a woman to be named as head of the household. Furthermore, a woman's adultery could be punished by imprisonment for two years in a convent. If a family council declared her legally dead, she would then lose all rights to her fortune, which would be divided among her children or relatives and the convent. There were no such penalties for male adultery. Married women had no power in the matter of decisions affecting the education and marriage of their children (Rogers, 1984).

The limited scope for women in careers within the church, military and legal professions was viewed as a natural consequence of their physiological inferiority. A few, exceptional women gained positions and qualifications in the Academies. Women were regarded as unreliable witnesses in courts of law and their common, legal occupations included midwifery and the retailing of lingerie, grains and clothes.

EXERCISE   Read *Woman (Natural Law)* by de Jaucourt, and find evidence which bears on the following questions, supporting your answers with reference to specific parts of the text.

1   In what respects are natural and civil (or 'positive') laws on women contrasted?

2   Identify the techniques of persuasion used by de Jaucourt to urge support for a change of attitude towards women.

DISCUSSION 1 The article first takes for granted, it seems, that the 'authority of government' within a marriage must belong to one of the partners. 'Positive law in civilized nations' is immediately characterized as adopting a categorical stance on this: the male, 'assumed to possess greater strength of mind and body', must have this authority. The Codex Fridericianus is cited as a recent example of codified civil law which upholds this view. Furthermore, this document justifies its position 'according to nature itself'. Finally, this view is sanctioned by 'the Scriptures'.

The article goes on to question whether such a rigid view of the legal position of men and women within marriage 'comes from nature' or is part of natural law. Declaring the 'natural equality' of men (i.e. both sexes in this case) it presents a structured undermining of the assumptions made about the 'greater physical strength, wisdom etc.' of men and of the speedy leap in logic from 'fitness to command' to the 'right to do so'. As Scriptural authority on this matter relates to a context of crime (original sin and Eve) and punishment, it can be related only to 'positive law' and, implicitly, not to the dictates of natural law or to formulations of what is truly just.

The suggestion then made is that 'there is nothing to prevent particular conventions from changing civil law' as long as there is no offence against natural law. The latter is therefore given priority over civil law. Women who knowingly enter into a civil marriage contract ('what civil law dictates') must abide by its rules because they have given tacit consent, but those who, 'by virtue of natural law', choose a different set of rules, should be free to do so: the paths of the 'civil' and the 'natural' may diverge.

2 There is a judicious balance between, on the one hand, respect for God ('The Supreme Being') and the establishment ('the laws and customs of Europe') and, on the other, 'bold' statements about the need for reform. This balance urges a shift in attitudes without alienating the orthodox. De Jaucourt proceeds slowly with his arguments and, in politic manner, begins by giving prominence to the formal legal situation as it exists in France. He does not attack his country openly but stresses that its views are shared by 'all jurisconsults, ancient and modern'. The 'enemy's' claims are put forward with a reasonable objectivity which makes the reader more receptive to the objections which are then listed methodically.

There are other techniques of persuasion, such as the use of emotive vocabulary ('irrefutable to the humane') and of rhetorical questions ('… should she not enjoy …?'). The references to female monarchs further suggest a context in which the family unit might be regarded as a microcosm of a state, thus adding status and the force of 'legitimate' precedent to his reformist views.

This is not the only context in which you will meet 'Nature' and 'natural law' as the underwriters of enlightened reason and humanity (see the Rousseau study, *Studies,* II). The challenge to authority in the name of Nature, reason and humanity, made in this article, is a typical Enlightenment strategy.

5.2.5 *Woman (Morality)* by Desmahis

Joseph François Desmahis (1722–61) contributed only two articles to the *Encyclopédie*. Born in Sully-sur-Loire of a *famille de robe* (nobility of the robe) he was a poet and playwright. His first comedy, *L'Impertinent*, had a first run of 15 performances at the Comédie Française in 1750.

EXERCISE   Now read *Woman (Morality)* with the following questions in mind. Support your answers to these questions with reference to the text.

1   How do we know that this is a male-centred view of woman?

2   How do we know whether Desmahis felt sympathy or antipathy for women?

DISCUSSION   1   First, there are the obvious notes of despair. Women reduce a philosopher – assumed to be male – to 'a lover with dreams'. It is difficult (for men, presumably) to achieve a 'good likeness' or accurate understanding of women because they seek an enhanced, 'unfaithful rendering' of themselves. (Compare this view with Reynolds's, discussed in *Studies,* I.) They are described by the writer in impersonal terms ('this half of the human race') which underline their distance from him. There is a feeling that the male writer is constantly cheated, deceived and out-witted – 'the more observations one makes, the fewer conclusions one draws' – in his quest to understand women. Women are viewed as objects of art, along with 'painting, music': a lovable enigma. Would a *woman* describe and discuss other women in this way? Are women's judgements of one another, 'prejudiced by love or hate'?

2   In a sense, the opening scenario of despairing incomprehension can be said to reveal neither sympathy nor antipathy. With the introduction of words such as 'dissimulation', 'duplicity', 'vengeance', however, a negative impression of the moral potential of women is generated. If women are virtuous, it is implied that this is very much against the odds and therefore to be admired: 'How I admire virtuous women …'

I think it would be unfair to characterize this entry as totally antipathetic, however, despite the 'outsider' viewpoint. There is a suggestion that the 'colours' of women, which 'change with the light', are an object of beauty: their 'complex, ambivalent or variable character' is a sensitive mirror to the world around them. Women are influenced by their education ('has changed their natural disposition'), or by their 'physiological delicacy' or their environment (their vengeance is generated by 'weakness' or lack of power). Nature has endowed them with positive attributes: 'grace and beauty, subtlety and sentiment'. The final sentence implies a link between vice and lack of education: do you perceive any sympathy here?

At the end of the course you will see a similar conflict imaginatively explored from *within* a woman's mind, by a male writer, Laclos. You may not find it so easy to identify Laclos's viewpoint as male-centred. Rousseau, Wollstonecraft and Laclos, writers you will be meeting later, share, however, a concern to expose the effect of the mechanisms of society on human (including female) nature. Attempts to identify the mechanisms of society and to formulate the general laws governing human nature were common in Enlightenment thought. Voltaire and Fréron (a literary critic), criticized Desmahis' entry on *Woman*. Fréron described it as a dull, flat, 'gutter-press' contribution dealing with titillating facts. Is this true? It will be interesting to see whether Voltaire does a better job in his treatment of women in *Candide*, which you'll look at in Part C.

5.3 Morality and religion

It was the anti-clericalism of the *philosophes* which got them into most trouble with the authorities. Although few *philosophes* were out-and-out atheists, they had little patience with the Roman Catholic Church, and they were roused to fury when, in the name of orthodoxy, people were tortured. The most celebrated case of what the *philosophes* saw as cruel bigotry was 'the Calas Affair'.

In 1762, in Toulouse, the son of a Protestant committed suicide. The father, Jean Calas, reported the melancholy incident, but was accused of having murdered the boy. The allegation was that the father was determined, at all costs, to resist the boy's alleged inclination to become a Catholic. The father was found guilty and was executed by being 'broken on the wheel' – a loathsome instrument of execution, described in TV3 'Humanity and the Scaffold'. Voltaire was revolted by this piece of judicial murder and wrote to a colleague:

> Three judges protested against the decision; the father called on God as witness of his innocence as he died, summoned his judges to face God's judgement, and wept for his son while on the wheel. Two of his children are in my neighbourhood, filling the district with their cries: I am beside myself; I am concerned as a man, even a little as a *philosophe*. I want to know on which side this horrible fanaticism lies. (Voltaire to Fyot de la Marche, 25 March 1762, in Lentin, 1985, p.100)

Four years later, in 1766, a young nobleman, the Chevalier de La Barre, was tortured as part of his trial for blasphemy, and then executed. A copy of Voltaire's *Philosophical dictionary* was ordered to be burnt, alongside de la Barre's mutilated body.

As you will see, the *philosophes'* attacks on the Church appear witty, and even playful, but, as the fate of de La Barre indicates, to attack – or even to be thought to attack – the Church, was no laughing matter.

On matters of morality the *philosophes* were not libertines, but they denied that human life is a vale of tears (a view commonly held by some sections of the Catholic church, which emphasized the penalties to be paid for sin). They did not believe that austerity was a necessary condition of virtuous conduct, and they were generally opposed to the asceticism of monastic life. They believed that happiness is the natural human condition, and they took an unashamed delight in pleasure, including sexual pleasure. Above all, they argued that a purely secular moral code could be established. Rational argument and the promptings of Nature were all that were needed. Morality needed no religious or theological underpinning.

5.3.1   *Priests* by Baron d'Holbach

Baron Paul Heinrich Dietrich d'Holbach (1723–89) was born at Edesheim in a German state, the Palatinate. He came to Paris to study, and stayed, becoming a naturalized Frenchman. *Philosophes* often ran '*salons*' – informal, convivial meetings of intellectuals. D'Holbach's *salon* was the most radical and freethinking in the city. D'Holbach's own views were more atheist than deist. He wrote some hundreds of articles for the *Encyclopédie*, many on chemistry and mineralogy, but also on politics. In 1770 he published (under the pseudonym of Mirabaud) *The System of Nature*, which gave a largely materialist picture of the universe. Given his own views, d'Holbach must have enjoyed writing the article on priests; you will notice how the words 'fanaticism' and 'superstition' recur in it.

EXERCISE   Read the article now and consider how d'Holbach manages to express fierce hostility to priests without writing anything which could be censored as being offensive to the Church.

DISCUSSION   D'Holbach shows how priests gain power, what kind of power and how they abuse it. He chooses literary techniques often used by the Encyclopedists when they were writing on controversial subjects.

His first technique is to disguise his attack by not writing about priests in any specific religion, time or place. He argues that they acquired power by exploiting superstition, became 'a separate order', an élite who ' shared with the divinity the respect of all human beings … favourites of the gods … mediators between them and mortals.' With this power they could ' make profitable the high opinion which they cultivated.' The power was reinforced by cruelty to the people 'subjugated by fear and intoxicated by superstition.' They kept the majority in ignorance of '… the secrets of nature, mysteries unknown to the average man.' And finally they achieved temporal power – ' fanaticism and superstition held a knife suspended over the heads of monarchs.'

Only then does d'Holbach refer to ' priests of paganism' and mention Egyptians, Druids and Mexicans. Yet a reader, at least a sympathetic, perceptive or else suspicious reader, could see that a lot of what he says could well apply to the Catholic Church in France. Indeed he does then point out that in the medieval, Dark Ages of Christian times, priests had challenged the power of the monarch – no doubt a point not lost on those who felt that the Church still had much too much temporal power.

The other technique which d'Holbach uses is that of irony. Look at the last two sentences. Does he mean what he says, or does he invite us to suppose that he means the exact opposite? There is an obvious use of exaggeration here: 'countries enlightened by …' alerts us to the possibility that he is being ironic.

5.3.2   *Adore* by Diderot

EXERCISE   This is a short, pithy, entry.

1   Imagine you are an official censor, employed to protect the eighteenth-century French Catholic Church from criticism. Can you find passages here that ought to be suppressed?

2   What does the entry reveal about Diderot's view of the common people?

DISCUSSION   1   Diderot taunts the orthodox by daring to compare – albeit in the guise of studious etymology – the adoration of God with the adoration of a mistress. And he pursues this comparison of the sacred and the profane systematically. Further, he declares, seemingly piously, that 'the manner in which we *adore* the true God should never part company with reason, because God is the author of Reason.' This is hard to object to, ponders the imaginary censor, but what's happened to *faith* – shouldn't it be mentioned somewhere?

2   It seems to be a lofty, patronising attitude. Or could it be that Diderot was being ironic? What are we to make of 'the common people do not know what it is to *honour* one another; that is a feeling reserved for their superiors'? Was it intended that the reader should be shocked into acknowledging that the common people indeed do know what it is to honour one another, or is Diderot merely giving an offhand expression of what he takes to be a perfectly uncontentious view of the lower orders? Given the general tone of the *philosophes*' writing, it's probably wiser always to assume that irony is in play.

There is a further point that can usefully be drawn from this entry. It concerns the distinction between the deist belief in God, and the fully Christian belief in the Revelation of God's purposes through the life of Christ, history, scripture, miracles and Church tradition. Diderot is keen to exhibit God as 'the author of Reason': Diderot wants believers to disentangle themselves from such irrational practices as saint worship, and to rest content with no more than a formal, civilized respect for a remote, rational God.

5.3.3   *Agnus Scythicus* by Diderot

Although this entry declares itself to relate to botany and natural history, it has a quite different purpose. *Agnus Scythicus* translates as 'Scythian lamb' (Scythia was an ancient province north of the Black Sea.) The entry, then, is nominally an earnest account of a plant, described by a number of earlier botanists, which has many of the characteristics of an animal. Diderot soberly recounts the descriptions of this plant and then, without a hitch, moves into quite different territory – territory upon which the religiously orthodox might be made to feel very uneasy. To appreciate the impact of this otherwise puzzling article, you need to know, first, that *Agnus Scythicus* would instantly have evoked in readers the term for Christ, the Lamb of God, in Latin, *Agnus Dei*, and secondly, that the entry on *Agnus Dei* directly preceded the entry on *Agnus Scythicus*, thus further prompting a comparison.

EXERCISE   Read the entry and tease out its implications for Christian belief, being careful always to support your discussion with textual evidence. This is a difficult exercise, for what Diderot *doesn't* say is as important as what he does say, and if you are not familiar – as Diderot's readers certainly would have been – with the Bible's account of miracles, Diderot's strategy will not be obvious. But it's a richly ironic and witty piece, so have a go.

DISCUSSION   Having worked through early accounts of the plant, Diderot comes to the conclusion that 'all the wonder of the Scythian Lamb is reduced to nothing, or at least to very little'. He then seizes the chance to set up general criteria for assessing the likely truth of improbable historical events. He suggests that the less probable an event, the more numerous and reliable must be the witnesses to it, if we are to believe that the event indeed happened. Now, what has this to do with Christianity, about which Diderot says nothing? Here we have a particularly subtle form of irony in which the author's intention is conveyed by the *absence* of things that he might have been expected to say. The implication of Diderot's studious account is this. Christianity could be said to be, to a large extent, dependent on the truth of a set of highly improbable historical events – events like the dead being raised, water's being turned into wine, the sky's turning dark at the crucifixion, the Resurrection itself. Now, if the testimony to these events turned out to be as unreliable as the testimony concerning the Scythian Lamb, then the wonder of Christianity, along with the wonder of the improbable plant, would be reduced to nothing.

Of course Diderot does not say that the testimony to the miracles upon which many people founded their belief in Christianity would indeed turn out to be unreliable. He points out, for example that if witnesses to an improbable event 'imperilled their lives to maintain their depositions, [as early Christians did] we must agree that their testimony would acquire great strength'. But the point and force of Diderot's argument is to expose miracles to the sort of rational scepticism that had despatched *Agnus Scythicus* to the realms of fable.

There is a remarkable similarity between Diderot's criteria for establishing the probability of miracles and those elaborated both by the Scottish philosopher David Hume, whose work you will be studying later in the course, and by the English historian, Gibbon, whose *Decline and fall of the Roman Empire* you will also be studying. Along with the *philosophes*, with whom they associated when they visited Paris, Hume and Gibbon took a sceptical view of miracles. To venture a very general point, it is the overlap in outlook, together with evidence of actual friendships, between intellectuals from different countries, that permits us to speak of a *European* Enlightenment.

5.3.4 *Consecrated Bread* by Diderot

Here is another example of Diderot's irony. As with *Agnus Scythicus*, much of the irony depends on what Diderot does *not* say. In this case, he completely, and surely deliberately, neglects to mention what it is that makes consecrated bread special to Catholics. Diderot treats it as if it is just plain bread, or a fancy version of it. But according to the Catholic doctrine of transubstantiation, as the priest consecrates the bread – the 'host' – it is turned into the body of Christ. Diderot, therefore, is probing to the very heart of orthodox Christian belief. But, as you'll see, he manages to withdraw his ironist's scalpel without leaving clumsy, obviously heretical, marks behind him.

EXERCISE You should, by now, be getting a feel for how writers like Diderot operate, and we can leave you to find out how this particular piece works. But the piece perhaps reveals a side of Diderot that we haven't seen before. Towards the end of the entry he seems to make some sort of profession of his own religious beliefs. What do you make of it? Is Diderot being ironic, or is he speaking from the heart?

DISCUSSION Irony is in play throughout his attack on elaborate and expensive Church ritual, but the final paragraph reads, to me, like an utterance of an undogmatic Christian humanitarianism. My guess is that Diderot, who was a mercurial character, believed it at least at the moment he wrote it. Perhaps, though, it is just the humanitarianism he approves of: the Christianity might be detached from his praise.

5.3.5 *Enjoyment* by Diderot

EXERCISE Bearing in mind earlier comments that the *philosophes* sought a secular moral code which placed more emphasis on happiness in this world than in the next, would you now read *Enjoyment* and try to answer the following questions, supporting your answers with specific references to the text:

1 How does Diderot legitimize sexual pleasure?

2 How does he characterize spontaneous sexual impulses on the one hand, and notions of selective courtship and fidelity on the other?

DISCUSSION 1 Having defined enjoyment in general as 'to experience, to feel the advantages of possession', Diderot goes on to suggest that those who possess (a magnificent palace, for example) without enjoyment are missing the opportunity for self-fulfilment. Sex is not named or discussed explicitly (note the circumlocution 'pleasure that perpetuates the chain of living beings') but this was in accordance with the demands of eighteenth-century polite taste. An impassioned invocation to the sensitive, human reader ('you who have a soul') is used to trigger an emotive rhetorical question ending 'that bound you together'. The accumulation and repetition of short clauses beginning with 'who' has a breathless quality which helps to emphasize the excitement and urgency of sexual pleasure. The entire human life cycle is encompassed in this one sentence, with sexual attraction as its main, dramatic impetus. (The article has been described as an 'erotic poem in prose' (see Spitzer (1948).) Adjectives with negative connotations are then used to pour scorn on all those who do not share in such experiences ('crude', 'insensitive') – an eighteenth-century reader might establish links with monasticism and asceticism? Anyone who dares to disagree with Diderot is classed as 'perverse' – an attempt to generate a complicity with the reader which is typical of the writings of the *philosophes*. Finally, Nature (or Natural Law?) is personified and lends her august authority to Diderot's cause by hurling an impressive series of rhetorical questions ('why do you blush ...') at the reader who might still dare to refute the legitimacy of sexual pleasure. A sharp command ('Be quiet ...') bludgeons the reader into consent. Sexual pleasure brings 'ecstasies' *and* has social utility as it creates life and propagates the species, and besides, your children 'protect you in old age.'

2   The sentence beginning 'A vague and brooding restlessness' poetically evokes the beginnings of sexual awareness. A series of rapid clauses ('the heart palpitates; the limbs tremble ...') then expresses the act of sexual arousal, culminating in the climax of the sex act itself: 'nature is satisfied'. To Diderot, this is a universal process, common to all men in all times and places ('This is the way ... cave'). He goes on to suggest, however, that human relationships inevitably become more complex and transcend the level of brute instinct. The act of courtship, in which a man's imagination is 'inflamed' by a woman's modest conduct, adds the 'delicate illusions', 'divine enthusiasm' and 'indiscreet oaths' characteristic of a more sophisticated form of love. Enjoyment or sexual pleasure can bring happiness of a less complex nature before the lovers fuse their souls into one. The final sentence adds a slight note of foreboding: innocent love may eventually be corrupted by 'mistrust or remorse'.

This article, which is hardly a piece of objective information, gives an idea of the stylistic and polemical scope of the *Encyclopédie*. Its inclusion in the work was controversial. In a slightly more moderate form, it was originally destined for the dedicatory epistle to a play written by Diderot, *The father of a family*. The lady to whom it was addressed, however, the Princess of Nassau-Sarrebruck, was reportedly embarrassed by the epistle, which was censored, in any case, by Malesherbes, the state censor. The decision to discuss physical pleasure in such an unapologetic manner in the *Encyclopédie* was therefore a bold one. (There were at least 70 articles on sex.)

Enjoyment was also a challenge to established Church morality. By suggesting that sex should be valued for its pleasures, it undermined the theological view (see *Woman (Natural Law)*) that women must submit to the advances of their husbands as a punishment for the sins of Eve. Genesis (2: 24) declared that bodily union had a sacramental and symbolic value. The birth of children was regarded by the Church as a sign of the resurrection to come. The Catholic church saw the pains of childbirth as an act of penitence. *Enjoyment* sweeps aside such considerations in order to view sexual pleasure in a secular and utilitarian manner: a form of disrespect for authority and championship of a 'healthier' approach to human nature which was typical of the *philosophes*. Many of the latter turned a sceptical eye on the institution of marriage and many (including Diderot) had mistresses. Fidelity in love was not a major requirement for the eighteenth century in general or for the enlightened in particular, and Voltaire attacks this ideal in *Candide*, through the relationship of Candide and Cunégonde. Compare, later, *Les Liaisons Dangereuses (Dangerous Acquaintances)*, and also the study of Catherine the Great, which you will read next in this volume.

5.3.6 *Epicureanism* by Diderot

EXERCISE   Read *Epicureanism* and answer the following questions, with specific references to the text.

1   How would you describe Diderot's treatment of the classics (or 'the Ancients') in this article?

2   How does Diderot-Epicurus treat the relationship between religion and morality?

3   What method is advocated for the pursuit of truth?

DISCUSSION 1   Diderot instantly sets himself up as a champion of the 'slandered' philosophy of Epicureanism and rebels against the stereotypical view that Epicurus was a debauched atheist, a charge often levelled at the *philosophes* themselves. He then brings Epicurus to life by placing him in an idyllic situation, under the 'shade of some trees', and allowing him to speak with the voice of an impassioned orator. If we were to judge the accuracy of Diderot's representation of Epicurus's views we would have to engage in a detailed comparison of the works of the two writers and there is not room for this here. Note, however, that Diderot allows himself to 'cast between his [i.e. Epicurus's] principles some of the most direct consequences that can be deduced from them' – perhaps to emphasize and develop those points with which he sympathizes, in an opportunist manner? When 'Epicurus' does express his ideas he does so forcefully: he asks rhetorical questions (e.g. 'Is there anything more ancient than truth?' and utters invocations ('O pleasure!') which coerce any reader of sense into agreement. As you'll see in a footnote of the text, however, there were those among Diderot's contemporaries who suspected that 'Epicurus' was really Diderot in disguise.

Although Epicurus receives Diderot's whole-hearted support, it is made clear that a judicious, critical approach is essential in the use and interpretation of classical sources. The Stoics are berated for giving the Epicureans 'the worst kind of reputation' and the way in which the 'dialectic' of Socrates has been abused and exaggerated is criticized. The enlightened must approach all sources, even those which, like the Ancients, were revered, with a critical spirit ('scorn all authorities'). The use of classical sources is raised, later in the course, in the studies of Hume, Reynolds, Adam, Lind and Diderot's *Salon of 1765*. For Johnson's refutation of Epicureanism, see the Johnson study, also in this volume.

2   This article reinforces the view that religion and morality have, in reality, very little connection. The section *About morality* speaks of 'guiding the tendencies of nature' and stresses the secular, human dimensions of virtue and happiness. Pleasures of all kinds ('of the body' and in 'the soul') are seen as desirable, but all excess (e.g. 'the lusts of passion') is to be avoided as it may upset the delicate balance provided by nature. Natural law is equated with 'public usefulness' and achieves an elevated status as a guide to human conduct (including the power to punish or deter would-be criminals, who would be condemned by 'common consent'). There is no room or need for religion in such a moral code: the virtues of 'friendship' and 'decency' can survive without its assistance as they require only a just appreciation of the workings of human nature and of the common consent of all rational beings. Religion can, in fact, act as a distraction from human virtue, as gods are not men. It can encourage people to 'bow down before any piece of carved stone' without enquiring into the nature or merits of the gods. ('Do you believe in God?' can become a more important question than 'what is God?') As a materialist Epicurus cannot depict the gods in a spiritual, non-material realm: they are rational hedonists seeking the means of maximum self-gratification. However, they are composed of physical matter of a more perfect kind ('a superior combination of atoms') than that which constitutes human beings. Models of 'perfection and happiness', the gods inhabit 'the empty spaces between adjoining worlds'. Their very perfection and inactivity render them irrelevant to human affairs. They are unaffected by the plight of human beings on earth and cannot therefore be seen as a source of authority: their existence is 'sterile'. The eighteenth-century reader-in-the-know could not fail to make a connection with the God and morality of Christianity.

3   Philosophy, in its quest for the truth, must have a practical bias: it should concern itself with 'what we must avoid and do'. It should be firmly grounded in a 'study of nature' and in evidence gained by the senses, upon which man's reason may then set to work in an inductive manner (i.e. working from observable facts to broader conclusions). 'Preconceptions' or creative conjecture should be used in conjunction with empirical (i.e. derived from observation or experience) evidence. This was a methodology advocated by many *philosophes*. (See below, the discussion of d'Alembert's article *Experimental*, and, later, compare Lind and Rousseau on methods of enquiry.)

Epicurus, like Socrates, was often regarded as a hero by the enlightened thinkers of the eighteenth century. They identified with the way in which he had been persecuted as a bearer of light and knowledge. Like them, he was a materialist who legitimized pleasure on this earth: this pleasure consisted of a moderate balance of physical pleasure ('appetites and requirements of nature') and virtue.

5.3.7   *Pyrrhonian Philosophy* by Diderot

The last ten volumes of the *Encyclopédie* were all published together in 1765. It was not until 1764 that Diderot discovered that the publisher Le Breton had himself made cuts in a number of articles, after Diderot had received the corrected proofs. Diderot was outraged. He wrote to Le Breton: 'I wept with rage in your presence. I wept with grief at home, in front of your associate M. Briasson, in front of my wife, my child, my servant – I shall bear this wound until I die.'

This article, as Diderot wrote it, never appeared in any edition of the *Encyclopédie.* What follows is a version of the article which includes most of the passages which Le Breton cut out. Why did he do it? Writers and publishers could be prosecuted for producing works 'contrary to Religion, the State or morals', so he could have had good reasons for being apprehensive.

EXERCISE   Read the article now and consider what you find in the censored passages (which are printed in italics) that Le Breton might have thought dangerous to print.

DISCUSSION   Diderot attacks the Catholic Church for its persecution of Protestants; '… the most sacred laws of humanity were violated and religion was dishonoured.' He claims that the *philosophes* are 'the only truly tolerant men.' Bayle was writing against some proofs on the existence of God' and Diderot praises his sincerity in doing so, while remaining uncommitted about whether or not Bayle was in error.

His demand for tolerance and his attack on censorship of writing on religious and political matters is put in pretty strong terms for the time: 'Wherever civil power supports religion or seeks its support the progress of reason must necessarily be retarded.'

These, and statements like them, could easily qualify as being contrary to religion and the state. And morals?

'Ignorance and falsehood are the causes of man's troubles … the principles of natural morality … are clear, evident and true.' Is there an implication here that the Church should not dictate morality? He has just said that 'questions of metaphysics' are 'obscure and false' and this, though indirectly, seems to reinforce the implication.

Le Breton may have thought his cuts were justified, but in making them he was betraying the very principles which Diderot so vigorously defends in the article.

EXERCISE   Relying only on what is said in this extract, consider what Diderot thought was good about the sceptical approach?

DISCUSSION   'Doubt is the first step along the path of knowledge and truth; he who doubts nothing discovers nothing'.

EXERCISE   After his discussion of Bayle, Diderot gives some more of his own ideas on sceptics. What are the main points which he makes about scepticism here?

DISCUSSION   Sceptics may have different motives, but '... there are some who have sincerely doubted because in most questions they saw only reasons for uncertainty.' The main reason for this is the limitations of human knowledge, '... there is nothing of which man can have perfect, absolute, complete knowledge ...' You are bound, he says, to reach a point when you simply do not know and have to accept this.

Diderot has no use for anyone who will not accept the self-evident facts and values which are needed in order to make some kind of sense of the way we live. So he draws a distinction between the scepticism which is not only valuable but essential (the necessary preliminary step towards knowledge) on the one hand, and 'frivolous' scepticism on the other. The latter is an insincere pretence (the sceptic in question 'does not hold' the opinions he expresses, does not have the doubts he professes.) This important distinction between different forms scepticism may take comes up again at the beginning of Hume's *Dialogues Concerning Natural Religion*, which you will meet later in the course.

5.4   Science and technology

As you have seen, the writers of the *Encyclopédie* tended to be destructively critical when they were writing about religion. Destructiveness and antagonism, however, were only one side of the *philosophes'* programme. A much more positive, even jubilant and celebratory side to their work appears when we turn to their writings on science, medicine and technology. In a sense, a belief in progress, through the humane application of science, *was* the religion of the *philosophes*. If this religion had a god at all, it was the remote, rational god of the deists: a god whose first and last act of creation was to have set in motion the colossal, intricate machine of the universe, and to have ensured both its smooth working, and its intelligibility, by the imposition of inviolable laws of nature. Such laws – like the law of gravity, for example – were to be discovered by the rational scientist. For the *philosophes*, therefore, the heroes of civilisation have been, not the Christian saints, but the scientists, and a heroic lineage was established, stretching from Aristotle, in fourth century BC Greece, to Sir Isaac Newton, who had died in 1727, having formulated the fundamental laws which hold the universe together.

The *philosophes'* respect was not reserved exclusively for high-level, theoretical science. They were determined to exalt the humble craftsman and to exhibit the benefits of technology as well. The writers of the *Encyclopédie* toured workshops, and consulted artisans, in order to guarantee that the many entries on trades and crafts would be both up-to-date and accurate.

This section of your work on the text is tied in closely with TV1 'The *Encyclopédie*'. In the programme you will see something of the eleven volumes of plates, many of them illustrating industrial, medical and agricultural technology. The programme also moves out, beyond the pages of the volumes to look at a particular surgical technique illustrated in the plates.

5.4.1 *Craft* by Diderot

The *philosophes*' interest in technology comes through clearly in the *Encyclopédie* article on *Craft*. It was written by Diderot – himself the son of a master cutler.

EXERCISE   Earlier, you looked at texts, in which a rather élitist or disdainful attitude towards the common people was revealed. Read *Craft* and consider the attitude that is revealed there.

DISCUSSION   There is surely no irony in play here. Diderot is perfectly earnest in his respect for the craftsman – though of course this does not commit him to an equivalent respect for the great mass of the labouring poor.

5.4.2 *Experimental* by d'Alembert

Jean d'Alembert (1717–83) was one of the founding fathers of the *Encyclopédie*. He was the illegitimate child of a woman of fashion and an artillery officer, and had been abandoned, as a baby, on the steps of a church. He was brought up by, and remained deeply attached to, the wife of a glazier. From these unpromising beginnings, and helped by a small annuity left by his father, he gained an education and went on to become one of the foremost mathematicians and physicists of his age, obtaining a post at the Academy of Sciences in 1741.

When the *Encyclopédie* was launched, he was appointed as associate director, and he made a number of important contributions to the work. The most important is the *Preliminary Discourse*, which was published in 1751, along with the Volume 1 of the *Encyclopédie* itself. In this long discourse, d'Alembert shapes history in order to present the *philosophes* in an impressive light: he constructs a lineage for them which goes back, through the scientific giants of all the ages, to Greece. (Such was the enduring, vital legacy of the Classics that it was second nature for intellectuals in the eighteenth century to trace their roots back to Athens).

D'Alembert contributed the *Encyclopédie* entry on *Experimental* and, since it offers a neat summary of the lengthier *Preliminary Discourse*, it is this text that we'll be examining. It is a longer extract than most of those you have been working on, but it should present no problems. Since he is establishing his and the *philosophes*' intellectual ancestry, he needs to introduce quite a few names. You may be unfamiliar with the philosophers and scientists in this roll-call, but all you need to grasp is a sense of the scientific tradition within which d'Alembert wants to locate himself and his colleagues.

D'Alembert's chief concern in *Experimental* is scientific methodology. He was trying to establish sound principles for the conduct of scientific research: he wanted to find reliable procedures which would stop science going up blind alleys. He was well aware that the history of science and medicine is littered with fanciful and mistaken theories, and with projects that came to nothing. One of his aims was to write history in a way which threw into prominence the men who, in his view, had been using sound method and who had therefore passed the bright torch of science and learning from the Greeks to the men of the eighteenth-century scientific academies.

D'Alembert's discussion of scientific method attempts to resolve a dilemma which besets enquiry. When opening up a new area of scientific enquiry, should researchers start by piling up a series of observations relating to the subject of the enquiry, or should they start by devising a theory, and then go out to see if observations will fit in with it? The dilemma is about the roles of theory, hypothesis, observation, experiment and scientific law. Which should come first?

Common sense dictates that *observation* is the heart of the matter: if you want to contribute to astronomy, surely you start by sweeping the skies with a telescope, observing and recording the paths of the heavenly bodies? If you want to contribute to botany, surely you stride off to the fields and hedgerows collecting wild flowers? If you want to contribute to chemistry, surely you conduct experiments in boiling up substances together to see what happens? The problem quickly arises, however, that piles of random observations and experimental results do not automatically turn themselves into neat scientific laws: they tend to remain frustratingly as piles of observations and experiments.

Perhaps it's better to start the other way round: perhaps it's better for scientists to start by sitting still, thinking and calculating, trying to come up with theories, or better still, predictions, which they can then go out and test. Only later should they go out and observe whether the orbit of a particular planet follows the prediction, whether the flower germinates in the way predicted, whether a gas is given off when certain substances are boiled.

This is a simplified version of the debate you will encounter in d'Alembert's article, but should be sufficient to give you a lead into it. If his concerns seem abstract, remember that what the *philosophes* were trying to do was to hammer out rules for the systematic explanation of the universe. And they believed that it was upon a scientific understanding of the world, rather than upon authority or faith, that progress depended.

This is not to say that every theory produced by eighteenth century scientists was as solid and as enduring as d'Alembert's programme promises. Much of the *content* of eighteenth century science has now been discarded, but the concern with *method* endures.

EXERCISE   This is lengthy and difficult article, so take your time, and go over it several times.

1   D'Alembert makes distinctions between 'observation', 'experiment', 'conjecture' and 'calculation'. How does he define each of them, and what is the relationship between them?

2   What does he say about the role of scientific academies and universities in fostering science?

DISCUSSION 1 'Observations' are, obviously enough, the results of simply looking at the world. To make observations, you do not interfere with nature, or manipulate it in any way: you just look. As d'Alembert puts it, it is a matter of 'accurately seeing and cataloguing all the different kinds of phenomena which the spectacle of Nature presents to us'. So far so good. But science is much more than this. Nature won't casually yield up all her secrets to the observer. If you want to formulate scientific laws, you have to 'interrogate' Nature. To establish the laws which describe the vertical fall of heavy bodies, or the weight of air, for example, you must devise *experiments*, procedures whereby you control and regulate natural operations in order to get at the principles behind the appearances. The relationship between observation and experiment is close. One smoothly graduates into the other. Experiments extend 'the field of observation ... experiment and observation can in one way be looked upon as the consequence and complement of each other.'

What is the place of 'conjecture', though? Does it have a role at all? D'Alembert says that it can be a snare: 'the idle pleasure of meditation and even of conjecture ensnares great spirits'. It's easy to sit and dream up scientific theories, but quite another to go out and establish them by observation and experiment. But although d'Alembert wants to banish fanciful dreaming, he is 'far from wanting to banish that spirit of conjecture, which, at one and the same time timid and enlightened, sometimes leads to discoveries'.

Lastly, what of 'calculation'? Newton is credited and praised by d'Alembert for 'uniting experiment with calculation'. (D'Alembert tends to use 'geometry' and 'calculation' interchangeably: 'mathematics' might be the general modern equivalent.) However, there is always a danger of seizing on just one element in the scientific enterprise and giving it a disproportionate emphasis, and d'Alembert later gives examples of what he sees as 'the abuse of calculation'. When 'geometrical figures have been put into treatises on the soul', then the scientific sense of proportion has been lost.

Overall, d'Alembert rules no procedures out of order. His aim is to celebrate those scientists who, like Newton, have managed to keep a creative tension between the quartet of 'conjecture' (imagining what might be the case), 'calculation' (abstract mathematical reasoning), 'observation' (noting the ordinary operations of nature) and 'experiment' (intervening and manipulating nature in order to observe phenomena not ordinarily visible). Furthermore, he has firm views on what sort of institutions are likely to serve the cause of science. This brings us to the second point.

2 D'Alembert notes that the Royal Society in England, and the Academy del Cimento in Italy, had fostered science. But his chief purpose here is to lobby for the expansion of French university scientific education. He is naturally delighted that 'the King has just established a chair of experimental physics in the University of Paris.' The *philosophes* were not always critical of authority. It is interesting too that he lobbies for the endowment of three further chairs, one in moral philosophy, one in history, and one in public law. This is not a philanthropic gesture on behalf of jobless academics in Arts

and Law Faculties. The divisions within learning that we now take for granted are comparatively recent. In d'Alembert's view, history and moral philosophy are disciplines which need to be animated by the scientific spirit no less than disciplines like physics and chemistry.

We can turn now from these considerations of the foundations of science and look at a single application of scientific reasoning.

5.4.3   *Inoculation* by Tronchin

Eighteenth-century medicine was more a matter of expectation than of achievement. It is by no means clear whether a visit to the doctor's enhanced or diminished a sick person's chances of recovery. Historians of medicine have yet to conclude a debate on the question of whether eighteenth-century hospitals were 'gateways to death', or to recovery.

But the century did see at least one material advance – or perhaps *potential* advance (for it met with a deal of public and official resistance). By the end of the century – in 1798 – Edward Jenner published, in England, *An enquiry into the causes and effects of variolae vaccine,* and thereby established a means of preventing smallpox, a scourge which killed or disfigured thousands. Louis XV died of it in 1774. The research Jenner had done was based firmly on folk practices common among dairymen and women, who inoculated themselves with the milder cowpox as a way of establishing a resistance to the more serious smallpox. But for decades before Jenner published, forms of inoculation had been practised throughout, and beyond Europe. The English intellectual and traveller Lady Mary Wortley Montague, for example, had her three-year old son successfully inoculated in Turkey, in 1718. And Catherine the Great of Russia and Frederick the Great of Prussia were enthusiasts for the practice. (The way in which inoculation was performed during the eighteenth century is demonstrated in TV1 'The *Encyclopédie*').

Tronchin (1709–81), like de Jaucourt, studied medicine at Leyden, the premier medical school in Europe. He settled in Paris in 1756 as the doctor of the Duke of Orleans, whose children he inoculated. He wrote just this single entry for the *Encyclopédie,* on a topic about which he was a national authority.

EXERCISE   To inoculate somebody is to perform a sort of experiment. In his article, Tronchin is trying to establish a way of judging the success of experiments in inoculation. Read the entry and find Tronchin's recommendations.

DISCUSSION   Tronchin goes for a purely statistical test. Take two hundred patients, and inoculate one hundred of them. Leave the other hundred as an uninoculated control group. Then watch the result. 'Compare the register of deaths on both sides and give the results to the people.' It's a good example of the rational, objective spirit of Enlightenment science.

You'll meet a closely similar approach when you come to Lind's *Treatise of the scurvy*, and you'll see more of the practice of inoculation in the study of Catherine the Great and Frederick the Great.

6 Conclusion

Your encounter with these entries from the *Encyclopédie* should have alerted you to many of the issues that run through the period, and through this course. First, you'll have picked up the metaphor of light and enlightenment: the *philosophes* saw themselves as bearers of a cool, rational, shadowless light, which would dispel ignorance and superstition. Secondly, it's plain that, although the *philosophes* regularly made approving references to a remote God, or to Nature, they regarded Christianity as a shadowy region of superstition, cruelty and the abuse of power. But thirdly, you may have been surprised by their relatively tender attitude to absolutist government and by their ambiguous relations with the French State. On one hand they mocked authority, and were locked up, from time to time, as a consequence. Yet, on the other hand, they came to occupy prominent places in the state's grand academies.

Fourthly, their enthusiasm for scientific, medical and technological progress comes through, in entry after entry, plate after plate. Fifthly, and perhaps paradoxically, this forward-looking frame of mind was coupled with a veneration for the Classics. The paradox can be resolved though, if we see the *philosophes* as reaching back, beyond the Christian Dark Ages to – as they saw it – a rational, scientific, civic pagan world, and finding there models for the building of a modern world.

Sixthly, in sifting through the layers of irony in these passages, we hope that you have begun to enjoy a characteristic mode of eighteenth-century discourse.

Finally, we hope that this study, together with TV1, has given you a sense of the *Encyclopédie* not simply as an intellectual undertaking, but also as a prodigious commercial venture. To handle the huge volumes is to realize that the abstract ideas of the Enlightenment were expressed concretely and practically.

7 References

Darnton, R. (1979) *The Business of Enlightenment*, Belknap Press of Harvard University Press, Cambridge, Mass.

Darnton, R. (1984) *The Great Cat Massacre*, Allen Lane, London, chap. 5, 'Philosophers trim the tree of knowledge', pp.191-213.'

D'Holbach, P. (1773) *La Politique Naturelle (Natural Politics)*.

Diderot, D. (ed.) (1755) *Encyclopédie*, vol.5, Paris.

Diderot, D. (ed.) (1771) *Encyclopédie*, Plates, vol.8, reprinted in C. Gillispie (ed.) (1959) *A Diderot Encyclopedia of Trades and Industry*, 2 vols, Dover, New York, vol.2, plate 382.

Lentin, A. (1985) (ed.) *Enlightened Absolutism (1760–1790). A Documentary Source Book*, Avero Eighteenth-century Publications, Newcastle-upon-Tyne.

Lough, L. (1971) *The Encyclopédie*, David McKay Co. Inc., New York.

Proust, J. (1962) *Diderot et L'Encyclopédie*, A. Colin, Paris.

Rogers, A. (1984) 'Women and the Law', in S. Spencer (ed.), *French Women in the Age of Enlightenment*, Indiana University Press, Bloomington.

Spitzer, L. (1948) *Linguistics and Literary History. Essays in Stylistics. 4: The Style of Diderot*, Princeton University Press, Princeton, New Jersey, pp.137–43.

8   Further reading

The *Encyclopédie* has never been translated as a whole into English, but the French text, with its magnificent plates, is to be found, in one or other of its several editions, in many large libraries. There are, however, English translations of individual articles (for example, Schwab, 1963), and a number of useful single-volume selections of entries.

Gendzier, S.J. (ed.) (1967) *The Encyclopaedia: Selections*, Harper Torchbooks, New York. (A good, compact selection.)

Gillispie, C.C.(ed.) (1959) *A Diderot pictorial encyclopedia of trades and industry*, 2 vols, Dover, New York. (An excellent selection of the plates.)

Hoyt, N. S. and Cassirer, T. (eds) (1965) *Encyclopedia: Selections*, Library of Liberal Arts, Bobbs-Merrill. (An excellent and extensive paperback selection in English translation, with notes and commentary.)

Lough, J. (ed.) (1954) *The Encyclopédie of Diderot and d'Alembert: Selected Articles*, Cambridge University Press, Cambridge. (This selection, in French, is shorter than Gendzier (1967).)

Schwab, R. N. (trans.) (1963) *(Discours Préliminaire) Preliminary Discourse to the Encyclopedia of Diderot*, Library of Liberal Arts, Bobbs-Merrill.

8.1   Studies on the Encyclopédie

Cranston, M. (1986) *Philosophers and Pamphleteers: Political Theorists of the Enlightenment*, Oxford University Press, Oxford. (Helpful chapters on Voltaire, Rousseau, Diderot and Holbach.)

Darnton, R. (1979) *The Business of Enlightenment*, Belknap Press of Harvard University Press, Cambridge, Mass. (A publishing history of the *Encyclopédie*.)

Lough, J. (1968) *Essays on the Encyclopédie of Diderot and d'Alembert*, Oxford University Press, Oxford. (A lengthy but well-organized book, covering many aspects of the *Encyclopédie*.)

Lough, J. (1971) *The Encyclopédie*, David McKay Co. Inc., New York.

8.2   Studies of Diderot

Diderot's main works, in French, are readily available in the Pléiade edition, Gallimard, Paris. Among studies of his life, and commentaries on and selections from his works, consult:

France, P. (1983) *Diderot*, Oxford University Press, Oxford. (A very good short study.)

Furbank, P.N. (1992) *Diderot: A Critical Biography*, Secker and Warburg, London.

Mason, J. H. (ed.) (1982) *The Irresistible Diderot*, Quartet Books, London. (This contains translated extracts with a commentary.)

Tancock, L. W. (trans. and ed.) (1966) Diderot's *Rameau's Nephew* and d'Alembert's *Dream*, Penguin Books Ltd, London.

Wilson, A. M. (1972) *Diderot*, Oxford University Press, Oxford. (A long but fascinating biography, which contains invaluable information about the whole French literary and social scene.)

8.3   Studies of d'Alembert

Grimsley, R. (1963) *Jean d'Alembert*, Clarendon Press, Oxford. (A general narrative of d'Alembert's life which includes some interesting material on his relationships with Voltaire, Rousseau, Diderot and other *philosophes*. A short account of d'Alembert's philosophy is also included.)

Frederick the Great, King of Prussia (1740–86) and Catherine the Great, Empress of Russia (1762–96)

Prepared for the Course Team by Antony Lentin

Contents

Frederick the Great and Catherine the Great (Study weeks 2–3)

Studies/Texts	Radio	TV	AC	Set books
Studies, I	R2	TV2	–	–
Texts, I	–	–	–	–

The object of this study is:

1   to introduce you, through primary sources, to Frederick and Catherine as they presented themselves to their contemporaries; and

2   to assist you to judge for yourself in what ways, and how far, their reputation for enlightenment was deserved.

The main primary sources appear in *Texts*, I, pp.41–92, and consist of extracts from letters and other documents. They also include two portraits, reproduced in the *Texts*, and other visual evidence shown in TV2, 'Frederick the Great and Sans Souci'. The Broadcast Notes include some further sources.

You have one week each to study Frederick and Catherine. In each case I suggest you quickly read the brief historical introduction and outline chronology for background (pp.53–4, 55–9, 75 for Frederick, and pp.75–8, 93–4 for Catherine) before plunging into the exercises and discussions. (For fuller understanding, consult some of the suggestions in 'Further reading'.) You should attempt to give independent answers to the questions in the 'exercises'. Supplementary questions appearing in the 'discussion' sections are there to provoke further thought, but formal, written answers, though highly desirable, are optional.

Acknowledgements

My thanks for comment and advice, to Professor Tim Blanning, Dr Colin Chant, Dr Simon Dixon, Professor Paul Dukes and Professor Isabel de Madariaga.

Frederick and Catherine

1 Introduction

Frederick II, King of Prussia 1740–86, and Catherine II, Empress of Russia 1762–96, were eminent contemporaries. Both were known as 'the Great'. They were regarded as two of the most charismatic as well as the most controversial rulers of the age. The philosopher Kant called the eighteenth century 'the age of enlightenment, the century of Frederick' (*What is Enlightenment?, Texts*, II). Another contemporary described Catherine as 'she who made one third of the eighteenth century her own epoch' (quoted in Alexander, 1989, p.330).

Figure 6
D. Therbusch: Frederick the Great. *(Musée de Versailles)*

Historical verdicts on them have fluctuated wildly and continue to do so. (See, for example, Born, 1986; Raeff, 1972; Dukes, 1990.) Their long-term significance is as rulers of two states – Prussia and Russia – which rose to the forefront of European affairs under their dynamic rule. Their military victories astounded and alarmed contemporaries. Frederick, both as diplomatist and as an inspired commander in the field, Catherine as a politician of spectacular ambition, made their influence felt across Europe and profoundly altered the balance of power.

But they were also known, perhaps best known, as the two rulers in Europe steeped in the thought of the Enlightenment and avowedly intent on ruling in accordance with the principles promoted by the *philosophes* in the *Encyclopédie* and elsewhere. It is primarily this aspect of their careers that you are invited to consider in this study. To the delight or indignation of observers, both monarchs enthusiastically espoused Enlightenment aims in their copious writings: Frederick, (who styled himself the *philosophe* of Sans Souci)[1] in such published works as his *Essay on the forms of government and on the duties of sovereigns* (1777); and Catherine (described by the historian G.P. Gooch as 'the only intellectual who has sat on the Russian throne' (Lentin, 1974, p.29)) in such documents as her celebrated manifesto of political principles, the *Nakaz* or *Instruction* to her Legislative Commission (1767). Based largely on Montesquieu and Beccaria, the *Nakaz* was banned in France as dangerously subversive and was hailed by Voltaire as 'the finest monument of the age' (Lentin, 1974, p.18).

Figure 7
S. Torelli: Catherine the Great. *(Russian State Museum, St Petersburg)*

Both rulers corresponded at length with d'Alembert, Voltaire and other contributors to the *Encyclopédie*. Both professed veneration for Voltaire as the embodiment of the Enlightenment. But during Voltaire's visit to Sans Souci (1750–3), Frederick and Voltaire got on each other's nerves; and Catherine, while profiting from Voltaire's promotion of her image in the West, evaded his pleas for an invitation to Russia – 'for God's sake, advise the old octogenarian to remain in Paris', she told Grimm[2] (Lentin, 1974, p.31). She did receive Diderot at St Petersburg but they did not see eye to eye on all her policies.

---

[1] Sans Souci ('free from care'): the park and miniature palace outside Potsdam which Frederick designed and used as his principal residence after 1747, and which features in TV2, 'Frederick the Great and Sans Souci'.

[2] Friedrich Melchior, Baron von Grimm (1723–1807). He contributed an article on music for the *Encyclopédie* and acted as Catherine's agent in the West for the purchase of books and paintings.

How far did Frederick and Catherine merit the acclaim of the *philosophes*? With his political authoritarianism, his ruthless militarisation of society, his retention of the existing governmental and social structure, did Frederick really deserve a reputation as an 'enlightened' ruler? And what of Catherine, whose reign witnessed the Pugachóv Rebellion (1773–4), the century's greatest social upheaval before the French Revolution? Serfdom in its crudest forms remained firmly entrenched under Catherine, whose outlook perceptibly hardened after the French Revolution. How far, moreover, did either Frederick or Catherine share the pacifist convictions of Voltaire, Rousseau and Kant, for whom war between Europeans was a supreme offence against humanity? Both rulers sent tens of thousands to their death in war for the sake of territorial expansion. And both extended their frontiers at the expense of Poland, whose territory they gradually gobbled up.

Not all the *philosophes* joined in the applause. Rousseau and Diderot detested Frederick, denouncing him as a tyrant and warmonger, even though Rousseau briefly enjoyed asylum in Prussia. Two enlightened Frenchwomen, the Duchesse de Choiseul and Mme du Deffand, dismissed Catherine as an ostentatious adventuress. 'She is all show', said Mme du Deffand. The duchess rebuked Voltaire for promoting Catherine's cause: 'he sullies his pen by praising that infamous woman' (Lentin, 1974, p.29).[3] Among modern historians, M.S. Anderson also takes a critical stance. He argues that Frederick's 'policies in practice were hardly affected at all by the new intellectual currents of the age', and agrees that 'vanity and *amour propre* played a greater role in her [Catherine's] policies than in those of any other ruler of the period' (Anderson, 1987, pp.191, 193). T.C.W. Blanning, on the other hand, reviewing the arguments on both sides, insists that 'the Enlightenment did have a discernible influence on Frederick's policies' (Blanning, 1990, p.265), and Roger Bartlett declares that 'Catherine II was clearly a representative of Enlightened Absolutism' (Bartlett, 1991, p.8).

How genuine, how significant and how effective (if at all) was their attachment to the Enlightenment? This question, in one aspect or another, forms the basis of this study. You are required to tackle it first and foremost by hearing Frederick and Catherine and their contemporaries speak for themselves in the comprehensive selection of documents (*Texts*, I, pp.41–92). As Frederick wrote (document 8): 'As for those ... who are in charge of government, I think one should hear them before condemning them'. You should make up your own mind, and draw such inferences as the evidence warrants, bearing in mind the kinds of evidence available and its reliability or lack of it: take careful note of the author, date, context and purpose of each document, and to whom it is addressed. You are expected to be active investigators in this enquiry. (If you have studied A102, the *Arts Foundation Course*, you may find its History section helpful in approaching the source material here.)

---

[3]   There was also the notoriety of her personal (but very public) life. An English biographer wrote in 1800 that Catherine 'contrived to blend the most daring ambition that ever distinguished the male character, with the grossest sensuality that ever dishonoured the vilest of her sex' (Henry Hunter, 1800, p.xix).

2   *Prussia in the age of Frederick the Great*

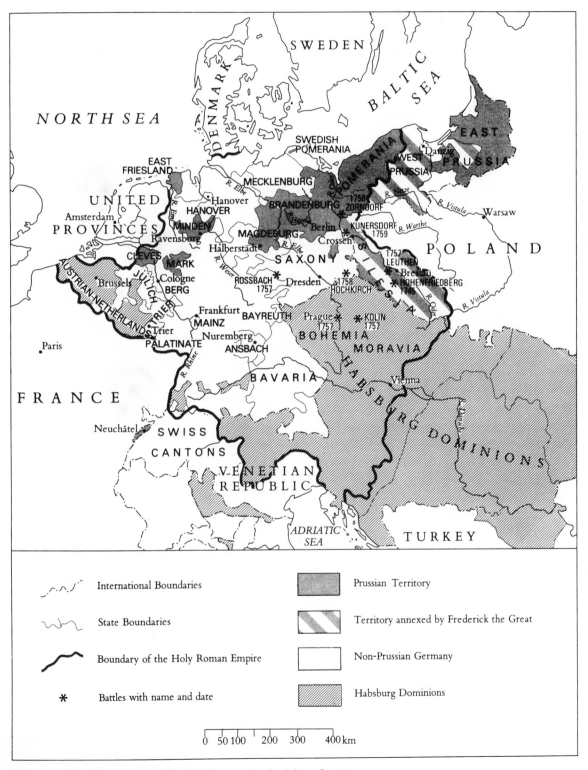

Map 1   *Germany in the eighteenth century.*

2.1 *'Germany' in the eighteenth century*

'Germany is undoubtedly a very fine country', wrote Hume in 1748, 'full of industrious honest people; and were it united, it would be the greatest power that ever was in the world.' (quoted in W.H. Bruford, 1965, p.1). In the eighteenth century, however, 'Germany' was little more than a geographical expression, covering a patchwork quilt of sovereign states, some 350 in number, ranging from large 'electorates',[4] like Hanover in the north or Bavaria in the south, to so-called Free Cities, like Frankfurt or Nuremberg, and tiny ecclesiastical principalities, like Mainz or Cologne, and other minute independent territories.

Nominally, all German states owed allegiance to the 'Holy Roman Emperor' of Germany, a title invariably now conferred by the 'electors' on the male head of the Austrian house of Habsburg. The Habsburgs – (Maria-Theresa ruled 1740–80, from 1765 as co-regent with her son Joseph II, who reigned 1780–90) – ruled over their own extensive polyglot dominions, most of them outside Germany. (In 1740 these dominions – which included Austria, Hungary, Bohemia, Silesia, Belgium and Milan – were five times the size of Prussia.) In the eighteenth century, the Holy Roman Empire of Germany was, as Voltaire quipped, 'neither holy, nor Roman nor an empire', but a somewhat sentimental and toothless anachronism, to which much pious lip-service was paid – though never by Frederick. The underlying reality was a complex mosaic of independent states with clashing political, economic and even religious interests: mainly Protestant in the north-east and south-west, mainly Catholic in the north-west and south-east, often mutual rivals, often under foreign influence, and pawns on the chessboard of European diplomacy. Until the end of the century there was little 'national' feeling in Germany: 'the fatherland' usually meant the individual's own state.

2.2 *The rise of Brandenburg-Prussia*

Brandenburg-Prussia was a relative upstart in Germany. It consisted of separate chunks of territory dispersed across the North German plain: on the Rhine – Cleves and the Mark; on the Weser – Minden and Ravensberg; on the Elbe and on the Oder – Magdeburg, Halberstadt, and the traditional heartland of Brandenburg, sandy, infertile and underpopulated; and East Prussia, which actually lay outside the Holy Roman Empire, cut off from Brandenburg by a wedge of Polish territory (West Prussia). Voltaire called Frederick 'king of the border-strips' *('roi des lisières')*, alluding to Prussia's long straggling frontier-lines, unprotected by natural geographical boundaries.

Prussia, though neutral, had nevertheless been invaded and devastated in the Thirty Years War (1618–48). Frederick-William, 'the Great Elector' (1640–88), was the founder of modern Prussia, building up a large army and reducing the independent powers of the nobility in his various lands in order to bring them under central control. His grandson, Frederick-William I (1713–40) known as 'the sergeant-king', reverted to these policies, increasing the military build-up, setting finances to rights, depriving the nobility of the last vestiges of political independence and

---

[4]   In the eighteenth century there were nine electorates: Brandenburg, Hanover, Bavaria, Cologne, Mainz, Trier, Saxony, the Palatinate, Bohemia.

creating a centralized bureaucracy controlled by himself. Frederick-William's son, born in 1712, was the future Frederick the Great.

Frederick-William was coarse, brutal, philistine and devout, Frederick was francophile, artistic and sceptical. Relations between father and son were appalling, culminating in Frederick's attempted flight and the execution of his friend and fellow-escaper. Frederick was forced by his father into a loveless marriage with an unfortunate woman from whom he in fact lived apart. He began his reign with a variety of acts pleasing to the *philosophes*: reopening the Berlin Academy of Sciences under the French scientist, Maupertuis, abolishing judicial torture and proclaiming freedom of religion and of the press.

2.3 Prussia under Frederick the Great

2.3.1 War and administration (see Map 2, p.59)

Despite an enormous build-up of troops under Frederick-William I, Prussia had played a passive role in German affairs as little more than a tool of Austria. Frederick immediately reversed this: beginning with his unprovoked grab for Austrian Silesia in 1740, Prussia took the initiative in Germany. Contemptuous of the Holy Roman Empire, Frederick saw the Habsburgs merely as obstacles to Prussian expansion. In 1740 and again in 1756 he sparked off general war between the European Great Powers (the War of the Austrian Succession (1740–8) and the Seven Years' War (1756–63) in order to seize, and then to keep, Silesia.

Frederick retained Prussia's basic administrative structure – a hierarchy of executive boards – as created by his father, but he exploited its potential to the full. His system was characterized as 'cabinet rule', not in the English sense of government by the king's ministers, but in quite the opposite sense of personal rule by the king himself from his 'cabinet', or study at Sans Souci. This was the nerve-centre of the administration, from where Frederick alone formulated policy, coordinated the work of the various branches of government, issued directives or 'cabinet orders' to his 'ministers' and supervised their implementation. Frederick acted with unremitting energy, detailed knowledge of the matters in hand, decisiveness, and a strict, military precision, undistracted by family or court life. He kept his bureaucracy under tight control, discouraging individual initiative and personally supervising its activities by annual tours of inspection. He took personal charge of finances. His 'ministers' were little more than accountants, responsible for individual areas of revenue and finance, but without knowledge, let alone control, of the overall budget. Prussia was the only major continental state to balance its budgets and produce a growing surplus. Her revenue in 1762 was as great as Russia's, with a *per capita* basis of taxation no greater than Austria's and much less than that of France.

2.3.2 War and society

Frederick's social policy was to maintain rigid class divisions. He regarded the nobility as the natural governing elite. He reserved the officer ranks in the army and administration for nobles far more strictly even than was the case in France. He consolidated and increased the privileges of the nobles. They were already exempt from taxation in most provinces. He jealously protected their monopoly of land ownership, subsidizing them with special State mortgages and outright gifts, and encouraged an entail system to preserve their estates intact.

The heaviest burdens in Prussia were borne by the peasants. The common soldiers were nearly all peasants (though up to a quarter after 1763 were recruited outside Prussia). They bore the bulk of direct taxation, which has been calculated as some forty per cent of the average peasant's income. They were obliged to provide billeting for officials and troops in transit and to undertake road works, canal construction etc, as well as to perform feudal services for the noble landowners. Degrees of peasant dependence on the landlord varied widely across Prussia. West of the Elbe, there were freehold or tenant farmers performing customary services, but legally free; east of the Elbe, conditions became progressively harsher. Freeholders were rare: there were 'protected' peasants, performing services, but free to leave the estate, and serfs, bound to the land and inheritable. In East Prussia, the most numerous class of peasants was legally free, employed as casual labourers by the local nobleman, who provided them with a cottage and a few acres, from which he could, however, dispossess them at will.

2.3.3   War, reconstruction and the economy

In the Seven Years' War, Prussia was repeatedly overrun from all sides: by Russians, Swedes, French, and Austrians. Berlin itself was twice occupied by the Russians. There was massive devastation. Frederick's principal internal achievement – what he called his 'peaceful conquest' – was the 'Reconstruction' *(rétablissement)*, Prussia's spectacular recovery and development in the two post-war decades. Land reclamation and resettlement had been traditional policy since the Great Elector, but Frederick encouraged them far more intensively than his predecessors. Particularly impressive was the reclamation of marshland along the rivers Oder, Warthe and Netze (including territory annexed from Poland in 1772). Altogether some 300,000 immigrants, mainly non-Prussian Germans, were resettled. By 1786 one in every five of the population was of immigrant origin. As a result of resettlement and (principally) annexations, Frederick doubled Prussia's population to some 5.5 million.

Frederick followed the mercantilist policy of his predecessors – the direction, subsidizing, regulating and coordinating of industry, agriculture, trade and finance by the State in the interests of the State. Prussia was an agrarian state, exporting, prior to 1763, a small amount of linen, grain and wool. While the mainstay of 'Reconstruction' remained agricultural development, Frederick put enormous effort into creating and fostering industries. These were financed and directed by the state, which was, through the army, the largest single consumer. The principal industries were the manufacture of silk, woollens, paper, glass, iron, steel and porcelain. As well as supplying army requirements, Prussian industry was required to produce an export surplus, and was protected from foreign competition by high tariff barriers. By the annexation of Silesia, Prussia acquired an area rich in mineral resources; and in addition to the trade routes of the Oder, with the annexation of West Prussia she also controlled the Vistula. Considerable effort went into improving communications, particularly by the construction of canals. By 1786, in production of manufactured goods, Prussia came next after the leaders, Britain, France and Holland.

The most important single institution in Prussia was the army. Its growth in the eighteenth century, and particularly under Frederick, was phenomenal: from 40,000 to 80,000 men under Frederick-William I, and from 150,000 in 1763 to 200,000 by 1786. Relative to its population, Prussia had an army nearly four times larger than France's. In 1786 Prussia came thirteenth in Europe in terms of population and tenth in terms of area; but in terms of the size of its army, no less than fourth. Even after the Seven Years' War, Frederick devoted 70% of his budget to the army. A contemporary observed that Prussia was 'not a country which has an army, but an army which has a country in which, as it were, it is just billeted' (quoted in Blanning, 1989, p.270).

Map 2
Administrative boundaries of Prussia in 1779.

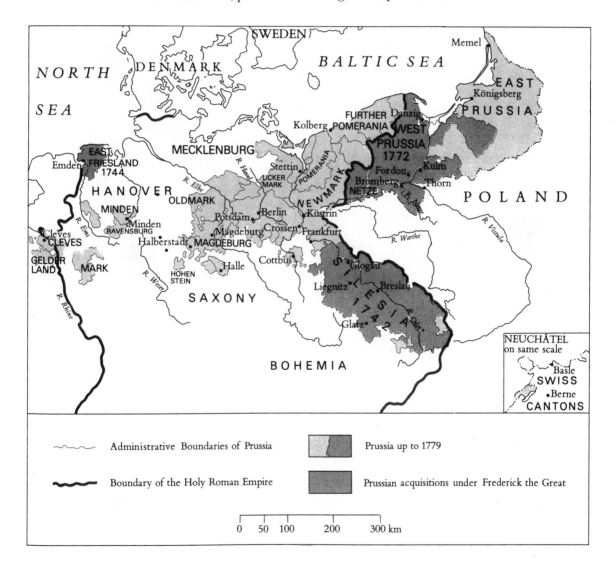

Administrative Boundaries of Prussia

Boundary of the Holy Roman Empire

Prussia up to 1779

Prussian acquisitions under Frederick the Great

0   50   100   200   300 km

2.4   Frederick and monarchy

2.4.1   Frederick – image, appearance and role

EXERCISE   What, briefly, is the overall impression of Frederick conveyed in the portrait by Franke (*Texts*, I, Fig. 1)?

DISCUSSION   The artist portrays him in the dress-uniform, sword and medal of a military commander. The face is highlighted, the expression dour. (What, by the way, do you make of Frederick's gesture with his hat?)

EXERCISE   1   What type of source is Fig. 1?
2   How reliable is it?

DISCUSSION   1   As a contemporary artefact (or, strictly speaking, a photographic reproduction of an artefact), it is a primary source.
2   Assuming that Frederick 'sat' for the original (i.e. that Franke painted from personal observation) we may make a further *prima facie* assumption that the portrait is a reasonable likeness. Although Frederick wished to be depicted formally, 'on parade', the portrait does not seem designed to flatter, and is therefore all the more likely to be a good likeness. Frederick was 52 in 1764 (compare *Study*, Fig. 6): Franke's portrait does not disguise the hollowed cheeks and deep wrinkles which marked Frederick after the Seven Years' War, nor his stern, penetrating gaze which we know about from other sources (e.g. portraits shown in TV2, 'Frederick the Great and Sans Souci', and document 1, where Moore also holds that 'his countenance, upon the whole, is agreeable'. (What do you understand from 'on the whole'?)

EXERCISE   Now read document 1 and compare it with the portrait.
1   What kind of source is Moore's account?
2   How reliable do you consider it?
3   Does Moore corroborate Franke?
4   Does Moore add to Franke?

DISCUSSION   1   Again, a primary source, this time a written one, recording the author's first-hand personal observations.
2   Moore's account seems a reliable description of Frederick's appearance and habits. Moore records his observations very shortly after the event (how do we know?) He is detailed and circumstantial. He is careful to separate verifiable fact from personal opinion (examples?).
3   Moore's account confirms Frederick's 'fine eyes', penetrating expression, military dress. The last paragraph confirms Frederick's military demeanour and habits: he was an unusually strict and active disciplinarian. (Can you suggest why? Compare your answer with Moore's in document 35, last paragraph).

4   Moore reveals Frederick's short stature, voice and liveliness in conversation, addiction to snuff, love of his dogs, and customary indif-
ference to dress (contrast *Texts,* I, Fig. 1).

EXERCISE   Define and consider critically document 2 as a piece of historical evidence.

DISCUSSION   Again, a primary source, this time by Frederick himself, written in a terse
and lucid style at a critical moment during the Seven Years War. He states
that if he is captured, this must in no way affect the pursuit of the war.
Does this suggest that Frederick was consciously striking a heroic pose?
Note the nature of the document, and its purpose: a secret cabinet-order
to a deputy minister in the Foreign Office, i.e. a top-level state document
not intended for publication. This suggests that Frederick meant to be
taken seriously and meant his order to be obeyed: note the reference to
'on pain of death'. (What does this suggest about his view of his own
importance as king, and the importance of the state?)

EXERCISE   What does document 3 indicate about Frederick's view of monarchy?

DISCUSSION   While scathing about individual monarchs and recognising the basic
inherent weakness of hereditary monarchy (what is it?), he accepts the
institution as such in defending it to Voltaire.

2.4.2   'The first servant of the State'

EXERCISE   In document 4 Frederick amplifies his views on monarchy.

1   How seriously should we take him?

2   What are his views?

DISCUSSION   1   We should take Frederick very seriously, given the nature of the
document.

2   Frederick takes a rational utilitarian view of government – 'a well-
run government must have a system as coherent as a system of philosophy'. The crucial importance of the king is immediately apparent. No mere figure-head, he is the hub and nerve-centre of the
entire administration, civil and military. Standing above faction and
private interests, he systematically directs, co-ordinates and super-
vises every aspect of government. The king thus has the key function in the running of the state, and a set of obligations which he is
paid to discharge, like a salaried employee. (But if the king is 'the
first servant of the State', from where does he derive his authority?)

EXERCISE   Answer the following questions with reference to the text.

    1   What, in Frederick's view, is the ultimate object of government?

    2   What is the place of foreign policy in Frederick's scheme?

    3   Does Frederick attach importance to other aspects of government?

DISCUSSION   1   'The consolidation of the State and the increase of its power'.

    2   Frederick asserts (a) that foreign policy is of prime importance (though he does not here explain why), (b) that it cannot be carried out in isolation from the other branches of government, and (c) that the ruler must conduct it 'in person'.

    3   He stresses, at the beginning, the need for social control (note his contrasting attitude to nobility and clergy and his disparaging reference to the latter), and at the end, the balancing of social interests, for the good of the state. The king also exists to do justice to individuals and to prevent exploitation. (We shall consider later the concern he expressed for the lower classes).

EXERCISE   Document 4 is from a confidential memorandum, written by Frederick in 1752 for the use of his heir. He is likely therefore to be in earnest, as we have seen. Document 5, by contrast, is from an essay published 25 years later. Do you detect significant differences of style, content or emphasis?

DISCUSSION   Style and content are similar in both. In document 5, Frederick repeats the expression 'the first servant of the State'. He again gives priority to law-enforcement, justice and defence, and reiterates the interdependence of all parts of the administration and the ruler's personal non-delegable responsibility for directing and co-ordinating them 'according to a fixed system'. On the evidence of documents 4 and 5, therefore, we may conclude (a) that Frederick's political philosophy remained consistent across his reign, and (b) that he wished to make it known to the reading public. He explicitly states in his title that monarchs have 'duties'. (To whom are they answerable for their discharge?)

    Frederick takes particular pains in his public essay to present a rational justification of his version of monarchy as 'superior' to other conventional 'forms of government' (*viz.* oligarchy, democracy and despotism). He provides it with an ideological underpinning drawn from contemporary political theory.

EXERCISE   What is that 'contemporary political theory'?

DISCUSSION   In the first sentence, Frederick relates monarchy to the 'social contract' theory of government (also discussed by Diderot in the article *Political Authority* in the *Encyclopédie, Texts,* I, p.12). This theory postulates an original implied agreement between ruler and people: 'the citizens only granted pre-eminence to one of their fellows in return for the services which they expected from him'. Since sovereignty derives ultimately from 'the citizens', the ruler must justify the authority vested in him by demonstrating his competence in government, 'as if at any moment he were accountable to his citizens for his stewardship'. (How literally did Frederick take this accountability?)

Frederick thus seeks to present his rule as inspired by modern enlightened principles. Traditionally, absolute monarchs like Louis XIV defended their authority in terms of God-given 'divine right', by virtue of which kings ruled absolutely, above the law, beyond control or criticism. Frederick-William I had stoutly asserted a divine-right claim, insisting that 'We are lord and master and can do what we like' (Blanning, 1990, p.277). Frederick scorned to justify his own rule in these terms. (We shall consider his religious views later.) He admits that the king is 'a man, like the least of his subjects'. He argues on utilitarian grounds that the sole justification of monarchy is to contribute to 'the greatest good of the state'.

2.4.3   Absolutism and 'republican virtue': reactions to classical antiquity

EXERCISE   Document 4 ends with a reference to 'a king of Epirus'. In document 5, Frederick compares monarchy with republican government, and in the last paragraph he refers to the Stoics and Marcus Aurelius. Read document 6, from another of Frederick's published essays.

1   Can you suggest why Frederick introduces classical allusions; and

2   Why, in particular, he refers to republicanism and Roman history in his discussion of his own government?

DISCUSSION   1   Classical examples and analogies (as you have have noted in the *Encyclopédie*) provided a common cultural frame of reference in the eighteenth century (a theme to be explored in Part B). Classical statuary at Sans Souci included a bust of Marcus Aurelius (TV2, 'Frederick the Great and Sans Souci').

2   Frederick's reference to republics also raises a question much canvassed at the time: is absolute monarchy compatible with civil liberty? The issue was of fundamental importance to political thinkers (e.g. Diderot, in article *Political Authority* in the *Encyclopédie*) and acquired particular topicality at the time of the American Revolution in the 1770s (see date of document). Traditionally, Prussia was reputed to be a 'despotism', characterized by arbitrary and tyrannical rule.

In document 28, Riesbeck confirmed that 'the Prussian government is generally considered the most despotic that exists', and Lessing complained (document 45) that Prussia was 'the most slavish country in Europe'. Frederick here defends his rule from the charge of 'despotism'. Drawing on examples from the Roman empire, which produced 'enlightened' rulers like Marcus Aurelius, or 'true citizens' and staunch patriots 'who put the interest and the advantage of the public good before their own', he argues that 'republican' freedom is compatible with absolutist rule, and that absolutism in Prussia is to be sharply distinguished from despotism, especially 'oriental despotism' of the Turkish variety – ('the Ottoman Empire') – a byword for tyranny and misrule (see Diderot's article *Political Authority*, last sentence, *Texts*, I, p.13.).

EXERCISE   How else does Frederick distinguish his rule from 'despotism' in document 6?

DISCUSSION   He claims that the distinction is to be found (a) in the supremacy of the rule of law – 'it is the laws alone that rule'; and (b) in the administrative, provincial, military, judicial and other institutions, which 'share a part of the sovereign authority', so that 'the ruler is not a despot ruling merely according to his own whim'. (We shall consider these claims later.)

2.5   Frederick and war

The *philosophes* denounced war between Europeans as the worst of contemporary evils and saw Frederick's Prussia as Europe's most militaristic state. Voltaire bitterly satirized Prussian militarism in *Candide* (1759). Frederick could not deny that his aggressive actions against other German states (his invasion of the Austrian province of Silesia in 1740 and of Saxony in 1756) twice ignited general war in Europe, nor that Prussia gained from his aggression (see Map 2).

He strenuously denied, however, being a war-monger by temperament.

2.5.1   The Anti-Machiavel

EXERCISE   Read document 7, from Frederick's *Anti-Machiavel*, a treatise on morality in international relations whose publication (with Voltaire's help) at the Hague in 1740 immediately preceded his unprovoked attack on Silesia. Both Voltaire and Rousseau came to see the *Anti-Machiavel* as a stratagem designed to deceive Europe and put Frederick's victims off their guard. Do you agree, on the basis of this extract?

DISCUSSION   Subterfuge can obviously not be ruled out: Frederick did after all go on to annex Silesia from the Habsburgs. But the *Anti-Machiavel* may genuinely express an aspect of his political philosophy already noted: his sense of responsibility for his people. In the last two sentences he again alludes to the social contract theory. But does he condemn war in general? Or only 'unjust wars'? (Is there a difference, in his view?) He asserts (in documents 4 and 5) that the welfare of the people is premised on an active foreign policy. (Or does he refer there only to defensive wars?)

2.5.2 Frederick a war-monger?

EXERCISE Read documents 8 and 9. How does Frederick defend himself from the charge of war-mongering in

1   his letter to the Electress Maria Antonia and

2   his letter to Voltaire?

DISCUSSION 1   He agrees with the Electress that justice in international affairs is no less desirable than in society. But in international affairs, he points out, justice and international law are 'nearly always crushed by the law of the heavy guns'. The ruler's duty is to his own country; it is to further its interests, to do which he must necessarily 'act in a different way from that which his natural inclination would dictate', i.e. by following policies that he might consider immoral as a private individual, but which are mandatory in a ruler, given his primary obligation under the 'social contract' 'to further ... the interests of the nation'. Frederick sees Prussia not as his own personal or dynastic property, to be disposed of at will, but as something akin to a trust property, to be managed selflessly on behalf of the citizens. (And enlarged?)

2   He claims that war is among the 'inevitable evils' of the human condition. Nothing can be done about it. 'If you have any cures, let us have them.'

EXERCISE Read document 10.

1   Assess its reliability as evidence of Frederick's intentions.

2   What is Frederick advocating?

3   Is Frederick an amoralist?

DISCUSSION 1   This is from a top-secret state document, Frederick's confidential memorandum to his heir on the policies to be followed in the event of his death. Here he deals with foreign policy, which, as we know, he regards as of prime importance. Written in 1752 after the War of the Austrian Succession (1740–8) and Frederick's annexation of Silesia, the advice is based on his own experience ('I have endeavoured to deal with my enemies on this basis'). We may therefore take it that Frederick is deadly serious.

2   Frederick stresses the need for the utmost tactical flexibility and guile in the conduct of foreign policy. Dissimulation, duplicity, trickery towards enemies and betrayal of allies are all permissible, indeed essential, ploys.

3   Maria-Theresa was one of many who regarded Frederick as a 'wicked man'; but note his contrast (also drawn in document 8) between the ruler as private and public man. Frederick sharply distinguishes 'your personal inclinations', which must be ignored,

from 'the strategy which your real interests dictate', i.e. interests as ruler of Prussia. The king must be guided by *raison d'état*, for the good of the state. Even so, his single-minded pursuit of *raison d'état* should be 'moderated and tempered by justice'. (What do you suppose he means by this?)

EXERCISE   Read document 11, from Frederick's advice to his heir in 1776. Has his advice changed since 1752?

DISCUSSION   Frederick's advice remains the same a quarter of a century later, despite his territorial gains in Poland meanwhile. He stresses the geopolitical vulnerability of Prussia, still surrounded and outnumbered by hostile neighbours (see Map 1). (Did Frederick's acquisitions make Prussia easier to defend?) Even with a disproportionately large standing army of around 200,000, if attacked on several fronts simultaneously, Prussia's forces are outnumbered. He again emphasizes the need for constant readiness for war, and for the king's active participation, numbering Prussia among the 'small states', in need of 'far greater strength and better frontiers'.

EXERCISE   Now read document 12, also an extract from Frederick's advice to his successor, 1776. What conclusions do you draw from it?

DISCUSSION   The document shows that even after the Silesian Wars, the Seven Years War and the first partition of Poland (see Map 1), Frederick's territorial ambitions remained unsatisfied. He casts his eyes on Saxony, regarding it as 'most appropriate' and indeed 'absolutely essential'. One method of acquiring it would be 'to conquer Bohemia and Moravia (Habsburg territories) and exchange them for Saxony'. Proof, surely, of undiminished aggression? (Or is it? *Why* does he regard the acquisition of Saxony as indispensable?)

EXERCISE   Read document 13, from a letter to d'Alembert. Summarize Frederick's argument.

DISCUSSION   Frederick contends (a) that modern standing armies are beneficial in their effects on civilian life: they provide employment and stimulate the circulation of money, (b) that modern wars are short and seasonal ('seven or eight annual campaigns'), and (c) that most civilians are unaffected by them. (But see footnote to document 21).

2.6   Frederick and society

2.6.1   Noble and peasant

EXERCISE   Read documents 14–16 as evidence of Frederick's social attitudes.

DISCUSSION   Frederick holds to a static and hierarchical view of society in his aristocratic predilections and active support of the nobles' monopoly of land
ownership. Note the dates and official character of documents 14 and 15
as evidence of his consistently high regard for the nobles as officers and
administrators. In his corresponding disdain for 'commoners', he pursued a 'reactionary' policy in comparison with his father. He takes it for
granted that the nobles are the only class qualified to officer his armies.
On the other hand, his exalted view of the aristocratic military caste (over
which he presided), though extreme, was not idiosyncratic. This is indicated by the independent testimony of von Riesbeck (admittedly, himself
a nobleman), who visited Prussia in the 1770s and also attributes 'the
excellence of the army' to 'the high birth of the officers'.

EXERCISE   Read documents 17–20. What do you see as the main elements in Frederick's policy towards the peasants?

DISCUSSION   Both in his published essay (document 17) and his confidential memorandum (document 18), he expresses sympathetic understanding of 'the
state of the poor' and a commitment to the principle of standardising
peasant conditions throughout Prussia. He regards serfdom as
'abominable' and 'repugnant to humanity' and agrees that 'no man was
born to be the slave of his fellow'. In both documents, however, he is
clear that to introduce root-and-branch reform would be 'to upset the
agricultural system' (document 17) and he expressly forbids social
mobility in his Code of Law (document 19). On the other hand, he pro-
tects land occupied by peasants from enclosure by the noble landowners
(a process taking place unhindered elsewhere in Germany). He reduces
the amount of compulsory labour, introduces emancipation of the serfs
on his own estates, and gives orders for the abolition of serfdom in
Pomerania (document 20, though this remained a dead letter). In the
last resort, despite the strong language of his cabinet-order (document
20), he was not prepared to provoke a confrontation with the nobility,
and though he mitigated peasant conditions, he undertook no radical
reform. (Was this a departure from the principles of the *Encyclopédie?* –
see de Jaucourt's article on *Natural Equality, Texts,* I, p.13.)

2.6.2   Post-war reconstruction

EXERCISE   On the evidence of the extracts from Frederick's letter to the Electress of
Saxony and from his letters to Voltaire (documents 21–3), make a short
list of Frederick's peacetime priorities.

SUGGESTED LIST

1   land reclamation, resettlement and other steps to increase population

2   exploitation of Prussia's natural resources

3   boosting agricultural and industrial output

4   introduction of modern techniques

(What weight do you give to the anti-war sentiments expressed in these letters?)

2.7   Frederick, law and justice

EXERCISE

In document 6, Frederick claimed that in Prussia 'it is the laws alone that rule'. What do Fig. 8[5] (below) and documents 24–7 indicate are the characteristics of the rule of law?

DISCUSSION

Figure 8
Title page of Frederick's Code,
1751. (By permission of the
British Library Board)

1   In all his declarations in this section, Frederick enlarges on his ideal of Prussia as a state in which 'the rights of man', specifically the 'protection of his person and property' (document 27), as laid down in the *Code of Laws* and *General Code*, are guaranteed.

2   All citizens are subject to the law, though not necessarily to the same law, since the rights of each individual 'derive from his birth (and) his class' (document 27). (And from the individual's sex?)

3   The rule of law demands a clear, concise and humane code of law. Frederick's *Code of Laws* is described as 'founded on Reason' (Fig. 8) and is characterized by logic, clarity and simplicity, and (document 26) moderate punishments.

4   The rule of law means that 'arbitrary force must never be applied in place of the law' (document 26). The law must be protected from interference by 'the powerful' (document 25), including the judges, and above all, the ruler himself (document 24). For the position where a dispute arises between king and subject, see document 27. (An instance of this, involving Frederick and a miller at Sans Souci, is described in TV2, 'Frederick the Great and Sans Souci'.)

---

[5]   Translation: 'Frederician Code, or Legal Code, for the states of his majesty the king of Prussia, founded on Reason and on the country's basic laws, in which the King has set out the Roman law in logical order, has removed the foreign laws, has eliminated the hair-splitting distinctions of Roman law, and has completely resolved the doubts and difficulties which that same law and its commentators had brought into the legal process, establishing in this way a clear and universal body of law.' Translated from the German by A.A.de C., the King's privy councillor, with a short account by M. Formay of the King's Plan for the Reform of Justice, 1751.

EXERCISE   How does Frederick see his own role as king in regard to the law?

DISCUSSION   In document 24, he states that 'the laws alone should rule and the monarch's duty is confined to protecting them'. The king's role is (a) supervisory: to check by personal inspections that justice is properly administered; (b) appellate: to receive petitions and hear complaints, and to review sentences.

2.7.1 The case of the miller Arnold

Riesbeck (document 28) argues that the rule of law did prevail under Frederick, asking 'what instances are there of the king's ever having allowed himself anything that bespoke arbitrary sentiments?' Frederick's critics' answer was: the case of the miller Arnold (document 29). His admirers, on the other hand, hailed Frederick's intervention in that case as a splendid instance of 'enlightened absolutism', overriding class prejudice and judicial bigotry. Who was right?

EXERCISE   Now read document 29. 'It is not at all proper for the monarch to interfere in the process of the law', Frederick wrote (document 24). Was his role in the case of the miller Arnold a denial of the rule of law by his own definition?

DISCUSSION   As the courts decided at the time (and confirmed, after Frederick's death), Arnold was a vexatious litigant and Frederick was wrong on the facts. His intervention was a violation of the rule of law. (Behrens, pp.111–15.)

    It is arguable, however, that in his capacity as the supreme source of justice in an absolute monarchy, Frederick was entitled under his own laws to review decisions of the courts – a prerogative he certainly exercised in criminal cases (documents 32 and 33). (What does the courts' persistence suggest about judicial independence in Prussia?)

2.7.2 Penal reform

It seems clear that in his attitude to the administration of criminal justice, Frederick was influenced by the Enlightenment. This influence shows itself in various ways in documents 30–2.

1   *Torture* was the conventional continental method of exacting evidence from the accused. In 1742 Frederick restricted its application to the most serious capital offences, and abolished it outright in 1754.

EXERCISE   Read document 30. How does Frederick justify the abolition of torture?

DISCUSSION   On both humanitarian grounds ('outrages which revolt humanity') and rational grounds. Torture is 'as cruel as it is useless'. As a means of discovering the truth, it is arbitrary and inefficient. (Frederick's policies were well in advance of the rest of Germany and of France. Beccaria's book *On Crimes and Punishments* (which you will be studying later in this part of the course) did not appear until 1764.)

2   *The presumption of innocence* (documents 30 and 31) 'it would be better to pardon twenty guilty men than to sacrifice one innocent one'.

3   *The death penalty*

EXERCISE   Read documents 31 and 32. Outline Frederick's attitude to the death penalty.

DISCUSSION   Frederick is familiar with Beccaria's arguments (which you will be introduced to later) against capital punishment. He is not himself a total abolitionist (what are his arguments against Beccaria?), but reserves the death penalty for the most serious offences (note his examples). Even then, he personally reviews all sentences (documents 25 and 33) and commutes the death-sentence whenever possible (on what grounds? – e.g. document 32).

4   *unmarried mothers and infanticide*

EXERCISE   Read documents 33 and 34.

1   Assess Frederick's treatment of unmarried mothers.

2   Why did he retain the death-penalty for infanticide?

DISCUSSION   1   Frederick shows a tolerant, sympathetic and practical view of unmarried mothers, deploring the stigma attaching to them and 'the unnatural prejudice that makes them do away with their children'. He puts a stop to their victimisation: 'these poor girls used to be forced to do public penance in church', and provides practical measures for the relief of mother and child. How far he was in advance of public opinion, even outside Prussia, is indicated by the Comte de Guibert's indignant reaction.

2   Frederick sanctioned capital punishment in proven cases of infanticide as a deterrent (see his justification of capital punishment for murder in document 31) and in order to protect the children. Were his motives humanitarian (most murders in Prussia were infanticides)? Or practical: as de Guibert puts it, 'to promote the propagation of the species in his territories'. (cf. document 21)

2.7.3 Military discipline

EXERCISE   Read document 35 . Describe Frederick's attitude to the rank-and-file as compared with his policies in civil and criminal justice.

DISCUSSION   His scrupulous concern for the rights of civilians seems to contrast sharply with his retention of the institutionalized brutality of military discipline (introduced by Frederick-William I and taken as a model elsewhere in Europe). Moore explains Frederick's reasons for adhering to the latter as: (a) to ensure the effectiveness of the Prussian army in the field and (b) to prevent desertion. (What do you make of Moore's argument that Frederick had no practical alternative? Compare Frederick's own comments on discipline in document 11.)

2.8   Frederick on religion

Frederick was admired by the French *philosophes* above all for his toleration of religious minorities. This contrasted sharply with the discrimination practised to a greater or lesser extent against Protestants in Catholic France and Austria (under Maria-Theresa) and, for that matter, against Catholics in Protestant Britain. However, religious toleration in Prussia predated the Enlightenment: it had been official policy since the Great Elector and Frederick-William I (see p.56), both in the Rhineland provinces, where Catholics were in a majority, and in Prussia generally, as part of the policy of encouraging immigration. With the annexation of mainly Catholic Silesia (1740) and West Prussia (1772) toleration became even more desirable. It was also essential in an army which included large non-Protestant contingents. Was there anything new, then, in Frederick's attitude to toleration?

EXERCISE   Read documents 36–41. What do they suggest about

1   Frederick's own religious beliefs;

2   his religious policy?

3   his attitude to the Jesuits?

DISCUSSION   1   Though formally 'head of the Protestant Church' in Prussia (document 38), Frederick is evidently not a conventional Christian. Is he a Christian at all? Not just in his letter to Voltaire (document 36) but in his public documents (37, 40) he is openly sceptical and disrespectful of all religions. (Was he a believer in any sense? What do you make of his reference to 'theism' in document 36 (compare the discussion of Deism in the General Introduction above) or his instructions concerning his burial at Sans Souci, mentioned in TV2, 'Frederick the Great and Sans Souci' and cited in the Broadcast Notes?)

2   He does not accept the need for a state religion, or for religion at all as a form of social control. Religion is a matter of individual preference. In document 37 he argues that freedom of religious

belief and practice is part of the social contract, laying this down 'as an unalterable principle of his government' in his cabinet order. (Note and describe his attitude to divorce, marriage within the 'prohibited degrees' and monasticism in document 38.)

3   His policy towards the Jesuits exemplifies his pragmatism: he invited them to Prussia as pedagogues. In allocating French Jesuits to (formerly Austrian) Silesia, he also sought to offset the anti-Prussian sentiments of the local Jesuits.

2.8.1   Frederick on the Calas affair and the case of de La Barre

EXERCISE   For these notorious French cases, taken up by Voltaire, see p.33. Read document 39, and compare Frederick's attitude to each.

DISCUSSION   Frederick shared Voltaire's hatred of religious intolerance and fanaticism as manifested in the Calas affair. However, while he agreed that the French blasphemy laws applied to de la Barre were 'bloody', he insisted here, as in his confidential memorandum (document 38), that 'one must show the people enough respect not to scandalize it in its religious beliefs'. (Did he follow his own maxim in document 40?) Thus while he denounced the Calas affair out of hand, he felt that de la Barre had partly provoked his own fate by insulting the established religion – 'tolerance … should not extend to condoning the effrontery and licence of young hooligans'. (What is do you make of his remarks about the *philosophes* in paragraph 3?)

2.9   Frederick, education and enlightenment

EXERCISE   Read documents 42–4. Assess Frederick's views on education in

1   document 42, and

2   documents 43–4.

DISCUSSION   1   Frederick wrote this letter to d'Alembert, who, as co-founder of the *Encyclopédie*, saw education as the principal key to enlightenment and progress. Frederick at once rules out all but 0.5% of the population as incapable of benefiting from education. He then halves this figure by eliminating women. He regards mass education (beyond an elementary level) as 'a waste of time' and 'sometimes dangerous' (why?). Education is the preserve of 'a tiny minority' of 'the nobility and the upper middle class'. At most one in 10,000 men are capable of enlightenment (i.e. about 500 in Prussia).

Frederick's apparently casual dismissal of the need and worth of educating women needs to be discussed in the context of the enlightenment period: (a) how far was he out of step with other *philosophes*, e.g. de Jaucourt on *Woman* in the *Encyclopédie?*; (b) is Frederick perhaps exaggerating here in order to shock and tease? Is his attitude here consistent with that of his correspondence with the Electress of Saxony (documents 8, 21, 41, 51)?

2   Frederick's published Instruction for the Noble Academy at Berlin indicates his hopes of the future nobility. If his attitudes to class and sex are conventional (and de Guibert's account suggests that they are), his views on education and corporal punishment are not. While the first object of the Academy is vocational training 'for war or administration', Frederick also seeks to encourage a high degree of independent judgement, as well as training in modern languages and gentlemanly accomplishments. Contrast his prohibition of corporal punishment with the 'shocking' discipline imposed on the rank and file (document 35).

2.9.1   *Freedom of speech and the press*

EXERCISE   Critically compare documents 45 and 46 on freedom of expression at Berlin. What weight do you attach to the testimony of each, and why?

DISCUSSION   The German playwright, Lessing (author of *Nathan the Wise*, which you will be studying later) was not welcome in Prussia. Frederick excluded him from the Berlin Academy and tried to have one of his plays suppressed. As a slighted intellectual with a personal axe to grind, not present in Berlin, his evidence should be approached with caution. (Even he admits that there is freedom to criticize religion, however.)

Moore, on the other hand, gives full and detailed evidence of what he has seen and heard at Berlin over a period of time. His first-hand account implies that political censorship was not rigorously enforced. (And, Moore points out, the criticism, satire, etc. did not really threaten the authority or power of the king.)

(For a third view, see Kant's *What is Enlightenment?*, *Texts*, II.)

2.9.2   *Aesthetics, science, progress and enlightenment*
Frederick was a ruler of marked cultivation. Flautist and composer, architect and designer, art connoisseur, poet, playwright and prolific man of letters, he wrote (in French) on history, politics and literature.

EXERCISE   Read documents 47–50. Define Frederick's aesthetic tastes.

DISCUSSION   Frederick is a devotee of the classical standards of Greece and Rome and
             of modern France. He has no time for contemporary German as a literary
             language, or for the German literature beginning to emerge from provin-
             ciality around the mid-century. While welcoming somewhat second-rate
             francophones to his Academy, he spurned German writers like Lessing
             (note his remarks on drama in the last sentence of document 47) and the
             distinguished Prussian art critic Winckelmann (document 49), whom he
             also excluded from the Academy. Note his conservative tastes in music:
             assuming Frederick knew the work of Haydn and Mozart, what do you
             suppose his attitude to it would have been? (For his architectural tastes,
             see TV2, 'Frederick the Great and Sans Souci'.)

EXERCISE   Read document 51. Why does Frederick champion inoculation?

DISCUSSION   Inoculation demonstrably works: 'of a million people who have been
             inoculated at Berlin, no one has died'. Inoculation is a triumph of scien-
             tific method applied for the betterment of mankind, and is specifically
             recommended in the *Encyclopédie* (article *Inoculation, Texts,* I, p.36). Its
             success proves the absurdity of its prohibition at Paris, based on 'old
             ignorant prejudices' and irrationality.

EXERCISE   Read documents 52–3. What is Frederick's purpose in his *Discourse on the
             Usefulness of the Arts and Sciences*?

DISCUSSION   Frederick vigorously and publicly defends the concept of civilisation and
             the doctrine of human progress through scientific method and techno-
             logical advance – the main thesis of the *Encyclopédie* (cf. article *Experimen-
             tal, Texts,* I, pp.32–6).
                  He also attacks the ideas of Rousseau, who, in his *Discourse on the
             Arts and Sciences* (1750) and *Discourse on Inequality* (1753) produced a rad-
             ical critique of these central beliefs in civilisation and progress. (You will
             learn more about Rousseau later in the course.) Frederick is unequivo-
             cally on the side of science and civilisation: 'compare a Canadian savage
             with any citizen of a civilized country of Europe' (p.66). (How would *'any*
             citizen' of Prussia benefit *equally* from enlightenment? – see his remarks
             on 'the riff-raff' in the last paragraph.) Can Frederick's defence of edu-
             cation and enlightenment be squared with his scathing denial, in docu-
             ment 42, of the possibility of the 'masses' either contributing to, or
             benefiting from, education and enlightenment?

RECAPITULATION   Re-read the list of the five main concerns of the *philosophes* (*Studies,* I,
EXERCISE   pp.14–15). Using this as a check-list, assess how far Frederick shared these
                 concerns, on the evidence of his speech to the Academy of Sciences.

2.10 Frederick the Great: Outline chronology

1712	Born
1736	Begins correspondence with Voltaire
1740	May: accedes to throne
	Autumn: *The Anti-Machiavel*
	December: invades Silesia
1740–8	War of Austrian Succession
1751	*Code of Laws* (Civil)
1752	*Political Testament* (i)
1754	Total abolition of torture
1756–63	Invades Saxony, Seven Years' War
1765	Founds Noble Academy
1768	*Political Testament* (ii)
1772	*Discourse on the usefulness of the arts and sciences in a state*
	First Partition of Poland (annexation of West Prussia)
1776	*Political Testament* (iii) (*Account of the government of Prussia*)
1777	*Essay on the forms of government and the duties of sovereigns*
1779	Acts in the case of the miller Arnold
	Essay on love of country
1780	Work begun on *General Code*
1786	Death of Frederick.

3 Russia in the age of Catherine the Great

3.1 Russia in the eighteenth century

The enormous Russian empire, stretching from the Baltic to the Pacific and occupying one sixth of the world's territory, did not impinge on modern European history until the forceful and dynamic rule of Peter the Great (1696–1725). By a programme of accelerated 'westernisation', particularly of the armed forces, Peter ousted Sweden from Russia's Baltic provinces, displaced Poland as a Great Power, and began to challenge Turkey for access to the Black Sea. Henceforth Russia was a force to be reckoned with in the west, as Frederick the Great found to his cost in the Seven Years' War (1756–63). In 1762, Russia had a population of some 20 million, second only to France, but the lowest population density in Europe. The nobility, some 50,000 males, comprised the tiny minority who officered the army and administration. There were about one million town dwellers. The remainder, the overwhelming mass of the population, were peasants. Of these, over half belonged to the noble landowners. The remainder belonged to the church (but were secularized by Catherine in 1764) or were state peasants, a mobile labour-force, liable to be conscripted for building or engineering works, in foundries, mines or canal construction.

The legal position of agricultural peasants belonging to the landowners was akin to that of the black slaves in the New World. Serfdom was a lifelong and hereditary condition. The serf was as much a part of his master's property as his cattle or horses. In law, he was simply a moveable chattel: the noble could buy or sell serfs, with or without land. Serfs were commonly put up for auction. They required their master's permission to wed, and were forbidden to complain to the authorities against their masters. Serfs either paid money dues or performed compulsory labour services for the landowner, or both. On average the compulsory labour was three days a week, though nothing prevented the landowner from demanding more. In addition, the serfs were also liable for military conscription, and paid a poll-tax and other taxes to the state.

There were no institutional restraints on the traditional 'autocracy', or absolute power, of the czar (after 1721 – 'emperor'), though Peter reorganized the governmental machinery on functional western lines. The emperor ruled with a co-ordinating body of officials, somewhat misleadingly called the Senate. This channelled imperial directives to a hierarchy of executive 'colleges' or ministries. While there was considerable continuity of overall policy after Peter's death, the succession to the throne between 1725 and 1762 was randomly determined half-a-dozen times by a sequence of palace-revolutions, backed by the imperial guards. Those raised to the throne in this way included Peter's widow, his niece and his daughter.

Map 3

Russia's westward expansion under Catherine II and the course of the Pugachóv Rebellion

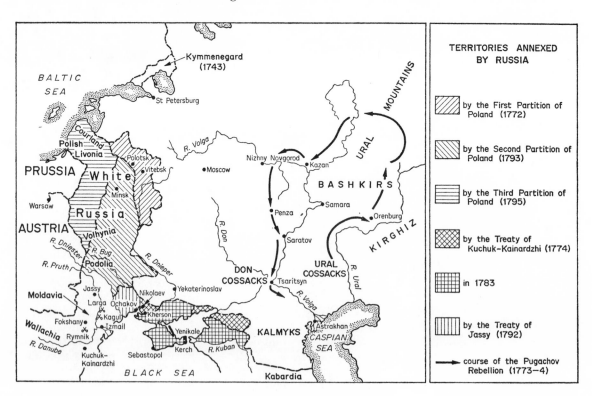

3.2 Catherine the Great

Catherine's own accession came about as the result of another such *coup d'état*. German by origin, born at Stettin into the minor princely house of Anhalt-Zerbst (her father was in Frederick's service), she had no legal claim to the Russian throne. In 1744 at the age of 14 she was brought to Russia simply in order to marry the Grand Duke Peter and produce an heir to the throne. Catherine, however, had other ideas. Unlike her boorish and unbalanced husband, who succeeded in 1761 as Peter III, she did all she could to win popularity and support, building up her own party at court, and making sure of the loyalty of the imperial guards, one of whom, Alexei Orlov, was her lover. After six months of misrule, Peter III was overthrown and murdered in a palace revolution engineered by the Orlovs. Passing over the claims of her son, Paul, Catherine was proclaimed Empress in her own right.

Catherine was self-possessed, single-minded and enormously ambitious. As a child, she believed she was plain, and strove to compensate for this by showing intelligence and sympathy. A critic describes her as 'clever, affable, magnanimous and compassionate on principle' (document 13). As Grand Duchess, she read widely, and immersed herself in the works of the *philosophes*, particularly the *Encyclopédie*. Catherine, like Frederick, was the heart and soul of her government, (though her court, unlike his, was spectacularly grandiose). Methodical and hardworking, she ruled the empire from her study in the Winter Palace at St Petersburg, advised by a small Imperial Council of personal advisers, most of whom she retained for decades, supplemented by occasional *ad hoc* commissions. Her right-hand man was the Procurator-General, who conferred with her daily and passed on her instructions to the presidents of the collegiate boards and provincial governors, whose activities he kept under surveillance through a staff of procurators.

In 1766 Catherine announced the establishment of a so-called Commission for the Drawing-up of a New Code of Laws, at which 500 elected representatives of the nobility, the towns, the state peasants, native peoples and cossacks, and the central organs of government, were to convene in Moscow the following year, to prepare for the task of updating the code of laws, last undertaken in 1649. Catherine outlined her own principles in her celebrated *Nakaz* or *Instruction for the Commission*. Despite hopes by some that it might lay down some sort of constitution for Russia or become a permanent representative assembly, the Commission was never intended by Catherine to share or dilute her absolute power. She favoured consultation and co-operation within a firmly absolutist and centrist framework. The Commission (which was prorogued on the outbreak of war with Turkey in 1768 and not reconvened) did begin discussion of draft bills on the rights of various social estates and was thus a sounding-board for the expression of social views. Catherine used its materials in much of her subsequent legislation.

The Pugachóv rebellion of 1773–4 was the greatest popular upheaval in Europe before the French Revolution of 1789. Beginning as a rising among the Ural Cossacks and oppressed non-Russian peoples north of the Caspian, the rebellion spread north to the Urals, gathering support (see Map 3). It veered west, and, with the capture of Kazan in July 1774, attracted large numbers of Russian peasants along the Volga, spreading terror among landowners and officials. Some 1,500 nobles were massacred. The rebellion was ruthlessly repressed. The scale of the disorders suggested chronic weaknesses in provincial government. Catherine pored over the minutes of the Legislative Commission, studied the English jurist, Blackstone, compared notes with experienced administrators, and produced the Provincial Statute (1775) and Municipal Charter (1785), which shaped the course of Russian provincial and urban administration until 1864. She redrew the administrative map according to density of population into new provinces (50 by 1796), each under a governor, directly answerable to herself. Administrative functions were decentralized. Provision was made for schools and hospitals, and a hierarchy of courts was organized on a class basis, which included access for state peasants. More reforming absolutism followed in various fields, including the Charter of the Nobility (1785) and the Statute on National Education (1786), all devised and drawn up by Catherine herself.

Catherine's successes in foreign policy were spectacular. Her drive to the Black Sea opened up important economic prospects, and enormously enhanced Russia's Great Power status. Of Russia's 50 provinces, into which Catherine gradually redivided Russia after 1775, 11 consisted of new acquisitions. These included extensive annexations from Poland (see Map 3).

Catherine's first priority remained the maintenance and supply of the armed forces, more than ever vital in view of her energetic foreign policy. The army (numbering half a million men by 1796) and navy were self-supporting in armaments. Industry was a creation of the state, which backed non-competitive enterprises with capital and loans, and guaranteed profits by bulk purchases and high protective tariffs. Most Russian exports consisted of traditional Muscovite wares – iron, timber, flax, hemp, pitch and tallow. Flax and hemp, in heavy demand by the British admiralty for sail-making and cordage, made up two-fifths of all exports.

State expenditure under Catherine tripled, the combined result of the new machinery of provincial government after 1775, huge increases in expenditure on the internal administration, warfare and imperial expansion. Even in peacetime the armed forces absorbed a third of the national revenue. Catherine raised costly loans abroad leaving a national debt, amounting at her death to some 200 million roubles, in the form of unsecured paper roubles, foreign loans and unpaid bills. Unlike Frederick, she resorted to deficit financing with inflationary consequences, which spiralled after 1786. Traditional expedients which she adopted included increasing the poll-tax paid by all non-nobles, and raising indirect taxes on spirits.

Catherine retained the organs of state security established by Peter the Great as a safeguard against opposition, which ranged from plots by guardsmen to dethrone her, to the Pugachóv rebellion. State security agencies also investigated the activities of social critics, notably Radíshchev and Novikóv at the time of the French Revolution.

3.3   *Catherine, enlightenment and the ruler*

3.3.1   *Catherine – image, appearance and role*

EXERCISE   Consider *Texts,* I, Fig. 2, Van Vilk's portrait of Catherine, and compare it with Franke's portrait of Frederick and with document 1. What impression of Catherine does it convey?

DISCUSSION   This portrait, though more intimate and engaging than the 'public' portrait of Frederick, does not seem particularly flattering and is apparently realistic, to judge by de Ligne's description of Catherine in her fifties ('one could see that she had been handsome rather than pretty' (compare *Studies,* I, Fig. 7), and note his comments on her chin, face, waist, hair). What stares out at us intently is a plump, middle-aged matronly bookworm, informally dressed, her arms bared, bent over some weighty, dog-eared tome and a map, presumably not light reading in any sense. The fact that Catherine consented to be thus portrayed offsets, perhaps, the common charge that vanity was her predominant characteristic. Normally, she was depicted in the grand manner. Here, at least, she was content to be shown as an unglamorous bluestocking. Put more positively, she clearly intended to be portrayed as an intellectual.

For intellectual she certainly was, widely read in ancient and modern literature. Her favourite reading-matter included the *Encyclopédie* (document 4) and other works of the *philosophes*. She also did 'an enormous amount of scribbling', as she put it (document 7). She corresponded with d'Alembert, Diderot, Voltaire and Grimm. Her interests were as wide as Frederick's, and she wrote on many of them. She invited Beccaria to Russia. She received Diderot at St Petersburg in 1774. Other visitors to Russia included the English prison-reformer, John Howard (of whom you will learn more later in this part of the course).

EXERCISE   Does de Ligne's description of Catherine (document 1) add anything not apparent from the portrait?

DISCUSSION   De Ligne brings out what the picture does not fully reveal: (a) her large waist and shortness of stature; (b) her impressive appearance and imposing manner, combined with a sympathetic and good-humoured personality; (c) her consciousness of playing a 'role'; and (d) his opinion that 'the role of Empress' suited her.

EXERCISE   Read document 2. What does it suggest about

1   ideals of conduct in Catherine's role-playing, and

2   the source of such ideals?

DISCUSSION 1   Catherine's concept of her role as Empress combines political authoritarianism with a 'humane' and 'liberal' outlook (i.e. what modern historians call 'enlightened absolutism'). The ruler should empathize with her subjects, but from above, without losing her 'authority' or their 'respect'. (How far do you feel that the qualities which Catherine lists for emulation in the first paragraph of document 2 are suggested in the portrait?)

2   Catherine's 'classical taste for honour and virtue' recalls Frederick's emulation of Marcus Aurelius. (Catherine especially admired the works of Tacitus and Plutarch's *Lives*.) Her conduct, or at least her style, as Empress, was perhaps partly shaped by her admiration for classical antiquity. (Do documents 1 and 2 suggest an insincerity about Catherine's role-playing? Or a contemporary acceptance of 'the role of Empress' as a *genre* of conduct expected of rulers, with accompanying conventions of classical 'greatness'?)

3.3.2   Catherine and the encyclopedists

EXERCISE   What do documents 3 and 4 suggest of Catherine's attitude to the encyclopedists?

DISCUSSION   Catherine expresses enthusiastic commitment to the encyclopedists and their cause. She presses d'Alembert to accept the post of tutor to her son, Paul. She invites the encyclopedists to Russia, contrasting a welcome there with the 'opposition and unpleasantness' they suffer in France (document 4). (How seriously do you think these documents should be taken, and why?)

EXERCISE   Consider documents 5 and 6, from Catherine's letters to Grimm, written five months after Voltaire's death, as evidence of Catherine's attitude to Voltaire.

DISCUSSION   Catherine's enthusiasm for Voltaire, and the impact of his ideas on her intellectual development seem genuine enough. Given the relatively short time-lapse since Voltaire's death, Catherine's account *may* be fairly spontaneous and she could no longer be motivated by the intention of flattering Voltaire. In document 5, she avers that 'it was he, or rather his works, that formed my way of thinking'. In document 6, ordering through Grimm 'a hundred complete sets' of his works for distribution in Russia, she professes her belief in the beneficial formative effects of Voltaire's works on her own subjects – effects which she, as Empress, is in a position to promote.

3.3.3   *Catherine and the Enlightenment – was she serious?*

Catherine's historical reputation has suffered (far more than Frederick's) from the basic charge of insincerity in her attitude to the Enlightenment. (She has also aroused hostility among Russian historians as a woman and as a non-Russian). She is criticized for failing to abolish serfdom and for allegedly violating her own professed principles, particularly after the French Revolution. (These claims will be considered later). She is commonly dismissed as a hypocrite, who sought to enhance her reputation in the West by bamboozling the *philosophes*. But how could such a policy serve her cause? How could a reputation for sharing the advanced ideas of the *philosophes* (which, as you know, incurred a high degree of suspicion and suppression even in France) stand her in good stead *in Russia*? Making full allowance for undoubted elements of vainglory in Catherine's character, it seems illogical to dismiss out of hand her attachment to enlightenment values, particularly since (like Frederick) she devoted most of her long reign to reading, thinking and writing about them, even if (as you will see later) she appears to have had some second thoughts in her final years.

Document 6, then, suggests a conviction on Catherine's part as intellectual and ruler that books and ideas can have a creative impact on society generally, as on individuals such as herself, if once assimilated by an educated minority, and, more broadly, if spread across society through legislation (cf. document 7). In this she shares a fundamental credo of the *Encyclopédie*.

Her prolific and detailed legislation – on which she worked long and hard and on which she prided herself (see documents 7–8) was inspired by this conviction of the efficacy of sound principles and clear ideas, and a characteristic enlightenment belief that good laws can produce good men and women and a good society – 'one should aim at instilling good conduct in the citizens through legislation' (document 34, article 83).

3.4   *Catherine and war*

EXERCISE   Consult Map 3 and read documents 9–12. What impression do they give of

1   Catherine's foreign policy

2   her motivation

3   the reaction of the *philosophes*?

DISCUSSION   1   They suggest an ambitious, large-scale, expansionist foreign policy at the expense of Turkey and Poland. (The gains from Turkey were won by war, 1768–74 and 1787–90), those from Poland by military and diplomatic pressure, culminating in the three partitions (1772, 1793, 1795)). Radíshchev's complaint (document 12) suggests that Catherine's wars were not universally popular in Russia (note her reaction).

2   Catherine denies the charge of personal ambition, and proclaims her longing for peace (document 9). She does not deny, however, her satisfaction at Russia's enhanced reputation. (Note her reference to 'heroes' (cf. document 6). Another classical echo?)

3   As a '*philosophe*' and spokesman of 'the friends of peace', Diderot voices reservations (document 11). (He also secretly hoped to promote France's interests as an ally of Turkey). Voltaire on the other hand, urges Catherine on against both Poles and Turks (document 10). (Why?)

3.4.1   Catherine's wars – aggressive or defensive?

Catherine claims that Russia was 'unjustly attacked' (document 9). It is true that both in 1768 and again in 1787, Turkey declared war on Russia (and in 1788 Sweden launched a surprise attack). But Turkey's reaction was provoked by Catherines's increasingly aggressive policy. Her object was a resumption of the drive to the Black Sea initiated by Peter the Great. Having by her victories gained a foothold on the northern shore of the Black Sea in 1774, Catherine could henceforth claim to be defending her gains. This may explain her impatient reaction to Radíshchev's protest (document 12). Even so, in the annexation of the Crimea (1783) and the Second Turkish war (1787–90), Catherine was also inspired by the grandiose 'Greek Project', aimed at expelling the Turks from Europe (significantly, her second grandson, born in 1777, was named Constantine, after the Roman emperor, of whom more in Gibbon's *Decline and Fall*).

EXERCISE   Compare briefly Catherine's outlook on foreign policy with Frederick's.

DISCUSSION   Despite her comments in documents 9 and 12, it is surely harder to justify Catherine's expansionist policy (as Frederick defended his) on the grounds of size and alleged strategic vulnerability (though see Raeff, 1972, pp.197–246, for a closely argued explanation of that policy). And neither ruler could justly complain of being threatened by Poland, their common victim.

3.5   Catherine and religion

EXERCISE   Nominally, on her arrival in Russia, Catherine became a convert from Lutheranism to Russian Orthodox Christianity.

1   Consider critically document 13 as evidence of her attitude to Christianity.

2   Is your answer to (1) affected by documents 14–17?

DISCUSSION 1 As his tone suggests, Shcherbátov was among Catherine's most hostile critics. We should therefore be alert for bias in his account. How reliable are his allegations, e.g. that 'her moral outlook is based on the modern philosophers' (i.e. the *philosophes*) and that 'she thinks nothing of the Christian religion'? Note that Shcherbátov substantiates these charges with facts. He instances (a) Catherine's own remarks in conversation (b) her enthusiasm for books with an anti-religious slant, like Voltaire's *Candide*, and Marmontel's *Bélisaire* (banned in France for its promotion of a classical, non-Christian code of ethics); (c) her attitude to marriages within the 'prohibited degrees'(cf. Frederick, document 38).

2 Documents 14–16, by Catherine herself, two addressed to Voltaire and one to foreigners in general, corroborate Shcherbátov's view of her 'moral outlook'. They illustrate her eagerness to associate herself with the cause of enlightenment and religious toleration in France (note her allusions to the Calas affair), and her insistence on toleration in Russia, in respect both of her own subjects, with their variety of religions, and of foreign immigrants, whom she encouraged to settle in Russia (why?). Document 17, on the other hand, from Catherine's private notes on her readings, gives a more subtle version of her attitude to 'prejudices'. While approving the exercise of *private* judgement and scepticism, 'where the people at large is concerned' she asserts the need to respect popular beliefs, particularly in matters of religion, where they 'must be upheld'.

EXERCISE Thus while a sceptic and disciple of the *philosophes*, who, according to Shcherbátov, 'pretends to be quite devout' (document 13), (though how do you interpret the last sentence of document 2?), Catherine begins the *Nakaz*, one of her most important public statements, by invoking 'a [Christian] religious precept' which, she states, 'is or ought to be, rooted in the hearts of the whole nation' (document 21). Is this hypocrisy? Or can you suggest another explanation for this dichotomy between Catherine in her private and public roles?

DISCUSSION Documents 13 and 17 suggest that Catherine sought, by outwardly respecting her subjects' religious convictions, to win their support, both for herself personally and for her reformist aspirations as outlined in the *Nakaz*. (Since Peter the Great, however, the administration of the Church had been under state control, a process which Catherine extended by secularizing church and monastic lands in 1764, again to the plaudits of the *philosophes*).

EXERCISE Looking at the first sentence of document 13, can you suggest another, more personal reason why Catherine should have taken pains not to offend what she privately called 'religious prejudices' (document 17) in Russia?

DISCUSSION   As a foreigner (who never lost her German accent), and a usurper, Catherine had a dubious title to the throne; and she had a son, Paul, with a superior claim. Paul became a figurehead for those who (like Shcherbátov) favoured constitutional rather than absolutist rule. Her position was thus inherently far more vulnerable than that of Frederick, who had no rivals, and she made correspondingly greater efforts to achieve acceptance and 'legitimacy'. The czar was traditionally associated with religious piety (document 13), and Catherine, whatever her private beliefs, took pains to show respect for the externals of her adoptive faith.

3.6   Catherine and her favourites

In document 18, Shcherbátov condemns Catherine's 'long and frequent succession of lovers'. He complains of the effect of her example on society, and sees her conduct as particularly scandalous in a middle-aged woman. (After Potémkin, from 1776, the disparity in age between Empress and favourites increased: all were in their twenties and early thirties. The last, Zúbov, became favourite when he was 22 and Catherine 60). Shcherbátov complains of their 'ascendancy' and 'power'; but apart from Potémkin, whose administrative genius she found invaluable, their activities were normally confined to the boudoir.

EXERCISE   Now read documents 19–20. How does Catherine attempt to rebut the charge of promiscuity?

DISCUSSION 1   In her letter to Potémkin (document 20), Catherine says that the number of her favourites has been exaggerated, at least at the time of writing. (In all, there were probably twelve; and with five of these, notably Potémkin, the relationship was, as it were, monogamous).

2   She argues that a love-match, instead of a dynastic marriage, would have solved the problem, given her affectionate, emotional and outgoing nature.

3   She appears to regret her own conduct, and thus to share the moral viewpoint of her critics.

4   On the other hand, in document 19, she holds frankly that sexual attraction is integral to human nature and ultimately irresistible. Diderot in his article *Enjoyment* in the *Encyclopédie*, suggests that sexual pleasure is a legitimate and natural source of enjoyment for both sexes, irrespective of marital status. Frederick, you will recall, was notoriously open-minded about unmarried mothers (Frederick documents 33–4). And Laclos' novel, *Les Liaisons Dangereuses (Dangerous Acquaintances)*, which you will be reading later, contains views similar to Catherine's. (Should she be seen therefore as a victim of circumstances? Or as a heroine of the Enlightenment, emancipated from prejudice?)

3.7   *Catherine, law and absolutism*

In 1767 Catherine published her *Nakaz* or *Instruction for the Commission for the Drawing-up of a New Code of Laws,* much of it avowedly borrowed from Montesquieu's *On the Spirit of the Laws* (1748), Beccaria's *On Crimes and Punishments* (1764) and the *Encyclopédie.* The *Nakaz* was banned in France, adding further to her reputation as an enlightened reformer. Voltaire acclaimed it as 'clear, concise, just, strict and humane' (Lentin, 1974, p.56).

EXERCISE   Read documents 21 and 22, extracts from the *Nakaz.* What do they suggest about Catherine's aims as ruler?

DISCUSSION   Catherine aspires to turn a Christian precept to secular ends: the 'prosperity, glory, happiness and stability' of Russia. She also hopes to see her subjects enjoy the rule of law. (How do you interpret article 6?)

In extract 22, she defines her ideas of the rule of law, equality before the law and civil liberty. Her aim is to lay down a code of laws, guaranteeing individual security and freedom. (How does her policy compare with Frederick's? cf. p.68)

EXERCISE   Like Frederick (cf. pp.63–4), Catherine was at pains to dissociate her absolute rule from the charge of 'despotism', with its connotations of tyranny and abuse. How does she do so in the *Nakaz,* (document 23)?

DISCUSSION   She justifies absolutism on strictly utilitarian grounds (i.e. without invoking religion or tradition): the size of Russia and the need for 'speed in decision-making'. She denies that 'the object of absolute government' is 'to deprive men of their natural freedom': like Frederick, she claims that absolute rule limits their freedom only as much as is necessary in the interests of the general welfare. She argues (like Frederick) that the power of the monarch is in fact checked and counterbalanced by the courts and by the regulations under which the organs of government operate. If a particular imperial decree is contrary to law, the Senate and other organs of governments have the right to make representations to the monarch, and thus protect the people from 'arbitrary whims and caprices'. Freedom, or at any rate a 'spirit of freedom' can coexist with absolute rule (clause 16).

EXERCISE   Read Shcherbátov (document 24) and Diderot (document 25) and summarize their reactions to Catherine's claims about absolutism.

DISCUSSION   Unlike Voltaire, both Shcherbátov and Diderot reject Catherine's justification of absolutism. However 'enlightened', they find it essentially indistinguishable from 'despotism'. Comparing the clauses of the *Nakaz* with their originals in Montesquieu's *On the Spirit of the Laws,* Shcherbátov argues that Catherine perverts Montesquieu's argument. In particular, she makes no provision for the separation of legislative and executive power. She pays only lip service to the social contract theory and the ideal of freedom under the rule of law, regarding herself as 'above the law' (cf. document 26). He denies that her absolute power is checked by the Senate and other organs of government; and notes the absence of any intention on her part to draw up 'fundamental laws' which might limit her own authority.

Diderot takes a similar view. He stresses a basic objection to hereditary absolutism (cf. Frederick, document 3) and also concludes that Russia needs a constitution to protect the laws from violation by the ruler.

3.7.1 Absolutism and 'republicanism'

Read document 27, written towards the end of the reign. Experience has mellowed Catherine. She has not abandoned her general principles of conduct (as set out in document 2), but she has lost some of her optimism about reform, given what she sees as the intractability of human nature. (What do you take her to mean by 'people like us'?)

EXERCISE What do you make of her claim in the last paragraph about her 'republican' convictions?

DISCUSSION Catherine admits that her claim sounds paradoxical, contrasted with her 'unlimited political power'. Evidently, like Frederick, she believes that '"republican" freedom is compatible with absolutist rule' (p.64). As for her claim that 'no-one in Russia will be able to say that I have abused that power', Shcherbátov (document 26) makes precisely that charge, citing particular cases. (How seriously should his accusations be taken, given his hostility to Catherine, and to women in general (see his first sentence and cf. document 13).)

3.8 Catherine and serfdom

Serfdom has been traditionally seen by Russian historians as the acid test of Catherine's 'enlightenment' and she has been found wanting for failing to abolish it. (The same criterion is not normally applied to Frederick). It is true that serfdom remained far more widespread and more deeply entrenched in Russia under Catherine than in Frederick's Prussia, and that the agricultural serfs, who comprised most of Russia's peasant population, remained the property of the noble landowners and lacked any civil rights. Catherine was well aware of their condition. What was her attitude to it? In 1766, she publicized the problem by setting and judging an essay competition on the serf question. She awarded the prize to an essay which recommended granting the peasants small freehold plots. In 1767, she followed this up in the *Nakaz*.

EXERCISE   Consider document 28 as evidence of Catherine's attitude to serfdom.

DISCUSSION   If Catherine appears somewhat tentative about serfdom in the *Nakaz*, this is because the *Nakaz* was a public document and the question was extremely controversial. As document 31 makes clear, serf-ownership rather than land-ownership alone was the index of wealth among the nobility, so that (as with Frederick in Prussia, cf. Frederick, document 17) any attempt at peasant reform was seen as prejudicial to the interests of the nobles. Catherine was, however, well aware of the frequency of serf revolts, and publicly indicates her wish to 'remove the causes'. She sought to test public opinion (which in practice meant noble opinion) in the *Nakaz* and to carry it with her. The *Nakaz* underwent successive drafts and the wording here is the result of watering down by her advisers. Articles 260–3 may sound indirect and allusive. But article 260 is lifted from Montesquieu, and Catherine's meaning is surely unmistakeable? Is it significant that she refers to the serfs as 'slaves'? What emerges is that Catherine is opposed to serfdom as a moral and social evil, contrary to 'natural law', that she seeks to mitigate its rigours, to allow serfs to possess 'personal property' and (article 260) to contemplate some measure of emancipation. (Is she more or less radical than de Jaucourt in his article on the *Slave Trade* in the *Encyclopédie* (*Texts*, I, p.13)?

EXERCISE   Consider documents 29–32. Do you detect evidence of a change in attitude to serfdom on Catherine's part and in Russian society, and if so, can you account for it?

DISCUSSION   All three documents postdate the Pugachóv rebellion. (a) Shcherbátov's thoughts (document 30) express the hostile reactions (in his case, totally hostile) which Catherine's liberal ideas provoked even among some of the most educated nobles. In Shcherbátov's view, the Pugachóv revolt should rule out all further discussion of emancipation. (b) Baroness Dimsdale's factual account in 1781 (document 31) indicates that no changes have been brought about in the condition of the serfs. (c) Catherine's own attitude in her memorandum to Diderot (document 29) appears to be one of resignation (in contrast to her earlier aspirations in the *Nakaz*). Having tested public opinion, and finding it hostile to reform, and having experienced the trauma of the Pugachóv rebellion, Catherine (like Frederick) abandoned her original hopes as unrealistic. Both English visitors are shocked by the social contrasts between noble and serf; but Coxe (document 32) accepts that change must be the work of time. Should Catherine be blamed for reaching similar conclusions?

3.9   Catherine and penal reform

EXERCISE   Summarize briefly what documents 33–5 from the *Nakaz* suggest about Catherine's views on law reform generally.

DISCUSSION   The *Nakaz* clearly demonstrates Catherine's up-to-date and humane views on criminal law reform. She closely follows the ideas (and the language) of Beccaria's *On Crimes and Punishments* (1764) (compare, e.g. document 33 (articles 240–1, 243–5) and document 35 (article 206) with Beccaria (*Texts*, I, pp.97; 104–5; 106). She calls for crime-prevention rather than punishment. Her general principle is: 'Do you wish to prevent crime? Spread enlightenment in society' (document 33, article 245).

EXERCISE   What specific legal principles does she advocate?

DISCUSSION   (a) Due process of law, (b) equality before the law, (c) trial by one's peers, (d) a simple and readily available code of laws, (e) punishments proportionate to the crime, and (f) the abolition of torture and physical mutilation.

3.9.1   Capital punishment and torture – theory and practice
In the present state of our knowledge of Catherine's Russia, it is difficult to ascertain how far Catherine's ideas on penal reform (items (a) to (f) above) were implemented, despite her good intentions. The *Nakaz* was a set of principles, not a code of law. There was no complete code of laws until the nineteenth century. The death-penalty had been suspended by the Empress Elisabeth in 1754, and was not activated by Catherine except in cases of treason, as in Pugachóv's case. Catherine almost invariably commuted death-sentences. There is no evidence that physical torture was ever officially sanctioned, and Catherine forbade it in the case of Pugachóv (document 38 refers to this).

EXERCISE   Read (1) document 36, and (2) documents 37 and 38, as evidence of Russian penal procedure in practice. (You might also compare Russia with Britain and France when you come to view TV3, 'Humanity and the Scaffold'.)

DISCUSSION   1   Archdeacon Coxe's eyewitness account clearly exposes a discrepancy between Catherine's ideals and actual penal practice in Russia. Under Peter the Great's unrepealed *Military Statute* (1715), the punishment for murder was knouting, accompanied by mutilation and branding, as in Coxe's account of 'this terrible operation' (despite Catherine's strictures in the *Nakaz*, document 34, article 96). The statute prescribed a so-called 'merciless' knouting, with an unspecified number of blows to be decided by the judge. It was common knowledge that more than 50 blows could prove fatal, as in this case.

               2   Documents 37 and 38 show that Catherine was prepared, reluctantly, to sanction brutal punishment in the suppression of the Pugachóv rebellion. However, the massacre of nobles who fell into

the rebels' hands was obviously felt to demand exemplary punishment (see document 30); and as Catherine's letter to Panin makes clear, his proclamation was intended as a deterrent, rather than to be carried out in full. Of a possible 200,000 rebels, over 300 were executed, 400 were knouted and had an ear cut off, and 7000 suffered other forms of physical punishment. (Do documents 37 and 38 belie Catherine's good intentions in the *Nakaz*?)

3.10 Catherine, education and enlightenment

In the *Nakaz*, Catherine insisted that 'Russia is a European power (document 21, article 6). She lavished funds on the purchase of masterpieces of European art, and embellished the architecture of St Petersburg in the neo-classical style popularized in the West by Robert Adam (whom you will study in Part B). She energetically promoted the spread of Western ideas and norms in Russia (cf. document 6). Unprecedented numbers of books, classical and modern, were systematically translated at her order (including the works of the *philosophes*, as Shcherbátov complained in document 13). Catherine herself edited a journal modelled on the *Spectator* of Addison and Steele, wrote satirical social comedies, historical essays and dramas, opera libretti and children's stories. Unlike Frederick, she generously patronized native writers including Radíshchev, Sumarókov (document 42), Novikóv (document 49), and Shcherbátov. In 1783, she proclaimed freedom of the press, subject to registration with the local chief of police and a limited degree of censorship. (The chief of police was authorized to check works privately printed for material subversive of the monarch, the Orthodox faith and public decency).

3.10.1 Catherine, Voltaire and inoculation

Catherine, like Frederick, made a point of undergoing inoculation, as recommended in the *Encyclopédie* (*Texts*, I, p.36). She wrote to Voltaire to inform him (document 39).

EXERCISE   Consider document 39 as evidence of Catherine's commitment (or lack of it) to enlightened values, commenting specifically on (1) style (2) content.

DISCUSSION   1   Catherine's style may seem flowery and contrived. (But 'thank you' letters are notoriously hard to write. And this one is six months late). It is certainly larded with flattery (examples?). But the evidence surely suggests, as we have seen elsewhere (pp.80–1) that her admiration for Voltaire and his works was perfectly sincere.

2   You may also be alienated by Catherine's probable ulterior motive in notifying him of her inoculation (and forwarding a copy of the *Nakaz*): the widespread publicity which Voltaire lent her reputation in Western Europe.

But was this letter merely a publicity exercise? Or was undergoing inoculation a demonstration of her genuine commitment to the cause of scientific advance, and, as she claims, 'a personal example which might be of use to people?' (see Voltaire's reply, document 40).

3.10.2 *Education*

In the *Nakaz* Catherine declared that 'the surest but most difficult method of improving men is by perfecting their education' (document 33, article 248). She was closely concerned with educational reform. She was assisted by Count Betskoy, an enthusiast of the educational theories of Locke and Rousseau (you will be studying Rousseau's ideas later in the course) with their stress on the formative effects of environment. Betskoy's schemes, published with Catherine's approval, were based on the theory that by educating young people in isolation from society and exposing them to humane influences and stimuli, a 'new type of people' might emerge. These ideas inspired the establishment of Foundlings' Homes, the reorganisation of Russia's main educational institute for boys, the Cadet Corps at St Petersburg (partly modelled on Frederick's Noble Academy) and the Smol'ny Institute at St Petersburg, founded in 1764 as Russia's first school for girls. Catherine patronized and generously financed these institutions. Like Frederick, she forbade corporal punishment.

EXERCISE   Read documents 41–3. Compare Catherine's educational ideas with Frederick's (Frederick documents, section 6, *Texts,* I, pp.61–67).

DISCUSSION 1   Catherine's Cadet Corps, like Frederick's Noble Academy, was a vocational training-school to prepare young men for the army and administration. Catherine shares his belief in exercise and outdoor activities.

2   While Frederick's Noble Academy is exclusively for nobles, Catherine admits non-nobles to both her institutions (note the proportion of non-nobles at Smol'ny).

3   Unlike Frederick, Catherine makes public provision for female education.

4   Catherine shares Frederick's attitude to monasticism (cf. Frederick, document 38). For both, the educational curriculum is secular, and includes social accomplishments (though, like Frederick, Catherine also welcomed the Jesuits (from provinces newly annexed from Poland as instructors).

EXERCISE   Re-read documents 42–3 and define Catherine's views on the aims of female education.

DISCUSSION Catherine differentiates between the education of boys and of girls. The avowed purpose of female education is to train girls for family, domestic and social life (and as governesses, in the case of non-nobles). Note the emphasis placed on amateur theatricals and social graces. Catherine's aims for girls seem to preclude a career, such as her own, on equal terms with men.

Document 44 suggests Catherine's commitment to a wider educational reform, on modern lines and on a national scale from primary school to university level. (In the event in 1786, she modelled her primary and secondary education system on the Austrian pattern, and did not found any new university).

3.11 Catherine, literature and revolution

3.11.1 The case of Radíshchev

Unlike Frederick, Catherine lived through the period from 1789 to 1796, from the outbreak of the French Revolution to the Revolutionary Wars. In documents 46–50, written between 1790 and 1794, when Catherine was in her sixties, a sharper tone emerges, and an increasingly critical attitude towards ideas which she had previously championed.

Documents 45–7 relate to the unauthorized publication in 1790 of Alexander Radíshchev's *A Journey from St Petersburg to Moscow.* Ostensibly a travelogue, Radíshchev's *Journey* criticized almost every aspect of Catherine's rule, including foreign policy (see document 12), censorship, serfdom and absolute monarchy.

EXERCISE Read document 45, two extracts from Radíshchev's *Journey.* Do you see anything to provoke Catherine's reactions in document 46?

DISCUSSION Radíshchev's strictures on censorship in themselves seem to echo Catherine's own earlier open-mindedness in the *Nakaz* (as he points out). Is it his disrespectful tone that Catherine resents? What about the tone of his remarks on serfdom: do you agree with Catherine (document 46) that he is 'quite outspoken'? (Note the timing of the book's appearance, which coincided with the second Turkish War, war with Sweden, and the French Revolution).

EXERCISE Read document 46. Do you detect a significant change in Catherine's tone? What are her main objections to Radíshchev's *Journey*?

DISCUSSION Catherine's tone is furious. Contrast her professed hatred of cruel punishment (documents 34, 35, 38) with her angry comment on Mirabeau (last sentence). She sees Radíshchev's book as a threat to the social and political order, and Radíshchev as manifestly subversive. She believes his aim to be to stir up mass discontent among the peasantry and the military – 'he places his hopes in a peasant rebellion'. She sees him as inspired by contemporary events in revolutionary France ('the French madness') and by the works of certain radical *philosophes*, especially Rousseau and Raynal. She denounces his egalitarian principles, his belief in the 'supposed' rights of man, and his religious views. He is outspokenly anti-monarchical: according to Catherine 'these pages are of criminal intent, absolutely seditious'. (Do you agree?)

EXERCISE Read document 47 from Catherine's interrogatory. What is its value for the historian of Catherine?

DISCUSSION The questions clearly indicate Catherine's acute preoccupation with Radíshchev and his book: his intentions in publishing; his supposed relationship with masonic circles, his religious and political views, particularly his attitude towards serfdom, censorship and monarchy. Indirectly this document attests to Catherine's respect for the power of books and ideas (cf. p.80–1) and is thus a telling piece of 'unwitting testimony'.

Catherine's complaints of religious unorthodoxy are also to be noted. Whatever her private religious beliefs (or lack of them), she evidently regards religion as an essential instrument of social control (cf. document 17). (How do you account for Radíshchev's somewhat cringing replies under interrogation? There is no evidence that physical torture was used).

EXERCISE What does document 48 indicate about Catherine's state of mind in 1792?

DISCUSSION She is clearly incensed by the progress of the Revolution, the threats on her own life by the revolutionary militants, (who declared war on all monarchs), their misrepresentation of the ideas of Voltaire, and the inaction of her fellow-monarchs. She calls for counter-revolution; (her own intervention took the form of the second and third partitions of Poland – 'I shall give those scoundrels a drubbing'. She professed to see constitutional reform in Poland as part of an international revolutionary conspiracy).

3.11.2 *The case of Novikóv*

The social satirist, Nikolai Novikóv, published educational books, including popularisations of the *philosophes*, for which, with Catherine's approval, he was granted a lease of Moscow University Press. However, Catherine twice suspended his activities for unauthorized publication of masonic works. Freemasonry was common among the nobility in Catherine's Russia (*The Magic Flute* was the first of Mozart's operas to win popularity there). Catherine, who at first tolerated masonry as harmless mumbo-jumbo, became increasingly suspicious and hostile, particularly after Novikóv joined the Rosicrucians, a mystical order of masonry with foreign connections. In 1792, after seizing Novikóv's papers, she had him held without trial and sentenced to 15 years' imprisonment. The nature of the charges against him emerges from document 49.

EXERCISE Read document 49. What are Catherine's objections to Novikóv's masonic activities?

DISCUSSION

(a) Catherine now sees freemasonry as a form of religious sectarianism, and as such unlicensed. It troubles her that Novikóv had operated outside state control, and she condemns his work as 'subversive activity' (question 3).

(b) She suspects the Rosicrucians as a conspiratorial secret society in league with influential hostile foreigners (Prussia at this time threatened Russia with war).

(c) The document suggests Catherine's growing fear of independent sources of opinion, unofficial activities, publication of unauthorized (masonic) books.

(She also feared opposition from circles who put their hopes in the Grand Duke Paul and aimed to initiate him into masonry.)

EXERCISE Compare document 50 with document 4 and explain the contrast.

DISCUSSION We seem to see a complete reversal in Catherine's attitude towards the *Encyclopédie* and what it stood for. At the beginning and throughout most of the reign, enthusiasm for and active promotion of enlightened ideas; at the end, outright condemnation of the *philosophes* and the *Encyclopédie* as destructive and revolutionary. She has become increasingly defensive of her own authority, fearful of social upheaval in Russia, and suspicious of independent thought and action among the *intelligentsia* whom she had earlier encouraged. What has changed her is the impact of the French Revolution and its open defiance of established government and absolute monarchy throughout Europe. (She was also influenced in this by the British commentator, Edmund Burke, whose *Reflections on the Revolution in France* (1790) you will be introduced to in your study of Mary Wollstonecraft).

3.12 Catherine the Great: Outline chronology

1729	Born in Stettin, as Princess Sophia of Anhalt-Zerbst
1744	Comes to Russia to marry heir to throne, Grand Duke Peter (rules 1761–2)
1762	Accedes to throne after overthrow of Peter III
1766	Essay Competition on serfdom

1767	*The Nakaz*
1767–8	Legislative Commission
1768–74	First Turkish War
1772	First Partition of Poland
1773–4	Pugachóv Rebellion
1775	Provincial Statute
1783	Annexation of Crimea
1785	Municipal Charter
	Charter of the Nobility
1786	Statute on National Education
1787–90	Second Turkish War
1788	War with Sweden
1790	Trial of Radíshchev
1793	Second Partition of Poland
1794	Imprisonment of Novikóv
1795	Third Partition of Poland
1796	Death of Catherine

4   *References*

Alexander, J.T. (1989) *Catherine the Great. Life and Legend*, Oxford University Press, Oxford.

Anderson, M.S. (1987) *Europe in the Eighteenth Century*, 3rd edition, Longman, London.

Bartlett, R. (1991) 'Catherine II of Russia, Enlightened Absolutism and Mikhail Gorbachev', *The Historian*, No. 30, pp.3–8.

Behrens, C.B.A. (1985) *Government and the Enlightenment. The Experiences of Eighteenth-century France and Prussia*, Thames and Hudson, London.

Blanning, T.C.W. (1989) 'Frederick the Great', in H.M. Scott (ed.) *Enlightened Absolutism. Reform and Reformers in Later Eighteenth-century Europe*, Macmillan, London, pp.265–88.

Born, K.E. (1986) 'Die Wirkungsgeschichte Friedrichs des Grossen' in Leuschner (1986), pp.205–31.

Bruford, W.H. (1965) *Germany in the Eighteenth Century. The Social Background of the Literary Revival*, Cambridge University Press, Cambridge.

Dukes, P. (1990) 'Why Peter? Why not Catherine? Some reflections on the development of Russian absolutism', *Study Group on Eighteenth-Century Russia Newsletter*, No.18, pp.45-8.

Hunter, H. (1800) *History of Catherine II, Empress of Russia*, London.

Lentin, A. (1974) *Voltaire and Catherine the Great. Selected Correspondence*, Oriental Research Partners, Cambridge.

Raeff, M. (ed.) (1972) *Catherine the Great. A Profile*, Hill and Wang, New York, pp.301–21.

5 Further reading

5.1 Documents

Aldington, R. (trans.) (1927) *Letters of Voltaire and Frederick the Great*, Broadway Library of XVIII century French Literature, London.

Budberg, M. (trans.) (1955) *The Memoirs of Catherine the Great*, Hamish Hamilton, London. (Fascinating on Catherine's early life, the memoirs end before her accession.)

Lentin, A. (ed.) (1974) *Voltaire and Catherine the Great. Selected Correspondence*, Oriental Research Partners, Cambridge.

Lentin, A. (ed.) (1985) *Enlightened Absolutism (1760–1790). A Documentary Source Book*, Avero Eighteenth-century Publications, Newcastle-upon-Tyne. (This has a fuller collection of documents on Frederick and Catherine than could be presented in this study.)

5.2 Secondary studies: Frederick

Asprey, A. (1986) *Frederick the Great. The Magnificent Enigma*, Ticknor and Fields, New York. (A full, up-to-date, reliable and readable biography.)

Behrens, C.B.A. (1985) *Society, Government and the Enlightenment. The Experiences of Eighteenth-century France and Prussia*, Thames and Hudson. (A detailed comparative overview.)

Blanning, T.C.W. (1989) in H.M. Scott (ed.), *Enlightened Absolutism. Reform and Reformers in Later Eighteenth Century Europe*, Macmillan, pp.265–88. (A well-argued brief discussion of Frederick and the case for and against his 'enlightenment'.)

Hubatsch, W. (1973) *Frederick the Great of Prussia. Absolutism and Administration*, Thames and Hudson. (A detailed study of Frederick as an enlightened administrator.)

Leuschner, H. (1986) *Friedrich der Grosse. Zeit. Person. Wirkung*, C. Bertelsmann Verlag GmbH - Bertelsmann Lexikothek Verlag GbmH, Gütersloh. (More compendious than Ziechmann (1985), and including an invaluable lexicon of persons, topics and events.)

Paret, P. (ed.) (1972) *Frederick the Great: A Profile*, Macmillan. (A useful collection of essays.)

Ritter, G. (1968) *Frederick the Great: an historical profile* (translated by P. Paret), University of California Press. (This older study is a useful supplement to Asprey (1986); it has a most thoughtful discussion of its subject against the background, never directly mentioned, of the Third Reich.)

Ziechmann, J. (ed.) (1985) *Panorama der Friedericianischen Zeit. Friedrich der Grosse und seine Epoche. Ein Handbuch*, edition Ziechmann, Bremen, (An exhaustive collection of 90 scholarly essays in German.)

5.3 Secondary studies: Catherine

Alexander, J.T. (1989) *Catherine the Great. Life and Legend*, Oxford University Press, Oxford. (A full, up-to-date, scholarly and readable biography.)

Madariaga, I. de (1981) *Russia in the Age of Catherine the Great*, Yale University Press, New Haven.

Madariaga, I. de (1990) *Catherine the Great. A Short History*, Yale University Press, New Haven. (A close study of Catherine and her achievements, which is shorter than Alexander (1989), and draws on de Madariaga's magisterial earlier work (1981).)

Raeff, M. (ed.) (1972) *Catherine the Great. A Profile*, Hill and Wang, New York. (An excellent collection of essays, mostly by Russian historians.)

For Radíshchev and Novikóv, see:

Jones, W. G. *(1984) Nikolai Novikov, Enlightener of Russia*, Cambridge University Press, Cambridge.

MacConnell, A. *(1964) A Russian Philosophe. Alexander Radishchev*, Mouton, The Hague.

Radishchev, A.N. (1958) *A Journey from St Petersburg to Moscow*, translated by L. Wiener, edited by R.P. Thaler, Harvard University Press, Cambridge, Mass.

Beccaria, Howard and Penal Reform

*Prepared for the Course Team by
Clive Emsley and Colin Cunningham*

Contents

Beccaria, Howard and Penal Reform (Study week 4)

Studies/Texts	Radio	TV	AC	Set books
Studies, I		TV3	AC1632 (blue)	–
Texts, I	–	–	–	–

The principal aim of this unit is to introduce you to Enlightenment ideas of penal reform and the work of Cesare Beccaria and John Howard. In particular we will be focussing on two pamphlets, Beccaria's *Dei Delitti e delle Pene (On Crimes and Punishments)* and Howard's *An Enquiry into the Present State of the Prisons in England and Wales.* Two secondary aims arise out of the need to contextualize Beccaria and his work: first, to introduce you to eighteenth-century Italy and the nature of the Italian Enlightenment; and secondly, to introduce you to some of the modern academic debate over possible reasons why ideas for penal reform emerged in the period of the Enlightenment.

The unit is divided into five sections:

1   Eighteenth-century Italy

2   The Enlightenment in Italy

3   Beccaria and his work

4   The impact of *On Crimes and Punishments*

5   Prison reform: The architecture of repression in the Enlightenment.

When you come to sections 4 and 5, you will probably find it useful to refer to the historical surveys on France and England at the end of this volume of *Studies*.

Beccaria, Howard and Penal Reform

1 Eighteenth-century Italy

EXERCISE: Start by looking at the map of Italy after the treaty of Aix-la-Chapelle in 1748 (Map 4). What strikes you immediately about the political structure of Italy?

Map 4
Italy in 1748 at the conclusion of the Treaty of Aix-la-Chapelle. (From D. Carpanetto and G. Ricuperati, Italy in the Age of Reason 1685-1789, *Longman, London, 1987)*

SPECIMEN ANSWER   Italy was not a single political unit in 1748; it was a collection of separate kingdoms (Sardinia, the Two Sicilies), or republics (Genoa, Lucca, San Marino, Venice), duchies (Mantua, Milan, Modena, Parma, Tuscany), and stretched across the centre were states owing allegiance to the Pope.

DISCUSSION   Note that this map is dated 1748 – after the Treaty of Aix-la-Chapelle which ended the War of the Austrian Succession. Among other things, this treaty settled the boundaries of the Italian states which had been shifting as the result of wars and diplomacy for half a century and more. The new boundaries were to last until the 1790s and the wars of the French Revolution in the 1790s. Some of the Italian states were autonomous: the two kingdoms and the republics are the obvious examples, though the Bourbon monarchy, which had taken over the Two Sicilies in 1734, was from the same family as the ruling house of Spain. The duchies of Mantua and Milan were part of the Austrian Empire; occasionally they are described as Lombardy, yet the true Lombardy was rather bigger and included territory controlled by the Venetian Republic. The Grand Duchy of Tuscany had been ruled by the Medici family until the line died out in 1737; the great powers of Europe agreed to the duchy's then passing to the Duke of Lorraine, but since the duke was the husband of Maria Theresa of Austria, Tuscany became an autonomous region of the Austrian Empire.

Within the complex and shifting political divisions of eighteenth-century Italy, the population grew from about 13 million in 1700, to just over 15 million in 1750, and to almost 18 million by 1800. This rate of increase was rather less than that calculated for Europe as a whole but was, nevertheless, significant. As elsewhere in Europe, the overwhelming majority of the population of Italy were peasants. However, again as elsewhere, the term 'peasant' masks considerable variations – from landless labourers (*bracciante*) whose numbers increased during the eighteenth century, to small farmers. In the south the situation remained semi-feudal; there were great grain-producing *latifundia* worked by poor, landless daylabourers who eked out their earnings by the customary usage of common land for pasture, wood, chestnuts and hunting. In the centre the peasants were often sharecroppers, but the annual contracts between landowner and tenant varied greatly from place to place. The short-term nature of the contract militated against the peasant seeking to make any significant improvements to the land. Share-cropping (*mezzadria*) was also to be found in Lombardy. However, in the north, agriculture was becoming more modernized: here the peasants might also be day-labourers, though less likely to be subject to feudal jurisdiction than peasants in the Two Sicilies.

Italy had more great towns than any other European state, though only a small percentage of her population was urban. In 1700 Naples was the third largest city in Europe, after London and Paris. In all, at the beginning of the century, six Italian towns had populations in excess of 100,000 – Messina, Milan, Naples, Palermo, Rome and Venice – and many others were large by the standards of the day. In part, this was a legacy of the great days of the Italian city-state and of Italy's past primacy in Mediterranean trade. But every small state had to have its administrative and judicial centre, and its ruling elite demanded the buildings and services which only an urban environment could provide – large numbers of town dwellers were servants, clients or providers of goods and services for the nobility. The towns attracted migrants – both permanent and seasonal – but there was no single great metropolis which acted as a cultural centre for the whole of the peninsula: Italian cities during the eighteenth century remained essentially parochial and provincial.

While some of the towns continued to be significant trading centres, the eighteenth century was generally a period of decline for the once great ports of Genoa and Venice, and of economic stagnation for Italy in general. The trade with the Islamic East, which had been dominated by the Venetian Republic, had begun to decline in the seventeenth century, while the merchant ships of the Dutch, the English and the French had begun to squeeze the Italians out of the trade with northern Europe. While agriculture in the north of Italy was modernising, there was little change in the south and the *mezzadria* system with its short leases positively discouraged improvements by the tenants. The whole economy of the peninsula was also checked by the variety of different currencies, by different weights and measures, and by local tolls and customs barriers between the states which were only partially and very gradually dismantled during the century. The unfavourable economic climate impeded the growth of any entrepreneurial middle class. Indeed, such a social group scarcely existed in eighteenth-century Italy. Such industry as there was, continued to be based in the small workshops of artisans and their journeymen.

The ruling elites in the duchies, the kingdoms and the republics were generally nobles. They were relatively few in number; it has been estimated, for example, that they comprised just over one percent of the population in northern Italy. But 'noble' is as wide a term as 'peasant'. There were urban patricians, especially in the republics, and feudal lords in the countryside. In Lombardy the nobility was made up of three distinct groups: the old feudal families; the patriciate of Milan which had originated in the town's mercantile elite; those families who had been ennobled during the Spanish domination of the duchy between 1535 and 1714. But this was not a closed caste; it was prepared to co-opt wealthy families by conceding grants of nobility or by intermarriage. In Piedmont a situation developed somewhat similar to that in France; from the late seventeenth century the dukes of Savoy kept their feudal nobility at court but increasingly denied them access to the principal offices of state, which were filled by men with mercantile and financial origins; successful administrators were then often rewarded with titles of nobility.

2   *The Enlightenment in Italy*

There was press censorship in eighteenth-century Italy and, although greatly in decline, the Inquisition still had an influence; even so, in general, the intellectual climate was favourable to debate and receptive to new ideas. The political divisions and the reluctance of states to cooperate with each other probably greatly limited any restriction on the circulation of ideas. There were a large number of universities and academies, another legacy of the past. There was an educated elite which, although Catholic, was generally open to the rational and sceptical ideas of the age. Governments, keen to maximize their revenues, were prepared to give employment to men of ideas and ability either in the state administration or in the universities, sometimes creating chairs especially for particular individuals.

At the close of the seventeenth century, Italian intellectuals recognized that hopes for the unification of the peninsula were unrealistic. But they feared that, even though Italian thought and example had played a significant part in the development of European civilisation and culture, it was now in decline. Such fears led to attempts to stimulate Italian intellectual endeavour and to link scholars with one another. The first such attempt was the *Arcadia*, an academy established in Rome in 1690 which succeeded, over the next thirty years, in creating a network of intellectuals, between 1500 and 2500 strong, spread through all the states of Italy. However, the *Arcadia* was strongly influenced by the Roman Curia (the Papal Court); and it has been argued that, rather than encouraging free thought, the thrust of the organisation was to undermine the rationalist trends in contemporary ideas. In 1704 Ludovico Antonio Muratori, a young priest working as keeper of the archives in the ducal library at Modena, published *Primi disegni di una repubblica letteraria d'Italia (First Sketches for an Italian Republic of Letters)* which outlined his ideas for a 're-public of letters'. Muratori wanted an organisation that would be both a centre for research and for the dissemination of all that was best in Italian culture. Furthermore, he had positive ideas about the kind of research that he wished to see pursued; above all, it was to have positive and material value by concentrating on scholarship and science rather than the literature which was the focus for the *Arcadia*.

Muratori's proposal excited much discussion and, while his 'republic of letters' was never established, his ideas prompted a group of Venetian intellectuals to publish *Giornale de' letterati d'Italia (Italian Literary Journal)*. This new journal, aimed at educated men across Italy, also fostered collaboration between intellectuals and governments in both Naples and Piedmont. Muratori himself went on to publish a large number of books and pamphlets, particularly on historical subjects, and these were to have a profound impact on the next generation of intellectuals. His work was informed by an enlightened Catholicism, often focussing on the conflict between reason and superstition, and seeking to overturn the restrictions of a backward and traditionalist society. He urged Pope Benedict XIV to reduce the number of religious feast-days which he considered as a potential threat to agricultural and industrial work. He studied medieval superstitions and suggested that these, together with a defective legal system permitting torture, were instrumental in enabling the accused to be found guilty in cases of diabolical practices and witchcraft. In 1749 he published *Della pubblica felicità* (literally, *On the public happiness*), a manual of enlightened reform for princes which proposed that general well-being and happiness was a valid and realisable objective for rulers and their ministers, and which urged freedom of trade, as well as agricultural and fiscal reform. There is evidence for believing that this book, which achieved considerable recognition and success throughout Europe, was the first introduction to policies for enlightened government for the future Joseph II of Austria as well as his brother, and successor, Leopold.

The long period of peace which followed the Treaty of Aix-la-Chapelle was beneficial to Italian intellectual development. Italian gentlemen travelled elsewhere in Europe, while foreign travellers came to Italy and foreign books circulated widely. The courts, particularly those of Naples and Milan, attracted savants and artists, often from France. The enlightened thinkers who emerged in Italy in the third quarter of the eighteenth century cannot easily be characterized as a group, though it is fair to say that, in general, they were concerned with immediate Italian problems. In the time and space available, it is impossible to give you anything other than a brief introduction to their thought, and I think that the best way to proceed is to concentrate on two influential figures, one from the south and one from the north.

Antonio Genovesi came from a modest background in Salerno. With some misgivings, he had entered the Church to secure an education; but his religious rationalism, which drew on the work of Muratori and John Locke, brought him into conflict with the Church authorities and this led, ultimately, to his being banned from teaching theology. He continued to hold a chair in ethics at the University of Naples, but his interests shifted away from philosophy and theology to subjects more in keeping with the spirit of the Enlightenment – the progress of human reason, the arts, trade and the economy. In 1753 Genovesi published an introduction to a recent treatise on agricultural reform. *Discorso sopra il vero fine delle arti e delle scienze (Discourse on the true ends of the arts and sciences)* was, in essence, a manifesto for developing the economy of southern Italy. Genovesi criticized abstract scholarship and, appealing to reason and experience, stressed the need for a rational education, for young people to be aware of the value of economics and technology, for the creation of an agricultural academy with branches throughout the kingdom, for the improvement of the living and working conditions of those engaged in manual labour, and for an increase in the active population. Also, as part and parcel of the latter, he urged that the clergy should not be allowed to live idle lives. The year after the *Discorso* was published, Genovesi was appointed to a chair of political economy at the University of Naples. The chair was created for him by a special endowment which also stipulated that in future the post must be filled by competition and that clerics were to be excluded. He continued to develop his ideas while holding the chair, most notably in the two volumes (1765 and 1767) of *Delle lezioni di commercio o sia di economica civile (On the understanding of commerce or civil economy)* which were essentially concerned with economic debates, particularly the importance of luxury in civil life, but which also challenged Rousseauist ideas about the 'noble savage' and egalitarian utopias. Genovesi recommended reformist governments which would correct the most glaring abuses in society. He died in 1769, but directly and indirectly, his work influenced intellectuals in the south for many years afterwards.

The most important single figure of the Enlightenment in Lombardy was a nobleman, Pietro Verri, who, after a youth spent in wild love affairs, ferocious family arguments, and a distinguished career in the Austrian army during the Seven Years' War, finally settled down in his early thirties to encourage literary, political and social reform. Verri saw that northern Italy had the potential to be economically rich and strong. This led him to support, and indeed to go beyond the Habsburg plans for centralising Lombardy by bypassing and undermining the independence of the Church and the nobility. Such ideas brought him into conflict with his father who was typical of the conservative nobility. Verri wanted to change the ideas of his class. In 1763 he published *Meditazioni sulla felicità (Meditations on happiness)* in which he asserted that it was the task of the intellectual to ensure the good of all and argued that the ethical basis for all political action should be utilitarian. Verri's morality was based not on religion but on a material calculation of pleasure and pain. He saw human history as progress, often interrupted, but always able to benefit and to grow from experience; new ideas could not be ignored; enlightened princes, dedicated to reform, were needed.

Verri, and his brother Alessandro, attracted around themselves a group of young, like-minded Milanese and formed a society known as the *Academia dei Pugni* (The Academy of Fists). They published *Il Caffè (The Café)*, which, although it lasted only two years, 1764 to 1766, was the most important journal of the Italian Enlightenment. Among this group was the one member of the Italian Enlightenment who achieved a major and overnight impact on European society – Cesare Beccaria.

3   Beccaria and his work

Figure 9
*Cesare Beccaria
Portrait. (Courtesy of Civiche
Raccolte delle Stampe, 'Achille
Bertarelli', Castello Sforzesco,
Milano)*

Cesare Beccaria was born on 15th March 1738 into a noble Milanese family. He was educated at a Jesuit college in Parma for eight years, and graduated with a degree in law from the University of Pavia in 1758. Beccaria became a close friend of the Verri brothers; they encouraged him to marry, against his father's wishes, in 1761, and subsequently arranged the reconciliation between father and son. He joined the Verris in the *Academia dei Pugni* and it was as a result of their promptings and asssitance that he began writing, first, in 1762, a treatise on the financial problems of his native Milan, and two years later, *On Crimes and Punishments*. The Verri's role in the production of the latter was crucial: they proposed the topic and discussed it with Beccaria as he was writing it; Pietro transcribed it and arranged for it to be published in Leghorn by the man who had brought out his own *Meditazione sulla felicità*.

The success of the book led to an invitation from the Encyclopedists for Pietro Verri and Beccaria to visit Paris. Pietro was himself unable to go, but persuaded a very reluctant Beccaria to make the trip in company with Alessandro. Beccaria could not cope with the adoration heaped upon him in Paris. He seemed permanently anxious to his hosts and, after about a month, he fled back to Milan and never left it again. The hasty departure from Paris was against Pietro's advice and led to strained relations between the two, but the success of *On Crimes and Punishments* brought Beccaria the patronage of the ruling Habsburgs. In 1768 he was appointed to a specially created chair of economics at the Palatinate college of Milan. Three years later he exchanged this for a post in the public administration where he continued to serve until his death in 1794.

During the last thirty years of his life Beccaria did not publish anything else of note; he did write a significant study of economics, *Elementi di economia pubblica (The Elements of public economy)*, but this was not published until 1804. The long silence helped to create a myth. For many in

England and France who admired his work, it seemed that the silence was the result of repression at the hands of a tyrannical government. After his death this notion also gained credence in Italy, particularly when, following the conquest of Milan by the French Revolutionary armies, 'Citizen' Pietro Verri forgot the long breach which had existed between him and his old friend and urged that the municipality erect a monument to 'the immortal Beccaria'.

I want now to take you through the extracts from *On Crimes and Punishments* which are included in *Texts*, I. Turn to this now (p.93).

EXERCISE   Read I. 'Introduction' and consider:

1   How, according to Beccaria, laws were made in the past; and how they should now be made.

2   Where, earlier in this study, you have come across ideas approaching Beccaria's suggestion that laws should be made to ensure the greatest happiness of the greatest number.

SPECIMEN ANSWERS   1   According to Beccaria, in the past, laws were not made rationally but were the products of passion or emergencies. He does not give a precise statement of how laws ought to be made here, but he suggests that there should be a detailed and dispassionate analysis, using 'geometrical precision', of certain key questions.

2   The idea was, perhaps, implicit in Muratori's *Della pubblica felicità* when he spoke of 'public happiness' as being a valid and realisable aim for princes; it was similarly latent in Verri's *Meditazione*.

DISCUSSION   These questions should not have given you too much trouble. If your answers were wildly different from mine, I suggest that you go back over the passage with my suggestions in mind. Rationalism, and developing ideas with 'geometrical precision' were at the core of much Enlightenment thought. The idea of *felicità pubblica* was central to the Italian Enlightenment; you will find it recurring throughout *On Crimes and Punishments*, though generally for eighteenth-century Italian intellectuals, and reforming administrators it was understood with reference to economic improvement.

EXERCISE   Now read the next page or so under the heading, II 'The Origin of Punishments, and the Right to Punish', and note down answers to:

1   How, according to Beccaria, did society come about?

2   How did punishment come about?

SPECIMEN ANSWERS   1   Society, Beccaria states, came about as a result of men coming together for mutual protection; in so doing they were sacrificing some part of their liberty to enjoy the remainder in peace and safety.

2   Punishment was the way of enforcing the laws that enable society to function.

DISCUSSION   What Beccaria is presenting here is a form of contract theory: men coming together to form society in place of a state of nature. Beccaria's state of nature was clearly an unpleasant one – 'a continual state of war'. Not every thinker of the Enlightenment would have agreed, although you have already encountered the notion of the contract theory in government in Diderot's entry on *Political Authority*, in the *Encyclopédie* (*Texts*, I, p.12). The issues of contract theory, and what rights men renounced when they entered society were hotly disputed by both eighteenth-century thinkers and by activists in the American and French Revolutions.

EXERCISE   Read on to the end of the extract and note down answers to the following questions:

1   What, according to Beccaria, should be the purpose of punishment?

2   What is wrong with very severe punishments?

3   What is wrong with the death penalty?

4   On whom, and on what, does Beccaria place his faith for improvement?

5   What should be the key factors governing punishment?

6   Do you detect anything in Beccaria's discussion about who he believes criminals are, and why they commit crimes?

7   What part, if any, does religion play in Beccaria's arguments?

SPECIMEN ANSWERS   1   Punishment should be designed to prevent criminals from committing new offences and to deter others who might possibly offend.

2   Too severe punishment might encourage criminals to commit additional or more serious crimes to avoid capture (a thief, for example, might commit murder to ensure that he could not be identified by his victim).

3   The death penalty gives an example of barbarity on the part of the authorities which, to Beccaria's mind, was a bad thing as it could suggest coldness and despotism. Moreover the execution of an offender was over in a moment and to Beccaria's rational mind it must therefore have had far less impact on both the public and on potential offenders than a life of penal servitude.

4   Beccaria hoped that enlightened monarchs – 'fathers to their peoples … crowned citizens' – would carry out reforms; he also believed that enlightened education would lead to improvement.

5   Generally speaking, Beccaria believed that individual punishment should be relevant to the crime for which it was given; it should also be both prompt and certain.

6 It is in the passage where he attempts to think through the thought processes of criminals contemplating the death penalty that Beccaria identifies the origins of his criminals: they are the poor and the hungry, who reason that it is better to have a good life for a few years before being caught, than to continue suffering passively. The same passage is implicitly critical of the rich who have no idea of how the poor live. Again, perhaps, there is evidence here of the influence of Pietro Verri who was keen to reform the ideas of his fellow nobles.

7 The tone of the pamphlet is almost completely secular, though there is a reference to a 'first cause' at one point. This is something which underlines Beccaria's links with the concerns of the *philosophes*.

DISCUSSION The extracts are, I think, straightforward and readily comprehensible but again, if you got very different answers from mine you should go back to the extracts with my comments in mind. I do not intend to discuss each of these questions and answers in detail, but we will return to most of the issues raised in the next section, which looks at the impact of Beccaria's book.

4 The impact of On Crimes and Punishments

Beccaria was concerned about the kind of reaction that his book would provoke. He therefore published the first edition anonymously. There was some hostile criticism. A monk, Ferdinando Facchinei, accused him of attacking both monarchy and the Church:

> Almost all that our author puts forward rests only on two false and absurd principles – that all men are born free and are naturally equal, and that the laws are no more, nor should be, than the voluntary pacts between such men.

In 1766 the book was put on the Catholic Index of forbidden books because of its rationalistic presuppositions. But the overwhelming reaction to the book was favourable, especially among the *philosophes* and the enlightened despots. Frederick the Great admired Beccaria's work; see, for example, his letter to Condorcet and his decision that two arsonists be reformed rather than executed (Frederick documents 31–32). Catherine the Great drew heavily upon it in preparing her reform of the Russian criminal law (*Studies*, I, p.88), and she invited Beccaria to her court to supervise the reform. Partly as a result of reading the book, Maria Theresa abolished torture in her hereditary lands of Austria and Bohemia; ironically, the conservative nobles in Milan, through their Senate, prevented her from doing the same in the duchy, insisting that torture was a necessity of government. Only when her son, Joseph II, abolished the Senate could Beccaria's native Milan abolish torture. Maria Theresa's second son, Leopold, used the book extensively when, as Grand Duke of Tuscany, he drew up a new legal code in 1786 and astonished Europe by abolishing both the death penalty and the crime of lese-majesty (treason).

It would be possible to chart the interest and excitement generated by the book in every country touched by the European Enlightenment, but I want now to look in detail at its impact in two states, England and France.

In England, concerns for a more effective (in the sense of crime-preventing) and a better regulated system of punishment went back at least to the beginning of the eighteenth century. Today, prison is generally regarded as the principal kind of punishment for serious offenders, but this was not the case during the eighteenth century. Prisons were usually considered as places where the accused might be held before trial and where the convicted might be held before physical punishment or execution; some petty offenders were given gaol sentences, but the law did not designate prison as the place of punishment. The idle or vagrants might be set to work in a 'house of correction', but few thinkers considered prisons as places for the reform of serious offenders . The English criminal system of the eighteenth century is often described as 'the Bloody Code'. The principal punishment for felony was death, and more and more capital statutes were made as the century wore on. By 1800, there were upwards of two hundred. Several qualifications need to be made to this ostensibly barbaric system: first there was no categorisation of crime as we know it today, consequently capital statutes were invariably tied to particular types, or items, of property – there was, for example, one statute which made it a capital offence to attempt to pull down Westminster Bridge, and another for attempting to destroy Fulham Bridge, and arguably any general attempt to pull down either might also have been covered by the Riot Act of 1714 or possibly the Black Act of 1723; thus at least four, and probably more statutes, covered what was, to modern eyes, the same kind of offence. Surprisingly, although the number of capital statutes increased during the eighteenth century, the number of executions did not, and most of the offenders who were hanged were sentenced under legislation dating back to the Tudors. The new legislation might have appeared 'bloody', but it was not often used. Large numbers of those found guilty were released after pleading benefit of clergy – a relic of the middle ages when clergy claimed to be outside the jurisdiction of the temporal courts, and which, by the late seventeenth century enabled a judge to exercise a discretionary leniency to any offender who could read a particular passage from the Bible. Also, following legislation of 1718, it was possible to have an offender, male or female, transported to one of the British colonies (generally in America) for a fixed term or for life. The less serious offences could be punished by flogging, by fine, by the pillory or, occasionally, by prison.

While, in the middle of the century, it was possible to find judges and legal theorists who insisted that it was necessary to be able to make the occasional, terrible example on the gallows, there appears also to have been a feeling that something was needed between the sentence of death and that of transportation. This feeling affected prosecutors and juries as well as judges and theorists. It was common practice for prosecutors (and in the eighteenth century, cases were generally brought by victims as prosecutors) to undervalue property which had been stolen so as to avoid the possibility of bringing about the death of the accused; and if the prosecutor did not down-value any goods stolen, then a jury bring-ing in a verdict of guilty might. There was also increasing disquiet among many judges, legal theorists and politicians, about the effect of public executions. These were supposed to discourage potential offenders by making a terrible example, yet too often the events around 'Tyburn Tree' seemed more reminiscent of the fair-ground. (Public execution is one of the topics covered in TV3, 'Humanity and the Scaffold'.)

Public executions were also supposed to have a didactic purpose in France, but as in England they were often taken to be holidays, and satur-nalia triumphed over solemnity. The eighteenth-century French penal system was based on the Criminal Ordinance of 1670 which concentrated overwhelmingly on the procedure of the courts rather than on specifying particular punishments for particular crimes. This meant that magistrates and judges had considerable discretion when it came to sentencing, though they were tied to a particular code of practice for a trial. Secrecy was the watchword in eighteenth-century French trials; there was no pub-lic gallery and no trial by jury. The idea was that the panel of experts, the judges and magistrates, should get at the truth by a careful, and private, investigation first of witnesses and then of the accused. It was possible, unless he had been 'caught in the act', for the accused person to be com-pletely unaware, during initial questioning by the court, of the charges being brought. The Ordinance of 1670 had modified the law of proof which reduced the need for *la question préparatoire* (torture to induce a confession), but torture remained a weapon in the judicial armoury both in this form as well as in the form of *la question préalable* (torture to make an offender reveal the names of accomplices). Punishments were as varied as in England, ranging from death for the most serious crimes to banishment from a town or district for petty offences. Again, prison played an insignificant role in punishment and people thought in terms of 'punishment' rather then 'reform'. Rather than being transported across the seas, male offenders not sentenced to death were sent to the galleys of the French Mediterranean fleet, and when these were decom-missioned in 1748, they were sent to the *bagne*, shore-based prisons, often situated on moored ships, in the great seaports and naval arsenals, where they served the needs of the navy as forced labourers. Female offenders might be executed, but were imprisoned in workhouses rather than sent to the galleys or the *bagne*. Executions were rather more varied than in England; hanging was common, so too was breaking on the wheel, and for what the authorities considered particularly heinous crimes, such as Robert Damiens's attempt to assassinate Louis XV in 1757, the most appalling public tortures were concocted.

Criticism of the system went back to the seventeenth century, but became more strident as the Enlightenment developed. Montesquieu attacked the use of torture in his *Lettres Persanes (Persian Letters)* (1721), and the entire system of criminal justice in France was criticized in *De l'Esprit des Lois (The Spirit of the Laws)* (1748). These ideas were taken up and developed in the *Encyclopédie* during the 1750s. The beginning of the following decade witnessed Voltaire embarking on his three celebrated judicial crusades on behalf of Jean Calas (a Protestant executed in 1762 for allegedly murdering his son when the latter became a Catholic), the Sirven family (accused of a similar offence), and the Chevalier de La Barre (tortured and executed for failing to remove his hat and kneel in the presence of a religious procession and for using profane language). (See *Encyclopédie* study, p.33.)

Beccaria's book, appearing in French translation in 1766 and in English translation in 1767, excited debate in both countries. There were some who condemned his arguments out of hand - an example was the French jurist and royal counsellor, Muyart de Vouglans, who insisted that the French legal system had reached perfection and that Beccaria's ideas were dangerous for both government and religion. But increasingly, even members of the legal establishment in France began to be receptive to Beccarian ideas. Young lawyers in particular, like Joseph Servan and Charles Dupaty, began to speak out in favour of reform. In 1780 a royal edict abolished *la question préparatoire*, eight years later a further edict abolished *la question préalable*. Also in 1788, the royal government announced a major reorganisation of the system established by the Ordinance of 1670. This reorganisation was cut short by the Revolution, though reform of the criminal law and penal system was high on the agenda of the early revolutionary legislatures. Bearing in mind the discretion in sentencing allowed to judges and magistrates under the 1670 Ordinance, it is also worth noting the comments of the magistrate Pierre-Louis Roederer that Beccaria's book

> had so changed the spirit of the old criminal courts in France that ten years before the Revolution they had been completely transformed. All the young magistrates – and I can attest to it since I was one of them – handed down their judgements, more in accordance with this work than with the laws. (Maestro, 1942, p.143)

The changes in the criminal law carried out in the early years of the Revolution (1790–91), involving the recognition that prison should be the standard punishment, were eloquent testimony of the extent to which reformist ideas had won the debate.

In England Beccaria's work influenced the great judge and jurist Sir William Blackstone. The fourth volume of Blackstone's *Commentaries on the Laws of England* appeared in 1769, two years after the English translation of *On Crimes and Punishments*. Among other things, it addressed the question of punishment. Blackstone believed that there was still a need for the death penalty, but condemned its indiscriminate use in Beccarian terms:

> ... punishments of unreasonable severity, especially where indiscriminately inflicted, have less effect in preventing crimes, and amending the manners of a people, than such as are more merciful in general, yet properly intermixed with due distinctions of severity. (Beattie, 1986, p.556)

From here Blackstone went on to contemplate new forms of punishment which were not simply deterrents but which also set out to reform offenders. Such ideas, drawn probably from reading both Blackstone and Beccaria, were taken up by MPs like Sir William Meredith, who, in November 1770, moved for an enquiry into the criminal laws. He expressed his concern that, as the law stood, a man, who has privately picked a pocket of a handkerchief worth thirteen pence, is punished with the same severity, as if he had murdered a whole family of benefactors.

This, Meredith believed, served only to make petty thieves more dangerous. He urged

> that none should be punished with death, but those who could not be made safely useful, except in cases of murder, where a capital punishment, as it would be less common, would operate more forcibly *in terrorem* [as a deterrent], and consequently more effectually answer its end. (Meredith, 1771, p.147).

The following year saw another M.P., William Eden, publish the influential *Principles of Penal Law* challenging the 'Bloody Code's' reliance on the death penalty, querying the value of transportation, and suggesting the need for some kind of punishment which would be continuous, lasting and public. Eden had doubted the value of prison since he feared that close confinement often only made offenders worse; but, like many others, he was converted to the idea of reforming offenders in regulated, orderly penal institutions by John Howard's *The State of the Prisons in England and Wales*, discussed in the final section of this study.

Together Blackstone, Eden and Howard prepared a parliamentary bill providing for the construction of two prisons in London: one for 600 men, the other for 300 women. The inmates were to be incarcerated for up to two years. They were to be uniformed, put to hard labour with each other during the day, and shut in solitary confinement by night. The aim was specifically to reform the offenders and teach them 'Habits of Industry'; the prisons were to be known as 'penitentiaries'. Parliament passed the bill in 1779, but the financial situation, particularly because of war against the American colonists and then against the French Revolution, meant that it was thirty years before work was started on a government-funded penitentiary in London. Debate and discussion continued during these years, however. In 1791 Jeremy Bentham, the Utilitarian philosopher who made Beccaria's phrase about 'the greatest happiness of the greatest number' his own, published *Panopticon*, an architectural and theoretical plan for a prison which would enable constant supervision of convicts working, and thus being reformed, for up to sixteen hours a day. At the same time, in the provinces, a clutch of reformers – notably the Duke of Richmond in Sussex, Sir George Onesiphorus Paul in Gloucestershire, and Thomas Butterworth Bailey in Manchester – established county gaols with regimes designed to inculcate 'Habits of Industry', and to prevent the contagion of criminal habits by separating those convicted from those awaiting trial, first offenders from recidivists, and men from women.

The debates about crime and punishment in the second half of the eighteenth century were not, however, confined to questions of prisons and the death penalty.

One of the key elements of Beccaria's plan was the certainty of punishment. But before an offender is tried, he or she must be caught.

Today, the apprehension of criminal offenders is usually regarded as a task for the police. France was generally considered to have the best police in eighteenth-century Europe. In Paris there were some 3000 men, about half of whom patrolled the city streets and maintained guard posts. Provincial towns and cities had a variety of watchmen and guards, generally dependent upon how much money the municipality was prepared to invest in policing. The main roads were patrolled by the *maréchaussée*, a military-style police force of about 3500 men. It was the police in Paris and the *maréchaussée* that other monarchs sought to emulate; the English being the notable exception. One English commentator, Sir William Mildmay, who was himself most impressed with the French police system, explained,

> I am aware particularly, that the *maréchaussée* in the provinces, and the watch-guard at Paris, go under the name of military establishments, and consequently cannot be initiated by our administration, under a free and civil constitution of government.

England, in contrast to France, was a

> land of liberty, where the injured and oppressed are to seek for no other protection, but that which the law ought to afford, without plying for aid to a military power; a remedy dangerous, and perhaps worse than the disease. (Mildmay, 1763, pp.iv, 41).

In England there were no centralized policing systems: there were local parish constables and watchmen – the former were generally non-professionals and part-time, the latter were paid. But when a local authority did not pay much, it did not get very good watchmen. There were professional thief-takers, like the celebrated Bow Street Runners, though the dubious practices of some thief-takers led many to view them all with suspicion.

Though the French policing system looks to have been more efficient, it should be noted first, how thin the *maréchaussée* were on the ground, and second, that efficient English night watches (of which there seem to have been several) patrolled with the same care and competence as later policemen. Furthermore, whatever the apparent efficiency of the one and inefficiency of the other, in the second half of the eighteenth century, concerns were expressed about the levels of crime and the standards of policing in both countries. In France these concerns focussed especially on the countryside, where population growth was forcing more and more impoverished young people on to the roads looking for work; to the respectable, however, these unfortunates were simply vagabonds and beggars, and it always appeared a short step from vagabond to thief and murderer. The government tried strengthening and reorganising the *maréchaussée*; but others called for the force as a whole, or for individual companies, to be disbanded and for the army to be deployed in its place. The major strengthening and reorganisation of the *maréchaussée* had to await the French Revolution when it doubled in size and was rechristened the *gendarmerie nationale*. In England the sense of insecurity focussed primarily on the sprawling metropolis – the largest city in Europe with a population of one million by the end of the century. There was too much gaming, drinking, debauchery and 'luxury'; the poor sought to emulate their social superiors in these pursuits, and theft was the easiest way for them to secure the necessary money. Henry Fielding, magistrate and novelist, caught the tone in 1751 when he lamented

> the vast Torrent of Luxury which ... hath poured itself into this nation ... It reaches the very Dregs of the People, who aspiring still to a Degree beyond that which belongs to them, and not being able by the Fruits of honest Labour to support the State which they affect, they disdain the Wages to which their Industry would intitle

them; and abandoning themselves to Idleness, the more simple and poor-spirited betake themselves to a State of Starving and Beggary, while those of more Art and Courage become Thieves, Sharpers and Robbers. (Zirker, 1988, p.77)

Henry Fielding and his brother, Sir John, were key figures in developing the police system in Bow Street. The idea of 'police' was discussed increasingly as the century wore on with piecemeal changes being made in London and with borough and county magistrates making their own local improvements; but hostility to the idea of a uniformed, centralized police force – something which seemed to the English to be peculiarly foreign to their ideas of liberty – was kept at arm's length until the second quarter of the nineteenth century.

Beccaria's work then contributed to existing debate within England and France (as well as elsewhere). It crystallized the thoughts of many already arguing for change, it converted others. But the major question has yet to be faced: how do we explain the interest in and demand for reform in the criminal systems of different countries during the second half of the eighteenth century?

The traditional view has stressed 'great men' with far-sighted ideas winning converts by the common sense and humanitarianism of their arguments, and in many respects this has been the view that you have encountered so far in this course during discussion of the *philosophes*. But this does not explain what it was that made these great men turn their attention to criminal justice and penal reform in the first place; nor what made others susceptible to their arguments at that particular time.

EXERCISE   Looking back over what I have said in the last two or three paragraphs, can you think of anything which might have led people to be interested in these questions in the second half of the eighteenth century?

SPECIMEN ANSWER: There were fears in the French countryside about beggars and vagabonds; and there were fears in England, particularly about the poorer elements of society in London. These arguably led men to question how better to prevent crime and to consider and debate new proposals.

DISCUSSION   In more general terms and looking back to the work you have already done on the *Encyclopédie*, as the principle of scientific explanation by natural causes gained wider acceptance, the notion that human crimes are often the result of adverse circumstances and a bad environment probably gained ground at the expense of old religious explanations. This trend was strengthened by philosophical optimism, and the notions of philosophers like Rousseau that human beings were basically good. If they were rational beings, then the sense of reasonable, good behaviour could be made clear to all but the most incorrigible.

Some historians have also stressed the role of great economic and social changes in contributing both to these fears and the desire to reform the penal system. Georg Rusche and Otto Kirchheimer related different systems of punishment with different social structures and argued that, during the Enlightenment, change came about not through an altruistic desire to make punishment more humane, but as a result of the twin desires of first, protecting the rising bourgeoisie from arbitrary punishment by their social superiors, and secondly, preventing upheaval by their social inferiors brought about by brutal and unequal punishment (Rusche and Kirchheimer (1939). The French philosopher-historian, Michel Foucault, argued that within the Enlightenment there was a growing trend towards establishing a disciplined society; the prison was just one element in the development of this new, controlled society, along with asylums, barracks, factories, hospitals and schools (Foucault, 1977). Writing after Foucault, Michael Ignatieff posed the question:

> why it came to be considered just, reasonable, and humane to immure prisoners in solitary cells, clothe them in uniform, regiment their day to the cadence of the clock, and 'improve' their minds with dosages of scripture and hard labour (Ignatieff, 1978, p.xiii)

He concluded that prison was one of the new ways that the elite of capitalist, industrialising England sought to control the poor; and he emphasized the economic, ideological and social connections between prison reformers and new industrial employers.

All of this is taking us along way from Cesare Beccaria, writing in economically backward Italy, a land with virtually no emergent middle class in the eighteenth century. But then weren't Beccaria and other Italian thinkers of the Enlightenment also concerned to improve the Italian economy? Weren't they concerned about changing the attitudes of the nobility? – and at times this meant (as with Henry Fielding) urging them to limit their luxury as an example to their social inferiors. Didn't Enlightenment figures everywhere see 'criminals' as coming overwhelmingly from the poorer sections of society – peasants, beggars, 'the very Dregs of the People'? This is not to say that any of the above historians are right – you should approach us all with a critical mind. But what you need to remember is that people do not think or write in an economic, political, and social vacuum. Teasing out the links between the content of a text and its context is not always easy, but if you want to pursue the debates over crime and punishment during the eighteenth century, I have provided a reading list at the end of this study.

5   *Prison reform: the architecture of repression in the eighteenth century*

It is difficult to remember that writers like Beccaria were not working in a vacuum, and there can also be problems relating a theoretical text such as *On Crimes and Punishments* to the actual life of individual societies. Yet you will be aware, from your study of the *Encyclopédie*, how much emphasis the *philosophes* put on the practical utility of their work. Section 4 of this study demonstrated the way in which Beccaria's thinking fitted into, and fostered, the movements for penal reform in Europe. To complete this study, I am going to ask you to read some extracts from another, rather different, text, John Howard's *Enquiry into the Present State of the Prisons,* published in 1777, and to look at the way prison buildings themselves developed.

Both the written text and the architecture are evidence for this study. I hope that you are now beginning to develop some confidence in analysing written texts and teasing out their meanings (though you will not find much irony in Howard). Architecture likewise has its meanings – aesthetic, expressive and functional – and you will need to give yourself some time to practice 'reading' these from illustrations. (You will be using these skills again for the Adam study in Part B, and they are related to skills of visual analysis that you will use in studying Reynolds's portraits and the *Salon* painters. There is a study cassette, 'An Introduction to Architecture', for use with the Adam study, and you may find it useful to work quickly through the first two exercises on the tape if you find the architectural elements of this study difficult.)

5.1 The state of English prisons

I would like you to begin by reading some extracts from the *Enquiry* to get a picture of what Howard was reacting to.

EXERCISE Read the extracts from Sections I and II, then look at Fig. 10. Ask yourself what it was that so appalled Howard, and what were his principal concerns? How did the unreformed prisons he describes differ from our concept of prison?

DISCUSSION It is important to come to terms with the huge difference from today. I think the Strangeways riot of 1990 brought home to many of us the indignities of twentieth-century prison life; but the sheer squalor of Fig. 10. and the evils described by Howard still have the power to shock. In Howard's day there were evidently considerable local variations in treatment; though lack of proper food seems to have been widespread. In fact, the practice of the allowing prisoners to beg from passers-by was common. Most prisons were effectively privatized, and run at a profit by the gaoler who could even 'farm' the official allowances of food. Prisoners were expected to pay for improved conditions, even for choice of irons, and there were also unofficial charges, 'garnishes', extracted by the other inmates. Almost all prisons were divided so that there was a *masters' side* for the better sort of prisoner and a *common side* for all the rest or those who could not afford to pay. There were also different categories of prisons. Bridewells, or houses of correction were for minor offenders, who were supposed to undertake work as a part of their punishment. Gaols held those imprisoned for debt, the small proportion of offenders committed to terms of imprisonment and the much larger proportion of detainees awaiting trial or the carrying out of sentences of execution. In some cases conditions were appalling.

Howard was much distressed by the failure to segregate 'debtors and felons; men and women; the young offender and the old offender'. He divided his criticisms under two headings. His horror of the evils affecting the health and life of the prisoners comes across clearly. Some gaolers refused to go into the felons' wards and even Howard's vinegar deodorant was not strong enough! His second category was the evils affecting the morals of the prisoners. Here, perhaps, there is some echo of his nonconformist zeal for he clearly saw criminality as a sort of contagion from which those who admitted their guilt and showed remorse could and should be rescued.

You have already seen (in section 4) how people like Blackstone, Meredith and Eden were already calling for improvement in the penal code that would include punishments that were not just deterrents, but which could reform the offender. This is something of a development from Beccaria, who saw punishment as aimed only at preventing further crime and as a deterrent. The problem was that there was no satisfactory alternative to the principal punishments of death or transportation. Prison was generally for holding felons awaiting trial or execution. Debtors were imprisoned but, otherwise, imprisonment as a punishment was reserved for the most minor offences: and, as Howard discovered, the existing prisons were in no state to act as places of humane, reforming detention.

5.2 Continental precedents for reform

Although the whole system of policing and the administration of justice was totally different on the Continent, Howard was impressed by several of the Continental gaols he visited.

EXERCISE   Read the extracts from section IV of the *State of Prisons*. What aspects of imprisonment in France and the Austrian Netherlands most impressed Howard?

DISCUSSION   The two aspects which strike me most forcibly are Howard's emphasis on the cleanliness and the management of the French prisons. These were state institutions, and the gaolers were paid, rather than having to make a living by selling food and favours to the inmates. The emphasis throughout is on the humanity with which the prisoners were treated; though there were still underground dungeons, and those in the private prison of St. Peter's Abbey in Ghent were apparently a cause for some embarrassment to the gaoler. The prisons appear to have had a strict daily regime, and care seems to have been taken to ensure that prisoners were both fit and fed. The prisoners were not kept in irons, though there is still the mixture of debtors and other detainees.

There is an interesting contrast between the quality of the continental gaols and the barbarity of the punishments inflicted particularly in France. The contrast between French and English attitudes to execution is discussed in TV3, 'Humanity and the Scaffold', but it is important to recognize that the element of the theatre of punishment was important in both societies. Only slowly did the idea of imprisonment as a means of reform gain ground; and you will see from several of the prison buildings how powerful the imagery and drama of punishment remained.

You will remember from section 4 that under the French system condemned criminals were removed and taken to the galleys or to the *bagnes* in the naval ports. These were desperate places where inmates were used as forced labour on the most menial dockyard tasks. It is worth having a look at one to see how one such building functioned, and how the architecture expressed the immediate and wider social purpose of imprisonment.

EXERCISE Study Figs 11–13 and try to work out how the plan relates to the elevations and sections. What does the elevation to the port (Fig. 12) suggest about the effect of the external treatment? Can you work out from the detail of the section (Fig. 11) exactly where the convicts slept? (If you are worried about reading plans and elevations, this would be a good moment to break off and study the first two exercises on the architecture cassette.)

Fig. 13 shows two plans, one of the basement, and one of a main floor and was originally supplied with an extensive key (61 items) of which I have translated some of the most interesting features. Fig. 12 consists of a long section in four parts, the front elevation of the building and a transverse section through the middle of the prison, its yard and freshwater cistern. This last image also contains (bottom left) a separate part section through the left hand side of the cistern, showing the stairs, and the water channel to the prison itself.

DISCUSSION You can see from the plan that the prisoners are kept in pairs of parallel halls, and that they live communally, not in individual cells. There are still a few of the dreaded *cachots*, or punishment cells, without light and, according to the description, fitted with manacles and the bastinade. The communal latrines (I count 7 or 14 for each section containing 280 convicts) and kitchens seem to me barely adequate for the numbers. This *bagne* held 2000 convicts – the written entry in the *Encyclopédie* says 20,000, but you can calculate from the numbered sleeping benches each of which accommodated 20. So, I think, there is little evidence of humanitarian concern in this model prison, although there is careful attention to the provision of fresh water.

The section (*profil*) and elevation show that convict accommodation was on two floors with further rooms in an attic, which were used as barracks for the soldiers of the guard. From the plan you can see that the officers were separately quartered in pavilions at each end and in the middle: this enabled them to provide easy and constant surveillance of the convicts.

The elevation from the port shows how these officers' quarters are treated. The centre block looks just like a country mansion, with an elegantly curved entrance ramp. If you count the windows you will see that this part is eleven bays wide – quite sizeable even on its own. Then it has rusticated quoins (deeply bevelled stones in a strip at each corner) giving the impression of columns; and there is apparently sculpture in the curved pediment. Evidently, the officers quarters are designed to express the grandeur of the state machine. The convicts' apartments are totally plain; but since they are constructed as parts of a single building, the whole thing has something of the grandeur of a palace. The scale gives an indication of the size. The overall length is given as 130 fathoms (Fr. *toises*) or 780 feet. On its sloping site by the sea, the whole building would have been clearly seen from across the water, a constant reminder of the scope and power of the judicial arm of government. However if you look at the transverse section, you can see that the whole of the rear and the court are enclosed by a wall reaching to the roof of the prison, so that the convicts themselves and the working side of the prison were carefully concealed from the land like a fortress.

Finally, the detailed section shows a side view of the sleeping benches. There are no separate beds; instead, there are sloping benches on each of which 20 convicts slept head to head. The architect explained that they were chained at night, though it appears that they were able to move as far as the latrines.

I have spent more time on this example, so as to give you a chance to practise the close visual analysis you will need to get the best out of the architectural evidence. If you have found this section difficult, I suggest you look at the figures again with my analysis in mind. Not all illustrations are as complicated or as detailed as these; but they seem to me important as the first example because this *bagne* was selected for illustration in the *Encyclopédie*, with an article on *Bagnes* by the architect, A. Choquet de Lindu, who built it in 1757. The article seems to me one of the straightforwardly informative ones; but the choice of this *bagne* as the main illustration suggests that it was seen as the classic example of its type, and the type was new in that the *bagnes* were designed to replace transportation to the galleys after their decommissioning in 1748 (see section 4). Choquet claimed that this *bagne* had been given 'every degree of perfection of which it was susceptible'; but the impression I get is that, while the external form of the prison had been carefully thought out, and the arrangements for control and surveillance are efficient, there is little concern for reform as opposed to punishment. The idea that it was possible to win privileges and access to workshops and trading does suggest some acknowledgement of progress; but I do not think it really constitutes an attempt at reform. However, as the architect explains, the prime object was to divide and subdivide the convicts so that they had no chance of combining to organize an escape. You might consider whether this building would not satisfy Beccaria while still appalling Howard.

5.3   The English problem and its practical solutions

Howard's horrific descriptions might seem enough to spark a movement
for reform. Yet he was by no means the first or only reformer. The campaigns for prison reform involved much more than mere humanitarian
concern. You can follow these up through the works listed in the recommended reading. Howard in his *Enquiry* mentions gaol fever, and quotes
Dr. James Lind (whose work you will study in Part C) to illustrate the
damage this might do when prisoners were forcibly drafted into the army
or navy. Gaol fever was in fact typhus, and there had been the famous
Black Assize at the Old Bailey in 1750 when the fever caught from the
prisoners carried off 50 members of the court including four judges and
several members of the jury. A cynical view would see straightforward fear
of contagion as a motive for reform, and it undoubtedly was a factor in
the decision to rebuild Newgate gaol in London.

There were, as you saw in section 4, problems with the penal system
as a whole. The extension of the Bloody Code gave rise to the increasing
tendency for juries to acquit offenders or accept a false valuation of their
crimes in order to avoid execution or transportation. The American War
of Independence brought transportation to a virtual halt in 1775 (the
first convicts did not leave for Australia until 1787); so there was
increased pressure on the existing gaols. And there was a general fear of
violence and the spread of crime, for instance when, after the war, many
discharged soldiers and sailors ended up driven to, or more likely returning to, a life of crime in the growing metropolis. The prison population
in England and Wales very nearly doubled in the fifteen years from 1775,
rising from 4084 to 7082, and there was an immediate problem of overcrowding.

Reformers might well recognize that such criminals were mainly
from the lower classes and see them as unfortunates in need of reform;
but the immediate problem of space was coupled with a recognition that
many existing gaols were unsuitable. Apart from being unsanitary and
badly run, many were set up in old houses and other buildings that had
been modified over the years. Compare, for instance Figs 14, 15 and 16
with the *bagne* at Brest. The Marshalsea is clearly made up of a row of
houses, which do not appear to have been radically altered, and a public
building of some sort with a first floor hall. Old Newgate is no more than
the gate tower of its name fitted up for prisoners internally, and equipped
with a primitive ventilation system to cope with the overcrowding. With
gaols like these, some reform was essential, and it involved both new
buildings and a reorganisation of the prison regime.

Almost the first response was action parallel to the French *bagnes*. In
1776 a licence was granted for those sentenced to transportation to be
used for river works. They were housed in the hulks (Figs 19–20), which
were rightly infamous. One in four of those sent there died in the first
twenty months. The other *cause célèbre* was the rebuilding of Newgate
which caught the public eye because of its situation in the centre of London. This had first been proposed, as the result of the fever scare, in 1775
but was not completed until 1780.

EXERCISE   Look carefully at Dance's plan (Fig. 21) and try to decide how far it meets
the concerns of Howard.

DISCUSSION   The three separate courts segregated debtors, men felons and women felons, but not young offenders. You may also have noticed the number of privies (each linked to a semicircular vent). These would have been an attempt to provide fresher air and cut down gaol fever (although, incidentally, typhus is spread by lice and not by aerial contagion).

EXERCISE   Now compare the designs for Newgate (Fig. 21) with those by Howard himself (Fig. 22) for a country gaol. How do they differ? What is the impression created by the architectural form?

DISCUSSION   James Lind, like Howard, recognized the need for ventilation and recommended a wind sail like the one installed on Newgate.

The plan of Newgate shows a mass of buildings with small, and probably rather airless courtyards within it. Howard's plan is for a set of yards with separate buildings in them. Both gaols show a concern for hygiene in the provision of privies; though it may seem odd to us that in Howard's plan these are set next to the oven, copper and bath. The ground floor of Howard's prison is almost entirely clear of buildings, which instead are set up on columns, providing sheltered spaces (he called them *piazzas*) in the yards and good circulation of air. There are three large courts for men debtors, men felons and young criminals, with a smaller court for women felons and an even smaller one for women debtors. At first glance it seems as though he did not expect so many women to be committed to gaol; but if you compare the size of the women's buildings (by looking at the columns on the plan) you can see that they occupy well over half the space of the young criminals' ward and two-thirds that of the men debtors' ward. This is a passing indication of a limitation in the scope of the reforms which you may like to bear in mind when you consider the role of women later in the course.

I am very struck by the architectural similarities. Howard's gaol is surrounded by a wall whose appearance we can only guess at, but his buildings are classical in form, with pediments. His gaoler's house and debtor's ward have all the careful symmetry of conventional classical urban architecture. Much the same symmetry is apparent in Dance's Newgate; but the size and treatment of the walls makes it look much more massive and fortress-like (Fig. 17). This effect is gained partly by the lack of windows, but also by the use of rustication for the whole wall surface. You can see how the joints in the stonework are deeply cut, and in the lower walls the surface of the stone is roughened. This is the classic means of expressing solidity and massiveness in buildings. It was usually reserved for the basement or the ground floor of buildings; but in both these gaols the rustication is carried right to the roof, a forceful expression of the might of the law and the security of the gaol.

However, Newgate when completed was already out of date compared to Continental prisons like the Maison de Force at Ghent (Fig. 29). It lacked the rows of single cells that were to become the hallmark of reformed prisons. What made Newgate famous was its outside appearance and its associations as the beginning of the route to 'Tyburn Tree' where criminals were hanged (see section 4).

5.4 The shaping of reformed prisons

The emergence of the new *genre* of planned prison architecture was a feature of the eighteenth century. For the most part prisons were built by cities, counties or states, and so were the results of corporate public patronage, itself a relatively new phenomenon. Their size made them significant features of the developing townscapes. Their new architecture had to be both the instigator of virtue, in the way it controlled the inmates, and an expression of the power and security of the state. Prison architecture, if you like, had to have two aspects, the internal organisation of spaces that allowed for the mechanisms of reform and control, and the external aspect of power and security. It resulted from the need to accommodate new theories of punishment, in particular the reform of criminals with imprisonment considered as the active means of punishment, and the consequent need to find an appropriate form for these buildings expressive of their function.

One of the earliest custom-built reforming prisons was Pope Clement XI's San Michele house of correction of 1704 (Figs 23–24). Howard was impressed when he saw it and noted there his favourite prison inscription 'it is of little advantage to restrain the bad by punishment, unless you render them good by discipline'. Internally, although there were galleries with individual cells, it looks a bit like a church. There was even an altar at one end. The image is of the charity of the Christian church, and both the medal and Howard's engraving simply ignore the fact that there were two lower floors containing dyeing vats and all the equipment of the cloth manufactory for which the young inmates were to be the labour force. Nonetheless, the great hall, onto which all the cells opened, with ordered rows of young offenders spinning provided a telling spectacle of reform through labour and discipline.

Reform and charity were not, however, the whole story. There was also a need to contain prisoners and to inculcate a sense of terror and awe. The image of the dungeon with prisoners securely shut away by massive architecture was very much part of the public perception (justified by the existence of many prisons in castles, and by the infamous *cachots* of French gaols). Perhaps the finest example of this genre is the series of engravings by the Italian artist Piranesi (Fig. 25). Piranesi drew inspiration for his dramatic visions from the ruins of classical antiquity, such as the great broken vaults of the Roman baths. This conception of the drama of punishment was also found in settings for opera; and I think you can trace an important link between the drama of incarceration and the theatre of punishment that went with the public executions (see TV3 'Humanity and the Scaffold').

A similar dramatic imagery occurs even in Francis Wheatley's painting of John Howard (Fig. 26). Though not directly connected with prison architecture, this imagery was nonetheless influential and inspired the exaggerated rustication and the massiveness of Dance's Newgate (Fig. 17). Massiveness and rustication are features that recur time and again in prison architecture (Fig. 27). This sort of expressive architecture of repression reaches its apogee in French visionary designs (Fig. 28). Old dungeons seem to have inspired castellated shapes (Fig. 34), though Piranesian classicism (and classicism was the usual choice for important buildings) seems to have been more common.

The other side of prison architecture has to do with control.

EXERCISE   Look at the plans for the Maison de Force at Ghent and for Liverpool Borough Gaol (Figs 29, 30) and see how this is achieved.

DISCUSSION   Both prisons use radiating blocks of cells in which prisoners could be kept in solitary confinement. The difference is that in the Liverpool gaol the blocks are isolated so as to increase the efficiency of the systems of control. At Ghent this was less necessary since the prison was intended only for minor offenders. In both cases the cells face onto communal but segregated yards. The separate blocks of Liverpool also facilitated the free flow of air that was such a concern to the reformers of the time. But the gaol is entirely surrounded by a massive wall which provided the security. Various arrangements of separate blocks encircled by massive walls were built up and down Britain, many by William Blackburn (Fig. 27). The effect of the walls was not only to prevent escape but also to cut the offenders off from public gaze – a far cry from the begging of New-gate prisoners from their grille on the street. Besides, as the new prisons needed more space, they were usually built on the outskirts of towns, which increased the sense of isolation even further.

The element of control led to further refinements in the attempt to convert the prisoners into useful citizens. The utilitarian philosopher Jeremy Bentham (see p.112) developed what he called his *Panopticon* as a sort of manufactory for the creation of morality. On his system, individual cells were arranged in a ring around a central observation core. This would have the effect of providing continual observation while at the same time reducing the number of guards required. The prisoners, confined in solitary cells, would provide cheap labour - Bentham even contracted to run such a prison for profit.

Such a wholly theoretical prison was never completely built in Britain, though Bentham did begin one (Fig. 31). However, these ideas, which went far beyond Howardian principals of reform, had a considerable effect on later prison architecture. A comparison of the designs by Robert Adam for the Edinburgh Bridewell show this clearly (Figs 32–33). His first plan is a symmetrical arrangement of four courtyards with open loggias. Between design and building he showed his plans to Bentham, and the redesigned prison was on four floors with workrooms and cells arranged around a central observation tower (Figs 34–36). As such it was a significant feature of the townscape at the east end of the Edinburgh new town, which you will see in TV4, 'Scotland and the Enlightenment'.

You may feel that these buildings are a very far cry from the careful theorising of Beccaria. However, given the importance he attached to the certainty of punishment and the barbarity of execution, an increasing interest in the building of appropriate prisons was surely to be expected. You will have to make up your own mind whether the drama of these buildings merely signifies a continuance of the theatre of punishment or whether the new systems of reform they housed represent a more humane, or more enlightened, attitude on the part of society.

6   References

Beattie, J.M. (1986) *Crime and the Courts 1660–1800*, Oxford University Press, Oxford.

Foucault, M. (1977) *Discipline and Punish: The Birth of the Modern Prison*, Penguin Books Ltd, London.

Ignatieff, M. (1978) *A Just Measure of Pain: The Penitentiary in the Industrial Revolution 1750–1850*, Macmillan, London.

Maestro, M. T. (1942) *Voltaire and Beccaria as Reformers of Criminal Law*, Columbia University Press, New York.

Meredith, W. (1771) *Gentleman's Magazine*, vol. 41.

Mildmay, W. (1763) *The Police of France*, London.

Rusche, G. and Kirchheimer, O. (1939) *Punishment and Social Structure*, Columbia University Press, New York.

Zirker, M. R. (ed.) (1988) *Henry Fielding, An Enquiry into the Causes of the Late Increase of Robbers*, Clarendon Press, Oxford.

7   Further reading

Emsley, C. (1983) *Policing and its Context 1750–1870*, Macmillan, London.

Emsley, C., (1987) *Crime and Society in England 1750–1900*, Longman, London.

Evans, R. (1982) *The Fabrication of Virtue: English Prison Architecture 1750–1840*, Cambridge University Press, Cambridge.

Farge, A. (1991) *Fragile Life: Violence, Power and Solidarity in the Eighteenth Century*, Polity Press, *Paris*.

Freeman, C. (ed.) (1978) *Prisons Past and Future* (papers to celebrate the bicentenary of John Howard's book for the Howard League for Penal Reform), Heinemann, London.

Hay, D., Linebaugh, P. *et al.* (1977) *Albion's Fatal Tree: Crime and Society in 18th-century England*, Penguin, London.

McLynn, F. (1989) *Crime and Punishment in 18th-century England*, University Press, Oxford. (A cautionary note: OUP have brought out a paperback of this book which may look attractive but is unbalanced and seriously flawed.)

Morris, R. (1976) *Prisons*, Batsford, London.

Rosenau, H. (1970) *Social Purpose in Architecture: Paris and London Compared, 1760–1800*, Studio Vista, London.

Sharpe, J. A. (1984) *Crime in Early Modern England 1550–1750*, Longman, London.

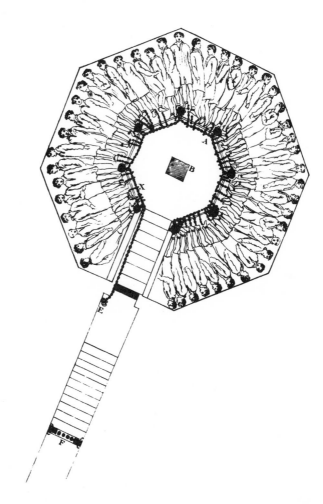

Figure 10
The pit at Warwick gaol from a drawing of 1818. This underground dungeon remained in use until 1797 for confining prisoners during the night. X marks the chain passing through the prisoners' ankle irons and fixed rings (A) fastened to the wall outside (E); B marks the central privy and drain. (Howard League Collection, Warwick University)

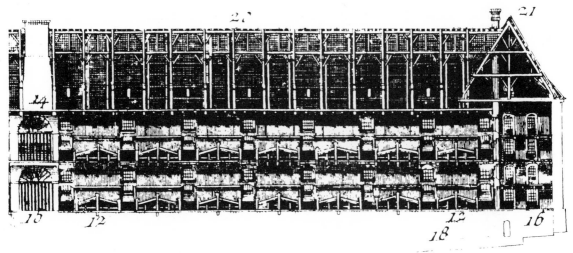

Figure 11 Encyclopédie: *Plate of the Bagne at Brest: part section, detail of Fig. 13, showing the sleeping benches.*

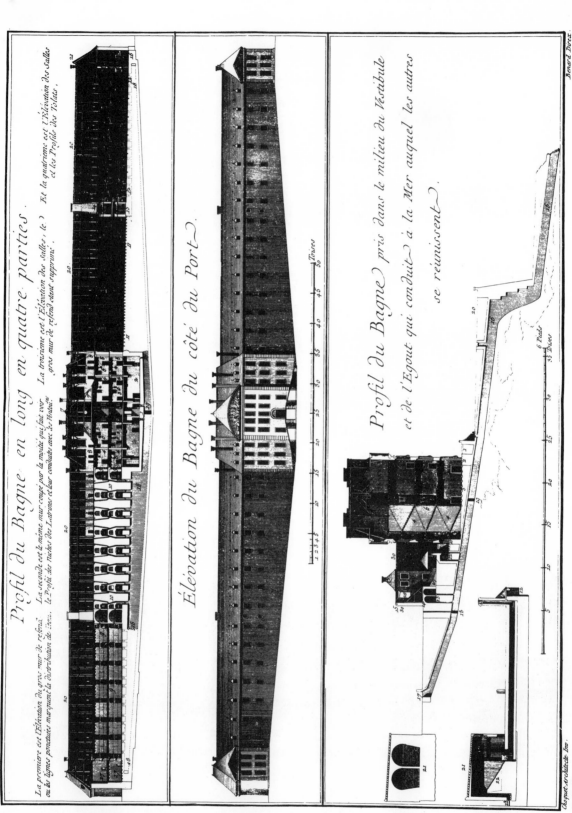

Figure 12 Encyclopédie: Plate of the Bagne at Brest. Top: longitudinal section. Centre: elevation facing the port. Bottom: transverse sections. The caption translates: 'Profile of the Bagne in four parts. The first is the elevation of the stout dividing wall where dotted lines mark the distribution of water. The second is the same wall divided in the centre which renders visible the latrine niches and ventilating conduits. The third is the elevation of the prison halls with the main wall removed. And the fourth is the elevation of the prison halls with sections of the sleeping benches'

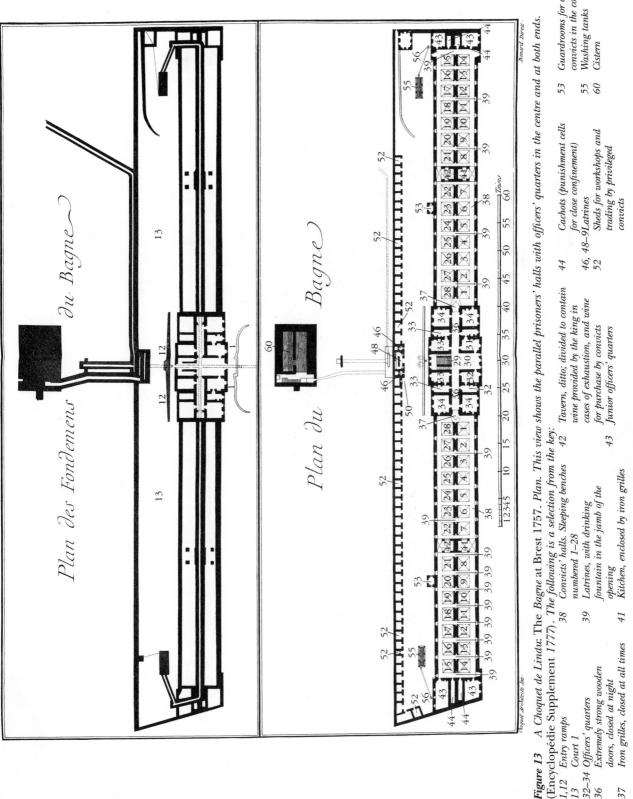

Figure 13 *A Choquet de Lindu: The Bagne at Brest 1757. Plan. This view shows the parallel prisoners' halls with officers' quarters in the centre and at both ends. (Encyclopédie Supplement 1777). The following is a selection from the key:*

1, 12 Entry ramps
13   Court 1
32–34 Officers' quarters
36   Extremely strong wooden doors, closed at night
37   Iron grilles, closed at all times

38   Convicts' halls. Sleeping benches numbered 1–28
39   Latrines, with drinking fountain in the jamb of the opening
41   Kitchen, enclosed by iron grilles

42   Tavern, ditto; divided to contain wine provided by the king in cases of exhaustion, and wine for purchase by convicts
43   Junior officers' quarters

44   Cachots (punishment cells for close confinement)
46, 48–9 Latrines
52   Sheds for workshops and trading by privileged convicts

53   Guardrooms for overseeing convicts in the court
55   Washing tanks
60   Cistern

Figure 14 The Marshalsea, from a survey taken in 1773. (Mary Evans Picture Library)

Figure 15
Old Newgate Gaol, from an early
nineteenth-century engraving. The
windmill on the roof is a part of the
ventilation system installed by Dr. Hales
in 1752. (Victoria and Albert Museum)

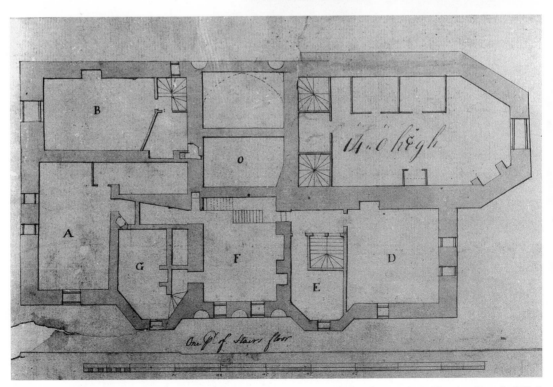

Figure 16   *Old Newgate Gaol, plan of the first floor from a survey of 1767. (Corporation of London Records Office)*

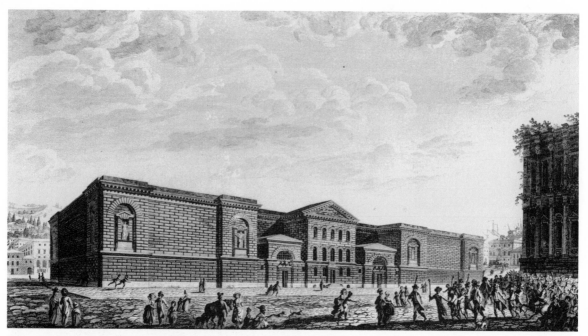

Figure 17 *George Dance the Younger: Newgate Gaol in 1790. The landscape setting is imaginary. (Guildhall Library)*

Figure 18 *View of one of the hulks. Two elderly sailing ships, The Justicia and the Censor, were converted by the insertion of iron cages (see Fig. 19) below decks and moored in the Thames near Barking Greek. (Mary Evans Picture Library)*

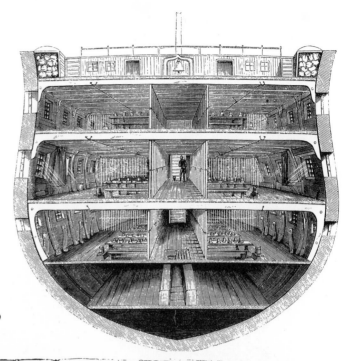

Figure 19
Sectional view of a third hulk, 'Defence'.
(Mary Evans Picture Library).

Figure 20   *Prisoners entering the cages in one of the hulks. (Mary Evans Picture Library)*

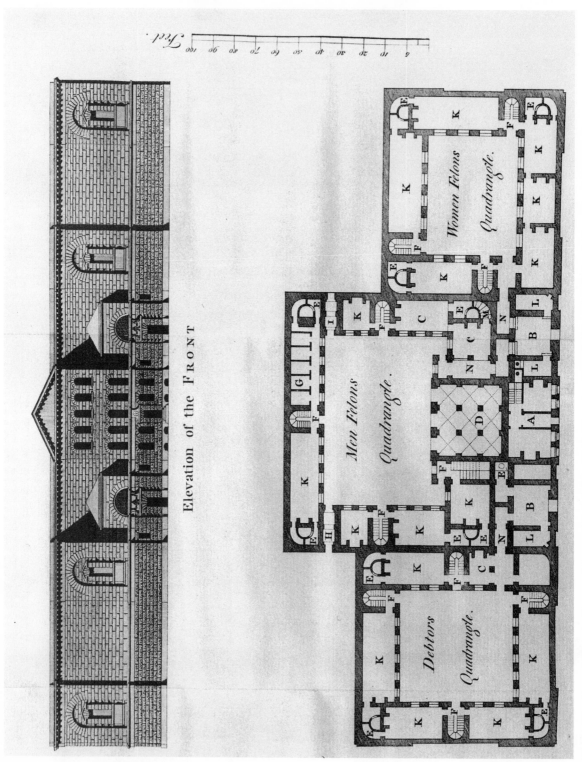

Figure 21 *George Dance the Younger: Newgate Gaol, design, 1769. Plan. A = Keeper's House, B = Prisoners' reception, D = Covered area, E = Privies, G = single cells, K = wards or prisoners quarters. (British Library)*

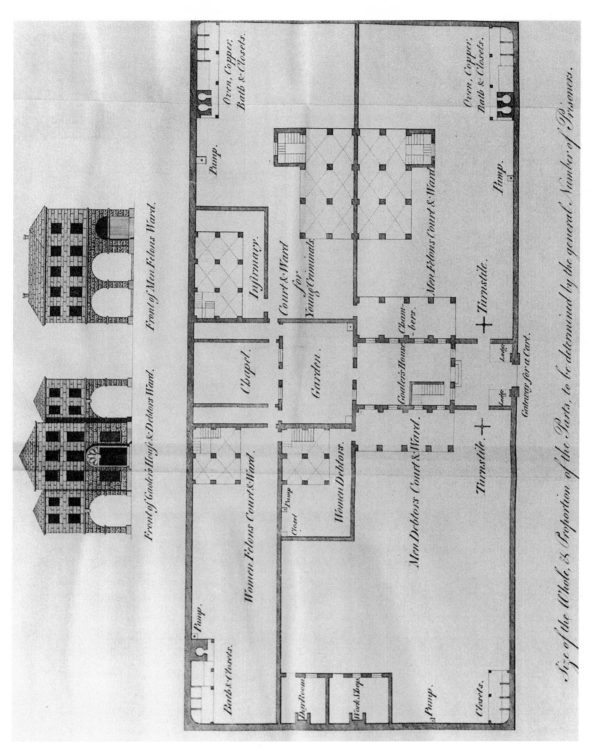

Figure 22 *John Howard: Design for a country gaol. (From* The State of the Prisons, *1777).*

Figure 23 *Carlo Fontana: Rome, S. Michele House of Correction, 1704, sketch for a commemorative medal. (Royal Library Windsor, c.1990, by courtesy of H.M. the Queen)*

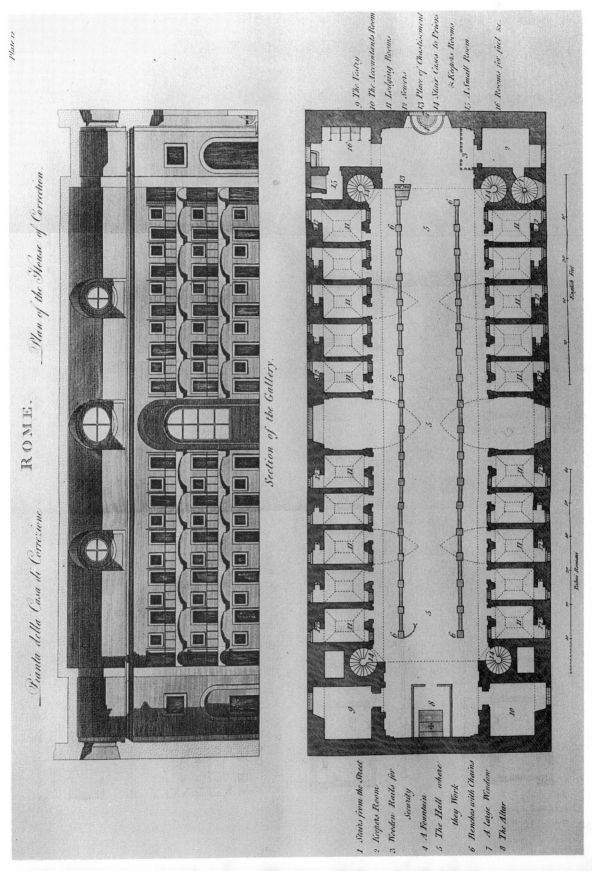

Figure 24 Section and plan of the Rome House of Correction. (From John Howard The State of the Prisons, 1777)

Second State.

Figure 25 *G.B. Piranesi: Carceri (Imaginary Prisons), 1745, Plate 16. One of a series of views of imaginary prisons.*

Figure 26   *Francis Wheatley: John Howard offering relief to prisoners, 1787. (By courtesy of the Earl of Harronby)*

Figure 27   *William Blackburn: Littledean Bridewell, Gloucestershire, design of entry lodge, 1785. (Gloucestershire County Records Office)*

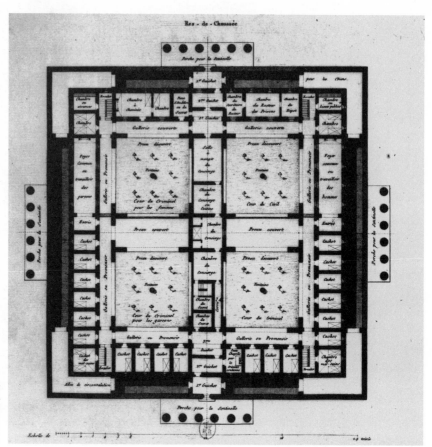

Figure 28a
C.N. Ledoux: Projected design
for a prison at Aix, plan,
1784. (Bibliothèque Nationale,
Paris)

Figure 28b   *Projected design for the prison at Aix, perspective view, 1794. (Bibliothèque Nationale, Paris)*

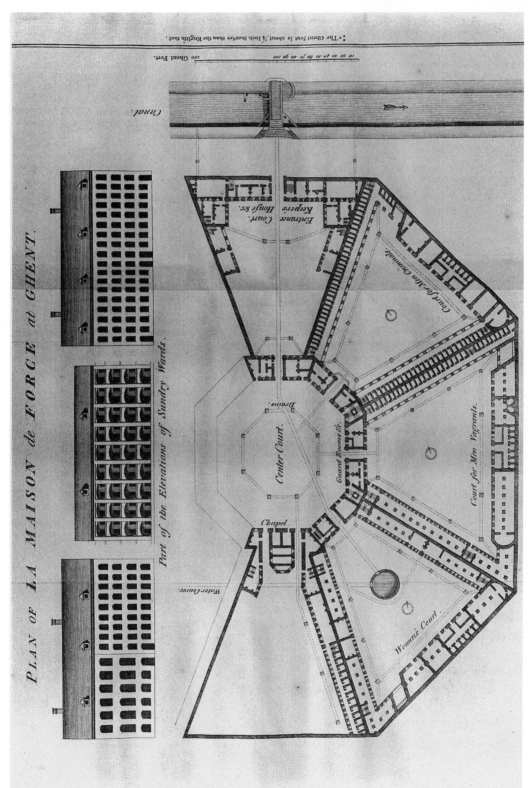

Figure 29 *Maison de Force, Ghent, begun 1772. It was intended to build a complete octagon, but only five of the eight courtyards were ever completed. (From John Howard* The State of the Prisons, *1777)*

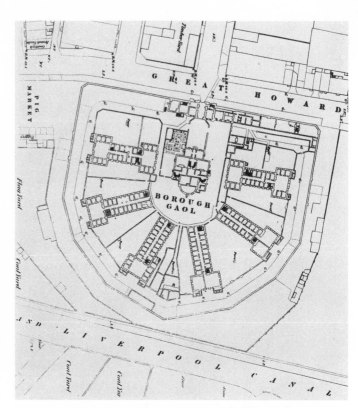

Figure 30
*Plan of Liverpool Borough Gaol by
William Blackburn 1785–9. (From the
Ordnance survey 1849. (Liverpool Central
Library Records Office.)*

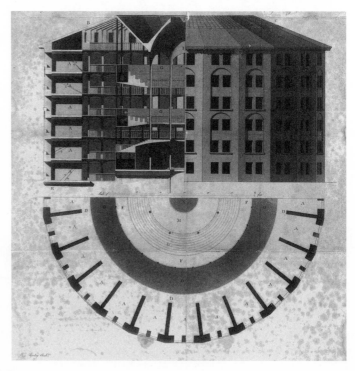

Figure 31
*Jeremy Bentham, Samuel Bentham and
Willy Revely: The Penitentiary Panopticon,
1791. Half-plan section and elevation.
(Bentham Papers, University College, London)*

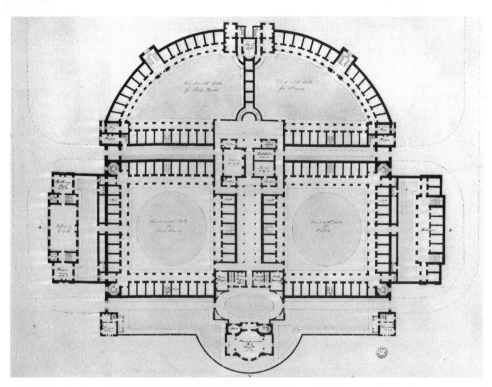

Figure 32   *Robert Adam: design for the Edinburgh Bridewell, 1790. Plan. (Royal Commission on the Ancient and Historical Monuments of Scotland)*

Figure 33
Robert Adam: south elevation of the Edinburgh Bridewell as built 1791–5. (Sir John Soane's Museum)

Figure 34 *Robert Adam: section of the central part of the Edinburgh Bridewell (1791–5), looking south. This view shows the galleries onto which the cells opened. (Sir John Soane's Museum)*

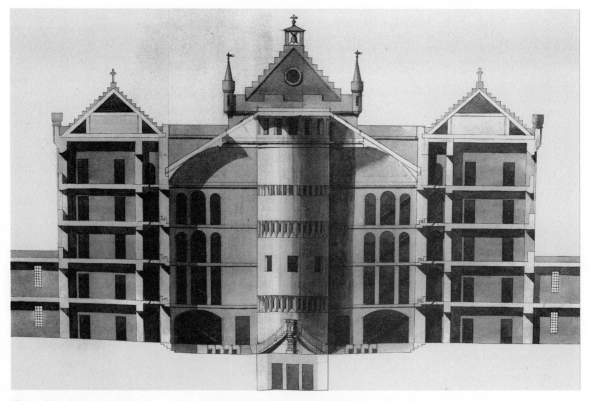

Figure 35 *Robert Adam: section of the central part of the Edinburgh Bridewell (1791–5), looking north. Note the central tower with slit windows for unseen observation. (Sir John Soane's Museum)*

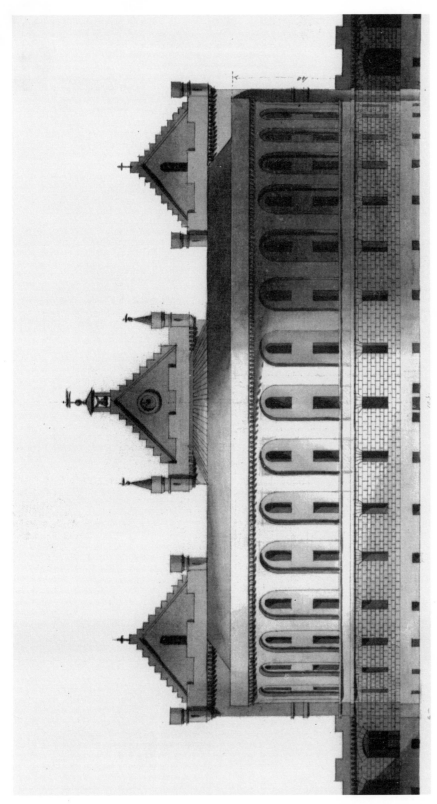

Figure 36 *Robert Adam: south elevation of the Edinburgh Bridewell as built 1791–5. (Sir John Soane's Museum)*

Johnson and Boswell

Prepared for the Course Team by Angus Calder, Simon Eliot and Keith Whitlock

Contents

Johnson and Boswell (Study weeks 5–6)

Studies/Texts	Radio	TV	AC	Set books
Studies, I		TV4	AC 1633 (green)	*Samuel Johnson*
Texts, I	–	–		

Johnson and Boswell

Figure 37
Sir Joshua Reynolds:
Samuel Johnson, *1769.*
(Knole Estates, Sevenoaks)

1 Introduction

You will be spending the next two weeks studying some aspects of the character and works of Samuel Johnson. Johnson's life was an extraordinary one and, despite endless battles with his self-proclaimed laziness, very productive. In two weeks we can do no more than give you a taste of this extraordinary man.

This study covers three very different aspects of Johnson. The first section, 'Dictionary Johnson', introduces you to Johnson through consideration of one of his works, the *Preface* to the *Dictionary*. It shows Johnson both as a practical man of letters operating in the business world of eighteenth-century publishing and patronage, and as a typically Enlightenment figure, the systematizing lexicographer trying to map the English language in his *Dictionary* (just as the *philosophes* tried to map human knowledge in the *Encyclopédie*). However, the section then goes on to suggest that Johnson's work on the *Dictionary* was in tension with an underlying belief that such systems were ultimately impossible, as human imperfections would always bring them down. In his pessimism about purely human endeavours, and in the intensity of the Christian beliefs which underlay it, Johnson was a far from typical Enlightenment thinker, and the section explores the way in which Johnson was different from many of the other writers you have studied so far.

The second section, picks up some of the ideas discussed in the first, in particular the concept of *genre* (that is, of different forms of writing and the style, tone and vocabulary proper to each). This section considers such ideas in relation to Johnson's poetry, in particular *The Vanity of Human Wishes* and discusses the influence of the classics in both Johnson's education and in his literary output.

Johnson is now popularly known, not through his own writings, but indirectly, through Boswell's biography of him. Boswell's *Life of Johnson* is a masterpiece in its own right, but it was written after Johnson's death and firmly promoted a particular view of the man. The fact that it's one we all instantly recognize should not blind us to the fact that it's a partial and highly edited account. The third section looks at the relationship between the two men through their very different accounts of the same experience: Johnson's *A Journey to the Western Islands of Scotland* (1775) and Boswell's *Journal of a Tour to the Hebrides with Samuel Johnson LL.D. 1773* (1785). Here we can see Johnson, the English city-dweller, trying to make sense in his own terms of an unfamiliar landscape and culture. We can also see Boswell observing Johnson, and trying to make sense of him. Finally, through the intriguingly distorting mirrors of both texts, we can just make out something of Scotland and the Scottish Enlightenment.

Almost all your set texts are contained in *Samuel Johnson*, edited by Donald Greene (The Oxford Authors, Oxford University Press, 1984). Excerpts from Boswell's *Journal of a Tour of the Hebrides* are included in *Texts*, I. The set texts are:

Preface to *A Dictionary of the English Language* (Greene, pp.307–28).
The Vanity of Human Wishes (Greene, pp.12–21).

A Journey to the Western Islands of Scotland (Greene, pp.593–641) and *Journal of a Tour to the Hebrides* (*Texts*, I, pp.115–24). You are recommended to consult, at the end of this volume of *Studies*, the *Historical Background to Scotland in the Eighteenth Century*.

All three sections of the study set brief exercises based on other examples of Johnson's writing in Greene.

You are encouraged to browse through Greene as a whole, for without a broader experience of Johnson's literary output it will be very difficult for you to understand the range, depth and versatility of his writing or the impact he had upon his contemporaries.

You should now read Greene's Introduction and take a quick look at his Chronology – these should give you a good overall picture of Samuel Johnson's life and works (Greene, pp.xi–xxvi and xxix–xxx).

2   'Dictionary Johnson'

SIMON ELIOT

2.1   Introduction

EXERCISE   Read the following two comments on Johnson's *Dictionary*, both written before it was actually published. What were both writers expecting the *Dictionary* to do?

> However, it is hoped that our language will be more fixed and better established when the public is favoured with a new dictionary, undertaken with that view … (William Strahan, 1749)[1]

> Toleration, adoption, and naturalisation have run their lengths. Good order and authority are now necessary. But where shall we find them, and at the same time the obedience due to them? We must have recourse to the old Roman expedient in times of confusion, and choose a dictator. Upon this principle, I give my vote for Mr. Johnson to fill that great and arduous post. (Lord Chesterfield, 1754)[2]

DISCUSSION   They were expecting a great dictionary which 'fixed' the language, defining what each word meant exactly so that no-one henceforward could misuse or distort a word without running foul of its authority.

---

[1]   William Strahan (1715–85): Scottish printer and bookseller who was involved in the production of the *Dictionary*.

[2]   Philip Dormer Stanhope, 4th Earl of Chesterfield (1694–1773): statesman and man of letters.

Behind this desire is that great influence on Enlightenment thinking –
Classical Rome – and, in particular, the Latin language. To many of the
most cultivated, the problem with any modern language was that it lacked
certainty and stability. A dead language didn't change, and thus seemed
stable and secure. Note that this is no abstract or trivial argument. Stable
and precise language was seen as necessary to accomplish the Enlightenment aim of finding truth and grasping certainty.

EXERCISE   In many ways, therefore, the new *Dictionary* promised to be another
monument to the rationalizing, systematizing nature of the Enlightenment. Indeed, Johnson himself seemed initially to view his dictionary as
something more than a lexical tool. Read the fourth paragraph on p.318
of Greene (beginning 'When I first collected ...'). What sort of book
would it have been had he been able to realize his ambition?

DISCUSSION   It sounds almost as though he were hoping to create a general encyclopedia in which words in science, philosophy, history and so on would be
explained by their best practitioners. Its original aim seems to have been
to create a universal system in which the definition of words led to a discussion of processes which in turn led to the understanding of things
themselves. As Johnson wryly noted, 'Such is design, while it is yet at a
distance from execution'.

Johnson may have retreated from this grand systematization of knowledge, but he did not abandon entirely the idea of a dictionary as a pre-
scriptive rather than purely descriptive device. He wanted to offer the
best examples of language use, the ones which would improve the reader's style. Read the fourth and fifth paragraphs on p.319 (beginning 'So
far have I been from my care ...'), noting what period he is going to take
most of his illustrative quotations from, and why.

Johnson intends to choose his illustrations roughly from Sir Philip
Sidney (1554–86) to the Restoration (1660), because he believed that
that period represented the golden age of English, the 'wells of English
undefiled', being after the time of 'rudeness' and before the period of
'false refinement and declension'. Although Johnson felt himself living in
the latter age, he believed he could partly restore the language by offering his reader improving examples from the past. As Johnson said in
another context, 'The only end of writing is to enable the readers better
to enjoy life, or better to endure it' (Greene, p.536).

Johnson explains his abandonment of the 'encyclopedic' approach
by arguing that 'the bulk of my volumes would fright away the student'
(Greene, p.318). He might more accurately have said that the bulk (and
therefore the cost) would have frightened away the publishers and potential customers. The issue of cost was not a trivial one, because Johnson's
Dictionary was financed, produced and sold in ways which marked it out as
a book of its period no less than Chesterfield's ambitions for it.

2.2 *Johnson and the Booksellers*

What made Johnson's *Dictionary* a characteristically Enlightenment publication? We can best answer this by comparing it with the ways in which most learned books had been produced since the invention of printing in the fifteenth century. Such books were frequently written by aristocrats or gentlemen with substantial private incomes who would have been insulted had you offered them payment for their writings. Alternatively, they were the products of clergymen, lawyers and doctors, whose profession would have provided the income, or of Oxbridge scholars secure in their college fellowships. In seventeenth-century Europe (most notably in Italy and France) great dictionaries of the national language were initiated by kings or cardinals, and were the product of decades of work by scores of scholars working under the protection of well-funded national academies (such as the Académie Française). The *Dictionnaire de la langue française* had first been proposed by the Académie Française in 1635; its first edition was finally completed in 1694.

Johnson's *Dictionary* was not commissioned by the Archbishop of Canterbury or King George II, but by a collection of booksellers. It was not conceived as a glorious national monument, but as a commercial speculation. It did not assemble a galaxy of academic stars, it hired shambling Sam Johnson, a professional writer without a degree, whose only income came from his pen. It did not allow him the half-century it had taken the French to produce their dictionary, it contracted him to do the job in three years for a set fee (1,500 guineas). In other words, it was a commercial and individualistic enterprise.

Just how commercial it was can be understood only if we know a little more about the eighteenth-century book trade. Until the early nineteenth century, there was no clear distinction between someone who commissioned a book from the author, paid him, had the book printed, advertised and distributed (in other words, a publisher), and someone who sold books. Commonly the same person did all these jobs, and was usually called a 'bookseller'.

Book production was expensive in the eighteenth century. There was no powered machinery for the cheap, mass production of printed texts. Everything printed was produced sheet by printed sheet through hard manual labour on a wooden press that hadn't changed much since its invention in the 1450s. Type was expensive, and no one printer would ever have had enough to set even half the *Dictionary* at one go. Good paper (made from linen rags; see TV1 'The *Encyclopédie*') was frequently the most costly single item in the making of a book. For these reasons, booksellers tended to form co-operatives, called 'congers', which allowed them to spread the investment and the risk. Booksellers in a conger had a share (or shares) in the joint enterprise according to their investment and would draw profits or bear losses according to the size of the share. (In later years these shares were bought and sold enthusiastically: a half-share in Ben Jonson's collected works was worth £60 in 1767 and a two-thirds share in Shakespeare's works was worth £1,200 in the same year.)

Such hard-headed men of business needed someone who could do a thorough, authoritative job but who, at the same time, could appreciate that time was money and that the market had to be served. This paradoxical combination of qualities they found in Samuel Johnson.

EXERCISE   Consider these two statements by Johnson:

'I respect Millar,[3] Sir; he has raised the price of literature.'

'No man but a blockhead ever wrote, except for money.'

What do these seem to tell us about Johnson's attitude to literature?

DISCUSSION   They suggest that he had, to our minds that have been so heavily influenced by Romantic ideas of art, a rather mercenary attitude to literature.

I used the word 'seem' in the question, however, because I think such a reaction might be a rather naive one. In fact, Johnson frequently wrote introductions, prefaces, sermons and lectures for less talented friends with no return in mind other than their friendship. Johnson here is arguing a rhetorical case which he does not expect to be taken literally. In his writing and in his speaking he often adopted the role of an advocate or an actor. We do not expect a lawyer always to believe what he is saying, we expect him to do the best job possible for his client. We do not require that an actor be as wicked as Shakespeare's Richard III in order to play the part. Johnson always made a point as effectively and as unanswerably as he could at the time he was making it. But the next day he could make a quite opposing point, just as an actor might perform a tragedy one night and a comedy the next. It was this view of art as advocacy that allowed Johnson, an enthusiast for London life, to write 'London: a poem' which satirically denounced that very city (Greene, pp.2–8).

If we cannot take the comments about writing for money literally, we can at least see that Johnson regards earning money from literature as legitimate and, indeed, honourable. In the centuries before Johnson, those who earned money from writing were regarded as contemptible, downmarket scribblers with no pretensions to gentility or seriousness. In the century afterwards, when writers were expected to express an individual vision of truth and nature, money was held to be a corrupter of inspiration, and was to be shunned (a view held commonly by Romantic readers, though not necessarily by the writers themselves). In holding to the middle ground, in not regarding money as dishonourable and in viewing writing as a craft to be practised, as acting or the law might be practised, Johnson held the rational middle position, as so often the Enlightenment did, between classicist restraint and individualist self-expression.

2.3 Johnson and Chesterfield

Let us now compare Johnson's attitude to the booksellers with his attitude to a would-be patron. Robert Dodsley, a member of the conger which was to publish the *Dictionary*, had encouraged Johnson to dedicate

---

[3]   Andrew Millar (1707–68): Scottish printer and bookseller who worked with William Strahan and others on the *Dictionary*.

his plan of it to Philip Dormer Stanhope, 4th Earl of Chesterfield, in 1747. Dodsley was a friend of both men, and no doubt felt that, with Chesterfield as its patron, the *Dictionary*'s success would be assured. There was much to justify Dodsley's hopes. Chesterfield was no boneheaded booby, but an intelligent and cultivated man who had counted among his friends Swift, Pope and Bolingbroke. Despite Johnson's reluctance, the relationship started well with an interview and the gift of ten pounds.

But something went wrong between the late 1740s and 1755. Chesterfield made no further attempts to communicate, and Johnson began to resent 'his Lordship's continued neglect'. It therefore must have been a considerable surprise to Johnson to find Chesterfield, a few months before the publication of the *Dictionary*, writing two essays promoting the *Dictionary* in a journal called *The World* (28 November, 5 December 1754). The quotation on page 148, which you have just read, comes from the issue of 28 November. Although flattering, the essays were frivolous, throwaway pieces which, while they praised Johnson, seemed to undermine the importance of his work by their very flippancy. As their styles, so the men: the cool, slightly mocking Chesterfield and the passionate, magisterial Johnson (both proud men) could never have understood each other, however good their intentions. Chesterfield's essays were the sort of thing that a patron was supposed to do, but they must have struck Johnson as a bitter irony. The *Dictionary* had taken nine years of hard, poorly rewarded toil with no one but Johnson and his small, irregular band of amanuenses working at it in the attic of his house in Gough Square. During its preparation Johnson's wife Tetty had died (1752). Yet all this time Chesterfield had said and done nothing. Then, at the moment of completion, he sailed in with two complimentary essays. What was Johnson to do? He could have been quietly pragmatic, written the usual fawning dedication for inclusion in the *Dictionary* and sat back to wait for the inevitable monetary gift from a pleased patron. Chesterfield clearly admired Johnson, there was no question of insult, just an unfortunate breakdown of communication, and there was no doubt that Johnson needed the money. In the past, writers of talent had commonly put up with much more from patrons than Johnson had suffered.

EXERCISE   Having pondered for a couple of months, Johnson wrote to Chesterfield. Read the letter on pp.782–3 of Greene. Who or what is the main target of this letter?

DISCUSSION   One might say Chesterfield, but in fact it could be thought of as a more general attack on patrons and patronage. Notice how Johnson implies his innocence: 'being very little accustomed to favours from the great' and 'a retired and uncourtly scholar'. It is this assumed innocence that allows him, when he had listed all his deprivations ('without one act of assistance, one word of encouragement, or one smile of favour'), to come out with the apparently ingenuous 'Such treatment I did not expect, for I never had a patron before'. Like so many writers of the period Johnson was a skilled practitioner of irony. Is it true, for instance, that Johnson does 'know not well how to receive, or in what terms to acknowledge' Chesterfield's articles? Of course not. He knows exactly, and that's what he proceeds to do in the rest of the letter. Irony allows Johnson to act the role of a puzzled innocent while ruthlessly exposing the absurdities of patronage.

Did you notice, when reading the letter, that it is made up of two quite distinct tones? One could be described as ironic and even light-hearted, and the other as unambiguously serious, even sad. Take another look at the fourth paragraph of the letter, and see if you can pick out an example of each.

The image of the patron as encumbering a person with help when he doesn't need it is an apt but, on the whole, a light-hearted image; however, when Johnson moves from the general to the particular, and talks about his own circumstances, the tone darkens and he expresses himself unambiguously: 'it has been delayed till I am indifferent and cannot enjoy it, till I am solitary and cannot impart it ...'.

Perhaps the most characteristic feature of the Johnsonian vision of life is the recognition that the comic and tragic are inextricably linked in human experience; that the human condition is a bizarre mixture of the silly and the serious, and that any account of human beings which was purely tragic or purely comic was false because it wasn't muddled enough. Many eighteenth-century critics, particularly French ones (Voltaire was an example), had objected to Shakespeare's tragedies because the plays were not 'pure': the tragedies often had comic scenes in them which undermined their seriousness. In 1773, after many years of work, Johnson published a new edition of Shakespeare's plays, another example of the Enlightenment drive to systematize and structure knowledge. In the Preface to his new edition, Johnson defended Shakespeare against the criticism of writing 'impure' tragedies.

EXERCISE   Read Greene, pp.423–4, from 'His adherence to general nature ...' to '... in the general system by unavoidable concatenation'. How does Johnson defend Shakespeare?

DISCUSSION   On p.424 Johnson says: '... there is always an appeal open from criticism to nature'. In other words, Shakespeare may offend against the rules of criticism, but if you look at what really happens in human life ('nature') you will find that the tragic and comic, the high and low, great plans and silly tricks do mingle together. In writing plays in which tragedy and comedy are mixed, Shakespeare got closer to real life than either straight tragedy or pure comedy could have done ('approached nearer than either to the appearance of life').

The letter to Lord Chesterfield was not, as we may tend to assume in the late twentieth-century, a private document; a closer parallel would be an open letter, or a letter to *The Times*. Johnson kept at least one copy which he showed to various friends, and, more surprisingly (but in keeping with his own advice in *Letters to his Son*), Chesterfield kept it on a table and showed it to visitors with the comment, 'This man has great powers'. In other words, the letter is a literary form, a *genre*, which therefore has its own rules and regulations (just as a satire or epic poem would). One rule of the eighteenth century was the valediction, the flowery farewell. Look at the various letters printed between pp.781–7. What is the most common form of valediction?

Most of them are variations on the 'most obedient and most humble servant' theme. Almost always, when there are two adjectives, 'humble' is used second. It was an expected, conventional end. Like all conventions, it tended to be taken for granted, and thus did not have much impact. This is, of course, the problem with all formal literary conventions: use them too often and they lose their punch. But notice how, although using the convention, Johnson slightly alters it, and places it in a different context, thus reviving its impact. Notice that the 'humble' and 'obedient' are in an unconventional order, with 'humble' coming first to emphasize one of the themes of the letter: Johnson's apparent lowliness in relation to Chesterfield; and 'obedient' in a subordinate position because he is patently not being obedient. More significantly, see what the last paragraph of the letter does to the meaning of the valediction.

The 'I have been long wakened from that dream of hope in which I once boasted myself' completely undermines its conventional meaning. He was *once* Chesterfield's 'most obedient servant' but, he implies, he is no longer.

The retention of conventional forms, the conformity to the rules of a given *genre*, did not stop Johnson from saying what he wanted to say. By reversing the conventional sequence of elements in the form he can get the valediction to mean the opposite of what it usually meant. The valediction appears to say one thing, but it means the opposite. By ironically playing with literary conventions, writers were able to express unconventional views while still using conventional forms.

Johnson's letter to Lord Chesterfield is often considered to be a turning point in literary history, the moment at which the aristocratic patron was rejected in favour of a more 'democratic' source of support: the market or, even more vaguely, 'the People'. In reality the process was slower and more complicated than that; it began before Johnson, and was to continue long after him. Nevertheless, as an expression of the independent dignity of the man of letters, relying on his own talents and efforts to gain reward and fame, it is an important moment in the English Enlightenment.

2.4 Preface *to the* Dictionary

EXERCISE   You have already read a few paragraphs from the *Preface*. Now, giving yourself time enough to do it at one sitting, read all of it (Greene, pp.307–28). However, before you do, remind yourself of Strahan's and Chesterfield's hopes for the *Dictionary* (p.148 above) and, as you work your way through, keep asking yourself how these hopes of 'fixing the language' match with what Johnson has to say about the same subject. Don't worry too much about the technical discussions of language in the earlier part of the *Preface*; read them, but concentrate your study on pp.318–28.

DISCUSSION Strahan and Chesterfield seemed to believe that language could be purified and fixed, Johnson was under no such delusion. Look at the third
paragraph on p.324 (beginning 'Of the event of this work ...'). Johnson
began by thinking that a dictionary would 'put a stop to those alterations
which time and chance ... make in it ...', but now '[I] begin to fear that I
have indulged expectation which neither reason nor fear nor experience
can justify'. Note here that he is suggesting that, despite appearances, the
systematizing rationality of a Chesterfield, who wants language to become
a precise instrument, is actually unreasonable: it is so because language is
a human product, and experience tells us that all things human are
imperfect and subject to change.

Did you notice, by the way, as you read through the *Preface*, that Johnson
had a tendency to move from the particular to the general? Of course,
compiling a dictionary is all about language, so you would expect the
Preface to move from talking about a specific dictionary to talking about
dictionaries in general and the language they are attempting to describe
(as Johnson does on p.324). But it goes further, doesn't it? Language
itself is quintessentially a human product, one of the things which make
us different from all other animals. Through a discussion of language
Johnson moves to a discussion of human nature, and of the human condition.

For instance, on p.321 (beginning 'Thus I have laboured ...') Johnson starts by detailing how he has tackled the definition of each word; he
then moves on to comment more generally about his own performance
('I have not always executed my own scheme ...'). By the final paragraph
on p.321 he is generalizing at the level of all humanity (from 'To have
attempted much ...' to 'because he can conceive little').

In all his writing Johnson displayed this very eighteenth-century
habit, that of moving from the particular to the general. In *Rasselas* (see
Greene, p.xxi) the particular circumstances of the characters are used to
illustrate broad human truths (that wishes are vain, that all men are self-
deluded). In the Preface to his edition of Shakespeare Johnson praises
the poet for his general truth to nature. To us in the late twentieth century, generalizations (unless they are scientific laws) are often suspect:
they smooth over important differences, they don't allow for individual
variations, and so on. But, to the classically educated minds of the eighteenth century, the only truth worth knowing was general, because that
was the only one which fitted the idea that everywhere and at all times
human beings were the same. This, of course, also suited the contemporary Christian mind which itself believed in the universal and unchanging
truth of God. As Johnson said of Shakespeare:

> Nothing can please many, and please long, but just representations
> of general nature ... the pleasures of sudden wonder are soon
> exhausted, and the mind can only repose on the stability of truth
> (p.420).

And that truth was general, rather than individual.

EXERCISE   So, for Johnson a study of the English language would reveal general truths about the human condition. Looking back over the *Preface* to the *Dictionary*, can you pull out one or two characteristics of language that Johnson discusses. (Spend about 10–15 minutes on this exercise and concentrate on pp.312–17.)

DISCUSSION   There are a number, but the two that struck me are:

1   the wild exuberance of language which stops it being fixed or controllable.

2   the universal tendency for language to become degenerate and corrupt.

On the very first page (p.307), Johnson views the language as though it were a wild garden 'itself been hitherto neglected; suffered to spread, under the direction of chance, into wild exuberance ...'; in the next paragraph he sees himself as a gardener: 'there was perplexity to be disentangled, and confusion to be regulated ...'. On p.312 he talks of 'the boundless chaos of a living speech', on p.315 of a 'maze of variation', on p.316 'the perplexity cannot be disentangled', on p.317 of 'the exuberance of signification', and so on.

To us, in a post-Romantic world, this sense of growth and plenitude is exciting, but to the classically trained mind looking for order, stability and calm, it was a nightmare, the nightmare of trying to fix that which will not stay still:

> while our language is yet living ... these words are hourly shifting their relations, and can be no more ascertained in a dictionary than a grove, in the agitation of a storm, can be accurately delineated from its picture in the water. (p.316)
>
> to enchain syllables, and to lash the wind, are equally the undertakings of pride, unwilling to measure its desires by its strength (p.324).

Language, like the human beings who created it, is subject to storms; is battered about with such ferocity that no permanent order can be imposed upon it. Again, we must remind ourselves that this was written a generation before Wordsworth and Coleridge, when nature was still best appreciated in a formal or landscaped garden, and when zephyrs were usually preferred to storms.

EXERCISE   Human language and human life battered by tempests, and amazed by confusion and complexity. Not quite the Enlightenment vision we might have expected, is it? It is neither confident nor optimistic. It is a view of human life as transitory and muddled. As Johnson says on p.327: 'no dictionary ... can be perfect ... some words are budding and some falling away'. If this does not come from an Enlightenment view, from where do you think Johnson might have got it? Think for a moment of the emphasis on falling away from perfection (to see how rich the image of 'falling away' is, check the *Dictionary's* definitions of the phrase between numbers 37–41 in Greene, p.330).

DISCUSSION   There is a very strong tradition in Christianity that views the world in this way. To many Christians, the human condition was determined by original sin, the Fall of Adam and Eve, and everything in this world was done in its shadow. The permanent, general truths, the certainties which did not change, dwelt elsewhere with God.

Johnson was a Christian; not in the polite, respectable, decent way in which many of his fellow intellectuals were Christian, but in an intense, often guilt-ridden, self-torturing way. Until the age of nineteen Johnson was, in his own words, 'a lax talker against religion', very much the Enlightenment sceptic. Sometime around 1728–9, while still an undergraduate at Oxford, he read William Law's *A Serious Call to a Devout and Holy Life* (1728). Following the model of *Ecclesiastes,* Law explored each human hope or ambition in turn, and found each ultimately futile or illusory (Johnson's theme of the 'vanity of human wishes' in part derives from Law and will be discussed in greater detail in the next section); only religion offered a hope which was stable and sure. As a Protestant writer, Law put a tremendous emphasis on the individual soul finding its own salvation by the full use of all its talents. From this time on, as Boswell observed, 'religion was the predominant object of his thoughts'.

Johnson's Christianity had two quite separate effects. To others he was endlessly generous with money (when he had any), time and help: on his way to a convivial evening in one tavern or another, he would frequently give all the silver he had in his pockets to the poor he passed; and on returning late at night he would be observed putting pennies into the hands of destitute children asleep in doorways so that they should be able to buy themselves breakfast when they awoke. To himself he was harsh: constantly castigating his indolence and lack of application (see, for instance, the comment on his life written 14 April 1775, Greene, pp.777–8), and haunted by a fear that on the day of Judgement he would be found wanting by a wrathful God:

> The day in which every work of the hand and imagination of the heart shall be brought to judgement, and an everlasting futurity shall be determined by the past. (Greene, p.306)

If we now return to Johnson's ideas about language, and recall that one of the features we noticed was the belief that English was becoming more corrupt, we can begin to understand the extent to which all Johnson's thinking was finally governed by the idea that the human life was transitory, vain and sinful.

EXERCISE   Look at Greene, pp.307–12. Can you find examples of this idea that language, like the beings who used it, was imperfect and corrupt?

DISCUSSION   On p.308 Johnson talks about language being part of 'the imperfection of human things'; on p.309 we have 'spots of barbarity impressed so deep ... that criticism can never wash them away'; on p.310 Johnson wishes that 'the instrument [language] might be less apt to decay, and the signs might be permanent, like the things which they denote'; and on p.312 'for it is incident to words, as to their authors, to degenerate from their ancestors'.

The 'vanity of human wishes' theme is also evident in the *Preface*, and gives a personal dimension to these broad moral generalizations about language and the human beings who use it. On p.318 Johnson explains his original intention of turning the *Dictionary* into an encyclopedia by use of copious quotation, and how that proved impossible. On p.319 he states that he would not use any quotations from living authors, and then promptly admits that he has broken his own rule. Take a look at pp.321–2. Can you find a couple more examples of the vanity of Johnson's wishes?

On p.321 he admits that 'I have not always executed my own scheme, or satisfied my own expectations'. At the bottom of p.321 and top of p.322 he describes vividly his hopes of producing an ideal dictionary, and then punctures the whole performance with the wry comment 'But these were the dreams of a poet doomed at the last to wake a lexicographer' (p.322).

On p.324 the parallels between the rampant profusion of language, which grows and shrivels like the shallow-rooted corn in the parable, and the energy and folly of mankind is made explicit in the middle paragraph. With one eye on the misguided ideologues, like Chesterfield, who want a fixed language, Johnson writes: '[no lexicographer] shall imagine that his dictionary can embalm his language, and secure it from corruption and decay ...'.

But Johnson's argument goes further. There is a paradox which questions the projects of the great Enlightenment systematizers.

EXERCISE   On p.325 Johnson, still apparently looking for a fixed language, or at least one which will not corrupt too fast, gives examples of cultures in which language will remain relatively stable, and then goes on to contrast them with those which will tend to accelerate language change. See if you can identify the two types.

DISCUSSION   A static society with a subsistence economy would, Johnson argued, tend to have a more stable language. An economically developed society with a cultured, leisured class will constantly be developing new ideas and new knowledge which will distort old words and require new ones.

The paradox of this is that it is precisely the cultures which see the need for rational, systematized dictionaries (i.e. the advanced, European, 'enlightened' nations) that will not be able to produce them because their language is changing faster, under the pressure of new ideas, than language in a primitive culture. Underlying this paradox is Johnson's

Christian belief that, in any case, since the Fall, the pursuit of knowledge has tended to lead to more sin and confusion.

This sounds like a counsel of despair. But, as a Christian, Johnson was enjoined never to despair, and on pp.326–7 he turns to what the lexicographer can do, despite the turmoil of a living language:

> It remains that we retard what we cannot repel, that we palliate what we cannot cure. Life may be lengthened by care, though death cannot be ultimately defeated.

It is an heroic vision: not of achieving victory but, for a time, of staving off defeat. Notice how Johnson equates the death of language with its human equivalent. It is not irrelevant to know that of his own death Johnson was to say 'I will be conquered; I will not capitulate'.

2.5 Johnson's achievement

Despite his apparent 'frigid tranquillity' (p.328), Johnson was well aware of what he had achieved in his *Dictionary*. In response to Boswell, who had suggested (rather rashly) that he had not known what he was undertaking when he had started on the work, Johnson had replied, 'Yes, sir, I knew very well what I was undertaking, – and very well how to do it, – and have done it very well.' He had. The *Dictionary* contained more than 40,000 entries and included 114,000 illustrative quotations. Although the etymologies were not always reliable (Johnson's classical education had equipped him to deal with words derived from Greek and Latin, but not the words from Germanic languages), the definitions were copious, clear and sometimes witty. More importantly, words with multiple meanings had each sense separately defined and very often illustrated: there are, for instance, sixteen definitions of 'in', sixty for 'make', sixty-five for 'fall' (see pp.331–3).

As Johnson had anticipated (see p.327), the *Dictionary* was not an overnight success. It was published on 15 April 1755 in two large, folio, volumes at £4.10.0, and sold its 2000 copies slowly. In an attempt to boost sales, the booksellers offered a second edition in 165 weekly parts at 6d each. This was not a success: if you had wished to look up a word beginning with 'A', you could have done so after the first month or so; if you had wanted a word beginning with 'Z', you would have had to wait no less than three years and nine weeks! The sales of the *Dictionary* really took off in 1756 when a new smaller, octavo, abridgement, stripped of all the illustrative quotations and with fewer words, but selling for just 10 shillings, appeared. Between 1756–86 this version sold over 40,000 copies. Like the *Encyclopédie*, the *Dictionary* achieved its full impact only when it was stripped down and re-packaged in a cheaper format.

Perhaps one measure of Johnson's achievement was that his *Dictionary*, despite his fears of its transience, was still in general use in the mid-nineteenth century when work first started on the *New English Dictionary* (which was later to become the *Oxford English Dictionary*). Astonishingly enough, scholars began in 1857 with a firm intention of writing a supplement to Johnson's work, rather than a replacement for it.

3 *Johnson's* Vanity of Human Wishes

KEITH WHITLOCK

The staple of Samuel Johnson's education at Lichfield Grammar School and Stourbridge was the classics, within which Latin predominated over Greek. He read Latin with an ease that would surprise us today, perhaps the ease with which we would read a quality newspaper article. This ease was not uncommon at that time: a reading facility in Latin and familiarity with classical Latin authors were part of the structure of the minds of the many educated men, and some women too. On his visit to France, Johnson conversed in Latin rather than French.

Johnson regarded human nature as universal and unchanging. Imbued as he was with the literature of ancient Rome, he was inclined to see Roman men and women not as strange, remote figures, but in essential respects, his contemporaries. He was pleased to find that Shakespeare took the same view. In his own Preface to *Shakespeare* he wrote:

> But Shakespeare always makes nature predominate over accident and if he preserves the essential character, is not very careful of distinctions superinduced and adventitious. His story requires Romans or Kings, but he thinks only on men. He knew that Rome, like every other city, had men of all dispositions; and wanting a buffoon, he went into the senate house for that which the senate-house would certainly have afforded him ... a poet overlooks the casual distinction of country and erudition, as a painter, satisfied with the figure, neglects the drapery. (Greene, p.423)

For 'senate-house', Johnson invites us to understand 'Houses of Parliament'. Given this assumption of the unchanging universality of human nature, and given too an intimate familiarity with, and respect for the classics, it was natural for Johnson, when he wished to write a poem on the eternal theme of human vanity, to have chosen a classical model for his work. With neither false modesty, nor any sense of incongruity, he called his poem 'an imitation' of the tenth Satire of the Roman poet Juvenal (AD.60–*c*.130). Juvenal's satire itself has no title, but Johnson chose, for his own poem, the title *The Vanity of Human Wishes*, and published it in 1749.

You may well have already looked at the opening lines of the poem and experienced an initial strangeness. I suggest that you now listen to the poem on your audio-cassette (AC1633 green) with the text in front of you (Greene, pp.12–21). Remember that in the history of human literacy, to read aloud has been far commoner than to read silently. Poetry can be felt before it is understood.

We have space to discuss in detail only four sections. I hope this will stimulate your appetite to read the whole. Let us start with the first twenty lines of the poem, attending to the content of what Johnson is saying and the poetic form in which he says it. (The Greene edition contains helpful notes, including in this case an excellent one on China and Peru.)

Johnson sees mankind as a whole, a unitary human nature, with common vices: pride, ambition, revenge and neglect of reason. He does not allow illustrative examples to break the moral force of his initial survey and generalizations. Johnson believes that whoever thinks rationally must also think morally.

Johnson uses a verse form called iambic pentameter. This is a common form in English verse and drama. Each line has ten syllables with five stresses. See, for example, line 55:

> Where wealth unloved without a mourner died.

If every line followed this strict pattern of ten syllables with alternate stresses, the verse would quickly become wooden. Johnson, like all poets who use iambic pentameters, subtly shifts the pattern of emphasis to vary the rhythm and add weight to particular words. He often writes lines with more than or fewer than ten syllables. The lines of iambic pentameters are often arranged, as in Johnson's poem, in rhyming couplets: each pair of lines has its own rhyme. The verse form lends itself to pithy epigrams and trenchant statements:

> How nations sink, by darling schemes oppressed,
> When vengeance listens to the fool's request. (lines 13–14)

Compare this with his playful parody of a banal ballad:

> I put my hat upon my head
>   And walked into the Strand,
> And there I met another man
>   Whose hat was in his hand.   (Greene, p.25)

The language of *The Vanity of Human Wishes* is deliberately abstract and generalized. Juvenal's original 'households', in Johnson's hand-written draft became 'families', only finally to become 'nations'. Johnson's sentence structure and grammar, which may at first puzzle you, enforce reflection and re-appraisal: 'observation' is the subject of 'survey', but it is also the subject of 'remark', 'watch' and 'say'; the first fourteen lines are one sentence; you should reflect upon the breathing control of commas, colons and semi-colons and the way they achieve a crescendo effect, in short a very self-conscious technique. Such literary technique is often termed 'rhetoric'. Rhetorical writing may be high-flown, declamatory and oratorical. And what about the last four lines of the section? Johnson has disrupted the expected ordering of the thoughts expressed by the lines. The reader might have expected:

> With fatal heat impetuous courage glows, ...
> And restless fire precipitates on death';

followed by

> 'With fatal sweetness elocution flows, ...
> Impeachment[4] stops the speaker's powerful breath.

Johnson has ordered thus: courage, eloquence, speaker, fire; he might more naturally have ordered them: courage, fire, eloquence, speaker. This technique, intended to deny us easy listening or reading, and to make us stop and reflect, is a typical rhetorical device. Further, 'strife' means 'striving'; and adjectives are chosen to force both intellectual and emotional reaction: 'restless toil', 'wavering man', 'treacherous phantoms', 'fatal heat', 'fatal sweetness'. The reiterated adjective 'fatal' means

---

[4]   Impeachment was a judicial prosecution by the House of Commons before the House of Lords.

'deadly', 'destructive' and 'ruinous'. Johnson's hand-written rough draft confirms the attention he paid to adjectives; at first he experimented with 'eager toil' and 'anxious toil'. Johnson makes us conscious of his use of language.

EXERCISE   From the detail of the opening section, turn to the poem as a whole, its overall structure. Without dwelling at length over particular sections, identify the features of human vanity that he discusses.

DISCUSSION   In order to expose the vanity (that is, emptiness) of human wishes, Johnson has singled out wealth (line 37), political power (line 273), learning (line 135), military glory (line 175), long life (line 255) and beauty (line 319); to add vividness, he has provided historical examples.

EXERCISE   Two of the most famous and memorable passages of the poem are the examples of Cardinal Wolsey and Charles XII of Sweden (lines 99–128 and 191–222). Read these sections and listen to them on tape. Do they have structural similarities? Is there an overriding tone?

DISCUSSION   You may have been familiar with some of these lines before, even though you may not have known their origin. The examples have a common parallel structure, that of the progress of fireworks:

They mount, they shine, evaporate, and fall. (line 76)

The examples seem implicitly shaped by this metaphor; explicitly the whole poem contains many verbs of sinking and falling; and the examples are rhetorically speaking, highly organized; the listener or reader is carried by the pace and rapid acceleration to a pitch; there is then a subsidence into controlled bathos (a rhetorical trick that deliberately sinks or deflates), and thereby exposes the emptiness, the insubstantial nature of the particular human aspiration. The second of these examples ends in one of the most famous couplets in English literature:

He left the name, at which the world grew pale,
To point a moral, or adorn a tale. (lines 221–2)

Let us now look a little more closely at both passages. You may find the glossary in the 'Notes to *The Vanity of Human Wishes*' where some of the more difficult words and phrases are explained, pp.169–70 below, helpful.

EXERCISE   First, the passage on Cardinal Wolsey. Having now re-read the section a couple of times, consider its rhetorical construction. Why is the vignette of Wolsey's fate such a powerful example of the vanity of human wishes?

DISCUSSION   My own response is that Johnson directs us to Wolsey with an imperative 'see Wolsey stand' (line 99), with standing contrasting with his later sinking or falling. Verbs are in the present tense for greater vividness. Wolsey's success is built up with a series of short sentences, again reminiscent of blocks or bricks: 'claim leads to claim, and power advances power'.

Where is the climax or turning point? Surely the couplet 109–10.

> At length his sovereign frowns – the train of state
> Mark the keen glance, and watch the sign to hate.

The 'train of state', courtiers and attendants, has a plural force, hence 'mark' and 'watch'; and notice the condensation of meanings in 'sign to hate' – not just 'evidence of hatred' but a signal that sycophants should hate Wolsey too, a powerful way of capturing court life under a tyrant like Henry VIII.

The second part mirrors the first, an itemized deconstruction of power based on royal favour. Finally, Johnson addresses the reader directly in order to enforce an evaluation and a response.

EXERCISE   Let us now move on to our second example, Charles XII of Sweden, lines 191–222. Examine this passage, identifying its rhetorical organization as I have done in the Wolsey.

DISCUSSION   Obviously there is a parallel structure: a crescendo to a rhetorical climax that turns out to be an anti-climax, all in the present tense:

> Hide, blushing Glory, hide Pultowa's day (line 210)

and the vividly itemized collapse of military heroism.

The parallelism is not however mechanical. Charles' unrestrained military ambition is put in direct speech; and the final pungent couplet of the passage (lines 221–2) surely requires no gloss.

You may be interested to know that in the Juvenal original, Wolsey was Tiberius' favourite Sejanus, and Charles was Hannibal. Bearing in mind that so many of Johnson's readers knew the classical models, you will appreciate that the effect was to reinforce Johnson's generalization of human conduct. However, like Juvenal, Johnson dealt not with the living but the dead; he left his readers to supply contemporary parallels, as doubtless we could too.

Johnson's section that exposes the futility of scholarship and learning (lines 135–64) was not modelled on Juvenal. The description of the scholar is substantially autobiographical:

> Should no disease thy torpid veins invade,
> Nor melancholy's phantoms haunt thy shade; (lines 153–4)

and

> There mark what ills the scholar's life assail,
> Toil, envy, want, the patron and the jail. (lines 159–60)

Johnson originally wrote 'garret' and deleted it in favour of 'patron'. You have already read Johnson's famous letter to his former patron Lord Chesterfield (p.152–4, above and Greene, pp.782–3).

EXERCISE   Let us now consider the poem's ending. Read and listen from line 343 to the end. Here are a few notes that may help:

'suspense': not of judgement, but of hope, fear, and other emotions

'sedate': settled and resigned

'darkling': in the dark

'attempt': try to obtain

'ambush': can mean 'crafty device' in the Latin

'secure': calmly sure (literally 'apart from care')

'seat': abode

'she' (final line): probably refers to 'mind' in previous line (which is feminine in Latin).

DISCUSSION   You should reflect upon this final section, asking yourself how far its moral position is pagan or Christian.

> Johnson puts the question:

> > Must helpless man, in ignorance sedate,
> > Roll darkling down the torrent of his fate?

This question directly challenges Juvenal's paganism. Johnson will have no truck with the pagan Lady Luck ('fortuna'); he equally rejects Greek Stoicism (Greene has a useful note, p.796) since it gave no assurance of personal survival. As Johnson wrote elsewhere: 'Real alleviation of the loss of friends, and rational tranquillity in the prospect of our own dissolution, can be received only from the promises of him in whose hands are life and death.' (*The Idler*, 41) The 'him' is plainly the God of Christianity.

Johnson believed in the value of religion and a personal God. He was not a mere satirist, cynical about human life: 'a happy life *is* possible for those who adopt the higher values of faith, hope, and love rather than the merely 'human' ones of fame, wealth, and power' (Greene, Introduction, p.xviii).

> I suspect that Johnson's omission from *The Vanity of Human Wishes* of explicit reference to God, Christianity and revealed religion is a concession to avoid anachronism, and to achieve a statement that will be culturally universal or transcendent. Such a statement accords with his conception of poetry: '[the poet] must divest himself of the prejudices of his age and country' (Greene, pp.352–3). However the poem conveys that Johnson regarded life as a probation. Indeed, the poem expresses a belief in Hell, as we have seen:

> > Why but to sink beneath misfortune's blow,
> > With louder ruin to the gulfs below? (lines 127–8)

Love, patience, faith, obedience and resignation, invoked in the last lines, constitute a constellation of values that is very Christian indeed, though by no means exclusively so. Johnson wrote in a tradition of Christian humanism. You will find several of his prayers and expressions of religious fervour in Greene, pp.775–80.

The title of Johnson's poem comes from the book *Ecclesiastes* in the *Old Testament:*

> Vanity of vanities, saith the Preacher, vanity of vanities; all is vanity … One generation passeth away, and another generation cometh: but the earth abideth for ever. (*Eccl.* 1: 2,4)

In its melancholy, Johnson's poem is a meditation on this Biblical text. The ending abandons satire and offers an ecumenical or universal prayer; but its spirit is that of the *New Testament* not of the *Old.*

We are now in a position to address the following broad questions:

1   what was Johnson's general concept of poetry?

2   what did he understand by an 'imitation'? and

3   how are we to understand the word 'satire'?

3.1 Johnson's concept of poetry

How Johnson conceived of poetry and of the activity of poetry is best answered by Johnson himself:

> Nothing can please many, and please long, but just representations of general nature (Greene, p.420)

> [Shakespeare's characters] are the genuine progeny of common humanity, such as the world will always supply, and observation will always find (Greene, p.421)

> The end of writing is to instruct; the end of poetry is to instruct by pleasing (Greene, p.424)

> There was therefore before the time of Dryden no poetical diction: no system of words at once refined from the grossness of domestic use and free from the harshness of terms appropriated to particular arts. Words too familiar or too remote defeat the purpose of a poet. From those sounds which we hear on small or on coarse occasions, we do not easily receive strong impressions or delightful images; and words to which we are nearly strangers, whenever they occur, draw that attention on themselves which they should transmit to things.' (Greene, pp.722–3)

A full statement of these views can be found in *Rasselas,* chapter X.

> 'The business of the poet,' said Imlac, 'is to examine, not the individual, but the species; to remark general properties and large appearances: he does not number the streaks of the tulip, or describe the different shades of the verdure of the forest. He is to exhibit in his portraits of nature such prominent and striking features as to recall the original to every mind; and must neglect the minuter discriminations, which one may have remarked, and another have neglected, for those characteristics which are alike obvious to vigilance and carelessness.

> But the knowledge of nature is only half the task of a poet …
> He must write as the interpreter of nature, and the legislator of
> mankind, and consider himself as being superior to time and
> place.' (Greene, pp.352–3)

The history of poetry contains many manifestos, statements of a broadly
aesthetic kind, which seek to inculate the taste with which a particular
sort of poetry is to be savoured. Johnson's is a very old one, in certain
respects reaching back to the Roman poet, Horace, and the Elizabethan,
Philip Sidney. Paramount is a concern that poetry should both teach and
delight; the subject matter of poetry should be general: and particular
examples should be representative. The language of poetry should be
purified from harshness and grossness.

In the arts today other values hold our esteem, values like originality, authenticity, individuality, the projection of personality. For these
reasons we admit an enormous range of diction into poetry. Johnson's
stress upon common humanity and dignified language may seem restric-
tive. Perhaps he would have found much twentieth-century poetry embar-
rassing or undignified; he destroyed many private papers before his
death. The opening lines of *The Vanity of Human Wishes* force generalization about the human condition upon our attention, even at the risk of
tautology; and the same point is reinforced throughout the poem: 'each
grace' (16), 'each gift' (17), 'general massacre' (22), 'general cry' (45),
'every state', 'every prayer' (72), 'every stage' (77), 'every room' (83), and
so on.

3.2 'Imitation'

So dominant is the value attached to originality today that we are, I suspect, immediately suspicious of collaborative art. Imitation is a sort of
trans-historical collaboration, for Johnson 'a kind of middle composition
between translation and original design, which pleases when the thoughts
are unexpectedly applicable, and the parallels lucky' (Johnson, 1958a,
p.192). Johnson believed that a successful imitation employs the structure
of an existing work as the basis for an *original* and *contemporary* composition which a common reader may enjoy. Knowledge of the original may
enlarge the pleasure but it is not a prerequisite for enjoyment.

Johnson was aware of earlier attempts to render Juvenal in English,
notably Dryden's. Johnson wrote:

> The general character of [Dryden's] translation will be given when
> it is said to preserve the wit, but to want the dignity, of the original.
> The peculiarity of Juvenal is a mixture of gaiety and stateliness, of
> pointed sentences and declamatory grandeur.(Johnson, 1958b,
> p.249).

In saying that Dryden's translation lacked dignity, Johnson meant that he
allowed Juvenal's obscenity to pass into English. Johnson did not.

Johnson was attracted to Juvenal's poetry in part because there
existed a long tradition which held Juvenal as a moralist whose savage
attacks on a decadent pagan society had made him acceptable to Christian readers. There was also a tradition that cast Juvenal as a sort of 'opposition satirist' and thereby a defender of Roman liberty against tyranny.

Furthermore, Juvenal was a rhetorician (a term which originally signified someone who is trained and expert in the presentation of briefs in a law court). This training shaped Juvenal's satiric practice and clearly delighted Johnson. Johnson too could have proved a brilliant barrister and, unofficially, was often involved with the law (see Greene, pp.570–9).

The Johnson scholar, Paul Fussell, has argued that since many eighteenth-century writers had close knowledge of the law, 'From this proximity of the law to Literature stems the very eighteenth-century idea that the act of literature is necessarily an act of argument, that the writer, even when he assumes the role of poet, is most comparable to a barrister arguing a case' (Fussell, 1972, pp.45–6).

Certainly Johnson, like Pope, saw himself as living in a period when many parallels with ancient Rome could be drawn. If you read Johnson's other published imitation of Juvenal, *London* (1738; Greene, pp.2–8), you find Johnson adopting an oppositional posture but without Juvenal's cynicism. The later *Vanity of Human Wishes* parallels a change in Juvenal's satires: the first nine are characterized by savage and often obscene wit; the remainder, of which the tenth is the first, achieves a higher moral tone, more like moral essays in verse.

3.3 'Satire'

What are we to understand by satire? A quick modern definition is a poem or prose composition in which prevailing vices or follies are held up to ridicule (OED). Johnson was well aware that satire had evolved during the Roman period. In Latin the word for satire, 'satura', probably meant a 'medley', possibly originally meaning 'a dish with many ingredients.' It took the early form of rudimentary drama, improvised dialogue of rude and unpolished verse, presenting scenes which had little or no connexion with each other. These scenes might be drawn from common life and contain gross and offensive banter. In time Roman satire incorporated philosophy and fable, became autobiographical and then, especially in its comments upon the corruption and incapacity of the governing class, acquired the character of invective, deploring the decay of old Roman virtues, the growth of luxury, avarice and selfish ambition. In his *Dictionary*, Johnson drily defines satire as a 'poem in which wickedness or folly is censured'. When a reader knows that a particular piece of writing is both satirical and imitative an horizon of possibilities and expectations opens up. We should therefore endeavour to see *The Vanity of Human Wishes* within particular literary conventions and share the expectations of the first readers.

To conclude I want you briefly to reflect on Johnson as an Enlightenment figure. Does *The Vanity of Human Wishes* support Johnson's inclusion in a European Enlightenment course? Does he fit easily with the authors of the *Encyclopédie* who used irony and satire to evade censorship? Or should we enlarge our conception of the Enlightenment?

By the end of the course you will be better able to respond; these are early days. Amongst the many authors you study in this course, Johnson was untypical because he was a sincere and committed Christian who wrote prayers, meditations and sermons. (See his *Dictionary's* definition of 'faith', Greene, p.329). Most authors of the French *Encyclopédie* were deist, agnostic or atheist. Both Johnson and authors of the *Encyclopédie* sought the spread of knowledge and humane reform; they did not advocate political revolution or a new social order. True, Johnson shocked Boswell by toasting 'Here's to the next insurrection of the negroes in the West Indies' (Boswell, *Life of Johnson*, Tuesday, 23 September 1777). However, Johnson regarded support for oppressed slaves as moral, not political: 'it may be doubted whether slavery can ever be supposed the natural condition of man ... It is to be lamented that moral right should ever give way to political convenience.' We have already encountered his view of patrons. Johnson saw the human condition as needing a moral rather than a radical political cure. In his *Preface* to his *Dictionary* he put usage above rules (see above, pp.154–6 and Greene, pp.307–8 and 310). Johnson was deeply suspicious of abstract systems, and of intellectuals who pursued paradox for the sake of challenging accepted beliefs or controverting common sense; he was therefore closer to Voltaire than to Rousseau. (See his Preface to *Shakespeare*, Greene, p.419.)

Johnson can seem ruggedly independent and free-thinking, yet politically quiescent and, from an Anglican viewpoint, religiously guilt-ridden. He reminds us that most Europeans during the Enlightenment believed in and practised Christianity. He may be associated both with Haydn for his Christian belief and with the *Encyclopédie* for breadth of intellectual curiosity. His moral principles arose from his Christian convictions, not, as with Hume, from notions of benevolence and a theory of social utility:

> The privileges of education may sometimes be improperly bestowed, but I shall always fear to withhold them, lest I should be yielding to the suggestions of pride, while I persuade myself that I am following the maxims of policy; and under the appearance of salutary restraints, should be indulging the lust of dominion, and that malevolence which delights in seeing others depressed. (Greene, p.529)

This utterance is a far cry from Diderot's justification for the *Encyclopédie*, but both Johnson and Diderot hoped that knowledge would make mankind virtuous and happier.

After these explorations and reflections, you should read the poem through again in its entirety – now, I hope, with a fuller understanding of its context and of Johnson's intentions.

3.4   Further reading and a note on the text

Johnson gave excellent advice on coping with the difficulties of Shakespeare: 'Notes are often necessary, but are necessary evils ... when the pleasures of novelty have ceased ... [then] read the commentators.' (Greene, p.445) You might take his advice by reading the poem in one of its excellent, annotated, scholarly editions, notably those published by Yale (1964) and Oxford (1974).

The hand-written draft of *The Vanity of Human Wishes* was recovered at Malahide Castle, near Dublin, after 1945, being part of papers originally in the possession of Boswell. Johnson claimed to have the whole in mind before committing a single couplet to paper. The surviving draft has only a moderate number of corrections. These may be found in Rudd, pp.91–101.

3.5 *Notes to* **The Vanity of Human Wishes**

99   'in full-blown dignity': suggests both corpulence and conspicuous display.

100   'fortune in his hand': gestures of the hand determine the fates of others.

102   'rays of regal bounty': Wolsey is compared to a sun, dispensing royal favours and outshining King Henry VIII.

113   'aweful state': awe-inspiring pomp.

115   'regal palace': the repetition of 'regal' suggests usurpation of the role of head of state and contrasts with Wolsey's humble birth as a butcher's son and his fall from grace.

121   'repine': fret, complain.

123   'safer pride': contrast with line 113.

124   Trent: this river flows by Lichfield where Johnson was born.

125   'steeps of fate': precipices, the first meaning in Johnson's *Dictionary*. Wolsey's misplaced ambition is conveyed by the image of a huge object toppling into an abyss.

126   'th' enormous weight': this echoes 'full blown' (line 99), Wolsey's physical bulk and ambition are conflated into a huge edifice, perhaps a colossus.

128   'gulfs below': abyss, but with an implication of Hell. Not the usual fate of a Churchman? Johnson returns to the image in line 312.

191   'warrior's pride': military glory.

192   'Swedish Charles': Voltaire's *History of Charles XII*, published in 1732 was well known in England. Johnson had intended to write a play about him.

194   'frame of adamant': powerful physique (literally as hard as diamond).

195   i.e. Charles extends his sway indifferently over those who love or fear him.

196   'unconquer'd: undefeated.

197   'pacific scepters': rulers who avoid war by making peace treaties gave Charles no pleasure. 'Scepters' means Kings who nowadays hold such objects at their coronation. This figure of speech, whereby a part refers to the whole, is called synecdoche. Compare 'hands' and 'sail' for sailors/workers and ship.

198   'trump': trumpet.

198   'field': battlefield.

202   'resign': abdicates.

202   i.e. until nothing remains to be done, by tradition a maxim of Julius Caesar.

203   'Gothic': i.e. Swedish.

204   'be': 'is' in present day English. Johnson preserves a subjunctive voice as with 'remain' in line 202. Latin would have required this grammatical voice now almost defunct in English.

207   'solitary coast': presumably the Baltic coast of present day Poland and Russia.

210   'blushing Glory': military glory, Johnson imagines, blushes at defeat.

211   'distant lands': Charles took refuge in Turkey.

213   'needy supplicant': penniless beggar.

214   i.e. Charles, the embodiment of heroic manly aggression, is reduced to depending upon the intervention of women (in fact the Empress Catherine I, Peter the Great's consort) and Eunuchs, slave officials of the Turkish Sultan, an important figure then in European power politics.

215   'Chance': compare 'fate' in line 125.

216   i.e. Charles died an obscure death.

219   'barren strand': deserted coast.

220   'petty' insignificant. Charles probably died from a chance cannon ball.

4   *Johnson and Boswell*

ANGUS CALDER

In 1773 two of the major writers in the English literary tradition as we now conceive it set off together from Edinburgh intending to visit the Hebrides. Dr Johnson was 63. James Boswell was 32. They had known each other, firm friends, for about a decade, and had long discussed this particular scheme. As early as 1764, when Boswell had thrust himself into the dwelling of Voltaire at Ferney, he had mentioned this 'design' to the Deist sage. Voltaire 'looked at me', Boswell wrote, 'as if I had talked of going to the North Pole, and said, 'You do not insist on my accompanying you?' 'No, Sir'. 'Then I am very willing you should go' (Pottle and Bennett, 1963, pp.3–4).

The friendship of Johnson with Boswell is the chief reason why we still read the prose of both. Without Boswell, Johnson would still be regarded as a major poet, and the historical significance of his *Dictionary* would be appreciated, but his other writings would interest only scholars. Without his huge *Life of Johnson* (1791) Boswell would be seen as a minor eccentric: the author of a spirited book about Corsica, and an unsuccessful lawyer on the fringes of the Edinburgh Enlightenment. His journals were discovered and printed in the twentieth century. They provide a fascinating example of the 'Jekyll and Hyde' mentality associated with Edinburgh, his native city. Respectable married man and habitual drunkard, devoted father and fornicator with prostitutes, Boswell was a would-be-virtuous Christian who nevertheless sought out the company of the 'infidel' philosopher Hume.

But in fact Boswell without Johnson is unimaginable. That great man – as he always, sincerely, saw him – was second father to Boswell and best friend from his early twenties. If he kept a diary, it was largely so as to record what Johnson said. His bouts of virtue owed much to fear of Johnson's disapproval. And the young friend of 'Dictionary Johnson' won enduring fame himself in the end as, so to speak, 'Biography Boswell': pioneer of a new genre of literature; a vast influence on the nineteenth-century novel; and the creator of a 'character', 'Johnson', whose sayings have become proverbial and whose eccentricities are literary folklore.

It has been disputed whether this vain, 'pushy' Scot described 'the real Johnson'. This question would have amused both men, since Boswell shared, despite large differences, one set of traits with his hero. Both were depressive: they could understand each others' mood all too well. Both, aspiring to fame and Christian virtue, saw clearly how happiness and good character were things to be achieved, if at all, only by daily effort. Johnson, at the time of their tour, drank nothing but water and tea, fearing what alcohol would do to him: Boswell, a ferocious bout drinker, flagellated himself in his diary for his own bad behaviour. The 'real' Johnson or Boswell, for either man, would have been a shapeless mass of sin and misery, product of Adam's fall and the world's decline. Together they set about creating the realistically flawed, yet ultimately heroic and dignified, character: 'Johnson'. The venerable Doctor read his young friend's diaries while they were on the Hebrides, knew exactly what

Boswell was trying to make of him, talked to him about his own biography – and so conspired in the result.

EXERCISE

The aim of this section is to examine this joint construction, 'Johnson', through excerpts from Johnson's own *A Journey to the Western Islands of Scotland*, published in 1775, and from Boswell's journal of the tour. We have this in two forms: the original diary entries written by Boswell as they travelled, and the tidied-up version published by him as *The Journal of a Tour to the Hebrides* in 1785, when it formed a kind of 'trailer' for the full *Life*, to which Boswell had long been committed.

To begin with, read the extracts from Johnson's book (about a third of the whole) which you will find in Greene, pp.593–642. Either beforehand, or immediately afterwards, read our essay on Scotland (at the end of this volume of *Studies*). While engaged with both items, reflect on the following questions, and finally, from your notes, try to answer them in your own words.

1 Would you say that Johnson was prejudiced against Scotland and the Scots? Did his attitudes to Lowlanders and Gaelic-speakers differ?

2 Does his attitude towards Macpherson and his *Ossian* seem, on the face of it, justifiable?

3 What examples can you produce to support Simon Eliot's point (p.155, above) that 'In all his writing Johnson displayed this very eighteenth-century habit, that of moving from the particular to the general'?

DISCUSSION

1 Edinburgh, Johnson says (Greene, p.593) is 'too well known to admit description' so he does not record his meetings there with some very notable thinkers and scholars, including William Robertson, whose work as a historian influenced Gibbon. Instead, he makes it seem as if St Andrews – then an intellectual and social backwater – represents the state of Scottish learning and that Scottish universities are being allowed to 'moulder into dust' (p.597). His bizarre remarks about the lack of trees in Scotland would take more pages to unravel than we (or Earth's forests) can afford here.

Johnson was a Tory, yet he had 'Jacobitical' sympathies: however, when he says (p.605) that Cromwell 'civilized' the Scots by 'conquests', he for once applauds the regicide usurper whose memory was hateful to him: at least the man was *English*. The passage which follows, on p.606, is, as you know from the essay on 'Scotland', at best debatable, at worst nonsense.

On the other hand, he found plenty to praise in the *Gaelic* character – the piety of an old woman (p.609), the kindness of a local laird (p.617), the surprising plenty of books (p.621), the elegant hospitality of MacLeod of Raasay (as we now spell the name; p.627). Here, his Tory and Jacobite proclivities lead to warm sympathy with the plight of Gaels after Culloden, and concern about the erosion of their clan system.

On balance, most informed Scots, then as now, would find Johnson perceptive (up to a point) but condescending. In *theory* he is prepared to doubt that 'civilized' Londoners are really better off than Gaels living in the traditional way. Read, to confirm this point, his powerful Latin poem *Skye* (Greene pp.30–1): despite the setting and climate, 'from these dwellings/worry is banished'. You might also now read *The Idler, No 81* (Greene, pp.296–8) in which, in 1759, he impersonates a native American chief denouncing the intrusion into a 'primitive' but happy way of life by European colonialists. In *theory* Johnson could flirt with the 'primitivism' of Rousseau and his co-thinkers which will be discussed in Part E (*Studies*, II) and elsewhere. But *in practice* he holds that Highlanders, and Scots in general, must be 'civilized' up to the *English* norm, and enter fully into the world of modern commerce and 'improved' agriculture. Many Scots, including Boswell, agreed with him, but even some of these must have winced at the comparison which concludes Johnson's book: 'after having seen the deaf taught arithmetic, who would be afraid to cultivate the Hebrides?'

2   History has up to a point vindicated Johnson's insistence that Ossian was a 'forgery': it now seems abundantly clear, from the work of scholars sympathetic in general towards Gaelic literature, that Macpherson constructed his 'epic' out of bits and pieces of folk tradition and that it had never existed as a whole in anything like the form which he gave it. On the other hand, if Johnson's own 'imitation' of Juvenal's satire was valid, if Pope's translation of Homer into eighteenth-century couplets imposed an English form remote from the original metre, was it ever fair to castigate Macpherson for treating his oral and manuscript sources as others used the 'classics'? Johnson does not seem to have fully realized that the reticence and apparent shiftiness of his Gaelic respondents on the subject of *Ossian* must have been due to their own complex appreciation of their very ancient culture. The tradition of Gaelic verse, in song and script, survives and even flourishes in our own day though Johnson assumed that it would collapse with the clan society which had sustained it. The 'very learned minister in Sky [sic]' would have refused to commit himself on *Ossian* because, while he knew that Macpherson *had* used manuscripts and genuine oral sources, he himself had reservations about the result: an 'epic' in sentimental *English* prose. (Stafford, 1988, p.169: 'Gaelic speakers' when challenged, mostly 'preferred to dwell on the beauties of the original poetry rather than on Macpherson's version.')

3   Johnson's overall method in *A Journey* ... is characteristic of his empirical age. One *should* seek out particular facts. The motivation of Johnson's journey may have been rooted in part in boyhood reading and Jacobite sympathies, but undoubtedly he believed that it represented a kind of 'experiment'. He would bring theories, derived from the ancient classics and modern travel books, to the test. He would be resolutely sceptical in any case where testimony was dubious, would make careful enquiries, observations and measurements (his stout oak stick, which sadly he lost in the islands, performed double duty as a support in walking and as a measuring

rod.) He would then advance to confirmed, modified, or 'revisionist' generalization.

The passage on 'The Highlands' (Greene, pp.613–17) exemplifies this three-part process. We begin with generalizations about 'mountainous countries', though in this case we know that they have already been tested by 'particular' observation. What Johnson says might equally well apply to Wales (which he visited between his Highland trip and publication of his book) or, as he says, to Northern Spain or to upland Sweden. What he has heard – in particular – in the Hebrides about clan traditions from men who remembered the old way of life – confirms the generalization. Indeed, it turns out that a particular instance – the Gaelic clan – typifies completely the 'family' character of all societies in rugged regions. Less schematically, Johnson's thoughts at 'Ostig' (Ostaig; Greene, pp.628ff), move from very specific observations about weather, fauna, agricultural practices, to broad generalizations. See p.630 for an instance: Johnson observes that most Hebrideans are of 'the middle stature' and moves thence to the (dubious) generalization that 'in regions of barrenness and scarcity, the human race is hindered in its growth by the same causes as other animals'.

Before you read the extracts from Boswell's *Journal* in your *Texts*, I, pp.117–24, a few words about the text. The first extract is from Boswell's published book, *The Journal of a Tour to the Hebrides*: it describes Johnson's arrival in Edinburgh as if in distant retrospect, though we know that Boswell kept notes at the time. The text of the second extract, where Dr Johnson is entertained at Ullinish and Fernilea, is from the original diary. Boswell revised this considerably for publication. On p.123 of your text for instance, the published volume omits the obscurely personal reference to the Will of Langton, another member of Johnson's Club and also, rather sadly, the quirky, very Boswell-ish, comparison of the variegated flagstones at Fernilea to the varied forms for concluding English letters, which takes up again a topic discussed at Ullinish the previous night (p.124).

EXERCISE Read through the following paragraph from the published book and then compare it with Boswell's diary entry which is printed in *Texts*, I, pp.121–22. What is the general effect of Boswell's revisions? For what reason might he have made them?

When Dr Johnson came down, I told him that I had now obtained some evidence concerning *Fingal*; for that Mr M'Queen had repeated a passage in the original Erse, which Mr M'Pherson's translation was pretty like; and reminded him that he himself had once said, he did not require Mr M'Pherson's Ossian to be more like the original than Pope's Homer. JOHNSON. 'Well, sir, this is just what I always maintained. He has found names, and stories, and phrases, nay passage in old songs, and with them has blended his own compositions, and so made what he gives to the world as the translation of an ancient poem'. If this was the case, I observed, it was wrong to publish it as a poem in six books. JOHNSON. 'Yes, sir; and to ascribe it to a time too when the Highlanders knew nothing of *books,* and nothing of *six;* or perhaps were got the length of counting six. We have been told, by Condamine, of a nation that could count no more than four. This should be told to Monboddo; it would help him. There is as much charity in helping a man down-hill, as in helping him up-hill'. BOSWELL. 'I don't think there is as much charity'. JOHNSON. 'Yes, sir, if his *tendency* be downwards. Till he is at the bottom, he flounders; get him once there, and he is quiet. Swift tells, that Stella had a trick, which she learned from Addison, of encouraging a man in absurdity, instead of endeavouring to extricate him.

DISCUSSION   Apart from the fact that Boswell awards his friend the title of 'Dr', given him by Oxford University in 1775, *after* the *Journey,* other revisions also enhance the hero's dignity. The Latinate 'endeavouring to extricate him' replaces, for instance, the plain-English 'strive to pull him out of it'. The characteristic 'Johnson' opening of a remark with 'Sir' is present only once in the original, twice in the published version. It looks as if Boswell wanted to make Johnson grander, more eloquent and more definite.

But it's a well known fact among diarists that very often one does *not* note down some circumstance which later haunts the memory. Boswell didn't take shorthand notes while Johnson was talking – he 'gleaned' what he could remember at whatever time afterwards proved to be convenient for writing. From years of friendship he would have retained a vivid *general* impression of Johnson's tricks while talking, such as his 'polite' yet imperious 'Sir'. Adapting slightly what he had noted in diaries was a perfectly valid procedure – 'yes, *he'd* have said it like *this,* of course'. Since a person can rarely remember exactly what she or he 'really' said half an hour ago, there is no more reason to dispute the authenticity of Boswell's published text than that of any other 'primary' source for speech before the epoch of sound recording.

EXERCISE   Read both the extracts from Boswell's *Journal.* Note any contrasts which strike you between Boswell's 'discourse' – his way-of-writing – and Johnson's. In case you are tempted to say flatly that one's a philosophical traveller, the other's a diarist, so their purposes in writing are obviously quite different – look at the specimen of *Johnson* as diarist in Greene (pp.775–80) and his letter to Mrs Thrale from 'Ostig' (pp.787–9).

DISCUSSION   Johnson's discourse is generally detached from the immediate human foreground. When he records a silly remark by a scholar at St Andrews about the Divinity College library, he does not 'characterize' or particularly describe the 'doctor', let alone reproduce his statement as speech (Greene, p.597). The old woman in her hut on p.609 is made more immediate for us, but the description of her is very general, and one might (unfairly) deduce that Johnson was only interested in her for the information which she could supply relevant to his study of society in the

Highlands. Even the letter to his dear friend Mrs Thrale, always in his thoughts during his journey, is full of geographical information drily presented, and the tribute to 'Young Macleod', while warm, gives one no clear sense of his appearance, let alone his 'personality'. As for the intimate Diaries, Johnson contents himself with topographical description and general meditation (July 25, 1774); with a brief record of a holy (hence 'awe-full') day with Boswell giving none of their talk (April 14, 1775); and, in other entries, with prayers, self-castigations and suchlike spiritual exercises.

I am not suggesting that Johnson *ought* to have written otherwise. It is as valid to keep a diary for bare notes ('aide-memoires') of things seen, which was Johnson's practice in Paris in 1775, as it is to do so for Boswell's more lavish purposes. Johnson's *A Journey to the Western Islands*, while primarily concerned to make and support generalizations, is much more immediate and 'personal' than, say, Adam Smith's *Wealth of Nations* (1776), a pioneering work in economics concerned with questions such as interested Johnson on his tour.

But with Boswell's discourse, surely, we feel much more 'immediately' at home? Even in the considered, retrospective first paragraph of our first extract there is an atmosphere of twinkling improvisation: having used the nautical words 'convoys', he makes it the pretext for a remark about Johnson's delight in the rapid motion of postchaises. This is not as 'artless' as it might seem. Discomfort at sea and on roads unfit for carriages will be a frequent topic in this journal: Johnson's, and Boswell's, pleasure at returning at last to a carriage will be stressed near the end of Boswell's account of their tour, when they have reached Loch Lomond:

> We were favoured with Sir James Colquhoun's coach ... Our satisfaction at finding ourselves again in a comfortable carriage was very great. We had a pleasing conviction of the commodiousness of civilisation, and heartily laughed at the ravings of those absurd visionaries [e.g. Rousseau] who have attempted to persuade us of the superior advantages of a state of nature. (Levi, 1984, p.386)

Leaving for later the measured overall characterization of Johnson which follows, look at the paragraph on p.119 beginning 'I am, I flatter myself ...' It is characteristic of Boswell in its disarmingly open boastfulness. He has told us how much he venerated 'that Wonderful Man', now he remarks that he sometimes treated him like a child, humouring his absurd prejudices. This is no static master-disciple relationship: as Boswell will show us, for all their 'love' for each other, he and his friend quarrelled, had huffs, 'put each other down' (as we would now say) and disagreed about important subjects. Boswell does not scruple to bring the intimate informality of his journal fully into play at once. The anecdote which tells about the lump of sugar reveals Johnson's latent physical violence. The account of his short walk with Boswell from Canongate to James Court has been quoted in book after book to illustrate the sanitation problems of Edinburgh's Old Town: it is characteristic of Boswell that he not only freely admits to an unfortunate feature of his home city, he also recounts a fine joke of Johnson's against himself: 'I smell you in the dark ...'

Later on, when they have reached Skye, after the notable moment when Johnson bursts out with an Elizabethan ballad, Boswell comments on their fellow guest MacQueen (p.121) 'He has not firmness of mind sufficient to break' – with terse 'wit' of Johnson's own variety.

But this is not *ex cathedra*, like Johnson's judgement on Orrery (p.120). 'That his conversation was like his writing, neat, elegant, but without strength'. This is Boswell prompted, in some exasperation, to an extempore judgement on a good, likeable man. He continues to watch MacQueen, even when he and Johnson (with amazingly bad manners?) are teasing him about the figure he would cut as a suspect on trial: 'Mr Macqueen stood patiently by while all this passed'. Unlike Johnson's handling of the old Highland woman (Greene, p.609), Boswell's of Mac-Queen is 'open': we are conscious of the minister as an intelligent and polite man guarding his own thoughts from these boisterous outsiders. While Boswell danced reels in houses where they were entertained, Johnson sat reading or lecturing those who wished to hear the great man's opinions. He did not close himself to fresh experience, or ignore the personalities of those he met, but he was not universally sociable and inquisitive, like Boswell.

What Boswell's *Journal* (in printed form as well as in manuscript) often produces are effects like those found in the 'stream of consciousness' novelists of the early twentieth century. Events, scenery, meditations, conversations, and surprising fancies, tumble over each other. See the paragraph about Isay (p.123). Boswell, recalling recent conversations, remembers MacLeod's jocular offer of the little island to Johnson. He relates Johnson's reaction to other episodes in their years of acquaintance which had involved similar wild, 'astonishing' glee on the Doctor's part. He remembers a tale of Langton's involving Garrick, then some kind of joke at the expense of 'poor Langton'. Though we realize on reflection that Boswell must have composed some time later the whole entry for that day, it is as if these memories run through his head as they sail agreeably on Ullinish's boat; the loud voice of Johnson dies away, Boswell falls into reverie and reminiscence. Then he observes the seascape: a fine harbour, a varied shore. Then arrival at Fernilea, their host's broad Scots greeting, sudden pleasure at the shapes of the flagstones in his parlour, simple delight over a good hot dinner.

To say that the novelist Lawrence Sterne, who became immensely popular with his *Tristram Shandy* (1759–67) at a time when Boswell was forming his own style, anticipated 'stream of consciousness' before Boswell, is merely to emphasize that the latter brings into 'serious non fiction' (as we call it) techniques developed by fiction writers. In turn, his characterization influenced novelists who read his Hebridean *Journal* and his *Life of Johnson*: notably Walter Scott whose influence, in turn, touched every fiction writer in Europe in the middle decades of the nineteenth-century. Through Boswell's prose medium, changeable as the weather, Johnson, his moods, his caprices, his physical presence, come to our minds with extraordinary vividness.

EXERCISE   Try to sum up in your own words the character of Johnson as it appears in these writings by Boswell. How does it square with the impression which you derived from Johnson's own writings?

DISCUSSION   One recognizes a 'discourse' common to Johnson the writer and to Johnson the talker (as recorded by Boswell.) It is pithy, terse, marked by well formed sentences and authoritative-sounding judgements.

But it *is* hard to 'square' the author of Johnson's magisterial book on his *Journey* with the figure displayed by Boswell, rapt in glee over his Isay fantasy (or, elsewhere in Boswell's account, flirting happily when a pretty woman boldly sits on his knee.) The judgements on *Ossian* which seem so finely pondered in Johnson's book (Greene, pp.636–8) are developed and expressed in context, on Skye, with a churlish obtuseness which puts me (for one) off them. What *that* squares with is Boswell's memorable summary of the man in the first extract in your text.

Boswell freely admits that his friend and hero was 'impetuous and irritable', that he was susceptible to flattery, that his prose was stiffer in style than his poetry, that he had a loud voice and a ponderous way of talking to match his large physical frame, now grown 'unwieldy from corpulency'. Such a man we might think a pompous bully if we met him, and even if we were glad enough to submit, for a time at least, to his 'lecturing' manner, his '*bow-wow* way', we might be less than allured by his ugly scars and his aggressively plain way of dressing.

Yet Boswell (whose familiar, easy manner suggests that he sees his own reader as a friend, to be introduced with pride to his greatest friend) balances disagreeable and comic features of Johnson's personality against wholly admirable ones: he is sincere in religion and politics, 'humane and benevolent' in heart, immensely learned, 'most logical'. Intriguingly: 'he might have been perpetually a poet'. Boswell delights in his friend's 'fertile imagination'. Mention of 'constitutional melancholy' is also important in establishing that a sensitive, suffering man was not very well disguised by Johnson's overbearing façade as he 'talked for victory'. No doubt Highlanders meeting him respected and even loved Johnson for his gallant attempts to control an unreliable temperament, as well as for an extraordinary range of learning which included minute practical knowledge of everyday, useful trades.

This 'encyclopedic' coverage, combined with a zeal for 'improvement' of the lives of people great and small with the help of better technology, brings him curiously close to the French *philosophe*, Diderot, whose free thought about religion Johnson would have execrated. He was a practical human being, concerned to help others, with, as Boswell puts it, 'a stratum of common clay under the rock of marble'.

Boswell, who loved him, succeeded in making him both lovable, and formidable, clay and marble. One hopes that as Boswell lay dying, aged only 54, a worn out alcoholic whose ambitions in law and politics had long since been sabotaged by his own waywardness, he remembered that moment on Skye the morning after he had lapsed from the abstemiousness which he had maintained in Johnson's constant company and, as his published *Journal* records with candour, had succumbed to Highland hospitality till 'near five in the morning'. He had awoken at noon, 'afraid of a reproof from Dr Johnson. I thought it very inconsistent with that conduct which I ought to maintain while the companion of the *Rambler.*

About one he came into my room and accosted me, 'What, drunk yet?' His tone of voice was not that of severe upbraiding: so I was relieved a little. 'Sir', said I, 'they kept me up'. He answered, 'No, you kept them up, you drunken dog' ... Finding him thus jocular, I became quite easy ...' (Levi, 1984, p.315.) Even such, the inveterate sinner Boswell might have hoped, would be the forgiveness of God.

5 Conclusion to the study on Johnson

In his views on publishing and on writing Johnson was pragmatic and rational; in his rejection of patronage he was at one with Voltaire; he shared his zeal for the 'improvement' of the common lot through better technology with Diderot; in his desire to organize and systematize what was known he resembled the Encyclopedists; and in his admiration for, and use of, the classics he displayed a characteristically Enlightenment approach. But the intensity and centrality of the Christian religion in his life separates him from many of the other figures we have studied so far in 'Varieties of Enlightenment'. Johnson saw humanity not as striding rationally ever forward and upward on the path to perfection, but as a poor, ambivalent creature, as often motivated by passion and blind selfishness as by reason, stumbling about in a decaying world besmirched by sin. Yet Johnson was too great to despair. He did stay and fight, and in the face of all the imperfections in language, all the uncertainties of knowledge and all the insecurities of his own personality, produced a host of works which honestly acknowledged human limitations and, by doing so, speak to us, two hundred years and more later, with greater conviction and humanity than do many other, more facile, works of the Enlightenment.

6 References

Boswell, J. (1980) *Life of Johnson*, Oxford University Press (The World's Classics), London.

Johnson, S. (1958a) *Life of Pope*, vol. 2, Everyman Library, London.

Johnson, S. (1958b) *Life of Dryden*, vol. 1, Everyman Library, London.

Levi, P. (ed.) (1984) Boswell, J. and Johnson, S., *A Journey to the Western Islands of Scotland* and *The Journal of a Tour to the Hebrides*, Penguin, London.

Pottle, F. and Bennett, C. (eds) (1963) *Boswell's Journal of a Tour to the Hebrides*, Heinemann, London.

Rudd, W.J.N. (1988) *Johnson's Juvenal*, Classical Press, Bristol.

Stafford, F. (1988) *The Sublime Savage: James MacPherson and The Poems of Ossian*, Edinburgh University Press, Edinburgh.

7 Further reading

Bate, W. J. (1955) *The Achievement of Samuel Johnson*, University of Chicago Press, Chicago and London.

Bate, W. J. (1975) *Samuel Johnson*, Harcourt Brace Jovanovich, New York and London.

Brooks, H.F. (1949) 'The 'Imitation' in English poetry, especially informal satire before the Age of Pope', *Review of English Studies*, vol.25, no.98, pp.124–40.

Clifford, J. L.(1979) *Dictionary Johnson: Samuel Johnson's Middle Years*, McGraw-Hill, New York.

Fussell, P. (1972) *Samuel Johnson and the Life of Writing*, Chatto & Windus, London.

Hardy, J.P. *(1979) Samuel Johnson: A Critical Study*, Routledge & Kegan Paul, London.

Humphreys, A.R. (1957) 'Johnson' in *The Pelican Guide to English Literature*, edited by Boris Ford, vol.4, Penguin Books Ltd, London.

Kernan, A. (1987) *Samuel Johnson and the Impact of Print*, Princeton University Press, Princeton.

Mackail, J.W. (1952) *Latin Literature*, J. Murray, London.

Nichol Smith, D. and McAdam, E.L. (eds) (1974) *The Poems of Samuel Johnson*, Oxford University Press, Oxford.

Reddick, A. (1990) *The Making of Johnson's Dictionary* 1746–73, Cambridge University Press, Cambridge.

Rudd, W.J.N. *(1991) Juvenal: The Satires*, Clarendon Press, Oxford.

Wain, J. (ed.) (1976) *Johnson on Johnson*, Dent, London.

Music and the Enlightenment and Haydn's Creation

Prepared for the Course Team by Patricia Howard

Contents

Music in the Enlightenment and Haydn's Creation
(Study weeks 7–8)

Studies/ Texts	Radio	TV	AC	Set books
Studies, I	–	–	AC 1628 (red)	–
Texts, I	–	–	AC 1626 (red)	–
–	–	–	AC 1627 (red)	–

The following two essays introduce music into your Enlightenment studies. The first aims to provide a general, non-technical discussion of musical language in the late eighteenth century; the second focuses on Part One of Haydn's oratorio *The Creation*. Cassette references, for both essays, will be found on the first page of the Study (p. 183). For the first essay you will also be asked to read from Section 5 of the *Encyclopédie* text (*Texts*, I, pp. 37–40) and for the second you will need to read the Haydn section in *Texts*, I and also refer again to the extracts from the *Encyclopédie*.

Music and the Enlightenment and Haydn's Creation

1   Music and the Enlightenment

This first part of the study is in two sections:

1   Music in the age of Enlightenment
2   The language of Enlightenment music

The two sections are illustrated on the red Cassette AC 1628, side 1, 'The Techniques of Enlightenment Music' and side 2, 'Enlightenment Composers Represent Light'. You will need to have the cassette set up and ready to play before you begin to read the study, and several times in the course of the study, you will be asked to stop reading and listen to a short section of the cassette. You may find it useful to take a counter reading each time you use the cassette, so that you can easily replay any section you wish to hear again. You will also need to have the relevant Cassette Notes to hand.

1.1   Music in the age of Enlightenment

You have already met some Enlightenment musicians. Frederick the Great was a flautist and the composer of music which is still occasionally played today. Catherine the Great was an enthusiastic patron of opera who drew French, German and Italian composers to her court. Many members of European ruling families were keen amateur musicians: among the Habsburgs, for example, the Empress Maria Theresa, her son the future Joseph II and her daughter Marie Antoinette, all took part in amateur opera productions in mid-century Vienna. Rousseau was a composer of rather higher standing than Frederick and a distinguished analyst of music. Grimm, Voltaire and de Jaucourt were music critics. D'Alembert was a theorist, who explored both the philosophy and the physics of music. Diderot's interest was music theatre; he strove to bring realistic scenery and costume to opera and ballet. He was also a historian of musical instruments.

Music was a hotly debated topic among the *philosophes*. If we look up musical topics in the *Encyclopédie* we find well-researched, factual articles on almost every known musical instrument from *Archlute* to *Violin*, every current musical form from *Air* to *Vaudeville*, and many aspects of style from *Accompaniment* to *Variation*. There are also polemical articles: the personal antagonism between Rousseau and the composer Rameau brought about a thorough investigation of acoustic theory in dauntingly technical articles on *Harmony* and *Fundamental Bass*. Other authors argued for a reform of ballet along Enlightenment lines, advocating in articles on *Choreography*, *Gesture* and *Pantomime* the use of natural gestures and a coherent plot. Many articles vigorously assert another obsession of the Encyclopedists: the superiority of Italian over French music: 'Let us consider our contemporaries the Italians, whose music is the best in the world according to everyone except the French, who prefer their own,' wrote Rousseau, in *Music*. But a pro-Italian bias is not sustained in the articles which investigate the meaning of music. When the Encyclopedists questioned the capacity of music to make sense without reference to the other arts, they were able to relate theory to practice only in the context of French music.

For the Encyclopedists music had one purpose only – to paint: 'A concerto or sonata must depict something or it is nothing but noise' (*Expression*). Scenes from nature were regarded as ideal subject matter for music: 'There is truth in a *Symphony* which has been composed in imitation of a storm, when the melody, harmony and rhythm of the *Symphony* make us hear a noise like the howl of winds and the roar of the waves as they crash together or break against the rocks' (*Symphony*). An important extension of this was to depict the reactions of a human observer of the natural scene, and so to attempt a portrayal of human nature itself, by representing a range of emotions, the more heightened the better: 'The composer would do well always to keep in mind the idea of some person, some situation or some passion and to concentrate so completely on this idea that eventually he seems to hear speaking the very person who is in the situation ... all composition which does not communicate intelligibly the language of feeling will be nothing but vain noise' (*Instrumental music*). In short, 'Music is an imitative art' (*Sonata*). In the middle of the eighteenth century, French critics either had no concept of music as an autonomous language or did not know how to criticize it as such. In the most famous musical pronouncement in the *Encyclopédie*, Rousseau recounts the words of 'the famous M. de Fontenelle, who, finding himself at a concert and exhausted by an endless symphony, called out loud in a fit of impatience, 'Sonata, what are you trying to tell me?" (*Sonata*).

You can find these quotations in context in Section 5 of the *Encyclopédie* text. Read the articles on *Expression*, *Sonata* and *Symphony* now, to catch something of the flavour of French musical theory (*Texts*, I, pp. 38–9).

The French position is an extreme one, but throughout Europe musicians and critics were attempting to understand the meaning of music, particularly instrumental music which lacked the support or justification of words, in terms of the emotions it represented. Johann Joachim Quantz, who taught Frederick the Great to play the flute, claimed that 'Instrumental music, quite as much as vocal music, should express certain passions and transport the listeners from one to another' (J.J. Quantz, 1752, p.583).

Quantz's colleague at Frederick's court, Carl Philip Emmanuel Bach (son of J.S. Bach), also took an interest in the expressive power of music. Starting from the conviction that 'Nature has wisely provided music with every kind of appeal so that all might share in its enjoyment', he gave this advice to performers:

> A musician cannot move others unless he too is moved. He must of necessity feel all of the affects [passions] that he hopes to arouse in his audience, for the revealing of his own humour will stimulate a like humour in the listener. In languishing, sad passages, the performer must languish and grow sad. Thus will the expression of the piece be more clearly perceived by the audience. (C.P.E. Bach, 1974, p.152. The spelling has been anglicized.)

(Various contemporaries confirm that Bach practised what he preached. The composer and theorist Marpurg reported that 'I know a great composer on whose face one can see depicted everything that his music expresses as he plays it at the keyboard' (C.P.E. Bach, 1974, note 9, p.152).)

Haydn, too, admitted that his instrumental music sometimes carried an extra-musical meaning. In an interview towards the end of his life:

> He said that he oftentimes had portrayed moral characters in his symphonies. In one of the oldest, which, however, he could not accurately identify, 'the dominant idea is of God speaking with an abandoned sinner, pleading with him to reform. But the sinner in his thoughtlessness pays no heed to the admonition.' (G.A. Griesinger, 1810, p.62)

Beethoven's servant and biographer, Anton Schindler, recounts an anecdote which, if true (Schindler is not the most reliable of biographers), would suggest that that composer held a similar view. In 1814, Beethoven dedicated his Piano Sonata Op. 90 in E minor, to Count Moritz Lichnowsky, who had recently scandalized his family by marrying an actress. The count, struck with the beauty and the intimate passion of the sonata, asked Beethoven whether it had any specific meaning. Beethoven replied that 'he had set the count's love-story to music, and if he wished to have names for the movements, the first could be 'Conflict Between Head and Heart', and the second 'Conversation with the Beloved' (Anton Schindler, 1966, p.210 footnote).

We should note that both Beethoven and Haydn referred to the ability of music to describe feelings rather than to paint events or objects. Beethoven made clear his view of the nature of the descriptive role of music when he subtitled his Pastoral Symphony 'More an expression of feeling than tone-painting.' This was the German approach. Tone-painting – the use of music to evoke a scene – was regarded as a typically French process. Although the distinctions between French music and the Italo-German style prevalent throughout the rest of Europe persisted to the end of the century, many attempts were made to bring the national styles together. One of the most deliberate internationalists was the composer Christoph Gluck, who set out to devise a music 'fit for all nations' (Gluck, 1773). And in writing *The Creation*, Haydn made a more reluctant attempt towards the same end when he incorporated French tone-painting into his German instrumental style.

Now read the short articles from the *Supplément* to the *Encyclopédie* on *Vocal Music* and *Instrumental Music*, noticing how far the authors were able to concede that music might be 'more an expression of feeling than of tone-painting' (*Texts*, I, p.40).

We have now accumulated a good many opinions on meaning in music. The time-span of the above quotations, ranging from Quantz and the Encyclopedists writing at the beginning of the 1750s to Beethoven in 1814, requires explanation; the 65-year period extends well beyond the content of the rest of the course. The reason for this is the curious fact that artistic movements in music tend to occur a generation later than similar movements in the other arts. Julian Rushton points out the disconcerting relevance for the Enlightenment of Beethoven, who produced all his significant music well after the French Revolution:

> The arts do not work in phase … Connections between politics, philosophy and the arts, and among the arts, are seldom straightforward, nor do they necessarily have much importance for the understanding of musical works. In retrospect the vision of a better future for mankind in charge of its own destiny finds a belated artistic consummation, in a period of renewed despotism, in the music of Beethoven. (Julian Rushton, 1986, pp.17-18)

But there is another difference between music and the other arts besides chronology: it is not, I think, possible to talk of an enlightened composer in the same way that we can identify an enlightened writer, philosopher or artist. The nature of meaning in music is such that, at least in the eighteenth century, music written at the same time and in the same place and for the same function will tend to sound similar (and therefore, arguably, mean the same) regardless of the intellectual attitudes of the composer. To a greater extent than is the case with art or literature, 'Enlightenment' describes a period style, the period of greatest overlap between the 'Classical' and 'Romantic' tendencies in music. There are, perhaps, Enlightenment *genres* rather than Enlightenment composers: in 1791 Mozart wrote both his popular opera *The Magic Flute*, which is an enlightened work by any definition, and, for church performance, the Requiem Mass, which is not. Not that it was impossible to write enlightened liturgical music: Beethoven's *Missa Solemnis*, 1823, places humanity at the centre of the work and was, I believe, unprecedented in creating a triumphant musical climax out of the phrase 'et homo factus est' – 'and [Christ] was made man'. With the odd exception, however, music written in the second half of the eighteenth century and the first two decades of the nineteenth shares common characteristics which relate to qualities in the art and literature which it narrowly post-dates. There would be no point in using the term 'Enlightenment music' unless there were some connection between the music created, performed, listened to and discussed by Frederick, Catherine, Rousseau, Voltaire, Diderot and their immediate successors, and the more concrete ideas pursued by these men and women of the Enlightenment.

1.2   *The language of Enlightenment music*

Music engages with Enlightenment ideas most obviously when it sets a text. The texts of Enlightenment works – operas, oratorios, songs – focus typically on the human race, its creation, its nature, its relationship with the natural world, and how it engages with and overcomes the vicissitudes of life on this earth. Haydn's *Creation*, for example, places man and woman at the pinnacle of the created world. There is a marked limitation in the representation of the supernatural in this period. In serious opera, the gods still appear, but their role becomes increasingly perfunctory. To grasp how opera was subjected to a process of 'Enlightening', we can compare two settings of the story of Orpheus, one from the seventeenth century and one from the eighteenth. In both operas Orpheus loses his wife and rescues her from the underworld, only to lose her a second time. In Monteverdi's opera (written in 1607) he is then taken up into the heavens where he can eternally gaze upon the image of his wife among the stars; in Gluck's *Orpheus* (1762) his wife is restored to him in the flesh, and they continue their married life together on this earth.[1]

Whether or not it is associated with a text, Enlightenment music gives a high priority to the exploration of human character and situation, especially through the representation of feelings. It is the fluidity of human emotions which seems to have been the discovery of musicians in this period. The character of Cherubino in Mozart's opera *The Marriage of Figaro* delights in exploiting music's new-found ability to switch from one passion to another:

> What I am feeling …
> Is all new to me and hard to understand.
> I have a feeling full of strange desire,
> Which one moment pleases, and the next is full of pain.
> I freeze, and then I find my soul all burning.
> Then in a moment I'm freezing again.

> (From *The Marriage of Figaro* II.3, 'Voi che sapete'. P. Furbank, 1980, p.18)

Such a riot of transient emotion is equally present in much instrumental music of the period.

Enlightenment music is also associated with the pursuit of pleasure. (You will remember the popular if inaccurate account of Epicurus mentioned in the *Encyclopédie* as one who 'legitimised pleasure'). The box-office element began to make itself felt. In this age the public concert gradually displaced the princely court as the principal venue for the performance of music, and composers had to appeal to a wider and less discriminating audience. It is no coincidence that the genre of comic opera originated in the mid-eighteenth century. Further, a lightness of manner and an intention to entertain informs even the most serious context – Haydn re-used the idea of a sudden loud chord, initially thought up to amuse the bourgeois audience at his public concerts in London, for the most solemn moment in his oratorio *The Creation*.

But music of the Enlightenment period also has its own, purely musical characteristics, which relate only metaphorically to more concrete Enlightenment themes. In the musical language of the period there is an underlying sense of progress. Continually moving from one state to another, it is concerned with the process of transition, always developing from something less to something more. It tends to grow from soft to loud and from minor to major; it can also be described as progressing metaphorically, from depth to height, and from darkness to light. All Enlightenment music will make a feature of some of these transitions. To get closer to its language we shall have to attempt to see how they work.

---

[1] The recurrence of themes throughout the period of the musical Enlightenment can be illustrated by comparing Gluck's *Orpheus* with Beethoven's opera *Fidelio* (1805). The plot is structurally the same. Only the sex of the protagonist is changed: in *Fidelio* a wife descends to the underworld in the form of a prison dungeon to rescue her husband. Again she nearly loses him for a second time, but he is restored to her by a higher agent. You will be able to hear this rescue scene on the cassette.

In the century before the musical Enlightenment, composers were much concerned with loud and soft. This contrast was achieved partly through the restricted range of dynamic notation in use at the time, with soft passages marked 'p' *(piano)* and loud passages marked 'f' *(forte)*. They also exploited contrasted vocal or instrumental groups (notably a choir pitted against a few solo singers, or a full orchestra with an instrumental soloist or soloists); these opposing forces were often spatially separated to enhance the effect (for example, placed on opposite sides of a church). The simple contrast of loud with soft, known aptly as the echo effect, was a favourite technique in the seventeenth century. It is illustrated with particular and literal appropriateness by the chorus of witches in Purcell's opera *Dido and Aeneas* (1689):

> *Witches (f, and accompanied by the orchestra)*
> In our deep vaulted cell,
> *(p, accompanied by a smaller group)* – ed cell,
> *(f, with orchestra)* the charm we'll prepare,
> *(p, with smaller group)* prepare …

(This example, and other music referred to in this study, is played on Cassette AC 1628, Side 1, 'The Techniques of Enlightenment Music'.)

The idea of contrasting loud and soft music is still, of course, an ingredient of eighteenth-century music, but a new effect came into use around the middle of the century which called for a gradual increase in sound. Notated with the word *crescendo*, or with a typographical symbol that looks like an expanding 'hairpin' ⟨ , the effect was regarded as an exciting novelty. The music historian Charles Burney, who travelled throughout Europe during the 1770s, reporting on contemporary developments, enthused over the crescendos (and their opposite, the diminuendo, or diminution of volume) which he heard for the first time at the court of Mannheim:

> It was [at Mannheim] that … every effect has been tried which such an aggregate of sound can produce; it was here that the *Crescendo* and *Diminuendo* had birth; and the *Piano*, which was before chiefly used as an echo, with which it was generally synonymous, as well as the *Forte*, were found to be musical *colours* which had their *shades*, as much as red or blue in painting. (Burney, 1969, vol.1, p.96)

The crescendo demonstrates in miniature the sense of progress which underlies Enlightenment music. The music grows from a state of something less to something more. (It was not until the nineteenth century that the opposite procedure, the diminuendo, was fully exploited.) It is also part of the new rhetoric used to captivate the wider public which eighteenth-century music addresses. The crescendo is an intrinsically exciting sound, and helps the composer to manipulate the audience's emotional response. (You can hear several crescendos on the cassette, including one written in Mannheim, perhaps the very passage to which Burney refers.)

Sudden contrasts between *piano* and *forte* were, as Burney notes, still to be found in the mid-century, but instead of forming the essentially predictable echo effect, they were used more informally, to create surprise.

As Haydn said when he wrote the famous loud chord which has given his 'Surprise Symphony' its nickname, 'I was interested in surprising the public with something new' (Griesinger, 1810). (He is also quoted as saying, 'That will make the ladies jump!' (Gyrowetz, 1848, p.75).)

Play section 1 of the cassette before reading further.

A sense of progress also describes the innovative treatment of major and minor keys in Enlightenment music. Unlike the contrast between soft and loud, the opposing colours of major and minor keys have not always been a part of Western European music. They affect only a comparatively short span in its history, emerging towards the end of the sixteenth century and facing serious challenge, perhaps even extinction, in the works of early twentieth-century composers (although the major/minor contrast still flourishes in popular music). The eighteenth century can, however, be described as the heyday of major-minor tonality, and composers of Enlightenment music made great use of this potential source of contrast.

I'm anxious to avoid going unnecessarily into technical matters, so I'm going to ask you to take on trust the fact that Enlightenment composers differed in their use of major and minor keys from both earlier and later composers. You may, however, be interested in a summary of changing theoretical attitudes to major and minor across four centuries:

Table 1

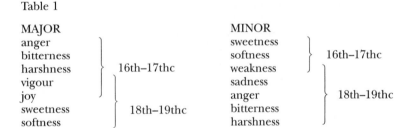

(Adapted from Lorenzo Bianconi, 1987, p.55)

You can see how some emotional states crossed over completely between the seventeenth century and the eighteenth – 'sweetness', for example, being attributed to the minor key in Purcell's day, but to the major in Haydn's. A particularly striking reversal is shown if we compare Purcell's ecstatic minor-key marriage hymn *(Epithalamium)* from *The Fairy Queen* (1692) with the major-key celebration of the union between Adam and Eve in *The Creation*, written a century later. (You can hear Purcell's music in section 5 of the cassette.) In music of the Enlightenment period, then, we find a reassessment of the expressive content of major and minor.

Detecting the difference between major and minor is the one aspect of this study which you may initially find a little daunting, but you will have plenty of chance to practise this skill as you listen to the red Cassette AC 1628. You may be encouraged to realise that the new audience for this music, drawn from the general public, must have picked up the skill quite quickly, since so much music from the eighteenth century depends on this element of contrast. The point I hope you'll be able to observe is that in Enlightenment music, there is a strong sense of progression from minor to major. That is to say that in sonatas and symphonies, and also across the time-scale of whole operas, there is a marked tendency for a work which begins in a minor key to end in the major. This was a new approach.

For example, time and again we can find in Haydn's symphonies a short minor-key introduction followed by four major-key movements. In his last symphony, No. 104, the slow introduction exploits the full range of emotions which eighteenth-century theorists attributed to the minor key; the four subsequent major-key movements respond to this disturbing opening with a mood change which even the most cautious of verbal analogues must describe as a 'happy ending'. Beethoven provides similar happy endings for his symphonies but with significantly changed proportions: he invariably defers the change to the major key to a much later stage in the piece. In his Fifth and Ninth symphonies, for example, the turn to the major – the happy ending – is delayed until the last movement.

Mozart's opera *Don Giovanni* makes the same tonal journey from minor to major, from its powerful minor-key overture, associated with the supernatural element in the drama, to its down-to-earth, moralising, major-key ending. However Mozart, as I suggested earlier, is a non-conforming figure in the musical Enlightenment. The extent to which he avoids the major-key solution in the majority of his mature minor-key works suggests how much closer he is to the practices and attitudes of his nineteenth-century successors, some of whom, significantly, used to cut the major-key finale from *Don Giovanni*.

The concepts of major and minor make more sense when you can hear them. Listen now to section 2 of the cassette.

The third transition technique we shall examine is from depth to height. 'Depth' and 'height' clearly relate to musical pitch, and one way in which Enlightenment music exploits this transition is in melodies which climb from a low note to a high one. A certain type of rising tune became enormously popular in the period – so much so that it acquired the nickname of 'Mannheim rocket' ('Mannheim' because it originated at the same court where the crescendo was first exploited. Look back to p.188.)

Here are some 'Mannheim rockets', though they were written in Vienna! You don't need to be able to read notation to see how the music shoots upwards. You can hear these tunes on section 3 of the cassette.

Mozart, Symphony No. 40, Finale

Haydn, Op 64 No. 4, first movement

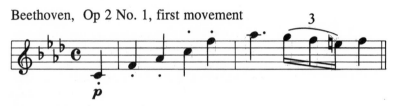

Beethoven, Op 2 No. 1, first movement

Music Example 1

The opposition of depth with height is applied in another sense in the medium of opera. Enlightenment operas, like Enlightenment symphonies, have happy endings. Their underlying theme is survival, and there are few deaths on or off the stage. And while happy endings are by no means exclusive to eighteenth-century opera, the vertical structuring of the action is particularly characteristic of the period. Typically, a potential tragedy is set up on one level (earth) and averted by a character from a higher plane (heaven).

We can see this structure most clearly in the serious operas of the period: the neo-classical dramas of Gluck and the so-called 'historical event' of Beethoven's *Fidelio*. In the former, the drama is always resolved from above, by the intervention of an appropriate supernatural being. (When Orpheus loses his wife for the second time, it is Cupid, the god of love, who steps in to restore her to life and to her husband.) Far from betraying an unenlightened dependence on supernatural aid, such plots in fact show a severe limitation of supernatural elements in comparison with seventeenth-century opera. And there are signs that in his last operas Gluck was beginning to rebel against even this token appearance of the gods. He tried to leave one opera *(Iphigenia in Aulis)* with an ambiguous ending, so that it could be understood as being resolved by purely human

ingenuity, until the Parisian public objected and he was forced to introduce the conventional descent of a goddess to bring the drama to a conclusion.[2]

As we have already seen, Beethoven's *Fidelio* has interesting parallels
with Gluck's operas. Here, too, the opera occupies different levels and is
resolved from above, but now all the levels are human. A threatened
murder in an underground dungeon is averted by the arrival of the king's
representative (a strange embodiment of power and virtue in a French
post-revolutionary tale!). Just as Gluck sometimes enhanced the vertical
structure of his operas (for example *Orpheus*) by representing three levels
of action, the underworld, earth and sky, so Beethoven's librettist,
Treitschke, expanded the depth-height dimension of *Fidelio* by having the
arrival of the king's minister announced by a trumpet call from a high
tower above the prison.

Fidelio is only one example of a rich vein of operas, written in the
last decade of the eighteenth century and the first decade of the nineteenth, which featured rescue from underground imprisonment and a
happy ending at ground level. This structure is the complete opposite of
that which we find in later nineteenth-century opera. In the later period,
the resolution is usually on a lower plane than the main action: characters leap down to their death (Tosca), or are buried alive (Aida), or end
up underground in other ways (Don Carlos is drawn down into a tomb).
And happy endings are conspicuously avoided.

Although comic opera in the Enlightenment period keeps, on the
whole, both feet firmly on the ground, the human-supernatural relationship is often imitated in the vertical structure of society. In Mozart's *Marriage of Figaro* a happy ending is handed down to the servants by the
Countess. Mozart's magic opera, *The Magic Flute*, is full of vertical aspects:
the sky-borne Queen of the Night is opposed by earth-bound Sarastro.
But the significance of the images is confused because of a late change of
plot which turned a (high soprano) benevolent fairy queen into a she-
devil, and a (low bass) evil wizard into a wise ruler. And though we are
aware that height and depth matter very much in this opera, they do not
speak as unambiguously as in more conventional Enlightenment works.

*Now turn to the cassette, section 4, and listen to the climax of perhaps the
greatest of Enlightenment operas, Beethoven's* Fidelio, *first performed in 1805,
but revised and finally completed in 1814. There is a resumé of the story, and a
translation of the words of this scene, in the Cassette Notes. You should have no
difficulty in hearing the rescue signalled by the trumpet on the tower.*

The sense of growth, which we have traced in the crescendo from
soft to loud, the transition from minor to major, and the ascent from
earth-bound tragedy to heaven-brought happy ending, is also illustrated

---

[2]   The opera deals with the dilemma of the Greek general, Agamemnon, en
route to Troy, to take part in the Trojan war, but becalmed at Aulis. His high priest, Calchas, has declared that the goddess Diana will let the fleet go only if Agamemnon sacrifices his daughter, Iphigenia. The original version of the opera avoids
the sacrifice. Calchas (it has been suggested that he notices an imminent change
in the weather) suddenly announces that the goddess has been appeased by
Agamemnon's readiness to sacrifice his daughter, and the fleet departs for Troy.
In the revised version, the sacrifice goes ahead, but Diana descends at the last
moment and spirits Iphigenia away.

by another metaphor of progress, and one peculiarly appropriate to the period in question. This is the contrast between darkness and light, or rather, because Enlightenment music is characteristically concerned with the happy ending, the movement *from* darkness *to* light.

There is nothing mysterious or fortuitous about the fact that composers in the age of Enlightenment were fascinated by the phenomenon of sunrise. Their musical style and the conventions of their drama led them to write music which tended always to represent movement from the more subdued (soft, minor, low) to the brighter (loud, major, high). At the same time, their tendency to write descriptive music, prompted them towards the most apt context for this musical process.

Haydn's oratorio *The Creation* makes the phenomenon of light its central theme. The work taken as a whole traces the progression from chaos to order. And not only does the whole one-and-a-half-hour stretch of music travel from impenetrable darkness (minor key, of course, and for substantial stretches very quiet indeed) to the ecstatic love scene between Adam and Eve (major key, and culminating in a loud, brilliant chorus), but there are many smaller-scale dark-into-light progressions within the work. There is the memorable initial creation of light (Haydn clearly adhered to the 'Big Bang' theory of the universe!). Additionally, and most beautifully, the first sunrise and moonrise. Haydn returns to the same phenomenon a third time to represent Adam and Eve's first morning.

The portrayal of light in music is such a large topic that I have given it a whole cassette-side to itself. Before reading further, play side 2 of the red Cassette AC 1628, 'Enlightenment Composers Represent Light.'

Enlightenment music is music which displays contrasts in order to represent a state of progress towards a happy ending. In the middle of the century, the happy ending in opera or oratorio is usually brought about by supernatural means; by the end of the century the agency which produces happy endings is identified both with the nature of the physical world and the abilities of man. Such works will always tend to move from a lower level to a higher, and from darkness to light. The same transitions are evident in instrumental music, where a sense of progress is represented as a crescendo, from soft to loud, and by movement from minor to major.

We can observe the process becoming less facile as the period develops. The gentle and inevitable tendency towards a happy ending which is typical of early Enlightenment composers (J.C. Bach, Sammartini, Boccherini) becomes an arduous journey or well-argued debate in the mature works of Gluck and Haydn; and throughout the whole of Beethoven's life, it cost a titanic struggle to reach the light, a struggle which composers who followed him often seemed disinclined to undertake. Underlying the entertaining surface of Enlightenment music we can trace, towards the end of the period, an increasing seriousness, arising from a growing awareness that music has the power to represent the most elemental oppositions in nature. What distinguishes Enlightenment music from the music which follows it is that the outcome of these oppositions – the happy, loud, light, high, major ending – is pre-determined.

2 *Haydn's* Creation

This second part of the study is in eight sections:

1   The making of *The Creation:* the words

2   The making of *The Creation:* the music

3   Performing *The Creation*

4   Imitation (i): 'The music all by itself described ...'

5   Imitation (ii): producing 'the appropriate feeling in the heart'

6   *The Creation* as Enlightenment music

7   Listening Guide

8   Outline chronology of Haydn's life

Part I of *The Creation* is your text for the course (see *Texts*, I, pp.127–34). We shall be looking in detail at just three numbers; the Listening Guide at the end of the block will guide you through the remainder of Part I. I have also suggested that you play Parts II and III at least once, taking counter readings, so that you can dip into them from time to time. Before reading the first section of this study, listen to Part I on the red Cassette AC 1626. Remember to take counter readings at the start of each number, and write these into your libretto.
    LISTEN

2.1 *The making of* The Creation: *the words.*

In the Autumn of 1795, after two triumphant visits to England, Haydn returned to Vienna, where he was welcomed as 'that universally esteemed and indeed very great composer whose excellent compositions are everywhere received with the greatest approbation' (*Haydn Yearbook, 8* (1971), p.278). During the last decade of the eighteenth century, Haydn became a legend in his own lifetime, being commemorated by a monument erected in the village where he was born. At 63, Haydn was by eighteenth-century standards elderly. Yet his creativity seemed inextinguishable. An English admirer, Rev. Thomas Twining, had expressed the fear that 'he must soon get to the bottom of his genius box' (quoted in Landon, 1976, p.49). But in the last years of the century Haydn constantly reached out for new types of music to stamp with his highly individual personality. A substantial body of major works dates from these years, each one contributing something new: the last string quartets and piano trios, the much-loved trumpet concerto, the six last and greatest masses, and two oratorios, *The Creation* and *The Seasons*.

Figure 38
*Portrait of Haydn. (Royal
School of Music)*

It is not by chance that choral works play a substantial role in the music from this period. During his visits to London Haydn had been profoundly impressed by performances of Handel's oratorios, and their reception by the large, ticket-buying, middle class audiences who flocked to hear them. Handel's music was by no means unknown in Vienna, but there the oratorios were performed semi-privately, before an invited, learned and aristocratic audience, and they did not have the same impact on the wider musical scene that they had in London. Witnessing the reverence and affection which Handel's music – and especially the great choruses – inspired in English audiences, Haydn made a conscious decision to turn his own energies to choral music.

England provided not only the stimulus for *The Creation* but also the source material. There are numerous anecdotal accounts of how Haydn came by his libretto. The most charming, though not necessarily the most reliable, is told at third hand by the minor nineteenth-century composer C.J. Purday:

> During Haydn's stay in England he was so much struck with the performance of Handel's *Messiah* that he intimated to his friend Barthelemon [a leading violinist, who told this story to Purday's father] his great desire to compose a work of a similar kind. He asked Barthelemon what subject he would advise for such a purpose. Barthelemon took up his Bible and said, 'There, take that, and begin at he beginning.' (Edward Olleson, 1968, p.152)

Other accounts make it clear that, rather than merely receiving good advice, Haydn was given a complete pre-existing text, possibly prepared for Handel in the 1740s. Haydn brought his English libretto home to Vienna, where it was translated into German by Baron Gottfried Van Swieten, an influential patron of Viennese music.[3] Haydn set this German translation and it was in German that the oratorio was first performed in Vienna in April 1798. However, when the score was published two years later, it was in a bilingual edition, with both English and German words.[4]

---

[3]   Van Swieten was a major figure in Viennese musical life, and a perfect example of the wealthy, cultivated patron. A diplomat, he became Prefect of the National Library in Vienna, then President of the Education Committee, charged with overseeing Joseph II's far-reaching reform bill. He promoted regular concerts on Sunday mornings at his own house, at which Bach's and Handel's music was featured – a taste considered old-fashioned in Vienna. He was useful to Mozart, and it was at Van Swieten's invitation that Mozart re-orchestrated *Messiah*. When Beethoven began to attract attention in Vienna, Van Swieten again played a major role in promoting this new talent, and Beethoven dedicated his first symphony to the Baron in gratitude. His relationship with Haydn was a little less smooth, but he was certainly a powerful force in bringing *The Creation* into being, so much so that it was sometimes known as his, the Baron's, *Creation*.

[4]   *The Creation* was first performed in London in 1800. The same year also saw its première in Paris; the occasion was marked by an assassination attempt made on Napoleon as he was on his way to attend the performance.

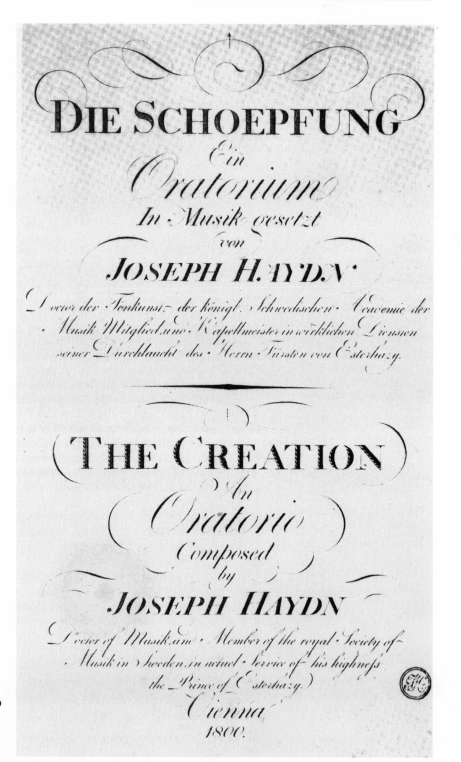

Figure 39
Title page of Die
Schöpfung. (Haydn
Museum – Vienna)

Van Swieten described his task as 'clothing the English poem in German garb.' His lack of precision has left a tantalizing puzzle for musicologists: we simply do not know whether the English text given in the first published score corresponds to the original text Haydn was given in England (now lost), or whether it constitutes a third version of the text, a translation back into English from Van Swieten's German. It is for this reason that you will find a variety of English versions of *The Creation* where later editors have felt free to eliminate some of the awkward inversions. For example, the chorus which concludes Part I appears in the score of 1800 as:

Und seiner Hände Werk zeigt an das Firmament

The wonder of his works[5] displays the firmament.

Many modern vocal scores reverse the English to give:

The firmament displays the wonder of his work.

One reason for cherishing Purday's account of the origin of *The Creation* is that the oratorio does indeed take the Bible and 'begin at the beginning'. Parts I and II tell the story of the six days of creation, and Part III celebrates the place of man and woman in a newly-formed world, created, ordered and arranged for their benefit. The structure of Parts I and II is particularly clear. Each day begins with a narrative (called 'recitative') of the act of creation, which is followed by a lyrical description or reflection (usually in an 'air' or song), and ends with a chorus of praise.[6] The sources on which the English libretto is based are the Book of Genesis and the Psalms (both in the language of the Authorized Version of the Bible) and Milton's poem *Paradise Lost* (1667). (Notice that these are seventeenth-century sources, arranged as a text for musical treatment in the first half of the eighteenth century, and set in the very last years of that century.) That the libretto as literature often falls far short of these great originals is due in some measure to Van Swieten's need to manipulate both the German and the English texts to fit the same set of notes. However, the libretto in the edition we are studying contains some striking verbal correspondences with the English originals, and this is sufficient reason to think that it comes close to the version of the work first offered to Haydn.

EXERCISE The Miltonic and Biblical sources are identified in your libretto. Read it through now, and consider the following question: to what extent can the libretto of *The Creation* be called an Enlightenment text?

DISCUSSION It would be easy to dismiss the text as irrelevant to the Enlightenment on the basis of its religious subject matter. Leaving aside, however, the universality of the subject, which certainly transcends the doctrines of that

---

[5] This is changed to 'work' in all subsequent editions, probably to secure a less hissing performance!

[6] You may have met a discussion of recitative, song (= air or aria) and chorus in A102, Unit 9, Section 3.

bugbear of Enlightenment thinkers, the allegedly corrupt Catholic Church, it seems to me that each part of the oratorio makes a distinct and deliberate connection with Enlightenment themes. Part I expounds the created world as a system: 'Now chaos ends and order fair prevails.' Part II continues the idea of order with the classification of plant and animal species; in both parts the phenomena of the natural world are unfolded with the same sense of wonder which informs the intricate detail of the *Encyclopédie* plates. The world is also presented as a political structure, created and maintained by an absolutist ruler for the benefit of his subjects. Adam enjoys delegated power: he is 'lord and king of nature all'. He is also rational man: 'His large and arched brow sublime / Of wisdom deep declares the seat!'

Part III raises other issues. Unless you know *Paradise Lost* you are not in a position to detect how the librettist manipulated the seventeenth-century poem to harmonize with later attitudes, though you may have noticed that here Adam and Eve's paradise is not 'lost'. By cutting short the story before the fall of man (and excluding any reference to original sin) the librettist has represented happiness as the natural, attainable human condition: 'With thee is life incessant bliss.' The result of this is to manufacture the happy ending dispensable in Milton's (more realistic) century, but essential for a work of the musical Enlightenment. Moreover, although we in the twentieth century may be disturbed by the implication of man's dominance over woman, suggested in Adam's last recitative, there is nothing in this passage to disturb an enlightened audience. And while few *philosophes* would have endorsed Uriel's final words, the librettists's contention that happiness is threatened by knowledge would have found a receptive reader in Rousseau.

There is perhaps another elusive connection with the Enlightenment, though its importance is still a matter for debate. From an early point in its history, *The Creation* has been regarded as a masonic text, though less overtly so than *The Magic Flute*. Haydn, like Mozart, was a freemason; he wrote six symphonies Nos. 82–7 for a Parisian Lodge, and six string quartets (opp. 54 and 55) for a brother mason. It is very likely that Van Swieten was a mason also, though no records of his membership survive. The clues for a masonic reading of *The Creation* are both textual and musical (– the discussion which follows is based on Joachim Hurwitz (1985), which is also the source of the quotations given). The theme of 'the victory of Light against the darkness of the superstitious Middle Ages [signified] an equally definitive historical advance of mankind.' The 'ordered, reasoned, logical' act of creation is shown (particularly in the German text) as an act of workmanship as well as of divine decree. The German text translates the Miltonic phrase 'the glorious hierarchy of heaven' as 'the citizens of heaven' – an expression which has republican implications besides coming close to articulating the masonic theme of the brotherhood of man. Man is presented as 'the noble savage … the summit of creation, and given powers of reason to continue intellectual, scientific and technological creation'. Then there is emphasis on the number three – a masonic symbol. The oratorio is in three parts, unusual in late eighteenth-century Vienna, (though common enough in early eighteenth-century England where the libretto originated); there are three soloists, and they are often used in a trio-texture; the work begins (like *The Magic Flute*) in a key with three flats.

The appeal of *The Creation*, however, is universal. It is a religious work, but it celebrates this world not the next. It gives an infinitely optimistic view of human potential. Robbins Landon links the oratorio, as we have linked it in the previous section, with *The Magic Flute* and *Fidelio*, as 'representatives of a great humanitarian era in Central Europe, a golden age of freedom, cultivation and true sophistication which were soon to disappear for ever' (Landon, 1977, p.349).

Now listen to Part II, remembering to take counter readings where indicated in your libretto.

LISTEN

2.2   *The making of* **The Creation**: *the music*

Haydn began work on *The Creation* in October 1796 and completed it on 6 April 1798 – an unprecedented length of time for him to spend on a single work, though he did, of course, complete a number of other shorter compositions during this period. He did not work unaided. Van Swieten's translation of the libretto was annotated with suggestions for the music, particularly about how it could best 'paint' the images in the text (Van Swieten was clearly influenced by the Encyclopedists' view of the function of music). Haydn occasionally followed this advice, but as often ignored it. An example from Part II of the oratorio, which you have just heard, occurs in No. 16, the air 'On mighty pens'. Beside the line 'No grief affected yet her breast', Van Swieten wrote: 'N.B. Because of the last three lines only the joyful twittering, not the long held notes, of the nightingale can be imitated here.'

EXERCISE   Did Haydn take Van Swieten's advice? Play the final section of No. 16 again and decide.
LISTEN

ANSWER   There are plenty of 'twitterings' in both the voice part and the orchestral accompaniment, but Haydn also gives long held notes to the singer whenever he sets the word 'soft'.

The Creation marks a new departure for Haydn. Its forms are innovatory, it displays the latest techniques in harmony and in writing for a large orchestra, and in contrast to his liturgical music from this period, which represents the troubled face of war-torn Europe *(Mass in Time of War, Mass in Time of Trouble)* it displays a deep spiritual joy not to be touched on in music again until Beethoven's very last works. Listen now to Part III of the oratorio, in which Haydn gives free rein to the evocation of this joy.

LISTEN

2.3   *Performing* The Creation

Some Viennese had their first opportunity to hear *The Creation* on 29 April 1798, when the customary semi-public final rehearsal was given. The real première was a day later. On both occasions the oratorio was performed before a select invited audience in Prince Schwarzenberg's palace: Vienna did not share the London tradition of numerous public concerts open to anyone who could afford a ticket. The excitement at these performances was immense. Such a crowd, both of invited guests and of casual spectators, was assembled in the market square in front of the Schwarzenberg Palace that the Prince was forced to give orders for the market stalls to be cleared away, and mounted police were drafted in to control the crowds. Yet inside the palace the audience listened in total silence – a sufficiently unusual event for it to receive widespread comment – until the sudden *forte* at 'And there was light' when the entire audience rose to its feet, applauding. Listen to this moment again: play from the opening recitative, 'In the beginning God created the heaven and the earth', Part I, No. 1.

LISTEN

The first truly public performance was given on 19 March 1799 in the Burgtheater. (Haydn's oratorio has always tended to be given in secular surroundings, theatres and concert halls, as befits its universal appeal). On this occasion enthusiasm reached new heights. The concert was to begin at 7 o'clock. A member of the audience revealed that the theatre had never seen such crowds:

> I was standing at the door by 1 o'clock, and only at the risk of life and limb did I get a little seat in the last row of the 4th floor ... My wife reserved 2 seats – she likes things comfortable – and so she got to the theatre about 6 o'clock, and she couldn't get to her seats any more, so the usher was kind enough to let her sit on his seat by the door ... there was a noise and a yelling so that you couldn't hear yourself think. They yelled: Ow! My arm! My foot! My hat! ... A small child was almost crushed ... Finally the music began, and all at once it became so quiet that you could have heard a mouse running ... in my whole life I won't hear such a beautiful piece of music ... for the life of me I wouldn't have believed that human lungs and sheep gut and calf's skin could create such miracles. The music all by itself described thunder and lightning and then ... the rain falling and the water rushing and even the worms crawling on the ground ... I never left a theatre more contented and all night I dreamed of the Creation of the World. (Letter from Joseph Richter 'Eipeldauer', written in broad Viennese dialect, quoted in Landon, 1977, p.455)

The choral and orchestral forces at this performance probably totalled about 180, though wildly exaggerated numbers, up to 400, are also quoted. Haydn certainly added extra parts for bass trombone and double bassoon for this big public occasion. It seems likely that there was an orchestra of about 120 players and a choir of about 60 singers. The choir was all male, with boy trebles on the top line, but the soprano solos (Gabriel and Eve) were sung by a seventeen-year-old soprano, Thérèse Saal, making her debut on this occasion. The performers were arranged in a dramatic pyramid:

> Down below at the fortepiano sat [the director] Weigl, surrounded by the vocal soloists, the chorus, a [cello] and a double bass. At one level higher stood Haydn himself with his conductor's baton. Still a level higher on one side were the first violins ... and on the other the second violins. In the centre, violas and double basses. In the wings, more double basses; on higher levels the wind instruments, and at the very top: trumpets, kettledrums and trombones. (Contemporary account by Johann Fredrik Berwald, quoted in Landon, 1977, p.455)

A poster announcing the performance requested the audience not to call for encores: 'If the opportunity for applause arises, [Haydn] will be permitted to receive it as a much-appreciated mark of esteem, but not as a request for the repetition of an individual number, or else the true connection between the separate parts ... would be lost and the audience's pleasure would be substantially reduced.' The same poster announced that 'the prices of admission are as usual'; however an account in the music journal *Allgemeine Musikalische Zeitung* told of huge receipts ('a sum that has never before been taken in any Viennese theatre') owing to the unprecedented size of the audience and raised seat prices.

Figure 41
The Interior of the Old
Burgtheater. (Plate 27 in
Landon, 1977)

2.4   Imitation (i): 'The music all by itself described ... '

There can be no doubt that the appeal of *The Creation* for ordinary
listeners was its ability to describe 'all by itself' the wonders of the natural
world mentioned in the words. As we have already noted, the ability of
music to describe was one of its most discussed qualities in the Enlightenment period. The diarist 'Eipeldauer' seems to have been affected on the
simplest level, identified by de Jaucourt (see *Encyclopédie* text, p.38, *Symphony*). He 'heard the rain falling and the water rushing' – that is, he
heard music which he thought sounded the same, or nearly the same, as
the object it imitated. We can easily identify the passages of music which
impressed 'Eipeldauer' so deeply. The thunder and lightning come in
No. 4, the rushing water in No. 7, and the worm crawls most effectively at
the end of No. 22.

EXERCISE   Find No. 4, 'And God made the firmament', on the cassette and in the
libretto; (*Texts*, I, p.128, 147). Listen to it twice, following the first time in
the libretto, the second time in the score; then answer the following
question: do the words precede or follow the music which describes
them?

ANSWER   The descriptive music precedes the words to which it applies.

DISCUSSION   It may have taken you a little time to realise this, since the first four passages of music are all more or less 'stormy'. But by the time you hear drum rolls imitating thunder, there can be no doubt. The following table shows the structure of the movement:

Table 2
' ... and it was so.'

storm music
'Now furious storms tempestuous rage'

wind music
'Like chaff by the winds impelled are the clouds'

lightning music
'By sudden fire the sky is inflamed'

thunder music
'And awful thunders are rolling on high'

rain music
'Now from the floods ... showers of rain'

hail music
'The dreary wasteful hail'

snow music
'The light and flaky snow'

Each natural phenomenon has its musical counterpart. But we need to examine them more closely to determine just how descriptive each passage is. De Jaucourt required music to 'make us hear a noise like the howl of the winds'. Do any of the passages create this degree of realism?

EXERCISE   Listen to No. 4 again, and decide whether any of the passages actually sounds like the natural phenomenon it aims to imitate.

ANSWER   Some are more imitative than others. The storm and wind music attempt to reproduce the pitch differences we hear in the swirl of sound during a storm. The thunder music gets even closer to the natural sound, with its grumbling drum roll. Lightning is primarily a visual not an aural phenomenon. The sounds of rain and hail are imitated, but, of course, not snow (which is silent!).

DISCUSSION   By the time Haydn came to write *The Creation*, composers had built up a vocabulary of sound images, conventions, with which such common experiences as storms, gales, thunder and lightning could be represented. (Both Vivaldi's *The Four Seasons* and Beethoven's *Pastoral Symphony* exploit this common imitative code.) Any storm music written in the seventeenth, eighteenth or nineteenth centuries will share certain techniques: it will be fast and use short notes, and these will probably run up and down scales (next-door notes), more often than not in a minor key. Lightning has its own convention, too: the music will run up and down not a scale but a chord (that is, there will be gaps – jumps – between the notes). Haydn may well have invented this convention: it appears in one of his earliest symphonies, called 'Evening', which ends with a representation of a storm. The musical notation of the code for lightning more or less produces a visual image of a lightning flash. Listen to the lightning music again and try to pick out the sound of flutes playing up and down a chord.

LISTEN

Now look for this shape in the score at bars 19–20:

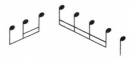

There are, however, no ready-made conventions for imitating rain, hail or snow.

EXERCISE Listen once more to No. 4, concentrating on the last three instrumental passages. If you were a creature from another planet who had never felt rain, hail or snow, what kind of experience would this music prepare you for? Add a sentence or two about how the music achieves its effect.

ANSWER AND DISCUSSION In all three passages, Haydn represents something which falls, and which falls in separate drops. (It is unreasonable, I think, to expect music to convey the quality of wetness!) The melodic lines all descend, though in different degrees of urgency. The notes are separated, so that we get an impression of rain *drops,* hail *stones,* snow *flakes.* The different intensities are represented by different rhythms, which you can pick out in the score – you really do not need to be able to read music for this: just look at the patterns. The rain is painted by this continuous pattern:

(bar 27)

The hail uses shorter notes which look like this:

(bar 34)

For the snow, Haydn creates a gentle, floating effect by separating the notes from each other by rests:

$$> \wp > \wp > \wp > \wp$$

(bar 38)

If you would like to hear more imitative music, this time representing animals, listen to No. 22, 'Straight opening her fertile womb', from Part II of *The Creation*. Try to decide for yourself how much of the imitation is a direct copy of a sound you might hear in nature, and notice that for a countryman, Haydn is remarkably unconcerned at the difference between cows and sheep!

LISTEN

2.5   Imitation (ii): producing 'the appropriate feeling in the heart'

The more perceptive writers were not satisfied with the simple level of imitation indulged in in the descriptive passages we found in No. 4. Rousseau refined the idea of imitation to include a different aim for music. Re-read his *Encyclopédie* article on *Sonata* in *Texts*, I, p.38.

Rousseau wrote his article as part of an impassioned attack on instrumental music, which he held to be literally unintelligible, because its content was not defined by words. ('Sonata, what are you trying to tell me?') He was, however, forced to concede that the aim of music was not only to make the listener visualise the object which is being represented, but to experience 'the appropriate feeling in the heart' which the object itself would evoke.

This difference is precisely that between Haydn's representation of the lion and the cows in No. 22: we hear something very like the roar of a real lion, but we do not hear the cows moo; instead the music evokes the pleasant, peaceful feelings we might have on seeing a landscape with cows in it. We can usefully call the lion's roar, like the rolls of thunder, 'direct imitation', and the manipulation of the listerner's emotional response, in the cow music, 'indirect imitation.'[7]

It seem unlikely that Haydn concerned himself with aesthetic debates. He did not need Rousseau to give him permission to write a sonata or a symphony. Also, we know from their correspondence that while it was Van Swieten who urged him to please popular taste by writing passages of direct imitation (as in No. 4 and No. 22), it was Haydn himself who preferred to 'produce appropriate feelings' in his listeners. *The Creation* contains many passages which are designed to go beyond the direct imitation of objects, and which have the production of 'appropriate feelings' as their aim. To this end, in most of the airs and choruses, the representation of individual words or ideas is less important than the impression given of the whole text.

EXERCISE   Read in your libretto the text of the air No. 9, 'With verdure clad'. Put yourself in the place of Haydn and assess the task before you; write down in a few sentences what picture you have been asked to paint, and what feelings you think are appropriate to the observer.

---

[7]   In Enlightenment texts, you may find what I have called 'indirect imitation' referred to as 'the imitation of an imitation'. I've tried to avoid such a cumbersome label.

ANSWER   The verse describes the creation of vegetation; there is an expanding progression from grass through plants (flowers, herbs) to trees, in groves and
forests. The composer's task is to find some way of representing growing
things. The poem also makes appeal to the senses of sight and smell, and
perhaps less directly to taste (the 'copious fruit'), and the sensation of
welcome shade in a sunny landscape. These cannot be directly imitated
and so it will be important to evoke the feelings of sensuous pleasure.

EXERCISE   Now you become the audience! Listen to the music, and try to follow the
words in the score (if you find this confusing, follow them in the libretto.) My question is, how does Haydn attempt to paint the scene and create in you the appropriate feeling of delight? If you find it hard to put
this answer into words, remember that music is composed of *melody,
rhythm, harmony* and *timbre;* try to write a sentence about each of these
elements. Most of your comments will relate to the evocation of feelings,
but there are a couple of touches of direct imitation: see if you can spot
these.

ANSWER AND   Your answer may differ widely from mine, and will almost certainly be
DISCUSSION   shorter. If you have used some of the same adjectives, you are probably
on the right lines.
       The *melody* is peaceful, tuneful, lyrical, and seems appropriate to
conjure up a pastoral scene: it does not leap about or have violent contrasts, it just flows. There are moments when the voice takes off in quite
elaborate decorative passages ('Here shoots the healing plant' bars 24–
28) but these flourishes do not disturb the peaceful mood.
       The *rhythm* can hardly be separated from the melody: it underlines
the gently rocking feel of the music, though you may have noticed that it
changes – it seems to solidify – when 'majestic forests' are mentioned
(bars 47–51).
       The *harmony* is similarly straightforward and unsurprising. If you
listened particularly carefully you may have picked out the fact that it seemed to be richer and more varied in the middle of the air, between 'With
copious fruit' and 'majestic forests wave' (bars 39–48); you may even have
detected a touch of minor key here and there in this section. But on the
whole, the feeling is placid – very like the cow and sheep music in No. 22,
but expanded into a whole piece. (Did you perhaps notice that the
rhythm is the same as in the cow and sheep music?)
       Within such uneventful music, you are free to give all your attention
to the *timbre*, the colour of the sound. Wind instruments are important
throughout, though I would not expect you to identify them individually.
At the very beginning of the air (bars 1–4, before the voice comes in) you
can hear a duet for clarinet and bassoon, accompanied by quiet strings.
Just before and during the words 'Enhanced is the charming sight' (bars
11–13) you may have heard twiddles on the clarinet – a touch of direct
imitation of birdsong, even though it is not mentioned in the text. The
next prominent colour is a brief fanfare on the horn just before 'Here
fragrant herbs' (bars 16–19), This is another piece of direct imitation: the
reference is to a hunting horn (to the eighteenth-century mind, hunting
was as much a part of the countryside as birds and trees). Both the use of

wind instruments and the particular rocking rhythm used in this air are part of the conventional code for pastoral music.[8]

I felt there was one more instance of direct imitation, though I cannot be sure that Haydn intended it: find in your score, towards the end of the air, the music for 'Here shoots the healing plant' (from bar 71). Look at the pattern made by the twiddles on the word 'plant': this long, horizontal twining looks to me remarkably like a visual and aural representation of the growth of the vine, with its curling tendrils perfectly drawn in the separate twiddles in bars 73 and 74. If I am right, we have here an excellent joke on Haydn's part, since the words refer to the growth of medicinal herbs, but Haydn has substituted a picture of a different kind of healing plant.

There was a lot to notice here. Write as many points as you can into your score, and listen to the air once more.

LISTEN

2.6   The Creation *as Enlightenment music*

Haydn's biographer describes a meeting between Haydn and the Emperor Francis II at which the Emperor asked the composer which work he held in greatest esteem. *'The Creation,'* replied Haydn, 'because in *The Creation* the angels speak and tell of God.'[9] To conclude our study of Part I of *The Creation,* we shall focus on a chorus in which the angels spoke for Haydn. All the choruses are splendid (and in supplying you with the score, I must confess to the hope that you will be drawn to sing along with some of them) so my choice is an arbitrary one, but I think you will not be disappointed to spend some time with 'The heavens are telling', No. 14. Listen to it now.

LISTEN

Haydn fitted his music to the expectations of all his audience. He satisfied both the Viennese adherents of the *philosophes* and the popular audience by his descriptive music. Using indirect imitation throughout this chorus, he represented feelings appropriate to one who had witnessed the first four days of creation by marking the progression from dark to light with all the techniques of Enlightenment musical language – more of this in a moment. And as always, he set out to please his listeners with an engaging melody: in spite of the exalted mood of the words, the chorus is based on the simplest of tunes, deliberately written to imitate a folksong. Sing, hum or whistle for yourself the opening lines:

The heavens are telling the glory of God.
The wonder of his work displays the firmament.

---

[8]   You may have read about pastoral conventions in music in A102, Unit 9, Section 3. The rhythm, melody and overall mood of 'With verdure clad' are similar to those elements in the movement called 'Pifa' from *Messiah*.

[9]   Albert Christoph Dies, quoted in Vernon Gotwals (1963), p.188.

Haydn also catered for his popular audience by providing enough sur-
prises to make it hard to nod off during this chorus! The moment of
greatest drama occurs towards the end, where unanimous shouts of 'ever,
ever' are followed by silence (and we read with what excitement these
silences were received in the early performances), then a slowed-down
delivery of the same words before the speeded-up last section. Turn now to
p.180, of the score and look at the passage between bars 84–105 to see if
you can relate any of my description to the symbols on the page. The sign
⌢ is a pause, and directs the conductor to hold the music up at that point.
A tempo means back in time again, and *Più Allegro* means faster. Play this
section of the chorus again before tackling the following exercise.

EXERCISE   In 'The Language of Enlightenment Music', we identified four tran-
sitional techniques or progressions which we expect to find in music of
this period. Jot them down now.

ANSWER   The four transitions were from soft to loud, minor to major, depth to
height, and darkness to light.

EXERCISE   Has Haydn used any of these transitions in this chorus? Listen to the
chorus *four times*, each time looking out for evidence of one transition:
loud/soft, minor/major, depth/height, dark/light. 'Depth' and 'height'
here will refer to low and high musical pitches. 'Dark' and 'light' are
indicated in the text: you have to decide whether the music is appropriate to them. Work with the score or the libretto, whichever gives you
more support, and clearly mark the passages which contain the relevant
transitions.

ANSWER AND   The chorus is predominantly *loud*; there is only one *soft* passage, at the
DISCUSSION   words 'The night that is gone' (you may correctly have marked a passage
starting either at the end of bar 26 or the end of bar 29).
    The same passage contains the most obvious use of the *minor* key
(there are also fleeting touches of minor between bars 120–143). The rest
of the music is in the major.
    The passage of soft, minor-key music which we have just identified
('The night that is gone') also uses the voices in a *low* register. Perhaps
more important than this, I hope you heard (and saw, if you were working with the score) that most of the vocal lines *rise*; in particular, the little
scale on 'The wonder of his work' keeps coming back to give the whole
movement a feeling of upward movement.
    The contrast between *dark* and *light* is of course the subject matter
of the chorus, since it deals with day and night. Haydn has concentrated
his loud, high, major-key effects appropriately on the representation of
day, and made the brief reference to night sound dark by writing music
which is soft, low-pitched and in the minor key. Contrast was a problem
for him throughout *The Creation*. It is a continuously 'light' work, and the
few areas of darkness have to be carefully marked in order to produce the
contrast necessary for a sense of drama.

SUGGESTIONS FOR FURTHER WORK   If you would like further practice in this kind of analytical listening, try to work through a similar exercise with No. 3, 'Now vanish before the holy beams', or No. 7, 'Rolling in foaming billows'. Begin by reading the words and assessing the composer's task. (*What is he required to represent?*) Then listen carefully to the piece, looking out for instances of the four transition processes. (*How has he used loud/soft, minor/major, depth/height, dark/light?*) Finally relate these musical techniques to the text (*How has he succeeded in representing the text?*)

2.7 Listening guide

Part I of *The Creation* is your text for the course, though by now you have listened to the whole work at least once, and studied three numbers in detail. I now append a brief guide to Part I, which you can use as you work through this music again.

No. 1   *Representation of Chaos:* don't worry if you find this difficult and mysterious: Haydn intended it to have just that effect. Its chief function is to provide a long enough stretch of dark music – soft, minor-key, predominantly low – to prepare for the brilliance of the remainder of the work. If you are intrigued by it, listen for the thrilling and totally novel orchestral effects – the rising figure which is passed from one instrument to another near the opening, the bubbling swirls of sound for the clarinets and the stabbing orchestral chords which accompany them.

No. 2   *Recitative with Chorus:* this contains the stunning explosion of sound and light at 'and there was light'. The effect of this when it was first heard is described above on p.200.

No. 3   *Air with Chorus:* listen for Haydn's use of contrast between dark and light and depth and height – that is, between falling phrases in a minor key ('Affrighted fly hell's spirits black') and rising phrases in the major ('A new-created world springs up').

No. 4   *Recitative:* analysed in detail on pp.203–4.

No. 5   *Chorus with Solo:* more bright music, opening with a brilliant oboe solo. This is one of several numbers containing masonic clues in the text: Van Swieten translated 'The glorious hierarchy of heaven' as 'Himmelsbürger' – citizens of heaven. There is in the last phrase for the soprano (the angel Gabriel) an extreme example of high pitch matched appropriately to the text: the last time she sings 'And to th'ethereal vaults' the solo voice soars up to a top C.

No. 6   *Recitative:* simple narration.

No. 7   *Air:* this number has always been a hit in concert halls and drawing rooms. Robbins Landon informs us that even the light ballad singer, Nelson Eddy, made a popular recording of the piece. It is full of imitation – the 'boisterous sea', mountain tops, the winding river and the deep valley. Try to follow this air in the score, and listen out especially for depth and height portrayed in the music.

No. 8   *Recitative:* simple narration.

No. 9   *Air:* analysed in detail on pp.205–7.

No. 10   *Recitative:* simple narration.

No. 11   *Chorus:* a brilliant chorus to remind you that it was Handel's choruses which inspired Haydn to write this work. To discuss this number you may need to use the terms 'homophonic' and 'fugal'. (These terms are used in the music block of the Arts Foundation Course, A102.) The first three lines of text are set homophonically (all voices singing the same thing at the same time); the two lines beginning 'For he both heaven and earth' are set as a fugue (one voice chasing another).

No. 12   *Recitative:* simple narration

No. 13   *Recitative:* the first 15 bars of this are, quite simply, the most beautiful music I know. Try to work out how Haydn brings out the difference between the quality of sunlight and moonlight.

No. 14   *Chorus with trio:* analysed in detail on p.207–8.

Recommended listening from Part II:

No. 17   *Recitative:* one of the most thrilling sounds in the oratorio. On one level this is an imitation of whales or perhaps all the 'finny tribes' (fish) swimming sonorously through the deep. I find it, however, touched with a wistful sadness: the words proclaim the command 'Be fruitful all, and multiply' and on hearing this, I cannot forget that it was Haydn's great grief that he had no children.

No. 22   *Recitative:* you have already enjoyed this naïve example of direct imitation.

No. 25   *Air:* Haydn's tribute to the human race, man as the 'lord and king of nature'. Most unusually for a work of the musical Enlightenment, it ends with a long diminuendo: Haydn devised this quiet ending as part of his representation of woman in relation to man (compare moonrise with sunrise in No. 13). In the last year of his life, when Vienna was being bombarded by Napoleon's army, Haydn's house was under special protection, and a young French officer on sentry duty asked to be allowed to sing to the dying composer. He sang this air, and the men embraced, both in tears. This air deserves closer study than we have time for. Play it again at the end of the course and see how far you think Haydn has succeeded in representing 'Enlightenment man.'

Recommended listening from Part III:

No. 28   *Introduction:* this is the moment in *The Creation* when Haydn's style most closely approaches Mozart's in *The Magic Flute.* Play this richly coloured orchestral piece when you come to the Mozart study in the course. The rest of Part III confronts the problem mentioned above: in representing unfallen creation, Haydn had few opportunities for contrast – there is hardly a moment of darkness in the whole sequence. You may find this sustained ecstasy less interesting than the earlier parts of the work.

2.8   *Outline chronology of Haydn's life*

1732 Franz Joseph Haydn born 31 March or 1 April at Rohrau; second child of Matthias and Anna Maria Haydn.

1740 Enters the Cathedral Choir School of St. Stephen's Vienna.

1749 Leaves Choir School.

1755 Invited by Baron von Fürnberg to Weinzierl.

1756 Returns to Vienna.

1759 Enters the service of Count Morzin at Lukaveč, as Kapellmeister.

1760 Marries Maria Anna Aloysia Apollonia Keller, 26 November.

1761 Enters the service of Prince Paul Anton Esterházy in Eisenstadt as deputy Kapellmeister.

1762 Death of Prince Paul Anton; succeeded by his brother Nicholas.

1766 Becomes full Kapellmeister on the death of Gregor Joseph Werner. The Esterházy family moves to the palace of Esterháza.

1790 Death of Prince Nicholas Esterházy. Johann Peter Salomon invites Haydn to London.

1791 Arrives in England, 1 January.

1792 Returns to Vienna in June. Beethoven becomes his pupil.

1794 Second visit to England, arriving 4 February.

1795 Returns to Vienna in August.

1809 Dies in Vienna, 31 May.

3   References

Bach, C.P.E. (1974 edn) *Essay on the True Art of Playing Keyboard Instruments (Versuch über die wahre Art das Clavier zu spielen)*, translated and edited by W.J. Mitchell, Ernst Eulenberg, London.

Bianconi, L. (1987) *Music in the Seventeenth Century*, translated by David Bryant, Cambridge University Press, Cambridge.

Burney, C. (1969) *The Present State of Music in Germany, the Netherlands and United Provinces*, facsimile of 1775 original, Broude Brothers, New York.

Furbank, P. (trans.) (1980) Mozart's *The Marriage of Figaro*, Open University, Milton Keynes.

Gluck, C. (1773) Letter (1 February) to the *Mercure de France*.

Gotwals, V. (trans. and ed.) (1963) *Joseph Haydn, Eighteenth-Century Gentleman and Genius*, University of Wisconsin Press, Madison.

Griesinger, G.A. (1810) 'Biographische Notizen über Joseph Haydn', in V. Gotwals (1963)

Gyrowetz, A. (1848) *Autobiography*, Vienna.

Haydn Yearbook, 8 (1971) Theodore Presser & Co., Paoli, Pennsylvania.

Hurwitz, J. (1985) 'Haydn and the Freemasons' in *The Haydn Yearbook, 16*.

Landon, H.C. R. (1976) *Haydn in England*, Thames & Hudson, London.

Landon, H.C. R. (1977) *Haydn: The Years of The Creation*, Thames & Hudson, London.

Olleson, E. (1968) 'The Origin and Libretto of Haydn's *Creation*' in *Haydn Yearbook, 4.*

Quantz, J.J. (1752) *Versuch einer Anweisung die Flöte traversière zu spielen* in O. Strunk (ed.) (1950) *Source Readings in Music*, W.W. Norton, New York.

Rushton, J. (1986) *Classical Music: A Concise History from Gluck to Beethoven*, Thames & Hudson, London.

Schindler, A. (1966) *Beethoven as I knew him*, edited by D. MacArdle and translated by C. Jolly, Faber, London.

Strunk, O. (ed.) (1950) *Source Readings in Music*, W.W. Norton, New York.

4   Further reading

Landon, H.C.R (1977). (See 'References' for full details. This 656-page volume is the fourth part of a five-volume documentary and analytical study of Haydn. It is the major scholarly study of *The Creation*, and addresses readers on a variety of levels. I would not suggest that you attempt to read it through, but for browsing in, for a chance to read far more primary sources (letters, journals, criticism) surrounding the early years of *The Creation* than I have been able to include, it is an inspiring source.)

Open University (1990) A102 *Arts Foundation Course*, Units 7, 8 and 9, *Introduction to Music*, The Open University, Milton Keynes. (Do refer back to these units if you feel you need to revise specifically musical skills. The music on A206 is less demanding than A102, and if you could cope with music then, you should have no problems now.)

Rushton, J. (1986). (See 'References' for full details.) (Although heavier than Zaslaw (1989), this paperback is also intended for the general reader. It is non-technical and does not include music examples. Moreover, it is particularly relevant for the course, since it discusses music in terms of the Enlightenment. (Rushton's periodization of 'Enlightenment music' coincides with mine.))

Temperley, N. (1991) *Haydn: The Creation*, Cambridge University Press, Cambridge. (This new short study, in the Cambridge Music Handbooks series, is a useful summary of the most recent research, set out in a particularly clear, easy to consult format. It contains a handful of elementary errors over dates, but the 'Outline chronology' should enable you to correct these.)

Zaslaw, N. (ed.) (1989) *The Classical Era*, Macmillan, London. (A recent paperback, which supports the excellent Channel 4 series *Man and Music*, and which, like Rushton (1986), aims to be useful to non-specialist students. It takes different areas of Europe and describes the place of music in each. The language is entirely non-technical and the studies are chiefly historical and social. The introductory chapter, 'Music and Society in the Classical Era' is very accessible, and subsequent chapters on Vienna, Paris and London are especially recommended.)

Conclusion

Prepared for the Course Team by
Simon Eliot

Conclusion

As you have only just begun your work on the Enlightenment this is hardly the appropriate time to ask you to come to conclusions about anything, so we won't. Instead we will take a few paragraphs to recall the purpose of Part A, to highlight one or two questions it should have encouraged you to ask, and to remind you that, although the Enlightenment was in many ways the product of a very small group of people spread thinly over Europe and beyond, its eventual influence was substantial, if frequently indirect.

The aim of this first section was, as explained in the *Introduction*, to give you some idea of the variety of the Enlightenment and its productions. At the same time, however, you should be aware that most of the texts we have looked at so far are bound together by certain common characteristics (the application of reason, the admiration of classical cultures,and so on) and that very different texts frequently make use of the same devices (such as irony, for instance).

Whether these common features are strong enough to draw all the texts we have chosen into the magic circle of the Enlightenment is for you to decide. In what sense, for instance, are Frederick and Catherine Enlightenment figures? How possible was it, given political exigencies, for either to act as though he or she were a *philosophe*? Were they making genuine attempts to follow the practical implications of Enlightenment thinking, or was it just a matter of intellectual affectation? Was the Enlightenment merely a cultural hobby for despots to while away the time between one piece of oppression and the next?

Was Samuel Johnson an Enlightenment figure? His version of Christianity, with its vision of mankind's inevitable folly and imperfection, seems miles away from the Enlightenment, and yet in his use of classical models, in his desire to systematize knowledge and in his deployment of irony Johnson seems at one with the Encyclopédists. Oddly enough, even Johnson's grim vision of the human condition was not as exceptional as you might think: when you come to read Voltaire's *Candide* in Part C you will find that this arch-*philosophe* shares some of his world view with Johnson, but without the latter's confidence in the redemption promised by Christianity. As in many intellectual movements that were widespread geographically and long-lasting in time, you will find that the same materials are used for different purposes, and very different materials are employed for the same purpose.

In one sense, of course, despite the diversity and spread we have been at pains to illustrate, all this activity was occurring in a very narrow world: that of a smallish number of highly-educated people drawn from the middle and upper sections of society. The overwhelming majority in all ranks in all the countries that we have visited would not, for instance, have questioned the value and status of the Christian religion, nor would they have spent their time attempting to relate the forms of classical culture to their everyday lives. Those who were doing so formed a small élite, but it was an important and influential élite, and its ideas frequently percolated down through cheap and popular versions of the works that we are studying. After all, it was not the folio first edition of the *Encyclopédie* that was widely distributed and read, but the much cheaper quarto and octavo editions that were to be found later in the century in many European homes. It would not be the original four pounds ten shillings edition of Johnson's *Dictionary* that would nestle next to the Bible and *Pilgrim's Progress* on innumerable British bookshelves, or be thrown out of the carriage window by Becky Sharp in Thackeray's *Vanity Fair*, it would be one of the many cheaper versions (some costing only a few shillings) that were produced in the years after Johnson's death. It was not only through the design of grand country houses that Greece and Rome were to have an influence on the visual world of our period but also through the average architect, builder, carpenter and plasterer who, in running up and decorating the thousands of eighteenth and early nineteenth-century town houses, villas and banks, spread these ideas, albeit in a diluted form, far and wide.

Part B
Reactions to Classical Antiquity

Contents

Study Timetable

Below is a timetable detailing your study schedule for Part B. Each section reproduces in detail its own study requirements.

Hume's Of the Standard of Taste *(Study week 9)*

Studies/Texts	Radio	TV	AC	Set Books
Studies, I	R3	TV5	–	–
Texts, I				

Reynolds and the Royal Academy (Study week 10)

Studies/Texts	Radio	TV	AC	Set Books
Studies, I	–	TV6	AC1632 (blue)	–
Texts, I				
Illustration Book				

Robert Adam: Architectural Theory and Practice (Study week 11)

Studies/Texts	Radio	TV	AC	Set Books
Studies, I	–	TV7	AC1632 (blue)	–
Texts, I				
Illustration Book				
Folder of Engravings				

Gibbon's The Decline and Fall of the Roman Empire *(Study weeks 12 and 13)*

Studies/Texts	Radio	TV	AC	Set Books
Studies, I	–	–	AC1633 (green)	–
Texts, I				

Introduction

Prepared for the Course Team by
Colin Cunningham

'The only way for us to become great, even inimitable, is through imitation of the ancients.' This statement by the art historian and arbiter of taste Johann Joachim Winckelmann (1717–67) sums up a basic presupposition of much eighteenth-century culture. Whatever the reason for this attitude, it was, quite simply, so pervasive in eighteenth-century thought and manners as well as in the arts that it needs special consideration, and forms the common theme of this Part.

Pervasive though it was, the influence of the classics on the culture of Europe in the eighteenth century does not mean we can call that period 'classical' in any simple sense. Consider for instance what is meant by calling an object a 'classic'; and our loose term 'classical' with reference to music has little to do with the eighteenth century, and certainly does not imply that it is derived from antiquity. In fact the modern use of the word 'classical' is often imprecise and contradictory. In the eighteenth century terms such as 'the ancients' and 'the antique' were used as often as, if not more often than, 'the classics'. The texts chosen for this block allow you to explore some of the complex reasons why the ancient world was such a fruitful and powerful source of inspiration in the period of the Enlightenment.

The influence of the classics on western culture is continuous, and has a long history, although attention began to be closely focused on the pagan and classical world at the time of the Renaissance. Latin and Greek texts were translated and, with the advent of printing, widely circulated; Roman ruins provided exemplars for architects; Greek and Roman gems and sculptures began to be excavated and collected by the great families of Italy; and classical myths inspired painters, writers and musicians.

This new flowering of classical influence in the fifteenth, sixteenth and seventeenth centuries was a part of the inspiration of eighteenth-century classicism. Precise explanations of why that century was so mesmerized by the classics are impossible to find. We get, I think, some hint from the way in which English noblemen liked to think of themselves as living by the best standards of the ancients, and ruling as senators in their own republic. And the British system of government (in which a constitutional monarch, an aristocracy and an element of strictly limited democracy achieved a supposed harmony) was widely admired for similar reasons. Roman values, as described by Cicero, were praised; and the myths and stories of the classical world proved a rich and lasting source of inspiration in the arts.

The myths of the ancient world had long been a source of interest and were widely read, frequently depicted in the arts, and above all valued for the way they illustrated the human condition. With their many stories of heroism, faithfulness, divine protection and nemesis, the Greek and Roman myths and historical tales provided an alternative language of moral obligations and values to that offered by the traditions of Christianity.

Equally important was the way in which the culture of the classical world had grown to influence the forms of production. A western tradition of epic poetry, derived largely from Homer (*The Iliad* and *The Odyssey* – see Open University course A295, *Homer*) and Virgil (*The Aeneid*). Pastoral and lyric poetry, some of which you will study in Part E of this course, derived from Horace (*The Odes*), from Ovid (*The Metamorphoses*) and from Virgil (*The Eclogues*), and was important from the Renaissance on. Dramatic literature was derived from the tragedians of Greece (such as Sophocles) and the Roman comedians (such as Plautus). Many modern dramatic conventions such as the length of plays (from two to three hours as a norm), the division into acts and the use of a chorus (particularly in opera) can be traced back to the classics; and the so-called unities (that a dramatic story should deal with one action, one period of twenty-four hours and be set in one place), thought to be based on classical notions, were still largely adhered to. There was also satire, a Roman form used extensively in the early eighteenth century by poets such as Alexander Pope, who even adopted rhythmic patterns similar to those of Latin for his work. Prose, too, was affected by both the style and content of the ancient orators, historians and philosophers. You will see some of this in your study of Gibbon, and it is evident in Johnson's work as well.

In painting and architecture the influence was slightly different. In architecture the textbook by the Roman engineer Vitruvius (*On Architecture*) was widely studied, and actual classical monuments were sometimes copied, as at Shugborough Park in Staffordshire. But buildings also had to serve eighteenth-century needs, and so directly classical elements were largely confined to decoration. Besides, needs and tastes varied from country to country, so that, for instance, the fanciful rococo style was more popular in France and Germany than in Britain. Also some elements were copied at second hand, since eighteenth-century architects were also influenced by the fine buildings of the Renaissance that they saw as well as by the ancient ruins.

Classical influences in painting could take various forms, in the subject matter, the techniques adopted, in incidental details in the image or through allegorical or mythological associations of the theme. In portraiture direct classical references tended to be part of the background, as in Alan Ramsay's portrait of the 3rd Earl of Bute (see TV4, 'Scotland and the Enlightenment'), or in costume, when the likeness was linked to an associative role that could be drawn from mythology. One reason for this was that practically no classical painting, other than on pottery or in the house decorations of Pompeii and Herculaneum, was known to survive in the eighteenth century. There were no painted portraits from the ancient world at all. Sculpture, however, was altogether different in that more and more actual sculptures from the antique world were being discovered, collections were being established and there was even a thriving trade in restorations and forgeries as well as the production of casts (see TV5, 'The Grand Tour and the Rediscovery of the Classics'). These works of sculpture, besides being collected in their own right, were a source of influence in paintings and portraiture.

The case was very different with music, since no ancient music at all survived. None of the instruments used in the eighteenth century derived in any meaningful way from such ancient ones as were known. Nonetheless the myths of the ancients were a fruitful source of inspiration for composers, particularly of opera. Mozart's first major opera, *Idomeneo*, recounts a classical myth; and the dramatic organization of opera itself owed something to ancient drama, as we have seen. However, music such as Haydn's *Creation* reminds us of the other mainspring of western culture, Christianity. In a world where Christian, and particularly Roman Catholic, traditions were still very much alive, there was an important place for religious music in the form of masses and oratorios.

The classical world, of course, was essentially pagan and so unrelated to the religious dimension of the eighteenth century, and it is important to remember that while the pagan classical tradition was very pervasive, this other Hebrew-Christian strand was also powerful. Equally if we pay too much attention to the Classics, we are in danger of ignoring the essential fascination of the thinkers of the Enlightenment with the world around them. This element has been described in your study of Haydn's *Creation*, where it is linked to religion. It is also present in the rationalist approach of thinkers such as the authors of the *Encyclopédie*.

The influence of the ancients, then, was pervasive, but not all-pervasive in the eighteenth century. So we need to consider how it achieved the hold it had on the creative imagination of the times, and how it developed over the period. In the first place education was very largely tied to the classics. Schooling, as you have seen from Donald Greene's introduction to Johnson, was essentially a matter of learning Latin and Greek, and those languages and their authors were still the staple diet of the Universities along with theology. The interest in archaeology, or rather in the hunt for antique remains, grew apace in the eighteenth century with the discovery of the Roman towns of Herculaneum in 1738 and of Pompeii in 1748. Much of the excavation was done by burrowing into the volcanic ash and lava, so that the treasures were only to be seen in underground caverns, adding an air of awesome exoticism to the intrinsic charm of the art objects. Robert Adam acknowledges this when he speaks of the grottoes as the source of the grotesque details he uses in his decoration.

Knowledge of the ancients spread with the growth of tourism. It was increasingly the practice, especially among the British nobility, to complete one's education by a Grand Tour into Italy. This was usually accompanied, if finances allowed, by collecting samples of antique art to display on one's return home. To meet this demand there developed in Rome a thriving art market which included portrait painters to record the tourist's visit (see TV4, 'Scotland and the Enlightenment'), and, more importantly, a tradition of scholarly study that produced guides and critical works. The Italian Artist G.B. Piranesi was one of the leading figures, producing some rather exaggerated but compellingly romantic views of the ruins of ancient Rome as well as a series of imaginatively derived works. However, it was soon recognized that the influence on the Romans of the Greeks, and especially of fifth century Athens, had been particularly important (see Open University course A294, *Fifth Century Athens*). One result of this was a greater interest in Greek art and architecture. The British Society of Dilettanti, whose members had to have completed a Grand Tour to qualify for election, actually sponsored an expedition under the architects James Stuart and Nicholas Revett, to study the remains. Their publication of *The Antiquities of Athens*, from 1762 on, was of considerable importance.

However, the real protagonist of the taste for Greek art was the theorist and art historian Winckelmann, whose words open this introduction. Although he never actually visited Greece, his persuasive arguments in works such as *Gedanken Über die Nachahmung der Griechischen Werke* (Reflections on the Imitation of the Greek Works) (1755) were central in establishing the 'noble simplicity and sedate grandeur in gesture and expression' of Greek art as the ideal. In fact there developed something of a battle between the lovers of Roman antiquity, led by Piranesi, and the devotees of the Greeks under the banner of Winckelmann. The outcome was effectively a victory for the Greek faction, seen in the severely sculptural paintings of artists such as the French painter Jean Jacques-Louis David and the purer more archaeological Greek-revival architecture of the last years of the eighteenth century and the early decades of the nineteenth.

The continuing history of classical influence is no part of this course. However, the brief outline I have provided gives you some idea of the extent of the influence of the ancient world, and one or two reasons for its importance. In this block you will be studying a series of texts dealing with philosophy, art, architecture and history, each of which reveals a slightly different, though related, reaction to the ancient world. These are not the only texts you will study that rely heavily on or reflect the importance of the ancient world; but they do allow you to concentrate on the ways in which writers, artists and thinkers of the Enlightenment reacted, often in different ways, to this very powerful influence.

David Hume's essay *Of the Standard of Taste* is a good place to start because he is facing the problem caused by the notion of a learnable correct taste. The influence of the ancients was so widespread that the *cognoscenti* of the day were quite sure that correct taste was founded on the example of classicism. Taste, however, had also been defined as the inner sense which allowed the appreciation of beauty. Hume tries to reconcile the firm conviction that classical taste is the only correct taste with the belief in an individual inner sense. As you will see the attempt is far from successful, though the philosophical quagmire that Hume enters did nothing to overthrow what later generations saw as the tyranny of the classics. That revolution was not successfully achieved until the cult of sensibility and the early stirrings of romanticism in the closing years of the century focused attention more on the uniqueness of the individual. You will return to this theme in the studies of Part E.

The theme is developed in your study of the *Discourses* and portraits of Sir Joshua Reynolds. You will see how Reynolds worked within the generalized cultural influence of the classics; but portraiture was not fully susceptible to classical inspiration. There was in any case the important influence of earlier portrait genres; and the lack of actual classical portraits tended to produce a confusion between renaissance and antique classical influences. There was a further important problem for portrait painters in reconciling the requirement for likeness and the desire to show an ideal form related to those described in the philosophy of Plato. There was a great deal more to portrait painting than merely recording the features of an individual, and it was important to consider very carefully exactly which aspects of a persona were to be displayed to the public. Associative meanings were central, and the adoption of classical, or pseudo-classical dress was felt to add dignity to a figure. Finally Reynolds and his contemporaries were well aware of the traditions of allegory that were rooted in classical mythology.

In his *Discourses* Reynolds acknowledged that 'Greece and Rome are the foundations from whence have flowed all kinds of excellence'; but he, like Hume, had to accommodate the power of individual genius even when, as in the work of Gainsborough, it did not appear to conform to the classical rules. Establishing the importance of these 'rules' was a fundamental part of his attempt to raise the status of the work of art and of the artist. It is always important to remember that artists, writers and thinkers do not operate in a vacuum; and Reynolds was very much involved in the struggle to achieve professional recognition for painters which led to the founding of the Royal Academy in 1768. The relation between Reynolds's practice, his theories and the institutions of art forms the concluding section of this study.

In your study of Robert Adam you will see the same rather mixed motives at work in another field, that of architecture. Adam had studied the ruins of antiquity at first hand and was keen to use them as a resource for designing. He justified his design theory in a publication, *The Works in Architecture of Robert and James Adam, Esquires,* illustrating many of his works and explaining his aims in a series of prefaces. He, like Reynolds and Hume, began from the assumption that the work of the ancients constituted the only standard of taste; but he was also concerned to provide novelty and variety for different clients. The study examines the ways in which he rearranged an eclectic collection of Greek and Roman sources into harmonious decorative schemes that suited the status of his noble clients. The search for variety, however, soon led him to use other forms than classical, and several of his later houses are designed in a castellated style, although generally with a classically symmetrical plan. You will also see how the architecture of country houses serves more than the function of housing a nobleman and his family. The house contains a suite of parade rooms as well as all the rooms for the family and servants; but the whole park could also be designed, and landscape architecture reveals yet another reaction to classical antiquity in the way that powerful men, usually holders of important public appointments, liked to recreate for their pleasure surroundings based on the concept of Arcadia described by the classical authors (and often coloured by the landscape of the Italian Campagna they had seen on their Grand Tour).

The final study in this Part broadens the approach to antiquity in that Gibbon's *Decline and Fall of the Roman Empire* is very much more than a mere history of what happened in antiquity (and you certainly do not have to study that in addition to the eighteenth century). The importance of Gibbon for the Enlightenment lies very much in his attitude to the civilization of antiquity and the way in which he mobilizes the classical world as a sort of paradigm of human progress. In discussing the barbarians it becomes clear that for Gibbon there is an implication that the best traditions of antiquity are what constitute civilization. He sees the virtues of civilization as being law, discipline, the arts and writing, all of which were present in Rome. The way these are portrayed by Gibbon as declining at the same time that the Roman empire embraced Christianity, is a striking testimony to the value he placed on the ordered society of Rome. His reaction to classical antiquity is parallel to that of the other writers in this Part you have studied in the acceptance of antiquity as a sound model. Gibbon adds a political dimension to this adulation, though he is very far from uncritical acceptance of all the ancients had to offer. There were many in the eighteenth century who took quite a critical view of the ancients. Gibbon is the only author you will study in this section who is determinedly critical of some aspects of ancient civilization; but you should look out for elements of criticism and parody of the ancients in other texts.

Admiration of antiquity on aesthetic and on political or moral grounds, and a lasting delight in pagan mythology, in fact run through a great deal of Enlightenment thought. The influence of classical writers such as Cicero and Tacitus is strong throughout the writing of Johnson; and you may already have noticed that your collection of his works contains several items written in Latin, as well as direct translations and works based on Latin authors (see the Johnson set book, pp.1 and 2–8). You have already seen how the Encyclopédistes included entries on *Epicureanism* and *Pyrrhonian Philosophy*. The study of *Agnus scythicus* begins with a historical description rooted in antiquity; and you will find many other references in the *Encyclopédie*, though you need to remember that classical references in the *Encyclopédie* often had a propagandist function. Look again at the entries on *Priests, Natural Equality* and *Men of Letters*. Not surprisingly, in the light of this concentration on the ancients, the authority of Roman political systems appealed to the rulers of the period as well. Catherine acknowledged the power of the precedent in her reference to the Roman Senate in section 26 of the *Nakaz* (Document 24). Frederick referred to the philosopher emperor Marcus Aurelius on several occasions (Documents 5, 6, 52) and accepted the aesthetic dominance of classical antiquity (Documents 47, 48).

It seems to be symptomatic of the reaction to classical antiquity in the age of Enlightenment that Frederick's letter to Voltaire (Document 48) professes sentiments so close to those of Winckelmann: 'Taste will only spread in Germany after careful study of the classic writers, Greek as well as Roman and French'. You do not need to be a classicist to study the works of the Enlightenment[1] but you can hardly escape noticing that classical antiquity was a major influence as you study the four texts of this Part.

Further reading

Highet, S. (1949) *The Classical Tradition: Greek and Roman Influences on Western Literature*, Oxford University Press, Oxford. (Still a useful compendium.)

Honour, H. (1968) *Neo-Classicism*, Penguin, Harmondsworth. (An outstanding guide.)

Irwin, D. (1966) *English Neoclassical Art: Studies in Inspiration and Taste*, Faber and Faber, London. (An excellent survey of one aspect.)

---

[1] You may find some of the names confusing at first, though you will not be expected to remember many classical names or terms. However, if you are interested you may like to consult one of the many classical dictionaries available.

Radice, B. (1971) *Who's Who in the Ancient World*, Penguin, Harmondsworth.

Royal Academy (1972) *The Age of Neo-Classicism*, Catalogue of the Fourteenth Exhibition of the Council of Europe.

Hume's Of the Standard of Taste *(1757)*

*Prepared for the Course Team by
Robert Wilkinson*

Contents

Hume's Of the Standard of Taste *(Study week 9)*

Studies/Texts	Radio	TV	AC	Set Books
Studies, I	R3	TV5	–	–
Texts, I				

For this week of study you will need to refer to *Texts,* I. TV5 and Radio 3 will also complement your work on this study.

Hume's Of the Standard of Taste

1 Introduction

Hume's *Of the Standard of Taste* is an essay in aesthetics, that is, the philosophy of art. This is the branch of philosophy which deals with such questions as: what is art? What is a work of art? When I experience a work of art, do I take up a special attitude toward it? What do critics do when they criticize a work of art? Why should someone want to say that works of art are produced by people with special talent, and want to call those people creative, or in exceptional cases, a genius? Are aesthetic properties (such as beauty) subjective ('in the eye of the beholder') or objective (features of the aesthetic object itself)?

In this short piece, Hume does not deal with all these questions, and I will consider the issues that do concern him shortly. It is, however, worth pointing out that this list of topics – if clothed in a different vocabulary – would have been perfectly intelligible to Hume and would have struck him as a statement of serious questions also. This is because aesthetics as it is currently understood was shaped in the eighteenth century, by thinkers from both Great Britain and Europe. Prior to this period, the questions asked by those who thought generally about art were rather different. Roughly speaking, the goal of aesthetic endeavour was described as the creation of beauty, and such general treatises of art theory as there were consisted largely of rules and recipes by following which artists could create beautiful things. The creation of beauty remained as *one* issue in aesthetics in the eighteenth century, but it was no longer *the* issue: it was one among many addressed by those thinkers exercised by aesthetic problems, and in no period of European history other than our own has more time and energy been devoted to problems of aesthetics than in Enlightenment Europe.

Something must have occurred to change and expand the agenda of aesthetics in this way, and I will try to explain some of the reasons for this in the next section, which gives the relevant historical and philosophical background to Hume's essay. I suggest that, in dealing with Hume's text you should (i) read the following historical section before reading Hume; (ii) then read Hume's text right through once; (iii) re-read Hume's text in conjunction with the commentary on it in section 3 below (please note that section 3 is written on the assumption that you *have read* Hume once and have his text in front of you); and (iv) read the Conclusion, section 4.

2 *The background to Hume's* Of the Standard of Taste

There is no concept more central to the thought of the Enlightenment about aesthetics than that of taste. The thinkers of the period did not *invent* its application to aesthetics – it had been thus applied since ancient times – but they investigated this concept in a new way, placing it in a new framework of ideas. Throughout the century, almost every major practitioner and theorist in all the arts, and almost every philosopher, felt obliged to say something about taste, and bibliographies of the period are packed with 'essays', 'enquiries', 'treatises', 'conjectures', and so on,

Figure 42
Portrait of David Hume.
(Hulton/Deutsch Pictures
Collection)

about taste. The persistence of interest in a concept in this way for almost a hundred years, with such constancy and intensity, is not to be accounted for in terms of intellectual fashion alone. It indicates that the concept was felt to be both indispensable and yet in some way problematic. The aim of this section is to show how it came about that the concept of taste was thought to have these two properties (i.e. being indispensable and problematic). To understand this is to understand the context in which Hume was writing, and of which he could take it for granted his readers were aware. My argument will be as follows: the concept of taste was considered to be indispensable by the thinkers of the time because it was the best way of describing certain aesthetic phenomena within the framework of empiricist philosophy; but their conception of taste was problematic because it apparently invited a lack of agreement in aesthetic matters which seemed to them undesirable, chiefly because the *cognoscenti* of the time were quite sure that there was a correct taste and that they knew what that correct taste was, i.e. a taste founded on the example of the classics. This is a complex proposition, the meaning of which should become much clearer in the next few pages.

Hume was writing within the philosophical tradition known as empiricism. This type of philosophy made its first serious impact with the publication of John Locke's *An Essay Concerning Human Understanding* (first published 1690), and has remained a major element in British philosophy ever since. Locke set out in his work to examine the extent of human knowledge (Locke, 1975 edn, pp.43–4; *Essay* I,i,2 in Locke's numbering). This was not an unusual task for a philosopher; what was new was the key assumption he made at the start of his project, namely that there are no ideas at all in the mind prior to experience. As he puts it, the mind before experience is like a sheet of 'white Paper, void of all Characters' (Locke, 1975 edn, p.104; *Essay* II,i,2). Every idea that the mind ever has is furnished either by sense experience of the external world, or by introspection on its own operations. Again, as Locke puts it:

> Our Observation employ'd either about *external, sensible Objects; or about the internal Operations of our Minds, perceived on and reflected on by our selves, is that, which supplies our Understandings with all the materials of thinking.* (Locke, 1975 edn, p.104; *Essay* II,i,2)

Locke then sets out to examine all our ideas, with a view to establishing their ultimate derivation from one or other of these sources, i.e. sense experience or introspection.

Although Locke himself says next to nothing about aesthetics – he was temperamentally a man to whom aesthetic experience was unimportant – the effect of his philosophical principles and method on thought about aesthetic matters was profound. As I noted in section 1, above, before the eighteenth century, general works on art theory were largely composed of sets of directions for the construction of beautiful works of art, and no thinker had scrutinized in detail the *effect* these works had on the beholder. Generally, aesthetic experience (the experience provided by works of art and nature) would be characterized by some blunt catch-all term such as 'pleasant'. The central assumptions of Locke's empiricism, however, caused a major shift in the way aesthetic experience was considered. As we have seen, Locke asserts that all ideas can be traced back to a foundation in sense experience or introspection, and so it became essential for philosophers to pay the closest attention to the quality of their experiences (to determine what precisely was *given* and what was *inferred* from that). The upshot of this in aesthetics was that detailed attention was paid to what it felt like to be in the presence of beauty. There continued to be (as we shall see) interest in what it is about beautiful things that makes them beautiful; but this was no longer the only question to be considered. It was equally important to describe as precisely as possible what aesthetic experience felt like to those in the presence of beauty. The effect of empiricism was for the first time to make the subject in aesthetics (the person experiencing beauty) as much a topic for study as the object (the beautiful thing).

The next step is to consider what was found when serious attention was given to the question of what it feels like to have aesthetic experience. I will now set out what were in the eighteenth century Britain the most widely accepted views in this subject, all from writers who wrote before Hume, whose works were influential and were known to Hume. The ideas put forward by these writers make clear what was meant by 'taste' in this period, and indicate why the notion should have been so problematic. The writers are Shaftesbury, Addison and Hutcheson.

Anthony Ashley Cooper, third earl of Shaftesbury (1671–1713) was for a time a pupil of Locke, but came to disagree with his teacher on the fundamental principles of philosophy. His chief work, *Characteristicks of Men, Manners, Opinions, Times* (1st edition 1711, revised 1713 and reprinted regularly in the eighteenth century) is not an empiricist work. Rather, it exhibits a philosophical outlook chiefly formed by the older philosophical tradition of Platonism. Yet the pages of this long, rhapsodic book contain some remarks on aesthetic experience which are the reports of very sharply observed introspection indeed, and which set the agenda for many thinkers in the eighteenth century.

The first feature of aesthetic experience to which Shaftesbury draws attention is that (to use a slightly later term for what he means) it is *disinterested*. This point is made in a section of the *Characteristicks*, called *The Moralists: A Rhapsody*, which is cast as a dialogue. Shaftesbury's spokesman Theocles is addressing his guest and pupil Philocles:

> Imagine then, good Philocles, if being taken with the beauty of the ocean which you see yonder at a distance, it should come into your head, to seek how to command it; and like some mighty admiral, ride master of the sea, would not the fancy be a little absurd? ... [Again] to come nearer home ... Suppose (my Philocles!) that, viewing such a tract of country, as this delicious vale we see beneath us, you should for the enjoyment of the prospect, require the property of possession of the land. (Shaftesbury, 1773 edn, pp.396–7; punctuation modernized.)

Shaftesbury's point is this: enjoying something for the sake of its aesthetic properties (its beauty, as he puts it) is incompatible with the desire to possess it. He does not mean, of course, that we do not desire to own beautiful things, but is making a rather subtler observation which is this: *while* you are enjoying a beautiful object because of its beauty, while you are *actually experiencing* its beauty, you consider it solely *for its own sake*, entirely independently of its relations to your own practical purposes. The source of your pleasure in beauty is entirely distinct from any question of ownership or other utility: what makes the object beautiful has nothing whatever to do with who owns it or what it is (financially) worth.

What makes the object beautiful are properties entirely *intrinsic* to it. His point can also be phrased as a conceptual one: if (to use his own example) someone were to say 'I find this land beautiful *because* I own it', they would be saying something logically odd. This view was taken over by many subsequent theorists, up to the present day. It is now usually stated in the form that aesthetic experience involves an attitude which is (to repeat the term used above) disinterested.

Shaftesbury's second and third assertions concerning aesthetic experience are closely linked. He contends that aesthetic properties are experienced *immediately*, and that these qualities (like beauty) are discerned by means of an *inner sense*. The best approach to an understanding of what these claims mean is again via his own words:

> No sooner the eye opens upon figures, the ear to sound, than straight the beautiful results, and grace and harmony are known and acknowledge'd ... an inward EYE distinguishes, and sees the fair and shapely, the amiable and admirable, apart from the deforme'd, the foul, the odious, or the despicable. How is it possible therefore not to own, 'that these distinctions have their formation in nature, the discernment itself is natural, and from nature alone'? (Shaftesbury, 1773, pp.414–5)

Let us deal with the idea that aesthetic properties (beauty and so on) are apprehended or experienced *immediately*. What Shaftesbury is pointing out is this: when an object or sound (etc.) strikes you as beautiful, it does so as directly as if it had struck you as being red, or smooth, or sour, or loud. You do not *reason* yourself into judging that something is beautiful, any more that you *reason* yourself into judging it to be red (etc.). You do not say to yourself, for instance, something like this: 'Ah yes, this painting has a balanced composition, has a colour range suited to its theme and subject; has elegant lines, and so on, and *therefore* I will regard it as beautiful.' The beauty *strikes you first*, and only after it has struck you would you set about trying to say why it had done so. This is what Shaftesbury means when he says, in the passage quoted: 'No sooner the eye opens upon figures [i.e. shapes, forms] ... than *straight* the beautiful results.'

This conclusion generates a further problem for Shaftesbury. He thinks that experiencing beauty is like experiencing sensations of colour, sound, taste, smell or touch, because, like these other sensations, beauty is experienced immediately; but there is no bodily sense, like sight, hearing etc., devoted to beauty alone. By what means, then, do we experience it? His answer is bold and straightforward: he concludes that there must be a sixth sense by means of which beauty is experienced. It cannot be a bodily sense, since it has no sense organ, and therefore it must be what he terms an *inner sense*. This is what he means when, in the passage quoted above, he speaks of an 'inward eye'. (He also thinks that this inner sense, when directed at human action and character, also distinguishes moral right and wrong, but this aspect of his theory lies outside the present subject.)

EXERCISE   Before going on, write down what were in Shaftesbury's view the three most important features of aesthetic experience. For the answer see the first sentence of the next paragraph.

The three assertions about aesthetic experience which Shaftesbury made – that it is disinterested, immediate, and apprehended via an inner sense – were accepted by many leading thinkers of the period. One of these was the Scottish philosopher Francis Hutcheson (1694–1746). In his work, *An Inquiry into the Original of our Ideas of Beauty and Virtue* (first published in 1720), he repeats Shaftesbury's views in a systematic way, and adds a second argument in favour of the view that beauty is apprehended via an inner sense:

> It is plain from experience, that many men have, in the common meaning, the senses of seeing and hearing perfect enough … in figures they discern the length, breadth, wideness of each line, surface, angle; and may be as capable of hearing and seeing at great distances as any men whatsoever: and yet perhaps they shall find no pleasure in musical compositions, in painting, architecture, natural landskip [i.e. landscape]; or but a very weak one in comparison of what others enjoy from the same objects. In musick we seem universally to acknowledge something like a distinct sense from the external one of hearing, and call it a good ear … (Hutcheson, 1738 edn, pp.8–9; capitalization modernized.)

Hutcheson can use the idea of an extra, inner sense to account for an obvious but odd fact about beauty: while those who do experience it find it strikes them directly, it strikes some human beings very weakly and some not at all. An inner sense, like bodily ones, can be supposed to be acute or feeble, according to nature's gift.

It might seem that in all this talk of inner sense we have lost sight of the idea of taste from which we began, but the link could not be more direct, since taste is no more than another name for this inner sense by means of which we apprehend aesthetic properties. In 1712, the year after Shaftesbury's *Characteristicks* was published, the essayist Joseph Addison (1672–1719) wrote a series of a dozen essays for *The Spectator* under the general heading 'The Pleasures of the Imagination' (by which he meant what we mean by 'aesthetic pleasures'). These essays are the first attempt by any English writer to deal systematically with the nature, varieties and causes of aesthetic experiences. Addison takes over Shaftesbury's view that the experience of beauty is disinterested and immediate. The faculty which discerns beauty is taste, which he defines as follows: 'That Faculty of the Soul, which discerns the Beauties of an Author with Pleasure, and Imperfections with dislike' (Addison, in the first essay on 'The Pleasures of the Imagination', *The Spectator*, no 409, 19 June 1712). These are much the same words used by Shaftesbury and Hutcheson when speaking of 'inner sense', and this sense of the word 'taste' rapidly became accepted usage in intellectual circles of the time in Great Britain.

Moreover, it was no accident that the word 'taste' was the one used to refer to this special aesthetic sense or faculty. The word was used precisely to stress the discovery of the immediacy of the apprehension of aesthetic properties, since of the senses, bodily taste is the most obviously immediate: no one is tempted to argue that food is judged sweet or sour on the basis of *reasoning*. It is worth remembering that the aesthetic or inner sense was called taste not to stress its subjectivity (since, as we shall see, the majority of thinkers did not accept that taste is subjective) but to stress its *immediacy*.

EXERCISE   Say in your words why the term 'taste' was felt so appropriate to describe the aesthetic sense.

SPECIMEN ANSWER   Because the apprehension of aesthetic properties is immediate: beauty just strikes us: we do not have to reason to work out that something is beautiful. However, taste was not taken to imply subjectivity of aesthetic standards.

We can now turn to the second strand of the argument, that is, why this notion of taste, albeit indispensable, was also deeply problematic. The thinkers I have been discussing, together with many others, including leading artists, believed not only that they knew what taste was (i.e. inner sense), but also that they knew what sort of works of art were uniformly preferred by those whose taste was working correctly, and these were works, as the other studies in this Part of the course will make clear, which were either the classics themselves or suitably modelled on them. Thus when Addison poses the question, 'How can I tell whether or not I have correct taste?', he can provide an answer which is unhesitating, clear and typical:

> If a Man would know whether he is possessed of this faculty [i.e. taste], I would have him read over the celebrated Works of Antiquity, which have stood the Test of so many different Ages and Countries; or those Works among the moderns, which have the Sanction of the Politer Part of our Contemporaries. If upon the Perusal of such writings he does not find himself delighted in an extraordinary Manner, or if, upon reading the admired Passages in such Authors, he finds a Coldness and Indifference in his Thoughts, he ought to conclude, not (as is too usual among tasteless Readers) that the author wants those Perfections which have been admired in him, but that he himself wants the Faculty of discovering them. (*The Spectator*, no 409, 19 June 1712)

The kernel of the problem of taste which Hume is addressing in *Of the Standard of Taste* is generated by the need to try to find a logical link between this conviction as to what correct taste consisted in, and the theory of taste as inner sense. The aim was to try to make the theory of inner sense guarantee or underwrite the intuition of the classical preferences of correct taste; the problem was that the theory of inner sense did not seem readily to entail that there was a correct taste, that is, it did not seem to provide any obvious *standard* of taste. I will now try to explain why there was no obvious link.

On the basis of what I have said so far, it might appear that there was unanimity on the theory of taste: Shaftesbury, Addison and Hutcheson all agree that taste is an inner sense. Yet when they move on to the next stage of their enquiries, this unanimity disappears. When they ask the question, 'What must aesthetic objects be like, what qualities must they have, in order for them to give us aesthetic pleasure?', the answers they give are all different. Shaftesbury's answer is this:

> What is BEAUTIFUL is harmonious and proportionable; what is harmonious and proportionable is TRUE; and what at once both beautiful and true, is, of consequence, agreeable and GOOD. (Shaftesbury, 1773 edn, p.180)

(The idea that beauty consists in harmony and proportion was not at all new, going back to ancient times. Shaftesbury's source, as he makes clear in a note, is Vitruvius.) Addison takes a different line, identifying three sources of aesthetic pleasure: greatness (roughly what later writers came to call 'the sublime'); novelty, and beauty (*The Spectator*, no 412, 23 June 1712). Hutcheson claims that the objects which give us aesthetic pleasure, 'seem to be those in which there is uniformity amidst variety' (Hutcheson, 1738 edn, p.17). By the middle of the century, another 'inner sense' theorist not so far mentioned, Alexander Gerard (1728–95), produced the following list of features of objects which give us aesthetic pleasure: novelty, sublimity, beauty, imitation, harmony, the ridiculous, and virtue (Gerard, *An Essay on Taste*, 1st edn 1759; 3rd edn 1780, III, i, p.147). Gerard has copied Addison's list and added four other categories to it. Now these writers did not set out to disagree with one another: they were reporting, as accurately as they could and as they were bound to by their empiricist principles, what they found when they came to try to classify features of aesthetic objects which pleased them. The result is a number of sets of different ideas, some of which overlap and some of which do not. Moreover, as time went on, the list grew longer and more complicated, as exemplified by Gerard. Instead of indicating *one* set of properties as *the* set which makes objects aesthetically valuable, detailed empirical scrutiny of these objects tended instead to show that the features which make objects aesthetically pleasing are many, varied and irreducible to one another.

The variety of outcome exhibited in these enquiries was doubly a problem for defenders of the inner sense view who also held classically inspired aesthetic ideals. In the first place, it goes no way at all to vindicating their sincere preferences for the classical; and secondly it indicates a central difficulty in the inner sense view itself, which is this: if aesthetic qualities are experienced via an inner sense, how can it come about that disagreements about what qualities please, and about whether a given object has them, are so common? And how does it come about that these disputes are so notoriously difficult to settle? Disagreements about the other five senses are much rarer, and when they do happen there are ways of deciding whose view is to be preferred and how the dispute arose. For example, jaundice can cause odd perceptions of colour; ageing or illness can diminish the sensitivity of the ears and so account for perceived differences in loudness and timbre, and so on. If the inner sense is indeed a *sense* at all, how can it be so prone to generate different reports? Inner sense theorists were aware of this difficulty from the start. Shaftesbury states the problem, and indicates what was to become one of the standard lines of reply. He contends that in effect everyone accepts that there is *one* standard of beauty; confusion arises only when we try to *apply* the standard in the course of ordinary experience.

> [W]ithout controversy, 'tis allow'd, 'There is a beauty of each kind.' This no-one goes about to teach: nor is it learnt by any; but confess'd by all. All own the standard, rule, and measure: but in apply-

ing it to things, disorder arises, ignorance prevails, interest and passion breed disturbance. (Shaftesbury, 1773, p.416)

Shaftesbury is suggesting that disagreements over taste arise, not because we take aesthetic pleasure in radically different things with irreducibly unlike properties, but because the inner sense is confused and deflected from the path of right judgement by ignorance, interest and passion. Could these features be eliminated, he contends, we would all make the same judgements.

We can leave this assertion unassessed for the moment, since Hume develops a subtle variant of it in *Of the Standard of Taste*, where he spends some time describing obstacles to the exercise of correct taste.

Taken together, the views set out above generate a serious logical problem: the best theory of taste available, that of inner sense, failed to provide a basis for the deeply-felt preference for the classical, the surrender of which was unthinkable. The search for some way of showing that these two central elements of the aesthetic outlook of the time could be made to cohere was, unsurprisingly, a priority for all those thinkers and artists to whom general aesthetic matters were important. It was feared that, if no way of arbitrating between different tastes could be found, then subjectivism in taste (the thesis that there is in principle no such thing as a 'correct' taste) would follow, and preference for the classical would have no respectable intellectual grounding. Moreover, and very importantly, it was generally assumed that the only way to arbitrate between different tastes was to compare them to a standard.

This is the point from which Hume begins. He was not only a philosopher but, by the time he wrote *Of the Standard of Taste*, one of the leading men of letters of the day, and the issues described concerned him deeply. It is clear from the philosophical masterpiece he wrote as a young man, *A Treatise of Human Nature* (1740), that he accepts the substance of the views we have been considering. Notably, he accepts that aesthetic and moral distinctions are derived from a special aesthetic or moral sense (let me repeat that the 'inner sense', for all these thinkers, also functioned, when directed to human action and character, as a moral sense) and that these distinctions are felt immediately.

To have the sense of virtue, is nothing but to *feel* a satisfaction of a particular kind from the contemplation of a character. The very *feeling* constitutes our praise or admiration. We go no further; nor do we enquire into the cause of the satisfaction. We do not infer a character to be virtuous, because it pleases: But in feeling that it pleases after such a particular manner, we in effect feel that it is virtuous. The case is the same as in our judgements concerning all kinds of beauty, and tastes, and sensations. Our approbation is imply'd in the immediate pleasure they convey to us. (Hume, 1978 edn, p.471)

Hume also shared the genuine admiration for the classics felt by the *cognoscenti* of his day, as many remarks in *Of the Standard of Taste* make clear.

EXERCISE   Say briefly why Hume and others were concerned to find a standard of taste.

SPECIMEN ANSWER Because it seemed the only way to arbitrate in disputes of taste, and so harmonize the notion of taste as an inner sense with the conviction of the superiority of classical standards.

Please read Hume's text through once now, before going on to the next section.

3 *Commentary on* Of the Standard of Taste

My examination of Hume's essay has two main subdivisions: (a) notes on each of the steps in Hume's argument in his essay and (b) a concluding review of that argument. I suggest that you have Hume's text in front of you, re-reading it piecemeal as suggested below. Hume is a very subtle and a very exact thinker, and there is no quick way of getting to grips with what he says. However, he is hardly ever obscure, and patient, careful reading does make clear what he is driving at.

1   Opening remarks (*Texts*, I, pp.195–6, up to '... to be perverted or mistaken'). Hume begins with a statement of one of the major and obvious difficulties in the theory of taste which I discussed in the previous section, that is, the evident and immense variety of tastes which human beings evince. Notably, he goes out of his way to stress that this variety is even greater than it is usually taken to be in aesthetic and moral matters. The variety, he argues, is partially masked by the use of the same words to ascribe praise or blame. When we take account of the objects and actions to which these epithets are applied, the variety of tastes which emerges is even greater than casual observation would suggest.

EXERCISE Can you think of a reason why Hume should try to make the problem of aesthetic disagreements seem even graver that it was generally taken to be?

SPECIMEN ANSWER Though Hume does not say so explicitly, he has a good reason for beginning his essay by making the problem look as grave as he can. If he can find a way of arbitrating between these different tastes, his solution will be definitive, since he has started from the worst possible form of the difficulty.

2   Statement of the aim of the essay (*Texts*, I, p.196: the brief paragraph beginning 'It is natural...'). For reasons given in section 2, above, Hume takes it for granted that the state of affairs he has just outlined is undesirable, and he takes it to be, as he exactly puts it, *natural* for us to seek a standard of taste. That seems clear enough, but there is something odd about the next two clauses, which appear to be intended as a general definition of what a standard of taste might be. The oddity lies in the fact that they are not equivalent: *reconciling* different tastes by means of the application of a rule is not the same as *confirming* some sentiments and *condemning*

others. This should be borne in mind from now on: it will be interesting to see whether Hume tries to do the one or the other. Equally, he has implied that the standard of taste will take the form of a *rule*: again, this should be borne in mind. Does he, in the course of the essay, produce anything that looks like a *rule*?

3   Next two paragraphs ('There is a species ...' to '... are compared together', *Texts*, I, pp.196–7). Hume next has to refer to a theory about the nature of beauty which, if it is true, entails that the attempt to find a standard of taste is in principle doomed to failure. This is the view that beauty is not a quality of objects at all, only an affection of the mind. If this is true, it follows that all our judgements about beauty are only statements about how we feel, and are logically like our statements about whether, for example, we like the taste of jam. This philosophical view accords well with the proverb, 'There is no disputing about taste'. Hume does not at this point make any philosophical comment on this view. Instead, he points out (very justly) in the next paragraph that, however ready people are to claim that there is no disputing about taste, nobody acts as if they really believed it. We *do* dispute about tastes. We think that anyone who maintains that Ogilby is as great a poet as Milton is making a mistake. Hume leaves this issue at that for the moment: his philosophical comment on the subjectivist view of beauty occurs later on.

4   Long paragraph: 'It is evident ... and unaccountable' (*Texts*, I, pp.197–8). Though it may not seem so on first reading, this paragraph is the start of Hume's positive argument towards finding a standard of taste. He does this via some remarks on the nature and status of what he calls 'the rules of composition', about which he makes two comments.

The first is that the rules are not abstract deductions from first principles concerning the nature of art; on the contrary, they are a summary of observations of 'what has been universally found to please'. He is saying that the only justification for the rules is that they have been found to work. He is also advancing for the first time a notion to which he will return repeatedly in this essay and which is important in its argument, namely that there is a body of art which has pleased ever since it was created (that is, the classics) and has passed the test of time. This body of work, and any principles derived from it, constitute something *constant* amid the many superficial vagaries of taste.

His second point in this paragraph is that where works of art break the rules and yet please us, they do so not *because* they break the rules, but *in spite of* doing so. Such works can please only because they have *other* aesthetic virtues (this is the point of the Ariosto example). His reason for making this point is clear: he is going to rely very heavily on the assertion that the classics have always pleased, and he must therefore have an account of successful works which are not cast in a classical mould.

5   Next paragraph: 'But though ... and envy' (*Texts*, I, p.198). Hume now announces a second important thesis in his argument to find a standard of taste, namely that the operations of taste (the inner

sense) are delicate and easily deflected. If he can prove this, and can classify the chief types of factor which impair taste, he will have gone some way to being able to discount many judgements of taste as aberrant. If he can show that there is a correct way for taste to function, he will have found a second constant underlying the apparent disunity over taste.

6 Three paragraphs: 'The same Homer ... sentiment and perception' (*Texts*, I, pp.198–9). These paragraphs set out Hume's central argument in favour of there being a 'standard of taste', which is as follows:

(a) There are works which have stood the test of time. They have been found to be aesthetically pleasing ever since they were created. (They are the classics of the ancient world.)

(b) The only plausible way to explain their having been found to be of continuing aesthetic value is to suppose some constant feature of human nature which they satisfy. Cast in terms of the vocabulary of the 'inner sense' theory, this emerges as follows: the organs of inner sense ('the internal fabric') have an 'original structure' which is constant over time. This structure is such that only certain 'particular forms and qualities' in works of art (or nature) occasion aesthetic pleasure in these organs.

(c) Since there is an invariant structure of inner sense, the only way to explain instances of divergent aesthetic judgement is to suppose that the operations of the inner sense have been disrupted by other factors. (If on a given occasion you judge Virgil to be dull, the fault is in you, not Virgil.) I shall leave the issue of assessing this argument for the moment, and return to it in the Conclusion, below.

Having stated this key argument, Hume turns to consider ('Many and frequent ... ' etc.) factors which interfere with the correct operation of taste. Given the stress placed on the variety of judgements of taste at the outset of the essay, it is to be expected that he will spend some time on these disrupting factors, and this he does.

7 Next four paragraphs: 'One obvious cause ... nations and ages' (*Texts*, I, pp.199–200). This section concerns the first taste-disrupting factor, that is, want of delicacy. The example from *Don Quixote* is used to define delicacy, in effect, as the capacity for exact discernment of nuance. There are two points of philosophical interest in what he says here. The first is that here he gives his comment on the view that beauty is only a matter of sentiment. (He stated this view earlier (*Texts*, I, p.196), but made no comment on it.) Having established the 'test of time' thesis to his own satisfaction, he can now point out that the 'beauty-is-only-a-sentiment' view is only half the story. The sentiment (of aesthetic pleasure) is caused only by objects with certain properties, because the inner sense has an invariant structure; and so subjectivism in the theory of taste can be avoided.

The second point is that the use Hume tries to make of the *Don Quixote* example is very odd indeed. He returns to the notion of the rules of composition drawn from the classics. He argues that the rules of composition are of great use in settling disputes in criticism. If you can show your opponents that a work which you admire but they do not, is constructed according to rules which work elsewhere, then they will be convinced that the work under discussion is aesthetically successful. Hume thinks that 'To produce these general rules or avowed patterns of composition, is like finding the key with the leather thong ...' (*Texts*, I, p.199). The difficulty is that finding the key (etc.) is not in the least like finding a general rule, nor is critical reasoning conducted as Hume here suggests it is.

Finding the key (etc.) is a rather good analogue for what a successful critic does, that is, to discern what gives a work of art its particular quality, and to describe these features in such a way that we come to experience them too. However, this is the reverse of discerning *rules*: it is discerning what is *unique* to a given work. Nor is anyone ever likely to be convinced by a form of critical argument of the kind Hume here outlines, for example, 'Paintings A and B have a principal figure with blue robes and are failures; therefore painting C, which also has a blue principal figure, is a failure'. The problem is that no such rules have been found to work (witness Gainsborough's *Blue Boy*, a work painted to disprove the 'rule' that blue is a recessional colour and so cannot be used successfully for foreground figures). Works of art are more like persons than like machines: they cannot be understood simply by following rules, and *general* descriptions tend to miss out everything individual and important about them. What a critic does is to make us experience what is unique to them. One can agree with Hume's description of delicacy, but his attempt to link delicacy with rules of composition is unconvincing.

EXERCISE Say briefly what is curious about Hume's use of the incident from *Don Quixote*.

SPECIMEN ANSWER What Sancho's kinsmen do is to describe exactly the unique flavour of the wine, which is a reasonable analogue for what a good critic does. What they do not do is to try to make their description the basis for any general rules, whereas Hume says that what they do *is* analogous to finding rules.

8   Next four paragraphs: 'But though ... and authority' (*Texts*, I, pp.200–1). Next Hume describes two further factors which impede the correct operation of taste: want of practice, and prejudice. He describes with precision how taste is improved by experience of a range of aesthetic situations.

In his statement of what he means by an unprejudiced judgement, he describes the correct state of mind in which a critic should approach a work of art as one in which he has 'imposed a proper violence on his imagination, and ... forgotten himself for a moment' (*Texts*, I, p.201). To forget oneself is to put one's own interests aside, and this description of the correct approach to art as self-forgetfulness, is his restatement of the view (stated by Shaftesbury) that aesthetic experience is disinterested. (Hume had held this view for some time. cf. *Treatise*, p.472.)

9   Next paragraph: 'It is well known ... a sound understanding' (*Texts*, I, pp.201–2). The fourth and last factor which impedes the operation of taste is want of 'good sense'. Good sense is a function of reason, and Hume is here at pains to stress how great a role reason has to play in aesthetic experience: we need to be rational in order to grasp the overall form of a work of art, since to grasp form is to grasp a relation of parts; we need reason to estimate an artist's purpose in creating the work, and to assess the reasonings of the characters, and so on. This may initially seem a little odd, but it is entirely coherent with Hume's general line of argument in this piece. He is making use of a presupposition that he does not make explicit here, but which is extremely important to him, and that is that whatever is correctly discerned by the use of *reason* is universally true. He states this in a number of places, for example in another major work, his *Enquiry Concerning the Principles of Morals* (1751):

> [Reason] conveys the knowledge of truth and falsehood ... [it] discovers objects as they really stand in nature, without addition or diminution ... The standard [of reason], being founded on the nature of things, is eternal and inflexible, even by the will of the Supreme Being. (Hume, 1962 edn, p.294)

The truths of reason are impersonally true or objective. Therefore, the more Hume can demonstrate the involvement of reason in the operation of taste, the more taste will be shown to be objective. This strategy in the theory of taste is not by any means unique to Hume. When, for example, Hume's contemporary, the painter Sir Joshua Reynolds puts forward his argument to show that there is a real standard of taste, his initial assumption is identical. Reason, he says, 'is something invariable and fixed in the nature of things' and so:

> Whatever goes under the name of taste, which we can fairly bring under the dominion of reason, must be considered as equally exempt from change. (Reynolds, *Discourse VII*, 1965, p.98)

10   Next paragraph: 'Thus, though ... of taste and beauty' (*Texts*, I, p.202). This paragraph sums up the argument so far. Hume considers that he has shown (a) that there are universal 'principles of taste', and (b) that judgements of taste which fail to observe these principles can be explained in terms of the disruption of the inner sense by one or some combination of: want of delicacy, want of practice, prejudice, and want of good sense.

EXERCISE   Hume here refers to principles of taste. Can you find any examples of these in the text?

SPECIMEN ANSWER   My answer would be 'no'. Though he has spoken of 'rules' and 'principles', he has quite signally failed to provide any examples of such. Instead, he has produced a body of works (the classics) which has stood the test of time, and his one attempt to link delicacy of taste to rules is a manifest failure.

We must simply bear this point in mind for the moment, however, since Hume now has to face a logical difficulty which is potentially fatal to his argument. He concludes the current summary paragraph with this assertion: the joint verdict of correct critics 'is the true standard of taste and beauty' (*Texts*, I, p.202), the correct critics being those free of all the defects of taste Hume has described. The problem he must face is: how do we tell which critics *are* the correct ones?

EXERCISE   Can you say why you think this question is so important to Hume? (Think of the way Hume sets up the problem of taste at the opening of this essay.)

Don't worry if you find this difficult. My answer is contained in the next paragraph.

11   Next four paragraphs: 'But where … or tragic author' (*Texts*, I, pp.202–3). This question (how do we pick out the critics with correct taste?) is crucial for Hume. If he cannot answer it satisfactorily, he will be back where he began, simply faced with a bewildering variety of incompatible judgements of taste with no way of arbitrating between them. His answer to the difficulty has two stages. The first is the assertion that the question of whether or not any critic has correct taste is a question of *fact*, not of *sentiment*. We have already come across one example of what Hume means by a question of sentiment, that is, the theory that beauty is only a feeling in us. If the question of whether a critic has correct taste were only a question of our *feelings* on the matter, then there would in principle be *no correct answer* to the question at all. By contrast, if the question is one of fact, a question not about how we feel but about objective features of the world, then no matter how difficult it is in practice to find the answer, at least in principle there *is* a correct answer. Now Hume thinks he has shown in what the correct functioning of taste consists (that is, when it is delicate, unprejudiced, and so on): whether someone has such taste is a matter of *fact*, no matter how hard it may be to work out in practice whether or not someone has such taste, and if that is so, there is *in principle* a way of arbitrating in disputes over taste.

The second strand of Hume's reply to this difficulty is the assertion that, in practice, finding the standard of taste and identifying those who discern it is not so hard as it is made out to be. To begin with, he reiterates his 'test of time' argument: there is no plausible way of explaining the durability of the classics other than by the hypothesis that the aesthetic qualities they embody gratify our sense of beauty. Then, considering how we pick out critics we can trust (because they have 'correct' taste), he contends that these people inevitably acquire an ascendancy in society, because of 'the soundness of their understanding, and the superiority of their faculties above the rest of mankind' (*Texts*, I, p.203). This may seem to be rather a pious expression of faith in an aesthetic meritocracy not confirmed in practice, but what he has in mind is subtler than that (Hume was not at all naïve about the ways of the world). What he has to say in the rest of this paragraph is a reasonable description of how we do in fact assess critical remarks about the arts. What a good critic can do is to bring us in some way to accept their view of the work: to see in it what they have seen in it. They can point out 'fine strokes' to the rest of us, whose taste is usually smothered by the impediments Hume has described. Notably absent, however, from this description is any reference to the critic making use of *rules*.

12   Next four paragraphs: 'But notwithstanding … resemble them' (*Texts*, I, pp.203–5). Hume has now concluded his argument for the existence of a standard of taste, and the rest of the essay is made up of (a) one important qualification to it and (b) a number of corollaries or consequences which follow from it. The four paragraphs which we are concerned with here state the qualification Hume adds to his argument.

From what Hume has said so far concerning the standard of taste, it might appear to follow that, were all the eliminable defects in the operation of taste removed, everyone would concur in all their judgements of taste. This has never been the case, and is never likely to be the case, as Hume was well aware. One of the basic intuitions which underlies all Hume's thought is a conviction that the world is extremely complex, in some ways irreducibly untidy, and that consequently any philosophy which makes it look neat is bound to do violence to the facts. He states this explicitly at the start of his essay, *The Sceptic* (1742):

> Philosophers confine too much their principles, and make no account of that vast variety which nature has so much affected in all her operations. When a philosopher has once laid hold of a favourite principle, which perhaps accounts for many natural effects, he extends the same principle over the whole creation, and reduces to it every phenomenon, though by the most violent and absurd reasoning. (Hume, 1963 edn, p.161)

It is hardly surprising, then, to find than no sooner has Hume established a standard of taste to his satisfaction than he states that there are two irremovable and blameless factors which will always cause a variation in taste: personal temperament, and the local manners and opinions of our own time and place. His argument is that correct taste is as uniform as human nature, and human nature is reasonably but not perfectly uniform. He goes on to describe with great exactness how different works of art appeal to us at different stages in our lives.

13   Remaining paragraphs: 'But here there …' to the end of the essay (*Texts*, I, pp.205–7). Hume now uses the foregoing argument and its qualification and applies it to some aesthetic problems of his time, the first being what he refers to as 'the celebrated controversy concerning ancient and modern learning' (*Texts*, I, p.205). This was a controversy which had dominated artistic theory in the late seventeenth century in France. The party referred to as 'the ancients' advocated a strict adherence to classical models in art, because the classics had stood the test of time and were reflections in art of 'simple nature'. The 'moderns' regarded this imitation as slavish and debasing, and contended that modern works of art were better than

the classics: they believed in a form of the doctrine that there is something in the arts, as elsewhere, which can be called *progress*. Hume comments that we should not condemn the classics if the reason for doing so is simply a failure to allow for the differences of custom, which, he has just argued, are an irremovable and blameless cause of variety in taste. Only where morally vicious behaviour is depicted without condemnation by the artist should any work, ancient or modern, be condemned. Hume is here making only a brief comment on what is a very tricky issue in aesthetics, that is, to what extent the *aesthetic* merit of a work of art is vitiated by certain *moral* defects it is judged to have. The line Hume takes is by no means the only line one can take on this matter, but it is a subject in itself, and too big to tackle here.

The final paragraphs, from 'The case is not the same ...' are mischievous. The aesthetic point Hume is making is that the aesthetic merit of a work of art is not affected if the work embodies false beliefs of a speculative kind. For example if you believe that Catholicism is false, it does not follow that you regard the *Divine Comedy* of Dante as an inferior work of art for that reason. (This again shows Hume taking a short way with a very complicated problem.) The mischief lies in Hume's relegation of religious beliefs to the lowest level of importance in art. Though he is careful here to limit his recital of 'errors' to 'pagans' and Catholics, the implications for British Protestantism are perfectly clear and would have outraged the orthodox.

4   Conclusion

Having gone through Hume's text in detail, we can now stand back, view the argument as a whole, and try to assess it. Hume set out this essay to furnish a 'standard of taste', a phrase which he defined somewhat ambiguously, first as 'a rule by which the various sentiments of men may be reconciled', and then as something by means of which 'at least a decision [can] be afforded confirming one sentiment, and condemning another' (*Texts*, I, p.196). The reason for seeking a standard of taste in the first place is that Hume, in common with many other thinkers who have addressed this issue, takes it for granted that the only way to avoid subjectivism in matters of taste is to produce a standard. Subjectivism was intellectually very uncomfortable, since it would deprive the classics of any real authority. A standard is invariant or constant, and other things being equal, invariancy is *one* of the properties we are inclined to take to be a mark of what is *objective*.

What it seems to me Hume quite clearly does *not* do is to produce anything resembling a *rule*. His one attempt to claim to do so – the *Don Quixote* example – is a failure. Rather than produce rules, Hume chooses instead to refer repeatedly to a canon of works which has stood the test of time, and he is not tempted to try to draw neat rules or formulae of any kind from them: he does not, for instance, try to find a formula for beauty of the type we encountered in section 2, above, such as 'harmony and proportion' or 'unity in variety'. Since Hume does not tell us why he does not produce more rules, any explanation of this can only be surmise. My view is this: Hume was an acute observer, of both works of art and their effect on our inner life, and he was conscious that the aesthetic objects, both natural and artistic, which please us, do so for a wide variety of reasons. This variety is such as to render impossible the framing of any rule for aesthetic success to which exceptions cannot readily be found.

Instead, the main thrust of his argument is this: that taste is a very delicate faculty, whose operations are all too easily spoiled by factors such as prejudice, want of delicacy, and so on. There is a healthy, normal and unimpeded condition of the faculty of taste, and it is the judgements of taste made when in this state which furnish the standard of taste. He assumes that, although temperament and local custom preclude unanimity in taste, the judgements of those with normal taste will be convergent, and will converge in a preference for classics and classic-derived works of art. This convergence will occur because the classics have aesthetic properties that satisfy something deep and constant in human nature, and this explains why they have stood the test of time. If this line of argument is satisfactory, Hume would have fulfilled the second version of his aim in this essay, that is, to have found a way of confirming one sentiment and condemning another.

The difficulty is that one of the major steps in this argument – that all healthy taste will converge in a preference for something recognizably classical – is, with historical hindsight, simply not acceptable. Too many artistic styles which could not without abuse of the term be called remotely 'classical' have been and still are found deeply aesthetically satisfying. To argue in reply that all these non-classical tastes must be the result of impaired taste is just not credible, and runs the risk of making this thesis true by definition and therefore trivial: that is, the argument would be that correct taste is by definition a liking for the classics, and so non-classical preferences would, by definition, be defective. Hume would not for one moment wish to argue in this way. He wants his claims about correctly operating taste to be claims about matters of fact, not mere manipulations of definitions to which nothing corresponds.

Before finally concluding this examination of Hume, let me stress one point. Even if Hume has not been able to produce a standard of taste, it does not follow (as Hume feared it did) that subjectivism in matters of taste is unavoidable. Another way of putting Hume's assumption is this: that unless judgements of taste can be defended by reference to standards or principles, then they cannot be rationally defended at all. (That Hume accepts this is quite clearly shown by the example of critical reasoning he gives after the *Don Quixote* example. The critic is shown defending his judgement, 'Work of art *A* is good' by an argument of the form, 'All works of art with property *x* are good'; '*A* has property *x*', therefore '*A* is good', and this is not at all how critics reason.) If, as I suggested at various points above, critical discourse aims to convince you of its truth, not by reasoning from first principles, but by developing descriptions of the work of art which bring you to *perceive* it in the same way as the critic (and perception is different from reasoning), then critical judgements can be evaluated and argued about in a way which neither presupposes the truth of subjectivism nor involves the use of rules or principles. A less abstract way of putting the same point is this: rather than using chains of deductive logic to make their point, what critics do is more akin to persuasion. By a number of means, but chiefly by insightful description, they persuade us to see the work of art as they do. Now there is no reason to suppose that, when we are persuaded to accept something, what we accept is subjective and not rationally defensible (when a critic brings us to see something in a work, we have no reason to assume that what we now see is not there to be seen). It is just that the means we use to persuade and to defend what we are persuaded of, are varied, subtle, and often do not involve reasoning from principles.

One final point about Hume's essay: even if his argument is not acceptable for various reasons, it does not follow that studying this text is a waste of time. Very often in philosophy, progress can only be made by working out why the arguments of a philosopher, and especially one as great as Hume, have gone wrong. Deep philosophical errors are instructive. Let us take one example from this essay. Even if the argument will not quite work, there is something profoundly right in Hume's very sharp focus on the persistent aesthetic appeal of the classics. Perhaps the attempt to treat them as a source of rules or as patterns to copy is wrongheaded, and does not lead to artistic success, but the fact remains that artists have found them impossible to ignore, and they manifestly have played and do play a genuinely important role in artistic life. The same is true of non-classical works which have also stood the test of time. Yet if they are not sources of rules, what role do they play? The clue to this problem lies with the notion of a 'standard' from which Hume begins. This concept is ambiguous in an important way (perhaps this lies behind Hume's initial ambiguity in defining it): it can mean either a rule or set of rules or it can mean an *exemplar* (as in 'that sets the standard for future generations'). Exemplars are items which we do not try to imitate, but whose quality we try to emulate in our own, different efforts. This is how the canon of classic works functions in artistic life, not as items to copy, but as an instance of what can be achieved.

5   References

Addison, J. (1982) 'The pleasures of the imagination' in A. Ross (ed.), *Selections from the Tatler and the Spectator of Steele and Addison*, Penguin, Harmondsworth, pp.364–406. (First published in 1712.)

Gerard, A. (1780 edn) *An Essay On Taste*, Edinburgh.

Hume, D. (1962 edn) *Enquiry Concerning the Principles of Morals*, edited by L.A. Selby-Bigge, Oxford University Press. (First published in 1751.)

Hume, D. (1963 edn) 'The Sceptic' in *Essays, Moral, Political and Literary*, Oxford University Press. (First published in 1742.)

Hume, D. (1978 edn) *A Treatise of Human Nature*, edited by L.A. Selby-Bigge, Oxford University Press. (First published in 1740.)

Hutcheson, F. (1738 edn) *An Inquiry into the Original of our Ideas of Beauty and Virtue*, London.

Locke, J. (1975 edn) *An Essay Concerning Human Understanding*, edited by P.H. Nidditch, Clarendon Press, Oxford. (First published in 1690.)

Reynolds, J. (1965 edn) *Discourses*, edited by S.O. Mitchell, Bobbs-Merrill, Indianapolis, New York and Kansas City. (First delivered between 1769 and 1790.)

Shaftesbury, Lord (1773 edn) *Characteristicks of Men, Manners, Opinions, Times*, John Baskerville, Birmingham.

Reynolds and the Royal Academy

Prepared for the Course Team by
Gill Perry

Contents

Reynolds and the Royal Academy (Study week 10)

Studies/Texts	Radio	TV	AC	Set Books
Studies, I	–	TV6	AC1632 (blue)	–
Texts, I				
Illustration Book				

As you read this study you will need to have by you *Texts*, I and the *Illustration Book*.

Reynolds and the Royal Academy

Figure 43
Joshua Reynolds, Self-portrait, *127 × 101.6 cm on wood. (Royal Academy of Arts)*

1 Introduction

1.1 Reynolds and the Classical Ideal

In this study you will be working with two sorts of 'text': extracts from Reynolds's *Discourses III* and *VII* and a selection of Reynolds's paintings. Please read the extracts in *Texts*, I, pp.211–22 and look at the reproductions in the *Illustration Book* Pls 1–23 and Col. Pls 1–9. Much of the discussion which follows will focus on the relationship between these two sorts of 'text', between Reynolds's art theory and art practice. This week you should also be looking at TV6, 'Angelica Kauffman R.A. and the Choice of Painting', and you should listen to the blue audio-cassette (AC 1632).

In 1779 Sir Joshua Reynolds (1732–92), first president of the Royal Academy of Art, completed his painting *Theory* (Col. Pl. 1) for the centre-piece of the ceiling of the Academy's new library in Somerset House in

Figure 44 *Aquatint of the Strand Front of Somerset House, by Thomas Malton, c.1792, reproduced in* The History of the Royal Academy, *S.C. Hutchinson (1986), Robert Royce, London (sale source for* The Exhibition of the Royal Academy, Somerset House).

the Strand in London. With its imposing coved ceiling, this room was one of the focal points of the new design for Somerset House (Fig. 44). The architect Sir William Chambers had been given the commission to rebuild the premises to provide an environment deemed appropriate for the expanding activities and aspirations of the Royal Academy.[1] But why should this particular painting have been given pride of place within the new design, and what can this work tell us about the self-image of the Royal Academy at the time?

We can presume that the painting's central position in the library was at least partly in deference to Reynolds's presidency. In addition, the title and content of *Theory* were seen by contemporaries and academicians to hold important symbolic meanings. It is the range of literal and symbolic associations, some of which suggested classical values and sources, that I want to explore in this introductory section.

To a modern audience the subject matter could appear deceptively simple: a woman with a dreamy expression is shown sitting languorously on a cloud and holding a scroll. Yet to an educated eighteenth-century audience, versed in well-established pictorial conventions for representing abstract virtues, the superficial subject of the painting – that is, what is actually depicted – would have been less important than what it was intended to symbolize. In one of the earliest official guides to the Royal Academy, Reynolds's friend John Baretti (Pl. 1) described the work thus:

> The Centre-Painting represents the Theory of Art under the form of an elegant and majestik female, seated in the clouds, and looking upwards, as contemplating the Heavens. She holds in one hand the Compass, in the other a label, on which this sentence is written THEORY is the Knowledge of what is truly NATURE. (Quoted in Penny, 1986, p.284)

This painting, then, has an allegorical function. As the title and the writing on the scroll tell us, the female figure personifies a virtue that the Academy was founded to reinforce, namely a theory of art that would raise painting and sculpture to the status of a 'liberal' art (one directed towards the cultivation of the mind for its own sake). The Royal Academy received its royal charter and was founded in 1768, and during his presidency Reynolds produced his *Discourses*, a series of lectures delivered to students and Academicians between 1769–90 (and published in the 1790s) in which he sought to elaborate his theoretical aims. He and other founder members were anxious to establish painting firmly as a discipline comparable with poetry, which in its use of imagery, symbols, allusions and other established conventions should be seen to have a sound intellectual basis: according to Reynolds, a theory of art which gives painting the status of a 'Liberal Art, and ranks it as a sister of poetry' (*Texts*, I, p.215). Reynolds's use of the word 'liberal' then implied a theoretical content, an art imbued with great ideas, and was used to distinguish painting from a 'mechanical trade'. Reynolds's notion of painting contributed to the establishment of a nineteenth century notion of High Art, that is, an art which was elevated in both style and subject matter. Later in

---

[1] The building was also used to house the Royal Society, the Society of Antiquaries and some government departments. Today it houses the Courtauld Institute of Art and the Courtauld Galleries.

this study we will be considering a certain slippage in Reynolds's idea of a liberal art, but as a category it was opposed to the merely 'mechanical'. In *Discourse III* he argued that it is 'intellectual dignity ... that ennobles the painter's art; that lays the line between him and the mere mechanic' (*Texts*, I, p.212).

In eighteenth-century writings the 'mechanical' had immediately recognizable resonances of a servile process, a trade rather than a profession. The early Academicians were anxious to establish their status as professionals, to advertise their intellectual qualifications and thereby distinguish themselves from the more mechanical practices of engravers and printmakers, topographical and animal painters and wax modellers. It's also worth noting here that British artists had an important model to look to across the channel. The French monarchy had already established an Academy of Painting and Sculpture in 1648. This institution significantly affected the status accorded to the discipline of painting in France, and to the prestige and economic security of those French artists who belonged to it. An important source of inspiration for the more intellectual forms of art practised and encouraged by the French academy was classical antiquity, notably Roman and/or Greek sources. Historical and allegorical subjects which drew on classical models and themes were popular within French academic circles (although, as in England, there was also an expanding market for portraiture). These were considered to be more intellectual forms of art, and were placed at the top of the hierarchy of genres, an academic system of classifying different types of subject matter which will be discussed in detail in the study on Diderot's *Salon* (*Studies* II, Part E). Portrait painting, which was generally thought to hold little intellectual interest, and to be less susceptible to classical influences, was seen as one of the lower genres in this hierarchy. Although the founder members of the British Academy looked to France as their model, relatively few of the British Academicians were primarily history painters. As we shall see, Reynolds's attempts to correct this in his *Discourses* were rarely borne out in his actual paintings.

But how could classical sources, which were mostly in the form of Greek or Roman sculpture, influence the forms and practices of eighteenth-century painting?

EXERCISE Please look again at Reynolds's *Theory* (Col. Pl. 1), and at a history painting by another founder member of the Royal Academy, Gavin Hamilton's *Hector's Farewell to Andromache* (Col. Pl. 2).

Bearing in mind the preceding discussion, can you suggest any ways in which each work represents or is related to classical themes or interests? Do either or both of these works suggest a 'classical' mode of painting?

[Note: Gavin Hamilton (1723–98) was among the minority of founder members of the Royal Academy who worked largely on history painting. Moreover, his was a style of history painting heavily influenced by his own archeological excavations in Italy.]

DISCUSSION Hamilton's *Hector's Farewell to Andromache* depicts an incident from Homer's *Iliad*, the ancient Greek epic much admired by eighteenth-

Figure 45
Pergamene Laocoon,
Agesander, Polydorus,
Athenodorus, *2nd Century*
BC. *(Vatican)*

century writers and artists. The artist has also paid close attention to archeological details: the clothes, armour, furniture and architecture are based on Greek and Roman sources; even the temple on the right closely follows the original Greek classical style.

However, like most British artists in Italy on the Grand Tour, Hamilton never actually went to Greece, but his archeological work in Italy helped him to accumulate many Roman copies of original Greek sculptures.

It's not just the subject matter and the archeological detail which allow us to label this a 'classical' painting. The way in which the subject matter is interpreted draws on conventions associated with a classical style of painting. The figures are organized in a frieze-like composition across the foreground picture-plane, a pictorial device reminiscent of classical low-relief sculptural friezes. Many of the poses appear stylized and frozen, based on the idealized poses of antique sculpture. And among the male protagonists at least there is an air of restraint, a lack of expressive emotion which eighteenth-century observers (among them the German art critic Johann

Joachim Winckelmann) associated with antique sculpture.[2] The general restraint in the techniques employed, that is to say the somewhat linear style and lack of painterly flourish, was also associated with a classical style. In these respects *Hector's Farewell to Andromache*, like many other of Hamilton's works, was close to that of the French seventeenth-century painter Nicholas Poussin (Pl. 2). Poussin's reworking of antique sources was often regarded as a model for subsequent attempts at a classical style in painting.

The label *neo*-classical is often used to describe those styles and interests influenced by Graeco-Roman sources which emerged in eighteenth- and nineteenth-century art. It is useful, I think, because it carries with it the sense of a later culture *reconstructing* an image of antique civilizations. As will emerge from this group of studies, eighteenth-century uses of the labels 'classical' and 'antique' often masked inconsistencies and some confused and confusing reworkings of original Greek and/or Roman sources. These inconsistencies certainly emerge in the theory and practice of Reynolds, and are much in evidence if we compare *Theory* with Hamilton's painting.

The female subject of *Theory* is idealized, wearing a toga-like garment which seems to be vaguely influenced by, rather than an archeological copy of, classical dress. Her pose appears mannered and stylized, and is more likely to have been influenced by Italian Renaissance sources, rather than by earlier Greek or Roman sources. It has been claimed that the legs and the design of the drapery may have been derived from an angel by Raphael in his mosaic design for the cupola of the Chigi Chapel in S. Maria del Poplo in Rome, of which Reynolds probably owned a print. This was not a strictly classical source, but Reynolds greatly admired many Renaissance artists, including Raphael and Michaelangelo, and would have justified this on the grounds that such artists were themselves looking to antique sources for inspiration, and belonged to a Renaissance culture which was imbued with classical values. As we shall see, there are many other works, mostly portraits, in which Reynolds makes more direct quotations from Greek and Roman sources. The manner in which the work is painted also appears freer, less linear and less restrained than the Hamilton. If we can talk about the 'classicism' of this work, it must be in a more generalized sense, in terms of the cultural associations which the painting would have suggested to its audience. This is rather different from the precise antique references which can be identified in the Hamilton painting.

However, the very process of idealizing from nature, of producing a generalized image rather than a mechanical imitation, was seen to have a classical root. In his *Discourses*, Reynolds developed a concept of the 'Grand Style' (sometimes called the 'Grand Manner') in which the artist was encouraged to learn from classical sources, to abstract from the particular, selecting elements from nature to produce an ideal image or what he calls 'an abstract idea' (*Texts*, I, p.213) rather than a true likeness. This notion of ideal forms is partly derived from Plato, and the ideal and unearthly beauty of *Theory* would seem to embody this artistic aim.

---

[2]   Later discoveries, among them the Parthenon Marbles in the early nineteenth century, suggested that the range of emotions displayed in classical sculpture was less limited than had previously been thought. See Irwin (1966, pp.33–4).

But despite his theoretical ambitions, *Theory* was an unusual subject for Reynolds. Only occasionally did he produce historical and allegorical works (Pls 3–5); his more regular work was largely on commissioned portraits, which were regarded as a lesser genre than historical or allegorical subjects. In portrait painting, the client's demands and expectations necessarily involved some concessions to the problems of likeness. British patrons were less likely than their French counterparts to commission elevated history paintings. Thus when seen alongside his actual works, Reynolds's concept of the 'Grand Style' seems (in part) to be an attempt to produce a theory of historical portraiture, to raise the portrait genre to the status of High Art.

In *Theory* the artist also follows an artistic convention dominant since classical times: the representation of abstract virtues and desires through the female form. In fact *Theory* was the centrepiece of a series of allegorical works on the library ceiling. The four coves contained works by the Italian artist Cipriani on the themes of Nature, History, Allegory and Fable. Of these Nature and History are also represented as female figures. Baretti described *Nature* as 'a lady nursing one child and simultaneously exhibiting herself to infant, artists etc.', and *History* as 'a lady with a trumpet engraving on a shield etc.' (Penny, 1986, p.284). In eighteenth-century literature, popular mythology, painting and sculpture, women were frequently transformed into ideal allegorical figures representing concepts which they were rarely expected to practise or engage in. Thus the aesthetic principles symbolized by Reynolds's unearthly female in *Theory* were almost exclusively the preserve of male academicians. As Marina Warner has argued, women's suitability for these symbolic roles was usually directly related to their actual roles in society. When women were unenfranchised, generally less educated than men, and rarely in professional roles (as was the case in eighteenth-century Britain), they were more easily transformed into seductive allegorical images. Warner has shown that women are often 'the protagonists of the great allegorical dramas familiar in our own culture. Athena, goddess of wisdom and of war is the pattern for the armed maidens, invulnerable epitomes of the nation like Britannia, as well as the Renaissance's muse of muses, patroness of learning and the arts' (Warner, 1985). This Renaissance muse was also foreshadowed in the female muses of ancient mythology who represented History, Lyric Poetry, Love Poetry, Comedy, Tragedy and so on, and in medieval art, in which the Virtues and the Liberal Arts were traditionally personified by images of women, conventions which Reynolds was clearly reworking.

In a later study of Gibbon's *Decline and Fall of the Roman Empire*, you will encounter the view that Gibbon drew on the classics, and the classical, in order to assert the value and supremacy of his own culture. Gibbon, it is argued, believed that his own age had reached a vital stage in the grand narrative of western culture: The Graeco-Roman, classical past was represented by him as a paradigm of human progress, which could be used to marginalize other races and cultures. Although we need to be wary of generalizations, I think that we could apply a similar argument to some of Reynolds's interests and artistic ambitions. Like many eighteenth-century artists and intellectuals, Reynolds tended to represent the early history of art as a rise from barbarism to the cultured civic society of ancient Greece. To prevent another descent into barbarism, the modern artist, he believed, had a duty to follow the example of the ancients. In

Discourse VI Reynolds wrote: 'From the remains of the works of the ancients the modern arts were revived, and it is by their means that they must be restored a second time. However it may mortify our vanity, we must be forced to allow them our masters; and we may venture the prophecy, that when they shall cease to be studied, arts will no longer flourish, and we shall again relapse into barbarism' (Reynolds, 1981 edn, p.106).

The founder members of the Royal Academy looked to societies such as Periclean Athens and renaissance Florence as environments in which a superior aesthetic theory was publicly disseminated. The Royal Academy was founded as a public institution which could teach and disseminate a similar theory of art. The cultural historian John Barrell has suggested that it was the public rhetorical function of Greek art – particularly sculpture – which the founders of the Royal Academy were seeking to restore to art, believing that it had been lost after the classical period, when art degenerated into individual styles (Barrell, 1986). According to Barrell, Greek art was considered to be imbued with civic humanist values, which Reynolds's concept of the 'Grand Style' was implicitly seeking to revive. Hence Reynolds's persistent encouragement to his contemporaries to borrow from antique sources, for 'their works are considered a magazine storehouse of common property, always open to the public, whence every man has a right to take what material he pleases' (Reynolds, 1981 edn, p.107).

The idea of a public function for art also presupposes an *audience* for art who will understand its rhetorical function. Thus the various meanings of *Theory* which we have been discussing could be understood only by an educated spectator who could reflect on the values being expressed, and who could identify with them. A liberal art required a liberal audience. Reynolds's notional public was a somewhat restricted group. Those with the appropriate education and economic status came largely from the middle and upper classes, and Reynolds sold many of his portraits to the aristocracy and the landed gentry. The Academy was founded to attract 'men of taste' (a term used by Reynolds in the *Discourses*) with the appropriate classical education for the study and patronage of art. But as I shall argue, 'taste' could also be a *gendered* concept in eighteenth-century art theory, through which the production and understanding of High Art was seen as a predominately (though not exclusively) 'masculine' activity. Women then were more likely to be seen as the symbolic *objects* of academic art than as part of its intellectual audience.

2   Likeness and the Grand Style: Reynolds and portraiture

> The mere face painter has little in common with the poet; but, like the mere historian, copies what he sees, and minutely traces every feature and odd mark. 'Tis otherwise with the men of invention and design. (Shaftesbury, 1773, p.145)

Thus wrote the Earl of Shaftesbury in his influential *Characteristicks of Men, Manners, Opinions, Times* first published in 1711 (and which was referred to in section 2 of the study on Hume's essay on taste). Shaftesbury was canvassing the view, held widely at the beginning of the century, that portraiture involved a purely mechanical copying of nature and could not therefore qualify as a liberal art. As I suggested in the preceding section, it was precisely this view of portraiture which Reynolds qualified and implicitly challenged in his later attempt to raise portraiture to the level of High Art. The whole issue of the nature and function of portraiture became the subject of debate during the eighteenth century, a debate which largely revolved around the notion of 'likeness'. Implicit in the quotation from Shaftesbury is a derogatory concept of '*mere*' likeness which is to be obtained through meticulous and mechanical copying of what the artist sees.

Underlying his statement was a faith in an idealized or universal image rather than a detailed depiction of nature's imperfections, an attitude often associated with the culture of the Augustan era. You will recall Simon Eliot's discussion in the Johnson study of a similar attitude among the classically-educated, that is, the idea that the writer should move from the particular to the general, for universal truths were thought to be the only ones worth knowing.[3]

However, Reynolds's earlier position in relation to shifting concepts of likeness is not easy to pin down. In his *Discourses* he both represents portraiture as a lesser genre, inferior to the elevated genre of history painting, and advocates a style of portrait painting which follows the general principles of the Grand Style. In theory, at least, Reynolds plays down the value of minute observation, arguing in *Discourse IV*:

> Even in portraits, the grace, and, we may add, the likeness, consists more in taking the general air, than in observing the exact similitude of every feature. (Reynolds, 1981 edn, p.59)

As I suggested earlier, this need to 'take the general air' has a classical root. But Reynolds's attitude can be distinguished from that of Shaftesbury in that rather than dismissing portraiture as 'mere imitation', he seeks to instil into the genre some of the very same values with which Shaftesbury thought it was incompatible.

We have seen that despite his exhortations in the *Discourses* on the value of historical and poetic subjects, Reynolds, like most contemporary British artists, made his living largely through portrait commissions. Although he did receive a few commissions for history paintings, in mid-eighteenth century Britain there was a demand for portrait painting greater than anywhere else in Europe, bolstered by the growth of a moneyed middle-class anxious to commission works. In fact, even in the annual Royal Academy exhibitions, portraiture was the dominant genre exhibited. The most affluent patrons of both architecture and painting came from the British nobility (in comparison with France where the court itself was the most lavish patron). Reynolds produced large numbers of full-length portraits designed to hang on the walls of country seats. As you will see in the next study, many of Robert Adam's classical

---

[3]. With the development in early Romantic ideas towards the end of the century, 'likeness' acquired some rather different nuances of meaning. For some writers and artists it came to signify something more than recording the physical details of the sitter; it was also about capturing his or her essential character, a sense of the thoughts and feelings of the subject. The Romantic cult of individuality thus helped to give portraiture a higher status. William Hazlitt (1778–1830) developed this notion of 'likeness' – see Nadia Tscherny, 'Likeness in Early Romantic Portraiture', *Art Journal*, 1987, vol.46, No.3, p.193.

buildings included architectural space specifically designed to enclose the full-length portrait. Given this context, Reynolds's theoretical ambitions for painting had to be combined with a certain pragmatism. And if portraits were to be taken as the measure of his 'genius', Reynolds had to endow his sitters with something beyond 'mere likeness'.

His portraits, then, can be read as rich and complicated texts, as images in which a range of artistic, cultural and economic interests can be seen to converge. One of the challenges for us lies in sorting out the relationship between these commissioned images and the written theory as set out in the *Discourses*.

EXERCISE

Please read *Discourse VII* (delivered in 1776), *Texts*, I, pp.216–22 in which Reynolds discusses his concept of taste and its application to fashion and dress in portraiture, and look closely at the following illustrations of paintings by Reynolds:

    Commodore Augustus Keppel, 1752–53 (Pl. 6)
    Charles Coote, 1st Earl of Bellomont, 1774 (Col. Pl. 3)
    Lady Sarah Bunbury Sacrificing to the Graces, 1765 (Col. Pl. 4)
    *The Ladies Waldegrave c.*1780 (Col. Pl. 5)
    The Montgomery Sisters Adorning a Term of Hymen, 1773 (Col. Pl. 6)

Briefly outline the main arguments which Reynolds sets out in this part of *Discourse VII*. To what extent are his arguments borne out or undermined in the portraits listed? Can you identify any different (or similar) conventions in the portraits of men and women?

DISCUSSION

Reynolds seems to shift his position slightly from the emphasis of the earlier *Discourses*. In this lecture he reiterates his view that 'Greece and Rome are the foundations from whence have flowed all kinds of excellence'. But he also acknowledges that although the attainment of 'immovable principles' inherent in Greek and Roman art should still be the artist's presiding aim, these principles may be slightly modified by contemporary custom, by shifts in 'taste'. And these modifications, (Reynolds argues), are more excusable in portrait painting. Because Greek and Roman artists worked largely in the medium of sculpture, there are few ancient painted portraits which modern artists can use as models.

Reynolds goes on to cite the highly successful seventeenth-century portrait painter Sir Anthony Van Dyck (1599–1641) (Pl. 7), whose works 'we are not content to admire for their real excellence, but extend our approbation even to the dress which happened to be the fashion of that age'. Born in Antwerp, Van Dyck had become a successful court painter to Charles I, producing works which became models for a British tradition of portrait painting. In fact the so-called 'Van Dyck habit' was reproduced in many English portraits from the late eighteenth century, and Reynolds himself often followed Van Dyck's custom of showing his aristocratic subjects in elaborate ceremonial robes, which in contemporary French painting were more often reserved for royalty alone. Thus Reynolds's contemporaries would have viewed the extraordinarily lavish costume of *Charles Coote, 1st Earl of Bellomont* (1774) (Col. Pl. 3) as following the 'Van Dyck habit'.

Such elaborate costumes had important *public* functions to perform in that they could carry powerful political meanings, meanings which were rather more specific than the classical values signified by the use of Greek or Roman models. Lord Bellomont's gorgeous outfit complete with its hat of tall ostrich plumes, white satin breeches and matching silk coat was that of the Order of the Knights of the Bath. He had been made a member of this prestigious order in 1764 for his part in quelling an uprising in northern Ireland.

The painting was first exhibited in the Royal Academy in 1774, a year after Lord Bellomont had been shot in the groin in a duel, one of several controversial incidents which had brought him considerable notoriety. The political implications of the painting and its magisterial effects must have helped to counter a public image tainted by his more rakish exploits which had earned him the label of the 'Hibernian Seducer' (Penny, 1986, p.261). Through a portrait commission which could be exhibited in the Royal Academy show and subsequently hung on the walls of the family's country seat, an artist could help to construct the public image and values which a patron wished to convey.

Commodore Augustus Keppel, one of Reynolds's earliest portraits, is another male portrait in which the artist uses various conventions to suggest rank and status. According to an early biographer of Reynolds, this portrait 'attracted the publick notice' and established Reynolds as 'the greatest painter that England had seen since Vandyck' (quoted in Penny, 1986, p.182). Keppel's status, rank and achievements are represented in the painting through a variety of literal and symbolic references. The nineteenth-century writer and painter James Northcote claimed that the shipwreck in the background is a reference to one of Keppel's naval exploits when chasing a French ship in 1747, when his own ship was shipwrecked off the Brittany coast (Northcote, 1819). It is now well-established that the sitter's pose and the format of the work are very close to those adopted by the successful Scottish portrait painter Alan Ramsay in his *Norman, Twenty-Second Chief of Macleod* (1748) (Pl. 8). In both portraits the pose is reminiscent of antique sources, in particular the famous Apollo Belvedere from the second century BC. And the rhetorical gesture of the right arm echoes that commonly used in ancient Roman sculpture of public figures (Pls 9–10). This allusion is reinforced through the toga-like organization of Macleod's tartan robe. The Roman values of civic virtue associated with such sources would not have been lost on an educated contemporary audience. Reynolds's work thus draws on some of the same associations and meanings.[4] But they have become rather more diluted in *his* portrait. Keppel's pose and dress suggest a less direct quotation from an antique source and the figure appears more integrated with the background than in the Ramsay. Reynolds's figure, then, is less directly evocative of a sculptural model, which, because of its original three-dimensional sculptural form, would appear to be more separate from its painted landscape surroundings. The references in the Reynolds are more generalized and seem, I believe, to constitute some of the modifications which Reynolds later recommended in *Discourse VII*. The Keppel

---

[4]   This comparison has been developed by David Solkin in 'Great Pictures or Great Men? Reynolds, Male Portraiture and the Power of Art', in the *Oxford Art Journal*, 9 Feb 1986, p.46.

is neither rigidly tied to classical models, nor to the details of contemporary fashion, and as such could be seen as an early painted manifesto of the Grand Style in portraiture.

Towards the end of *Discourse VII*, Reynolds gives some detailed instructions on how the portrait painter is to negotiate a compromise between the artist's requirement 'to take the general air' and the need to produce some sort of likeness:

> He therefore who in his practice of portrait-painting wishes to dignify his subject, which we will suppose to be a lady, will not paint her in the modern dress, the familiarity of which alone is sufficient to destroy all dignity. He takes care that his work shall correspond to those ideas and that imagination which he knows will regulate the judgment of others; and therefore dresses his figure something with the general air of the antique for the sake of dignity, and preserves something of the modern for the sake of likeness. By this conduct his works correspond with those prejudices which we have in favour of what we continually see; and the relish of the antique simplicity corresponds with what we may call the more learned and scientific prejudice. (*Texts*, I, p.222)

I think it's significant that the conventions which Reynolds recommends are associated here with portraits of *female* subjects. While his male subjects are sometimes shown in contemporary dress, or in a political or military uniform, or in relation to their exploits, thus revealing their rank and/or their professional achievements, women are more likely to be shown in pseudo-classical dress and in the partial disguise of a goddess, muse or mythological figure. Without the public professional status or rank of their male counterparts, women more easily assume fictitious identities.

The rules for the Grand Style appear to be subtly different – or at least subject to some different interpretations – in their application to female subjects. Before we consider some of these differences in portraiture, we need to consider (albeit very briefly) some of the eighteenth-century ideals of femininity which flourished among the middle and upper classes of British society, that is, among the educated and patronizing classes to whom Reynolds was largely addressing his work. Much contemporary literature, art and educational theory encouraged and reinforced assumed oppositions between 'feminine' and 'masculine' virtues which, broadly speaking, identified female qualities as soft, sensitive, emotional and passive, as against strong, active, intellectual male qualities, values which were implicit at every level of social and cultural expression.[5] Such oppositions were rooted in the conventional sexual division of labour and in the educational and social restrictions and limitations experienced by women, and were challenged later in the century in the writings of Mary Wollstonecraft, some of whose works you will be studying in Part E of the course. Of course, we must be cautious when making generalizations about gender, despite social restrictions, for many middle-class women (among them Mary Wollstonecraft) were self-taught in literature and the

---

[5] These dominant ideals of femininity and the literature in which they abound are discussed and cited in V. Jones (ed.) (1990) *Women in the Eighteenth Century: Constructions of Femininity*, Routledge, London.

classics. My focus in this study is rather the extent to which the culture of the Royal Academy disseminated certain dominant attitudes towards women and their supposedly 'feminine' roles. I want to argue that these attitudes encouraged forms of social and cultural categorization which are implicit (and sometimes explicit) in Reynolds's aesthetic theory, and in his painted works.

The 'feminine' attributes of feeling, sensitivity and nurturing were generally associated with the *private* domestic sphere, while the 'masculine' attributes of strength, intellect, and so on, were more often associated with *public* and professional spheres. This public/private division is echoed in some of the assumptions contained in Reynolds's *Discourses*. They are addressed to a largely male audience and the artist is always referred to with the pronoun 'he'. During the eighteenth century, artistic creativity was seen as a predominantly male attribute, although there were two women painters – Angelica Kauffman and Mary Moser – among the founder members of the Royal Academy. Membership of the Academy was subsequently closed to women until 1922. While it's relatively easy to identify Reynolds's theoretical 'public' as predominantly male, I think it's more difficult to identify how some of these attitudes are mediated through his portraits of women.

In many respects *Lady Sarah Bunbury Sacrificing to the Graces* (1765, Col. Pl. 4) seems to correspond to the recommendations for painting 'a lady' quoted above. Lady Sarah is certainly not 'in the modern dress'. Her flowing robe is the artist's invention loosely influenced by classical robes. The protagonist makes her offering on the flames before a statue of the Three Graces, which may have been intended as symbolic representations of ideal friendship, or *Amicitia*. Although not identified as a specific classical figure, Lady Sarah is shown participating in a kind of mythological fantasy. Thus the work can be grouped with paintings such as *Mrs Hale as Euphrosyne* (1764), hung in Robert Adam's music room at Harewood House, and *Mrs Siddons as the Tragic Muse* (Col. Pl. 7 and Pl. 11) in which female sitters assume a mythological identity, conferring dignity on the subject and raising the status of the portrait genre. But it is also possible that Reynolds's employment of some of these mythological disguises was slightly tongue-in-cheek. Despite the publicly acknowledged heroic connotations of such themes, contemporary reports suggest that some members of Reynolds's public enjoyed the mock-heroic possibilities in these portraits. In the words of Mrs Thrale, a friend of Dr Johnson, Lady Sarah Bunbury 'never *did* sacrifice to the Graces; her face was gloriously handsome, but she used to play cricket and eat beef steaks on the Steyne at Brighton' (Penny, 1986, p.224).

As I suggested earlier, this dual identity was most often reserved for Reynolds's female subjects. As women rarely held professional roles or exercised any political power, they were more easily transformed into mythological or allegorical subjects and thereby lent themselves more easily to themes with mock-heroic possibilities. However, this group of female portraits could be seen to confuse the public/private opposition which I mentioned earlier. Although these are portraits of women, their heroic disguises suggest an imposing rhetorical function. Designed to hang in stately homes, these were commissioned as *public* works on grand (mythological) themes which could be understood by an educated spectator. I think that the point worth making here is that women were more often represented as the symbolic objects of a *public* rhetorical art, rather than regarded as a significant part of its audience.

This manner of representing female sitters co-existed in Reynolds's work with some other conventions of feminine portraiture. He also depicted female sitters in relation to the more *private* domestic sphere with which they were more traditionally associated. *The Ladies Waldegrave* (*c.*1780, Col. Pl. 5), for example, are shown in a relatively intimate domestic context, working together on embroidery and winding silk. Other ladies are painted with their children (Pls 12, 14, 16) or engaged in leisure activities such as reading, walking or listening (Pl. 13). *The Ladies Waldegrave* was commissioned by Horace Walpole, who described the painting in a letter of 1780.

> Sir Joshua has begun a charming picture of my 3 fair nieces, the Waldegraves, and very like. They are embroidering and winding silk. I rather wished to have them drawn like the Graces adorning a bust of the Duchess [their mother] as the Magna Mater [the goddess Cybele] – but my ideas are not adopted; however, I still intend to have the Duchess and her two other children as Latona [the Greek goddess, Leto] for myself. (Penny, 1986, p.293)

Walpole, then, explicitly opposes this portrait to those in the Grand Style. In this work, he suggests, likeness has come before the conventions associated with this style. If, however, his comment was ironic, it was probably intended as an implicit criticism of Reynolds's heroic manner, exemplified in another portrait of three sisters, *The Montgomery Sisters Adorning a Term of Hymen* (Col. Pl. 6). Walpole actually makes an ironic reference to this work when he claims he wanted to have his nieces drawn like the Graces 'adorning' a bust of their mother. The two portraits were frequently compared and could be seen to represent Reynolds's different approaches to the female group portrait. The Montgomery sisters are shown as modern-day Graces in what Reynolds called 'graceful historical attitudes'. They are decorating a statue of Hymen, the Roman god of marriage, with festoons of flowers, and are dressed in imaginary, flowing garments. In contrast, the Waldegrave sisters appear to be sitting in everyday poses and are wearing contemporary dresses of what was probably fashionable white muslin. They are engaged in a private domestic activity, while the Montgomery sisters are engaged in a stylized public display around the statue of Hymen, a piece of painted theatre which would have conferred dignity on its participants.

The Montgomery Sisters is also a reworking of a popular form of contemporary commission, the engagement portrait. As it was largely through marriage that women acquired public status and identity, this type of portrait was in great demand for women, though virtually unheard of for men. The eldest daughter Elizabeth (centre) had recently become engaged, and the painting was commissioned by her fiancé. And the symbolic significance of each sister's position in relation to the statue would not have escaped a spectator who knew the family. While Elizabeth approaches Hymen with her festoons, Anne – the only married daughter at the time – has passed the post and holds her festoons in triumph. Meanwhile the youngest daughter Barbara is placed on the left still gathering flowers.

Despite the obvious differences between the two paintings, I think it would be a mistake to see these two forms of female portraiture as revealing only incompatible conventions of feminine portraiture. Apart from the relative intimacy of the Waldegrave portrait, based on a British tradition of 'conversation pieces' (intimate group portraits), the work has several features associated with the Grand Style. The composition is made up of a group of balanced triangles and set against a typical Reynolds backdrop of (the base of) a classical column and a rich red drape, which give the work a certain monumentality.

In both portrait groups Reynolds also had to address the problem of likeness. Despite the mannered poses and artificial costumes of the Montgomery sisters, the faces were intended as portrait studies. Thus the heads in *both* works reveal individual portraits with hair and make-up in the contemporary fashion. Although the Waldegrave sisters appear rather more elaborately coiffured, the outdoor effects in *The Montgomery Sisters* have not disturbed their fashionable loops and plaits. In fact the requirements of a portrait commission would have made it difficult to avoid some concessions to likeness and to the display of contemporary fashions which this might involve. But it's also fair to say that Reynolds, like most other eighteenth-century portrait painters, combined a somewhat idealized contemporary face with an accurate depiction or 'likeness' of his sitter. Both the Montgomery and Waldegrave clients seem to share the fashionable pale oval face, straight longish nose and rosebud lips. The Waldegraves are also shown with powdered hair and rouge on their cheeks, cosmetics which became more popular in the late eighteenth century with the influence of French fashions. For women, as for men, the portrait commission was an ideal way of having yourself represented as you wished to look, and as the focus of beauty for women tended to be the face, this was where cosmetics or 'paint' could be useful. Although eighteenth-century portrait painters generally strove to make their clients' faces appear natural rather than painted, the use of cosmetics would have been commonplace for Reynolds's more affluent clients. As Aileen Ribeiro has suggested:

> Paint … was needed not just to gild the lily, but to remedy the effects of infrequent bathing and a defective diet (which caused eczema and scurvy), and illnesses like smallpox which pitted the skin. Ignorance of dental hygiene and fondness for sugar meant that women found it difficult to have the teeth like pearls which were praised in verse; early on the teeth decayed and had to be extracted, which is one of the reasons why sitters in portraits are rarely shown smiling. Until the end of the eighteenth century 'plumpers' of cork, wax or leather were inserted into the mouth where teeth were missing, to produce the rounded cheeks admired as part of female beauty. (Ribeiro, 1987, p.3)

The concessions to contemporary ideals of female beauty which Reynolds made in many of his portrait commissions of women might seem to conflict with the classical forms of idealization or 'abstraction' which he advocates for his Grand Style. Yet I think this is precisely the problem which Reynolds is trying to resolve in *Discourse VII* in his discussions on 'taste'. He advises *both* following 'the general air of the antique' *and* preserving 'something of the modern for the sake of likeness'. And by conflating the issue of the 'modern' (that is, contemporary taste or fashion) with that of 'likeness' he tries to get round the problem which I have been discussing, that concessions to contemporary fashion could also involve a reworking of reality, the construction of a modern ideal, rather than an accurate 'likeness'.

Most of the portraits we have discussed so far display a concern for decorum, that is for the rules of art which limited the range of poses, expressions and gestures deemed appropriate for portraiture. We have seen that the rules were often different for male and female sitters. The class and status of the client could *also* affect the rules adopted. Although it's not a hard and fast rule, a client from a less exalted social background than that of Reynolds's aristocratic patrons, was less likely to be represented in an heroic or grand context. Thus, wealthy but non-aristocratic landowners such as the Derbyshire squire *Philip Gell* (1763, Pl. 17) were painted (albeit early in Reynolds's career) in more 'natural' landscape contexts, as rural portraits which compare with those for which Thomas Gainsborough became renowned at the time (Pls 18–20).

Similarly, in his commissions for famous courtesans such as *Miss Kitty Fisher* or *Nelly O'Brien* (Pl. 21 and Col. Pl. 8) the virtuoso depiction of the textures and fabrics of their fashionable dress and the relatively informal poses contrast with the mannered poses and monumental style of many of his aristocratic portraits. Nelly O'Brien, for example, is shown in a relatively intimate pose,[6] without reference to a classical theme. Although much of the colour has now faded, this painting (now in the Wallace Collection) reveals Reynolds's ability to depict rich surface textures and delicate colours. The blue-striped silk dress, quilted pink underskirt, black lace shawl and lace trimmings are skilfully painted to suggest Nelly O'Brien's fashionable affluence. She was a well known courtesan who became mistress of the 3rd Viscount Bolingbroke, by whom she bore a son in 1764. O'Brien, who was also a friend of Reynolds, sat for the portrait between 1760 and 1761, and was probably the model for other pictures produced around this time.[7]

While certain upper-class and aristocratic interests and values could be reinforced through classical allusions and references to Renaissance models, commissions from less exalted clients often allowed Reynolds to develop those painterly and naturalistic interests which emerge increasingly in the text of the later *Discourses*. In *Discourse XIV*, written in 1788 as a tribute to Gainsborough, who had died earlier that year, he tries to reconcile his academic ambitions with his obvious taste for Gainsborough's relatively unacademic style. The result is a lecture in which Reynolds once again seeks to formulate some kind of aesthetic compromise, acknowledging that great art can (sometimes) be produced without recourse to antique models. (I want to develop this point in the following section.) What it reveals once again is that despite the theoretical ambitions of the

---

[6] These more intimate poses may also have art historical roots. Mannings (1973, pp.191–3) has suggested a link with Restoration portraits.

[7] See Ingamells (1985).

earlier *Discourses*, Reynolds was also a pragmatist, working in a climate in which there was increasing demand for the forms of naturalistic (or at least unacademic) rural portraits in which Gainsborough excelled (Pls 18–20). Given Reynolds's professional position and his personal interests, it is hardly surprising, then, that he should attempt to give Gainsborough's work, and portraiture in general, a theoretical basis, to represent it as worthy of academic debate.

In my discussion of the status of portraiture I have focused on the use of classical allusions, poses and costumes as means of conferring dignity and representing the class interests of the sitter. However, size and format were also recognizable indicators of status. During his career Reynolds adhered to five standard sizes of portrait, with prices fixed according to size:

1   Head, 24½in × 18½in in 1764, but changed to
     24in × 25in in 1782;

2   Bust, called the 'Three-quarter' because it measured approximately
     ¾yd, including one or both hands, 30in × 25in;

3   Kit-cat, or head and shoulders with one or both hands, 36in × 28in;

4   Half-length, 50in × 40in;

5   Whole-length, 94in × 58in.

Reynolds's prices rose over the years as he became more successful and established as an Academician. The following chart gives you an idea of how his prices rose.

	Head	Bust or ¾	Kit-cat	Half-length	Whole length
1742–8	3 guineas				
1753–5	12 guineas			24 guineas	48 guineas
1757	15 guineas			30 guineas	60 guineas
1758/9	20 guineas	20 guineas	30 guineas	50 guineas	100 guineas
1760	25 guineas			50 guineas	100 guineas
1764	30 guineas	35 guineas	50 guineas	70 guineas	150 guineas
1765–81	35 guineas	35 guineas	50 guineas	70 guineas	150 guineas

(*Source:* Penny, 1986, p.58)

This rise was way above a general increase in values because the art market had expanded much faster than the general market. By the 1770s Reynolds's portraits had become much more expensive than those of most of his competitors, and by the 1780s they were out of the reach of all but the wealthiest patrons. Some were sold for more than the fixed prices listed above. According to Reynolds's ledger, in 1769 or 1772, Sir Charles Bunbury paid 250 guineas for *Lady Sarah Bunbury Sacrificing to the Graces*, a very large sum at the time for a full-length portrait (Penny, 1986, p.225). Prices were also adjusted according to the number of extra figures to be included. The most popular extras included children, black servants, dogs and horses.

However, there was one aspect of Reynolds's artistic production which does not seem to have affected price. His work became renowned for technical problems such as the fading colours and cracking paint surface. (These problems are still evident in many of his paintings, although this cannot always be seen in reproduction.) Fading and cracking was caused by his constant, and not always successful, experiments in the mixing of colour and varnish. These caused problems which were evident to his contemporaries. In 1775 Horace Walpole is reported to have said that 'Sir Joshua Reynolds is a great painter; but unfortunately his colours seldom stand longer than "crayons" (Penny, 1986, p.55). Despite these technical problems Reynolds's status as a 'great painter' seems to have kept his prices high.

The full-length portrait, then, preferably with a few extras, was the ultimate demonstration of wealth and status. But what the list of categories and corresponding prices also tells us is that portraiture was still being produced according to certain rules of the trade. In terms of its production, therefore, portraiture in particular, and art in general, still carried with it some connotations of a mechanical trade. Hence Reynolds's desire to give it a theoretical basis which would allow it to claim the status of a liberal art. But given the conditions of the portrait genre, this was no easy aim to fulfil; hence my emphasis on some of the contradictions – or different interpretations – which emerged around the concept of 'likeness' and Reynolds's notion of the Grand Style.

3 Theory and the Institutions of art

In the preceding section we saw that portraiture could be a powerful medium for communicating and reinforcing the ideals, values and beliefs of a particular class or social group. It was through institutions of art that these values could be formally established and disseminated. Through its provision of teaching, lectures, exhibitions and distribution of prizes and awards, the Royal Academy of Arts became a powerful disseminator of artistic and cultural values. Although founded under royal charter, it was formed on the initiative of a group of British artists who were actually seeking to establish themselves as a respected body, membership of which might actually *reduce* their dependence on aristocratic patronage. They believed that the protection – or stamp of approval – from George III (who succeeded to the throne in 1760) would effectively allow them more control over the teaching and practice of art, thus limiting the interference by, and demands of, their aristocratic clients. But for this relative freedom to have any effect within an immensely hierarchical society, the institution still had to be seen to promote values and interests which were at least compatible with those of many of its patrons. Some of the founding aims were explained in Reynolds's first *Discourse*, and a document setting out the constitution and original membership was signed by George III in December 1768.

This charter (which you will find reproduced in the Broadcast Notes to AC1632) tells us that apart from the exhibiting facilities, great importance was attached to the organization and status of the Academy Schools. The establishment of a prestigious teaching institution with recognized pedagogic principles was essential for the ratification of the 'liberal' status of painting: hence the professorial appointments made in anatomy, architecture, painting, perspective and geometry. More significantly, the professor of painting was contracted to give regular lectures, to provide students with a theoretical basis for their work. And apart from course-based lectures, Reynolds himself delivered his annual *Discourses*. The Academy Schools were crucial, then, in elevating not only the discipline of painting, but also the study of, or training for, that discipline.

OΤΛΕΙΣ–ΑΜΟΤΣΟΣ–ΕΙΣΙΤΩ

THE EXHIBITION OF THE ROYAL ACADEMY, 1787.

Figure 46
Pietro Martini, Engraving after J.H. Ramberg, The Exhibition of the Royal Academy at Somerset House, 1787. *(Royal Academy of Arts)*

Although several private art academies, including Hogarth's St Martin's Lane Academy, had been established in London during the first half of the century, the study of art was still traditionally seen as a form of apprenticeship to a trade. The Academy was formed in the hope of raising that study to a form of intellectual labour: hence the important didactic and rhetorical function of Reynolds's painting *Theory,* positioned to look down on students and established academicians alike from the library ceiling.

The artists listed in the constitution include only two women, Angelica Kauffman and Mary Moser, among the founder members. Despite this, both women are absent from Johann Zoffany's famous painting of the first academicians, *The Academicians of the Royal Academy* (1771–2, Col. Pl. 9); or at least they are excluded from the group of male artists shown contemplating nude models and plaster casts. They are included, however, as painted portrait busts on the wall to the right of the assembled group of men. Zoffany's painting is to do with the pursuit of the academic ideal in art, and the copying from nude models which the pursuit of this ideal involved. But women were prohibited from studying the nude model and thereby excluded from the training which formed the basis of an academic art and the pursuit of genius which it involved. In this pictorial representation, then, both women are excluded from active participation in the academic life, and relegated to paintings (in the lower portrait genre) within a painting. We've seen that after Kauffman and Moser, women were actually barred from membership of the Royal Academy until well into the twentieth century.

Why, then, were Kauffman and Moser allowed to join the ranks of the founder members? Like most dominant social systems, the predominantly male academic culture which I have described would allow exceptions, particularly if the work of the women could compete on the same academic terms. Both Kauffman and Moser were daughters of foreigners and were closely associated with the founder members, and both had well-established reputations and artistic pedigrees. Kauffman had previously been elected to the famous Academy of Saint Luke in Rome in 1765, and Moser was a respected flower painter patronized by Queen Charlotte, the wife of George III. Moreover Kauffman was one of the leading British neo-classical painters, who made extensive use of historical and mythological themes and classical statues and reliefs in her work (Pl. 15). Such interests more than qualified her work for academic status. (Kauffman's form of classicism is discussed in TV6, 'Angelica Kauffman R.A. and the Choice of Painting'.)

EXERCISE Please reread the extracts from the *Discourses*, and consider Reynolds's discussion of genius and of taste. Can you detect any shifts between the ideas set out in *Discourse III* (1770) and *Discourse VII* (1776)?

DISCUSSION The concepts of 'taste' and 'genius' are, as Reynolds suggests in *Discourse III*, closely related in much eighteenth-century writing on aesthetics. He groups together the 'great style', genius and taste, claiming that these are different names for the same thing. He argues that the distinguishing factor of this art of genius is its pursuit of 'ideal beauty', which is superior to the many variations to be found in ordinary nature (*Texts*, I, pp.212–13).

In *Discourse III*, as in several of the earlier discourses (notably *VI* and *VII*), Reynolds seems intent upon anchoring his concept of genius in academic study. He argues that although the 'great qualities' of taste and genius are ultimately beyond rules – that is to say that there are no invariable rules for acquiring them – 'they always operate in proportion to our attention in observing works of nature, to our skill in selecting, and to our care in digesting, methodizing, and comparing our observations' (*Texts*, I, p.213).

Reynolds's attempts to define genius in the earlier *Discourses*, then, could be seen to demystify the concept, to undermine somehow the idea that this is an innately inspired gift. Reynolds seems to want to bring genius down to earth. In this respect, his theory was influenced by aspects of the late seventeenth-century empiricist philosophy which was discussed in the preceding study on Hume. In his *An Essay Concerning Human Understanding* of 1690, John Locke had argued against all forms of innatism, and hence any form of the belief that genius is innate or a gift. For Locke the mind was like a blank sheet of paper which acquired understanding and creative skills through experience, through the principal operations of the mind (which Locke lists as perception, thought, reason, belief and doubt).

Reynolds draws indirectly on some of these ideas, and in *Discourse VI*, written in 1774, he actually describes the mind as 'a barren soil' which will produce no crop 'unless it be continually fertilized and enriched with foreign matter' (Reynolds, 1981 edn, p.99). Rather than obey some divine inspiration, the distinguishing feature of 'genius' is its ability to discover and detect guiding ideas, which Reynolds sometimes refers to as 'rules':

> When we have continually before us the great works of Art to impregnate our minds with kindred ideas, we are then, and not till then, fit to produce something of the same species ... The greatest natural genius cannot subsist on its own stock: he who resolves never to ransack any mind but his own, will be soon reduced, from mere barrenness, to the poorest of all imitations. (Reynolds, 1981 edn, p.99)

This approach might seem to undermine what had been a traditional and crucial component of 'genius', that is the quality of 'invention', or as Reynolds sometimes calls it 'imagination'. Yet Reynolds manages to hold on to a concept of invention, albeit one which is always modified by experience. In *Discourse VI* he argues that it is 'by being conversant with the inventions of others that we learn to invent' (Reynolds, 1981 edn, p.99).

I want to argue that Reynolds's attempts to demystify genius, influenced as they were by aspects of empiricist philosophy, were an essential part of his attempt to raise the status of painting. If genius was the distinguishing feature of great art, it must be understood according to defensible intellectual principles. The Royal Academy was established to teach and encourage the production of High Art; thus artistic creativity had to be represented according to teachable academic principles. A notion of genius which could be seen to ignore or defy the rules, to be exclusively based on some innate capacity or divine inspiration, might undermine the rationale for teaching and disseminating academic theory.

But later *Discourses* suggest that Reynolds's ideas on genius were continually being modified and revised, partly to accommodate his own tastes and some of the practical constraints on his art (for example commissions for Grand Style history paintings were relatively few). In *Discourse VII* Reynolds reiterates the arguments on genius formulated in earlier *Discourses*. He regrets that it 'has been the fate of arts to be enveloped in mysterious and incomprehensible language' (*Texts*, I, p.216). At the same time he appears to be qualifying his ideas on taste and genius in his subsequent discussion. 'Taste' is defined as the power of distinguishing genius, and the difference between the two is that genius has the 'power of execution'. According to this distinction a person can have 'taste' to discern and recognize great art, but must be able to *produce* it in order to be called a genius.

As you have seen in the preceding study on Hume, 'taste' had emerged as a problematic concept in early eighteenth-century philosophy and aesthetics. As his career progressed Reynolds developed a more subtle argument about the extent to which rules were to be followed. He became increasingly aware that some of the eighteenth-century artists whose work he admired were not working to the rules of the academic textbooks. Gainsborough, whose work forms the subject of *Discourse XIV* delivered in 1788, is a notable example (Pls 18–20). In *Discourse VII*, you can see Reynolds trying to argue his way to a position from which he could, simultaneously, acknowledge the greatness of painters such as Gainsborough (and Rembrandt), yet insist that the greatest paintings will always be those which (unlike Gainsborough's or Rembrandt's) embody the most general, the least particular truths (see *Texts*, I, p.218–9).

Reynolds is concerned to resolve the problem that a knowledge of the rules *alone* will not produce genius. So in *Discourse VII* he affirms the belief that imagination is the faculty which ultimately distinguishes and organizes the rules. And this argument allows him to modify the extent to which 'taste' must be governed by Greek and Roman models. When applied to portraiture it allows him to qualify the need for classical models and dress, to introduce the value of ornament, and even to acknowledge the value of portraits, such as those of Van Dyck, which magnificently display contemporary fashion. As we saw in the preceding section on portraiture, Reynolds's pragmatism as a portraitist has once again encroached on his sense of responsibility as a teacher and theorist, to produce a form of writing about art which is both theoretical *and* rooted in the problems of an eighteenth-century art practice.

The language and content of those *Discourses* in which Reynolds considers the concepts of 'genius' and 'taste' raise another issue addressed earlier in this study, that is, the extent to which academic art theory was seen to be an essentially male form of intellectual activity. We have already seen that during the eighteenth century, artistic creativity was seen as a predominately male attribute. But these arguments can be extended to show that in Reynolds's writing, as in that of several other eighteenth-century theorists, the specific concepts of taste and genius are themselves implicitly gendered. They are seen as 'masculine' attributes, opposed to more unintellectual and 'decorative' qualities associated with the 'feminine'. When Reynolds is emphasizing both the superiority of intellectual activity in the production of painting, and the need to idealize from nature, he has in mind the male artist. And the conventions which Reynolds recommends for his 'Grand Style' are themselves represented in gendered terms. In *Discourse VIII* he discusses a distinction made in an earlier discourse between the 'sublime' and 'ornamental' styles which reinforced 'the more manly, noble and disguised manner of the former' (Reynolds, 1981 edn, p.153). The art historian Carol Gibson-Wood has argued that in other writings on art Reynolds identified the superficial with a 'feminine' form of art which was without intellectual insight.[8] These sorts of implicit oppositions between 'masculine' and 'feminine' judgement were to be found in other areas of eighteenth-century culture, and will be discussed further in the essays on Mary Wollstonecraft and Rousseau in Part E of the course.

4 Conclusion

The language of *art theory* in general, and Reynolds's *Discourses* in particular, then, had a powerful role to play in the dissemination of ideas and values which went beyond the field of painting and art history. I have discussed the way in which much of Reynolds's theory and practice show him to be engaged with some of the complexities and contradictions associated with the artistic and philosophical culture of the period. His

---

[8] For example, in his Notebook Manuscripts. Discussed in a paper to the Association of Art Historians, London, April 1991.

ambivalent relationship with the classical and antique sources, his appeal for a public rhetorical art, his early attempts to root the concepts of 'taste' and 'genius' in academic theory, and the contradictions within his theory and practice of the Grand Style, show him to be directly involved with some of the same aesthetic, moral and philosophical problems which preoccupied contemporaries such as Shaftesbury, Johnson, Hume, Adam and Diderot.

Throughout this study I have also tried to show that Reynolds's practical experiences as a painter were constantly causing him to adjust or modify his theoretical ambitions. Artists were dependent on patronage and commissions, and like most professional painters working in Britain at the time, Reynolds was most in demand for portrait commissions. Reynolds was keenly aware that his attempts to be both painter and academic theorist made both aspects of his work vulnerable to criticism. In his last lecture (*Discourse XV* delivered in 1790) he apologizes for any lack of skills in writing, but argues that the knowledge which an artist has of the practice of art 'will contribute more to advance the theory of our art, than a thousand volumes such as we sometimes see' (Reynolds, 1981 edn, p.267). Reynolds's contribution to eighteenth-century art theory, which was then a relatively new discipline, is partly this attempt to bridge the gulf between artist and critic, and thereby raise the status of art.

5   *References*

Barrell, J. (1986) *The Political Theory of Painting from Reynolds to Hazlitt,* Yale, London.

Hutchinson, S. (1986 edn) *The History of the Royal Academy,* Robert Royce, London.

Ingamells, J. (1985) *Wallace Collection: Catalogue of Pictures,* **vol.1,** London.

Irwin, D. (1966) *English Neo-Classical Art,* Faber and Faber, London.

Jones, V. (ed.) (1990) *Women in the Eighteenth Century: Constructions of Femininity,* Routledge, London.

Locke, J. (1975 edn) *An Essay Concerning Human Understanding,* edited by P.H. Nidditch, Clarendon Press, Oxford. (First published in 1690.)

Mannings, D. 'Reynolds and the Restoration Portrait', *Connoisseur,* CLXXXIII, July, 1973, pp.186–93.

Northcote, J. (1819) *The Life of Sir Joshua Reynolds,* Colburn, London.

Penny, N. (ed.) (1986) *Reynolds,* Royal Academy of Arts, London.

Reynolds, J. (1929) *The Letters,* edited by F.W. Hilles, Cambridge University Press, Cambridge.

Reynolds, J. (1981 edn) *Discourses on Art,* Yale University Press, New Haven.

Ribeiro, A. (1987) *The Female Face,* Tate Gallery, London.

Shaftesbury, Lord (1773 edn) *Characteristicks of Men, Manners, Opinions, Times,* John Baskerville, Birmingham.

Solkin, D. (1986) 'Great Pictures or Great Men? Reynolds, Male Portraiture and the Power of Art', *Oxford Art Journal,* 9 Feb.

Tscherny, N. 'Likeness in early romantic portraiture', *Art Journal,* 1987, vol.46, No.3.

Warner, M. (1985) *Monuments and Maidens: The Allegory of the Female Form,* Weidenfeld and Nicolson, London.

Waterhouse, E.K. (ed.) (1973) *Reynolds,* Phaidon, London.

Robert Adam: Architectural Theory and Practice

Prepared for the Course Team by
Colin Cunningham

Contents

Robert Adam: Architectural Theory and Practice (Study week 11)

Studies/Texts	Radio	TV	AC	Set Books
Studies, I	–	TV7	AC1632 (blue)	–
Texts, I				
Illustration Book				
Folder of Engravings				

As you read this study you will need to have by you *Texts*, I, the folder of engravings from *The Works in Architecture of Robert and James Adam*, and the *Illustration Book*. If you are not familiar with architectural plans or terminology, you should work through the exercise on AC1632 before you start.

Robert Adam: Architectural Theory and Practice

1 Introduction

The eighteenth century, the Age of Reason, or the Enlightenment period, saw a huge growth in the building and rebuilding of houses for the nobility and gentry. The vast majority of these are in one or another of the classical revival styles of architecture. So it is worth examining the nature of this taste for classicism, and its relation to the society in which it flourished. Of course, country houses are only one of many building types – the nobility had town houses as well, and there were public buildings, a few churches and also prisons, the architecture of which was a different thing altogether. Country houses, too, were only for a small élite group in society. Nonetheless that group was so powerful that it could command the very best in architectural design, and the houses form a sufficiently coherent group for me to choose a selection that is representative of Robert Adam's architectural theory and practice, and of its relationship to the Enlightenment.

2 Eighteenth-century architecture

In the second half of the century Robert Adam's version of decorative neo-classicism was, arguably, the leading taste in Britain. First, however, it is important to bear in mind that there were other architects and other styles that were popular. Sir William Chambers (1723–96), Adam's greatest rival, adopted a more severe Roman style, and was much more successful in obtaining official government commissions. James 'Athenian' Stuart (1713–88) was the originator of a taste for a more archaeologically-based style inspired by ancient Greek architecture. In France and the German-speaking states (as you saw in TV2, 'Frederick the Great and 'Sans Souci'') the rococo style was all the rage when Adam began, and gave way not to an Adam style but to a much severer Greek classical style. It is also as well to remember that the half century we are studying saw a rapid development of taste. In 1750 Adam had not even started the studies that were to lead to his individual style, yet by the time of his death in 1792 his version of classicism was almost completely *démodé* in England, though it lasted a little longer in Scotland.

The 'text' for this study consists of extracts from the Prefaces of the *Works* and 24 of the plates. I shall also consider three country houses, two from the 1760s, and one from the next decade in order to illustrate Robert Adam's aims and practice. (AC1632 deals with the technical aspect of studying architecture; and TV7, 'Kedleston', extends the study.) Begin by reading the biographical sketch of Robert Adam and the first five paragraphs of Preface I (as far as '... through all our numerous works') in the *Works* (*Texts*, I, pp.225–9). At this stage you do not need to read Adam's footnotes. Consider what sort of person Adam was, what sort of career he had, and what were his interests (and his achievements) as an architect. All these are basic issues that I shall discuss in the next section.

3   Adam and the Classical Sources

It is important to recognize that Adam's background in the world of the Scottish Enlightenment (see TV4, 'Scotland and the Enlightenment') was relatively privileged. He not only moved in intellectual circles and had access to his father's excellent architectural library, but was also sufficiently well-to-do to live like a gentleman. When he travelled to Italy he set out in company with Charles Lord Hope (see TV4, 'Scotland and the Enlightenment' and TV5, 'The Grand Tour and the Rediscovery of the Classics'), heir of the Earl of Hopetoun (though they soon quarrelled over their respective shares of the expenses). However, Adam was not a gentleman of leisure, and, like his father, was thoroughly versed in the craft of building. One important result of this was his concern that every detail of a scheme, down to the door knobs, should be designed by him (see Engraving 16). Many would argue that this is a key element in his success as a designer. Yet his very involvement in the business of architecture – in trade – set him apart from the landed gentry. In the eighteenth century, architects did not have the professional status they have now, and Adam was sometimes treated as little better than an upper servant. He was touchy about this, and was furious when the Earl of Bute, for whom he later built Luton Hoo, received him wearing riding boots and coat. Adam had called to solicit commissions and was anxious to be treated seriously.[1]

One way in which architects could establish their status and distinguish themselves from more lowly (though often equally wealthy) builders was by scholarship. It is in this context that Adam's publications were so important; but we have to consider whether they publicize the originality of his genius or his standard of taste, and which of these is the more important aspect of his work. Hume urged that standards and precedent were paramount; but I am impressed by Adam's stress on novelty and variety and his keenness to establish his own work as a source for others. His scholarship is first shown in the care with which he studied the monuments of ancient Rome.

EXERCISE   Read *Works*, Volume I Preface I, footnotes 3 and 5 (*Texts*, I, pp.227–8) and Prefaces IV and V (*Texts*, I, pp.234–7), and look at Pls 38 and 25–37. What sources does Adam refer to, and how does he assess them as precedents? (At this stage you should read the extracts quickly, without worrying too much about details.)

DISCUSSION   Adam refers to ancient Rome, and he is keen to show that he has read important literary sources such as Vitruvius' *De Architectura* (*On Architecture*) and other classical writers such as Horace and Suetonius. The general idea of the role of classical art is shown in the frontispiece of the *Works* (Pl. 38) where a young architect is led before the goddess Minerva, the Roman goddess of the household arts, who points to a map showing Italy and Greece. Fame, with wings and trumpet, is in attendance and the whole scene is set in a classical ruin. The frontispiece to his other book,

---

[1]   Adam's concern for the professional status of the architect was comparable with Reynolds's similar concern for painters, and with Johnson's for himself as a writer.

Ruins of the Palace of Diocletian at Spalatro (Pl. 35) shows the architect himself busily sketching; and the plates he drew (Pls 36–7) are clearly intended, with all their measurements, to be available for architects to copy. It is interesting, also, that in Volume I Preface II he claims to have found Desgodetz's *Les Edifices Antiques de Rome* (*The Ancient Buildings of Rome*) (Pl. 27), the standard guide to the monuments, inadequate, and intends to issue a new edition. Finally Adam is also impressed by the great architects of the Renaissance, and those of earlier generations in Britain (Pls 32–4).

Adam had clearly visited and studied the major monuments (Pls 25–9); and the collection of casts and drawings he made was a key resource for his later designing. He sketched the ruins of the palace of the emperor Diocletian for a publication intended to advertise his classical scholarship and to further his career. Yet both his scholarship and his taste were open to criticism. Turn to the extracts from Gibbon's *History of the Decline and Fall of the Roman Empire*, and read the two brief sections from Chapter XIII on Diocletian's palace (*Texts* I, pp. 265–7; see Pl. 26) and from Chapter XIV on the triumphal arch of Constantine (*Texts* I, pp.268–9; see Pl. 25) (a motif which Adam later adapted for the south facade of Kedleston Hall – Pl. 77).

Gibbon had used Adam's publication in working on volume one of his *Decline and Fall* (which came out in 1776), but he is rather scathing about both the quality of the building and of Adam's representation of it. By the 1770s, however, scholarship had moved on, and Adam's career had developed, not entirely successfully. Nonetheless, in 1764 Adam was certainly out to impress with the publication, and it is significant that his *Ruins of the Palace of Diocletian at Spalatro* included a long list of subscribers, many of whom were already his patrons.

4 The Works in Architecture of Robert and James Adam, Esquires

4.1 The Works as a text

EXERCISE   I would like you now to read all the extracts from the Prefaces in *Texts* I, and to look at Pls 39–47 and Engravings 1–24. As you read, I would like you to consider three questions:

What sort of document is the *Works*?

To whom is it addressed?

What claim does it make for the productions of Robert and James Adam?

Do not worry too much about the technical terms or the names of other architects. You will not be required to know details of those; but it is worth reading the extensive footnotes that Adam supplied, since they throw light on my three questions as well as explaining some of the technical obscurities. Although we shall return to a detailed discussion of the Syon plates later, it is worth spending some time now just looking at the plates, and reading the captions.

DISCUSSION   The *Works* is clearly not a literary document. You have only to look at the length of some of the sentences, which seem to be punctuated at a ration of two commas to a line, to see that. In fact I believe the first Volume at least was produced in something of a hurry. It is clear from the opening paragraph of Preface II that there were changes of plan. There are also a number of typographical errors (which we have retained) starting with 'tow' in the first paragraph of the first Preface. You may even have noticed careless and inconsistent spelling; for instance Adam uses both 'stile' and 'style', and he names Syon House as 'Sion'. Although the text is important in providing information about the plates and about Adam's artistic intentions, this attitude to the text is revealing. It seems to me that Adam was most interested in the plates since those actually demonstrated what he was capable of doing (but how much time did you spend on them compared to the written text?). Certainly later scholars, apart from a few select passages, have paid more attention to the plates than the text. It would not surprise me if you found much of the text rather a dull read, whereas some of the plates are both beautiful and fascinating.

4.2   *The purpose of the* Works

Text and plates together are a sort of manifesto for the production of the firm. They provide a defence for what Adam was doing, and are clearly aimed at marketing the partnership's works. Adam begins by recognizing that the Adam style is already widely copied. In Preface I paragraph 2 he talks of the extent to which his works have been imitated by other artists. This element of copying and competition is one that he returns to on several occasions. Engraving 3 (Volume I Pl. III in Adam's original numbering), for instance, seems quite explicitly to expect this. The amount of detailed explanation, for instance the attack on compartmented ceilings (Preface I footnote 3) or the set of rules for forming and disposing columns (Preface II), reads like instructions to other artists. However, I doubt whether the aim was principally, or even at all, to advertise the Adam style for copying.

You have to remember that in the eighteenth century, as now, the architect was virtually nothing without a patron. So I believe that Adam is much more likely to have been talking to potential patrons than to other architects. The fact that he is prepared to go into such detail in his text and to provide so many technical details in his drawings suggests that he assumed any worthwhile patrons would want to be properly informed about the architecture they might order, and would be as concerned as Adam was about the detail of the design. Such people, of course, are exactly those who, in Hume's opinion, would be most likely to possess correct taste.

From the contents list of the *Works* it is clear how Adam hoped to market his ideas. Of the eight houses illustrated in Volumes I and II the patrons include two Dukes and five Earls; and one whole section is given over to designs for the Royal family. Adam was firmly aiming at the very top. He offers designs for a screen for Carlton House (Pl. 39), which had long been one of George III's London houses. He was not always successful with these commissions; and you may have noticed that the birthday illumination for the king (Pl. 41) was only partly carried out. But if you look at Pls 42–3 and 46 you will see that Adam stresses these were not merely designs, but were actually executed. The same is true of the harpsichord (Pl. 45).

As a commission from Catherine the Great, this at last gave Adam a claim to important international patronage; though if you compare his buildings to Sans Souci (which you saw in TV2, 'Frederick the Great and 'Sans Souci''), you will see how different continental, or at least Frederick's, taste was. Adam does acknowledge (Volume I Preface I description of Syon House) the quality of French planning. He also includes captions in French as well as English, which suggests that he may have been hoping to impress foreign clients. However, it is a salutary reminder that though England, and English systems, were admired by Enlightenment thinkers, English taste was to some extent regarded as peripheral, and had little influence on the continent.

The status and influence of individual patrons was clearly important: and this even leads Adam to fudge his publication slightly. Engravings 8 and 16 were both published originally in sections headed 'Syon House', yet it appears that none of the furniture shown was actually made for Syon. It is possible that Adam hoped these designs would be bought for Syon, and he did design some furniture for the house (Pls 66 and 71–2). The door furniture was manufactured, and was used at Kedleston and Osterley, but those houses are not featured in the *Works*. Clearly it was important to Adam to establish that he was ready to design the whole of a house down to the last detail.

4.3 Adam's claim for originality in the Works

Adam had no false modesty in presenting his claims for attention. He asserts that he has 'in some measure ... brought about ... a kind of revolution' (Volume I Preface I) in taste. And he goes on to describe architecture as 'this useful and elegant art'. When we come to what was revolutionary, we find that he returns over and over again to concepts such as variety, novelty and gaiety. The emphasis is very much on the visual attractiveness of his schemes, which must then be seen as a sort of stage on which the patron could display his wealth, taste and presumably also his erudition in his understanding of the sources for Adam's designs.

That may seem a rather dismissive analysis of the architecture of what are often regarded as some of our finest country houses. And it ignores the common matters of servicing and structure. All the houses we shall study work well both from the point of parade – that is, the formal use of the state rooms – and in access for servants. Also, although Adam was most frequently at work altering older structures, his construction was invariably sound (which is more than can be said for some of his contemporaries). However, you have to remember that the principal rooms, which are often the only ones we see, were not so much the actual home of the owner as a place for the reception of visitors, tenants and dependants; and it is important to recognize that Adam was serving a wealthy and powerful élite for whom the display of wealth was often as important in advertizing their power and influence as was their concern to create beautiful surroundings for their own sake.

4.4   Adam's theory of classical design

Adam is at pains to stress the classical roots of his work. He cites Vitruvius (Volume I Preface I, footnote 5), quotes in Latin, and lists key buildings of the Augustan Principate (Volume I Preface IV, footnote 27). This is very much what one might expect given the extent to which Adam used Roman motifs in his designs. Compare, for instance the rather unusual Roman pilaster from Spalatro (Pl. 37) with the details of the Syon gateway (Engraving 2) or Kedleston (Pl. 84). He devotes the whole of Volume I Preface II to a discussion of the classical orders, and even claims to look to Greek precedents. This may have been some attempt to answer the popularity of 'Athenian' Stuart's work – he had published the first volume of *The Antiquities of Athens* in 1762. But you can see how much Adam relied on particular sources, some of which were Greek, if you compare Engraving 13 with Pl. 30 and the paragraph on the Grecian manner of forming the volute in Volume I Preface II (*Texts*, I, p.233). Nonetheless Adam is also at pains to maintain that the ancients 'courted ... variety and gracefulness of form' (Volume I description of the plan of Syon). In Volume I Preface II he gives himself a clear defence for breaking the 'rules' of classical architecture in search of that variety; and he uses that freedom to invent new orders (Pl. 39).

The classical rules had in fact been laid down by later architects such as Palladio (Pl. 31) reviving classical styles in the renaissance. Adam spends a good deal of time underlining the place of his architecture in that long tradition, which he claims to be developing. He is careful to name the main Italian Renaissance architects, and gives due credit to British architects of previous generations. I think the implication is that his own work is thereby legitimized. There are plenty of occasions, too, where he makes the claim that originality and genius are what are wanted to create new classical masterpieces, a claim which parallels Sir Joshua Reynolds's recognition of the need for individual genius as well as a proper understanding of the standards of taste in portraiture. This is linked to a degree of national chauvinism in his plea for more grand public buildings, which, of course, he hoped would mean more prestigious commissions. Preface IV in Volume I makes quite clear how important Adam felt major public commissions should be.

One final element of Adam's classicism is the conscious and careful search for unity in each decorative scheme. It seems to me that it is this above all that marks his work out. Look closely at the plates and you will be able to see how carefully he links the various motifs and elements in each of the rooms he designs. Notice, for instance, the way ceiling patterns are echoed in floors, at the way orders are related to each other and to the whole scheme, and at the way individual ornamental motifs are repeated.

At this point, if you have not already studied AC1632 on plan reading and architecture, you should do so before beginning a detailed study of Syon House.

5   Robert Adam and Syon House

Syon House at Brentford, near London, has been a noble house since 1547, and dates back even further to a fifteenth-century nunnery. It has belonged to the Percy family, Earls and Dukes of Northumberland, since

1594; and it was extensively reconstructed by the tenth Earl in the seventeenth century. However the title died out with his son, and was not recreated until 1750, when Sir Hugh Smithson became Earl of Northumberland (he was made a Duke in 1766). For him Robert Adam reconstructed the ancient house once again, creating at first floor, or *piano nobile*, level a complete set of parade rooms within the ancient structure. You will notice that the exterior (Pl. 48) does not look like the conventional eighteenth-century classical house (cf. Pls 93 and 130).

5.1   The Hall and Ante Room

The visitor to Syon in the 1770s, as now, would enter the Hall, and then pass through the Ante-room, the Great Dining Room and the State Drawing Room to the Gallery. You can check this progress from Engraving 6, and see how the Duke and Duchess themselves would probably follow a different route to their private apartments. The principal route leads through a sequence of splendid chambers, each different from the last. We shall concentrate on the Hall and Ante-room; but look first at all the rooms shown in Pls 50–63 and Col. Pls 10–11; then re-read the description of the plan of Syon that accompanies Engraving 5 (*Texts*, I, pp.229–31). See how the decoration varies from room to room. Each is different, yet all are related by similar uses of classical motifs. Then consider how the design of each space is related to the function of the room as described by Adam. Finally, ask yourself what effect Robert Adam achieves by his use of classical decoration in the Hall and Ante-room.

Both Hall and Ante-room are very grand, grander even than the State Drawing Room. Perhaps it would be more accurate to say that there is more moulded stucco decoration in the first two rooms than in the Drawing Room; and that, I think, adds to their air of grandeur and formality. The prevailing colours of the Hall are ivory and black (in the marble floor) but the Ante-room is gorgeous with gold and marble (Col. Pl. 10), setting up a tremendous contrast. Yet notice that both these rooms were for servants! (Servants out of livery may have been quite important people, secretaries, for example, or estate bailiffs, political agents, or even architects.) The attendance of liveried servants may have added a touch of living colour to the Hall. Horace Walpole gives a hint of the importance of this side of life to the newly-created Earl when, in expressing horror at the money that was being laid out, he said of the family, 'they live by the etiquette of the old peerage; have Swiss porters, the Countess [has] her pipers; in short they will soon have no estate'.

The gate lodge (Engraving 1) also has accommodation for Swiss porters, as the French version of the caption shows; and presumably they were also stationed in the inner lodges (Pl. 48). So the formality of the approach to this noble house began even outside. The hall itself was immense, about 49 by 30 feet, and higher than it is wide. Look carefully at Pl. 50 and Engravings 6, 7 and 9–11 to see how Adam assembles his classical elements. The floor echoes the ceiling, but I notice at once that Adam has abandoned his own advice about dispensing with heavy compartment ceilings. In the great height of this room, a bolder treatment was necessary. The room is given variety by the different shaped recesses at the ends (which, you will remember, allow for the adjustment to the level of the other parade rooms). One recess is cut off by a screen of columns, a novelty in English architecture but a favourite device of

Robert Adam's, for which he could cite precedents in Roman baths. Adam uses the entablature of this screen to give the space a unity by running it round the whole room, picking up the columns of the two major doorways. For this room he selects the severe Roman Doric order so that the effect is imposing rather than gay (novelty, variety and gaiety were, you will recall, the three characteristics he stressed). Instead the grandeur and formality of this space is emphasized by the over life-size statues. Adam's engravings specify casts of four of the most famous antique statues. Engraving 6 shows copies of the Dying Gaul and the Laocoon, Engraving 9 those of a portrait of Antinous and the Belvedere Apollo. You can see from Pl. 50 that only the Apollo and the Dying Gaul are there now. The spare pedestals support less famous but original antique statues. In the prevailing taste of the 1760s this probably represented an economy on the Duke's part.

There is no hint of economy in the Ante-room (Col. Pl. 10) where all is rich colour and gilding. Once again the floor echoes the ceiling pattern, but there are no heavy compartments. Instead the moulded plaster is more delicately handled. All the decoration is built in. There are no pictures on the walls; instead there are two plaster panels with trophies of Roman arms and another classical scene in plaster relief over the fireplace. There are twelve gilded statues, or rather plaster casts, set high up on the columns, which include the Venus de Medici and the Medici Faun, both well known antique works of the day (the set also includes a second Venus, another Antinous and another Apollo). The placing of these statues closely follows the arrangement of the Arch of Constantine in Rome (Pl. 25); but notice that Adam has used a different order, copied from the Greek temple, the Erechtheion (Pl. 30). Adam's classicism is certainly not archaeological, though as a matter of fact some of the columns are actually Roman originals dredged out of the Tiber, with the rest made to match in scagliola (imitation stone). What Adam has done here is to draw on a wide range of sources for attractive classical motifs, and then arranged them in a richly unified scheme.

Look at the plans (Engravings 5 and 21) to see how ingeniously this is done. The space Adam creates appears square, though the actual room is not. By dividing off the strip to one end, Adam is able to make each wall within the columns strictly symmetrical, and to conceal the awkward access to closets and turret stairs. (And you may have worked out from the plan that these turret stairs must have been used to bring the food from the kitchens in the basement to the Great Dining Room.) Finally, remember that this Ante-room was for servants out of livery and for tradesmen. Presumably those of the status of Robert Adam would be expected to wait here until the Duke was ready to see them.

5.2 The Long Gallery, Syon

EXERCISE I want you now to apply the sort of analysis I have used on the Hall and Ante-room to the Long Gallery at Syon. Read what Adam has to say about this room in the description of the plan of Syon, and look at the illustrations (Engravings 17–19 and Pls 56–61). Then try to answer the following three questions:

How does Robert Adam make a classical composition for this space?

How far does his composition accord with the principles set out in the *Works*?

Can we learn anything from the way this room is illustrated in the *Works* about Adam's likely attitude to this composition?

DISCUSSION The first thing to recognize, it seems to me, is the awkwardness of this space. Adam himself complains that it is too narrow and too low (Preface I description of Syon House). It is the former long gallery of the Jacobean house, and is far too long to be suited to the standard symmetrical classical decoration; yet Adam does manage to turn it into one of his most unforgettable spaces. The gallery is broken only by one large window recess at the mid-point, and the decoration is all kept quite flat and delicate, in comparison with the Hall. Yet Adam goes to some lengths to break up the apparent space. The ceiling is divided up by moulded ribs into a series of interconnecting hexagons with alternating roundels at their centres. The carpet makes no attempt to echo this, although the pattern shown in Engraving 17 does have interconnecting hexagons on a smaller scale. Presumably Adam recognized that the overall pattern of the floor in a space such as this would not easily be seen. This seems to me to be an extension of his principle that the scale of an order needed to be adjusted to its precise location.

When it comes to the walls, Adam is yet more ingenious. You can see from the plan and the section in Engraving 18 and Col. Pl. 12 how the long wall is divided up into a series of symmetrical tripartite compositions, rather echoing a series of Roman triumphal arches. Each door is flanked by square-headed niches (Pl. 59), and the fireplaces are flanked by semi-circular niches, filled with bookcases (Pl. 58), while in between are groups of three bookcases. This is essential for variety, which was another of Adam's principles. I think it also helps to give a sense of movement, though it is not quite the movement by advance and recess that he describes in Preface I footnote 1. The delicacy of the individual elements and the overall unity can be seen from Col. Pl. 11; and Col. Pls 12 and 13 show how Adam experimented with different colour combinations. The combination of fine detail with a uniform overall scheme seem to me to be vital to the success of this room. I think the small scale of the painted decoration is important in breaking up the space. The small classical pictures, for instance, can only be seen from fairly close up, and so would be best appreciated by small groups congregated round a fireplace – just how it might be used 'for the reception of company before dinner; or for the ladies to retire to after it' (Preface I description of Syon House).

There is still the usual ingenious manipulation of classical elements to create variety within uniformity, and to overcome the difficulties of space. The main order is a series of elongated Corinthian pilasters on pedestals, rising to the ceiling. Similar, though richer, pilasters without pedestals flank the doorways, and link to a continuous frieze that is supported by a minor order of Ionic pilasters that seem to hide behind the major order (Col. Pl. 12). These features all fit well with the usual rules for assembling classical ornament; but there was a problem in that the windows of the original structure did not fit with the pattern of bays that Adam had designed for his inner wall. Instead he simply adopted a different rhythm for the window wall. This would be fine, except that each of the major pilasters on the inner wall rises to meet one of the ceiling ribs. On the outer wall this link breaks down altogether. However, as that wall would always be in shadow, and one would be more likely to be looking out of the window than up at the ceiling, Adam clearly thought he could get away with it. The same goes for the end walls (see Col. Pl. 11).

It was perfectly acceptable to cheat in that way to achieve a balanced composition. Adam had done the same in the Ante-room. If you compare Pl. 60 with the plan, you will see just how far he went in this case. The lower three shelves of 'books' are false and conceal double doors to a window and steps to the garden. To the left is a completely concealed door to a closet in the turret. Pl. 63 shows the interior of the matching turret at the other end of the gallery, which you can see is a complex variation on the themes established in the Gallery itself. If you look at the plan you will see that it is a tiny room, less than nine feet in diameter. It would have been an ideal space for confidential meetings of two.

It may seem odd that such an ingenious scheme should be left for publication until after Adam's death. The three plates of the Gallery do not appear until Volume III of the *Works*. By then it was being described as the Library, and perhaps its function as a space for assembly had rather been taken over by the Great Drawing Room. Perhaps, too, the rarity and ingenuity of the scheme were, by 1822, recognized as worth publicizing in a way that would have been less appropriate for an architect setting out to impress potential clients. He might reasonably hope they would be building new houses that would not include old fashioned Jacobean long galleries. At any rate, if, like me, you are impressed by this room, you should remember that Adam himself chose not to illustrate it in either Volume I or II of the *Works*.

6 Robert Adam's practice and country house building

You may feel that Syon is entirely exceptional, and, of course, there would be some truth in that, for few of his commissions involved such a radical reworking of so intractable a structure. But as we have already seen it was not by any means his only important country house commission in the first decade of his practice. We need now to examine the principles of the *Works* against some other houses. In the next sections we shall look at Mellerstain in Lothian and Kedleston in Derbyshire, and in detail at Kedleston in TV7. You may also be able to visit a Robert Adam house in your area, or another eighteenth-century country house, and consider how far the principles of the *Works* are revealed there.[2]

I do not have space for a detailed discussion of all the rooms in each house. Instead I want to offer an analysis of key aspects of both houses, which I shall discuss in general terms. You will need to have the *Illustration Book* by you for this section.

---

[2] You will find useful information about houses in your area in the annual British Leisure Publications booklet, *Historic Houses, Castles and Gardens Open to the Public*, and in county by county guides, *The Buildings of England* (see References).

As you study each set of plates, ask yourself the following questions (not all the questions are applicable to every plate):

How is this house laid out?

How does this room function in relation to the house as a whole?

How is it serviced?

What order is used?

How does the finished item relate to the design?

What other decorative elements are used?

Are they typical of Adam's work as described in the *Works*?

What does this show about Adam's reaction to the ancient world?

I shall make some general points, and you will find the factual information you need in the captions of each plate.

1 House and Park. Every estate was founded on an individual basis. There were important government salaries for some, while other landlords, such as the Hopes of Hopetoun (see TV4, 'Scotland and the Enlightenment'), were engaged in early industrialization. However, most great men still drew the bulk of their wealth from agricultural land. The actual house was the chief glory of each estate; but the park and estate together were also crucial. Improvements and efficiency were vital in increasing income to pay for building. Adam's designs for a modern farm at Kedleston (Pls 101–2) indicate his readiness to link the need for improvement with the taste for classicism; though the lowlier status of the buildings is revealed in the lack of ornament. A part of each estate was generally laid out as parkland where client and architect could indulge the imagination more freely (Pls 103–8). Most park buildings had a genuine function (Pls 73–5); but there was less need for formality than in the principal public rooms of the house itself.

2 Plans. Begin by studying the plans (Engraving 5 and Pls 89–91 and 109). The main rooms of state are on the first floor or *piano nobile*, referred to by Adam as the principal floor. You will notice that both Syon and Kedleston have complete circuits of state rooms, which would be only for occasional use. At Mellerstain they open off one another *en suite*. In each house, almost the whole of the floor is given over to rooms of state: the family actually lived in private apartments, often in a separate wing (Pls 92–3 and 110). We do not have much accurate information about the sizes of households. Lord Scarsdale had five sons and two daughters, but not all families were as large. As for servants, plans at Kedleston show beds for about two dozen servants, but that number will have been much increased by gardeners, grooms and day servants, such as those working in the laundry. Presumably the household at Syon was substantially larger, while that at Mellerstain may have been about the same size. Although there were some grand or family rooms in the rustic, or ground floor, that would be largely given over to servants. Before you condemn this as discriminatory look carefully at Pl. 88, at the sizes of some of the service rooms, and at the exterior views of the houses, to see how well lit they were. Although the rustic was much lower than the *piano nobile* (Pl. 95) and in some cases sunk

into the ground (cf. Pls 110–11), it was always more like a ground floor than a basement.

3   Symmetry and variety. Symmetry was a key element in all classical designing. Check to see how this is achieved in the planning of houses, rooms and individual decorative schemes. You might think that such attention to symmetry would be too constraining for Adam to achieve 'novelty and variety'. Consider how successful he is in this, and whether you find the variety within the narrow range of classicism sufficiently interesting. You can certainly argue that endless variations on a relatively limited range of themes is bound to be boring (some would say this of eighteenth-century music too). Notice where Adam breaks out of the classical straightjacket in designs for ornamental buildings (Pls 103–5). Finally at Mellerstain, Adam rejects his father's classical design (Pl. 110) in favour of a castellated style, an atavistic echo of the baronial that is nonetheless strictly symmetrical.

4   Designs and designing. It is important to remember that Adam not only designed many more buildings and rooms than were actually built, but also provided alternative designs, particularly for the major features; for it was the client's taste, after all, that had to be satisfied. The various plans and elevations of Kedleston show you how a layout might be changed as the house progressed. A comparison of Pls 90 and 91 shows how the extent of Kedleston was reduced; and if you compare Pls 77 and 91 you can see that the two outer rooms on the plan were never built. Nonetheless Adam produced detailed designs (Col. Pls 16–19, 12 and Pl. 100) showing alternative versions of decoration. Pl. 125 shows how a room design was laid out, with the four walls and ceiling shown in plan and elevation. The sequence of fireplaces from Syon (Pls 67–70) shows how a design could be modified; and several of the ceiling drawings are only partly completed. These drawings, like designs for floors, could show two or more different decorative designs simultaneously. Did the clients always choose the most elaborate?

5   Colour. Several of Adam's drawings are painted or have colour notes on them; and he uses bright colours in his designs. You may remember that Adam had some copies of the *Works* coloured with 'the tints used in the execution'; so colour obviously mattered to him. His preference for low relief in his plaster work gave colour greater importance. However we have to remember that his own schemes were not always carried out precisely, and we must be careful when comparing his drawings with the present state of rooms, since decorations may have been altered in execution or been replaced.

6   Classical motifs. The use of plaster casts of antique sculpture was a regular feature, as were classical scenes in relief. Adam also used a wide variety of classical motifs. Two pages of designs for Mellerstain (Pls 126–7) show the way that these were drawn out before being decided on. Try and spot these motifs in the finished work. These were the sorts of details that Adam had collected in Rome. You can compare the different rooms and houses, and see whether you spot any repeats. (Of course there are a good many.)

You may not find precise answers to all the questions that I have listed above, but I hope you spend some time looking carefully at the plates. My discussion of the two main questions, on how they relate to the *Works* and how they reveal a reaction to the ancient world, is included in the following sections.

6.1 Adam and the classical sources

I think that Adam achieved in the Gallery at Syon one of his most imaginative and ingenious interiors. He managed to include references to ducal splendour and lineage in a series of portraits ranging from Charlemagne to the Duke himself (Pl. 56) and his wife, with other roundels left for completion with portraits of future Dukes. The classical scenes would be intelligible only to those with good knowledge of the ancient myths. And the ornamental motifs all had a firm ancestry in antique remains. The S-shaped flutes, for instance, below the bookcases, are derived directly from Roman sarcophagi. However, I think it is equally clear that the success of rooms such as the Gallery at Syon lies in the freedom with which Adam treats his classical sources, reassembling a variety of motifs and happily abandoning any so-called rules when his own composition demands. Although he is at pains in his book to stress his classical scholarship, and went to immense trouble to acquire drawings and casts of many antique remains, Adam is never in thrall to the tyranny of classical rules. His principle of variety ensures that, even when using strictly classical motifs, he always produces new combinations and novel compositions. He makes different uses of particular features such as screens and columns or motifs such as tripods, gryphons or garlands. Adam's success lies in producing varied and delightful spaces that suit the individual needs of patrons for attractive and/or imposing homes; one must not forget the function of these eighteenth-century country houses as both homes and centres of patronage and influence.

6.2 Adam and his patrons

It was no secret that for architects, patronage by the nobility was an essential prerequisite for success, and well over a quarter of Adam's 84 country house commissions were for peers. Not that all those were brand new houses; far from it. In fact only 7 of Adam's houses in England, Wales and Ireland were entirely or substantially new buildings, whereas 41 were alterations or extensions or minor works. The situation is reversed in Scotland, where he built 23 country houses almost entirely from scratch, and undertook only 10 commissions for alterations. To some extent this is a reflection of the political situation. In England, Adam was a member of the second generation of architects working for established families, many of whom had begun to build before he set up in practice. In Scotland, where there had been a great deal of building at the end of the seventeenth century, more of those with money to spend in the later half of the eighteenth century had become wealthy after (and in some cases because of) the Jacobite rising of 1745. But one must be careful not to take a simplistic view of this, and it is equally possible to argue that the Scottish nobility and gentry seem to have been readier to start afresh in their determination to achieve a complete work of art as the centrepiece of their estates. It is important to remember that each house and each patron had a history, and that the motives for building (and for employ-ing Robert Adam) were probably mixed.

In the case of Syon it easy to see how the wealthy Sir Hugh Smith-son was keen to celebrate his accession to the Earldom of Northumbria, recreated on the petition of his father-in-law the Duke of Somerset. Ked-leston was a new creation, replacing an old house for Nathaniel Curzon, and was begun almost immediately after he inherited the estate. His elev-ation to the peerage as 1st Baron Scarsdale in 1761, by which time he had given Robert Adam sole charge of the new house and park, may simply have confirmed him in his determination to go through with building a mansion that would also be a complete work of art. Mellerstain is perhaps more interesting, as it was not built for a nobleman but for George Hamilton Baillie who was only the second son of Lord Binning. He inherited the estate in 1759, and yet did not begin to build until 1770. So his house can be seen as simply the proper setting for an established gentleman of ample means and taste. In each case we can see that Adam has been true to his principles of novelty and variety, yet since all three houses are decorated in classical styles, it is clear that Adam and his patrons felt there were accepted standards of taste.

6.3   Design and craftsmanship

What is also abundantly clear in all these houses is that Robert Adam's firm was not only able to provide suites of rooms that offered novelty, var-iety and gaiety, but was able also to carry out the decoration, to the highest standards. Adam claimed to be able to design everything, down to the last candle-sconce and doorknob. In fact very few houses were designed *and* furnished by Adam. At Syon he is known to have designed some mirrors (or pier glasses) and tables (see Pls 64–6 and 71–2 and Col. Pl. 10), for which there are entries in the Syon House account book. He also probably designed the benches in the gallery and the carpet in the Great Drawing Room (Col. Pl. 13). Adam's furniture designs tend to rely on gilded and painted ornament, just like his room decoration. At Mellerstain the pier glass and table in the Music Room (Pl. 114) are so similar to those that Adam is known to have designed for Kenwood, that they are attributed to him, though it appears there is no other furniture by Adam in the house. At Kedleston, Adam certainly designed more fur-niture, especially in the Dining Room (Pl. 99); but it is also clear that he was working with other craftsmen designers, many of whom were inde-pendent, or, even if trained in Adam's office, continued to work for Lord Scarsdale after Adam had ceased to work for him (Col. Pl 22 and Pls 80 and 85–6).

Without consulting account books, which often do not survive, it is sometimes impossible to be sure exactly what was designed by Adam and what by others. This in itself is an indication of how all-embracing was this 'revolution' in taste that Adam claimed to have brought about. How-ever, another aspect of the completeness and homogeneity of an Adam scheme is the quality and range of craftsmen involved. To begin with, Robert Adam would not himself have done all the drawings. He may well have done some of the room designs, such as Col. Pl. 16, but there were, in addition, a great many detail drawings, such as Pls 64 and 128–9 which were produced by draughtsmen whom he trained. George Richardson, for instance, accompanied Robert's brother James Adam on the Grand

Tour and then worked in the office as a draughtsman for eighteen years before setting up on his own. He completed the decoration at Kedleston, and the fireplace (Pl. 79) is by him.

The designs then had to be turned into reality, and that involved a whole group of craftsmen. Some were independent workers, such as Joseph Rose the plasterer, who carried out most of Adam's plaster work. Often Adam commissioned work from other producers, such as Josiah Wedgwood or Matthew Boulton, who, between them, supplied pottery and ormolu (gilt brass ornaments) to Adam's designs. Several painters relied heavily on Adam for commissions for decorative work, such as Angelica Kauffman and, to a greater extent, her third husband Antonio Zucchi, who came to England at Adam's invitation, engraved plates for the Spalatro book and painted numerous ceilings for Adam. In addition Adam built up a reliable group of carpenters, joiners, carvers and modellers whose work is found again and again in his houses. You may like to look through the illustrations of any one of the houses and try to decide what range of craftsmen were involved in each room.

7 Architecture and society

It remains to consider how these houses worked, and how the classical taste, of which Adam was so much a part, was used by the nobility and gentry of Britain. Syon, Kedleston and Mellerstain all revolve round a sequence of formal rooms, and they were all created by great landlords as the formal centrepieces of their estates. The spaces, therefore are designed for a very formal lifestyle. Even the furniture was often designed for a particular place in a particular room, and was not intended to be moved. Adam describes the way Syon functioned quite carefully, though he provides no detail of the arrangements below stairs or of the upper floor. But then his interest, and that of his clients, was in the formal rooms, a sequence of connecting public spaces on three sides of the square, linked to a range of private rooms for the Duke and Duchess on two sides. At Kedleston the division between public and private was greater because the whole of the centre block on the *piano nobile* was given over to rooms of state, with separate wings for the family and for the kitchen. (This house is discussed in greater detail in TV7, 'Kedleston Hall'.) Kedleston was laid out in the most modern way with a circuit of connecting communal rooms round top-lit stairs. Mellerstain, with its single range of state rooms, follows an older layout, although it is the latest of the houses; so, obviously, one should be careful about discussing development from so small a sample.

In all three houses the upper floor is given over to guest bedrooms, though both Kedleston and Mellerstain retain the traditional State Bedroom on the *piano nobile*. It is difficult to be sure how often these were used, but they were reserved for really important visitors, who would sleep, eat and entertain there.

All three houses have grand stairs and service stairs, but these were more complicated to arrange. At Syon the service stairs are squeezed in wherever possible, and much the same is true of Kedleston. At Kedleston (Pl. 96) the grand stairs were originally designed to rise only to the *piano nobile*. At Mellerstain the grand stairs rise from the *piano nobile* to the upper floor, and have to be rather squeezed in, rising over the doorway from the hall to the main corridor and the state rooms; but Mellerstain seems to have much more efficient service stairs rising the full height of the building in each wing. Because it was mainly a new building with fewer formal rooms, perhaps there was more space and money for efficient and comfortable circulation.

It has been easy to find parallels between these houses, which were all created for members of the same narrow class. But Mellerstain also has one room of state, the Great Gallery (Pl. 124), which is not shown on the floor plan. It runs from front to back of the house on the top floor of the central block. If it looks slightly plain it is because it was never finished, and the patterned ceiling designed by Adam was never completed. However, in a cold, wet, northern climate, such a room with its fine views over the estate would be most useful, supplying a space for indoor exercise. It also allows access onto the roofs where the leads are spacious enough to permit walking about. In this sense, Mellerstain seems to me to be much more of a house to live in than are Kedleston and Syon. As at Syon, the floor below the state rooms is used for servants. To the north these rooms are in a semi-basement, but on the southern side they are well-lit ground floor apartments.

At Syon the arrangement of Dining Room and Drawing Rooms is well described (Preface I description of Syon). The effect of this segregation of the sexes was that the dining room came to be seen as a male preserve, and again at Kedleston it is well separated from the Drawing Room. Actually, at Kedleston, the whole of one side of the house is given over to elegant pursuits with the Music Room and the Library, the latter also being principally a male preserve. All three houses have libraries, that at Mellerstain being probably the finest room in the house, which is an indication of the importance accorded to an educated taste. I find it interesting that the Library at Mellerstain echoes the Gallery at Syon with its deep frieze containing roundels with portraits (busts this time, and not all of the family) and classical scenes. There is another echo too in the use of S-shaped fluting on the cupboards beneath the mirrors.

What strikes me in comparing the interiors of these three houses is the close similarity afforded by the Adam style of decoration. No two rooms are the same, even in one house; yet in each house we find similar motifs, and similar arrangements. A cynic might argue that Adam was adept at playing the changes on a limited range. The point, however, is surely that Adam, in composing in the classical style, was inevitably making 'new combinations of those images which have been previously gathered and deposited in the memory' (Reynolds, *Discourse II*). In that sense, one could regard the classical tradition as something of a straightjacket. This accords with the sentiments in the frontispiece to the *Works* (Pl. 38) where the young architect is directed to Greece and Italy as the fount of all knowledge. Adam's skill was to have ranged wide and collected models from a great variety of antique sources which he then assembled in combinations of his own inventing.

I have been chiefly concerned with interiors, that is, with controlled settings against which the owners and their guests mingled as members of the upper classes of enlightened Britain. The exteriors tell a different story, and they were always seen in relation to the specific estate on which the house was built. Syon retains something of its ancient aspect, while Kedleston is set down as a newly-created temple in Lord Scarsdale's own

Elysium. Mellerstain is built in the castle idiom, not unlike Syon. This was a style that Adam used more frequently in Scotland and in his later years. At first sight it contrasts rather oddly with the classical interiors, though you should notice how rigidly symmetrical his building is. Nonetheless this castle style, with its echoes of a baronial past, does represent a new taste that became increasingly popular as the century progressed. It has been linked to the rise of romantic sensibility which you will be studying later in the course. Certainly it is not a part of the ordered rational system of designing that was derived from carefully researched precedents in the architecture of the ancients. You will have to make up your own mind whether that classical architecture really constitutes Enlightened Architecture. The question is whether architecture, as opposed to the arguments of the *philosophes*, can truly embody abstract ideas. On the other hand, classical architecture does seem to centre on principles of rationality, veneration for the ancients, and so on, which are all characteristic of Enlightenment writing. However, if novelty and variety were among the tenets of Adam's Works, it should hardly be surprising that, after a decade or so of his classicism, a change of style was wanted.

8 Additonal note

Please note that this study was written in the bicentenary year of Robert Adam's death. That event has encouraged a new wave of research into his work; and it is already clear that there are likely to be major developments in Adam scholarship in the next few years. In particular, Eileen Harris is engaged on detailed work on household accounts and other archival material for Syon and elsewhere which may well reveal interesting differences between the description offered by Adam in *The Works* and what was actually built. If you enjoyed this study, you should keep an eye out for new publications on Robert Adam.

9 References

Cherry, B. and Pevsner, N. (eds) (various dates) *The Buildings of England*, Penguin, Harmondsworth. (County guides to the architecture of England. Parallel series are available for parts of Wales, Scotland and Ireland.)

Reynolds, J. (1965 edn) *Discourses*, edited by S.O. Mitchell, Bobbs-Merrill, Indianapolis, New York and Kansas City.

10 Further reaading

Beard, G. (1978) *The Work of Robert Adam*, Bartholomew, Edinburgh.

Fleming, J. (1962) *Robert Adam and his Circle in Edinburgh and Rome*, Murray, London.

Harris, E. (1963) *The Furniture of Robert Adam*, Tiranti, London.

Harris, L. (1987) *Robert Adam and Kedleston*, National Trust, London.

Summerson, J. (1963 edn) *Architecture in Britain 1530–1830*, Penguin, Harmondsworth.

Yarwood, D. (1970) *Robert Adam*, Batsford, London.

Gibbon's The Decline and Fall of the Roman Empire

*Prepared for the Course Team by
Richard Allen, Lorna Hardwick,
Anne Laurence and Antony Lentin*

Contents

Gibbon's The Decline and Fall of the Roman Empire *(Study weeks 12 and 13)*

Studies/Texts	Radio	TV	AC	Set Books
Studies, I	–	–	AC1633 (green)	–
Texts, I				

In the first week, you should complete the first four sections of this Study. In the second week, you should work on sections 5–7.

Gibbon's The Decline and Fall of the Roman Empire

1 Introduction

ANTONY LENTIN

Figure 47
Joshua Reynolds,
Edward Gibbon, *1779, oil
on canvas, 76 cm. × 61 cm.
(Photograph by Tom Scott;
reproduced by courtesy of the
National Galleries of
Scotland.)*

The aim of this study is to help you to enjoy and appreciate two selected chapters from Gibbon's *The History of the Decline and Fall of the Roman Empire*. Published between 1776 and 1788, it was acclaimed by, amongst others, Hume (himself a historian as well as a philosopher), both as a triumphant realization of eighteenth-century ideas on how history ought to be written, and as a literary epic, comparable to the works of classical antiquity which Hume (as a writer on aesthetics) held out as models for emulation in *Of the Standard of Taste*.

The work is a monumental one, beginning with the emergence of the Imperial form of government in Rome after the death of Julius Caesar, and continuing down to the collapse of the Eastern Empire with the capture of Constantinople by the Turks in 1453. We have chosen as your text Chapter IX, on the state of Germany in the middle of the second century AD (from volume I, published 1776), and most of Chapter XX, on the establishment of Christianity as the state religion of the Roman empire, by the emperor Constantine in the early fourth century (from volume II, published 1781). You are also referred to a short extract from the beginning of Chapter I (on the Roman Empire in the age of the Antonines (second century AD) and another from the end of Chapter XXXVIII (on the collapse of the western empire in the fifth century AD).[1]

Please note that you are *not* required to know anything about Roman history beyond the bare facts summed up in the outline headings and marginal notes to Chapters IX and XX. (Table 1, p.298 gives a basic chronology.) What matters for the purpose of this study is, in every case, Gibbon's *attitude* to his subject-matter and his *treatment* of it as writer and historian. It may help your understanding of Chapters IX and XX to know that Gibbon wrote of *The Decline and Fall*: 'I have described the triumph of barbarism and religion' (Gibbon, 1980 edn, p.553). Gibbon on 'barbarism and religion' indeed forms the main focus-points of this fortnight's work, together with his reactions to classical antiquity. While you should read the set text in its entirety, you should concentrate your close reading on those parts relating directly to these themes, and each week's study will include a section to help you develop your ability to do this.

---

[1] In the study of Robert Adam, reference is also made to brief excerpts from Chapters XIII and XIV on Roman architecture under Diocletian and Constantine. These excerpts appear in *Texts* I but are not required reading for the Gibbon study.

Edward Gibbon was born in 1737, the son of a well-to-do but eccentric and domineering Tory squire. He was almost entirely self-taught, an omnivorous and precocious bookworm. In 1752, his father sent him to Magdalen College, Oxford. Carried away by the study of religious books, he converted to the Church of Rome, a piece of 'childish revolt', as he later called it (Gibbon, 1891 edn, p.104).

Five years at Lausanne (1753–8) in the care of an educated Calvinist minister, had a crucial influence on his development. He returned to England cured, he wrote, of his 'religious folly'. He was an accomplished Latinist, had a perfect command of French, and combined a passion for French literature with an interest in the new school of 'philosophical' history represented by Voltaire (who settled in Switzerland in 1755). In 1761, he wrote his first work, an *Essay on the Study of Literature* (*Essai sur l'étude de la littérature*) in French.

Between 1763 and 1765 he travelled to the continent on the Grand Tour, meeting the *philosophes* d'Alembert, Diderot, Helvétius and d'Holbach at Paris, before proceeding to Italy. 'It was at Rome', he states in his *Memoirs,* 'on 15 October 1764, as I sat musing amidst the ruins of the Capitol, while the barefooted friars were singing vespers in the Temple of Jupiter, that the idea of writing the decline and fall of the city first started to my mind' (Gibbon, 1891 edn, p.151).

On his father's death in 1770, Gibbon moved to London, became known as a man of fashion, joined 'The Club' patronized by Johnson, Boswell and Reynolds, and even entered Parliament.

Volume I of *The History of the Decline and Fall of the Roman Empire,* which appeared in 1776, was an instant success, though the 'notorious' Chapters XV and XVI on the rise of Christianity provoked a furore in the Church of England. Gibbon pushed on with his work, pausing only to dash off his *Vindications* in 1779 – a defence of his scholarship and a devastating riposte to his clerical critics.

In 1781 he published the second and third volumes of *The Decline and Fall.* In 1782, he decided for the sake of economy to leave England and returned to Lausanne, where he set up house with his friend Deyverdun. Here he completed his last three volumes, returning to England briefly in 1788 to enjoy their reception. In Lausanne he wrote his *Memoirs,* itself a masterpiece in miniature. His last years were clouded by the death of Deyverdun, the outbreak of the French Revolution (which he abominated, and which threatened to spill over into Switzerland) and by his own declining health, aggravated by gross corpulence and a gigantic 'hydrocele' or swelling in the scrotum. In 1793 he returned to London, where he died in 1794, aged 56.

1.1 *Approaching Gibbon*

LORNA HARDWICK

One of the reasons that Gibbon is fun to read is that he can be approached in so many different ways. In the context of the eighteenth century he is not merely a historian but also first and foremost the writer of a sophisticated literary text, as well as a source of insights on philosophical, sociological and religious issues, a witty commentator on classical values and events and an iconoclast who positively enjoys 'putting down the proud' and dispelling certainty.

Exploring these aspects of Gibbon's writing requires an equal variety of approaches. In the first week's work on this we have kept these approaches clearly differentiated, to help you to get to know Gibbon gradually. So you will start with some quite detailed help with the sheer task of reading Chapter IX (section 2 of the study). Then, you will be helped to 'mine' the text of Chapter IX, to find out how Gibbon uses and refines classical antiquity in order to explore eighteenth-century ideas (section 3). Section 4 is about eighteenth-century attitudes and writings and will help you to relate Gibbon to ideas that you will encounter in other parts of the course. The 'voices' of the different authors in this part of the Study are quite distinct and each intentionally emphasizes his or her perspective on the material. Chapter IX is entitled *The State of Germany till the Invasion of the Barbarians, in the Time of the Emperor Decius.* We chose it because it introduces one of the reasons Gibbon gives for the decline of the Empire – namely, barbarism. Studying the rise of the 'barbarians' in western Europe also gives an additional and sometimes unexpected insight into the origins of the western European culture of Gibbon's day (and indeed of our own time). Our other chosen chapter is XX and this deals with the institution of Christianity as the state religion of the Roman Empire – the other main cause of decline, according to Gibbon.

You will study Chapter XX in your second week's work on Gibbon, which will aim to help you to integrate more closely the approaches introduced in Week 1. Gibbon will be discussed as a historian (section 5) and there will again be some preliminary help with reading (section 6), but then you will be asked to use the analytical skills you have developed and will join the debate about the extent to which Gibbon is subverting the conventions of writing about the past and whether he is questioning the basis of institutionalized religion (section 7). By the end of the Study you may find that some of your own assumptions about classical antiquity and reactions to it have been challenged.

As you work through the Study, you will find many references to wit and irony. Humour and laughter are personal to each of us, as well as being culturally defined. So don't worry if you don't laugh in the 'right' places. It is true that Gibbon often invites us to join a laughter of *superiority*. But don't be intimidated into sharing his social attitudes or feel excluded because you cannot respond to all his allusions (many of his eighteenth-century readers would not have known these either). Even if we could do the impossible and *recreate* eighteenth-century reactions, we would still bring additional present-day responses to the text. So make the most of these and of the laughter of *surprise*. This is partly created by Gibbon's manipulation of language but also partly comes from our own experience and understanding – which may even increase our enjoyment. Notice places where you smile and see how these increase and change as you read more Gibbon. Sometimes, too, you may be startled and shocked – just like Gibbon's eighteenth-century readers.

Table 1 Outline chronology

DATES	EMPERORS	EVENTS	DISCUSSED BY GIBBON
27 BC–AD 14	Augustus	Establishment of imperial form of government.	Ch.I
		AD 9 Varian disaster in Germany (defeat of Roman legions).	Ch.I
AD 14–68	Julio-Claudians	AD 43 Roman invasion of Britain.	Ch.I
AD 69–96	Flavians		Ch.IX
AD 96–180	'Golden Age' (Nerva, Trajan, Hadrian, Antoninus Pius, Marcus Aurelius)	Roman historian Tacitus (born *c.*AD 56) writes on Britain and Germany	Ch.I & Ch.IX
	Gibbon's 'happy period'		
AD 240–305	Includes 25 emperors in 47 years (only one died in bed!)	'Barbarian' invasions	
AD 284–305	Diocletian	AD 302 Great Persecution of Christians begins	Ch.XIII (on Diocletian's palace)
AD [306]–337	Constantine	AD 306 Begins progress through Imperial ranks	Ch.XIV (on arch of Constantine)
AD 312		Battle of Milvian Bridge and Conversion of Constantine	Ch.XX
AD 313		Edict of Milan (Regulations favouring Christians)	Ch.XX
AD 324		Foundation of Constantinople	
AD 410		End of Roman rule in Britain. Sack of Rome	
AD 476		Second wave of German invaders. Fall of Roman empire in the west. Eastern, Byzantine empire based on Constantinople continued for nearly 1,000 years	Ch.XXXVIII
1453		Conquest of Constantinople by the Turks	

2 Reading Gibbon I

RICHARD ALLEN

As you work through this section I hope you will develop your own sense of how Gibbon's style works in presenting his history to eighteenth-century and present-day readers; but three preliminary remarks may be helpful:

1   Despite the extraordinary length of *The Decline and Fall*, Gibbon's aim was to write as briefly as possible; his style can generally be described as 'condensed'.

2   Gibbon's aim was to be as objective a historian as possible, but this does not mean that his writing is impersonal. Throughout we should hear the sound of his voice and feel his personality. His sentences often gain from being read aloud. This is why we have included readings from parts of the work on the cassette.

3   Gibbon's mind was saturated with classical Latin and Greek literature. In his *Memoirs*, for example, he notes that between 1756 and 1758, 'I indulged myself in a second, and even a third perusal of Terence, Virgil, Horace, Tacitus etc. ... I always consulted the most learned of ingenious commentators, Torrentius and Dacier on Horace, Catrou and Servius on Virgil, Lipsius on Tacitus, Meziriac on Ovid, etc.' (Gibbon, 1984, p.98). Neither the admiration he felt for these writers, nor the effect this has on his style, can be exaggerated.

2.1 Chapter IX

EXERCISE   First try to make your own way into Chapter IX. Set aside 30 minutes and begin reading. (You might also like to listen to the opening to Chapter IX on AC1633). As you finish each paragraph look back to Gibbon's marginal heading and jot it down so that you gradually build up a sense of the meaning of the chapter. If you lose your way, or if you have not reached the end of the chapter as the 30 minutes come to an end, use the marginal notes to catch a sense of the remainder. Finally, try to condense Gibbon's marginal notes into as brief a summary of the chapter as possible.

DISCUSSION   My own summary is as follows:

Gibbon describes the extent and climate of Germany along with the origins of its people. He comments on their culture, or lack of it, and their wild character – all the opposite of what he finds in Roman culture. The crude political and religious structure is described and an account is given of their history, especially in relation to Rome.

Summarizing the content at this level of generality plainly leaves out a good deal of detail which may well have perplexed you as you read. A dictionary or a map will help sort out the geography, and a glance back to Table 1 will help you place the events chronologically; but in the paragraph with the marginal title 'Want of arms and of discipline' you might have faltered at the sentence beginning 'During the civil wars that followed the death of Nero …'. Faced with footnote 19 in the chapter most modern readers can only feel a sense of inadequacy before the text.

EXERCISE   What might this tell us about Gibbon's original readers and his expectations of them?

DISCUSSION   Gibbon's eighteenth-century readers had a different education from most of us, for whom classics no longer form part of the basic curriculum. Some original readers would have shared Gibbon's own impressive familiarity with the classics and at least one tried to trip him up on the accuracy of his use of sources, but we should not assume that all of them shared his level of erudition or that he addressed himself only to the erudite. Only the best educated would be able to move freely within Gibbon's historical world.[2] For many eighteenth-century readers, references such as 'that artful and intrepid Batavian', would be read simply as part of the flow of a historical narrative; the arrival of such characters on the scene would be akin to the arrival of a new character in a novel. Difficult footnotes first buttress the authority of Gibbon's account against the attacks of scholars, but secondly reinforce in the minds of other readers a sense of the author's wisdom and experience.

EXERCISE   How is our own present-day reading likely to relate to eighteenth-century readings?

DISCUSSION   Gibbon now often occupies an ambiguous place between history and literature, and approaches to the text are likely to be as concerned with the way he writes as they are with the accuracy of his history. This is reflected in this section of the study, where our aim is not to set out what classical literature Gibbon knew – following up lists of obscure names in large reference books – but to analyse how the text *works* and to begin exploring how the classics stand behind and influence the style of his writing and his judgement.

2.2 *Approaching the Gibbon sentence*

Let us now move from the argument of Chapter IX to look, slowly, at the sentences in a particular paragraph. I have chosen, fairly arbitrarily, the paragraph which has the marginal title 'Its effect on the native' (*Texts*, I, p.247). Listen to the paragraph on AC1633, then read it in your text.

---

[2]   Peter Gay refers to echoes of the classics as 'conventional flourishes imposed by the taste of the … time and the pretensions of … readers' (Gay, 1970, p.43).

EXERCISE   Mark and number the sentences in the paragraph for easy reference and then try to isolate a core of words in the first sentence without which it would make no sense.

DISCUSSION   To me the core consists of eleven words: 'difficult to ascertain ... the influence of the climate of ancient Germany'.

The sentence is built around this core as follows:

(a) *it is* — (a) a neutral opening rather than 'I know' or 'I think'

(b) *difficult to ascertain* — (b) first core words

(c) *and easy to exaggerate* — (c) core words immediately elaborated and qualified

(d) *the influence of the climate of ancient Germany* — (d) core words again

(e) *over the minds* — (e) sentence develops

(f) *and bodies* — (f) another qualifying phrase introduced

(g) *of the natives* — (g) sentence complete

Describing the sentence in this way perhaps makes it seem awkward and broken, but a clear sense of structure can quickly emerge if one imagines the sentence in a more diagrammatic form. Using the letter in brackets as labels the sentence might then look something like this:

$$(a) \cdots \begin{cases} \cdots (b) \cdots \\ \cdots (c) \cdots \end{cases} \cdots (d) \cdots \begin{cases} \cdots (e) \cdots \\ \cdots (f) \cdots \end{cases} \cdots (g)$$

Gibbon's writing and his sentence structure are very varied but this is quite typical of one kind of sentence. It achieves two things in my view. First it implants in the sentence the impression of a mind reflecting on the issues, turning back after (b) and (e) to add some qualification or elaboration before concluding the statement. In turn the reader is prompted to this kind of reflection. Second it is a very economical structure, testifying to the desire for condensation to which I referred above; disentangling the sentences into some simpler form would inevitably involve using more words and risk introducing repetition.

2.3   A classical style

Furthermore, the structure of this kind of sentence can be related to Gibbon's own reverence for the classics and to the way a 'classical' style developed as a model of good writing in English, geared to values embodied in *The Decline and Fall.* There is space only to touch on the issues here, and I should emphasize that I am selecting just one form of sentence structure from the many used by the authors to whom I refer. That said, there are immediate similarities between the sentence we have been examining and ones in Tacitus' *Germania*, which Gibbon used as a primary source for Chapter IX. As a simple example, this is a translation of how Tacitus describes the houses of the Germans which Gibbon describes as 'open on every side to the eye of indiscretion or jealousy' (*Texts*, I, p.257):

> They lived separated and scattered, [depending on whether] a spring, or a meadow, or a wood pleased: villages they laid out not in our way with buildings next to each other and connected: each house by a space is surrounded whether as a remedy against the mischance of fire or ignorance of building.[3]

The parallelism of 'separated and scattered' and the use of 'or' are both methods one can find repeated in Gibbon. Comparing the length of the translation above with the original Latin also shows how, given his desire for conciseness, Gibbon must have been constantly frustrated that English required more words than Latin.

Further evidence for the argument that the classics influenced both the thought of educated Englishmen and the style in which they wrote, can be found in the way Lord Sheffield finds it possible to express his sense of loss at the death of his friend Gibbon only by borrowing 'the forcible language of Tacitus'. Tacitus' sentence, which Sheffield quotes in the original Latin and which appears below in literal translation, shows again the structure I have been describing:

To me apart from the bitterness of a friend's loss

(a)   (b)

it is an added grief that to sit by his sick-bed,

(d)   (c)

to comfort his fainting spirit, to take our fill of gazing [at him]

(e)   (f)   (g)

and embracing [him], was denied [me].

(h)   (i)

The pattern of this sentence is

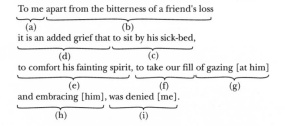

---

[3]   The translation here and in the next quotation purposely follows the word order of the Latin; both are adapted from that given in The Loeb Classical Library (Tacitus, 1970 edn) where the Latin texts can be found on pp.155 and 113. See also Gibbon, 1984, p.202 for Lord Sheffield's use of Tacitus.

The extent to which Gibbon himself might be said to have formed the style of others in this classical mould in the eighteenth century is difficult to judge. However some evidence for the case that the structure became more generally available within society may be offered by citing sentences from *The Old Manor House*, a novel by Charlotte Smith published in 1793, five years after the publication of the final volume of *The Decline and Fall*. Smith was by no means uneducated when she wrote this novel, but given that she was married at the age of 14 to a brutal husband, had two children before she was eighteen and seven altogether by the age of 25, she can hardly be said to have had the same opportunities as Gibbon to develop her educational career and her knowledge of Latin texts. Yet in *The Old Manor House* we still find many sentences following the pattern I have been describing. Here is an example:

> He read, however, in a lingering expectation of hearing of Warwick, which never wholly forsook him, the list of the killed and wounded in an engagement or rather skirmish which was related in that paper; and when he read that the American soldiers, fighting in defence of their liberties (of all those *rights* which his campaign as a British officer had not made him forget were the most sacred to an *Englishman*), had marked their route with the blood which flowed from their naked feet in walking over frozen ground, his heart felt for the sufferings of the oppressed, and for the honour of the oppressors.[*]

Smith even here adds a footnote,

> [*]The perusal of the history of the American Revolution, by Ramsay, is humbly recommended to those Englishmen who doubt whether, in defence of their freedom, any other nation but their own will fight, or conquer. (Smith, 1989 edn, pp.449–50)

The same highly patterned quality, particularly marked by the use of parallel phrases and a deferring of words, found in Tacitus, Gibbon and Smith, can also be seen in the far more influential work of Jane Austen, as here in *Sense and Sensibility*, begun in 1796 but not completed until 1811:

> The whole was tied up for the benefit of this child, who, in occasional visits with his father and mother at Norland, had so far gained on the affections of his uncle, by such attractions as are by no means unusual in children of two or three years old; an imperfect articulation, an earnest desire of having his own way, many cunning tricks, and a great deal of noise, as to outweigh all the value of all the attention which, for years, he had received from his niece and her daughters. (Austen, 1933 edn, p.4)

2.4 History and story

I began by presenting the first sentence of Gibbon's paragraph rather as if it were some kind of static thing and suggested that it may help in understanding the meaning. But the Smith and Austen examples and the fact that Gibbon was composing a narrative should alert us to the way a sentence, and ultimately a paragraph and a chapter, unfolds like a story as we read. In effect each of the sentences of Gibbon's history is a story moving from the beginning to some kind of conclusion. Words such as 'and ... though ... that' show the story unfolding, but as with any good story there are points where the forward movement is blocked. The narrative pauses or turns back and a sense of suspense is created. The effect is exactly as in the everyday stories we tell ourselves, for example:

> When I was at the bus stop today *and* by the way, I had to wait ages to get on a bus *though* I was there in plenty of time *because* one had broken down *and* the one that came was full, there was a man walking along the road *and do you know what* he fell right over into the road.

The 'stories' contained in the sentences of *The Decline and Fall* are seldom as simple as this, but understanding how each unrolls is important if we are to understand how Gibbon controls the judgements we make as we read, by controlling the flow of information to us. As an example let us look at the second sentence beginning 'Many writers ...' from the paragraph with the marginal heading 'Its effects on the natives' in Chapter IX (*Texts*, I, p.247).

EXERCISE   Try to work out how the story develops in the sentence, marking forward movement and points where suspense is created.

DISCUSSION   Many writers have supposed, and most have allowed, though,
begin story   *suspend*   *suspend*
as it should seem, without any adequate proof, that the
                    story still suspended
rigorous cold of the North was favourable to long life
story continuing
and generative vigour, that the women were more fruitful,
                              half suspended again
and the human species more prolific, than in warmer
fully suspended   *forward again*
and more temperate climates.
half suspended before final completion.

EXERCISE   What is the effect of the first part of the 'story', up to 'rigorous cold'?

DISCUSSION   By the time we reach 'the rigorous' in this sentence Gibbon has put three ideas in our minds without any indication of how important each is:

1   many people have actively 'supposed' what I am about to hear;

2   most other writers are prepared to allow that it is true;

3   but really there is no adequate proof.

We are caught up in the unrolling sentence and not able to weigh the issue here because we do not yet know what it is about. When we find that out, at the end of the sentence, the certainties of 'many people' etc.

are almost forgotten. When we finish the sentence we find footnote 24. This mimics the first part of the sentence; Rudbeck is an example of the 'many writers', and the assertion that his 'authority' is suspect parallels 'without any adequate proof'. We are now able to see that this story has two subjects (as my own was about catching the bus and the man falling). It is simultaneously about the effects of the German climate and the value of the work of other historians. Both stories unroll further in the next sentence, as Gibbon 'with greater confidence' asserts his own position, and brings forward evidence from Tacitus about the strength of the Germans. Sentences 2 and 3 together present an unfolding debate; sentence 2 sets out the position of Rudbeck etc. and this is answered by the case put by Gibbon himself, disguised as 'We' and supported by Tacitus. By contrast, the first and last sentences come from a more neutral and detached voice. The last sentence in the paragraph contains the conclusion to the story; through its factual opening and its footnotes Gibbon claims to avoid easy exaggeration and to show just what the historian can 'ascertain'.

2.5   *Figurative writing*

By 'figurative writing' I mean a way of writing in which something is written about 'as if' it were something else.

EXERCISE   Read the last sentence of the paragraph we have been discussing ('The severity ...') (*Texts*, I, p.247) and see if you can spot something described 'as if' it were something else.

DISCUSSION   You might have been tempted to pick on 'severity' but it would be safer to begin with the more obvious example 'chilled the courage'. Courage, being an abstract quality, cannot be chilled; Gibbon is describing bravery turning to fear 'as if' it were warmth turning to cold in winter. You might notice also that this creates a sense of unity in the sentence since 'chilled' picks up 'winter' in the first phrase. The value of the figurative phrase lies in the way it combines the fact that the battles were hard, with the idea that the Romans were as much affected by the weather as by the actual fighting.

The effect of this kind of language varies. Most often it creates a more highly coloured meaning which makes the text more pleasant and interesting to read. But it also draws our minds away from the specifics of what is being written about and cajoles us, almost without knowing, into a particular point of view. I hope I do not need to prove the first effect here. The argument Gibbon wants to make here is that neither Germans nor Romans fight well in a foreign climate; this is expressed through 'chilled the courage of the Roman troops' on the one hand and '[the Germans] ... dissolved away in languor and sickness' on the other. Gibbon has written admiringly of the 'large and masculine limbs of the Germans and their lofty stature', but in the end the Romans seem to have the edge. For while they are merely 'chilled' in the German winter, the Germans are 'dissolved' by the Italian sun. The final comparison takes place within the 'as if' language, moreover, so we are pushed away from a more literal balancing of the forces. The footnote stands ready to reinforce the point.

2.6 Irony

The notion that words can be used to describe something *as if* it were something else is the key to understanding Gibbon's frequent use of irony. When irony is used, the gap between the things referred to and the way they are described becomes so great and so obvious that it is this gap which we seize on as we read, and we are prompted to understand the opposite of what is said. To see this process in Chapter IX, I would like you to look at the paragraph beginning 'Such rational doubt ...', with the marginal heading 'Fables and conjectures' (*Texts*, I, p.248).

EXERCISE   Look at the section beginning 'The last century ...' to '... about twenty thousand persons', and look especially at the adjectives Gibbon uses. Mark points where you think that Gibbon's intended meaning is the opposite of what he writes; look particularly at the reference to Rudbeck who appeared in footnote 24.

DISCUSSION   The reference to Rudbeck is preceded by references to 'antiquarians of profound learning'; but almost immediately things become more difficult. The phrase 'easy faith' may remind you of 'easy to exaggerate' and a gap surely opens between 'easy' and the spirit of enquiry we expect of the antiquarian. Rudbeck may be 'judicious' but there is a gap between this and 'entertaining' as well as 'zealous patriot'; moreover the story of the paragraph has already set up a contrast between 'rational doubt' and the 'superstructure of fable'. Warming to his work, Gibbon spreads his mockery to Rudbeck's country. As the sentence 'Of that delightful ...' opens, Gibbon appears to adopt Rudbeck's perspective, but his own voice immediately is heard in the bracket '(for such it appeared to a native).' The bracket closes and Rudbeck's point of view might be expected to reappear; but the gap between his claims for Sweden and the truth as it would be known by *any* admirer of the classical world creates only irony at the expense of Sweden, for example in the phrase, 'a clime so profusely favoured by Nature ...'.

EXERCISE   What is the effect of this way of writing?

DISCUSSION   The immediate effect, I hope you will agree, is to make Rudbeck's position completely untenable. The use of short sentences without any of the layering we found in the earlier paragraph further reinforces the point and marks an absence here of reflection. But as before, we end up being absorbed into Gibbon's sense of values. The ironic words are planted in the sentence by the writer and picked up as ironic by the reader, and the result is that the argument takes place entirely on Gibbon's terms. No attempt is made to give any credence to Rudbeck's case or his character; the most favourable comment made about him is that he is a 'zealous patriot', and even this is tinged with irony. The classical point of view allows no opposition.

I hope you will agree that the ironies at Rudbeck's expense are hard to miss, even to those unfamiliar with eighteenth-century prose; however this is not always the case. The first sentence of this paragraph contains a more difficult example and raises important questions about the use of irony.

EXERCISE   Look carefully at the sentence and work out the meaning, paying particular attention to the phrase 'the genius of popular vanity'.

DISCUSSION   The essential meaning is that doubt based on reason does not fit with legends and stories which appeal to the vanity of the people. The phrase is placed in a prominent position in a very short sentence, balancing 'rational doubt'; its meaning is reasonably clear in its own sentence but becomes more so from the examples in the sentence that follows. The words 'popular vanity' in themselves already have a somewhat critical tone, but the irony rests more in the play of meanings in the word 'genius'. First there is the meaning which is now most common, that is, 'a man endowed with superior faculties'. But this meaning cannot easily fit with 'of popular vanity', so that the meaning within the phrase is one which is now less common, but was important in the eighteenth century, that is, 'the ruling power of men, places, or things'.[4] In this context the second meaning may be summed up in the phrase 'the guiding spirit of popular vanity' and in this respect the sentence can take on a more neutral tone. The play between this meaning and the alternative – that popular vanity might arrogantly assume itself to be possessed of superior faculties – creates the criticism Gibbon intends.

This example throws into relief the way in which irony can depend upon author and reader working within a shared sense of values and a shared sense of language. The ironic layers of meaning Gibbon might share with his eighteenth-century readers may not automatically be released to us as present-day readers, because our frames of reference are different, but one might query whether all Gibbon's contemporary readers automatically understood these ironies? In the Rudbeck example Gibbon seems to take no chances, but here one might ask how your reading would be affected if you were Swedish, and if the lake-filled countryside of

---

[4]   The definitions here are both taken from Dr Johnson's *Dictionary.*

southern Sweden did in fact strike you as 'the Fortunate Islands' or 'even the Elysian Fields'. You might well feel as excluded from the cultured values which fill *The Decline and Fall* as one who knew nothing of classical culture.

Irony, in its simplest form, is a way of expressing criticism, but almost more importantly it comes to operate here as an indicator of whether the reader is a member of what was, in the eighteenth century, the dominant cultural community. Like the consistent use of classical references, irony works to give order to a culture.

2.7 A note on reading

Working on sentences in the way I have asked you to do in Chapter IX is a time consuming process. To go though the whole text in this way would be impractical, and in any event, would risk losing a sense of the overall narrative flow. But looking in detail at a particular sentence at regular intervals is worthwhile: it fixes Gibbon's methods in your mind and helps you to see the sheer variety of sentence and language which exists within the classical style.

3   Gibbon and the Germans

LORNA HARDWICK

As you discovered from the very first paragraph of Chapter IX, Gibbon makes it plain that he is interested in the Germans, not only because they were vigorous enemies of the Romans, but also because he regarded them as the ancestors of the western European nations of his own day – 'The most civilized nations of modern Europe issued from the woods of Germany, and in the rude institutions of those barbarians we may still distinguish the original principles of our present laws and manners' (*Texts*, I, p.245). Thus we are straightaway confronted with the rather curious paradox that the Germans are both primitive barbarians *and* in some sense a source of improvement and progress. This means that although Gibbon stresses that he is using (and sometimes reproducing) evidence from ancient historians, the perspective from which he is assessing it is governed by his own time and place. He is also rigorous in distinguishing between what is and what is not to be regarded as historical evidence, showing a very proper disregard for fabulous inventions, while drawing every ounce of entertainment from them. (Look at footnote 29, for instance.)

I suggest that if you have not already done so, you complete your reading of Chapter IX. If you have time it would be good to read the whole thing straight through once, so that you can enjoy the way in which Gibbon both stuns us with his erudition and manipulates our response by his subtle use of language. Then make some notes on these topics:

1   What are the main terms in which Gibbon describes the barbarians?

2   What does he criticize or deplore about them?

3   What does he admire?

DISCUSSION   1   Here are a few examples:
                     'wretchedly destitute' of the arts (*Texts*, I, p.249).

'in a state of ignorance and poverty which it has pleased some declaimers to dignify with the appellation of virtuous simplicity' (*Texts*, I, p.249).

'their poverty secured their freedom' (*Texts*, I, p.254).

'conjugal faith and chastity' (*Texts*, I, p.257).

exposed 'naked and unarmed to the blind terrors of superstition' (*Texts*, I, p.259)

Did you notice how frequently there is a 'sting in the tail' to Gibbon's remarks?

He loves to use striking definitions (destitution is equated with 'lacking the arts') and to introduce paradox (poverty is not usually seen as a route to freedom) or to criticize implicitly an alternative interpretation. Some eighteenth-century writers idealized primitive people as Noble Savages, untainted by the corruption of material civilization (cf. *virtuous simplicity*) while others (such as Burke) identified the primitive with dangerous wildness and threats to order. Gibbon follows neither of these trends. As you will see later, for him the savage was 'naked both in mind and body' (*Texts*, I, p.301), and note his use of the term 'enemies of civilized society' (*Texts*, I, p.299).

2   Gibbon seems to be both attracted and repelled by the way of life of the barbarians. He makes close links between their environment, life-style, social traditions and religious practices. ('The religious system of the Germans (if the wild opinions of savages can deserve that name) was dictated by their wants, their fears and their ignorance' (*Texts*, I, p.258).) They are portrayed as crude, ignorant, indolent and unskilled. Gibbon seems to think that this is mainly because of their economic and technological limitations. ('Money, in a word, is the most universal incitement, iron the most powerful instrument, of human industry; and it is very difficult to conceive by what means a people, neither actuated by the one nor seconded by the other, could emerge from the grossest barbarism' (*Texts*, I, p.251).)

Gibbon clearly regards the barbarians' failure to exploit their environment as a sign of inferiority. When the Roman Empire was as its height, they could not challenge it, because they lacked developed military discipline and arms technology (*Texts*, I, p.261) as well as social cohesion and organization, and the ability to resist the blandishments of Roman diplomacy.

3   Nevertheless, the barbarians have certain attributes which Gibbon seems to admire. They 'found some compensation for this savage state in the enjoyment of liberty' (*Texts*, I, p.254). They also showed an almost heroic military vigour. (War is presented as preferable to indolence, but civilized discourse is a better alternative.) Gibbon also comments, somewhat ambiguously, on their single-mindedness which was reflected in a clear, if brutal, moral code. ('Adulteries were punished as rare and inexpiable crimes; nor was seduction justified by example and fashion' (*Texts*, I, p.257).)

3.1 Gibbon's perspective

Although Gibbon stresses that he regards the purpose of history as instruction (*Texts*, I, p.298) the precise 'lesson' in Chapter IX seems constantly to elude us. Certainly Gibbon's own criteria for judgement of the Germans are quite hard to pin down. He uses primary sources, and especially the Roman historian Tacitus (*c.* AD 56–117) for details about the government and for evidence about the 'facts' of climate, physical environment and social custom (for example, the footnotes on pp.248–9); but his footnotes also show that he maintained a healthy scepticism about the basis of the ancient historians' judgements. For example, footnote 87 (*Texts*, I, p.258) refers to the way Tacitus '*discovers* in Germany the gods of Greece and Rome' while he ironically comments that another later source 'is positive that, under the emblems of the sun, the moon, and the fire, his pious ancestors worshipped the Trinity in unity'.

Similarly, in his discussion of German chastity he draws on evidence from Tacitus but comments that Tacitus' approach is shaped by a desire to present a contrast between German austerity and the dissolute life of upper-class Romans of the second century AD. However, he then appears to support Tacitus by including 'universal' generalizations about the effect of civilization and luxury on sexual morality.

Look again at this section (*Texts*, I, p.257). It is quite difficult to sort out Gibbon's verbal technique, which moves from Romans writing about the Germans, to generalizations about social manners, and is punctuated by asides addressed to his contemporary audience. From these we can uncover some of his own underlying assumptions (and prejudices?). The overall effect is one of counterpoint of great versatility, but how easy would it be to argue with what he says, and on what basis?

In the opening paragraph of his essay *Of the Standard of Taste* (*Texts*, I, p.195) Hume asserted that 'we are apt to call *barbarous* whatever departs widely from our own taste and apprehension'. Hume's insight has been built on in recent academic work on the portrayal of barbarism in historical and ethnographical writings. Modern scholarship has tended to stress the way barbarians are depicted as marginal, irrational or unnatural (especially in religion, social custom, diet and sexual habits) and to locate the origins of this habit in the perspectives of writers in Greece and Rome, through which it was mediated to Western consciousness (Wiedemann, 1986 and Hall, 1989).

Tales of religious oddities, cannibalism, sexual promiscuity, and so on, have been shown to create stereotypes which lead to the characterisation of so-called barbarian peoples as 'other' and 'inferior'. Sometimes the habits attributed to marginalized peoples can be demonstrated to be directly *opposite* to those of the writer's own culture, rather than historically founded on independent evidence. Examples of polarities between 'barbarian' and 'civilized' peoples can certainly be found in Chapter IX (for example, ignorant/learned; primitive/artistic; religious/secular; rustic/urban; and you will find more in Chapter XX).

However, Gibbon's discussion of the barbarian Germans seems to be a special case, because he presents them as being both in opposition to the Romans (and hence to the eighteenth-century inheritors of Roman civilization), and also, in some sense, the ancestors of contemporary Europeans and their culture (since the barbarians eventually overcame the Romans). Can we discern any clear use of *opposition* between eighteenth-century and barbarian society? (Think about Gibbon's discussion of primitive religion and the Germans' lack of art and architecture, and their lack of towns. Think also about what he admires in the society of the Germans.)

This prompts a further question. To what extent is Gibbon's approach to barbarians a reflection of eighteenth-century attitudes to the 'foreign' and 'primitive', and to what extent is it a response to the attitudes he found in Roman writers, combined with his delight in irony and in wilful ambiguity of viewpoint?

In referring to 'barbarism' the course team has generally followed Gibbon's terminology. Recent scholarship has increasingly recognized that the use of the word 'barbarian' reflects the cultural perspective of the writer and is often an exercise in self-definition. The term 'barbarianism' is sometimes used to emphasize that what is being studied is how the concept of barbarism is being defined and used by a particular writer. 'Barbarianism' is therefore used in the title of section 4. It would also be useful to consider whether at other points 'barbarianism' rather than 'barbarism' could be used to analyze what Gibbon is saying. In taking over Gibbon's terminology do we run the risk of taking on his attitudes and values without realizing it?

4 Civilization and barbarianism in eighteenth-century writing

ANNE LAURENCE

Reading Gibbon sometimes seems to involve struggling with many different kinds of material, not least the assumptions with which he wrote and those which he might expect his readers to have. He at least acknowledged his sources so that we can see what kind of reading he did and what an educated reader of the late eighteenth century might be expected to know (or at least recognize). As you have seen, there were the classical writers such as Tacitus, Pliny and Strabo, but there was also more recent material. Gibbon was widely read in history and his curiosity led him to draw eclectically on many different types of writing with different ends in view, from the retelling of ancient legends by travellers, to their dismissal by contemporary scholars. (For example he was much influenced by Simon Ockley's *History of the Saracens,* one of the first European histories of Asian peoples written from Asian sources.)

Eighteenth-century attitudes to the boundaries between civilization and barbarism were in the process of change. In the sixteenth century, when the New World was being unveiled to Europeans, it had been taken as axiomatic that the inhabitants of those lands were barbarians. However, it was not long before some Europeans started to realize that the measures which were being taken supposedly to civilize the indigenous inhabitants of the New World outstripped anything that native Americans might do for savagery. In 1580 Montaigne wrote 'those which ourselves have altered by our artificiall devices, and diverted from the common order we should rather terme savage'.

Eighteenth-century writing about new peoples tended to fall into two different categories. First, there were the accounts of sailors and naturalists, such as James Cook (whom you will study in Part C of the course) and Joseph Banks, who wrote about their voyages and what they saw, or of people like Francis Moore, a factor to the Royal African

Company, who described his own travels in inland Africa along the Gambia river. There were many moral judgements implicit in what they said, but they tried to use their observations to question what was popularly believed. Moore, for example, wrote of the Mandingo people he came across that 'The Natives, really, are not so disagreeable in their Behaviour as we are apt to imagine' (Moore, 1738, p.120).

The second kind of writing was history written from sources uncovered by the author and dealing with the past as well as the present condition of the people described. A good example of this kind of work is Father P.F.X. Charlevoix's *History and General Description of New France*, published in 1743. Charlevoix weighed up the accounts of the earliest French travellers to North America and treated much of what they said with considerable scepticism. Of the writings of the traveller he said

> If he thinks fit to give a relation of his voyage, he finds all his readers on their guard; if he says anything in the least extraordinary he finds no credence. On the other hand, if the relation is utterly devoid of the marvellous, it lies unread. (Charlevoix, 1743, p.123)

The reason why Gibbon admired Charlevoix's work (which he cites in Chapter I) was that it was 'philosophical history', concerned to point up the moral lessons of the past while using the most rigorous means to investigate his sources. Neither writer was in any doubt as to the superiority of western Christian culture.

These two types of writing, the travellers' accounts and the histories, show the contradiction in Western European attitudes towards other peoples, and hence to barbarism.

On the one hand peoples outside Europe were seen as innocent and childlike (with an increasing recognition that their innocence had been destroyed by contact with Europeans). On the other hand it was said that they were wasteful of God's bounty of fertile lands and a clement climate, had no recognized religion, and treated their enemies with the utmost cruelty. Europeans had to 'justify' dispossessing the original inhabitants and appropriating their land, often in so doing desecrating venerated places and customs. They had also to glorify their own achievements by claiming to have subdued a 'worthy' (often war-like) enemy.

These contradictions may be seen in Gibbon. When he writes about the Germans, he is trying to convey the Romans' view of them, as people on the edge of the known world. Thus the Germans were for the Romans the equivalent of the non-European savages of Gibbon's day. So he also includes the perspectives of his own age about what constitutes civilization and draws on contemporary examples (note his reference in Chapter XXXVIII (*Texts*, I, p.301 and footnote 263) to Dampier's description of the inhabitants of New Holland (Australia)). Gibbon's attitude to the barbarians combines two elements. There is his attitude to the historical German tribes on the one hand and to the boundaries of civilization on the other. In the historical German tribes he is looking at the ancestors of the principal western European nations, and he firmly believes that they had eventually given rise to the best of all possible civilizations. In his autobiography he reflected upon his own good fortune in avoiding both slavery (the fate of the subjects of oriental despotism) and barbarism (the fate of the inhabitants of Africa, America and Australasia).

By what criteria does Gibbon define civilization, then? In Chapter I he suggests that laws and discipline are important ingredients. In Chapter IX he emphasizes the importance of writing, arts, towns and money. Lack of these things produced both what was praiseworthy in the Germans *and* what was detrimental. Lack of discipline was evidence of lack of moral development and gave rise to 'a supine indolence and a carelessness of futurity' which prevented the establishment of the institutions which promoted civilized society. Here there is a clear parallel with the South Sea islanders who had no written culture and bartered for goods or paid in cowrie shells.

Gibbon reflects other contemporary concerns in *The Decline and Fall*. For example he shows in Chapter I his interest in the effect of climate upon character. There was much debate in the eighteenth century about how human character is formed. Charlevoix, for example, produced various examples of how living in the extreme cold affected the characters and appearance of the inhabitants of Newfoundland. But there were also those who argued for the influence of the moral (rather than physical) environment in the development of character. Lack of civilization was equated with lack of moral development, with short-term gratification as the sole end of existence.

EXERCISE　Now look at the extract from Chapter XXXVIII (*Texts*, I, pp.298–303). What can you find in this passage which seems to embody Gibbon's ideas about the boundaries between barbarism and civilization?

DISCUSSION　Much of this passage is about the dissolution of a civilization rather than the nature of barbarism. We know from Gibbon's remarks about the Germans that he thought that cities were the real fount of civilized culture. We know, too, that Gibbon had a deep respect for proper laws and their administration. The replacement of a secular military state by one in which priests had some say over the government seemed to Gibbon a fundamental step towards decline: we see here his anti-clericalism and anti-monasticism as well as his objections to other aspects of established Christianity. There is something of a paradox here for, whilst Christianity was seen to have a debilitating effect upon the Roman empire, it was also said to have a beneficial effect upon the barbarians of the north.

'The rapid impulse of war' was one of the features of barbarian life which according to Gibbon prevented them from being civilized in the Roman sense. He sees this as coupled with an almost childlike desire for immediate gratification which prevented barbarians making progress in the arts and agriculture by settling down, building cities, cultivating the land, and making laws, but rather kept them in a perpetual round of war and roaming after their herds. Gibbon identifies the remnants of barbarian culture in the nomadic Kalmuks and Uzbeks. (The description of these people by John Baptista Tavernier who saw them in 1670 and whose account Gibbon knew, owes much to the description by the Roman historian Ammianus Marcellinus of the Huns in Scythia, probably the same part of the world.)

National freedom and military spirit seem to Gibbon to epitomize Roman civilization at its height, but these qualities came to be replaced by servility and oppression. The vigour and courage of the barbarians then overwhelmed the luxury and corruption of the empire. It was the absence of laws, arts and ideas for the generality which for Gibbon define a society without civilized values, even if in other respects it might be praiseworthy. Where we might differ from him is in recognizing how and where these things exist: we might not, for example, share his view of the paucity of Australian aboriginal culture. Though Gibbon did not believe the history of the human race to be one of inexorable progress, he did believe that a civilized people could not lose all its attributes, even if conquered by barbarians.

Perhaps the most difficult imaginative leap that is required of the present-day reader is to understand Gibbon's view that 'the savage nations of the globe are the common enemies of civilized society' (*Texts*, I, p.299). We have become so accustomed to the idea that the seeds of the destruction of the developed world lie in further development, that the idea of conquest by peoples with less developed economies and political institutions seems unthinkable. To some extent Gibbon is seeking to surprise the reader by posing the suggestion that Europe might be overrun by 'some obscure people, scarcely visible in the map of the world' (*Texts*, I, p.299). But he is also making a serious point: that the history of

Figure 48
Relief showing the beheading of German Prisoners; Rome, Colonna Antonina (Mansell Collection).
'In a civilized state every faculty of man is expanded and exercised.' (Gibbon, Decline and Fall, *Chapter IX)*

the human race has not simply been one of unimpeded progress towards a civilization defined as all that is best in western European culture. In that idea, he is very unlike his contemporaries.

Finally, to round off your first study week, please listen to Chapter IX, paragraph beginning 'If we contemplate ...', marginal title 'Their indolence' on AC1633.

5   Gibbon the historian

ANTONY LENTIN

5.1   Philosophical history

'Historians should be philosophers', Gibbon wrote in his *Essay on the Study of Literature*. Since he wrote the work in French, the word he used was '*philosophe*', and he meant it in the sense it is given in the article *Philosophe* in the *Encyclopédie*, a seeker after truth, objective, critical, dispassionate. In approaching the past, he 'takes as true what is true, as false what is false, as doubtful what is doubtful' (*Texts*, I, p.9). The 'philosophical' historian also aspires to be a contributing member of civilized society, not a mere antiquarian gathering information, or an '*érudit*', as the *philosophes* disparagingly termed it, an ivory-tower specialist writing for other specialists. A pioneering work of 'philosophical history' was Voltaire's *Essay on Customs* (1756), a critical survey of European history written in the spirit of the *Encyclopédie*. Its primary effect, according to Diderot, was to excite in the reader 'an intense hatred of lying, ignorance, hypocrisy, superstition, and tyranny'. Gibbon agreed. The 'philosophical historian' he believed, had the 'honourable office', not of studying history merely for its own sake, but of drawing out from it useful truths and lessons for his readers. 'This awful revolution,' he says of the fall of the Roman empire, 'may be usefully applied to the instruction of the present age' (*Texts*, I, p.298).

5.2   History as secular history

'Philosophical history' was above all secular. Therefore Gibbon's approach in Chapter XX was revolutionary, for the traditional historical approach to the emperor Constantine was theological. It was typified by the *Discourse on Universal History* (1681) by the seventeenth-century French Catholic ecclesiastic, Bishop Bossuet. Bossuet's conspectus of events from the Creation to Charlemagne presented history as the working out of God's purpose, first through Jewish and Christian history as recounted in Scripture, and then through the history of the Catholic Church. Political leaders such as Constantine, who established Christianity as the official religion of the Roman empire, were the agents of Providence, by which alone causation was to be explained, and to which all events were to be ascribed. Bossuet tells us:

> This long concatenation of particular causes which makes and unmakes empires depends on the secret decrees of Divine Providence. From the highest heavens God holds the reins of every king-

dom and holds every heart in his hands. At times he bridles man's passions, at others he gives them free rein, and this is how he moves all of mankind. Should he wish to see a conqueror, he will spread terror before him and will inspire his armies with invincible boldness. (Bossuet, 1976, pp.373–4)

'Philosophical' historians took issue with this approach, which they rejected as narrow, naïve, and uninformed. Voltaire accused Bossuet of 'telling lies with admirable eloquence', and wrote his *Essay on Customs* as a direct response to the *Discourse*. The *Essay*, significantly incorporating *The Philosophy of History*, became the manifesto of Enlightenment historians. (There are echoes of the *Essay* in *Candide*). Gibbon's purpose was to demythologize the traditional, hagiographic accounts of Constantine, and to explain, so far as he could, what really happened, and why.

5.3   Religion and secular history

Why, then, was the establishment of Christianity in the Roman Empire a theme worth examining in a 'philosophical history'?

Please read the first paragraph of Chapter XX (*Texts*, I, p.269). In the first sentence Gibbon tells us that the 'establishment of Christianity' in the Roman Empire was 'one of those important and domestic revolutions which excite the most lively curiosity, and afford the most valuable instruction'. His theme is the establishment of Christianity. Why is it worth examining? It is 'one of those important ... revolutions'. 'Revolutions' is a strong word. We have noted his use of it in connection with the fall of the Roman Empire. Gibbon here means 'revolution' in the sense of 'major historical phenomenon', the advent of a new order, a new historical epoch, as he shows in the next paragraph. Why does he describe the 'revolution' as 'domestic'? Gibbon means 'domestic' in the sense that the coming of Christianity affected the history of Europe, the common home of his readers. (There is a comparable use of the word 'domestic' at the beginning of Chapter IX, p.245.) True, Constantine's foreign and internal policy 'no longer influence the state of Europe'; but Christianity remained the dominant faith across eighteenth-century Europe; and the 'ecclesiastical institutions' founded by Constantine were directly related to themes which were still controversial, which still aroused strong feelings and which still affected 'the interests of the present generation'. Gibbon means 'interests' not in the sense of pastimes or amusements, but in the sense of real, material interests. Organized Christianity, that is, still matters. It is not merely of antiquarian interest. The first point to note about 'philosophical history', then, is that it is, or is felt by Gibbon to be, of the utmost relevance and contemporary importance. It affects 'the present generation' and it has something to teach it.

So in reacting to an event which was supposed to have changed the course of history, Gibbon treats it as a process in which the religious and the secular are intertwined. (You need not worry about the history of the early Christian church. We are concerned here only with how Gibbon handles his theme.)

Gibbon had already considered religious and social aspects of early Christianity in the famous (or infamous) Chapters XV and XVI. In Chapter XV (The Progress of the Christian Religion and the Sentiments, Manners, Numbers and Condition of the Primitive Christians), Gibbon elaborated and parodied the characteristics of early Christians. He took an almost voyeuristic pleasure in describing their zeal and their piety, their quietism and quarrelsomeness, their distaste for luxury and for learning, their embracement of celibacy and the passions of their martyrdom. Worse still (in the eyes of the orthodox) in Chapter XXXVIII Gibbon ascribed to the Christian religion a key role in the downfall of the Roman Empire. This, together with his depiction of Christian credulity and superstitious faith in miracles provoked, even in the rationalist eighteenth century, an outburst of rage and accusations of blasphemy. There is no doubt that Gibbon expected to shock – 'If the whole work was favourably received by the Public, I had the more reason to expect that this obnoxious part would provoke the zeal of those who consider themselves as the Watchmen of the Holy City' (Craddock, 1972, p.232). (Clearly, Gibbon had not forgotten the barefooted friars who had unwittingly prompted him to write; see *Studies*, I, p.296.)

In setting out the secular context for the triumph of religion, Chapter XX shifts the emphasis from the ordinary primitive Christians to the ruler who transformed Christianity into a state religion. Analysis of the relationship between religion and politics was always potentially controversial and subversive, even in an Enlightenment which combined reforming impulses with a belief in free enquiry (compare from Part I the devices adopted by the writers of the *Encyclopédie* in order to comment on issues which were 'out of bounds'). In addressing religion and politics in a fairly remote historical context Gibbon enjoys a relatively safe distance, but nevertheless as you read Chapter XX it is worth noting what he does not actually say outright, although he creates certain impressions in the reader. (Horace Walpole called him 'sly' and 'as accurate as he is inexact' in a letter to Rev. William Mason, 18 February 1776.) For example, starting from the apparent historical facts associated with Constantine's conversion, Gibbon progressively undermines the reader's certainty. After all, 'the obstacles which [Constantine] had *probably* experienced in his own mind instructed him to proceed with caution' (*Texts*, I, p.270) and 'he insensibly discovered his new opinions, *as far as he could enforce them with safety and with effect*'.

6   *Reading Gibbon II*

RICHARD ALLEN

As he became the historian of the later period of the Empire, Gibbon found himself facing difficult problems in his sources and his own judgements, and his style had to develop to meet these changes. But there are strong continuities, and again I suggest you begin work on Chapter XX by setting aside a period of time to read it through as a whole to fix Gibbon's argument in your mind. Again, use the marginal notes to help yourself here.

EXERCISE   Now please look in detail at the second paragraph of Chapter XX (*Texts*, I, p.269). Your work on Chapter IX picked out four features of Gibbon's style for special attention:

1   the pattern of each sentence;

2   the way the style embodies a mind characterized by reflection and strong opinion;

3   figurative language;

4   irony.

Are these elements useful in looking at this new paragraph from Chapter XX?

DISCUSSION   1   In the first sentence we find the same forward and backward movement, and the same method of deferring the subject of the sentence. Later in the sentence beginning 'It was ...', the use of parallels is very striking. Gibbon implicitly expresses more admiration for Constantine's artful balancing of the Christian and pagan worlds than for those historians who have attempted to drive him into a single track. The use of parallel clauses allows him to set almost exactly side by side and within a homogeneous framework a series of almost antithetical positions as in the sentence 'During the whole course ...'.

2   The whole paragraph shows Gibbon reflecting on a historical question and using the footnotes to set out and interrogate his sources.

3   Gibbon describes the development of Christianity 'as if' it were a 'stream' which 'flowed with a gentle, though accelerated, motion', etc. More powerfully, but perhaps only half figuratively, Constantine is described as possibly having 'imbrued his hands in the blood of his eldest son ...'

4   Irony is perhaps to be found first in the references to his sources: 'the eloquent Lactantius' and 'the learned Eusebius'. Later it occurs in a more subtle way as Gibbon begins to discuss the character of Constantine:

The obstacles which he had *probably* experienced in his own mind instructed him to proceed with caution in the momentous change of a national religion; and he *insensibly* discovered his new opinions.

6.1   *The condensed style*

Please now move on in the chapter to the paragraph beginning 'The passive and unresisting ...' (*Texts*, I, p.274). Here Gibbon reflects on the relation between ideals – the Christian 'Theory and practice of passive obedience' – and political motives and expediency.

EXERCISE First try to analyse the first sentence in the 'story' manner (see p.303–5 above).

DISCUSSION The basic story is simple: passive obedience appeared to an absolute monarch a most useful Christian virtue. The final sentence condenses this story and a set of parallel sentences. The reader is forced to store the beginnings of all the meanings Gibbon uses connecting words to layer together, i.e., 'passive *and* unresisting ... *which* ... *or even*', and so on.

6.2 *Taking a paragraph as a whole*

Finally, I should like you to consider how one might draw together the approaches we have used for sentences to deal with a longer section of Gibbon's prose.

EXERCISE Look again at the section of the paragraph from the beginning 'The passive and ...' to '... corner of the globe' (pp.274–5) and think about the points you would want to select for particular mention. Then go on and read my brief and far from exhaustive discussion of the passage.

DISCUSSION This passage consists of seven linked sentences, most of which are relatively short; the exception being the one beginning 'The humble Christians ...'. Hardly any of these sentences are free of phrases with double or linked words based on 'and' or 'or'. In the opening sentence there are 'passive and unresisting', 'authority, or ... oppression', 'conspicuous and useful'. Gibbon makes one sentence do the work of several in this way; he also shows himself to be concerned with precise shades of meaning. Thus 'passive' and 'unresisting' might be taken for synonyms but they create different nuances of meaning, and the juxtaposition of the two words should compel us not just to sense emphasis but to work to define one word against the other. 'Passive' here means 'not acting'; adding 'unresisting' to this adds further negative elements, particularly because of the negative prefix 'un-'. The pattern of the sentence may then lead us to construct a simple two-layer structure in which 'passive' goes with 'authority' and 'unresisting' with 'oppression'. The structure of the first sentence avoids mention of the Christian faith until the very end, so that the opening phrase is kept separate from any notion of positive Christian suffering, as demonstrated in the life of Christ or the martyrs.

The sentence structure generally in this passage is also typically complex, as can be seen by looking at the one beginning 'While they experienced ...'. The basic meaning here is 'they were never provoked'. To this Gibbon adds first an opening qualifying clause 'while they ...', in which 'persecution' is expanded as 'the vigour of persecution', and second a pair of consequential clauses 'either to meet ... or indignantly to withdraw'. One might equate this kind of concern for formal balance and symmetry with classical architecture in which simple and balanced forms predominate but where ornament exists to provide interest and a sense of humanity.

At the end of the sentence the description of the land is emphatic – 'remote and sequestered' – and attached to an image – 'corner of the globe'. Earlier in the passage Gibbon draws on the important Christian image of the sheep, guarded normally by the shepherd-priest. By shifting the image rather away from this context – 'as sheep among wolves' – he emphasizes both the defencelessness of the Christians and the lack of any kind of organized Christian church structure.

Given Gibbon's generally secular values, 'vain privileges, or the sordid possessions, of this transitory life', is to be read ironically. He also describes Constantine in a half ironic way, as in 'assumed the sacred character', and a similar strategy is used for the Christians, as in 'preserved their conscience pure and innocent'.

6.3   Style and history

Examining Gibbon's style can help us understand what he says; his style is also interesting in itself and repays formal analysis. But can it tell us anything about Gibbon as a historian? Working from the paragraph we have just been examining, one can conclude tentatively that seeing nuanced differences of meaning was vitally important to him. In the rest of the paragraph he sets out the parallel but different case of the more recent Protestants as a contrast to the Roman Christians, thus both seeing parallels, but refusing to simplify or schematize history. Alert reading will also help pick out the way Gibbon combines a close attention to particular facts with a desire to put forward his own personal hypotheses. Here we notice the use of 'perhaps', 'may be', and 'must have' as he speculates on the 'inevitable destruction' of the Christians; the progression between these words indicates also the conviction with which he advances his hypotheses.

A sense of the use of irony is crucial too. Here the ironies are spelt out: patience is a virtue but also a weakness, principles can stand apparently regardless of events or conduct. But often the irony is more embedded. Again if we notice the use of 'perhaps' we will be led to ask ourselves whether there is really any question that we should give 'applause' to 'the superior sense and spirit' of Gibbon's more recent ancestors.

Finally if we are alert to the voice that lies behind each sentence we will notice the shift in the final sentence of the paragraph as the historian enters the story to put words into the mouths of the Christians. If all citizens, like Christians, 'learn to suffer and to obey,' would not this make the imperial state 'fixed and permanent'? Such a state could not compete in excellence with that of the Antonines which Gibbon so reverently describes in Chapter I of *The Decline and Fall,* but it would surely not be without merit when the Roman world is moving through its decline and fall.

7   Gibbon on religion and classical antiquity

LORNA HARDWICK AND ANTONY LENTIN

By this stage you should have read Chapter XX in full. To confirm your 'feel' of how Gibbon approaches religious issues, listen to the two extracts from Chapter XX on AC1633.

7.1 Religion and the state in Chapter XX

EXERCISE Consider the paragraphs which Gibbon identifies by the following marginal summaries: 'AD 331. March. Edict of Milan', 'Use and beauty of the Christian morality' and 'Theory and practice of passive obedience' (*Texts*, I, pp.272–6). What do they suggest of Gibbon's interpretation of Constantine's motives in extending toleration to Christianity?

DISCUSSION Gibbon suggests that while Constantine, as a pagan before his conversion, might have been predisposed in any event to tolerate Christianity as a variety of polytheism or even of deism, he may also have had practical reasons of state for his religious policy: 'the counsels of princes are more frequently influenced by views of temporal advantage than by considerations of abstract and speculative truth' (*Texts*, I, p.274). Christianity might be socially useful to the emperor in that it preached as a religious duty the pursuit of a 'universal system of ethics, adapted to every duty and every condition of life' (*Texts*, I, p.274), underpinned by a theory of posthumous rewards and punishments. Furthermore, it preached the doctrine of absolute, unconditional obedience to the civil authorities. As the next section suggests, the Christian dogma that monarchs rule by divine right ('not from the consent of the people, but from the decrees of heaven'; *Texts*, I, pp.274–5) might be a useful instrument of political control.

In the paragraph with the marginal summary 'Loyalty and zeal of the Christian party' (*Texts*, I, p.277), Gibbon suggests that it was useful for Constantine to have an influential minority on his side in his wars against his rivals, Maxentius and Licinius.

In the paragraph headed 'The conversion of Constantine might be sincere' (*Texts*, I, p.285), Gibbon repeats the suggestion that 'in the choice of a religion, his [Constantine's] mind was determined only by a sense of interest' (*Texts*, I, p.285), though he again raises the possibility that Constantine may have been genuinely attracted to Christianity. But for what reasons? Gibbon's latest biographer insists that 'Gibbon is demonstrably *not* anxious to prove that Constantine's conversion was a cynical, callous, political move' (Craddock, 1989, p.110). Do you agree?

EXERCISE In the paragraph headed 'Propagation of Christianity' (*Texts*, I, p.290), how does Gibbon account for the rapid spread of Christianity after the edict of Milan?

DISCUSSION Gibbon's explanation is that it was in the material interest of the Romans to profess the now dominant religion. At every level of society, it paid to convert. The establishment of Christianity offered lucrative careers to 'the piercing eye of ambition and avarice' (*Texts*, I, p.290). Note how, according to Gibbon, the 'common people' were won over.

Recapitulation

All this is a far cry from Bossuet! Gibbon insisted on treating the establishment of Christianity 'with impartiality', as he put it (*Texts*, I, p.269), like any other historical phenomenon. He sought to explain it not as the reflection of the will of God, but in terms of its political, social and economic advantages to Constantine, to the church, and to the Romans. According to Gibbon, Christianity became the state religion not, or not only (or not at all?) because of its divine truth, but because of its perceived usefulness.

7.2   Gibbon and the miraculous

Constantine's cause is traditionally believed to have been aided by a miraculous occurrence: a mysterious cross appeared to him in a dream (or, according to another source, appeared in the sky) on the eve of a battle with Maxentius, the last of his political rivals. Constantine won the battle (the battle of the Milvian Bridge) and was allegedly inspired by the miracle to embrace Christianity. Gibbon agrees that the question was historically important: 'The real or imaginary cause of so important an event deserves and demands the attention of posterity' (*Texts*, I, p.278).

EXERCISE   What is Gibbon's attitude to the miracle of the cross? *(Texts*, I, pp.278–85).

DISCUSSION   He is sceptical in the extreme. Take the expressions which he uses to describe it – 'this extraordinary story' and 'artfully confounded in one splendid and brittle mass' (*Texts*, I, p.278). What image does the latter suggest? Surely that of a fabricated glass ornament that will shatter under investigation.

Gibbon questions the reliability of one primary source on the grounds of bias on the part of its author (Cæcilius) – 'Some considerations might perhaps incline a sceptical mind to suspect the judgement or the veracity of the rhetorician, whose pen, either from zeal or interest, was devoted to the cause of the prevailing faction' (*Texts*, I, p.281), that is, as an avowed partisan of the winning side, Cæcilius was either mistaken or a liar.

EXERCISE   How does Gibbon interpret Constantine's attitude to the miracle?

DISCUSSION   He suggests (*Texts*, I, p.282) that 'the dream of Constantine … may be naturally explained either by the policy or the enthusiasm of the emperor'. In reverse order, Constantine may genuinely have believed that he saw the vision, predisposed as he was in favour of Christianity, and being a man of vivid imagination ('active fancy'). 'Enthusiasm' is close to fanatical credulity in Gibbon's vocabulary, as generally among writers of the period. (Dr Johnson defined 'enthusiasm' in his *Dictionary* as 'a vain belief of private revelation'). Alternatively, the story may have been a deliberate fabrication on the part of Constantine, 'one of those pious frauds', the inventions of 'a consummate statesman' with everything to gain by exploiting his superstitious troops on the eve of his most critical battle.

7.3 Gibbon and irony

Following your work in sections 2 and 6 of this Study, you can hardly have failed to sense Gibbon's irony. Irony is not difficult to spot, but it is difficult to define.

Consider for example the following passage, from *Texts*, I, p.288 (also on AC1633):

> The sacrament of baptism was supposed to contain a full and absolute expiation of sin; and the soul was instantly restored to its original purity, and entitled to the promise of eternal salvation. Among the proselytes of Christianity, there were many who judged it imprudent to precipitate a salutary rite, which could not be repeated; to throw away an inestimable privilege, which could never be recovered.

EXERCISE   Where is the irony and to what effect does Gibbon use it?

DISCUSSION   The irony lies in the second sentence (though it may also be present in the first. 'Supposed' perhaps raises a doubt as to whether baptism really does 'contain' etc. And what do you make of 'instantly' and 'entitled'?) In the second sentence Gibbon ironically impugns the motives of the 'many' converts who 'judged it imprudent' to undergo such a 'salutary rite' prematurely. 'Salutary', because its effect was to expiate all previous wrongdoing. Many converts wished to postpone baptism as long as possible because it was a once-in-a-lifetime offer, and they (like Constantine) wished to make sure of having their fill of sin first! (Gibbon spells out his meaning in the following sentence.) Just before the quoted passage, he says (again with obvious irony) that converts 'were seldom impatient to assume the character of perfect and initiated Christians'.

1   The ironist, then, seems to be saying one thing but is really saying something quite different – maybe just the opposite, but in an exaggerated or incongruous form.

2   The reader is an accomplice of the ironist, sharing a pleasurable awareness of his true meaning. Gibbon refers to the 'philosophic readers of the present age' (*Texts*, I, p.285). Gibbon's 'victims' are the uncritical authors of his primary sources (or readers credulous enough to believe them). By pretending to take them seriously, Gibbon exposes their unreliability.

3   The effects of the irony are comic and aesthetic: comic in the sense that we smile at the unusual analogies, metaphors, and the like; aesthetic in that effective irony depends on the arrangement of a good setting for its display, good timing, the right tone of voice (often 'dry', 'deadpan') and so on. The ironist's attitude has something Olympian about it: it is distanced, detached, dispassionate, sceptical and there is an 'ironic' facial expression as he speaks or an 'ironic' tone of voice. (Reading Gibbon aloud and/or listening to readings on the cassette helps to bring out the irony.)

For another possible example, read *Texts*, I, pp.297–8 from 'Each bishop acquired' to the end of the Chapter (also on AC1633). The irony emerges in the long list of titles (in decreasing order of impressiveness) of church celebrants. What does Gibbon intend us to think of them? The sting comes in the last sentence: 'the swarms of monks, who arose from the Nile, overspread and darkened the face of the Christian world'. This makes us think of a plague of flying insects, locusts, perhaps. An unusual metaphor to apply to men in holy orders, and both apt and ironic to say that they 'darkened the face of the Christian world'. The irony is in the unexpected imagery (monks = loathsome insects). But what about the use of the word 'darkened' in the context of the Enlightenment? Does Gibbon mean what he says about the monks? And if so, can his description of them be called ironic? (Note that he uses the same metaphor in describing the barbarians of Germany – 'the innumerable swarms', *Texts*, I, p.253.)

7.4 *Gibbon's assessment of religion in the Roman Empire*

Another of the ways in which Gibbon undermines the miraculous aspects of Constantine's vision is by showing how conveniently this fitted in with the Roman tradition that rulers should claim legitimation by divine approval. Constantine's vision led, not to spiritual awakening, but to military success (*By this sign thou shalt conquer*). Thus Christian symbols fitted in with the pagan belief that keeping the gods happy ensured material prosperity.

According to Gibbon (who refers to early Christian sources, especially Eusebius who was Bishop of Caesarea *c.* 314 and Lactantius, a Christian apologist who was tutor to Constantine's son), the soldiers' shields were suitably inscribed, the battle of the Milvian Bridge won, and Constantine's dubious hold on the Empire triumphantly confirmed. But Gibbon was not merely uncritically reproducing Christian sources (see footnotes 184 and 219). The comment that Constantine 'used the altars of the church as a convenient footstool to the throne of the empire' (*Texts*, I, p.285) strikes home, only to be denied (or is it?) by reference to the capacity of 'artful statesmen' to feel religious enthusiasm when it is expedient. Nor is Gibbon's cutting edge felt only by Constantine. 'Personal interest is often the standard of our belief, as well as of our practice' and, even closer to home, 'nor can it be deemed incredible that the mind of an unlettered soldier should have yielded to the weight of evidence, which, in a more enlightened age, has *satisfied or subdued the reason* of a Grotius, a Pascal, or a Locke' (*Texts*, I, p.285, my italics). Gibbon uses the examples of three distinguished but very different philosophers to emphasize the conflict between reason and faith and to insinuate that those who subordinate faith to reason are comparable to an 'unlettered soldier'.

In Chapter XX (*Texts*, I, p.269), Gibbon cites the philosopher's role in exposing the fictive aspects of religious traditions. Is there an element of rhetorical one-upmanship in his insistence that the truly discerning reader will not be conned? Certainly, the aspects of religion that he addresses are all either concerned with political effect or are presented as discreditable in those who claim to be intellectually sophisticated. (Compare Hume's comments on the intrusiveness of religious principles in literature in *Of the Standard of Taste*, *Texts*, I, pp.206–7.)

First, Gibbon emphasizes the political effects of the passive obedience found in Christianity, which 'must have appeared, in the eyes of an absolute monarch, the most conspicuous and useful of the evangelic virtues' (*Texts*, I, p.274; note also the extended discussion on pp.25–60). A twentieth-century historian, G.E.M. de Ste Croix, has expressed this rather more brutally as 'the disastrous Pauline principle that the powers that be are ordained of God', citing St Paul's letter to the Romans 13:1–7, while Diderot's implied defiance of St Paul in *Political Authority* had provoked an outcry (see *Encyclopédie*, *Texts*, I, p.12–13). In the last section of Chapter XX, Gibbon shows how from this tradition of Christian obedience was derived Constantine's attention to the organization and doctrines of the Church, since these alone could either challenge the legitimacy of his authority or ensure that it was accepted by the faithful.

The second aspect of Gibbon's treatment of religion and politics in Chapter XX involves a change of emphasis away from the irrationality, credulity, ignorance and superstition with which he identified primitive pagan religion (in Chapter IX) and the Christianity of the lower classes (in Chapters XV and XVI). While it is true that the cross of Constantine is described in terms of a pagan emblem (*Texts*, I, pp.278–9), Gibbon also addresses the complexities and theological intricacies of established ritual (see *Texts*, I, pp.288–9 and footnote 216). His discussion of Constantine's participation reflects his verdict on the public rituals of the early Emperors in Chapter II, *Of the Union and Internal Prosperity of the Roman Empire, in the Age of the Antonines* – 'they approached with the same inward contempt and the same external reverence, the altars of the Libyan, the Olympian or the Capitoline Jupiter', 'the various modes of worship which prevailed in the Roman world were all considered by the people as equally true; by the philosopher as equally false; and by the magistrate as equally useful.' This is more trenchantly expressed in his discussion of Roman state religion but also underlies his analysis of its Christianized form. There seems to be a distinction in Gibbon's mind between the attitudes to religion of the people and those of the rulers. This parallels his distinction between the untutored rustic and the civilized, educated and Enlightened person.

However, there does seem to be a sense in which Gibbon is trying to have it all ways in his attitude to the historical role of Christianity. He portrays the primitive Christianity of the early Church as passive and unthreatening in political matters, and yet he suggests that Constantine was skilful in turning it to his use. He also suggests that the triumph of religion was responsible for the decline of Rome. Perhaps what he means is that the Christian religion contributed to this in two ways. The first was that early Christianity was a politically passive and even other-worldly presence, which (while it was attractive to the Emperor as a source of peace, harmony and obedience) nevertheless undermined the military vigour and desire for supremacy which Gibbon thinks was a major reason for the power of the Roman Empire. Secondly, however, when Constantine politicized Christianity by giving it a role in legitimizing his rule, he also had to set up a vast and expensive bureaucracy (including non-productive orders of clerics, monks and nuns), which eventually proved to be a crushing burden on an Empire which had neither the vigour nor the room to expand. Records show that estates settled on the Roman Church in Constantine's reign brought in an income of over 30,000 *solidi*, which was equivalent to more than 460 pounds of gold (de Ste Croix, 1981, p.495). Thus, ironically, while pietists (who wanted to remain faithful to the other-worldliness of the early Christians) blamed Constantine for the secularization of Christianity (for a discussion of modern version of this thesis, see Kee, 1982), Gibbon presents him as responsible for transforming and Christianizing Roman religious practice and, to some extent, social organization and values. In Chapter XXXVIII (*Texts*, I, p.298), Gibbon suggests that the Empire declined precisely because it rejected the values of paganism, while in his *Memoirs* Gibbon wrote, 'I still believe that the propagation of the Gospel and the triumph of the Church are inseparably connected with the decline in the Roman monarchy'.

For independent evidence about Constantine's use of public religious language look at Pl. 25 in the *Illustration Book*. This depicts the triple arch of Constantine of Rome. The inscription on the monument followed the traditional Roman form:

> To the Emperor Caesar Flavius Constantine Maximus, Pius, Felix, Augustus, the Roman Senate and People dedicated the arch, decorated with his victories, because, by the prompting of the Divinity, by the greatness of his mind, he with his army, at one moment by a just victory, avenged the State, both on the tyrant and on all his party.
> To the liberator of the city. To the establisher of peace.

Note that the sculptures on the arch do not show Christian symbols, even on the soldiers' shields. For Gibbon's comments on the monument see Chapter XIV (*Texts*, I, pp.268–9), Chapter XX (p.282) and footnote 189.

7.5 Gibbon's reaction to classical antiquity

Why does Gibbon make such frequent use of irony? Irony is among other things a means of conveying criticism. Gibbon *is* critical on the whole (and with important reservations) both of primitive peoples in Chapter IX and of the phenomenon and the effects of institutional Christianity in Chapter XX – 'barbarism and religion'. What values, then, does he champion?

EXERCISE   Please read the first paragraph of Chapter I and then re-read Chapter XX, *Texts*, I, p.289, the sentence beginning 'Instead of asserting his just superiority ...'. What does Gibbon mean by 'imperfect heroism and profane philosophy'?

DISCUSSION   'Trajan and the Antonines'[5] were to Gibbon models of enlightened rule. This is clear from the opening paragraph of Chapter I where, describing the second century AD, 'The age of the Antonines', as 'a happy period' of good government, Gibbon refers to their 'virtue and abilities'. In Chapter III he refers to 'the golden age of Trajan and the Antonines', and tells us there approvingly that Trajan and the Antonines were

---

[5] Trajan, ruled AD 97–117; 'the Antonines' were Antoninus Pius (138–161 AD) and Marcus Aurelius (AD 161–180).

followers of the Stoic philosophy. By 'his just superiority' Gibbon refers to Constantine's automatic superiority *as a Christian*. He is apparently saying: 'Since his religion was superior to that of the stoics, his conduct should also have been better'. (Which, he goes on to tell us, it wasn't.) But clearly Gibbon does *not* think that Christianity was superior to stoicism. And his reference to 'imperfect heroism' and 'profane philosophy' is, again, ironic. ('Imperfect' and 'profane' because not inspired by Christianity.) Gibbon believed that Christianity 'had some influence on the decline and fall of the Roman empire' (*Texts*, I, p.298). Read the rest of that paragraph for his view both of its negative and positive effects, and note how the latter relate to the theme of the barbarians.

'The classics', Gibbon records in his *Memoirs,* 'were my old and familiar companions ... The perusal of the Roman classics was at once my exercise and reward'. At Lausanne, he nearly completed a plan of rereading all the major Latin classics 'in a chronological series from the days of Plautus and Sallust to the decline of the language and empire of Rome'. 'Nor was this review', he assures us, 'however rapid, either hasty or superficial. I indulged myself in a second and even a third perusal of Terence, Virgil, Horace, Tacitus, etc. and studied to imbibe the sense and spirit most congenial to my own' (Gibbon, 1891 edn, pp. 91, 92, 161).

Gibbon's concern was with laws, manners and government, and he takes excellence in these as his criterion for civilization. Virgil wrote, 'Romans, never forget that government is your medium!' (*Aeneid* 6.851) and it is perhaps this characteristic which draws Gibbon to Rome rather than to Greece. What else did Gibbon find so congenial in the Roman writers? First, the 'beauties of the language' which he admired in Cicero and which finds its reflection in the long, rolling 'periodic' sentences of *The Decline and Fall*, with their carefully structured clauses. But he also asserted – without any irony – the absolute supremacy of the classics as establishing 'a standard of exclusive taste'. In Chapter LII, on the Arabs, he declares:

> Our education in the Greek and Latin schools may have fixed in our minds a standard of exclusive taste; and I am not forward to condemn the literature and judgement of nations of whose language I am ignorant. Yet I *know* that the classics have much to teach, and I *believe* that the Orientals have much to learn.

This puts Gibbon at one, aesthetically speaking, with Hume in *Of the Standard of Taste*. (And what does it suggest of his view of 'Orientals'? Ironically, it is now recognized that survival of classical texts and especially of Greek philosophy and science owed much to Arab scholars.) Gibbon was enraptured by Roman values generally. Note his reaction to Cicero: 'I tasted the beauty of the language; I breathed the spirit of freedom; and I imbibed from his precepts and examples the public and private sense of the man' (Gibbon, 1891 edn, p.92).

The achievements and values which caught his imagination and admiration were those of pagan scholars and ordered government. The paradox is that his huge work was devoted to the decline and fall of both.

In spite of his admiration of Roman civilization and administration, Gibbon knew there was always a price to be paid for the triumph of reason and ordered government. He found liberty in the lifestyle of the German barbarians, not in that of the Imperial order.

He also had the intelligence to know that things are rarely just what they seem, and had the inventive wit to convey this. That is why he was able to write from within the tradition of classicism without being swamped by reverence. In his writing, the spirit of *Candide* hovers alongside that of Marcus Aurelius, and frequently elbows it out of the way. Gibbon is both a proponent of the classical and a subverter of established orthodoxy. You have seen and heard how he conveys this apparent contradiction. Now you have to decide which aspect is dominant.

7.6 Tail-piece: Gibbon's influence

This is how a twentieth-century historian, Arnaldo Momigliano, summarized the *rise* of the Roman Empire in the west:

> The philosophic historian will never stop meditating on the nose of Cleopatra. If that nose had pleased the gods as it pleased Caesar and Antony, a loose Alexandrian gnosticism might have prevailed instead of the Christian discipline imposed by the two Romes, the old one on the Tiber, and the new one on the Bosporus. The Celts would have been allowed to go on collecting mistletoe in their forests. We would have fewer books on Queen Cleopatra and on King Arthur, but even more books on Tutankhamen and on Alexander the Great. But a Latin-speaking Etruscologist, not a Greek-speaking Egyptologist, brought to Britain the fruits of the victory of Roman imperialism over the Hellenistic system. We must face the facts.
>
> The victory of Roman imperialism can in its turn be described as the result of four factors: the new direction given by Rome to the social – that is the military – forces of old Italy; the utter inability of any Hellenistic army to match the Romans in the field; the painful erosion of Celtic civilization and its appendages which went on for centuries and ultimately enabled the Romans to control the resources of western Europe from the Atlantic to the Danubian regions; and finally the co-operation of Greek intellectuals with Italian politicians and writers in creating a new bilingual culture which gave sense to life under Roman rule. Only the Jews and the Iranians stood up to the Romans. (Momigliano, 1975, p.1)

Like an eighteenth-century reader of Gibbon, you might need a moment to spot the allusion to the Emperor Claudius (the Latin-speaking Etruscologist) or to puzzle over the 'Alexandrian gnosticism' which represented one aspect of early Christian controversy! But do the tone and sentence structure echo Gibbon? And what about the judgements in the second paragraph – to what extent is Gibbon's approach in general supported and to what extent is it undermined, especially by the last sentence?

8 References

Austen, J. (1933 edn) *Sense and Sensibility*, Oxford University Press, London. (First published in 1811.)

Bossuet, J.B. (1976 edn) *Discourse on Universal History*, translated by E.M. Forster, University of Chicago Press.

Charlevoix, P.F.X. (1743) *History and General Description of New France*.

Craddock, P.B. (ed.) (1972) *The English Essays of Edward Gibbon*, Clarendon Press, Oxford.

Craddock, P.B. (1989) *Edward Gibbon: Luminous historian 1772–1794*, Johns Hopkins University Press, Baltimore.

de Ste Croix, G.E.M. (1981) *The Class Struggle in the Ancient Greek World*, Duckworth, London. (See especially Chapter VIII 'The "Decline and Fall" of the Roman Empire: an explanation'.)

Gay, P. (1970) *The Enlightenment*, Wildwood House, London.

Gibbon, E. (1761) *Essai sur l'étude de la littérature* [*Essay on the Study of Literature*], London.

Gibbon, E. (1980 edn) *The Decline and Fall of the Roman Empire*, 6 volumes, Everyman edition, Dent, London.

Gibbon, E. (1984 edn) *Memoirs of my Life*, edited by B. Radice, Penguin, Harmondsworth.

Gibbon, E. (1891 edn) *Memoirs of Edward Gibbon*, edited by H. Morley, Routledge, London.

Hall, E. (1989) *Inventing the Barbarian*, Clarendon Press, Oxford.

Kee, A. (1982) *Constantine versus Christ*, SCM Press, London.

Momigliano, A. (1975) *Alien Wisdom: The Limits of Hellenisation*, Cambridge University Press.

Montaigne, M. de (1603) Essay XXX, vol.1 K. John Florio.

Moore, F. (1738) *Travels into the Inland Parts of Africa*, London.

Smith, C. (1989) *The Old Manor House*, Oxford University Press, Oxford. (First published in 1793.)

Tacitus (1970 edn) *Collected Works*, translated by M. Hutton *et al.*, Heinemann, London.

Virgil (1966 edn) *The Eclogues, Georgics and Aeneid of Virgil*, translated by C.D. Lewis, Oxford University Press.

Wiedemann, T.E.J. (1986) 'Between men and beasts: Barbarians in Ammianus Marcellinus' in I.S. Moxon, J.D. Smart and A.S. Woodman (eds), *Past Perspectives: Studies in Greek and Roman Historical Writing*, pp.181–201, Cambridge University Press, Cambridge.

Conclusion

*Prepared for the Course Team by
Gill Perry*

From your reading of the preceding essays and your study of the texts upon which they are based, you should have gained an idea of how many aspects of eighteenth-century culture were permeated by a sense of reverence for classical antiquity. The material in the preceding essays should also have helped you to see that there was no single fixed notion of the 'classical' which inspired or influenced eighteenth-century writers, artists and philosophers. It is rather the case that the notions of the 'classical' or 'neo-classical' which are now in common usage may mask some differences of interpretation in eighteenth-century culture.

However, as was suggested in the Introduction to this Part, the influence of classical antiquity was not all-pervasive in the eighteenth century. An interest in Greek and Roman culture depended on an education in the classics, and probably also on the resources to visit Italy on the Grand Tour, which, as you have seen, were usually the privileges of the upper and (some of) the middle classes. Although classical values could pervade many aspects of a culture, access to a classical education and the study of Greek and Latin which it involved was the privilege of a social minority. An understanding of the classical values and cultures which are the focus of the writers or artists studied in this Part would have depended on an audience trained to recognize erudite references to ancient mythology, history, architecture, sculpture and politics.

You will also have noticed that for some eighteenth-century writers and artists there was sometimes a blurring of the distinction between the cultures of ancient Greece and Rome, whereas for others this distinction became paramount. During the first half of the eighteenth century the city of Rome, with visible remains of its ancient past, tended to be seen as the cultural capital of the west. Much ancient Roman architecture, sculpture and literature had been based on or influenced by ancient Greek sources, hence the tendency to group the two cultures together under the label the 'antique'. As you saw in the Introduction to this Part, during the 1750s and 60s the distinction between the two increasingly became the focus of art and literature. For theorists such as Winckelmann, the supposed purity of Greek art was seen to be superior to the more derivative forms of later schools. This interest was encouraged by increasing archeological excavations not just in Italy, but also in Greece and the Near East.

An important aim of this Part of the course has been to consider what might constitute a classical style in the writing and production of literature, history, architecture, painting or philosophy. Although today we tend to see these disciplines as more distinct and exclusive than they would have appeared to an eighteenth-century audience, you should have some idea of how the conventions associated with different disciplines were used to express supposedly classical values. It is sometimes easier to see how these ideas are adapted or developed in the specific conventions of architecture, painting or literature, than to sort out how such ideas influenced philosophical thought or aesthetic theory, in which associations are necessarily more abstract.

In most branches of philosophy, both in Britain and on the Continent, Greek philosophical ideas, particularly from the work of Plato and Aristotle, had been an enduring presence in all periods, and were not in need of revival in the Enlightenment. However, as we see from Hume's *Of the Standard of Taste*, the position is a little more complex in British aesthetics. Thinkers in the British tradition, such as Hume, faced a common set of questions, generated by their acceptance of two sets of beliefs: first the empiricism inspired by Newton and Locke, and secondly their genuine enthusiasm for classical works. Put these sets of ideas together and you set the agenda which some eighteenth-century thinkers tackled: Why are the classics aesthetically satisfying? Or, put in another way: Why do they satisfy taste and how does taste operate? Why have the classics stood the test of time? Can we derive rules from them? How can a genius manage to disregard the rules? And if the mind is, as Locke said, a mere blank slate written on by experience, how are we to describe what it is that genius does?

Nor were such questions of pressing interest only to philosophers. They influenced many aspects of contemporary art, architecture and literature, and as you have seen consistently informed Reynolds's attempts to produce a theory of art in his *Discourses*. For Reynolds, the problems of what constituted 'taste' or 'genius' had to be addressed if he was to formulate an academic theory of High Art. Classical values, like classical sources, were often cited to evaluate the status of art. The problem for us is the extent to which such values were entangled with other ideas and beliefs, among them a growing interest later in the century in ideas of sensibility and emotion, which will be dealt with in Part E.

Part C
'The Best of all Possible Worlds'

Contents

Study Time-table
Candide *(Study Weeks 14 and 15)*

Studies/Texts	TV	Radio	AC	Set Books
Studies, I	–	R4	–	–
Texts, I				

Lind's A Treatise of the Scurvy *(Study Week 16)*

Studies/Texts	TV	Radio	AC	Set Books
Studies, I	TV8	–	–	–
Texts, I				

Cook and Equiano *(Study Week 17)*

Studies/Texts	TV	Radio	AC	Set Books
Studies, I	TV8	–	–	–
Texts, I	TV9			

Introduction

Michael Bartholomew

The theme of this part of the course is, to a fair extent, an improvization, passed off on the back of one of the most memorable phrases from the eighteenth century, in order to link together the four rather disparate texts which constitute this part of the course. The phrase 'the best of all possible worlds' is drawn from Voltaire's *Candide*, a text which is absolutely fundamental to any study of eighteenth-century culture, but whose stubborn and admirable particularity makes it impossible to classify. Voltaire's 'philosophical tale' is a supreme expression of the Enlightenment's scepticism, wit, urbanity and humanity, yet, simultaneously, it challenges some of the Enlightenment's most confident expectations: Voltaire ridicules the optimistic notions that the world has been intelligently designed, and that human affairs will steadily improve and progress. *Candide* opens this part of the course.

One of the areas of enquiry in which progress was generally and confidently expected, but which the sceptical Voltaire satirized, was medicine. This takes us to the second text in this part of the course, James Lind's *A Treatise of the Scurvy*. You will recall from your study of the *Encyclopédie*, and from TV1, 'The *Encyclopédie*', that a confidence in the methods of science and medicine was one of the marks both of the *philosophe* and of the Enlightenment. Lind's *Treatise* is a good example of the application of scientific method to the problem of an affliction which regularly disabled eighteenth-century navies. You will see, however, that, in this case, medical science did not march steadily forward in the systematic, triumphant conquest of the disease. Progress in medicine was by no means automatic.

The disease that Lind chose to study makes a bridge into the third text in this part of the course, Captain Cook's *A Voyage Towards the South Pole*. Cook is a fascinating character. On one hand, he is the plain, self-taught, no-nonsense, ex-mate of a Whitby collier, yet on the other, he is the enlightened, humane observer of Polynesian culture, and the scrupulous, scientific recorder of astronomical and topographic observations.

Cook takes us into the wider, non-European world, and in turn takes us to Olaudah Equiano, a West African who was sold into slavery, but who made his way into the British political and literary worlds, and who recorded his remarkable life in an autobiography.

The grouping of the texts in this Part grows more secure as the Part unfolds. There are real links between Lind, Cook and Equiano even though they never met. All three were experienced sailors who, literally and metaphorically, voyaged thousands of miles away from the polite society of the metropolitan *salons*. The voyages in *Candide*, by contrast, are imaginary: Voltaire was not part of the sub-culture that bound together all seamen. But *Candide* does imaginatively traverse non-European cultures, and raises issues that Equiano and Cook would certainly have recognized: issues concerning the uniformity of human nature, issues concerning human cruelty and stupidity, and yet issues concerning too, human indomitability and resilience.

The texts themselves are the primary focus of the course: themes and parts are secondary. With no more ado, therefore, turn the page and engage with *Candide.*

Voltaire, Candide

Prepared for the Course Team by Stephanie Clennell, with a contribution by Robert Wilkinson

Contents

Voltaire, **Candide** *(Study Weeks 14 and 15)*

Studies/Texts	TV	Radio	AC	Set Books
Studies, I	–	R4	–	–
Texts, I				

For the following two weeks, you will need the text of *Candide* in *Texts,* I, pp.307–61.

Voltaire, Candide

Figure 49
Portrait of Voltaire.
(Hulton Picture Company)

1 Introduction

<small>STEPHANIE CLENNELL</small>

Candide is one of the best-known works of the eighteenth century and Voltaire himself was one of the most famous, most quoted, most irrepressible writers of his age. The aim of this study is to help you to read *Candide* with enjoyment, to study it as a text of the Enlightenment and to understand its criticism of the philosophy of Optimism.

We suggest you begin by reading the short account of Voltaire's life in the Introduction of your *Candide* text, and then read the story itself straight through. It is very short. Let it make its first impression on you.

If you have not read *Candide* before you may find it quite unlike anything you have ever read. After this first reading you can now go on to study it more closely, to examine the qualities of this extraordinary little book, why Voltaire wrote it and how it achieved both an immediate effect on readers at the time and a lasting effect in the centuries which have followed.

2 Voltaire (François-Marie Arouet, 1694–1778)

'I had the satisfaction of seeing the most extraordinary man of the age', wrote Gibbon in his *Memoirs*. He saw Voltaire in 1757 and 1758, before the aptness of the adjective was reinforced by the appearance of *Candide*, and before Voltaire went to Ferney, his home for the last twenty years of his life, which became a place of pilgrimage for visitors to the 'patriarch of Ferney', as he came to be called. 'Patriarch' hardly seems to apply to the ever-active and iconoclastic Voltaire who, until the very end, worked as ferociously hard as he had always done. Yet it does suggest the acknowledged influence which Voltaire had in his own lifetime.

That lifetime spanned most of the eighteenth century. He was born when Louis XIV was still on the throne, lived to become a leading figure of the French Enlightenment and died just eleven years before the French Revolution.

EXERCISE Re-read the short article *Men of Letters* (*Texts*, I, *The Encyclopédie*, Section 1, p.11) and consider what this suggests to you about Voltaire.

DISCUSSION In his article *Men of Letters* (meaning the *philosophes*) in the *Encyclopédie* Voltaire could well be describing himself: '... a man familiar with geometry, philosophy, and general and particular history, a man whose special studies were poetry and eloquence. Today that is what our men of letters are.'

Voltaire himself was no narrow specialist; he excelled in many kinds of writing, published fifteen million words, wrote twenty thousand letters, was dramatist, poet, historian, *philosophe* and journalist – defying categorization. That he was 'more independent of mind than other men' could not be challenged. He was known for what he wrote, what he was and what he did; and was constantly in the public eye, constantly in trouble, and constantly making trouble in the cause of enlightened ideas, especially on religion and science, and on behalf of tolerance, justice and liberty.

Of all Voltaire's immense output the best-known work, still read, even more than 200 years after his death, is the short satirical tale *Candide*.

So far you have met Voltaire as a contributor to the *Encyclopédie* and as a correspondent of Frederick the Great and Catherine the Great. Voltaire did not join the *philosophes* in working for the *Encyclopédie* when it began; he issued encouragements and compliments, but did not contribute articles until 1755 in Volume 5, and even then on fairly non-controversial subjects. By then he was in exile and, as so often in his life, was alternately rash and cautious. It was a 'scoop' for the *Encyclopédie* when Voltaire did at last contribute. He had a European reputation and demonstrated in his own writing the power of reason to enlighten; and his credentials as being independent of mind were impeccable: two spells in prison, constant trouble with censors, the banning of some of his works, exile from Paris for some thirty years of his life. The Encyclopaedists were gratified and a little nervous. Even Diderot, whose relations with Voltaire were more distant and less cordial than those of some *philosophes*, was often respectful and addressed him later as 'illustrious and tender friend of humanity' (in 1766, writing to Voltaire about Le Breton's cuts in the *Encyclopédie*). D'Alembert's relations with Voltaire were more cordial and, ironically, contributed to the trouble which flared up as a result of d'Alembert's article *Geneva* in Volume 7 (1757) which was at least one factor in the banning of the *Encyclopédie*. It is generally agreed that Voltaire must have had some part in this article, which outraged Genevan pastors by suggesting that many of them were Socinians.[1] But Voltaire was adept at covering his tracks, or at least confusing the trail, when he got involved in trouble of this kind. He could be economical with the truth, and issued denials and fabrications, as well as indignant protests. We shall see these tactics at work when we come to 'the moment of *Candide*' in 1758.

First let us go back some years, for in *Candide* there is a kind of distillation of Voltaire's experience, knowledge and attitudes. There are paradoxes here. Though he wrote many unconventional works, Voltaire's command of the French language is rooted in the French classical tradition, formed in his case in the prestigious Jesuit school, the Lycée Louis le Grand. His main ambition as a writer was to succeed in the classical forms of drama, epic and shorter verse forms; and he did succeed. His first major success was with his tragedy *Oedipe* in 1718. The paradox here evidently is that he maintained a solid reputation as a classical writer among those very members of the establishment who were most incensed

---

[1]   See *Texts*, I, p.361 (Voltaire Glossary).

by his satirical works. (He was working on a tragedy, *Tancrède*, in 1759, the year in which *Candide* appeared.) A further paradox is that it was Voltaire who claimed, rightly, to have made Shakespeare known in France, translated him, recognized his genius, but deplored his 'barbarity'. As you will recall from Part A, Johnson, who had a similar grounding in the classics, also found much to criticize, but appreciated Shakespeare as the 'poet of nature' (Johnson set text, p.40). For Voltaire the plays were 'brilliant monstrosities'; '... his was a genius fertile and strong, natural and sublime, without the smallest spark of good taste ...' (*Letters Concerning the English Nation*, Letter 18).[2]

Voltaire's attitude to the French aristocracy was ambivalent; he delighted in his acceptance at court and in polite society, had friends at court, and even, as you will recall from the Introduction to your text of *Candide*; also held an official position as royal historiographer for a number of years. He was flattered by Frederick's attentions. Yet he managed to lose favour at the French court and, to put it mildly, at the Prussian court too. Already in 1734 he had attacked the aristocracy in his *Letters Concerning the English Nation*, gently enough at times: 'I don't know which is more useful to the state, a well-powdered lord, who knows the precise time at which the King rises and when he goes to bed and who assumes lofty airs while acting as a slave in some minister's antechamber, or a merchant who enriches his country...' (Letter 10). In the same book, despite its mask of irony, there was no ambivalence in his attitude to the Catholic Church, and his condemnation, indirect but quite clear, of its intolerance and bigotry. The result of this, you will remember, was that the *Parlement* condemned the book and it was publicly burned.

Yet Voltaire had no doubts about the greatness of French culture, of France as a nation, whatever its faults. Something of this emerges in the historical work *The Century of Louis XIV* (1752) which he completed during his stay in Prussia. In his introduction to this work Voltaire identified four happy ages '... when the arts were perfected, and forming an epoch in the greatness of human spirit, which are examples for posterity'; the golden age of Greece in the fifth century BC, the Rome of Caesar and Augustus, the Italian Renaissance, and the age of Louis XIV in France, 'the one which most nearly approaches perfection'. As you will recall from your study of Gibbon, Voltaire was writing as a 'philosophical historian', of whom Gibbon was to be the supreme disciple. 'It is humanity which deserves the attention of history', he said in his *Essay on Customs* (Voltaire, 1963, Volume 1, p.781).

Attachment to tradition and an interest in the past were combined, possibly paradoxically too, with Voltaire's pursuit of the new knowledge which played such an important part in the Enlightenment.

He shared the interest of many of his contemporaries in other peoples and countries, both primitive and civilized peoples, not only in past cultures, but also in the present new world which, as you will find in your study of Cook and Equiano, was becoming more widely known through exploration and writing. He quickly sensed and pin-pointed those areas

---

[2]   This work is usually referred to in French as *Lettres Philosphiques* (*Philosophical Letters*). It was in fact first published in its English translation, entitled *Letters Concerning the English Nation*, in 1733 before its first appearance in French as *Lettres Philosphiques* in 1734.

of knowledge where there were innovations likely to influence the development of ideas and the progress of society, notably in science and philosophy. He became the main populariser in France of the ideas of Newton and Locke, and was supremely gifted in presenting these with lucidity, wit and elegance. His letter 16 in *Letters Concerning the English Nation*, for example, *On Newton's Optics* is a model of exposition.

Voltaire also had very practical interests in the contemporary world; he had become rich through shrewd speculation and investment, particularly in trading ventures; Cadiz in *Candide* was more for him than a name in an adventure story, for he had financial interests there.

By temperament, and because of his standpoint on many controversial issues, Voltaire led an eventful personal life; he had many friends and not a few enemies. Some of this experience too lies behind *Candide*.

We need to say more now about the context of *Candide* and the philosophical ideas which it intends to challenge.

3   Voltaire and optimism

ROBERT WILKINSON

It sometimes happens that works of literature are written as much in response to the impact of an idea or set of ideas as they are in response, for example, to political events or changes in manners or moral or emotional dilemmas or a fascination with character and relationships. When this is so, the ideas in question are as much the subject matter of the work as are its characters or story, and works of this kind are not completely comprehensible unless the ideas in question are understood. Lessing's *Nathan the Wise* is an example of such a work, and so is Voltaire's *Candide*. The beliefs which are in this sense the subject of *Candide* are summarized in its sub-title: optimism. The optimism Voltaire sets out to question, however, is not merely a tendency to look on the bright side or to expect things to turn out for the best. Voltaire is attacking a much more complex and powerful set of ideas more properly referred to as philosophical optimism, roughly summarizable as the assertion that the world which exists (the world in which we live) is the best of *all possible* worlds, a belief widely canvassed in the first half of the eighteenth century. To appreciate fully what is involved in the assertion that this world is the best possible, it is necessary to say something about the two major sources of this view in the late seventeenth and early eighteenth centuries: Alexander Pope's poem, *An Essay on Man* (1732–4) and, more importantly, the thought of the great German philosopher Gottfried Wilhelm Leibniz (1646–1716).

Alexander Pope (1688–1744) was not naturally at home among the abstractions of philosophy and theology, and the ideas set out in *An Essay on Man* are neither as clear and consistent as they might be nor original to him. The immediate source of most of the ideas in the poem is its addressee, his friend Henry St John, first Viscount Bolingbroke (1678–1751), and through him, Anthony Ashley Cooper, third Earl of Shaftesbury (1671–1713: Shaftesbury's seminal influence in another field, that of aesthetics, has been discussed in Part B in the study concerning Hume's *Of the Standard of Taste*). The derivative nature of the content of this poem, however, is unimportant: the brilliance of the writing together with the topicality of the subject matter combined to make it immensely successful. Moreover, its success was not confined to England: it appeared in a French prose translation by Silhouette in 1736, and this was followed by two translations into French verse. French editions continued to be issued regularly until at least the middle of the century, making Pope the first English poet to be revered in France as well as England in his own lifetime. Voltaire admired Pope and wrote about him in his *Letters Concerning the English Nation* No.22.

Popular success of such an extent cannot be accounted for solely in terms of the poet's reputation, even though it was by then very considerable. What Pope had achieved was the production, in an aesthetically attractive form, of a distillation of ideas of great importance to his contemporaries: he had formulated a theodicy for his time. Getting to grips with the idea of 'theodicy' will lead us directly to the heart of the poem, and to Pope's version of optimism.

Pope opens his *Essay on Man* with a statement of what the poem sets out to do: he intends to examine all aspects of creation with a common aim in view, and that aim is 'to vindicate the ways of God to Man' (Butt, 1963, *EM*, I, 16). Such a vindication is a theodicy. The term itself derives from two Greek words, 'theos' (=God) and 'diké' (=right): to construct a theodicy is to demonstrate that God acts rightly or justly by his creatures. (The currency of the term 'theodicy' in the period was in no small part due to Leibniz, whose influential *Essais de théodicée* (*Essays in Theodicy*) appeared in 1710.)

The idea that theodicy needs to be undertaken at all was anything but new in the eighteenth century, and is a concomitant of any form of theism which includes a belief in a creator who is beneficent in intention. The reasoning behind the notion of any theodicy is this: the creator of the universe is omnipotent, and has only benevolent intentions towards his creatures; yet here on earth we witness, seemingly without end, both physical evil (natural disasters; disease; pain) and moral evil (all forms of oppression or torment of the good by the wicked; all forms of suffering brought about as a result of free action). If the creator is both all-powerful and entirely benevolent, how can this be permitted? The aim of a theodicy is to demonstrate that, despite all the sufferings of his creatures, the creator is benevolent, and therefore his 'ways' can be 'vindicated' to us. Put another way, the aim of a theodicy is to provide an answer to a very serious theological problem, the problem of evil.

Whilst Pope was born a Catholic and notionally remained one throughout his life (which was unusual among leading English writers of the period), the religious outlook of *An Essay on Man* is that of a deist. (The term 'deist' is fully explained in *Studies*, II, in the 'Introduction' to Part D of the Course, *Religion and Humanity*, and in the section on 'Lessing and Religion' in that Part.) For present purposes, it is enough to note that, for the deist as for the orthodox believer, the problem of evil, which generates the need for a theodicy, remains the most urgent of difficulties associated with religious belief, since deists retained the notion of an omnipotent and benevolent God and were faced with a world beset by calamity and suffering. Pope begins his theodicy with one of the central beliefs of optimism: if God is omnipotent, omniscient and benevolent, then, when he chooses to create a world (= universe; what there is), he must choose to create the *best* world:

> Of Systems possible, if 'tis confest,
> That Wisdom infinite must form the best ... (Butt, 1963, *EM*, I, 43–4)

The created world must be the best that there can be: to suppose otherwise is to deny either that God is omniscient, or omnipotent, or benevolent, or all three. The reference in these lines to 'systems possible' is verbally similar to the Leibnizian formulation 'best of all possible worlds' to which we will come presently; but it is important to stress the similarity is *only* verbal. Pope had not read Leibniz, was unaware of his metaphysics, and his philosophical mentor Bolingbroke held Leibniz in contempt. (Bolingbroke wrote of Leibniz that he was 'one of the vainest and most chimerical men that ever got a name in philosophy' (Bolingbroke, 1777, p.329).) Pope's immediate source for the idea that God would create the best world was Shaftesbury (cf. e.g. *Characteristicks* etc. 1773 edn, II, pp.204, 360, and 363) and the first occurrence of the idea itself long predates its incorporation into Christian apologetics, occurring in Plato's dialogue *Timaeus*, (29–30) written in the fourth century BC.

Granted the premise that this world is the best possible, Pope feels that he can explain the presence of both physical and moral evil. What appears to us calamitous or wicked seems so only because we have limited knowledge and cannot see the whole scheme of things. Could we but see the universe from the divine point of view, what appears to us as evil would be shown to be good (cf. Butt, 1963, *EM*, I, 51–5; 57–60). He sums up this aspect of his optimism as follows:

> All Nature is but Art, unknown to thee;
> All Chance, Direction, which thou canst not see;
> All Discord, Harmony not understood;
> All partial Evil, universal Good;
> And, spite of Pride, in erring Reason's spite,
> One truth is clear, 'Whatever is, is RIGHT'
> (Butt, 1963, *EM*, I, 289–94)

This optimism concerning the general order of things is reflected in a complementary optimism concerning the specifically human condition, especially with regard to the distribution of happiness amongst humankind. Human nature has been beneficently designed by God: we have passions to motivate action and lead us to pleasure, and reason to curb the excesses of the passions and to harmonize them (Butt, 1963, *EM*, II, 53–4; 91–2; 216–94). Of course there are inequalities of condition among human beings (Pope regarded a stable social order as impossible without inequality), but these are compensated for, in Pope's view, by the distribution of spiritual goods and evils: thus the pauper is blessed with hope and the rich man cursed with fear for the safety of his possessions (cf. e.g. Butt, 1963, *EM*, IV, 49–76; II, 261–74). True happiness does not lie in wealth or station or goods. Happiness consists in health and peace of mind; health derives from moderation, and peace of mind from virtue and a clear conscience, and therefore happiness is within reach of all (cf. Butt, 1963, *EM*, IV, 77–120; 167–92).

Pope's answer to the problem of the existence of evil and, therefore, the central tenet in his theodicy, is in effect to deny that there is evil: there is only the *appearance* of evil, an appearance generated by our imperfect and partial knowledge of the creation. Leibniz, to whose version of optimism we can now turn, produced a somewhat different answer, that evil is real, but is the minimum possible, though the two types of optimism were regularly confused by their readers.

Unlike Pope and Voltaire, Leibniz did not claim to be a deist: instead, he professed to accept conventional Christianity in many respects; but his version of Christianity was underpinned by a special metaphysics or theory of the nature of reality which was original to him. For reasons which need not detain us, Leibniz believed that the world as we ordinarily experience it via our senses and via introspection is a manifestation of a reality which, so to speak, lies behind it. All the objects and beings we are aware of, including ourselves, are manifestations of collections or aggregates of simple substances, which Leibniz calls monads, a term derived from the Greek 'monas' = a unit; one. Each monad has a nature which cannot be altered, and some possible monads have natures which are incompatible with one another, that is they could not exist simultaneously in the same world. A possible world, for Leibniz, is a world composed of monads whose natures are compatible with one another. There is an infinity of possible worlds (NB remember 'world' = 'universe') but only one actual world.

The actual world became actual because God (who is the supreme monad) chose to create it. Why did God choose this world to make actual? Leibniz's answer is as follows:

> (53) Now, as in the Ideas of God there is an infinite number of possible universes, and as only one of them can be actual, there must be a sufficient reason for the choice of God, which leads him to decide upon one rather than another;
>
> (54) And this reason can be found only in the fitness, or in the degrees of perfection, that these worlds possess, since each possible thing has the right to aspire to existence in proportion to the amount of perfection it contains in germ.
>
> (55) Thus the actual existence of the best that wisdom makes known to God is due to this, that His goodness makes Him choose it, and His power makes Him produce it. (Leibniz, 1898, pp.247–8)

What makes a possible world more 'perfect' or 'fit to exist' than a rival possible world, in Leibniz's view, is that it contains a greater variety of phenomena produced by simpler means (cf. e.g. Leibniz, 1898, section 58).

With the above in mind, it is possible to appreciate what was originally meant by a number of the turns of phrase Voltaire uses in *Candide*: this world is indeed in Leibniz's view, *the best of all possible worlds*. It is possible because its constituent monads are compatible with one another; it is the best because it combines the richest diversity of phenomena produced by means of the smallest number of laws; and it exists because God, who is omnipotent and benevolent, chose to create it. He did not do so by whim: he had what Leibniz calls a *sufficient reason* for his act of Will: God's wisdom allows him to see which possible world is best, and his goodness and power lead him to produce it. (The 'principle of sufficient reason', of which Leibniz makes use here, is one of the fundamental principles of his philosophy. He holds that there is always a reason why things are as they are and not otherwise: to deny this would render explanation impossible and phenomena unintelligible.)

Two other Leibnizian doctrines in particular are mentioned in the text of *Candide*, and a few words need to be said about each of them. The first concerns Leibniz's theory of space. In chapter 5, Pangloss remarks: 'For if there is a volcano in Lisbon, it could not be anywhere else. For it is impossible that things should not be where they are'. The thesis that spatial objects *can* only occupy the space which they do in fact occupy is one of the aspects of Leibnizian metaphysics to which Voltaire took exception. He favoured the alternative view of space put forward by Newton. For Newton, space is an absolute independent of what it contains, from which it follows that God could have placed the actual world in a part of space other than the part it in fact occupies. Leibniz objected that this consequence violates the principle of sufficient reason: God must have a reason for placing the world where it is, and, if space is an absolute, there could be no such reason. Space, in Leibniz's view, is not an absolute independent of things but consists instead in the relations of things to one another. This was a view Voltaire had on a number of occasions taken pains to argue against, and it is no surprise, therefore, to find it singled out for attack in *Candide*.

The second Leibnizian doctrine which is mentioned more than once is that of the pre-established harmony (*Texts*, I, ch. 28, p.356; Conclusion p.357). This doctrine is a consequence of Leibniz's assertion that the monads, which, it will be recalled, constitute the reality which underlies appearance, do not interact one with another, but only change internally to themselves. What appears to us a causal interaction, between minds and bodies for example, is therefore *only* an appearance. In reality, Leibniz contends, God has so chosen and arranged the monads which make up the world that in going through the unalterable sequence of internal changes which constitutes their nature, they develop harmoniously side by side, as it were. This arrangement was chosen by God before he created the actual world: hence the harmony is said by Leibniz to be pre-established, that is, arranged by God prior to the creation.

Other aspects of Leibniz's philosophy are mentioned in passing in the text of *Candide*, but they are merely named, rather than being singled out for particular ridicule, and it is not necessary to go deeply into these views in order to follow Voltaire's text. Thus, for example, there is a reference to the doctrine that the universe is a 'plenum' (lit.: 'fulness'), that it does not include a vacuum at any point; but no special play is made on this idea.

The extent to which Leibniz's views are attacked in *Candide* might lead one to suppose that his works were widely known in France in the years before Voltaire wrote this story, but the truth of the matter is rather less straightforward. Whilst Leibniz wrote a great deal, comparatively little of it was published during his lifetime. Only two substantial philosophical works by him were in print during the first half of the eighteenth century: his *Essays in Theodicy* (1710) and his correspondence with Newton's apologist Dr Samuel Clarke (1717: the source of Voltaire's knowledge of the disagreement over the nature of space). Voltaire certainly knew these works; and, by the time he came to write *Candide*, he had access to a Latin version of Leibniz's short work, *The Monadology*, a brief summary of his principal views written for the consumption of aristocratic patrons. More important, however, in the first half of the eighteenth century in the dissemination of Leibnizian ideas than that philosopher's own books were the works of a German academic, Christian Wolff (1679–1754).

As is often the way with academics, Wolff liked to deny that he owed extensive intellectual debts to others; but, while he did disagree with Leibniz on some technical aspects of metaphysics, there is no doubt that Wolff's philosophy is in effect an extended and systematized version of Leibnizianism. In the course of his professional life, Wolff published many volumes on subjects from metaphysics to international law, in both German and Latin. These works became the standard university textbooks of philosophy in Germany until late in the century, their continued acceptance secured by the accession to professorships of philosophy in Germany of a number of Wolff's former pupils.

Wolff's works were known to some extent in France, and there were a few attempts at popularization of his philosophy in translations into French made by Huguenot pastors exiled in Germany. (On this, cf. Barber, 1955, ch. VIII.) However, by far the most important follower of the Leibniz–Wolff philosophy in France was Emilie du Châtelet (1706–49), Voltaire's mistress between 1733 and 1749. Amongst the intellectual women of the time Mme du Châtelet was distinguished by her preference for mathematics and physics. All her published works are in this field, including what proved to be the most influential vehicle for the Leibniz–Wolff philosophy produced in France itself, her *Institutions de Physique* (*Fundamental Principles of Physics*; Châtelet, 1740). This work, ostensibly a textbook for her son, was initially conceived as an exposition of physics on largely Newtonian lines; however, in the late 1730s, Mme du Châtelet was influenced intellectually to a marked extent by a disciple of Wolff named König, through whom she became acquainted with some of Wolff's work. As a result she delayed publication of her book until she had added to it seven chapters of Wolffian metaphysics, which she placed at the start of the work. Most of the Leibnizian doctrines considered above appear in these new chapters, including the view that this is the best of all possible worlds (Châtelet, pp.43–8). The notable absentee is the doctrine of the pre-established harmony, which is not present in her Wolffian source. Quite typically for the period Mme du Châtelet both regards Wolff as an expositor of Leibniz and is unaware of the philosophical differences between them.

Voltaire greatly admired Mme du Châtelet's book, though he could not accept the Leibnizian viewpoint on many of the matters discussed. He prepared a reply of his own, *La Métaphysique de Newton* (*Newton's Metaphysics*, 1740) which he later incorporated into a longer work, *Eléments de la philosophie de Newton* (*Elements of Newtonian Philosophy*, 1741). In the early 1740s, therefore, Voltaire could discuss Leibniz's philosophy simply as a set of beliefs with some of which he disagreed. There is no suggestion at this time that Voltaire regarded Leibnizianism with the deep contempt evinced in *Candide*.

His outlook on life around 1740 was relatively untroubled. Only a few years before, at the age of forty-two, Voltaire had published his poem *Le Mondain* (*The Man of the World*, 1736) in which he describes life in civilized society as a paradise on earth. The poem exhibits an optimism of a non-philosophical kind, a rather sunny acceptance of the way things are. This is very remote from the outlook which informs *Candide*, and it is worth spending a little time noting how and why Voltaire changed his attitude to optimism so radically.

Of all Voltaire's significant works, *The Man of the World* is the least troubled in its outlook on the human condition. The philosophical stories of the period up to about 1750 show an increasing awareness of doubts and difficulties and a gradual disenchantment with optimism. The story *Zadig* (1747) shows Voltaire troubled by the concept of providence. Zadig is a Babylonian of exemplary character. Through no fault of his own he suffers repeated and undeserved misfortunes before he eventually wins the hand of his beloved and can live in peace. He is reconciled to the notion of a benevolent providence only by divine intervention in the form of the angel Jesrad. The angel replies to Zadig's doubts concerning providence; yet Zadig is not quite satisfied with his answers: he is still saying 'But ...' when Jesrad terminates the conversation by ascending to Heaven. Only the glory of the sight is enough to silence Zadig. Voltaire could just stifle his doubts. This same more informed acceptance is shown in the story *Le Monde comme il va* (*The World As It Is*, 1748). The angel Ituriel sends Babouc to report on the state of Persepolis (a thinly disguised Paris), so that a decision can be made as to whether the city deserves punishment. Babouc reports that the city displays both good and evil features, but that they are inextricably interwoven, and there is no simple way of separating the one from the other. Ituriel decides to leave Persepolis alone on the grounds that if 'all is not for the best, it is at least tolerable'.

The first significant indication that Voltaire no longer finds some sort of optimism a completely satisfying view of the world occurs in the story *Memnon, ou la sagesse humaine* (*Memnon, or Human Wisdom*, 1749). Memnon, like Zadig, is a good man, though a rather foolish one, who is despoiled of all his goods and blinded in one eye by worthless persons who get away with their crimes. After suffering these misfortunes, he is visited in a dream by his guardian angel. Memnon is assured that, looked at from the point of view of the universe as a whole, all is for the best. 'I will believe that,' replies Memnon, 'when I'm no longer one-eyed.' Voltaire's point is that optimism is worse than useless as a consolation to those who are in distress, a theme taken up again in *Candide*.

Yet while *Memnon* makes this point about optimism, it does not exhibit anything like the savage irony of *Candide*, nor the latter's bleak outlook on the world. A number of events, both public and private, took place between 1749 and 1759 which made it impossible for Voltaire to regard optimism as a viable world-view. Privately, Voltaire's domestic contentment was shattered when Mme du Châtelet died in September 1749 giving birth to the child of a man with whom she had been having an affair. In the public domain, two major events combined further to darken Voltaire's outlook and to focus his mind on the need for solutions of some immediate use to those oppressed or in pain. These events were the Lisbon earthquake and the outbreak of the Seven Years' War.

The Lisbon earthquake (described in ch. 5 of *Candide*) took place on 1 November, 1755 (the Feast of All Saints, a major religious festival), devastating the city and causing enormous loss of life. A natural disaster of such magnitude, and in Europe itself, presented a very serious problem for deists of all kinds, and especially for those who were optimists. No one realised this more clearly than Voltaire, whose response is expressed in his *Poème sur le désastre de Lisbonne, ou examen de cet axiome. Tout est bien* (*Poem on the Lisbon Disaster, or Examination of the Axiom: 'All is for the Best'*, 1756), a work which was extremely successful and which caused a very considerable controversy. The Voltaire scholar Theodore Besterman (1976, p.371) notes that over one hundred pamphlets dealing with the implications of the Lisbon earthquake and stimulated by Voltaire's poem were published in 1756–7 alone. The poem indicates another important stage in the sequence of changes in Voltaire's attitude to optimism. He now admits that he cannot accept that all is for the best: in the face of suffering of the just and the unjust alike, he cannot bring himself to believe it:

> From Leibniz learn we not by what unseen
> Bonds, in this best of all imagined worlds,
> Endless disorder, chaos of distress,
> Must mix our little pleasures thus with pain;
> Nor why the guiltless suffer all this woe
> In common with the most abhorrent guilt.
> 'Tis mockery to tell me all is well.
> Like learned doctors, nothing do I know. (McCabe, 1911)

Voltaire admits that he can find no satisfactory answer to the problem of evil: all he can in honesty propose as a consolation to suffering humanity is hope.

Even the Lisbon disaster, however, did not draw from Voltaire the bitter contempt for optimism expressed in *Candide*. At least the Lisbon disaster was not attributable to human folly and baseness: the same could not be said of the Seven Years' War. It broke out in 1756, and involved most of the major European states. By 1758, Germany, the birthplace and stronghold of Leibnizian optimism, presented a spectacle of devastation and suffering at least as terrible as Lisbon, and all the more appalling for being entirely the responsibility of human beings. Voltaire could not remain silent, and in the latter part of 1758 he wrote *Candide*.

After *Candide* optimism was finished as a world-view acceptable to leading thinkers. Voltaire had not in any sense *refuted* it: *Candide* is not an argument. Voltaire neither shows the falsehood of any of Leibniz's beliefs, nor that he makes invalid inferences from them. However, he had done something which is usually more effective: he had made it ridiculous. (Gibbon (Part B), you will recall, used ridicule as an effective weapon too). It is hardly surprising to find, then, that in works written after *Candide*, Voltaire has little to say about optimism and certainly nothing new. The article, *Bien [Tout est]* (*Best [All is for the]*) in his *Dictionnaire Philosophique* (*Philosophical Dictionary*, 1764) repeats the point of view of *Candide*, as do his few subsequent references to this subject.

Yet while he had effectively disposed of optimism, Voltaire had not disposed of the problem to which it was put forward as a solution, that is the problem of evil which lies at the centre of all theodicies. Voltaire was well aware of this, and there is a certain interest in his post-optimistic response to this problem. Part of this later response is set out in a story published when Voltaire was eighty-one, *Histoire de Jenni, ou l'Athée et le Sage* (*The Story of Jenni, or the Atheist and the Sage*, 1775). In this story, Voltaire's spokesman is an English Quaker called Freind (*sic*). Taxed to explain why God permits evil, Freind replies: 'It is impossible that God is not good; but men are perverse: they make atrocious use of the freedom which the Supreme Being gave them and had to give them, that is, the power to carry out their own wishes, without which they would be mere machines, created by an evil being solely in order to be broken by him' (Voltaire, 1966, p.72). This is a return to a proposed solution of the problem of evil which pre-dates optimism. What Voltaire means is this: a world in which God's creatures have free will is better or more perfect than one in which they do not. Moral evil is consistent with God's goodness because God cannot both allow a creature to be free and prevent it from doing wrong. Were God to prevent us from doing wrong, we would not be free. One might ask in reply why it is that God has so ordered the creation that some of the options open to human beings when they exercise their free will are options to do evil: this is to claim that the argument Voltaire advances, through the character of Freind, will not of itself explain or justify the existence of evil, and merely pushes the problem one stage back.

It would lead us too far from *Candide* to pursue this profound issue further. Voltaire himself would not have claimed to have produced a definitive answer to the problem of evil and would have regarded Freind's argument as only one part of any such answer. I suspect that Voltaire's own final position on this issue is the one at which he arrives at the end of the article *Best (All is for the)* in his *Philosophical Dictionary* (first published in 1764), to which I referred above. In this piece, he surveys solutions which have been proposed to the question: why is there evil in the world? His final remark is:

> Let us put at the end of almost all these chapters of metaphysics the two letters used by Roman judges when they could not reach an understanding of a case: N.L., *non liquet,* this is not clear. (Voltaire, 1964, p.72)

4   Candide, *a philosophical tale*

STEPHANIE CLENNELL

Theodore Besterman (1976) said that Voltaire invented the *conte philosophique,* or philosophical tale. There is some truth in this, for there is nothing quite like it. As you saw in the previous section the themes of some of the *contes* show trends in Voltaire's thinking. How did he come to use, even invent, this way of using light and witty narration to present philosophical ideas?

In the late 1730s when Voltaire was at Cirey with Madame du Châtelet he was working on *Elements of Newtonian Philosophy* in 1737; he was also reading Plato, with some scepticism. Voltaire took an idea from Plato's dialogue *Timaeus* and wrote a lively piece called *Plato's Dream* (Voltaire, 1979), whose subject is the creation of the universe. Plato dreams that the 'Eternal Geometer' gives to each of his subordinates, called 'geniuses', the task of forming a planet from a fragment of matter. The one who forms the earth is ridiculed for the poor job he makes of it; it is a bizarre mixture of good and bad; 'onions and artichokes are good things', but why so many poisonous plants? The human species has reason, but 'this reason is too ridiculous and is much too close to madness'; 'there is moral evil and physical evil'; and so on. In one derisive page Voltaire illustrates (as Van den Heuvel, 1967, has pointed out) what he had said in his *Treatise on Metaphysics* (1734, ch.2): 'As far as the miseries of men are concerned we have enough grounds for reproaching the divinity during the whole of our lives'. In the story he takes an even wider, quasi-Newtonian view, for the 'geniuses' who form the other planets fare no better than the one who created the earth. The Eternal Geometer, as he is called in the *conte*, tells them that their imperfect creations will last only a few hundred million years; in any case only he can make things which are perfect and immortal. 'And then', says one of Plato's disciples, 'you woke up'.

There is good evidence that this *conte, Plato's Dream* was written in 1737–8, and although it was not published until 1756, it can be considered as Voltaire's first *conte*; and it was written as a diversion for himself and friends, which gave a satirical view of a number of philosophical ideas. The next *conte, Micromégas* (1738), was subtitled 'a philosophical tale'; Voltaire sent it to Frederick the Great calling it *une fadaise philosophique* ('a bit of philosophical nonsense'). He did not see the *contes* as having any literary importance and had to be urged to publish them later. He wrote them at irregular intervals, and though they do not always have a similar pattern, they have in common the fact that they were an immediate expression of ideas which were preoccupying Voltaire at the time, as *Plato's Dream* shows, and as is very clearly the case in *Candide*. Though most of the *contes* are comic adventure stories, the essential plot is a philosophical one, a plot of ideas.

In order to appreciate Voltaire's valuation, or rather, as posterity has judged, his own undervaluation of the *contes*, we need to understand that in the scale of values of the French classical tradition novels were on a low level, and Voltaire did not have a very high opinion of works of fiction as a literary genre. 'Divide the human race in twenty parts. Nineteen are made up of those who work with their hands and who would never have any idea of the existence of a Locke; and in the remaining part how few people who read can be found, and amongst those who do read there are twenty who read novels to one who studies philosophy: the number of those who think is extremely small (Letter 13, *On Mr Locke*, in *Letters Concerning the English Nation*).

Voltaire in *Candide* was bridging this gap in offering a story which was about philosophy, and which even persuaded people to think.

Voltaire's philosophical tales do not fit neatly into a category, but they do have links with several kinds of eighteenth-century fiction. First the despised novel itself: Vivienne Mylne (1965) estimates that in France 1,200 novels were published between 1600 and 1699, and 946 between 1700 and 1750. Daniel Mornet (1916) estimates that about 800 novels were published between 1740 and 1760, so there is evidence of quite a large and increasing readership of novels. 'And what do we find in every novel?' was the question asked in the *Année littéraire* (*Literary Year*) in 1757 and answered: 'Thwarted loves, cruel fathers, parents in dispute, powerful rivals, jealous fury, abductions, sword and pistols, dangerous illnesses, miraculous recoveries, unexpected encounters, touching reunions, virtuous girls, women who are just the opposite, old husbands deceived by young wives, gossiping servants'.

Novels were usually long; and already in seventeenth-century French novels of adventure and romance the main plot was interrupted by characters who related past adventures – a kind of story within a story, a flashback.

The picaresque novel became popular in eighteenth-century France. The word 'picaresque' comes from the Spanish 'picaro', meaning a rogue; it is used to describe a novel which tells of a series of adventures, usually on a journey, of one main character, low-born, in low-life surroundings very different from the aristocratic milieu of the sentimental melodramas. It was a sixteenth-century Spanish tale which set the pattern: the anonymous *La vida de Lazarillo de Tormes y de sus fortunes y adversidades. Burgos* (*Life of Lazarillo de Tormes and his Fortunes and Misfortunes*, 1554). The most famous French picaresque hero of this kind is Gil Blas in Lesage's novel *Gil Blas de Santillane* (*Gil Blas of Santillana*, 1715–35). More or less the same formula of what amounts to a series of short stories strung together is found in erotic novels of the eighteenth century, such as Crébillon's *Le Sopha* (*The Sofa*, 1742), in which a sofa describes incidents which have happened on it, or Diderot's *Les Bijoux indiscrets* (*Indiscreet Jewels*, 1748), in which women are induced by a magic ring to tell stories 'not with their mouth but with the frankest part of their body'.

The reading public took to fairy tales and oriental fantasies. The fourteenth-century *Decameron* of Boccacio was translated into French and German in the eighteenth century, and you will see that Lessing used one story from this in his *Nathan der Weise* (*Nathan the Wise*); and the *Arabian Nights' Entertainments* or *Thousand and One Nights* was translated between 1704 and 1717 by Antoine Galland.

Rather on the margins of literature, but also widely read, were the accounts of travellers to foreign parts, especially to distant and exotic lands. Technically these do not qualify as fiction, but in practice it was difficult to check how strictly truthful the authors were.

You may find that this brief catalogue helps to increase your awareness that Voltaire was burlesquing some of these different kinds of fiction in *Candide*: the picaresque novel in some of the encounters of Candide and Cunégonde; melodramatic adventures (spiced with some bawdy touches) in the stories of the old woman and Cunégonde, and other shorter interpolated stories; fantastic tales or fairy tales in the Eldorado episode.

There were works well known to Voltaire which are similar in style to his *contes*: that is works which entertain, but above all make readers *think*. These works do not fit into neat categories, but they have in common the fact that they are, in their different ways, accounts of travellers who are searching, observing and learning. Cervantes's *Don Quixote* (1605–15) (*The History of the Valorous and Wittie Knight-Errant Don Quixote of the Mancha*; translated out of the Spanish, London 1613) and translated into French 1618, had been known for over a century. When Voltaire was in England he met Swift, whom he called, in letter 22, 'On Mr Pope and other writers' in *Letters Concerning the English Nation* (1734), 'the ingenious Doctor Swift who is called 'the English Rabelais'.[3] He continued: 'he is a Rabelais without a lot of hotchpotch and this book would be amusing in any case, because it is full of remarkable imaginative invention and

---

[3]   François Rabelais (1494?–1553), French physician, humanist and satirist, best known for his comic and satirical masterpieces *Pantagruel* (1532) and *Gargantua* (1534).

Figure 50
Title-page of the authorized
Geneva edition of Candide
and published in January
1759. (Courtesy of the Taylor
Institution Library, Oxford)

because of its lightness of style, even if it were not a satire of the human race as well'.[4] This book was of course *Gulliver's Travels*, which appeared in 1726. Another work which deserves particular mention is Montesquieu's *Lettres Persanes* (*Persian Letters*, 1721), which is a satire on French society as seen through the eyes of Persian visitors. Like Swift, Montesquieu used the device of an observer from far away, but unlike Voltaire, he avoided getting into trouble with the censors.

Of greatest interest to us is probably Samuel Johnson's *Rasselas* (1759) described by Donald Greene in his Introduction (p.xxi) to your Johnson text as '... similar in form and plot and written at almost the same time ...' as Voltaire's *Candide*. You will find the whole of this didactic tale, *Rasselas*, in your Johnson text (pp.335–418).

Much of Voltaire's own reading about foreign lands and voyages of exploration was done in his capacity as a serious historian. He needed it for his *History of Charles XII* (1731) in which he had to give an account of the Swedish king's journey through Poland and Russia to Turkey; but he had a much heavier research programme for his *Essai sur les moeurs* (*Essay on Customs*, 1756, 1769) – a modest sounding title, which quite fails to convey the immense scale of this work of sociological history, which starts from ancient civilizations and progresses to recent history. Even his plays which had exotic settings needed exploratory background reading. All of this was stored in his prodigious memory and slipped out smoothly when needed in *Candide*.

5   *The publication of* Candide

Voltaire kept very quiet about *Candide* when writing it, but there is clear evidence that this was in 1758 – indeed there are oblique references in it to things which happened in 1758. Precautions had to be taken about publication, including the not unusual one of creating ambiguity about where this was done and who wrote it, as you can see from the title page (Fig. 50).

---

[4]   In a letter to N. -Ch Thiriot in 1727.

The work had to be taken clandestinely to Paris; police inspector d'Hémery in February noted: 'Candide ... printed in Geneva. It's a bad joke about all countries and all established custom, and unworthy of the author to whom it is attributed – Monsieur de Voltaire'. The book was denounced and copies seized. Meantime it could not be printed fast enough to satisfy the demand in France, the Low Countries and England. Voltaire's friend the Duc de la Vallière wrote: 'Probably no book has ever been sold so fast. It is considered delightful; people are saying you wrote it. I deny this, no one believes me ... "Let's eat Jesuits" has already become a proverb'. Meantime the Swiss pastors had gone into action in denouncing a book which 'contains evil things, inspires inhumanity, is contrary to good morals and is injurious to Providence'. On the other hand Frederick the Great got his copy fairly soon and said that he read it seven times: 'the only novel which one can read and re-read'. Voltaire was playing his own part by writing in February 1759 to Cramer, his publisher: 'What is this little book called *Candide* ... I should like to see it'; and to a friend he wrote, 'Heaven forbid that I should ever have had anything to do with this work'. No one doubted, or could have doubted, who wrote it. Its brilliance made this obvious and its popularity increased.

6 *Reading* Candide

Voltaire wrote in 1753: 'Destiny plays with poor human beings as if they were tennis balls'. In 1754 – 'How small and stupid the middle of the eighteenth century is'. 'Destiny makes fun of us and carries us along. Let us live as long as we can and as best we can. Let us try ... let us try – what an expression! Nothing depends on us; we are like clockwork machines.'

Such was Voltaire's mood before the gloom was intensified by the great disasters of the Lisbon earthquake and the Seven Years' War. The philosophy of optimism and a belief in providence seemed absurd: 'This best of possible worlds is the maddest of worlds too', he wrote in 1756. Yet two years after the Lisbon poem he was able to stand back a little and ridicule optimism in a short, lively, outrageously comic tale. I hope that you found on a first reading, even perhaps without much knowledge of the background or understanding many of the allusions, that you were carried along by the pace of the story and the irreverent fun of it; and it keeps its freshness, even after repeated reading, even after being taken apart and analysed.

I suggest that you now read the text closely, looking at it from different points of view and noting what you find. The questions which follow are intended to help you to select certain aspects and then recombine them. It is a text which supports, indeed deserves, this kind of analysis, and in the end we appreciate the complex blend of techniques which Voltaire uses on every single page. We see better how he suggests ideas and attitudes, how he provokes thoughts and questions in his readers, especially about the philosophical and moral ideas.

EXERCISE   At a first reading *Candide* may seem to you a fast-moving tale in which adventures and episodes follow each other with no particular aim except that of keeping up the pace. But does the book have a plan? How could you divide it into a few main sections, and what heading would you give to sum up each section?

DISCUSSION I find it anything but a haphazard, picaresque story. There are three main sections:

1   The misadventures of Candide in Europe, where his mentor is Pangloss, and where Candide himself (with his companions) is a victim who suffers horrific misfortunes.

2   Candide goes to the New World, with a new companion, Cacambo, and for a while they enter the Utopian world of Eldorado.

3   Candide returns to Europe with another companion, Martin, and, empowered by wealth, he no longer suffers personally, but is an observer of many kinds of suffering and evil.

Pangloss the optimist is balanced by Martin the pessimist and in between them is Cacambo, the shrewd realist and practical man, who does not go in for philosophical speculation.

What is the purpose of this plan?
        We can see how the structure of the story is closely linked to the philosophical plot. In the first half Candide clings to Pangloss's creed of optimism; however grotesquely this is belied by experience, this is his one guide in a world of which he knows nothing; he has no 'innate ideas', he is Locke's *tabula rasa* or blank sheet; (Locke believed that human beings are not born with 'innate ideas', but acquire knowledge and ideas through their senses and their experience of life). Candide acquires experience, but is not equipped to learn from it. After leaving Eldorado and meeting the mutilated negro in Surinam, Candide for the first time seriously questions Pangloss's optimism, and after this his objections to Martin's pessimistic view become increasingly muted, though he is still hopefully trying to find some good in what he sees. While being entertained we are being skilfully led to balance the opposing views. The evils of the first part make a contrast to the fairy-tale world of Eldorado. When Candide and Cacambo leave Eldorado, some element of fairy tale remains, though paradoxically alongside Candide's sharpened awareness of evil. Like a fairy-tale hero, he now has power, the power of immense wealth, which for a while at least leaves him free to go where he likes, to seek Cunégonde, to bribe his way out of trouble, to become a privileged visitor in society, instead of being an outcast and a fugitive. From these adventures we get a cynical view of the power of money and of corruption: he is cheated by doctors, priests, prostitutes, gamblers, as well as in 'normal' commercial transactions.
        Voltaire, as a dramatist, knew how to grip an audience and take it with him, and how to give a work a firm shape; but no play could be packed, as is *Candide*, with so many incidents, surprises and proceed at such a pace and with such a huge cast of characters.

EXERCISE (Events) Voltaire sets *Candide* in his contemporary eighteenth-century world. What part do real events play in the story? Could we read it as a picture of the world today too?

DISCUSSION   Many of the events in the story actually happened: the Seven Years' War, the Lisbon earthquake, the Inquisition, the Jesuits' régime in Paraguay, the execution of Admiral Byng, some of the incidents in the Paris episode, to name only the main ones in which Voltaire had a particular interest. He had made a personal appeal for clemency for Admiral Byng. For his *Essay on Customs* he had already written the history of the communities set up by the Jesuit missionaries in Paraguay over a century before. (These were seen by some as military dictatorships and by others as an enlightened experiment in creating a well-organized and prosperous society for native peoples. In 1756 Spain sent a military expedition against the Jesuits who refused to obey orders from Spain. One of Voltaire's own investments was in a ship which took part in this expedition.) What is unrealistic is the pace at which the events happen and the exaggerated comic description of some of them. The answer to the second question depends on you. It seems to me that there are depressing parallels in the last decade of the twentieth century.

EXERCISE (Characters)   If many of the events in the story really did happen, can we say that the characters in it seem like real people? As you think about this you could make brief notes on the main characters, showing what we know about them, and how Voltaire presents them.

DISCUSSION   Clearly they are not the three-dimensional characters of a psychological novel. 'Voltaire does not analyse characters, he draws silhouettes' was the comment of a French critic, Gustave Lanson, in his biography of Voltaire (1906). Yet in a curious way there is some life in them; partly perhaps because the main characters are all actively involved in the philosophical plot as well as in the satirical one.

1   Candide and Pangloss

Candide's whole background and character is given in the first short paragraph of the story: '... a young man whom nature had endowed with the gentlest of characters. His face bespoke his soul. His judgement was rather good and his mind of the simplest. This is the reason, I think, why he was named Candide' (p.313) (a name which then stood for candour and integrity and always thinking the best of people; it suggested gullibility too, though in twentieth-century English 'candid' usually means 'frank and open'.) After that we know him only by what he does – always gullible, always kind – and by what he says. And in what he says we see his development.

These are just a few examples, and you can find many more:

'Doctor Pangloss was certainly right to tell me that all is for the best in this world ...' (p.316);

'If this is the best of all possible worlds, then what are the others? (p.320);

... I would feel strong enough to dare to offer him, respectfully, a few objections.' (p.327);

'... At last I shall have to renounce your optimism ... it is the mania of maintaining that all is well when we are miserable' (p.337);

'... Yet there is some good' (p.339);

and '... he reflected deeply on the Turk's remarks', is all we know of how he reaches his conclusion ... we must cultivate our garden' (p.358).

Pangloss's role is to be absurd, as the upholder of the philosophy of optimism, a comic caricature from his first introduction as teacher of 'metaphysico-theologo-cosmolonigology'; his ludicrous proofs: 'noses were made to wear spectacles and so we have spectacles ... ' (p.313); his mad logic: ' ... private misfortunes make up the general good; so that the more private misfortunes there are, the more all is well' (p.318), a pronouncement instantly followed up, you will recall, by a violent storm and shipwreck. His constant use, or more often misuse, of Leibnizian terms in unpromising situations is often followed by spectacular misfortunes; and, as fitting a farcical character, the rest of his troubles come from the pursuit of women. The things which happen to Pangloss in the story are the most unlikely of all, but he bounces back, quite incapable of learning from experience, not yielding an inch to the evidence of facts.

2   Cunégonde, the old woman, Cacambo, Martin, the Baron.
The other characters are even more lightly sketched, portrayed by a few characteristics which are repeated, with slight variations, whenever they appear. Cunégonde is sensual, showing interest in 'experiments', 'sufficient reason' and 'soft white skin', and is realistic in her acceptance of her various fates. The old woman is 'prudent', gives practical advice and, as she keeps reminding us, has 'only one buttock'. Cacambo is 'good', 'faithful', 'prudent', 'vigilant'. The brief profile of Cacambo, '... he had been choirboy, sacristan, sailor, monk, merchant's representative, soldier, lackey', (p.328) gives him a Figaro-like part as a quick-witted fixer, comic in his adroit manipulation and in his cynical comments. Martin is 'a good man', a Manichean ' ... I cannot think any other way' (p.339) and is always level-headed. The Baron is a Jesuit, a homosexual, and the embodiment of stiff-necked, aristocratic pride. They are not (except Pangloss, you may think) caricatures, but rather perhaps like cartoon characters who come to life through their role in the plot of ideas.

EXERCISE (Characters and Plot)   What is the part played by the characters in the plot of ideas?

DISCUSSION   Voltaire uses the characters to put points of view. I expect that you looked first at Candide and his three companions. We have seen how Candide learns from his experience of life to reject the philosophy of optimism, indeed all metaphysical systems, and how his mentor, Pangloss, patently and absurdly, does not. We can hardly miss the points being made through Pangloss, since almost every scene in which he appears is a memorable black farce. Although he appears in only ten of the thirty chapters, he is there in the many references to him made by Candide. We have the constant entertainment of Pangloss's variations on Leibnizian themes, invariably contradicted by events, but, more seriously, showing the heartlessness which results from adherence to rigid principles. We have only to think of Pangloss's callous attitude to the drowning of James the Anabaptist; and it is this incident which most clearly raises one of the most worrying questions of all: why should the good and innocent suffer? It is through Pangloss too that Voltaire first introduces the exploitation and corruption by Europeans of other continents, something which recurs later in the story (and which you will find again in your study of Cook and Equiano). 'If Columbus had not caught ... this disease ... we would not have either chocolate or cochineal' pronounces Pangloss; and for good measure another point is slipped in here: 'It should be noted that to this day this malady is peculiar to us in our continent like religious controversy' (p.317).

One way and another we get full value in Pangloss, but, as you have seen, this is not haphazard comedy. Candide's progressive disenchantment with his mentor's ideas is shown in his alternating attitudes of optimism and pessimism according to his immediate experience. The first serious crisis of confidence comes in Surinam, and it concerns the treatment of slaves. After this it is worth noting when Candide feels 'black melancholy'.

Martin's role is clear. He puts the pessimistic case that, if this is not the worst of possible worlds, it most certainly is not the best. If you re-read his speech on page 339 of your text you will find that he sets out his case in most detail there, and it may make you consider how many of the evils he mentions have already been shown in *Candide*. Yet it is also Martin who makes explicit qualifications. You will notice how he says: '... excepting Eldorado'; and it is Martin who speaks of hope: 'It is always a good thing to hope' (p.351); and Martin is not stupid or grotesque, but an intelligent foil to Candide.

It is clear that Cacambo plays an important part in the events of the story as the quick-witted servant and friend who copes with adventures and turns of fortune; but does he not have a part in the plot of ideas? He is no victim and no philosopher either, but a man who takes life as it comes or who tries to manoeuvre out of trouble. In him we see a pragmatic approach to the problem of evil.

An important point in the story is that Candide begins to think for himself; which of his three main companions is closest to him in his conclusions?

EXERCISE   Do the women characters play any part in the plot of ideas?

DISCUSSION   Cunégonde, the reason for Candide's travels, is ostensibly a conventional novel heroine, but as we have seen, Voltaire gives her an earthiness which is far from romantic: after her terrible story she says: 'You must be ravenously hungry; my appetite is good; let's begin with supper' (p.322). Her final ugliness gives a cynical twist to a possible happy ending, but does it also suggest something more? Candide's dream and ideal was a 'rosy complexioned, fresh, plump, appetising girl', and in real life instead of the ideal he has to accept a Cunégonde who is 'dark-skinned, eyes bloodshot, flat-bosomed, cheeks wrinkled, arms red and rough' (p.356) *and* 'shrewish and intolerable' (p.357). But what Cunégonde suffers is severe and, though comically and painfully exaggerated, shows man's inhumanity to woman. Paquette's story reinforces this.

It is even more marked in the old woman's longer recital of misfortunes, darkly comic, frankly bawdy, and containing many other targets of Voltaire's satire. The compression of so much into the women's stories gives particularly strong emphasis to the prevalence of evils, as well as emphasizing how women suffer so much as victims of men and yet can survive. With irony Voltaire makes the old woman say: '... these are things so common that they are not worth speaking of' (p.325); and Cacambo, the realist, says of Cunégonde: ' ... she will get along as best she can ... women are never at a loss' (p.328).

Do all these characters have hope? At least they are all survivors. The old woman expresses this best when she says: '... a hundred times I have wanted to kill myself, but I still love life. This ridiculous foible is perhaps one of our most disastrous inclinations. For is there anything more stupid than to bear continually a burden that we always want to throw to the ground?' (pp.326–7). The old woman is asking a very important question here, important in the plot of ideas. You will have noticed that it is placed at the end of the first part of the story in Europe, when we have had an account of a large number of disasters and misfortunes, and her story is the longest and most horrendous. At this point we surely ask the question: not only how, but why do people put up with such things?

Some characters suggest issues which are not directly relevant to the attack on the philosophy of optimism, but could be one of the means by which Voltaire pays off scores. The old woman is the daughter of a pope, Cunégonde and her brother are aristocrats, and Voltaire is very hard on these aristocrats. They are stripped of their rank, wealth, independence, health, are deprived and disfigured. Is there some malevolence here, arising from Voltaire's own ambivalent attitude to the aristocracy? He allows the Baron no saving graces at all and gets rid of him in the end: '... they had the pleasure of trapping a Jesuit and punishing the pride of a German baron' (p.357). Of course Pangloss is deprived and disfigured too, and he is no aristocrat, but he *is* a philosopher.

Let us not forget all the other characters in the book. There are hundreds of them; some appear for a page or two, a few paragraphs, a few sentences, and they draw attention to some issue: the King of the Bulgars (who represents Frederick the Great), the Dutch orator, 'two doctors whom he had not sent for', the abbé from Perigord ... and very many more. Philosophical or satirical points are made in human terms. Voltaire, like Diderot in his article *Encyclopedia*, puts man at the centre of the universe in *Candide*.

7 Story and style

We are never allowed to forget the philosophical questions, but we can enjoy an entertaining adventure story too. Voltaire tells a good story at a tremendous pace: he 'never relaxes his pressure on the accelerator and seldom touches the brake', says Besterman (1969, p.417). He varies his narrative techniques: there is straight narration, some description, some dialogue, but there is rarely any direct expression of his point of view. We have to keep our wits about us when reading *Candide*.

EXERCISE (Theme, *comedy and language in* *Chapter 1)*	What does Voltaire put into the first short chapter? What makes it comic? What effects does he create by his use of language?
DISCUSSION	We learn about the hero's background. We are introduced to the main theme of the philosophical tale. Candide's enforced parting from Cunégonde sets the story in motion.

    In the first sentence we are in Westphalia at Thunder-ten-tronckh, a name comic in itself, showing how German sounds to a Frenchman like Voltaire, still smarting and bitter after the unpleasant farce of his break with Frederick; and the name prepares us for the comic contempt for aristocratic pretentions: 'seventy-one quarterings' in dismal rural surroundings, where the castle 'had a door and windows'; five characters are introduced, and we go straight into the attack on the philosophy of optimism through Pangloss's ludicrous arguments (and notice that he is a *German* philosopher); then comes the 'lesson in experimental physics', showing Pangloss's other Achilles heel. The chapter ends as a parody of a sentimental novel: 'their lips met, their eyes glowed, their knees trembled, their hands wandered' (p.314), with an intended effect in the suggestively mocking last three words.

EXERCISE (Voltaire's *comic techniques)*	What are the main comic techniques which Voltaire uses in the book as a whole? What would you choose as the best examples of these techniques?
DISCUSSION	The choice is wide. Voltaire uses the whole range of comic techniques: there is bawdy humour, most obviously in the old woman's and Cunégonde's stories (even some of Voltaire's contemporary readers thought that this went a bit too far at times); there is repetition of catch phrases like the old woman's 'only one buttock'; the comic theme with variations of Pangloss's 'all is for the best'; black farce in the dissection of Pangloss; 'dramatic' irony in Candide's encounter with the recruiting officers and of Pangloss with the Inquisition's scouts (*we* as readers know what is happening, *they* do not); a whole comedy scene where Cacambo manipulates the Oreillons; exaggeration, grimly comic in Candide's military punishment, light-hearted in Eldorado; and all those brief dialogues which are crucial to the philosophical theme. But the prevailing device and weapon is irony of different kinds, above all verbal irony: '... the musketry removed from the best of [possible] worlds some nine or ten thousand scoundrels who infected its surface' (p.315). Clearly it is not the best of worlds where slaughter on this scale takes place, even if justified by killing 'scoundrels' who are people who are alive, and so 'infecting its surface'.

    '... both kings were having Te Deums sung, each in his own camp' (p.315).

    Voltaire and other philosophers covered many pages attacking hypocrisy, religion, and war, and here it is all expressed in part of a sentence.

    Or the irony may be less complex: 'Los Padres have everything and the people have nothing; it is a masterpiece of reason and justice' (p.328) says Cacambo; and there is irony of situation: '... it was decided by the University of Coimbra that the spectacle of a few persons burned by a slow fire in great ceremony is an infallible secret for keeping the earth from quaking, ... on the same day the earth quaked again with a fearful crash' (pp.319, 320).

For us, as readers, narrative and comic techniques, the author's meaning and his use of language are closely blended; but it helps us, I think, to savour the wit and understand how Voltaire conveys ideas and attitudes, if we look at his use of language. We can appreciate this even in translation, although we miss some of the resonances and allusiveness of the original.

EXERCISE *(Voltaire's use of language)*   What are some of the main points you would note about Voltaire's use of language?

DISCUSSION   It seems very simple. It is not only the economy, but the total assurance of Voltaire's style which creates effect with such apparent ease. The sentences are short and simply constructed, especially in the narrative passages. Background details are minimal, but precise: the right food for the country, the right coinage. Descriptions are given with classical economy: the Lisbon earthquake is described in eight lines, the aftermath of a battle in two sentences. Horrendous events and gross physical cruelty are mostly described without comment; or rather without direct comment. Voltaire creates effects and suggests attitudes by breaking down conventional associations of words and making paradoxical juxtapositions such as 'heroic butchery', 'regimented assassins', or by using blandly inappropriate phrases such as 'extremely cool apartments' for dungeons. Dialogue may be appropriate for the speaker or the situation, or ironically inappropriate for comic effect as in the formal courtesies of the brutes who recruit Candide or the inquisitors who trap Pangloss; or sometimes, one suspects, Voltaire speaks for himself, rather than as the character in the story, like the negro in Surinam when he says: 'It is at this price that you eat sugar in Europe' (p.337), and so makes his attitude to slavery unequivocal.

We are constantly reminded of the book's main target by the slipping in of philosophical phrases and reminders of philosophical issues in moments of extreme drama:

'In vain he told them that the will is free and that he wanted neither of these; he had to make a choice. By virtue of the gift of God that is called liberty he decided to run the gauntlet thirty-six times; he did it twice' (p.315).

8   Story and satire

EXERCISE (Targets of Voltaire's satire)

As a satirist Voltaire aims at many different targets in *Candide*. How many of these can you identify? If you make a list you will find that it is quite long.

DISCUSSION

The main target of Voltaire's satire is made very clear. We have seen how the whole story is organized to ridicule the philosophy of optimism. The attack on organized religion of many kinds is relentless too; on Catholics, Protestants, Muslims, Jews; murderers, fornicators, thieves are identified by their religion and most often turn out to be priests. The Jesuits get the most prolonged attack, particularly the Jesuits in Paraguay, a contentious subject at the time. The only religious man who escapes attack, the only really good man, James the Anabaptist, loses his life early in the story.

The folly and brutality of war is another major target; this too is a universal evil; it appears in *Candide* in England, the New World, including Canada, and in the Muslim world, as well as in the very precise attack on Frederick the Great's militarism and the carnage of the Seven Years' War. One of the few deadly serious passages is about the aftermath of a battle. Voltaire may have remembered here a letter from the Duchess of Saxe-Gotha in 1756 about what she had seen: 'I am horrified by the rivers of human blood which flooded the battlefield and by the groans of so many who were dying'.

But that is by no means all. In Voltaire's catalogue of evils we find the treatment of women as victims of exploitation, cruelty and rape; the misuse of power in greed and corruption; some of Voltaire's personal aversions: the incompetence and greed of doctors, the misuse of science, Rousseau's view of the noble savage (which is caricatured in *Candide* and which you will be able to re-assess when you read the study on Rousseau in Part E of the course). And there is some contemporary and very personal satire on Paris society. Voltaire was by now a long way away from the serene view of the *The Man of the World*.

9   Eldorado and after

When Candide and his companions sail for the New World it is with some feeling of optimism. 'We are going to another universe ... no doubt it is in that one that all is well' (p.323). 'It is certainly the new world that is the best of possible universes' (p.323).

First they find militant Jesuits exploiting the natives. People in the state of nature are cannibals: 'Let's eat Jesuits'. This new world is not a better one.

Is Eldorado at last the promised land? Light-hearted parody of tales of fantasy and adventure is combined with satire of the evil world outside, which has the strange customs of attaching value to pebbles and mud, of demanding payment for services, and of being discourteous.

But the tone becomes more serious in the discussion with the old man about religion. There is no satire of his natural religion, only of its opposite: 'What! you have no monks to teach, to dispute, to govern, to intrigue and to have people burned who are not of their opinion?' (p.335). We get a few glimpses of an ideal state where the king is treated like an ordinary human being, there is good town planning, there are no law courts or prisons, there is a Palace of Sciences, there is no tyranny, all men are free: a rather cursory parody of Utopias or a list of priorities?

Why did Voltaire include the Eldorado episode?

If Voltaire was demolishing the idea that the world as we know it is the best possible world, one of the things he could do was to compare it with the best possible world that could be imagined. (Why he located it in Eldorado is explained by the fact that for his *Essay on Customs* he had studied both the origins of the myth and the attempts, by Raleigh and others, to find Eldorado.) Candide is optimistically pursuing a dream. In the first part of the book he has first-hand experience of the evils of the world. If the story is to show how he learns from experiences, then it is fitting that he should also encounter an ideal world. 'Probably this is the country where all is well; for there absolutely must be one of that sort' (p.334).

Is Eldorado the place which can set the standards to which human beings can aspire? One difficulty which we have in understanding just what Voltaire was intending to convey arises partly from the fact that there are many changes of tone in the Eldorado episode. Before the strange journey which takes Candide and Cacambo into Eldorado Candide says: 'Let's go. Let us recommend ourselves to Providence' (p.333). At this point he still thinks a benevolent providence may well exist. Their first impression in Eldorado is of people in harmony with nature. Nature has been unpleasant, or positively malevolent, in the book so far, but here: 'the country was cultivated for pleasure as well as for need; everywhere the useful was attractive' (p.333). The *philosophes* would have approved of this; and we shall remember the word 'cultivated' when we reach the end of the story. Then, surely, Voltaire goes on to amuse himself, and us, by parodying fantastic tales in the exaggerations of the details of life in Eldorado, and at the same time satirizing the materialistic outlook of the real world. Is he also asking whether total freedom from material cares is one essential aspect of an ideal society?

The serious conversation with the old man is based first on material from the *Essay on Customs*, and then raises the questions for us of whether the old man's deist view was Voltaire's own, and whether an ideal world includes genuine religion.

Eldorado has a well-ordered society which is reasonable and humane, hierarchical, but ruled by an intelligent and benevolent monarch. Is this the *philosophes*' dream? Or is there a faint suspicion that Voltaire is teasing again; he did himself passionately believe in justice and liberty, had a strong interest in science. So did most *philosophes*, but is there just a touch of mockery, or self-mockery here?

EXERCISE   Why do Candide and Cacambo leave Eldorado?

DISCUSSION   I think the two reasons why they leave Eldorado are made clear:

First: 'Mademoiselle Cunégonde is not here', says Candide; then, 'If we stay here we shall only be like the others … ' (p.336), and to make quite sure we get this point Voltaire makes one of his rare direct comments: ' ... people are so fond of running about, showing off before the folks at home and parading what they have seen on their travels that the two happy men resolved to be happy no longer ... '(p.336). Is Voltaire saying that it is in the nature of human beings that they cannot live in an ideal society? Candide has not yet learned this lesson, but the Eldorado episode has changed his role and changed his perceptions in his subsequent adventures and it has provided a model, something to aspire to.

The Eldorado episode is an integral part of the book and it is not forgotten, as Martin reminds us. Candide is confronted with Martin's relentless pessimism in the last part of the story and has to abandon his dreams and face bleak reality. He has explored the old world and the new, looking for an answer to the question of how to live in an evil world. In the old world evil is omnipresent; the same is true in the new world, where the Europeans are still corrupt and the natives are not much better. Pangloss's view that all is for the best is totally destroyed by ridicule and by the overwhelming evidence of facts. Where is there any hope of a better world? In Eldorado? But this world is a Utopian dream and people are not yet ready for it, if they ever will be. 'There is a horrible amount of evil on earth' says Candide when they consult the dervish. 'What does it matter, said the dervish, whether there is evil or good? When His Highness sends a ship to Egypt, is he bothered about whether the mice in the ship are comfortable or not?' 'What should we do? said Pangloss?' 'Hold your tongue, said the dervish.' '... at these words the dervish shut the door in their faces' (p.358).

The dervish has shut the door on philosophy as a guide for living; providence, if it exists, seems malevolent; no conventional religion offers a solution. The Turkish farmer suggests more limited horizons.

10   Candide's garden

The philosophy of optimism, as embodied in Pangloss, is absurd, Eldorado is an illusion, Martin's patient acceptance of evil offers no better answer. Candide's solution is: 'We must cultivate our garden'. But what does this mean? In the end Voltaire leaves it to us, his readers, to speculate and give different answers. For example, the first question which Pangloss asks the Turkish farmer is about the latest political killing. The farmer's answer is: 'I presume ... those who meddle with public affairs sometimes perish miserably and that they deserve it; but I never inquire what is going on in Constantinople' (p.358). Does this suggest that ordinary people should not concern themselves with public affairs and simply try to look after their own interests? Voltaire at this time probably still felt bitter and disillusioned about his own experience, but as his later campaigns for justice show, did not believe in practice that individuals can live isolated from society. The end of *Candide* shows a society on a very small scale. Candide accepts what the Turk says: '... work keeps away three great evils: boredom, vice and need'. The old woman has already asked whether doing nothing is not the worst thing of all. Candide's 'laudable plan' means that they work and they co-operate: 'each one began to exercise his talents'. They do what they can within their own limitations – on a human scale. Pangloss continues to try to put things on a cosmic scale, but Candide has the last word. 'Work without reasoning', 'make life endurable' can be what 'we must cultivate our garden' means for some, and implies having really limited horizons; or the garden could mean whatever goals individuals set themselves; or perhaps it is a final note of mischief by Voltaire, leaving contemporaries and posterity something to think about.

11 The best of all possible worlds?

Candide was not Voltaire's last word, or only word, on the subject. You will remember that there are some remarks on this matter at the end of section 2, 'Voltaire and Optimism', where there is brief description of Voltaire's subsequent remarks on optimism and the problem of evil. In *Candide* he has ridiculed Leibniz's and others' view of the world as created by God as the best which could have been created. Does he, in *Candide* at least, seem to reject any idea of a relatively benevolent providence? Does *Candide* express his view of the world as an ant-hill peopled by human beings who are helpless in the face of natural disasters and disasters caused by the misuse of human capacities and human power? Does Voltaire, despite all the bitter satire on many types of religion, entirely reject the notion of God? The conversation with the old man in Eldorado suggests that he does not. Yet the conclusion of the story suggests that this notion is irrelevant. On what can human beings rely? On their will to survive, on hope, however limited both of these may be? On the fact that all people are not entirely bad, and can work together to make the best of the world as it is? Is there any hope of progress here?

The bleakness underlying the lightness of tone in *Candide* is not found in everything Voltaire wrote at this period of his life. He did believe in working for posterity, as his attitude to the *Encyclopédie* shows: '… you are making yourselves wings to fly to posterity' and '… I shall always be glad to add a few grains of sand to your pyramid …' he wrote to d'Alembert in 1758. In viewing the whole history of mankind as mostly a record of crimes, violence and folly he nevertheless conceded that there were happy ages in history; though this hardly goes as far as Gibbon's '… pleasing conclusion that every age of the world has increased, and still increases, the real wealth, the happiness, the knowledge and perhaps the virtue, of the human race' (*Texts*, I, p.303). Yet even in the comedy of *Candide* a deep concern for the human race emerges. Voltaire did not believe in giving in. His personal response to the problem of evil was not just, literally, to cultivate his own land and improve the lot of his tenants at Ferney, but actively to fight for the rest of his life against specific acts of intolerance and cruelty.

12 *Candide and the Enlightenment*

EXERCISE In what ways is *Candide* a text of the Enlightenment?

DISCUSSION Many of the questions raised by the book will be familiar to you by now. As a satirical tale *Candide* does not allow for any direct expression of opinion by Voltaire, but it is nevertheless a deeply personal book.

Distanced from the ills of the world by wit and humour, it takes a rational view of humanity. It was greeted with approval by Frederick the Great, the cynical pragmatist, and by Catherine the Great, the intellectual empress, with aversion by Rousseau, the subjective prophet, and with enthusiasm by the *philosophes* for its contribution to their campaign against philosophical systems, the church, religious and political intolerance, denial of liberty and human values, injustice, war. It provokes renewed consideration of the dichotomies of reason and sentiment, optimism and pessimism, and a review of human morals and values world-wide. You will find it relevant to your study of other possible, indeed existing, worlds in your study of Cook and Equiano, and even more relevant when we look at Lessing's view of providence and of religious and moral questions in *Nathan the Wise* (*Studies*, II).

13   References

Barber, W.H. (1955) *Leibniz in France*, Oxford University Press, Oxford.

Besterman, T. (1969 and 1976) *Voltaire*, Blackwell, Oxford.

Bolingbroke, H. St J. (1777) *Works*, III, London.

Butt, J. (ed.) (1963) *The Poems of Alexander Pope*, Methuen, London.

du Châtelet-Lomond, G. E. Le T. de B., marquise (1740) *Institutions de Physique*, Prault fils, Paris.

Lanson, G. (1906) *Voltaire*, Hachette, Paris.

Leibniz, G. W. (1898) *The Monadology and Other Philosophical Writings*, edited and translated by R. Latta, Oxford University Press, Oxford. (1968 edn used in this study.)

McCabe, J. (ed. and trans.) (1911) *Selected Works of Voltaire*, Watts and Co., London.

Mornet, D. (1916) 'Les enseignements des bibliothèques privées 1750–1780', *Revue d'histoire littéraire de la France*.

Mylne, V. (1965) *The Eighteenth Century French Novel: Techniques of Illusion*, Manchester University Press, Manchester.

Shaftesbury, A. A. C. third earl (1773) *Characteristicks of Men, Manners, Opinions, Times*, 3 vols, John Baskerville, Birmingham.

Van den Heuvel, J. (1967) *Voltaire dans ses contes*, Armand Colin, Paris.

Voltaire (1979) *Correspondence. The Complete Works of Voltaire*, vols 85–135, Voltaire Foundation, Oxford. (Quotations from correspondence are taken from this edition and translated for the text.)

Voltaire (1877–82) *Oeuvres complètes de Voltaire*, edited by L. Moland, 50 vols, Garnier Frères, Paris.

Voltaire (1911) *Poem on the Lisbon Disaster*, translated by Joseph McCabe, in S. Eliot and B. Stern (eds), *The Enlightenment*, vol. I, Open University Press, Milton Keynes.

Voltaire (1963) *Esssai sur les Moeurs*, edited by R. Pomeau, Garnier, Paris.

Voltaire (1964) *Dictionnaire philosphique*, edited by R. Pomeau, Garnier, Paris.

Voltaire (1966) *Romans et Contes*, edited by R. Pomeau, Flammarion, Coll. GF, Paris.

Voltaire (1979) *Le songe de Platon*, in *Romans et Contes*, edited by F. Deloffre and J. Van den Heuvel, Bibliothièque de la Pléiade, Gallimard, Paris.

14 Further Reading

14.1 Critical editions of Candide and other works by Voltaire

Deloffre, F. and van den Heuvel, J. (eds) (1979) *Voltaire: Romans et Contes*, Bibliothèque de la Pléiade, Gallimard, Paris.

Groos, R. (ed.) (1950) *Voltaire: Romans et Contes*, Bibliothèque de la Pléiade, Gallimard, Paris.

Morize, A. (1913) *Voltaire: Candide ou l'optimisme*, Nizet, Paris. (Revised 1959.)

Pomeau, R. (1959) *Voltaire: Candide ou l'optimisme*, Hachette, Paris.

Pomeau, R. (ed.) (1964) *Voltaire: Essais sur les moeurs*, Garnier, Paris.

Voltaire (1979) *Correspondence: The Complete Works of Voltaire*, vols 85–135, Voltaire Foundation, Oxford.

14.2 Works in English on Voltaire

Besterman, T. (1976) *Voltaire*, Blackwell, Oxford.

Lanson, G. (1906) *Voltaire*, Hachette, Paris, translated by R.A. Wagoner (1966), New York.

Wade, I. O. (1959) *Voltaire and Candide*, Princeton University Press.

14.3 Works in French

Pomeau, R. (1956) *La Religion de Voltaire*, Nizet, Paris.

Van den Heuvel, J. (1767) *Voltaire dans ses contes*, Armand Colin, Paris.

Voltaire en son temps (sous la direction de René Pomeau)

Recent detailed studies appearing in five volumes, Voltaire Foundation, Taylor Institution:

    Pomeau, R. (1985) *D'Arouet à Voltaire 1694–1734*.
    Vaillot, R. (1989) *Avec Madame du Châtelet 1734–49*.
    Pomeau, R. and Marvaud, C. (1991) *De la cour au jardin* 1750–59.
    To come: Volumes on 1759–70, 1770–78.

14.4 Works on Voltaire and Madame du Châtelet

Barber, W.H. (1955) *Leibniz in France*, Oxford University Press.

Ehrman, E. (1986) *Madame du Châtelet*, Berg Women's Series.

Mitford, N. (1957) *Voltaire in Love*, Hamish Hamilton.

Vaillot, R. (1978) *Madame du Châtelet*, Albin Michel, Paris.

14.5 English translations of works by Voltaire

Besterman T. (ed. and trans.) (1963) *Select Letters of Voltaire*, Lond & c.

Besterman T. (ed. and trans.) (1979) *Voltaire's Philosophical Dictionary*, Penguin Classics, Harmondsworth.

Redman, B. R. (1977) *The Portable Voltaire*, Viking Portable Library.

Tancock, L. (trans) (1980) *Letters on England*, Penguin Classics, Harmondsworth.

James Lind, A Treatise of the Scurvy

Prepared for the Course Team by Michael Bartholomew

Contents

James Lind, **A Treatise of the Scurvy** *(Study Week 16)*

Studies/Texts	TV	Radio	AC	Set Books
Studies, I	TV8	–	–	–
Texts, I				

For this week's work you will need this *Studies* volume and *Texts*, I. TV8, 'The Eighteenth-Century Seaman', is also tied in closely to the study.

Acknowledgements

Discussions with Dr Christopher Lawrence of the Wellcome Institute for the History of Medicine were extremely helpful during the preparation of this study. Jerome Satterthwaite suggested a number of improvements to the first draft.

James Lind
A Treatise of the Scurvy

1 Medicine in the eighteenth century

Medicine was one of the hopes of the Enlightenment. The educated and enlightened were no longer willing to regard life as a vale of tears, through which humankind trudged, afflicted by sicknesses sent by God. On the contrary, *health* was seen as the natural condition.

Eighteenth-century doctors drew on the legacy of Sir Isaac Newton, the great hero of the Enlightenment. Newton had bequeathed a confident expectation that the universe is fully explicable. He had shown that the heavens and the earth, from the orbits of the planets, to the fall of an apple, are governed by a single set of laws which can be formulated mathematically. This immense achievement inspired scientists, doctors, economists, historians – indeed thinkers in every field – to seek equivalent regularities in the workings of the particular part of the natural world, or the particular part of human society, that they studied. Science was widely held to be the chief agent in the progress of society.

For doctors in particular, however, the Newtonian legacy was a mixed blessing. It raised expectations that secure, elegant, scientific laws might be framed to account for the workings and the disorders of the human body, and perhaps even of the human mind, just as the great Sir Isaac had framed them in astronomy and physics. But the human body – let alone the human mind – stubbornly eluded neat, scientific formulations. Enlightenment doctors, with their commitment to a belief in the fundamental intelligibility of the human body, could not throw up their hands and concede that sickness and health were inherently mysterious conditions. Yet the object of their study – the human body – often seemed, in practice, to be bafflingly unpredictable.

Although secure, rational explanations of diseases were elusive, superstitious explanations were firmly ruled out. Early in the century, around the year 1710, the infant Samuel Johnson, who suffered from scrofula (or 'the King's Evil', as it was known), was brought to London to be 'touched' by Queen Anne. A monarch's touch, it was believed, could cure the affliction. By the middle of our period, educated people would have ridiculed such superstition, even though no medical cure for scrofula had been produced.

Other diseases, though, were starting to be brought under control. You may recall, for instance, the entry on inoculation in the *Encyclopédie*, and recall also that Frederick and Catherine the Great were enthusiasts for the practice. You may also recall from TV1, 'The *Encyclopédie*', the account of the brilliant surgical operation for the removal of bladder stones. But not everybody was impressed by the claims of doctors. Rousseau, for example, who suffered from a painful urinary complaint, for which doctors offered only agonising, useless treatment, eventually wrote off medicine altogether, dismissing it as a 'useless art'.

On one hand, then, we find eighteenth-century doctors proclaiming their skills, and pointing to their successes. Indeed, we can see them as a profession that was committed to taking charge of what they would have seen as the benign, rational management of human welfare. Yet on the other hand, we can find plenty of instances of people expressing well-founded fears of having a doctor come anywhere near them. There were large gaps between medical ambition and medical achievement. Your study this week takes you to a text which sought to bridge one particular gap, by applying rational, enlightened, scientific principles to the study of a disabling disease.

2   'This foul and fatal mischief'

The text associated with this study is *A Treatise of the Scurvy*, written by the naval doctor, James Lind, and published in Edinburgh in 1753. A 'treatise' is a systematic study of a subject (Hume, for instance wrote *A Treatise of Human Nature*), and 'scurvy' was an endemic disorder during the eighteenth century, especially in northern climates and among seamen.

Your challenge this week is to enter the world of Enlightenment medicine and to see one of its most eminent Scottish doctors addressing an excruciating and perplexing disorder – what he called 'this foul and fatal mischief'.

Scurvy had been known for centuries. If we turn first to the *Encyclopédie* (1765) for a mid-century, up-to-date description of the symptoms, published a dozen years after Lind's *Treatise*, we find this account:

> *The first stage:* the sufferer is extremely lethargic and torpid; he just wants to sit down or go to bed; he feels a spontaneous lassitude and a heaviness in all parts of his body, all his muscles ache, as if he were exhausted, especially in his thighs and loins; he has great difficulty in walking; on waking in the morning he feels shattered.
>
> *The second stage:* he has difficulty breathing and is out of breath, almost suffocating at the slightest movement. A swelling in his thighs comes and goes, marked with red, brown, hot, livid, purple blotches. His face is coloured a pale brown. His gums are swollen, aching, throbbing, burning, and the slightest pressure on them causes bleeding. The teeth are denuded of the gums and are loosened. He has vague pains in all parts of his body, both internally and externally and from these arise cruel torments in the lungs, the stomach, the ileum [part of the intestine], the colon, the kidneys, the gall bladder, the liver, the spleen etc. There is frequent haemorrhaging.
>
> *The third stage:* the gums give off a cadaverous stench. They are inflamed, and blood oozes out of them, drop by drop. The teeth loosen still further and become black, yellow and decayed. Varicose rings form on the ranine veins [veins of the tongue]. There is frequent haemorrhaging through the skin, without there being a wound, and through the lips, mouth, gums, œsophagus, stomach etc. Over all the body, but principally on the thighs, putrid, stubborn ulcers form, which respond to no treatment.
>
> Blood drawn from the veins is partly fibrous, black, clotted and thick, yet the serous part is fluid, salty, stale and covered with a mucus, the colour of which is yellow verging on green. The sufferer is tormented by gnawing, stabbing pains, moving quickly from one part of the body to another and increasing during the night in all limbs, joints, bones and viscera. Livid blotches appear on the skin.

The fourth stage: the sufferer is attacked by all kinds of different, hot, malignant intermittent fevers, vague, periodic and continuous, which cause atrophy, vomiting, diarrhoea and dysentery.
Stranguries [pains in the bladder] give way to lipothymia [loss of
consciousness], extreme anxieties, dropsy [accumulation of fluids],
phthisis [wasting of tissues], convulsions, trembling, paralysis,
cramps, vomiting and bloody stools. The liver, the spleen, the pan-
creas and the mesentery [abdominal membrane] putrefy. At this
stage the illness is very contagious. (pp.802–4, here translated by
J. Greenwood)

The writer goes on to say that sufferers commonly recover from the disease if it has reached only its early stages, but that if it reaches its fourth
stage, death is likely.

This was the disorder that James Lind had chosen to study. Why
should he have made this choice, from among the multitudes of ill-
understood disorders for which cures were needed? Scurvy had become a
matter of especial concern because it seriously affected navies – both
merchant and war fleets. And in an age when international trade, and
related international military rivalry, were developing, a disease which
regularly disabled ships' crews would equally regularly come to the notice
of a young naval doctor such as Lind.

The naval voyage which exhibited the impact of scurvy at its most
fearsome, and which focussed public and medical attention – including
Lind's – on the problem, was undertaken by a squadron commanded by
Captain George Anson in 1740. A war against Spain and France had
broken out in 1739. One of the tactics licensed by the war was the sending out of squadrons of Royal Navy ships to harass enemy merchant ships
and to plunder Spanish and French colonies. Anson was given such a
commission and set sail with a squadron of eight ships, so ill-equipped
and ill-manned that the complement of marines had to be made up with
Chelsea Pensioners. By the time Anson's own ship, *The Centurion*, had
staggered around Cape Horn and made port on the western coast of
South America, 200 of the crew of 400 were dead, mostly from scurvy, and
of the survivors, only about eight were fully fit for service. The squadron
had taken a tremendous battering at Cape Horn. One ship was wrecked
and three returned to England. The remaining four ships sailed up the
west coast of South America, raiding Spanish colonies, and then set sail
across the Pacific, where scurvy again raged among the crews. As one of
Anson's lieutenants put it, in a letter to his brother: 'our men by this time
died like rotten sheep, tossing overboard six, eight, ten or twelve a day'.
Eventually, the combined effects of scurvy and disintegrating ships
reduced the squadron to one vessel, which somehow still managed to
capture a Spanish treasure ship and limp leakily, unhealthily, but triumphantly back to England with a colossal fortune in gold. Over 2,000 men
had left on the expedition. From the crews of the four ships which
rounded the Horn, only 200 men returned with Anson. And it was scurvy
which had done the damage. Enemy action accounted for very few
deaths.[1]

---

[1] A fascinating collection of documents relating to this voyage has been collected
and edited (see Williams, 1967).

What precautions against, and treatments for, scurvy had been tried on the expedition? It seems that there was a general belief that diet had a lot to do with the disease, with 'bad air' as a subsidiary cause. What is perhaps more striking than the crew's precautions, however, is their general fatalism: they seem to have accepted that scurvy was something that just had to be expected by sailors. Their hope was that they would reach land before they were beyond hope, for they were convinced that *something* associated particularly with the land, would restore their health. When *The Tryal*, one of the ships in the squadron, made harbour in South America, in the words of its purser:

> We caught fish for the sick, which with the greens and other refreshments we met with here, together with the smell of the earth, recovered them in a miracle. (Williams, 1967, p.79)

The surgeon on board *The Centurion* made a systematic study of the disease, in an attempt to explain it completely. Another member of the crew, Pascoe Thomas, kept his own record of the voyage and wrote a sceptical and sardonic commentary on the surgeon's research. Pascoe Thomas was not at all impressed by this research; with grim satisfaction, he relates the downfall of the surgeon's pet theory:

> Since our passing Cape Horn our surgeon, Henry Ettrick (who was a very good practical surgeon, but in the theory part vain and pragmatical, making science to consist in a flow of words, with little or no meaning) had been very busy in digesting a theory of scurvies; wherein he enumerated many cases very particularly, having been allowed to open and examine as many bodies as were abundantly sufficient for that purpose. His system was principally founded on the observations made on a long passage, in a very cold climate. He took abundant pains to prove, by many instances, that the tone of the blood was broke by this cold nipping air, and rendered so thin as to be unfit for circulation, or any other of the uses of life; and being thus deprived of a proper force and vigour, stagnation and death must necessarily ensue. From this supposition, he laid it down as an infallible rule, that any food of a glutinous nature, such as salt fish, bread, and several sorts of grains, were alone proper on such voyages. As for liquids, I know not which he had pitched on as the most salutary on this occasion. But this passage, in a very hot climate, where the symptoms were not only more dreadful, but the mortality much more quick and fatal in proportion to the number of people, put our scheming doctor to a sad nonplus: he could not account for this, on the same principles with the other: Nay, they must be in a manner diametrically opposite. All this obliged him at last (though he was still endeavouring to reconcile contradictions) to own, that though some of the concurrent helps of this disease were plain enough, yet that the grand centre was certainly the long continuance at sea, or an entire secret; and that no cure but the shore would ever take place. (Williams, 1967, pp.86–7)

Pascoe Thomas here sounds a note which will reverberate when you study Lind's *Treatise*. Thomas's chief point is that there was a clash between the theory espoused by 'our scheming doctor', and the results of observing sailors who'd been struck down by scurvy. (You may recall that in the *Encyclopédie* entry *Experimental*, d'Alembert discusses the relationship between theory and observation. The case of scurvy is an excellent practical example of the problems of scientific method that d'Alembert was trying to systematize.)

Pascoe Thomas was evidently unimpressed by the efforts of the 'scheming doctor' on board *The Centurion*. As you will see, Lind wrestled with similar problems concerning the relationship between theory and observation.

Dispassionately, however, Thomas followed this record of the failure of medical theory with a brief note of the amateur treatment tried out by Captain Anson himself. In desperation, Anson issued the crew with a patent medicine called 'Ward's Pills' (and took them himself). They produced vomiting and diarrhoea, but failed to arrest the relentless attack of the disease. Thomas's sad conclusion was that the pills, 'together with the inefficacy of all our surgeons could do in the case, sufficiently showed the vanity of attempting the cure of this distemper at sea' (Williams, 1967, pp.86–7).

This was the challenge that Lind took up: in a treatise dedicated to Anson, he aimed to present a coherent account of the disease, and to attempt a cure for it at sea.

Lind was born in 1716 in Edinburgh, a city then on the brink of its golden age as a major European centre of Enlightenment thinking. The new spirit manifested itself in philosophy, science, the law, and of course, medicine. Edinburgh's medical school was staffed by professors who trained in the premier European medical school at Leyden, in the Netherlands, under the premier doctor in Europe, Hermann Boerhaave (1668–1738).[2] They brought back to Scotland a medical tradition of research and teaching which attracted students from all across Europe and America. The young James Lind, however, could hover only on the fringe of these exciting developments, for he entered medicine not by the prestigious route of the University's medical school, but by the lowlier route of apprenticeship to a surgeon.

His apprenticeship could not qualify him for a rich private practice. Instead, it led him to a job as a surgeon's mate in the navy. For ten years he served in the fleet, on deep sea voyages to Africa and the West Indies, and on blockading and patrolling cruises in the English Channel. The world of the eighteenth-century seaman – the world of Anson, Lind and Captain Cook – is explored in TV8, 'The world of the eighteenth-century seaman'.

In 1748 Lind left the navy and went back to Edinburgh to upgrade his medical qualifications. He wrote a thesis which gained him his MD, and spent ten years making the most of the social and professional opportunities that the capital presented. Drawing on his experiences as a naval surgeon, he researched and wrote his *A Treatise of the scurvy*. He followed this in 1757 with a more general book entitled *An Essay on the Most Effectual Means of Preserving the Health of Seamen*. In 1758, he left Scotland to take up another naval appointment, this time to the much grander post of Physician to the Haslar Naval Hospital at Portsmouth. (The establishment of large public institutions like hospitals, prisons, and asylums was a characteristic of the age, one you will remember from the study of the reforms associated with Cesare Beccaria and John Howard. The

---

[2]   It was said that a letter from China addressed simply 'Boerhaave, Physician, Europe', reached him without trouble. Dr Johnson wrote a brief life of him which is printed in the Johnson set text (pp.54–70).

Haslar hospital, incidentally, was the largest brick building in Europe at the time.)

Lind remained in the post at Haslar for twenty-five years. He retired in 1783 (passing on the job to his son in a way quite typical of the eighteenth century) and died in 1794.

3   *Lind's* Treatise

By plucking out just a few carefully selected passages from Lind's book, it is possible to make him look very modern. Scurvy is now completely understood, and Lind can be presented as the doctor who made the first major contribution to our understanding of the disorder. Indeed, Lind is revered by medical and naval historians as 'the father of nautical medicine'. The simple, heroic, but misleading story that can be told is this: Lind pioneered clinical trials for various potential cures for scurvy, and demonstrated the efficacy of one particular treatment – the one that present-day doctors would prescribe. He then published a report of these trials in his *Treatise*. Eventually, the Navy adopted his recommendations and, as a result, scurvy was soon eliminated from the fleet.

Taking this view, it is plausible to claim that Britain's victory in the Napoleonic Wars, at the beginning of the nineteenth century, owed less to Nelson than to Lind, for, by enabling the Admiralty to keep squadrons healthily at sea for long periods, Lind doubled the efficiency of the fleet.

However, by presenting Lind in this way – that is, in the light of modern medical knowledge – we get a seriously distorted view of what he was up to. In order imaginatively to enter his world and follow his researches into scurvy, we must try to set to one side our knowledge of modern treatments for scurvy. If you happen to know nothing at all about modern theories of, and treatments for scurvy, so much the better – you'll be ready to follow Lind's text wherever it leads. If you know something about scurvy, you'll be bound to want to cheer Lind when he looks as if he's getting close to our current beliefs, and to deride him when he goes down a 'wrong' track. If you do this you risk overlooking the fascinating mental set which governed eighteenth-century doctors' views of the human body and its operations. Rather, immerse yourself in what was thought in the eighteenth century. Take the theories of Lind and his contemporaries seriously. Don't let your twentieth-century medical knowledge overwhelm your encounter with eighteenth-century knowledge. Don't give way to feelings of superiority.

Lind opens his *Treatise* with a survey of everything that had ever been written about scurvy. You will not be surprised, given your work on the legacy of the ancient worlds of Greece and Rome, to hear that Lind starts his survey with Hippocrates, the first century BC Greek physician. The Classical tradition exerted as powerful an influence on science and medicine as it did on architecture, painting and philosophy. From ancient Greece, Lind moves on through medieval accounts of scurvy, through seventeenth-century voyagers' accounts of the disease, and up to the views of the eminent Boerhaave. Lind is scrupulous in giving each writer a fair hearing, and sets out their arguments on the causes, symptoms, and cure for the disorder.

From Lind's historical survey, a consensus emerges on the descriptions of the symptoms of scurvy. Writer after writer describes the same gruesome decline of the sufferer: gums rot, teeth fall out, the breath stinks, sores break out, old wounds reopen, the joints seize up. The entry in the *Encyclopédie*, which you have just read, is a reliable summary.

However, when it comes to the causes of, and the cure for the disorder, there is no consensus. The suggested causes can be roughly classified as follows, although many writers say that a number of causes act simultaneously.

First, there is what we might call the 'environmental view'. On this view, climate or weather has a great deal to do with the disease. Cold, damp weather, and long, dark winters, it is contended, bring on the scurvy.

Secondly, there is what we might term the 'dietary view'. Within this view, some writers contend that the disease is caused by eating *too much* of a certain type of food – smoked or salted meat, for example. Certain types of food, it is argued, have qualities which, when eaten in large quantities, over a long period, induce scurvy (rather in the way that we believe that too much sugar induces tooth decay, or too much alcohol damages the liver). But also within the diet view we can find the contention that scurvy is caused by *failing to eat* certain types of food – greens, for example. It's worth pondering this distinction: it is not at all sharply drawn by the writers whom Lind surveys, and common sense does not suggest that one view, rather than the other, is likely to be correct, but there might be a large conceptual gap between the belief that an illness is caused by eating too much of something that's bad for you, and the belief that it is caused by failing to eat enough of something that's good for you. It will be interesting to see what Lind himself has to say when he sets out his own views.

Thirdly, there is what we might call the 'psychological view'. On this view, scurvy assails chiefly the lazy, the indolent, the melancholic. States of mind, or natural disposition, seem to play a part in who goes down with scurvy and who remains healthy.

Fourthly, there is what we might call the 'lowered-resistance view'. On this view, scurvy assails people who, but for some other, unrelated indisposition, would be able to resist the disease's attack successfully. If they are recovering from another illness, for example, they are more prone than fully-fit people are to scurvy attacks.

Fifthly, we can group together suggestions which Lind mentions out of an obligation to be comprehensive, rather than because he sees them as fruitful research suggestions. He curtly summarizes, for instance, the views of Everard Maynwaringe, who, in 1668, had suggested that smoking and immoderate sexual activity were supplementary causes of the affliction.

Lastly, it is important to note possible causes which Lind never considers. Scurvy is never seen as a punishment from God. Nor is it ever seen as the result of witchcraft. Whatever his private religious beliefs (and they are not known), Lind's professional world is wholly secular. He is an entirely characteristic Enlightenment thinker in limiting his field of enquiry to the rational and the empirical. To anticipate somewhat, you will not be surprised to learn that he never considers prayer as a likely agent in the cure of scurvy.

No consensus on the cure for scurvy emerges from Lind's historical survey. Some authorities recommend bleeding – the practice common in the eighteenth century of opening a vein and drawing off a quantity of blood. Others suggest purgatives. Some suggest the need for warm, dry lodgings. As for diet, some recommend that salty meat should be eliminated from the patient's fare, while others recommend that vegetables, or 'green trade' as it was sometimes called, should be included. One writer in Lind's survey notes that seamen on a sixteenth-century expedition to Newfoundland cured themselves of the disease by following the practice of local inhabitants, who drank a brew made from the bark and green shoots of pine trees. The references, like this Newfoundland example, to local, folk remedies is striking. A number of writers note that the common people have their own ways of tackling the disease. One sixteenth-century authority, Ronsseus, while himself advocating bleeding and mineral waters, notes that seamen on long voyages cure themselves 'by the use of oranges', and that, on land, 'the vulgar' cure themselves 'by scurvygrass, brooklime, and water cresses' (Lind, 1953, p.265). The common name 'scurvygrass' (*Cochlearia*, a common plant, found near the seashore) is suggestive: was there perhaps an underlying folk tradition of cures for scurvy, possibly in tension with professional medical authority? Again it will be interesting to see what Lind himself thought.

Two further accounts from Lind's historical survey are worth singling out. The first is of the Dutch writer, Bachstrom, who wrote about scurvy in 1738, twenty-five years before Lind published his own *Treatise*. In Lind's own paraphrase, Bachstrom's unambiguous conclusion is

> that as abstinence from recent vegetables is altogether and solely the cause of the distemper, so these alone are its effectual remedies. (Lind, 1953, p.316)

The second account is of Hermann Boerhaave's views of the disorder. Boerhaave's views automatically commanded Lind's attention. The founders of Edinburgh's medical school, Lind's own teachers when he returned to Edinburgh to take his MD, had themselves been taught by Boerhaave at Leyden, and they brought back with them an allegiance to their eminent teacher's theories. Thus, Boerhaave's ideas dominated Edinburgh medicine. Boerhaave's explanation of scurvy is complicated. He does not approach the disease with a low-level, empirical, trial-and-error method. His aim seems to have been to assimilate scurvy to a very particular overall account of how the body works. He operates at the level of sophisticated physiological theory. To echo the discussion of scientific method in your study of the *Encyclopédie*, Boerhaave was not collecting random observations about what eases the pain of people with the scurvy: he was striving for a total account of the body's workings.

We needn't go far into Boerhaave's theory. All we need to note is that in the case of scurvy, the immediate focus of his attention is the composition of the patient's blood. His contention is that one constituent of the blood had become, as Lind summarizes it, 'too thick and viscid' (sticky), while another constituent of the blood has become 'too thin and dissolved'. Therapy, therefore, should be designed to rebalance the composition of the blood. Problems arise, however, because different patients have different imbalances in their blood, 'so it requires different and opposite cures; what is serviceable to one scorbutic [i.e. scurvy-ridden] patient, proving poisonous to another'. Because of these problems, Boerhaave 'thinks it the master-piece of art to cure the scurvy'. His recommendations are for purgatives, bleeding, baths, friction for stiff joints, sometimes medicines containing mercury, all to be varied according to the particular symptoms exhibited by the patient (Lind, 1953, pp.307–10).

(The 'scheming doctor' on *The Centurion*, we may suppose, was probably a follower of Boerhaave.)

Lind's survey of everything that had ever been said about scurvy – itself a characteristic eighteenth-century exercise in systematic classification – establishes scurvy as a painful, disabling disease, the symptoms of which were widely recognized. Its cause, and its cure, though, were the subject of wide disagreement. Lind's survey leads him on to the next part of his *Treatise,* in which he sets out what he calls 'the true causes of the disease, from observations made upon it, both at sea and land'. And it is at this point that we engage with the text.

4 *Reading the* Treatise

Three sections from the *Treatise* have been extracted and printed in volume one of the *Texts.* Shortly, you will be asked to read and re-read these sections, steadily familiarising yourself with Lind's world and his ways of thinking. Obviously, you will encounter both medical terminology and a number of medical theories which have long been since discarded. But Lind was not addressing a solely medical readership: he would have had a wide general readership as well. So it is perfectly possible for the modern general reader to get hold of Lind's ideas both of how the human body works, and of what goes wrong with it when it is assailed by scurvy. The initial strangeness of phrases like '*a saponaceous, attenuating, and resolving virtue*', will give way, as you become familiar with text, to the satisfaction of tackling a piece of eighteenth-century medical research at first hand.

The *Treatise* as a whole runs to about 100,000 words. The extracts you'll be studying come to about 12,000, so plainly, I have had to do a great deal of editing and compressing. But my aim has been to preserve some sense of Lind's grand attempt to be as comprehensive and scrupulous as possible about an extremely perplexing disease.

The exercises will ask you to read through each section a couple of times, and for each reading, you'll be posed a different question, starting with a fairly straightforward one, and moving on to more difficult ones.

EXERCISE Go through the first section of the text (*Texts,* I, pp.365–72) and make a list of the possible causes of scurvy that Lind discusses. Sort them into the five categories established earlier – environmental, dietary, psychological, lowered-resistance and miscellaneous.

You'll find all sorts of other issues being considered in this first section. For the moment though, just rough out a list of all the possible causes, using the five categories, and using Lind's terminology.

DISCUSSION Here's my list:

1   *Possible environmental causes:* 'polluted air', especially from bilge-water; 'filth, or want of cleanliness'; sea air; moist air; cold air; a combination of cold and moist air – 'a combination of moisture with cold, is the most frequent and genuine source of this disease'; poor air-circulation.

2   *Possible dietary causes:* salt from sea water; 'sea provisions' – the standard naval diet; lack of 'green herbage, vegetables, and fruits'; the drinking of spirits rather than beer.

3   *Possible psychological causes:* indolence and laziness; melancholy; skulking; being in a 'discontented state of mind' (e.g. by having been pressed, against one's will, into the navy by a press-gang).

4   *Possible sources of lowered resistance:* a 'preceding fit of sickness'; 'long continuance and constant use of any one particular source of food' – especially indigestible food.

5   *Miscellaneous possible causes:* 'unsound and obstructed viscera'; suppressed menses; sedentary occupations (e.g. tailoring, shoemaking).

There's no need to worry if your list doesn't correspond exactly with mine: the boundaries between my categories can't be very precise. But if you've not come up with something approximating to my list, have another go, doing the exercise in reverse: take my list and find the places in the text from which I've collected the examples.

You will have noticed that at no point in this section does Lind claim to have discovered the single, sure cause of scurvy. Rather, he is sifting through all sorts of frustrating evidence, evaluating it, eliminating some possible causes, and trying to draw significant distinctions among the rest. Our job now is to go back over this first section of the text and look more closely at Lind's presentation of his research. A second, careful reading should give you a secure grasp of his lines of argument.

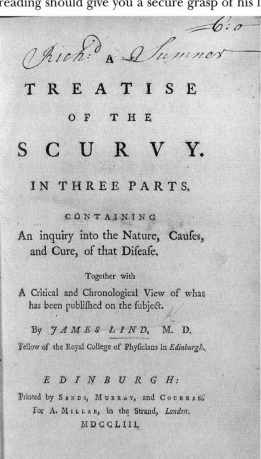

Figure 52
Title-page of Lind's
A Treatise of the Scurvy.
(Published by permission of the British Library Board)

EXERCISE   As you go through the section again, consider the following two questions.

1   *The elimination of some possible causes of scurvy.* Even if Lind does not establish a single, definite cause, does he rule out any contenders? Look closely at his evaluation of the evidence, and at his own observations, and see if he is able conclusively to eliminate some false leads from the enquiry.

2   *Lind's distinction between what he calls 'occasional' and 'predisposing' (or 'disposing') causes.* What he is trying to do here is to distinguish between, on one hand, conditions which might *predispose* people to go down with scurvy, but which won't, of themselves, bring about the disease, and, on the other, conditions which will actually *occasion* their going down with the disease. He is using the term 'occasion' in a now slightly archaic sense – in the sense in which I might say 'my drunkenness occasioned a fall from my bicycle'. That is to say, my fall was immediately caused by my drunkenness. To continue the analogy with Lind's terminology, I might also say that although my fall was occasioned by my drunkenness, I was *predisposed* to such an accident because I have weak eyesight, a poor sense of balance, and because the road was icy.

Get hold of Lind's distinction and apply it to the list of causes that was drawn up in the last exercise: which headings cover *occasional*, and which cover *predisposing* causes?

DISCUSSION   1   *The elimination of false leads.* It is evident that Lind has had wide experience of the disease, has made some acute observations, and has even conducted some clinical experiments upon patients. He seems to have good grounds for rejecting those theories of which he is critical.

His experiment on the effects of drinking sea water, for instance, seem pretty sound. He records his taking two scurvy-ridden patients and dosing them for a fortnight with sea water, in order to confirm that, at the end of the treatment, they were 'in the same condition as those who had taken no medicine whatever' (*Texts*, I, p.365). Notice, though, that Lind does not rule out the effect of salt altogether: brine seems to impair the digestibility of meat.

His observations on the effects of 'the confined and polluted air of a ship' seem sound too. If bad air were a definite cause, those who habitually spend time in the most noxious part of the ship would be specially prone to scurvy. But they are not.

Is sheer length of voyage a straightforward cause? Again, Lind is persuasive. Voyages of similar duration can end equally with healthy or with scurvy-ridden crews.

2   *Occasional and predisposing causes.* Lind's distinction is complicated, but you should have come up with something like this. All the headings on the list, save one, cover *predisposing* causes. The headings of environmental, psychological, lowered-resistance, and miscellaneous causes cover a range of conditions which make people susceptible to scurvy (although polluted air is ruled out, and the uniquely

female condition of suppressed menses is never followed up, since Lind is concerned chiefly with seamen). Lind makes a further distinction which you may have noticed, between what he calls, on one hand 'principal and main', and on the other, 'secondary' predisposing causes (p.368). The principal predisposing cause is cold, damp weather. The rest are secondary.

Moving now to what it is that actually *occasions* the disease, it is plain that it falls under the one remaining heading – diet. Something to do with diet occasions the outbreak of scurvy among those seamen who are already predisposed to it. Scurvy seems to be a digestive disorder. The regular sea diet is normally 'extremely wholesome' (p.370), but, Lind says, the predisposing causes – chiefly the weather – render the body incapable of properly digesting it. He promises (p.370) to explain this 'weakening of the animal powers of digestion' later. In this preliminary section, though, he is keen to establish just that diet occasions the disease and that adjustments to diet, mainly by the addition of 'green vegetables, and the fresh fruits of the earth' (p.372) can stave it off.

Lind is struggling a bit here, I think. He cannot nail down a single, invariable cause. Moreover, he can say neither that if all the predisposing and occasional causes are present, seamen are *certain* to go down with scurvy, nor that if the most promising anti-scurvy items of diet – fresh greens and vegetables – are present, seamen will *certainly not* go down with it. As a scrupulous and experienced observer, he is aware of so many exceptions and oddities in the incidence of scurvy that he is obliged to present a highly complicated account of the disease.

Has Lind made any progress at all in clarifying matters? This brings us to a final, consolidating exercise on this first section of the *Treatise*.

EXERCISE   Review your notes, look back at bits of the text, and write a couple of sentences which answer the question: 'What, according to Lind, are the causes of scurvy at sea?'.

DISCUSSION   Scurvy is a disease of faulty digestion and is caused by the conjunction of, on the one hand, *predisposing* causes, chief of which is cold, wet weather, and, on the other, the *occasional* cause of the regular ship's diet. This diet is normally perfectly adequate, but when the predisposing causes upset the body's powers of digestion, regular sea diet cannot be digested and the symptoms of scurvy break out.

We can now move on to section two of the text (*Texts*, I, pp.372–7) in which Lind sets out his recommendations both for preventing and curing the disease. This section contains the passage which, for most historians of medicine, is the most significant in the *Treatise*. The passage records what are possibly the first-ever controlled clinical trials of medicines.

Lind makes a clarion Enlightenment call when, in this next section, he says that he will 'propose nothing merely dictated from theory: but shall confirm all by experience and facts, the surest and most unerring guides' (*Texts*, I, p.372). Your job is to see whether he faithfully heeds his own call.

The section falls into three parts. Let us take each in turn.

EXERCISE Read from the start of the section up to the end of his account of his clinical trials of various medicines (up to '… might in all probability have been preserved', pp.372–4). Are his conclusions persuasive?

DISCUSSION Generally speaking, the conclusions are persuasive. Of the six potential remedies that Lind tried, oranges and lemons came out as clear winners. The experiments aren't absolutely conclusive, though. The sea-water remedy, for instance, was tried on 'two of the worst patients'. Can we be sure that the sample of 12 unfortunate sailors was reasonably uniform? But, given the undoubted difficulties of conducting rigorous clinical trials at sea, it is hard to resist the conclusions that Lind draws from his experiment, especially as he fortifies them by modestly claiming that the efficacy of oranges and lemons had 'stood the test of nearly 200 years', and by acknowledging that, centuries ago, common sailors had accidentally discovered that oranges and lemons were an effective remedy.

EXERCISE In the second part of this section, Lind sets out methods of preserving orange juice and fruit, and makes recommendations to commanders of ships concerning seamen's diet. Read from 'As oranges and lemons are liable to spoil', up to '… certainly become much more anti-scorbutic' (pp.374–6). Are his recommendations and his belief in the efficacy of his evaporated orange juice warranted by his trials with actual patients?

DISCUSSION The interesting point here is that having proved, seemingly to his complete satisfaction, that oranges and lemons rapidly cure scurvy, Lind launches into a wide-ranging series of medicinal and dietary recommendations, most of which are not actually warranted by his experiments. His discussion notably does not narrow down to a scheme for the regular supply of the items that cured his two patients, namely, oranges and lemons. Instead, he launches into a scheme for preparing and preserving evaporated orange juice – or 'rob' as it was called at the time. And then he moves on to a much more general review of sailors' diet, stressing the need for vegetables and fermented drinks. By the end, the link with his actual clinical trials has become very tenuous. He is relying, it seems, on more general observations.

EXERCISE Thirdly, Lind makes some recommendations concerning what he has identified as the predisposing causes of scurvy. Read from 'I proceed now …' up to the end of this section (pp.376–7) and again consider the basis upon which Lind makes these confident recommendations.

DISCUSSION   He wants ships to be clean, dry and warm, with a good circulation of air, possibly fumigated by a 'wholesome antiseptic vapour' produced by plunging red hot irons into buckets of tar. Seamen should be encouraged to sweat. Lind supplies no firm experimental evidence upon which these recommendations might be based.

You should now be in a position to judge whether Lind was indeed guided by 'experience and facts', and I guess that your judgement is likely to be 'only up to a point'. He seems ready to range well beyond the limits of his experimental results. Although it seems plausible that evaporated orange juice would preserve the 'virtue' of the real thing, Lind hasn't tested it experimentally.

He seems to have a lot on his mind that tends to blur the apparently straightforward logic of his own conclusions. He spends a deal of time on problems to do with digestion, excretion, sweating and fermentation. You'll probably recall odd passages in section one in which he argues, for example, that 'the glutinous viscidity and tenacious oils' of certain vegetables are 'broken and subdued' by fermentation (*Texts*, I, p.370).

The general question that now faces us is this: given that there was a good deal of rough-and-ready experience, dating back two centuries, of the value of oranges, and given that Lind experimentally confirmed their efficacy, why did Lind – one of the most committed and experienced researchers of his age – give them so little prominence in his *Treatise* as a whole? Why did he simply not write a brief tract, aimed at the Admiralty, arguing strenuously and single-mindedly, for oranges, oranges, and more oranges?

A clue lies in the third and last section of the extracts from the *Treatise*, to which we must now turn. This section, in which Lind sets out his 'theory of the disease', is the most difficult, simply because it deals with unfamiliar ideas. It will need to be read at least a couple of times, but it is perfectly coherent.

EXERCISE   Lind's account moves through four stages.

1   He gives a general account of how the body works, (up to '... death and putrefaction', p.377).

2   He outlines a theory of the processes of digestion and excretion, and says how they operate on regular ship's diet, (up to '... found to be imperspirable', p.380).

3   He explains what he sees as the particular digestive characteristics of 'vegetables' – by which, in this context, he means edible plants generally (as opposed to animal products), (up to '... exerted in its full force', p.380).

4   He makes some observations on the value of items of diet, like beer, in the preparation of which, *fermentation* has been involved (p.381).

Work through this section a couple of times, making careful critical summaries of each of the stages of the argument.

DISCUSSION

1   *Lind's general theory of the body.* His idea is that the body is serviced by a network of circulating fluids or 'humours' (an idea which, incidentally, is traceable back to the Greeks – another example of the continuing hold of the Classics on eighteenth-century thought).

    If the smooth circulation of these fluids and the excretion of their waste products is inhibited, the body starts to putrefy. The symptoms of scurvy, by implication, are manifestations of the body's putrefaction.

2   *Digestion and excretion.* Food is broken down into finer and finer particles which, in the form of *chyle*, renovate, via the blood, the whole body. The most important outlet for waste products is perspiration. If perspiration is prevented, waste products build up inside the body and putrefaction sets in.

3   *The sea-going diet and the importance of vegetables.* In ideal circumstances, sea-fare is digestible, but when cold, wet weather inhibits perspiration, and when the seaman is less than fully fit, the body can neither properly digest it, nor excrete its wastes. By contrast, vegetables 'are of a more tender texture': they are more easily digested. What is special about vegetables, and what makes them effective in the treatment of scurvy, is that they have '*a saponaceous attenuating, and resolving virtue*'. That is to say, they are characterized by the readiness with which they can be broken down by digestion and used by the body to restore a proper, healthful balance to its scorbutic – sticky, putrefying – fluids. Sea-fare on its own becomes indigestible, but if green vegetables are added to the diet, the combination can be digested efficiently and turned into the material necessary for the body's maintenance.

4   *Fermentation.* Another good thing about vegetables is that they ferment, and fermented drinks, such as beer – including 'spruce beer', made from the fermented sprouts of spruce trees – are held by Lind to be anti-scorbutic.

 You may have noted in the earlier extracts a number of references to fermentation. We don't have space to pursue them here, but briefly, digestion of food was held to *be* a process of fermentation: thus, foods which readily ferment are more easily digested. Accordingly, bread baked with yeast – which ferments – was held by Lind to be better than the unleavened ship's biscuit, which was the seaman's regular fare. Similarly, beer is better than spirits. And since fermentation gives off a gas, bottled fizzy water containing the gas might reasonably be thought to be anti-scorbutic – an idea you'll meet again in your study of Captain Cook.

    We are now in a position to stand back and review Lind's *Treatise* as a whole.

    Lind appears in histories of medicine as the champion of empirical observation. Here is how he is described by the editor of a standard work on the subject:

> [The *Treatise*] is one of the finest clinical studies ever written. It is excellent clinical research, combining careful observation of disease, penetrating analysis of possible factors involved, precise experimentation, cautious drawing of conclusion. (King, 1971, p.154)

The sections you have read will confirm many of these judgements: Lind's observations, experiments and analysis are indeed acute. But what strikes me about the *Treatise* is the way in which all Lind's observations are governed by his prior commitment to a particular theory of the body. Lind did *not* look at scurvy with an innocent eye. He was committed – probably via his Edinburgh, and hence, Boerhaavian background – to a theory which made him look more or less exclusively at digestion and excretion when he was framing his account of the disease. Any observations he made had to be conformable with this theory. This is not to criticise Lind. Like all scientists, he approached his material with a particular mental set – a cluster of expectations and conventions which simultaneously stimulated and restricted his research.

What preliminary conclusions can we draw about the *Treatise?* First, I suggest that the text opens an intriguing window into the period, and especially into the life and conditions of the seaman.

Secondly, I would argue that Lind exhibits wonderfully the tensions between two strands within the Enlightenment. On one hand he has the ambition to frame a grand general theory, and on the other he is doggedly determined to fulfil the obligation to make scrupulous, empirical observations.

Thirdly, it might be possible to argue that doctors like Lind, with their commitment to medical theory and professional prestige, paid relatively little attention to low-level, popular but effective cures. Lind could not rest content with the simple, provisional conclusion that, generally speaking, oranges cure scurvy. He was committed to explaining how and why they do, and this led him into chapters of theorizing which tended to muffle the force of his experiments on the twelve scurvy-ridden seamen on the *Salisbury*. The *Treatise* as a whole promises to sharpen and clarify understanding of the disease, but ends by diffusing and complicating it.

5   *The impact of Lind's* Treatise

To make headway in almost any field of endeavour during the eighteenth century, it was useful to have powerful patrons. Lind had made a hopeful gesture in this direction by dedicating his *Treatise* to Anson, who had risen to the rank of admiral. But Lind seems not to have been naturally adept at promoting his own cause. He did not spend time lobbying at the Admiralty or at the premier scientific society of the age, The Royal Society. Indeed, it's not easy to see exactly what Lind's cause actually was. He was transparently earnest in his wish to improve the lot of the seaman – he later, for instance, recommended that seamen be issued with uniforms, rather than being left to equip themselves as best they could. But his *Treatise* notably does *not* end with a ringing call to their Lordships to issue a regular ration of oranges and to include fresh vegetables in the diet of seamen. So muted are Lind's conclusions that another doctor, writing forty years later, could quote from the *Treatise* passages which indicated that fruit and vegetables are *not* an infallible cure for scurvy (see Beddoes, 1793, p.61).

Lind's *Treatise*, then, effected no immediate revolution. Indeed, in subsequent editions of his *Treatise*, Lind's theorizing became more, not less, diffuse. Scurvy continued to rage among the fleet. In 1781, for instance, 3000 cases were reported in the West Indies Fleet. The

Admiralty's Sick and Hurt Board, which was charged with the health of the fleet, put its faith not in oranges and lemons, but in 'wort' – a fermented malt extract. This was not blind prejudice. Even if fresh oranges and lemons had been proven beyond all doubt to be a sovereign cure for scurvy, how could the Navy possibly be supplied with them? Where would they come from? How could they be kept fresh? Lind's recommendation that, in the absence of fresh fruit, an evaporated extract or 'rob' of the fruit juice, would be an effective substitute, met with only limited success. Perhaps, it was thought, the process of evaporation by heating destroyed the very quality which made the fresh fruit effective. What was the point in the Admiralty's tying up scarce resources in an elaborate preparation of unproven success? Wort had no greater success rate, but at least it was cheap and readily obtainable, and it had the blessing of the remarkable Captain Cook, who, as you will see in the next study, achieved astonishing success in keeping his crews free from the scurvy.

However, Lind's successors and disciples in naval medicine, Gilbert Blane and Thomas Trotter, kept up a steady lobby for lemon and orange juice, and eventually, after further sea trials, the Admiralty, in 1795, agreed to issue crews with a daily allowance of three-quarters of an ounce of lemon juice per man. The incidence of scurvy fell, straight away, just as the fleet was to be put to its severest test, in the war with Napoleon's France. The final push for a regulation issue of lemon juice had come from Blane, and he should have the last word, for in 1785, while graciously acknowledging Lind's pioneering work, he frankly conceded that the disease was still as big a mystery as it ever was. He wrote that it was now certain that oranges and lemons both prevent and cure scurvy:

> This was first ascertained and set in a clear light by Dr Lind. Upon what principle their efficacy depends, and in what manner they produce their effect, I am at a loss to determine, never having been able to satisfy my mind with any theory concerning the nature and cure of this disease, nor hardly indeed of any other. (Lloyd, 1965, pp.159–60)

Lind, it seems, had wrestled only partially successfully with a disease whose elimination would have eased much pain and distress. His recommendations concerning oranges and lemons had somehow been stifled by the blanket of his theory, and the strategy of his disciples was to substitute their own theories, while salvaging some of his recommendations.

6   Postscript

At the outset of this study, I argued that an understanding of present-day theories of scurvy would hinder your approach to Lind: it would either prevent your giving him a fair hearing, or predispose you to hunt only for those bits of the *Treatise* that look modern.

However, an interest in what *really* causes, and what *really* cures scurvy cannot indefinitely be suppressed. After all, it is not a disease which will respond to *any* treatment, no matter how whimsical. Some treatments will cure it, and some won't. And it happens that Lind got it 'right' when he went (along with dozens of other writers) for oranges and greens, and 'wrong' in practically everything else – though I hope that you'll agree that he was perfectly rational in drawing the conclusions that he did draw, and that neither he nor his contemporaries were blind to solutions that were staring them in the face.

If you look back in this study to the summary of Lind's historical survey of writings on the subject of scurvy (pp.376–8) you'll find a fragment from Bachstrom. He gives what is, in modern terms, a completely accurate, common-sense estimate of the disease: fail to eat greens and scurvy will break out; start to eat them and it will clear up. Captain Cook took pretty much the same view. But neither Cook nor Bachstrom could unite their estimates with a full theory of the disease, and this, of course, was Lind's aim. In pursuit of it, and using the best authorities available to him, he was led down the tracks you have followed.

Two final points. First, Lind had been dead for over a hundred years before vitamins were discovered and vitamin-deficiency studied. Not until 1907 was it possible successfully to unite observations of the effects on scurvy patients of green vegetables, lemon and orange juice, with theories both of how the body works, and of what precisely it is within greens and citrus fruits that make them effective. Secondly, by a cruel twist, it was discovered, again after Lind's death, that evaporating orange juice destroys most of its anti-scorbutic properties.

7   *References*

[Anon] (1765) *Encyclopédie*, (Neuchâtel).

Beddoes, T. (1793) *Observations of the Nature and Cure of Calculus, Sea Scurvy, Consumption and Fever*, London.

King, L.S. (1971) (ed.) *A History of Medicine: Selected Readings*, Penguin, Harmondsworth.

Lind, J. (1953) *A Treatise of the Scurvy*, edited by C. P. Stewart and D. Guthrie, Edinburgh University Press, Edinburgh. (Reprint of 1st, 1753, edn.)

Lloyd, C. (1965) (ed.) *The Health of Seamen*, Navy Records Society.

Williams, G. (1967) (ed.) *Documents Relating to Anson's Voyage Round the World 1740–1744*, Publications of the Naval Records Society, vol. 109.

8   *Further reading*

Carpenter, K. J. (1986) *The History of Scurvy and Vitamin C*, Cambridge University Press.

Watt, J., Freeman, E. J. and Bynum, W. (1981) *Starving Sailors*, National Maritime Museum. (A generally fascinating collection including an article by J. Watt, entitled 'Some consequences of nutritional disorders in eighteenth-century British circumnavigation'.)

Captain Cook and Olaudah Equiano

Prepared for the Course Team by Angus Calder

Contents

Cook and Equiano (Study Week 17)

Studies/Texts	TV	Radio	AC	Set Books
Studies, I	TV8	–	–	–
Texts, I	TV9			

For this week's work you will need to consult texts by Cook (*Texts*, I, pp.383–402) and Equiano (pp.405–22). TV8, 'The Eighteenth-Century Seaman' and TV9. 'Slaves and Noble Savages: Equiano and the Enlightenment', are both central to this study.

Captain Cook and Olaudah Equiano

1 Introduction

The prowess of European seafarers since the fifteenth century was an important precondition for Enlightenment in Europe. Columbus in 1492 had accidentally bumped into America. Colonisation of the New World by Spaniards and Portuguese had followed. Seamen, traders and colonists from north-western Europe had invaded the Iberian monopoly, and by the mid-seventeenth century there were well-established British, French and Dutch colonies in North America and the West Indies, providing furs, fish, tobacco and a novel comestible, cane sugar, for European markets. The mines of Latin America gave Europeans the means of trading for tea, silks and porcelain with the ancient and opulent Chinese Empire. Meanwhile, fine cloths from India lured Europeans to the sub-continent, where they established small but rewarding trading 'factories'.

The rise of capitalism in Europe from the fifteenth to the eighteenth centuries was fuelled by the expansion of intercontinental trade. Around 1500, Chinese technology was more advanced than Europe's. Living standards for cultivators of the soil were as high, or higher, in India and Africa. Indian cotton textiles were covetably superior to lumpish European woollens. Sophisticated Muslims controlled commerce from Egypt to Indonesia. Three hundred years later, European naval technology and gunnery, clearly the best in the world, were the basis for European dominance in every ocean. Europeans made their own cotton textiles by new factory methods and were poised to flood Eastern markets with them. Through the eighteenth century Britain and France fought a series of wars affecting every continent: Britain emerged with a temporary near-monopoly of overseas colonies. Nowhere was British predominance more striking than in the slave trade, which the British Parliament piously outlawed in 1807.

Slave-grown sugar, moving into an endlessly expandable market among the growing middle classes and even the lower orders of Europe, had created vast fortunes. The slave trade itself had enriched Liverpool, the trade in slave-grown tobacco was crucial to the swift rise of Glasgow. In the hinterlands of these two ports, in the late eighteenth century, slave-grown cotton was the basis for industrial revolution capitalized from fortunes based, directly or indirectly, on slavery.

How, you may ask, did this impressive commercial expansion contribute to 'Enlightenment'? Very directly: the text of the Bible did not hint at the existence of America, and the revered writers of classical Greece and Rome had known nothing about that continent. Here, and in other unimagined regions, European traders, settlers and travellers encountered unsuspected fauna and flora and peoples of many skin hues with customs and beliefs of intriguing variety. Exploration and intercontinental trade fed on and encouraged the faith of enlightened persons in man's capacity to exploit to his own material advantage the various good things which Providence, or Nature, had distributed around the globe. News of strange sights in far places promoted scepticism about received authority, whether biblical or classical. The fact that Chinese and Indians lived by creeds, Confucian and Hindu, which supported ordered and complex civilisations but did not admit the Christian Trinity, fostered support for 'deism' – the belief that there was indeed one God, but that different peoples worshipped Him in different ways and that Christian 'revelation' had no overweening special status. Civilized Chinese gave Voltaire sticks with which to beat superstitious Europeans. And many educated Europeans transferred elements of the 'pastoral' dream of the Golden Age to largely imaginary versions of life among primitive peoples encountered by travellers: the myth of the 'noble savage' reached its apogee of influence in the late eighteenth century.

You have already heard something in Part A of the success, from the 1760s, of James Macpherson's 'Ossianic' poetry. Gibbon was moved to compare 'Ossian's' heroes favourably with the 'degenerate Romans polluted with the vices of wealth and slavery' who had lived at the same time. The Ossianic cult became closely related, in 'neo-classical' art, to the cult of the ancient Greeks. The important aesthetic theorist, Johann Joachim Winckelmann (1717–68) suggested that the superior beauty of Greek art derived from the superior beauty of the Greeks themselves, whose way of life was simpler and more natural than that of corrupt modern Europeans. And he saw the life of contemporary savages as analogous: 'Behold the swift Indian [Amerindian] outstripping in pursuit the hart: how briskly his juices circulate! how flexible, how elastic his nerves and muscles! how easy his whole frame!' (Winckelmann, 1755, extracted in Eitner, 1971, p.6).

The thinker above all associated with the cult of the 'noble savage' was, however, Jean Jacques Rousseau, whom you will meet extensively in Part E. His *Discourse on the Origin of Inequality* (1755) traced human society from man's primitive condition to his present state of depravity. Rousseau was not a naive primitivist – he believed that the Golden Age, when people had subsisted in small societies by hunting and gathering, was gone beyond recall, and his political writings extolled the small city-state, of which his own native Geneva was a modern model. But his *Discourse* presented a positive view of the 'savage' in his natural state, 'satisfying his hunger under an oak, quenching his thirst at the first stream'. Natural man, Rousseau says, is immensely robust and can put his body to 'all sorts of uses' of which ours 'for lack of practice are incapable' – so he can throw stones harder, climb trees more nimbly, and run faster than his civilized counterpart: without machines to aid him, he is 'complete' in himself (Rousseau, 1984, p.81ff).

A positive view of the 'savage' which assimilated him with the heroes of Homer and of Ossian conditioned both the production and the reception of the two texts which you are about to study. While accounts by himself and others of the voyages of James Cook in the Pacific were read (or misread) as providing evidence of the nobility and virtue of man in a savage state, the anti-slavery movements, of which Olaudah Equiano became a distinguished leader, made great play with the conception that Africans, happy amid the natural plenty of their homelands, were torn from them to suffer grief, torture and mutilation in the New World. A more simply and 'naturally' ordered world, or so many fancied, would be better than the cruel Europe of luxury, poverty, war, syphilis and injustice attacked in Voltaire's *Candide*.

EXERCISE   Read now the extract by Cook in your *Texts*, I, pp.383–402. As a first exercise summarize briefly, in, say, 150 words, Cook's attitude towards the islanders of Tanna. 'Noble savages' or just 'savages'? Reconsider your summary as you read the essay which follows here.

2 Pacific exploration and the 'noble savage'

The 'South Seas' of the Pacific and eastern Indian Ocean remained a mystery in the mid-eighteenth century. Galleons traversed regularly between the Spanish domains in Mexico and the Spanish Philippines, while Dutch and Portuguese dominated parts of Indonesia; but the vastness of the Pacific (which covers a third of the world's surface) was such that islands had been found, lost, 'discovered' again and given different names, and geographers continued to speculate about the existence of a second 'New World', a great Southern Continent in temperate latitudes, ripe for trade, mining and perhaps colonisation by the first European power to claim it.

In 1605 de Quiros, a Spanish pilot, thought he had found its edge. He had in fact struck one of the New Hebrides group, which he named Australia del Espiritu Santu. What we now call 'Australia' was known as 'New Holland', and its western coast was sometimes visited by European seamen. In 1642 a Dutchman, Tasman, had discovered 'Van Diemen's Land', now 'Tasmania', and part of the west coast of 'New Zealand'. Competition for empire world wide between Britain and France ensured that after their Seven Years' War (1756–63) fierce competition began over Pacific discovery.

In 1764, the British Government sent out Commodore Byron with 'a design of making discoveries and exploring the Southern Hemisphere'. He found some islands, and returned in 1766. From August of that year Captain Wallis and Captain Carteret voyaged. Separated as they entered the Pacific, each hit more islands. Wallis was the lucky one who landed on Tahiti, then called 'Otaheite'. Meanwhile, the French commodore Bougainville went to search the Pacific from November 1766, returning in May 1769. He too visited Tahiti. Diderot wrote in 1772 a fictitious 'Supplement' to Bougainville's account of his travels, richly symptomatic of the huge impact of the discovery of this apparently paradisal island.

In Diderot's imaginary account, an aged patriarch steps forward as Bougainville prepares to sail away. To his fellow Tahitians, he prophesies their enslavement and corruption by Europeans in the future. To Bougainville himself, he says:

> Quickly get your vessel away from our shores. We are innocent. We are happy. And you can only hurt our felicity. We follow the unsullied instinct of nature alone. And you have tried to erase its mark from our souls. Here everything belongs to everybody. And you have preached to us of I know not what distinction between *yours* and *mine*. We hold our daughters and our wives in common. You have shared this privilege with us. And you have come to ignite in them hitherto unknown frenzies ... We are free and here you have implanted in our earth the standard proclaiming our future slavery

... The Tahitian of whom you wish to take possession like an animal is your brother ... Leave us to our customs. They are wiser and more honourable than yours. (Manuel, 1965, pp.99–103)

Diderot's patriarch goes on specifically to denounce the Europeans' introduction of syphilis. Captain Wallis had found sandy beaches, lofty mountains, noble trees, pure air, abundant food, and girls wearing chaplets of sweet-smelling flowers who were very willing to give their bodies in return for an iron nail or two. Bougainville, soon after, concluded that Wallis' men had introduced syphilis: the islanders told Cook that the French had brought it, though they called the disease 'Apa no Britannia'.

2.1   *James Cook's voyages*

Cook was the Captain of an expedition sent by the British Government to the South Seas in 1768. Besides the general aim of forestalling the French in the Great Southern Continent, there were scientific objectives, chief among them the observation of the transit of the planet Venus across the sun in 1769. Tahiti seemed an ideal site for this. The significance of the transit was that it could help to determine the size of the universe: Venus provided a kind of stepping stone in calculating the distance between earth and sun. However, Cook and the scientists with him, despite enjoying perfect weather, found that the penumbra around the planet as it crossed the sun made agreement in their calculations impossible.

In other scientific aims, the expedition was more successful. After three months on Tahiti, Cook sailed on, visited the Society Isles which he claimed to have discovered, fell in with, explored and surveyed the coast of New Zealand, then proceeded to 'New Holland', Australia, and moved up the eastern coast of that 'vast country' also. He had cut a way through a very large part of the area where a Southern Continent might exist. Two naturalists with him, Sir Joseph Banks and Dr Solander, were able to bring back remarkable specimens and observations.

Banks, later President of the Royal Society, was a titled gentleman of 'ample fortune'. 'Cook's First Voyage' of 1768–71 brought much less prestige to the Captain than to Banks, who was given an honorary doctorate of Oxford University. The great Swedish naturalist Linnaeus suggested that 'New South Wales' should be named 'Banksia'. Yet Cook, as soon became clear, was the more remarkable man: a kind of self-made seaman-scientist.

Born in 1728, the son of a labourer who had emigrated from Scotland to Yorkshire, Cook worked on the farm his father managed, then in a grocer's shop. He went to sea later than most sailors, aged 18. But the Whitby collier on which he worked provided fine training. The Admiralty chose such a ship for his 1768 expedition. North Sea colliers were big (300 to 500 tons) and very strong, but their moderate draught meant that they could use the shallow waters along a coastline where sands stretched far into the North Sea and exacted great skill of the pilots. Cook studied mathematics and navigation in his spare time and became expert in coastal surveying – the skill which he applied to New Zealand and Australia.

In 1755, he decided to try his luck in the Royal Navy. His outstanding work in the charting of the St Laurence River for Wolfe's expedition which captured Quebec from the French in 1759 led to further such

Figure 53
Portrait of Cook by J. Webber.
(National Portrait Gallery,
London)

employment. In 1766, while working on the coast of Newfoundland, he made observations of an eclipse of the sun which impressed the Royal Society in London. So he seemed just the man for the Tahiti expedition.

His 'Second Voyage' (1772–5) was prompted by renewed concern over imperial hegemony in the South Seas. The 'Falkland Islands' in the South Atlantic were of no economic value in themselves but their large, secure harbours made them strategically useful as a 'gateway' to the Pacific. Spain claimed both 'Malvinas'. Bougainville put a French settlement on the eastern 'Malouine' in 1764, and soon after Commodore Byron set up a little British colony on 'West Falkland'. In 1770 the Spaniards expelled it. For a while war seemed certain, though Dr Johnson inveighed against such folly. But a compromise was patched up, and the British reoccupied the island on the understanding that they would soon quit (as they did in 1774).

The Admiralty bought two more colliers and gave Cook naval command of a new expedition. Banks was due to go again, as scientific leader, but made a fool of himself. He proposed to take a personal party of seventeen, and put an extra upper deck on the converted collier *Resolution* to accommodate his expensive ideas. This made it top heavy. When it was taken down, the sulking Banks refused to go.

Banks' withdrawal, as one contemporary wrote, put 'a check to the rising expectations of the literati' (Smith, 1985, p.53). His party was to have included able painters and scientists.

However, William Hodges was now appointed as painter – a very necessary role before the invention of photography – and John Reinhold Forster who, though German, was a Fellow of the (British) Royal Society, and his gifted teenage son George, went as naturalists, with two astronomers, William Wales and William Bayley. Cook's new expedition had so many scientific objectives that it might be compared to a present day space-probe. It carried, in order to test them, a large range of possible cures for scurvy (including 'Marmalade of Carrots' and 'Inspissated juice of Beer and Wort'). It settled the age-old problem of how to determine longitude at sea. Since the Renaissance, *latitude* had been established with increasing accuracy by observation of the stars. But *longitude* was far harder to settle and without accurate observation of *both*, the exact position of islands in the Pacific could not be established for future navigators – hence the geographical uncertainty which had sustained the myth of the Great Southern Continent, and hence the importance attached by the British Government and its 'Board of Longitude' to settling the matter. Cook took four chronometers: accurate measurement of Greenwich time was seen as the key. The instrument devised by John Harrison (1693–1776) accumulated an error of only about 10 seconds a day over three years and 20 days, and while Cook was still at sea the Board rewarded the old watchmaker for nearly half a century of work with its great prize of £20,000.

Cook didn't settle the problem of scurvy. Though he lost only four men from 112, and only one of them through disease, he carried so many anti-scorbutics that it was not clear which was the best answer, and his own commonsensical insistence that his men eat fresh fruit and vegetables whenever possible was without doubt the basis of his success. Nor was his testing of Harrison's chronometer truly epochal: its virtues had been increasingly clear for some time and meanwhile it was too expensive to be of wide naval use. What Cook's skill and courage did achieve, was the destruction of notions about a Great Southern Continent.

Leaving Plymouth in July 1772, the *Resolution* and *Adventure* crossed the Antarctic Circle from the South Atlantic next January: Cook was the first known commander to do so. Then he sailed east at an average latitude of about 60° – that of St Petersburg in the Northern Hemisphere – and found not so much as an island all the way from the meridian of Greenwich to that of New South Wales. With the Southern winter impending, he sought milder conditions in New Zealand, then sailed east from there to the centre of the Pacific. The ocean was still empty. After scurvy broke out on ship he turned to Tahiti for fresh provisions.

In November 1773, having lost touch with the *Adventure*, Cook took the *Resolution* eastward again from New Zealand, then sailed south to latitude 71° 10' S, where he found a solid ice barrier. No sailing ship, in that longitude, would ever get so far again. Cook then made a great sweep round the Pacific – back to New Zealand via the Marquesas Islands and Melanesia (the New Hebrides and New Caledonia). So, in August 1774, he came to the island which he called 'Tanna'.

2.2   Cook on Tanna

The Tahitians, whom Cook had got to know well, and whom he respected without any delusions that they were 'noble savages', belonged to that amazing seafaring group of peoples, the Polynesians, whose skill as navigators had enabled them to settle islands over a vast triangle. The apex was Hawaii; the base stretched from Easter Island in the east to New Zealand in the west. The western side ran up Fiji. Fijians, and the inhabitants of lands ranging from New Guinea to New Caledonia, were 'Melanesian'. Whereas Polynesians were light-skinned, Melanesians were darker, some black, and had frizzy hair and broad noses, reminiscent of Africans.

Cook was not the first European to visit the group which, for reasons unclear, he chose to call the 'New Hebrides'. As we have seen, a Spaniard, de Quiros, had mistaken one of them, early in the seventeenth century, for the Southern Continent. Bougainville had recently steered through the group. But the natives were unused to Europeans, and vice versa.

After a bloody skirmish with hostile natives on Eromanga, Cook then sailed on to the smaller, volcanic island of Tanna. During a month in the New Hebrides Cook, as was his wont, did wonders as a marine surveyor, putting on paper a remarkable chart which includes ten large islands, six or eight smaller ones and dozens of rocks and islets. Tanna was the only place where he anchored for more than two nights, and his fortnight there gave him almost all he knew about Melanesian people and their customs. Of these, some did, and some didn't correspond to Rousseauesque stereotypes.

Since the island was not visited again by a European ship for a quarter of a century (the Russian Captain Golovnin, in 1809, found Cook's glossary invaluable) and after that not till 1825, Cook's was the only systematic account of its people before British missionaries settled there in the 1840s. These zealous men were convinced that the Tannese were disgusting, superstitious cannibals who never stopped fighting each other,

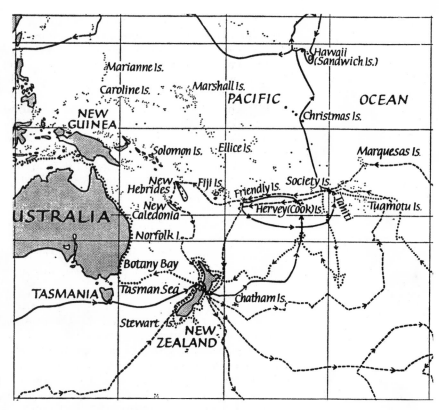

Map 5
Australia and Pacific islands.

and their deeply prejudiced accounts now make ludicrous reading. However, thanks to their statements and the observations of twentieth-century
anthropologists, it is possible to reconstruct the society which Cook
encountered.

The behaviour of the Tannese towards Cook and his men was conditioned by their belief that these were the ghosts of ancestors, figures
from the spirit world who were dangerous and had to be propitiated. Mis-
understanding affected even the naming of the island. If it had a native
name this was Ipari, which was what people in the surrounding islands
called it: the Tannese themselves gave it no name. When Forster pointed
at the ground, they said 'Tanna'. This was their word for 'land' or 'earth'.
(The 'New Hebrides', incidentally, are now independent as Vanuatu,
which means, simply, 'our islands'.)

On their mountainous island the 'Tannese' lived dispersed in several hundred small settlements. These had been created by different
waves of settlers, mostly Melanesian, some Polynesian, over a long period.
Cook identified two different languages: there were actually five major
languages. But a common social organisation secured equilibrium.

> The nuclear family formed a distant household, though it was
> usually linked with similar households belonging to the same
> patrilineage to form one settlement. Groups of hamlets shared com-
> mon territorial names: Europeans chose to call these 'tribes'. But it
> is not clear how much importance Tannese themselves attached to
> 'tribal' affiliation. Ongoing community life was tied to the more
> localized *yimwarem* – cleared spots in the bush ... sacred places,

shaded by ancient banyan trees ... where the men congregated each night to drink their *kava*. (Adams, 1984, p.7)

The daily exchange of *kava*, an alcoholic brew made from the root of *Piper methysticum*, was part of a regular system of ritual exchange of gifts, which ranged up to elaborate transfers of pigs, ceremonies and dances between super-'tribal' networks. A cycle of 'one-upmanship' rotated endlessly. The village or larger grouping which received pigs had to match or exceed the gift in its turn. Girls were assigned to marriage soon after birth, often to another lineage in the same 'tribe', sometimes to another 'tribe'. These matches related to political alliances. Any rights to land which a woman had were lost on marriage – but her husband's people had to provide a bride to her own people, reciprocally, sometime in the future.

Even warfare was essentially an exchange ritual. Battles were pre-arranged like cricket fixtures (in some parts of the Pacific, forms of cricket may today function as substitutes for warfare). They depended on suitable weather, and had to fit into the routine of daily work on the plots which provided food. Small war parties confronted each other, shouted and flung spears. If a man was by chance killed, the battle finished for the day to 'allow the losing side to examine whether any one had breached any of their "appointed observances", thus provoking the anger of the gods' – a kind of 'time out'.

The anthropologist W. Arens (1979) was unable to find any clearcut evidence in recorded history for cannibalism (meaning the habitual eating of people as food) in any part of the world: all reports were hearsay. If 'cannibalism' can be said to have existed in Tanna, it was part of the pattern of exchange rituals and was of political rather than dietary significance. Victorian missionaries would never be able to *name* any *individual* who was actually munching his neighbours because he liked the taste. 'For the whole island there were never more than twenty-eight families with the right to eat human flesh' (Adams, 1984, pp.10, 18). This was confined to the ritual ingestion of portions of the bodies of enemies fallen in battle, passed down to acknowledged flesh-eaters, ritually, from village to village.

The Tannese recognized a founding deity, Kwumesan. Various spiritual entities – dead ancestors, legendary heroes, later Jesus Christ – were intermediaries between them and Kwumesan. Keeping the spirits happy was an incessant preoccupation. All adult men performed rites to ensure success of crops. Society was 'acephalous'. There was no one 'high priest', and no one political chief. 'Given the number of dignitaries', a recent scholar concludes, 'it is difficult to find a system more flexible and more democratic at the same time ... a leader one day would be a follower the next – this one would practice [special] magic to make the yams grow, that one would lead the people into battle, another would bring rain' (Adams, 1984, p.21). If the yams failed, the rain didn't come, or the battle was unsuccessful, the leaders responsible lost authority.

Some men – called *yeremwanu* – wore impressive feathered headdresses – *kayoo* – on ceremonial occasions. But these *yeremwanu* were pretty commonplace – at least one or two in every village – and had different privileges. An anthropologist found 472 *yeremwanu* on Tanna in the 1950s. 140 had *only* the privilege of wearing *kayoos*. '235 could also feast on the head of the turtle, 27 could supervise the cooking of the smooth pig, thirteen were masters of the *nekawa topungu* ... [a special variety of the root used for making *kava*], three could take part in cannibal feasts [*sic*], and 106 were magicians' (Adams, 1984, p.15). The war chief, *yani en dete*, had just one material privilege – a black and red penis-wrapper. But in the assemblies where men argued for hours or days, employing elaborate oratorical skills, when war was at issue, the *yani en dete's* final say was potentially decisive.

If Cook's party had understood all this, they might well have been struck by similarities between this political system and those of ancient Athens and Republican Rome. (Analogies were drawn between the political arrangements of the Iroquois Confederation and those of the new USA; rather later, between Maoris and Ancient Greeks.) But Cook had scant time to attempt 'social science'. He made use of Paowang, who was, it seems, the man with some claim to leadership who worked out most quickly how to propitiate the returning ancestors, Cook and his men. The older men followed him and became polite and deferential. Younger men, in some cases, were ready to try different methods – threats and derision. The murder of a young warrior by a sentry brought Cook's fortnight to a sad close.

But the Tannese weren't fools, and thought they'd done pretty well out of Cook's visit – or so a tradition picked up by a missionary in the mid-nineteenth century suggests. 'Kuke' was indeed violent: he shot seven people, the tradition had it, though five recovered. His visit on 14 August to the house of a dead (or dying?) man received a positive construction. The man was ill because bewitched. Learning that 'certain persons were burning his rubbish and causing all the sickness', 'Kuke' went off and shot the offending sorcerer. So the Tannese had successfully controlled this dangerous ancestor for their own purposes: the young man who died had needed sorting out, and 'Kuke' zapped him, then sailed off, as if his mission had been accomplished (Adams, 1984, p.31).

EXERCISE   Could you now, please, look again over Cook's account of Tanna with the following questions in mind.

1   To what extent did 'scientific' considerations determine the length of Cook's stay: what other factors were involved?

2   In the light of the information you've just had, how would you now describe Cook's attitude to the Tannese? Was he prejudiced? Condescending? Quick to jump to conclusions?

3   What do you make of his comments (*Texts*, I, p.401) on a passage from Wales's journal? You might like to consider this alongside the reproductions of two engravings after Hodges made from the artist's on-the-spot drawings after his return to Britain, and included in Cook's published account of the Voyage.

DISCUSSION   1   It is evident that procuring wood and water was Cook's primary motive (p.388). Eromanga was abandoned for this purpose because of the hostility of the people: good reason for Cook to be careful in relations with the Tannese. However, Wales conducted astronomical observations, the Forsters studied local botany, and the expedition made careful study of the volcano: Cook is clearly pleased that the theory that volcanoes were always found on the highest peaks is disproved in this instance (p.398) – he displays the interest which a scientist takes in testing theory against observation.

Why is Forster so keen (15 August) to find the tree which bears the wild nutmeg which he finds in the craw of a pigeon he shoots (p.397)? This was of acute economic interest. The nutmeg gave a much-prized spice. If it were native to Tanna, this might be sufficient motive for European settlement, to organize plantations. There were in fact several species of wild nutmeg in Vanuatu.

2   Cook describes the incident on August 19 when a sentry (William Wedgeborough) shoots at a group of natives (p.398), but his printed account does not give the aftermath. He flung Wedgeborough in irons, and was intending to have him flogged, but his officers took the man's side and after a heated argument the flogging was remitted. Young Lieutenant Elliot remarked in his memoirs later '... with respect to the Natives, tho' I have several times said that Capt Cook was a most Brave, Just, Humane and good man, and fittest of all others for such a Voyage, yet I must think that here ... he lost sight of both justice and Humanity' (Holmes, 1982, p.34). Elliot and others believed that the sentry shot just in time to save himself from a poisoned arrow. Elliot clearly thought that 'justice' and 'humanity' were terms restricted to treatment of white people.

Not so Cook. And contrast Cook's tone with that of Dr John Paton who went as Reformed Presbyterian missionary to Tanna in 1858:

> My first impressions drove me, I must confess, to the verge of utter dismay. On beholding these Natives in their paint and nakedness and misery, my heart was as full of horror as of pity. Had I given up my much-beloved work and my dear people in Glasgow ... to consecrate my life to these degraded creatures? (Paton, 1893, p.66)

Cook could be fairly cynical about the motivations of Pacific peoples, but only because he assumed that they resembled his own unruly, light-fingered crewmen. Unlike the later missionaries, he is sceptical about the possibility of cannibalism, even though the 'natives' themselves first broach the subject: he doesn't see any proof (p.393). He is rightly convinced, after two weeks, that he is dealing with an 'acephalous' people without a king (p.402), though in his very brief contact with Eromanga he thought he had spotted such a personage. He does object to the Tannese 'making the females do the most laborious work' (p.400). Here he jumps unfairly to conclusions: men did in fact carry heavy burdens, but with a pole – either one at each end, or a man in the middle with load before or behind – never on the back or under the arm like a woman. However this is in a paragraph where he comments on the 'good features, and agreeable countenances' of these lazy-seeming men. To him their behaviour

Figure 54
*Man of Tanna. (The Trustees
of the National Library of
Scotland)*

(Sunday 7) is not 'savage', but 'inconsistent' (p.392). The young
men at first are 'daring and insolent' (terms perfectly applicable to
British sailors on occasion). But by Tuesday 9 the natives seem 'cour-
teous and obliging' (p.392) (terms which would compliment British
gentlemen). He respects the 'jealousy' with which they fix 'bounds'
to the whites' excursions (p.393). If his prejudice against the 'vile
custom' of homosexuality seems 'unenlightened' now, it is typical
that Cook should express his gladness that his men had misunderstood Tannese behaviour at first and that he need not charge the
islanders with sodomy (pp.395–6).

He admires what he can, reporting (Tuesday 9) the appreciative view taken by Forster's party of 'fine plantations' inland (p.393). He is far from idealising the islanders' stone age culture – their lack of interest (at first) in metal carried the very practical disadvantage that the British found it hard to trade successfully with them (p.399). He infers that they fight many wars from their constant carrying of weapons (p.399), but does not moralize over this: these people are neither Paton's 'degraded' natives – nor the 'noble savages' imagined by Diderot and other European philosophers.

3   Nevertheless, Cook defers to the cult of the 'noble savage' when he incorporates Wales's comments into his account (pp.401–2). The comparison with Homeric heroes elevates the Tannese. The same effect is seen in Hodges's oils. Hodges (1744–97) was, like Cook himself, of humble origins: he had began life as errand boy to a well-known artist. He had been a pupil of Richard Wilson, Britain's most

Figure 56
Landing at Tanna. (National Maritime Museum, London)

noted painter of landscapes in 'classical' style. He shared with the scientists in Cook's expedition a keen interest in the study of light and atmospheric effects – not only of interest in their own right, but of acute practical importance to seamen who could interpret such effects to forecast weather changes. Hodges made remarkable wash and water colour drawings of ice, water, mist and light in the Antarctic. In his work in the Pacific he breaks, as Bernard Smith puts it 'quite free from neo-classical formulas'; the roseate hue diffused over sea and sky is something quite different from the golden sunset glow of Claude and Richard Wilson.

But when he got home, Hodges – aspiring to a Fellowship in the Royal Academy – bowed to prevalent taste as he completed, for his employers, the Admiralty, the paintings and drawings he had brought back. He created Claude-like visions of Arcadian pastoral bliss, while accurately representing South Seas peculiarities.

Hodges employed other artists to draw figures for him, and they gravitated towards sentimental stereotypes of the 'noble savage' and heroic neo-classical images of 'Homeric' natives. Whereas Hodges's ethnographic depictions of Tannese, found in Cook's book, are direct and unidealized, the *View of the Island of Tanna* there is Arcadian: Hodges's painting in the National Maritime Museum of the *Landing at Tanna* gives the islanders Homeric physique and stances. Wales, his scientific friend, defended Hodges against the criticisms of George Forster, who complained in print about 'Greek contours and features' in depiction of the South Seas: he retorted that Forster himself used such phrases as 'elegant' and 'exquisitely proportioned' when describing the natives of the Friendly Islands (Smith, 1985, pp.53–80). This points to the fact that the language of painting, at any one time, is as conventional as the use of words.

People literally cannot understand paintings, or writings, which move outside accepted clichés. This will cause problems for us in interpreting the prose of Olaudah Equiano.

2.3   Cook's 'Second Voyage': the aftermath

Cook's remarkable feats were recognized on his return to England in July 1775. He was made a Fellow of the Royal Society, and was admired in more general society. James Boswell was duly attracted to him, and was temporarily seized with a burning desire to go with him on his next expedition to the Pacific. He found Cook 'a plain, sensible man with an uncommon attention to veracity. My metaphor was that he had a balance in his mind for the truth as nice as scales for weighing a guinea'. (Beaglehole, 1974, pp.451–2). Meanwhile, Captain Furneaux, whose ship had separated from Cook's long before, had returned to Britain in July 1774 with a real-life South Sea Islander, Mae, called in London 'Omai'. This young man, native of Ituahine in the Society Islands, was adopted into fashionable 'society' by Banks and the Earl of Sandwich (First Lord of the Admiralty), and was duly painted by Sir Joshua Reynolds, in a style quite distinct from the realistic, coarse-featured picture of him made by Hodges for the famous Scottish surgeon John Hunter (you see both in TV9). With Reynolds, bare feet and flowing robe evoke classical antiquity. 'Omai' was a cheerful, unintellectual, soul. 'How do, King Tosh!' he is alleged to have said when introduced to King George III, who made him an allowance which enabled him to live in some style in his own lodgings in London. Even Dr Johnson admired his good breeding, though Cook thought little of him, knowing more impressive Polynesians. 'He was not a man of much observation'. Cook took him back to his homeland on his 'Third Voyage', which set out in July 1776.

This was intended to solve another geographical puzzle, the whereabouts of a 'North West Passage' over and around America which might provide a shorter route on which to bring that increasingly popular beverage, tea, from China, than the immensely long haul around South Africa. Cook established that the Behring Strait was the only approach from the Pacific to the Northern Sea. At $70\frac{1}{2}°$N he ran into a wall of ice. He turned back to Hawaii, an island which he had just 'discovered' and was killed there in a skirmish with local inhabitants. His temper had not improved over the years, and his death was precipitated by his rash attempt to take a hostage to use for the return of a cutter stolen by islanders. Cook had been a remarkably 'just and humane' negotiator with Pacific people. The irony of his end, however, would not have shocked Voltaire. 'Providence', if it existed, had treated Cook harshly.

3   Olaudah Equiano and the campaign against black slavery

Olaudah Equiano who might well, as an experienced seaman, have served under Cook, perhaps felt that great Captain's death to be puzzling. As he saw it, God's Providence constantly intervened in naval matters to protect Equiano himself and other good people, or, perchance, to strike down the wicked.

Equiano's is one of the most extraordinary autobiographies to come to us from the eighteenth, or any other, century, yet what he recalled were mostly experiences shared by many others: enslavement in Africa, suffering on the 'Middle Passage' to America and as a slave in the New World, hard service below decks in the Royal Navy. What was unusual was that someone who had gone though all this wrote a polished prose narrative which became a best-seller, and died a respected middle-class person in England, with a white wife.

Before you read our set extract from his autobiography, which takes us only as far as the beginning of his service, aged about 12, in the Royal Navy, you should know the whole story. (It's vivified somewhat, we hope, in TV 9.)

Equiano was born an Igbo in what is now eastern Nigeria. His name, 'Equiano', probably signifies 'when they speak others listen'. Captured by slave traders when aged about 11, he was transported to the African coast and thence to Virginia via Barbados. After a short spell as a servant in this British North American colony (where his master was apparently one of the many Scots doing well in the tobacco business), he was purchased by a naval lieutenant, Michael Pascal, who re-named him Gustavus Vassa after a famous Swedish king.

With Pascal, 'Vassa' saw service in the Seven Years' War, in Wolfe's campaign to conquer Canada (where, as we have seen, James Cook was involved) and in fights and blockades off European coasts. Then, Pascal sold him to Captain James Doran, who took him back to the West Indies and disposed of him there. Under his new master, Robert King, a Quaker who was the chief merchant on Monserrat but also an unusually mild master, Equiano saved up £40 from petty trading, and so bought his freedom. Now in his twenties, he travelled widely, in Europe, Turkey and the New World. In 1772 he joined Constantine Phipps's expedition towards

the North Pole, aimed at finding a 'North East Passage' over Russia by sea to China. It got as far as Spitzbergen – further north, at 81°20', than any navigator had been before, or so Equiano could claim.

Thanks to white well-wishers, Equiano had been baptized as a child. Nearing thirty and still, despite his ability and experience, no more than a free servant, he went though a religious crisis, and identified himself with an evangelical form of dissenting Calvinism through the independent Westminster Chapter ('Congregationalist').

His confirmed piety was an asset, as he began to work on behalf of fellow victims of slavery, though the Bishop of London refused to ordain him as a clergyman to go as a missionary back to Africa. In 1786 he rose, for the first time, above the status of servant, as commissary of provisions and stores for the project to resettle destitute black people from London on the coast of Sierra Leone. He quarrelled with the white government agent, who he thought was abusing his position, and though the Navy Board vindicated his character, he was dismissed. He became a full-time campaigner for the abolition of the slave trade, trusted and admired by the middle-class evangelicals who funded the movement, travelling through England, Scotland and Ireland to promote the cause, and selling many copies of his *Narrative* of his own life. (In 1791, he disposed of 1900 during a tour of Ireland which lasted $8\frac{1}{2}$ months.) The book went through eight editions before his death in 1797, a further six in the next 22 years, during which, in 1807, the British parliament illegalized the slave trade. A Belfast abolitionist, Thomas Digges, averred that Equiano was 'a principal instrument in bringing about the motion for the repeal of the slave act'. He was certainly the first major political leader of black people resident in Britain.

In TV9 'Slaves and Noble Savages: Equiano and the Enlightenment', Dr David Dabydeen and Professor Paul Edwards give authoritative information about the history of black settlement in Britain. To summarize: black Africans were known in Britain from very early times, as Roman soldiers, and even on Viking longboats. From the 1560s, when Englishmen first became involved in the slave trade, black slaves entered the country as personal servants: this grew to something of a spate in the later seventeenth century with the rise of Caribbean sugar colonies. Black servants became items of fashion, and as such featured with rich clothes and fine horses in eighteenth-century portraits. Returning planters and North America colonists visiting Britain brought slaves with them for the practical reason that they didn't want the cost of employing free-born white servants. Slaves were openly offered for sale in London, Bristol and Liverpool, the chief slaving ports, and runaway slaves (their harsh treatment often signalled by conspicuous scars) were frequently the subjects of newspaper advertisements offering rewards.

Nevertheless, it remained unclear whether slavery was actually legal on British soil. As Equiano found, the position of black people was utterly insecure in the North American and Caribbean colonies: time and again, whether trusted slave or 'freeman', he was cheated and bullied by whites who knew that a black couldn't obtain redress against a European. Was it also the case in Britain that the law could give no support to a black person asserting a claim to freedom? Were masters entitled to ship black servants against their will, in bondage, back to the New World?

In 1729, the law officers of the British crown affirmed, in response to pressure from white planters, that a slave brought to Britain did not become free and might be compelled to return to the plantations. This so-called 'Yorke–Talbot' ruling was opposed by Lord Chancellor Henley when he ruled in 1762 that 'as soon as a man sets foot on English ground

Map 6
Slave trade.

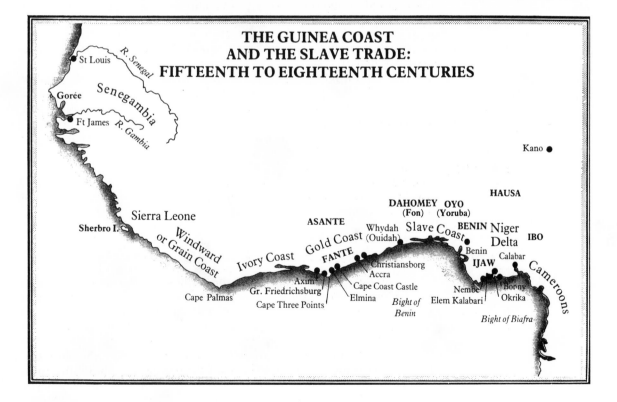

**THE GUINEA COAST
AND THE SLAVE TRADE:
FIFTEENTH TO EIGHTEENTH CENTURIES**

he is free'. In 1765, an eccentric, devout civil servant, Granville Sharp, was shocked to encounter Jonathan Strong, brought from Barbados as a slave, beaten savagely by his master, then thrown on the streets as useless. Sharp arranged for Strong's care in hospital and eventually found him work. But when his former master spotted him, he sold Strong to a Jamaica planter and employed two professional slave-hunters to kidnap him and jail him till he could be put on shipboard. Sharp took the case to the Lord Mayor of London, who set Strong free. The Jamaica man sued Sharp for damages, unsuccessfully. Sharp went on to fight a prolonged battle over the general issue – was slavery legal in Britain? – and over particular cases of kidnapping. In 1772 he secured what seemed a triumph in Lord Mansfield's judgement in the case of James Somerset. Somerset had escaped from his master, a Massachusetts customs official, in 1769. After two years he was recaptured and put on a ship. Mansfield, the Lord Chief Justice, eventually ruled that the laws of the colonies did not apply in England. The 'Mansfield judgement' did not mean, as many textbooks have held, that 'slavery was abolished' in Britain. Till the 1830s, when the status was done away with throughout the Empire, blacks might still enter Britain as slaves, be bought and sold, bullied and exploited. All that Mansfield said was that it was illegal to compel a slave to go by force out of England – and even this did not prevent further cases of kidnapping and transportation. The ruling in the case of *Knight vs Wedderburn* which came before the Scottish Court of Session in 1778 was, by contrast, quite decisive. Wedderburn's escaped slave must be free because 'The dominion assumed over this Negro under the laws of Jamaica, being unjust, could not be supported in this country to any extent'.

Momentum was building up for a campaign against slavery. Quakers in Britain, and more so in the USA, were very uneasy about slavery, though, like Equiano's master King, some were heavily involved in it. Sharp typified the movement of conscience among Christians – John Wesley emphatically to the fore – which drew on the growing 'evangelical' fervour of the period. All people, black and white, evangelicals said, were equal before God, equally sinful, equally open to conversion and salvation.

EXERCISE   You may wish at this point to pause and reconsider the general view of 'Enlightenment' which this course has been giving you. Would you still wish (if you ever did) to equate 'Enlightenment' with 'rationalism', 'scepticism' or 'paganism'?

DISCUSSION   There are, I think, two ways of looking at this.

1   Centrally important figures in the Enlightenment seen as an intellectual movement, were hostile or indifferent towards the Christian churches. A selection from the most famous texts produced in eighteenth-century Europe is bound to bring out the enormous influence of the pagan classics of Greece and Rome, the profound attraction for many of ideals of pagan 'noble savagery', the deep impression made on some by non-Christian Eastern civilizations (or, in the case of Mozart's Freemasons, the 'wisdom' of ancient Egypt). The scepticism of Voltaire about the claims of the churches and his

deep loathing of Christian intolerance was matched by Gibbon's contempt for Christian 'superstition'. Hume went further than any in questioning the central elements of Christian faith. So the generalisation that 'the Enlightenment undermined Christianity' is easily supported.

2 But only if we leave out of our definition of 'Enlightenment' such very substantial figures as Dr Johnson, Haydn, and the Christians who opposed slavery in Britain. *Chambers Dictionary* gives, amongst other definitions of the verb 'enlighten', these:

> to elevate by knowledge or religion: to free from prejudice and superstition.

You'll see the ambiguity of the term 'Enlightenment' when it isn't used (to quote *Chambers* again) to mean

> the spirit of the French *philosophes* of the eighteenth century.

Haydn's aim in *The Creation* might be called 'elevation by religion': Dr Johnson, while convinced of the truth of Christian doctrine, was notably free from prejudice against black people, and Equiano, like other evangelicals, wrote powerfully against such prejudice.

It's a fact that the *philosophes* of Paris and Edinburgh contributed important arguments against slavery. (You may recall the episode of the negro at Surinam in *Candide.*) But the mass movement against it was chiefly the work of Christian men – and women.

The first target of abolitionists was not slavery overall, but the trade in slaves. Equiano in his memoirs often wrote as if slavery itself could be tolerated so long as it was maintained without cruelty. On behalf of his master, King, he himself traded in slaves, and when a freeman he helped another master, Dr Irving, set up a plantation with slave labour in Central America: he congratulates himself on his kindness and efficiency as overseer of fellow Africans. But the trade was inherently brutal. In 1782, Equiano drew Sharp's attention to the appalling case where the master of the *Zong*, a Liverpool ship, threw 130 sick slaves overboard so as to claim insurance on them. Sharp strove to bring the murderous crew to justice. They went unpunished, but by the 'Dolben Act' of 1788 Parliament regulated the slave trade so as to counter such atrocities.

Meanwhile, in 1783, Quakers had presented the first large anti-slavery petition to Parliament. The lower orders in Britain, struggling in this period for their own political rights, saw a connection between slavery in the colonies and aristocratic dominance at home. This was the first modern 'mass movement' – in 1792, 500 petitions were sent in support of William Wilberforce's abolition bill, and the one from Manchester, where the population was less than 75,000, carried over 20,000 signatures.

It was under the general auspices of the highly respectable Society for the Abolition of the Slave Trade, founded in 1787, that Equiano made propaganda. But within the movement he was in touch with men like Thomas Hardy, from the artisan class, who were regarded by the authorities as dangerously radical. To Hardy he wrote from 'Edingburg' in 1792 about a successful current tour of Scotland – 'I have sold books in Glasgow and Paisley ... I was in the General assembly of the Church of

Scotland, now Convened, and they agreed unanimously on a petition, or an address, to the House of Lords to abolish the Slave Trade ... Thanks to God the Gospel is Plantifully preached here – and the Churches, or Karks is well filled' (Fryer, 1984, p.403). It will be seen from this that Equiano's spelling, like that of many of his educated contemporaries, was erratic. It will also be clear that he was a respected and effective agitator on behalf of Christian principles as he saw them, exemplifying in his own person the equality of black people with white before God.

In 'upward social mobility' he was typical of a section of the black community in Britain. In the 1770s and 80s, this may have numbered 15,000 or 20,000 people, largely concentrated in London. While most of its members were servants (if not beggars and street musicians) some were instrumentalists in the 'negro' bands which became *de rigueur* for British army regiments in this period, others were seamen. A few were in skilled trades (Equiano himself was a hairdresser on occasion) or owned shops. Equiano's literary predecessor, Ignatius Sancho (1729–80) born in slavery on shipboard, butler to the Duchess of Montagu, a skilled musician (and composer), befriended by Johnson, by the novelist Sterne and by the great actor Garrick, eventually opened a grocery shop in Westminster. His *Letters* were published posthumously in 1782. Whether poor or relatively well off, blacks at this time did not lack friends. The London 'mob' would commonly take the side of a black runaway against his master. That the quite large black minority in London tended to disappear early in the next century must in part relate to the simple fact that blacks married whites and their children and grandchildren were absorbed as 'British' into the general community. The story of Francis Barber, Dr Johnson's trusted black personal assistant, and eventual legatee, is relevant here: he set up a school in Johnson's home town, Lichfield. His son Samuel, by an Englishwoman ('eminently pretty'), became a Primitive Methodist preacher in Staffordshire and himself left six children when he died.

So, while Equiano's *Narrative* is a work of protest, and designed as such, it was not written in a cultural climate where racism in its present-day form was general. Racism became so only during the nineteenth century: in Equiano's day it was the palpably self-interested creed of the New World planters and their allies, who were losing ground to evangelical and humanitarian sentiment and to certain ideas emerging from the French and Scottish Enlightenment. When Equiano wrote, the economic ideas of Adam Smith, enunciated in the *Wealth of Nations* (1776), were making an enormous impact on politicians and other educated people. Smith argued that slavery was intrinsically *inefficient* (he was probably wrong, but that need not concern us). Free men, he said, would work harder. And 'free trade' with Africa, in consumer goods rather than human beings would, so Wesley, Equiano and other abolitionists argued, be a source of vast profit to British manufacturers. One need not cynically assume that the movement for abolition was 'really economic' in its motivations. Abolitionists used such arguments rather as Greens now point out that less-polluting cars are cheaper to run. Motor cars seem an inevitable part of modern life, just as plantation slavery did of the eighteenth-century economy. However, it was certainly important that the 'manufacturing interest' growing out of Britain's 'industrial revolution' had no respect for old-fashioned, quasi-feudal sugar production, or its friends in the aristocrat-dominated British parliament, and tended to align itself behind the cause of abolition.

3.1 Equiano's narrative: chapters one to three

Like Cook, Equiano probably took advice from educated friends on the style of his autobiography, though there is no doubt that years of dogged self-education had equipped him to express his own opinions, and to set his own story in wide perspective. Recent scholars, black and white, have found his account of the Igbo society of his childhood, in general, credible.

EXERCISE   Read Chapter one now and, as you do so, note down answers to these questions.

1   What features, of Igbo society, as Equiano describes it, remind you of Cook's account of the customs of Tanna? How do the Igbo here relate to the concept of the 'noble savage'?

2   Can you point to places where Equiano's expressions seem to mask rather than depict, what he describes – that is, to use 'stock phrases' of polite eighteenth-century usage?

3   How does he present the difficult topic of slavery *within* Africa?

DISCUSSION   1   The main similarity, apart from ancestor-worship, is the absence of regal, or state, authority over heads of households. In 'acephalous' Igbo society, the elders, of whom Equiano's father was one, 'decided disputes and punished crimes' in general assembly. This characteristic of certain 'savage' cultures was not unobserved by European radicals: the union of the fourteen colonies is said to owe something to the model of the Iroquois federation of upstate New York (which Benjamin Franklin admired), and the tribal assembly was a good model of direct 'democracy' (cf. Kiernan, 1990, p.96).

However, Equiano's Igbo are further from the model of the 'noble savage' than Cook's Tannese, though perhaps closer to the models of cultured, 'democratic' Ancient Greece or Rousseau's public-spirited Geneva. Theirs is a relatively complex and sophisticated trading society.

'As yet the natives are unacquainted with those refinements in cookery which debauch the taste ... They are totally unacquainted with strong or spirituous liquors' (p.407). Equiano certainly underestimates here the intoxicating power of palm wine. He may be consciously or unconsciously aiming to convince readers that his people are exempt from the corruptions of sophisticated Europe against which Rousseau had inveighed so powerfully. With their scrupulous cleanliness and their belief in 'one Creator of all things' (p.410), and their affinities with the Jews of the Old Testament, Equiano suggests that his people are 'naturally' moral beings. To their sensible habits can be related their general hardiness and good health. But their music and dancing are elaborate, like the art forms of ancient Athens: they combine honest simplicity with cultivated artistic expression.

2   When Equiano describes his native land as a 'charming fruitful vale' (p.406), he is using, whether knowingly or not, the linguistic conventions of pastoralism, which you will meet in Part E.

     Equiano's language is full of 'polite' eighteenth-century usages which have the effect of drawing his own people towards European norms. To compare the Igbo dress to a 'highland plaid' (p.407) is to evoke Macpherson's 'Ossian' and thus connect with 'noble savagery'. Had Equiano written 'Roman toga', an equally apt analogy, he would have implied urbane dignity. And this is exactly what he does with other usages. '... Our *women of distinction* wear golden ornaments ...' (p.407). The elders are '*judges and senators*' (p.406). Livestock constitute 'the chief articles of ... *commerce*' (p.407). In buildings the Igbo '*study convenience rather ornament*' (p.408). Such phrases assimilate the Igbo with genteel counterparts in Britain: with Mansfield in his court, with the Duchess of Montagu in her finery, with City merchants discussing trade and county gentlemen considering plans for new houses.

     Yet if one reads the vivid and authoritative novels of Chinua Achebe, *Things Fall Apart* (1958) and *Arrow of God* (1963), about pre-colonial Igbo society, it is clear that its customs were useful and dignified *on their own terms*. The Igbo outlook was not 'European', nor was it any the worse for that. A rich culture was sustained by religious beliefs and social ideology very different from those of post-medieval England. The tendency to generalize, universalize and homogenize all human experience found in the *Encyclopédie* and in much genteel prose in the age of Enlightenment may seem admirable in so far as it asserts the common characteristics of all creatures considered to be human. But it serves to obscure very important differences between cultures, to reduce rich variety into simple deistic formulae, to assimilate all cultural forms with the entertainments of Europe and all conceptions of valour with these prevalent in European armies. (For a comment on how Cook, in particular, is prone to 'universalize', see Porter (1990).)

3   Modern scholars fully support Equiano's view that slavery in Africa was usually far more humane than under Europeans in the New World (p.410). It had the same function – to retain hold of labour in country which was underpopulated though (as Equiano stresses) very fertile. (The same applied to serfdom in Catherine's Russia: free labour would be irresistibly drawn to the unexploited resources of the steppes and Siberia.)

     But slaves in Africa could and often did rise to positions of power and respect. What Equiano cannot really gloss over is the fact that some Africans, knowing of European demand for slaves at the coast, went beyond conventions that only criminals and prisoners of war could legitimately be enslaved, and kidnapped fellow-Africans, including, of course, Equiano himself. He canvasses, but only cautiously, the idea that wars between villages were started by African traders who brought in European goods (p.409). Why is he so cautious?

     I think this must be related to his devout Christianity. White traders might, he acknowledges discreetly, have destabilized an otherwise comfortable and equitable African culture by their demands. But Christianity, the religion of the whites, possesses truths which Igbo society does not acknowledge. Involvement in slavery is a sign of Igbos' sin, and its evil effects are due punishment for it, though the positive aspects of their way of life show how easily these people might be redeemed by Christian missionaries. While the institution of slavery is not solely the *fault* of Europeans, the redemption of Africa would be a *triumph* for them.

EXERCISE   Read now Chapter Two and the excerpt from Chapter Three (pp.412–22). Here Equiano describes how, torn away from familiar Igbo life, he responded to unfamiliar and frightening experiences. In a sense, he is like Cook and his seamen: faced with the challenge of understanding sights and customs, wholly out of his previous ken. As you read through, note the contrasts which strike you between his literary practices and Cook's, his situation and Cook's.

DISCUSSION   Cook, of course, while at risk of his own life and faced with difficult problems and decisions, has much power at his disposal. His expedition is large. His ships are well equipped. His weaponry will easily annihilate stone-age Melanesian opposition. Equiano, to state the obvious, is totally powerless once he has lost touch with his own people. Every new situation is fraught with dangers to which he has no prepared or adequate response.

A more radical difference still, however, is this: Cook leaves Tanna still guessing – he knows that he has *not* fully understood what he has seen and heard. To that extent, he is *less* in charge of his subject-matter than Equiano. Writing more than thirty years after the events he describes, Equiano is now in full possession of the apparent secrets of white society. He knows that whites rarely eat other people, that they don't practice human sacrifice, that some of them are kindly in disposition. He is familiar with horses, with watches, and with houses of more than one storey (though even near the end of his life he would complain, perhaps jokingly, to his friend Hardy that the famous tenements of Edinburgh were 'to tall' [sic]).

So his reconstruction of his own childish perplexity is a calculated feat of literary artifice. Amongst his calculations must have intruded his desire to stir the consciences of white readers in favour of Africans, whom they may casually despise as 'primitive cannibals'. Describing his long-held fears that the whites would eat *him* is a very neat way of teasing his readers' sympathies (p.416).

Likewise, the poignant passage in which Equiano is reunited with his sister and then deprived forever of her company (p.414) is skilfully worked up so as to play on such feelings as were aroused in readers by the 'Sentimental' school, which included Laurence Sterne, Henry Mackenzie and many followers of Rousseau. The same might be said of his touching relationship with Dick, the young American boy. In both cases, stress is laid on the young people sleeping in each other's arms, like the fairy-tale 'Babes in the Wood.' However phrases such as 'bathing each other with our tears' (p.413) and 'lain in each other's bosoms' (p.420) come not from folk-narrative but from the 'stock' of eighteenth-century 'sentimental' convention.

You may think that I am suggesting that Equiano's narrative is really nothing but a literary fabrication created for propaganda purposes. Not at all! While all writing from any period (including this OU teaching material) contains conventional elements, and much (e.g. Mills and Boon romance) contains very little *except* stock verbiage, Equiano's narrative is equal as a documentary source to any we have on eighteenth-century slavery. While his memory has been shown to be faulty in certain instances, his detail is so vivid, circumstantial and coherently patterned that we may believe his account of his experience, coloured though it is by the Christian gentility which he acquired. Look again, for example, at the short account of his time in Virginia (p.419). The muzzle on the head of the black cook is appalling yet all too convincing; the account of the narrator's fear that the watch on the chimney was spying on him, or was a sacred object incorporating an ancestral spirit, is wrily amusing and wholly convincing.

4   Equiano, Pangloss and 'providence': a conclusion

In his excellent history of black people in Britain, *Staying Power*, Peter Fryer writes:

> A history of Liverpool, written in 1957 by the city's then public librarian, and sponsored by the city council to celebrate the seven-hundred-and-fiftieth anniversary of Liverpool's charter, dismissed the slave trade in just 28 lines (in a book of 515 pages) that ended with this remarkable sentence: 'In the long run, the triangular operation based on Liverpool was to bring benefits to all, not least to the translated slaves, whose descendants have subsequently achieved in the New World standards of education and civilization far ahead of their compatriots whom they left behind.' Well might a city governed and memorialized by Panglosses display on its town hall, built in 1749–54, the symbolic heads of African elephants and African slaves. (Fryer, 1984, p.66)

The reference to Voltaire here is apt. Yet, curiously, Equiano would have been in partial agreement with the historian of Liverpool: he believed that he himself had been marked out by God's Providence for special good fortune, and that his own conversion to Christianity, while a slave, was Providential.

In Igbo belief, an individual was strongly fated: his personal *chi* had control of his destiny, and could not be defied. Equiano's childhood background therefore predisposed him to accept the Calvinist conception that God controls, through predestination, all that human individuals do. He further accepted the common notion, which Voltaire satirized through Pangloss, that God's Providence explained every event from the grandest to the most trivial.

If you have time to read the rest of Equiano's story you will encounter numerous instances of Equiano's 'Providentialist' interpretation of life. In 1761, for instance, he is assisting the Royal Navy in an attack on the French fleet at Belle-Isle. Another ship rams his early in the morning. A gunner named Mondle had been a man of 'very indifferent morals'. But the night before the ramming, he had awoken in terror from a dream in which St Peter has warned him to repent. He vows never to touch alcohol again, gives away all his liquor, and begins to read the Bible – but still, through 'agony', cannot sleep. Hence, he rushes out of his cabin as soon as he hears an alarm, and his life is thereby saved, since the other vessel smashes his cabin to smithereens. 'I could not help regarding this as an awful interposition of Providence for his preservation.' Equiano then goes on to recall how, at another time, he himself fell from the upper deck of a ship into the empty hold but 'received not the least injury ... I thought I could plainly trace the hand of God, without whose permission a sparrow cannot fall' (Edwards, 1988, pp.51-3). And so on. He concludes his autobiography with yet another invocation of Providence:

> If any incident in this little work should appear uninteresting and trifling to most readers, I can only say, as my excuse for mentioning it, that almost every event of my life made as impression on my mind and influenced my conduct. I early accustomed myself to look for the hand of God in the minutest occurrence, and to learn from it a lesson of morality and religion ...(Edwards, 1988, p.170)

Yet his conviction that he himself had been fortunate did not inhibit him from seeking to alleviate the lives of his fellow Africans in captivity. Providentialism, despite what you've read in *Candide*, did not necessarily generate acceptance of apparent evil. God might, in fact, Providentially choose individuals to struggle against evil in accordance with His will.

5 References

Adams, R. (1984) *In the Land of Strangers: A Century of European Contact with Tanna, 1774–1874*, Australian National University Press, Canberra.

Arens, W. (1979) *The Man Eating Myth*, Oxford University Press, London.

Beaglehole, J.C. (1974) *The Life of Captain James Cook*, A & C. Black, London.

Edwards, P. (1988) *The Life of Olaudah Equiano*, Longman, London.

Eitner, L. (ed.) (1971) *Neo-Classicism and Romanticism*, Prentice Hall, New York.

Fryer, P. (1984) *Staying Power: the History of Black People in Britain*, Pluto Publishing Ltd, London.

Holmes, C. (ed.) (1982) *Captain Cook's Second Voyage: the Journals of Lieutenants Elliot and Pickersgill*, Caliban Books, London.

Kiernan, V.G. (1990) 'Noble and ignoble savages' in Rousseau and Porter (1990).

Manuel, F. and Manuel, F. (eds) (1965) *The Enlightenment*, Prentice Hall, New York.

Paton, J. (1893) *John Paton D.D. – An Autobiography*, Hodder and Stoughton, London.

Porter, R. (1990) 'The exotic as erotic: Captain Cook at Tahiti', in Rousseau and Porter (1990).

Rousseau, G.S. and Porter, R. (eds) (1990) *Exoticism in the Enlightenment*, Manchester University Press, Manchester.

Rousseau, J-J. (1984) *A Discourse on Inequality*, Penguin Books Ltd, London.

Smith, B. (1985) *European Vision and the South Pacific*, (2nd edn), Yale University Press, New Haven.

6   *Further Reading*

Achebe, C. (1974) *Arrow of God*, (2nd edn), Heinemann Educational, London.

Beaglehole, J.C. (1955–69) (ed.) Cook's *Journals*, 4 vols, Hakluyt Society, Cambridge.

Blackburn, R., (1988) *The Overthrow of Colonial Slavery, 1776–1848*, Verso, London.

Calder, A. (1981) *Revolutionary Empire: The Rise of the English Speaking Empires from the Fifteenth Century to the 1780s*, Jonathan Cape Ltd, London.

Edwards, P. (ed.) (1969) Equiano's *The Interesting Narrative...*, (facsimile of first edn) Dawson UK Ltd, London.

Edwards, P. and Dabydeen, D. (eds) (1991) *Black Writers in Britain 1760–1890*, Edinburgh University Press, Edinburgh.

Edwards, P. and Walvin, J. (1983) *Black Personalities in the Era of the Slave Trade*, Macmillan, London.

Joppien, R. and Smith, B. (1985–88) *The Art of Captain Cook's Voyages*, 3 vols, Yale University Press, New Haven.

Tattersfield, N. (1991), *The Forgotten Trade*, Jonathan Cape Ltd, London.

Conclusion

Michael Bartholomew

This part of the course has surveyed four somewhat disparate texts. A conclusion which attempted to yoke them tightly together would probably be rather strained. However, at this mid-point in the course, it may be useful to reflect briefly, in the light of these four texts, on the validity, or otherwise, of the rough characterization of the Enlightenment that was ventured right at the beginning of the course (see General Introduction).

You will recall that it was suggested that the movement was characterized by a dislike of arbitrary power and of Christianity, a veneration for the ancients, a commitment to the methods of science, and a cooly sceptical general tone. You will by now have your own views on the extent to which the texts in the first two parts of the course conform to, and depart from, this characterization. How do the texts in Part C fare?

Voltaire epitomizes the Enlightenment. Dozens of books on the movement have images of his mischievous face on their covers. In a number of powerful senses, his position is unassailable. You will have found in his life and work plenty of the features listed in our characterization. But what about *Candide*? Surprisingly (but interestingly), the text presents challenges to neat formulations of the Enlightenment. What are we to make of the view that life is commonly a sequence of appalling misfortunes, some inflicted by cruel humans, and others by an ineptly designed universe? What are we to make of the novel's enigmatic last sentence? These questions have never been settled, but you should now be in a position to join the continuing debate.

Lind's *Treatise* is far less enigmatic. When offered up against our list of characteristics, it unambiguously affirms one of them, and takes no strong position on the others. There is no difficulty in assimilating Lind into the Enlightenment, but his work does raise interesting questions about the movement's confident programme for the amelioration of suffering by the humane application of science. His work perhaps indicates that the conquest of disease would be a longer haul than was anticipated in mid-century by the projectors of the *Encyclopédie*.

With Equiano and Cook a different sort of problem arises. It is a problem of definition. If we define the Enlightenment tightly, we can confidently exclude countless texts and say that whatever else they are, they are not products of the movement. This is to give no final evaluation of their qualities: their merits may be incontestable, on all sorts of grounds, but they just do not happen to belong in the Enlightenment. If, on the other hand, we are ready to accept a much looser and broader definition of the Enlightenment, we might find that we can usefully expand it in order to cover a text which exhibits some features which seem to run counter to the movement.

In this respect, Equiano and Cook are good examples. Their texts have an intrinsic appeal that may make questions of definition appear rather trivial. It is pointless simply to pick up a text and shake the life out of it just to find out if it is enlightened or not. Equiano and Cook are interesting in their own right; not just as exemplars of this or that movement. But if we are stock-taking, we need, at some point to test their relationship with the theme of the course. Neither of them tends to appear in standard surveys of the Enlightenment.[1] We have included them in order to open up two highly individual views of the wider, non-European world, and to raise the very question of the limits of the notion of Enlightenment.

Equiano's Christianity allies him with Dr Johnson, and it will be for you to decide whether the notion of Enlightenment loses, or gains coherence by including them. At the very least, you should be able to set out the arguments on both sides. Reading Equiano in conjunction with de Jaucourt's entry on the Slave Trade in the *Encyclopédie* would be useful (see *Texts*, I, pp.15–16).

At first sight, Cook may look as if he is barely connected to the other texts in the course. We certainly cannot imagine him bantering, in elegant French, with *philosophes* at a Parisian *salon*. However, try thinking about him in the light of Diderot's praise of the artisan in the *Encyclopédie* article *Craft (Texts,* I, p.32), and in the light of the *Encyclopédie's* general enthusiasm for the practical and technological. In the article on *Craft*, Diderot is thinking of rather humdrum, repetitive work, but it might be productive to see Cook as the supreme artisan, who by virtue of his excellence in the practice of such craft-skills as navigation, made his bluff way into the world of England's leading scientific institution, The Royal Society. When it comes, however, to Cook's humane views of non-European societies, however closely they correspond with the *philosophes'* views, it is highly unlikely that he derived them from reading their works.

This part of the course, as well as introducing you to four, very different sorts of text, should, incidentally, have opened up the notion of Enlightenment for review. The next part of the course, by contrast, raises few problems of definition: by general reckoning, Hume, Lessing and Mozart are somewhere close to the very heart of the movement.

References

Gay, P. (1970) *The Enlightenment: An Interpretation*, 2 vols, Wildwood House, London.

---

[1]   An exception is Peter Gay's two-volume study, *The Enlightenment*. Gay makes reference to Cook in his section on 'The Spirit of Age' (see Gay, 1970, vol. ii, p.41).

Historical Surveys

Prepared for the Course Team by
Clive Emsley and Angus Calder

Contents

1   France in the Eighteenth Century

CLIVE EMSLEY

The aim of this section is to give you a brief introduction to the administrative, economic and social structure of France during the eighteenth century which can act as some sort of historical anchor for your subsequent study of French Enlightenment art, literature and thought.

The frontiers of eighteenth-century France were not greatly dissimilar to the frontiers of modern France, but it is worth remarking that parts of the north, east and south of the country (notably Artois, Alsace, Franche-Comté and Roussillon) were added during the reign of Louis XIV (1643–1715), while Lorraine was not finally incorporated into France until 1766. These additions were made in the same manner that the French monarchy had been building up its territories since the Middle Ages – by war, diplomacy, marriage. But the outcome was that there were many people living in eighteenth-century France who had little idea of exactly what 'France' was, and who did not speak French. More serious for the government and for the workings of the French economy, the way in which the territories of the monarchy had been created over the centuries had left a legacy of internal customs barriers as well as a mixture of local administrations and privileges which the monarchy occasionally by-passed or over-ruled, but which invariably reasserted themselves when the opportunity arose.

1.1   Government and administration

Louis XIV had ascended the throne in 1643 at the age of four. The early years of his reign, when the country was governed by his mother and, more important, Cardinal Mazarin, were marked by external war and internal disorder – twice the court was forced to flee from Paris. When Mazarin died in 1661 Louis declared that in future he would rule without a principal minister, and from then on, while he did appoint some competent ministers, he presided over the government of his realm himself and made the crucial decisions. He created a court of which the splendour became legendary even before it was established in a permanent setting at Versailles. Louis's court was a centre for the arts and learning; it became the model for other absolutist monarchs in Europe. It was also a centre where the most powerful noblemen, those who might pose a threat to the monarchy, could be kept under a watchful eye and showered with honours and offices to maintain their loyalty. Other lesser nobles flocked to the court seeking favours, office or patronage either within the court itself, or back in their own provinces.

While the monarch was the embodiment of all power, there was no means of ensuring his capability in the exercise of power. Louis XIV was competent, but his protracted and exhausting wars, and the privileges which he gave his nobles, were to have disastrous long-term results. When he died in 1715 the cracks were already beginning to appear in the edifice which he had constructed. Louis had survived his own sons and grandsons, and was succeeded by a great-grandson. Louis XV was five when he came to the throne in 1715; the Duke of Orleans acted as

Regent until 1723, and for the next twenty years Louis was dominated in matters of state by his chief minister, and former tutor, Cardinal Fleury. Louis XV was not a great enthusiast for the business of state; he preferred hunting or his mistresses, notably the Marquise de Pompadour and later Madame du Barry. His costly and largely unsuccessful wars, together with the extravagance of his court, served only to encourage critics. His grandson, Louis XVI, who succeeded him in 1774, was well-meaning but of mediocre intelligence and ability. His participation in the American War of Independence had the short-term success of humbling the old enemy, Britain; but it finally bankrupted France and set in motion that chain of events which culminated in the Revolution of 1789.

The size and complexity of eighteenth-century France put the administration of the country beyond the capabilities of one man. Louis XIV may have made the decisions, but those decisions depended upon the information which his ministers put before him. Louis XV continued his great-grandfather's practice of ruling with councils of ministers. While a few ministers may have been guilty of misrepresentation, they did not all deliberately mislead their monarchs: however, they had to edit and filter the papers that were communicated to them, and sometimes these papers contained what men who wanted favours or higher office believed the king and his ministers wanted to hear, rather than what they needed to know.

Although France was nominally one country under an absolute monarch, one of the most crucial areas of the state – taxation – was 'farmed' out to a group of wealthy financiers. While the *fermiers* (tax farmers) do not appear to have been especially corrupt by the standards of the day, the system gave the impression of corruption. Also, the exemption from certain taxes enjoyed by the nobility and clergy gave the impression of unfairness. Perhaps the taxation system would have been more tolerable had it brought in sufficient money to pay for the court and for foreign adventures, but it did not, and its critics cast envious eyes on the successful fiscal system of England, often assuming that a strong currency and solvent government were the product of a balanced constitutional monarchy.

The variety of legal and customs divisions, and the different overlapping administrative areas did not make for efficient government. Perhaps the most obvious example of this complexity of overlapping areas is to be found in the fact that the divisions of the country, called *généralités* and directed by royal *intendants,* did not always share borders with the older administrative *gouvernements* with their royal *gouverneurs.* In most instances the *intendant* was able to make decisions and act on them but, particularly in those provinces where there were old elected ruling bodies, he might have to negotiate with these local 'estates'. The provincial estates, where they survived, were dominated by the nobility. So too were the *parlements.* There were twelve *parlements* until a thirteenth was created, for Lorraine, in 1775. Despite the name, you should not think of them as being like the British parliament. They were law courts which had certain additional powers relating to censorship, morals, religion, trade and industry. They also claimed the right to endorse all royal decrees, and it was this claim which led them into conflict with the monarchy during the eighteenth century.

The monarchy was aware that any rationalization of the complexities within France would require the limitation, or even abolition, of many privileges and that the people who enjoyed these privileges – the nobility and the higher clergy – were not likely to give them up without a fight. In the early 1770s, there was a serious confrontation between the *parlements* and the monarchy during which the former were replaced. However, on his accession Louis XVI restored them hoping, in this way, to secure the support of the nobility for his government.

Monarchy, nobility and higher clergy in eighteenth-century France did not share a common view of privilege and of royal absolutism; indeed many of the *philosophes*, and some of the sharpest critics of French absolutism, came from the nobility. Yet, in contrast to the rest of the population of France, monarchy, nobility and higher clergy did appear as a solid, if small, privileged block.

1.2 The three 'estates'

France had a larger population than any other European state in the eighteenth century. There appear to have been some twenty-one million people in France in 1700, and the numbers arose to about twenty-eight million by the beginning of the Revolution. Paris was the largest city in the country with between 600,000 and 650,000 inhabitants in 1789 making it roughly six times larger than each of its nearest rivals, Bordeaux, Lyon and Marseilles. But probably less than ten per cent of the French lived in urban areas; overwhelmingly, eighteenth-century Frenchmen and women were rural dwellers. Regardless of where or how they lived, however, the inhabitants were divided into three 'orders' or 'estates' – the clergy, the nobility, and 'the Third Estate'.

1.2.1 The first estate: the clergy

There were, perhaps, 130,000 clergy in eighteenth-century France. Over half of these were in regular orders, (the 'regular clergy') and two-thirds of these were women. The clergy were a privileged order being mostly exempt from direct taxation. They granted an annual subsidy, the *don gratuit,* to the monarch for this privilege. The Church as an institution was immensely wealthy with considerable lands and property. This wealth was controlled by the higher clergy, bishops, abbots and priors, who, generally speaking, were men, drawn from the ranks of the nobility. Some had, as well as wealth, considerable political power. There were also the secular clergy, that is those who were not in regular orders but who worked as *curés* (parish priests); there were also the *abbés* who did not take holy orders but belonged to the Church and were entitled to ecclesiastical benefits. The *curés*, though probably better off than the bulk of the peasantry, were not wealthy: they often shared the outlook and rustic speech of their rural parishioners.

The Catholic Church was far more dominant in the life of eighteenth-century France than the Anglican Church was in England. In 1685 Louis XIV revoked the Edict of Nantes, which had granted toleration to Protestants; this encouraged thousands to flee abroad; it also provoked the ferocious *Camisard* rebellion which continued for years in central Languedoc. The small number of Protestants who remained in France continued to be cruelly persecuted into the eighteenth century. The prosecutions brought against Jean Calas of Toulouse and the Sirven family of Castres, both in 1762, for allegedly murdering children who, it was asserted, wanted to become Catholics, were only the most notorious instances of this persecution. In fact, by the time these two cases were tried, the royal government had generally discarded its policies of overt persecution. It was unable, however, to carry many parish priests along with its policy of toleration. In the second half of the century several *curés* took action against Protestants in defiance of the orders of royal officials and even of their bishops.

Much of the Church's time was taken up with its social responsibilities within the state. Teaching in urban primary schools, in secondary schools and in the universities, was done largely by clergy. The rural schools, authorized by royal decree, were supposed to be lay, but even here the clergy generally had a say in the choice of teachers though they were not always able to get rid of men whom they considered undesirable once these were in their posts. The clergy also played a vital role in social welfare. By the middle of the eighteenth century all diocesan centres and all towns of at least 5,000 inhabitants had an *hôpital général.* These *hôpitaux* were run by nuns from orders like the Sisters of Charity or the Sisters of Providence. They varied greatly in size, and as the century progressed, their financial situation generally became more and more unstable. The result of this in Paris was that, increasingly, poor relief and supervision came to be taken over by the city's police. However, across the country as a whole, the Church and the *hôpitaux* continued to provide shelter for the many varieties of urban poor and indigent – for the old and infirm, for the insane, and for deserted or orphaned children. The rural *curé* generally supervised poor relief in his parish. Many *curés* put all their surplus income (i.e. after paying for their own maintenance, for a servant and for the minimal upkeep of their church buildings) at the disposal of the poor; many of them became highly critical of those who appeared able to help, but who refused to do so. Much of this criticism was directed against members of the upper clergy – bishops, abbots and priors who collected many of the tithes, leaving the *curé* with only a meagre emolument.

The first estate was by no means united in opposition to the development of the Enlightenment in France, although it was generally opposed to the *philosophes,* who were anti-clerical and held unorthodox views on religion. There was dissension, also, within the Church itself. The higher clergy were criticized by the lower, and there were some radical thinkers within the clergy. There were bitter and long-standing quarrels about Jansenists and Jesuits, which became mixed with political issues.

The Jansenists had been a subject of controversy since the seventeenth century, when the movement developed. Jansenism took its name from Cornelius Jansen, Bishop of Ypres. Its followers believed in salvation by grace, and denied freedom of will. Its doctrines were not unlike those of the Calvinists. Jesuit doctrines, on the other hand, asserted that man was a free agent who could resist grace, or else accept it, or achieve it by effort. The Jesuits, who were in a strong position at the French Court as advisers and confessors, and who had the ear of the Pope, succeeded in having the Jansenists branded as heretics in the 1650s. The differences later became political. The Jesuits and their supporters were Ultramontanists, accepting papal claims in France, while the Jansenists became associated with Gallicanism, which asserted French independence from Rome. In 1713, a papal bull, *Unigenitus,* condemned errors in the writing of a Jansenist, Pasquier Quesnel. The *parlements* supported the Jansenists, partly from the motive of asserting their own independence. The Jansenist cause also won popular, patriotic support. Jansenism developed a mystical element too, which appealed particularly to the poor. Miraculous cures were alleged to take place at the cemetery of St Médard in Paris, at the tomb of a Jansenist deacon. *Philosophes,* especially Diderot, were particularly scathing about this form of superstition, as they saw it.

The quarrel between Jesuits and Jansenists flared up in the 1750s after the Archbishop of Paris had introduced the so called *billets de confession* (certificates of confession). Priests were instructed to refuse absolution to dying Jansenists unless they produced a signed statement that they accepted *Unigenitus.* The *parlements* supported the Jansenists by fining priests who obeyed the instructions and by beginning proceedings against the Archbishop himself. As the King supported the bishops, the matter became a conflict between King and *parlements.*

The Paris *parlement* took further action against the Jesuits in the 1760s. It investigated their finances, condemned books written by Jesuits, and closed their schools. These moves had much popular support. A Jesuit enterprise in Martinique failed. This failure, along with other financial disasters, was due to the Seven Years' War (1756–63), but Louis XV reluctantly agreed to make the Jesuits scapegoats and issued a royal decree suppressing their order in 1764.

There were, then, bitter dissensions within the Church, but questioning of fundamental beliefs was firmly opposed. Both Jansenist and Jesuit journals published strong criticism of works by *philosophes* and of the *Encyclopédie.* Stronger action still could be taken by the condemnation of works (as was done, for example, by the Sorbonne, the Faculty of Theology of the University of Paris). Such condemnation could result in imprisonment, exile or death for the offenders. In England and Scotland, people like Hume and Gibbon met with strong criticism from Church authorities, but in France, the Catholic Church, with its supporters at court (and in spite of its different factions), could present a really dangerous threat to the unorthodox.

1.2.2 The second estate: the nobility

There are widely differing estimates of the size of the nobility in France during the eighteenth century; taking an average between the estimates there appear to have been about 250,000 nobles in 1789. There were considerable differences of origin, wealth and ideology among them.

The *noblesse d'épée,* the nobility of the sword, were the descendants of the old feudal nobility to whom military service had been a way of life. As the administration of the state had grown more complex and less reliant upon the sword, a new administrative nobility had been created, the *noblesse de robe.* This consisted of men, generally drawn from the middle, non-noble ranks of society, who had purchased government offices which carried with them privileges of nobility. Initially, the proud Sword families had looked disparagingly on those of the Robe, but by the middle of the eighteenth century many Robe families had been ennobled for generations and were inter-marrying with the Sword.

Furthermore, Sword families were sending their sons into magisterial careers (traditionally the reserve of the Robe), while Robe families were finding places for their sons in the army. In 1781 the Baron de Gaix, scion of an old feudal family, could tell his three sons: 'You have to choose between the robe and [military] service ... The first of these two states is no less respectable than the second'.

While distinctions between Robe and Sword were becoming blurred, there could still be a sharp hostility between the two as late as the 1780s, and there was always a very marked division between the rich and poor noble. The poor nobility were to be found in the provinces. Their 'poverty' was, of course, relative. A few of those who pleaded poverty were on the fringe of court life, while others do appear to have been genuinely poor. There was a popular saying about the gentleman of Beauce 'who stays in bed while his breeches are mended'. Brittany had hundreds of these *hobereaux,* some of whom took positions as stewards, gamekeepers, wig-makers, even muleteers. They brought their produce to market in baskets slung on their right side, leaving their left for the symbol of their pride and their nobility – their sword. They plagued *intendants* and central government with requests for army commissions or Church appointments for their sons, or places in convents for their daughters. Their pride prevented most of them from seeking a way out of their poverty through commerce. They pointed to the *loi de dérogeance,* the law which forbade such activity; though in fact this law had never been generally applied. After 1750 the government was encouraging nobles to participate in trade and industry.

The wealthy nobility, particularly those who were to be found at Versailles or (as the eighteenth century wore on) in increasingly fashionable Paris, had no such qualms about participating in large-scale industrial or financial enterprise. Nor had they any worries about rubbing shoulders with non-nobles, particularly intellectuals who made their names with their pen by their erudition and wit. In the Parisian *salons,* nobles and non-nobles met and talked; in Baron d'Holbach's salon particularly, no subject was taboo. Discussing the nobility in Paris and Versailles during the eighteenth century, Professor John McManners concluded that 'the overall picture' did not reveal 'a caste ... graded by antiquity and lineage'. There was, he suggested, 'an upper class unified by money' which was, in turn, subdivided, and men boasted of or sought after their noble titles 'as admission tickets to lucrative employments or favours, or for their snob value, or simply as collector's pieces' (McManners, 1967, p.28). Even some of the nobles who mingled with the *philosophes* advocated reform within France; indeed, some of the most significant and most radical thinkers of eighteenth-century France came from the nobility. When the Revolution commenced there were liberal nobles ready to make common cause with different elements in the Third Estate. But in general the nobility presented a barrier to reform in eighteenth-century France. The monarch could, and still did, create nobles; yet, at the same time he acquiesced in the nobles' demands that four quarterings of nobility be essential for most military commissions. The lucrative sinecures around the king were awarded only to nobles. The great offices of state became closed for the most part to all but nobles: of Louis XVI's thirty-six ministers, all but one were nobles; fourteen of his *intendants* were the sons of *intendants,* in some cases inheriting directly from their fathers.

There is a paradox in the behaviour of the nobility of eighteenth-century France. On the one hand they were creating barriers to reform by guarding their privileges and shutting off opportunities for non-nobles, but on the other hand they began to popularize terms like 'rights' and 'liberties', particularly the 'rights of the nation' and the 'rights guaranteed by Law' over which the monarch had no control. The *parlements* particularly argued in such terms. In 1776 the *Parlement* of Paris declared,

> The first rule of justice is to preserve for everyone what is due to him, a fundamental rule of natural right and of civil government, and one which consists not only in upholding rights of property but in safeguarding rights attached to the person and born of prerogatives of birth and estate. (Palmer, 1959, p.451)

Of course, the *parlements* were talking about the 'rights' existing in society in which nobles were privileged, and were using the terms to defend (or sometimes to advance) their privileges as nobles. They were playing with fire, for they looked for mass support from the Third Estate, and for a time enjoyed much support. But once the fabric of society had been weakened by aristocratic protest, members of the Third Estate could easily switch from supporting the rights of men as nobles to supporting the rights of men as men. The explosion of 1789 offered the opportunity.

1.2.3   The Third Estate

In pre-revolutionary France the Third Estate encompassed everyone who was not a member of the clergy or nobility: from the wealthiest bourgeois (who might own land and enjoy the seigneurial rights that went with that land) to the poorest, landless peasant – and many peasants were very poor. It has been estimated that about a third of the population of France in 1789 could be classified as poor or indigent.

The word 'bourgeois' immediately presents us with a problem of definition. The original meaning in France was simply 'townsman'. During the seventeenth and eighteenth centuries, however, it acquired a precise legal meaning and applied to non-nobles with sufficient wealth and leisure to live comfortably and who did not labour with their hands. Today, 'bourgeois' is used as a rather vague synonym for 'middle-class', but for our purposes, three points are important:

1   The legally defined bourgeois of eighteenth-century France was generally a person living off an income derived from property, sometimes land, which gave him seigneurial rights, though not noble rank; most 'bourgeois' employed domestic servants.

2   Although some members of the Third Estate made considerable profits from commerce, industry or financial speculation, so too did some nobles; and these pursuits were not exclusive to a legally defined bourgeois. Probably no one ever entered the bourgeoisie without being involved in trade, as this was the way to abandon manual work; but many also moved out of trade quickly to invest in land, in government stock, or in a venal office.

3   The holders of small administrative or judicial offices that did not carry noble status, and professional men, some of whom played significant roles in the ferment before the Revolution itself, were not necessarily legally defined bourgeois, though they would probably be encompassed by a broad, modern definition.

Below the bourgeois on the social scale of the Third Estate came the urban craftsman. Again, this was a broad category ranging from, for example, wealthy goldsmiths or tailors who worked primarily for the wealthy nobility, to modest shoemakers, tailors, masons, and so on. Master craftsmen employed the next level of urban worker, the journeyman. At the bottom of the social scale in the towns were the domestic servants (of the bourgeois or of master craftsmen), and then the day-labourers, men and women who had entered the towns either permanently, or on a seasonal migration from country to town looking for work.

Peasants were the largest single social group in eighteenth-century France, there were about nineteen million of them. But the word 'peasant' – *paysan* – covered an enormous range. Generally speaking, the peasant was free; Louis XVI abolished residual serfdom on his domains in 1779, condemning it as contrary to social justice. Only in a few central eastern areas did the peasant remain tied to the land. Peasants themselves owned about forty to fifty per cent of land. But land ownership did not mean freedom from the local *seigneur*, for the land was still part of his fief; if lands were sold, the *seigneur* could claim a proportion of the sale (*lods et ventes*); often he could tax certain basic commodities, and held the monopoly of indispensable economic instruments – mill, bakery, wine and oil presses. There were scores of similar 'rights' for the *seigneur* and burdens for the land-owning peasants. The peasant holdings varied greatly in size and were often fragmented; some peasants were landless, some were fairly well-off, though the genuinely independent owner-occupier was the exception rather than the rule. In France, it was the custom in many areas to divide an inheritance of property among all the child-ren, rather than, as in England, passing it all to the first born. Consequently, the holdings often grew smaller with each generation. Peasants were therefore obliged to ensure their livelihood by tenant farming, share-cropping, labouring or doing domestic outwork (usually weaving or spinning) for urban entrepreneurs.

Bad harvests resulted in food shortages and these, as in Britain, often led to popular disorder and riots about rapid price rises. Sometimes in France this kind of disorder also saw the creation of bands of brigands. But while food riots and the outrages of the brigands were a headache for the local authorities and the police, they never presented a threat to the social structure of France. Rural France, in spite of the inequality of taxation and the burdensome last vestiges of feudalism, remained essentially stable and inward-looking: the peasants' first loyalties were to family and neighbourhood. Many rarely travelled more than a few miles from their native village in their whole lives.

As in the less rigid social divisions in England, women were kept in a subordinate position, indeed they were scarcely considered as members of the three estates in their own right. Some of the *philosophes* developed the orthodoxy by perceiving women as governed more by feeling than reason and as imaginative rather than analytical. When they contemplated improvements in the position of women it was largely in terms of re-evaluation of their domestic role by which they might contribute to improvements within society.

1.3 References

McManners, J. (1967) 'France' in A. Goodwin (ed.), *The European Nobility in the Eighteenth Century*, A & C Black, London.

Palmer, R.R. (1959) *The Age of the Democratic Revolution*, vol. 1, Princeton University Press, New Haven. (Vol. 2 was published in 1964.)

2   *England in the Eighteenth Century*

CLIVE EMSLEY

The aim of this section is to give you some background information on the political, social and economic structure of eighteenth-century England. It cannot, of course, give you a complete history, but it will, I hope, be sufficient to contextualize the material originating in, or dealing with, eighteenth-century England elsewhere in the course.

To begin with we need to say something about the term 'England'. It is often used, rather carelessly, as a synonym for 'Britain' or the 'United Kingdom'. In what follows, 'England' is primarily used with reference to the political entity or 'state' governed from Westminster. This entity comprised what is geographically England, as well as Wales, Scotland and Ireland. By the eighteenth century Wales was very fully coupled with England, legally, politically and economically. By contrast, while there were Scottish MPs at Westminster following the Act of Union in 1707, the Scottish legal system remained completely distinct and independent. (There is a separate 'historical survey' of Scotland in the eighteenth century, see pp.442–50.) Ireland had its own parliament meeting in Dublin but was run from Dublin Castle by 'English state' officials. In 1714 the Elector of Hanover (a German principality) became George I of Great Britain; although he retained his former title, Hanover was not governed from Westminster but from Hanover, and by Hanoverian ministers resident there. The adjective 'Hanoverian' is applied, on occasions, to British ministers, society or possessions, after 1714. In certain specific contexts, for example in the phrase 'the freeborn Englishman', 'English' and 'England' are the most appropriate terms and, in any case, unavoidable.

2.1   *Population and the economy*

The population of England and Wales was growing during the eighteenth century. Initially it rose gradually from just over five million in 1700 to just over six million in 1750; but thereafter the pace quickened and by the first census in 1801 there was a population of a little over nine million. While there were very few people tied to the land and even fewer land owners with tiny plots (things that were common among the 'peasantries' of continental Europe), most people lived close to the land. Agriculture remained the largest single employer of labour throughout the century; even as late as 1811 one third of the labour force was employed in agriculture, forestry and fishing. But agriculture was changing; improvements and more intensive use of the land meant that crop yields increased by some forty per cent in the course of the century. These improvements brought profits to the farmers and landowners and the capital which they accumulated was subsequently used to finance other economic ventures. The agricultural improvements also helped feed the increasing population, particularly the growing urban population and those engaged in the new manufacturing practices which, in the second half of the century, contributed to the first industrial revolution.

Industrialization in the sense of production by new machinery in new factories was not a great feature of the economy until the last quarter of the century, when cotton manufacture, in particular, began to be revolutionized. But significant profits were made from manufacturing throughout the century, and several areas of the country flourished as a result of growing demand for their specialized products. Leeds and Nottingham, respectively centres of the Yorkshire woollen industry and the Midlands hosiery industry, increased from about 7,000 inhabitants each in 1700 to 24,000 and 16,500 respectively in 1775; in Birmingham and Sheffield – the former a metalwork centre, the latter famous for its cutlery – the increases over the same period were even more dramatic: 8,000 to 40,000 and 3,500 to 27,000.

Much of this population increase in the towns was the result of migration. There is a traditional, and lurid, picture of pathetic rural dwellers being forced off the land by improving landlords and compelled to look for work in the towns and cities. Such a picture is to be found, for example, in Oliver Goldsmith's poem *The Deserted Village* (1770). The reality appears to have been rather different. Where common land was enclosed during the eighteenth century, it was generally used for arable farming; this continued to be labour intensive and required no significant reduction in the local labour force. It was the prospect of higher wages and a better standard of living which attracted people to the towns. Moreover, the improved standard of living, and the increased disposable income available to the growing numbers of urban dwellers themselves, contributed to the growing demand for manufactured products.

The largest urban district in eighteenth-century England was London; it was composed of the City of London proper and the City of Westminster, but it sprawled increasingly into the counties of Middlesex and Surrey. In 1700 there were about half a million people in the metropolis; a hundred years later this number had doubled, and again the principal increase had come in the second half of the century. London in 1800 was the largest city in Europe. It was not an industrial city; it was a political and commercial capital. The court and parliament, together with the powerful and prospering business and financial houses in the City, attracted service crafts and trades – milliners, shoemakers, tailors, as well as builders, furniture-makers, victuallers and so forth. The port of London attracted other trades – caulkers, chandlers, shipwrights – as well as hundreds of seamen and the unskilled labourers who worked on the docks. The increasing size of the metropolis was a source of anxiety throughout the century; moreover, its people acquired a reputation for unruliness and a general lack of deference.

But if this feature of metropolis life gave cause for concern, another gave rise to an aggressive confidence. London was the centre of an expanding, thriving commercial empire trading in North America, Africa, the East and West Indies; while other ports were significant and growing themselves, at mid-century around three-quarters of all Britain's trade (imports, exports and re-exports) went through the port of London. The financial market in London flourished throughout the century. There were several private banks in the City involved with commerce and trade, lending for urban needs or to the landed aristocracy. These banks were linked with scores of counterparts in the provinces; between them, the London banks and their country cousins transferred funds from areas of the country where surplus capital was accruing – such as the profitable agricultural districts of the south and west – to the Midlands and the North where there was a growing demand for capital to finance industrial development. Gradually these financial networks came to be regulated by the Bank of England. (The Bank of England had been created as a wartime expedient in 1694 when the government, desperately short of money, came to an agreement with a group of leading financiers and merchants.) In the early eighteenth century its principal business remained with the government, but more and more it came to dominate the financial world in London. There were financial crises and scandals during the eighteenth century, and there was concern about the size of the national debt which increased with successive wars, but men continued to have confidence in both the developing financial system and public credit. As the taxation system in England was perceived to be fairer and far more competent than its continental counterparts, men were prepared to lend money to the government, confident that they would not lose by it: one-third of the money required to fight Britain's wars in the eighteenth century was raised by loans on government stock (see Table 1).

Table 1   England's wars and their cost 1689–1783

War	*Principal opponents*	*Expenditure (in ££s sterling)*	*Percentage of expenditure raised by loans*	*National Debt (in ££s sterling)*		*Full-time employees of fiscal bureaucracy at fixed dates*
				Beginning	*End*	
Nine Years' War 1689–97	France	49,300	33.6	–	16,700	2524 (in 1690)
War of the Spanish Succession 1702–13	France; Spain	93,600	31.4	14,100	36,200	4780 (in 1708)
War of the Austrian Succession 1739–48	Spain; France (from 1741)	95,600	31.1	46,900	76,100	6765 (in 1741) 6595 (in 1748)
Seven Years' War 1756–63	France; Austria	160,600	37.4	74,600	132,600	7478 (in 1763)
American War of Independence 1775–83	American Colonies; France (from 1779); Spain (from 1779)	236,500	39.9	127,300	242,900	8292 (in 1782–3)

2.2 Social structure

Not until the end of the eighteenth century was the term 'class' used to describe the divisions in Hanoverian society, but throughout the century people did tend to think of a social pyramid divided into three very broad groups. At the very top came the peerage, rather less than 200 men for most of the century; most of these possessed vast estates bringing them huge annual incomes, and their country houses – Blenheim, Chatsworth, Castle Howard, Woburn – rivalled those of many of the wealthiest European nobles and princelings. There were about 1,000 substantial landed gentry; these were often related to the peerage, some of them were as rich or richer than the peers while several thousand others had more modest holdings; and, of course, wealth was no shield against the debts which several profligate scions of the gentry incurred during the century. This upper stratum of society must also include the pseudo-gentry, that small number of rich men of leisure who lived off their investments in London or other large provincial towns. Throughout the century promotion to the peerage was generally given to men from the substantial landed gentry and most of these promotions (about 90%) involved men with direct family connections to the peerage.

Beneath the gentry came 'the middling sort'. The upper layers of this group often shaded into the landed gentry, or married their daughters into it since at the top of this group came some extremely wealthy merchants. The 'middling sort' was also recognized as including office holders in government departments or the customs and excise, some industrialists, professional men – most clergy, doctors, lawyers, – small owner-occupiers (often described by contemporaries as 'yeomen') who, as county freeholders, had the right to vote for county MPs. Shopkeepers and tradesmen formed the bottom layer of this group, some of them shading into the top of the third division sometimes described as 'the lower orders' or 'the poorer sort'. This bottom section of the social pyramid also encompassed an enormous range of people with a range of lifestyles and incomes, from artisans and journeymen, some of whom were little different from the less well-to-do shopkeepers and tradesmen, down to the unskilled labourers and the indigent.

It is difficult, and dangerous, to put numbers on these social divisions but contemporary estimates made at both the beginning and the end of the period suggest that the landed gentry made up something just over one per cent of the population, the middling sort were just under a third, and the lower orders about two-thirds.

The lower orders in England had a reputation for lacking deference to their social superiors. Many foreign visitors expressed surprise at the way English artisans and journeymen showed an interest in foreign news and politics. They noted how Englishmen, whether they had the right to vote or not, liked to attend the hustings to cheer or jeer the candidates. The eighteenth-century Englishman appears to have had an exaggerated consciousness of his 'rights' very different from that of his continental neighbours: he was born a free man; he was not subject to the 'slavery' or the 'wooden shoes' of Popery and absolutist monarchs; he could not be imprisoned without trial, and he could only be tried before a jury of his peers. These 'rights' brought him on to the streets to demonstrate, and such demonstrations were often fostered by members of the parliamentary opposition. The most striking example of this were the Wilkes disorders of the 1760s and 1770s. John Wilkes, a shrewd self-publicist and propagandist for the opposition, played unashamedly on the liberties of the freeborn Englishmen when his opposition to successive governments of George III landed him in court, an outlaw, a prisoner in the King's Bench prison, and denied the right to sit as an MP even though he had been duly elected. The most alarming of the eighteenth-century crowd actions were the Gordon Riots of 1780 when London was subject to a week of violence as a result of parliament's attempt to liberalize the laws debarring Catholics from civic life. The riots were put down by the army with

considerable loss of life; and prominent in organizing the defence of the
Bank of England was John Wilkes who, by 1780, had become Chamberlain
of the City of London. After the Gordon Riots the ruling elite were much
more wary of encouraging their street allies in demonstrations.

The gender distinction between men and women was regarded
similarly across all social groups. Women were the subordinate members
of the landed classes and the middling sort; and similarly among the
lower orders. In rural areas, women contributed to the family economy,
but their labours were generally restricted to work in and around the
house – spinning, managing a small plot of land and perhaps an animal
or two, helping at harvest time – the shift to wheat production, in the
south especially, meant that their employment opportunities on the land
declined. They were more liberated in the towns where there was a
greater choice of work; even here they usually earned less than men and
their jobs were prone to seasonal demand. Yet there were writers and
thinkers who, from early on in the century, were challenging the orthodoxy of a divinely ordained patriarchy and questioning the extent to
which a husband might have authority over his wife.

2.3   *Constitutional structure and politics*

When Queen Anne died in August 1714 she was succeeded by a German
prince, George Lewis, the Elector of Hanover and the first of the
Hanoverian monarchs who were to rule England until the accession of
Victoria in 1837. George was not the next in line to the throne; more
than fifty individuals had a stronger claim, but he was more acceptable to
that element of England's ruling elite which feared the Stuart claimants
to the throne for their absolutist ideas and, above all, for their Catholicism. The absolutist aspirations and Catholicism of James II, had led to
his deposition in the Glorious Revolution of 1688; the Act of Settlement,
passed in 1701, debarred Catholics from the throne and safeguarded a
protestant succession.

George's succession was not without difficulties. It came on the back
of ferocious party strife in which arguments about the succession had
played a significant part. There were many who believed that the rightful
heir to the throne was James Stuart, the son of James II then living in
exile in Lorraine. There were riots by 'Jacobites' (the name given to the
supporters of the Stuarts). In 1715 there was a rising in Scotland which
had support in England; there were plots and rumours of plots continuing throughout the early years of George's reign. His son, George II, who
came to the throne in 1727, had to contend with the Jacobite rising of
1745–6 – again largely a Scottish affair, but again with English sympathiz-
ers.

The powers and authority of the Hanoverian monarchs were limited
by Acts of Parliament and by practices which had developed in the aftermath of the Glorious Revolution. The Act of Settlement, for example, not
only required that the monarch be a Protestant, it also required that he,
or she, be an Anglican since the Church of England was the established
church. George I was therefore required to relinquish his Lutheranism for
Anglicanism. An additional clause in this act ensured the independence
of the judiciary: judges could not be removed on a royal whim, their ten-
ure was permanent, subject to their good behaviour. No legislation

required the monarch to summon parliament every year, but practicalities meant that this happened. There had been almost continual war with France since 1689 (see Table 1) and parliament was required to vote the annual Mutiny Act for the army; more importantly, it was required to vote the taxes necessary for the conduct of military operations, and when peace was eventually established, taxes were required to service the national debt. Parliament also voted an annual amount of money for the king's government, the Civil List. This financial dependence curtailed the monarch's sphere of action in respect of war, peace and the appointment of ministers.

The Hanoverian monarchs still remained very powerful; they could make peers of the realm, they chose their own ministers, but once appointed these ministers could not disregard, or act in defiance of, parliament. Eighteenth-century Englishmen spoke proudly of their balanced constitution. In their eyes it consisted of three elements, monarch, lords and commons, which checked each other. Classical political theory supposed that any single kind of government would ultimately degenerate into its worst form, but by balancing three kinds of government it was assumed that the English system avoided this – the monarch was restrained from becoming an absolutist tyrant, the lords were prevented from transforming themselves into a tyrannical oligarchy, and the commons could not degenerate into anarchy. Some observers, notably the French *philosophe* Montesquieu, detected a rather different but equally beneficial tripartite balance between the executive (the sovereign), the legislature (parliament), and the judiciary. Yet this is not the division which appears to have counted most with most eighteenth-century English theorists: they tended to emphasize the primacy of the legislative branch of the constitution. Some fifty years after the accession of George I the greatest English jurist of the eighteenth-century, Sir William Blackstone, described parliament as having:

> ... sovereign and uncontrollable authority in making, confirming, enlarging, restraining, abrogating, repealing, reviving, and expounding of laws, concerning matters of all possible denominations, ecclesiastical, or temporal, civil, military, maritime, or criminal: this being the place where the absolute despotic power which must in all governments reside somewhere, is entrusted by the constitution of these kingdoms. All mischiefs and grievances, operations and remedies, that transcend the ordinary course of the laws, are within the reach of this extraordinary tribunal. (Blackstone, 1982, vol.1, pp.160–1)

Parliament itself consisted of two chambers: the Lords and the Commons. There were usually about two hundred peers eligible to sit in the Lords during the eighteenth century; another sixteen were elected by the noblemen of Scotland; there were also 26 bishops who had seats in the chamber. Increasingly under the first two Georges, the Lords became dominated by a small group who regularly held principal posts in government – the Dukes of Bedfordshire, Devonshire, and Newcastle, and the Marquis of Rockingham. George III, who succeeded in 1760, infuriated these magnates when he looked outside this group and their supporters for his chief ministers.

There were 558 members elected to the House of Commons: 513 for England and Wales, 45 for Scotland. Every English and Welsh county sent two members elected by men possessing a county freehold; the borough members were elected by a variety of franchises, some very wide – such as 'pot-walloper' boroughs, where every man had the right to vote who had control of a separate doorway to his dwelling, who could provide his own sustenance, and had a fireplace where he could cook his meals – but most were very restricted. The distribution of borough seats, like the borough franchises, was the result of historical accident rather than rational planning: there were twenty-one parliamentary boroughs in Cornwall, a result of that county's population and strength during the sixteenth century; there were only twenty in Lancashire and the three Ridings of Yorkshire combined. A man needed property to the annual value of £300 to be eligible to stand for election for a borough, and double that to be able to stand for a county. This meant that MPs tended to be country gentlemen or else successful professionals or businessmen; large numbers of men in the Commons were often related to, or under the patronage of, members of the upper house.

Legislation of 1716 limited the life of any parliament to seven years. But not every constituency was contested at every general election. It was common for the leading members of a county elite to agree who should represent the county and thus obviate the need for an election; the same thing could happen in boroughs, especially where the franchise depended on ownership of a particular piece of land. There were many more contested elections at the beginning of the eighteenth century than in the middle years; and while the number of contests increased in the second half of the century, they were still not as common as at the beginning. Party strife generated elections.

The political parties of eighteenth-century England were not the structured, bureaucratic organizations that we recognize today as political parties. In the late seventeenth and early eighteenth centuries the Tories projected themselves as the party of the landed interest while the Whigs liked to portray themselves as spokesmen for the professionals and businessmen. In some respects these projections were justified: most country gentry and most clergy voted Tory; while the great financial and trading institutions like the Bank of England and the East India Company backed the Whigs. But such generalizations can distort as much as they explain. The divisions were very much based on religion and principle: the Whigs were much more keen on prosecuting the wars against Louis XIV; the Tories were strong supporters of the Anglican Church, and feared that the Whigs were too sympathetic to Protestant Dissenters; Tories also inclined to ideas of the monarch's divine right of succession. In consequence the Whigs were much more enthusiastic about the succession of George I, and while it would be quite wrong to tar the early eighteenth-century Tories with the brush of Jacobitism, this did become a feature of Whig propaganda and, following the Hanoverian succession and successive plots and scares, Tory gentlemen in the counties were systematically purged from positions of authority.

The divisions between Whig and Tory declined during the reigns of the first two Georges. Initially they were replaced by a different split between the factions of Court and Country: the former made up of the ruling Whigs led by Sir Robert Walpole; the latter a mixture of Whigs and Tories who considered that a group of plutocrats were systematically milking the country of its wealth and that Walpole and his cronies were abusing the patronage at their disposal to create majorities in parliament. In many respects the charges against Walpole were justified. He was a master of political management which, at the time, required the distribution of patronage to make the machinery of government and parliament function. He mixed with individuals whose financial dealings were often corrupt and he amassed a large personal fortune during his twenty years as prime minister. But it was never clear how his opponents were going to replace the system, other than by putting themselves forward as controllers of the purse and patronage strings. However, with the fall of Walpole in 1742 the friction between Court and Country factions subsided; politics began to be dominated by the small group of powerful Whig families, noted above, who disbursed the patronage of the state, at least in part, to their own advantage – another reason for their annoyance when George III turned his back on them and appointed his own men as ministers.

George III's favoured ministers are sometimes described as Tories; they were not – at least not until the early nineteenth century when the ruling faction, many of whom had served as ministers under William Pitt the Younger (Prime Minister 1783–1801 and 1804–5), acknowledged the name. George III's actions in choosing his own men also helped to rekindle party strife, since the opposition to his ministers – the old grandees and their supporters – took to glorying in the name of Whig, and went some way towards creating an organized party bureaucracy. But the conflicts of the last third of the eighteenth century were not conflicts of Whig against Tory. Rather they were conflicts between factions in which one group of faction leaders had the crucial support of the monarch. The opposition group revived the old complaints about corruption and demanded a reduction in the patronage available to the king and his ministers. Other demands also began to be heard for parliamentary reform; initially these concentrated on calls for a strengthening of the independent element within the Commons – the gentlemen elected by the counties who, it was believed, stood apart from the faction fighting and voted for the good of the country – and for annual elections so as to make MPs much more responsive to the will of the electors. But more radical calls also began to be made for an extension of the franchise and for the abolition of 'rotten boroughs', where elections, if they happened at all, were controlled by a very few.

2.4 Government and administration

From the viewpoint of the late twentieth century it is often difficult to comprehend how limited were the concerns of the eighteenth-century government at Westminster, and how tiny were most government departments. Central government was primarily concerned with foreign policy and domestic order. It had no departments of agriculture, industry, health, education, transport; and even at the end of the century the Foreign Office and the Home Office had staffs of only about two dozen individuals each, ranging from the secretary of state at the top, down through the permanent under-secretaries, the clerks who wrote letters, to the janitors and cleaners. Nevertheless, there was a marked overall expansion in the numbers of central government employees during the century and this was most apparent in the revenue departments which grew from some 2,500 full-time employees in 1690 to 8,300 at the close of the

American War of Independence in 1783; the increase was most marked in the Excise, and the increase was driven by the demands of war (see Table 1). In contrast to the fiscal bureaucracies of European powers, the government at Westminster was capable and efficient, and perhaps even more important, however unpopular taxation may have been, the administration of it seemed fair.

Government and government policy was in the hands of the sovereign and his or her ministers. The ministers had begun meeting in cabinet during Anne's reign and the system was developed under Walpole, notably as a result of George I's absences from the kingdom to deal with the affairs of his native Hanover. The cabinet became the main link between the crown and the two houses of parliament; throughout the century most ministers were drawn from the Lords, but Walpole set the precedent for the sovereign's principal minister's sitting in the Commons, something which contributes to the claim that he was Britain's first 'Prime Minister'.

Walpole liked to give the impression that he read the reports of his farm agents before dealing with the affairs of state; it was one way of appealing to the independent country gentlemen in the Commons and undermining the opposition of the Country Party. To make the system work, a minister had to be a shrewd politician capable of bestowing patronage carefully to build up and to maintain parliamentary majorities; but politics did not take up a minister's whole time, and certainly not an ordinary MP's. While parliament met once a year, there were long periods of recess, generally in the summer and autumn, when many gentlemen returned to their country seats or 'took the waters' in the increasingly fashionable spa towns. But the landed gentry ran not only the country, as ministers and MPs, but also local government, in their capacity as county magistrates.

Eighteenth-century English local government was far more decentralized than any of its European equivalents. The counties and parishes were responsible for fixing their own financial rates, for maintaining their poor, their roads, their law and order. These tasks were supervised by magistrates meeting in Quarter Sessions. Four times a year, at Epiphany, Easter, Midsummer, and Michaelmas, the magistrates of a county would meet, generally in the county town, to appoint, or to ratify the appointment of, part-time administrators such as constables or surveyors of the highways, and to hear cases against petty offenders – both those who had broken the criminal law and those who had infringed regulations about, for example, the payment of the poor rate or the upkeep and tidiness of the highways. The magistrates, of whom there were about 2,500 towards the end of the century, were drawn from the local gentry; they rarely possessed any formal legal training for their tasks but relied on the advice of the county clerk of the peace and the handbooks for their role, of which the most notable during the eighteenth-century was Richard Burn's *The Justice of the Peace and the Parish Officer* which ran through nineteen editions between 1755 and 1800. The boroughs were administered in a similar way; the mayor and aldermen generally acted as magistrates, but they usually met more often than the quarterly county sessions. Some of the tasks of the quarter sessions could be of national importance; they were responsible for recruiting and administering the county militia regiments whose role was internal defence in time of war.

But, except in times of emergency such as, for example, when magistrates feared riots and wanted troops, local government and the government at Westminster had little to do with each other.

2.5 References

Blackstone, W. (1982) *Commentaries on the Laws of England*, 4 vols, Professional Books, Abingdon, Oxford. (Reprinted from the 4 vols of the 15th (1809) edn.)

3   Scotland in the Eighteenth Century

ANGUS CALDER

3.1   Scotland

In the eighteenth century, as now, the term 'Scotland' denoted a very large proportion of the land of the British archipelago. Its borders, unchanged since the late fifteenth century, lay exactly where they do today. As with Sweden and Norway (and it is often helpful to compare Scotland with the Scandinavian countries) there was a 'far north' of difficult terrain, and population was quite small relative to geographical area.

The purpose of this essay is to help you to understand how a country which apparently stood on the periphery of European culture contributed so much to Europe's Enlightenment (and to the diffusion of it to America). Hume was a key figure in the philosophical awakening of the period, his profound influence acknowledged widely, and most gracefully in this compliment of Kant's: 'it was David Hume's remark that ... interrupted my dogmatic slumber and gave a completely different direction to my enquiries in the field of speculative philosophy' (Lucas, 1953, p.9). Burns was not the first Scottish poet of the century to gain international fame. Robert Adam's neo-classical architecture left an enduring mark on the surface of Britain. An Edinburgh lawyer, Boswell, wrote a biography, of his friend Johnson, on an unprecedented scale using 'novel' methods in both senses of that word. The pioneering excellence of medical studies at Edinburgh University is represented in this course by James Lind. To Scotland in an earlier century can be traced the origins of freemasonary, that favourite cult among 'enlightened' men, integral to Mozart's *Magic Flute* (see Stevenson, 1988). Historians of ideas find in eighteenth-century Scotland the onset of modern approaches to 'economics', 'social science' and 'history'.

Scotland produced, in 1755, one of the very earliest examples of the scientific 'census'. Dr Alexander Webster computed the country's population at rather over 1,265,000. The grander all-British census of 1801 gave a figure of 1,608,000. Such an expansion is wholly plausible: the rise of population all over Europe was a feature of the period, with important economic and social consequences. In Scotland's case, it accompanied a significant shift in north–south balance. 'In 1755 just over half the people had lived north of a line from the Firth of Tay to the Firth of Clyde: by 1820 this proportion had dropped to two-fifths, and almost half the Scots now occupied the central belt where only twenty-seven per cent had lived before. Edinburgh, Glasgow, and their satellite towns and villages had swollen. The population of Glasgow, soaring from 31,700 to 83,700, had outstripped rapidly that of Edinburgh (81,600 in 1801)' (Smout, 1972, pp.241–5). Such figures explain why we talk about an 'industrial revolution', since Glasgow was a centre of expanding industries, especially in textiles.

In his *Annals of the Parish* (1821), the novelist John Galt presented the history of a village in south-west Scotland over the half century following 1760, through the eyes of its Church of Scotland minister. The book remains an ideal introduction to the material and social life of that period. At the end of it, the old man speaks of 'the great spread that has been in our national prosperity' (Galt, n.d, p.273). Commerce and industry, within one lifetime, had transformed a country which traditionally regarded itself, and had been regarded by natives of others, as 'poor'. Along with pride in advancing prosperity – seen as a result of native enterprise and hard work – came a sense of loss: distinctively Scottish ways, it seemed, were being dissolved into the international culture of commerce and Enlightenment. No-one felt this so clearly as Walter Scott, author of an epoch-making best seller *Waverley* (1814), a novel set in the period of the '45 Rebellion (see below). The vision of Scottish history projected by Scott in his 'Waverley novels' was an astonishing achievement, based on saturation in relevant sources. But it has the effect, unfortunate from our point of view, of presenting the '45 as a watershed. Before then, Old Scotland, an arena of endemic violence, poverty, religious bigotry, and fatalistic attachment to doomed causes. After the '45 – a country of 'enlightened' thought, 'improved' agriculture, peace and general thriving. This over-simplification obscures the deep roots of 'enlightenment' and 'improvement' in Scottish culture.

Scotland in the fifteenth century had been a much more peaceful place than England, France or Italy. It had produced magnificent poets and internationally acclaimed philosophers. Two developments, within a few generations, obscured the effulgence of this 'Scottish Renaissance'.

Scotland became a factor in the rivalry between England and France, with phases of English and French occupation of the Scottish Lowlands. The Scottish Reformation of 1559 emerged under English protection, and its proponents adopted the English translation of the Bible. The young King James VI developed, nevertheless, a promising court culture of music, architecture and Scots poetry. But in 1603 he inherited the crown of England. His departure south with his courtiers robbed Edinburgh of cultural eminence. For over half a century, from the late 1630s, religious disputation inspired Lowland Scottish life at every level.

By 1689, it was, up to a point, settled: the defeat of James VII of Scotland and II of England at the hands of William of Orange, his daughter's husband, was the prelude to the establishment of a Presbyterian Church of Scotland, without bishops. But Episcopalians remained disaffected, and 'Jacobite' insurgency on behalf of the exiled King's son, 'James VIII', 'the Old Pretender', continued intermittently for more than half a century, till the 'Young Pretender', Charles Edward Stewart, leading a largely Highland army, was defeated at Culloden in 1746.

Meanwhile by the Treaty of Union with England in 1707, Scotland lost its own ancient parliament, in return for the right to send MPs to Westminster. In the 1690s, Scottish leaders had tried to bring their nation into the thriving world of 'commercial revolution'. England now led Europe in commerce: England had colonies: Scotland should have a colony. The Scottish attempt to found a trading colony on the isthmus of Panama, open to both Atlantic and Pacific commerce, wasn't daft but it didn't work. An enormous proportion of the nation's liquid capital was destroyed in the Darien colony's failure. English parliamentarians wanted to ensure that when childless Queen Anne, last of the Stewarts, died, her crown passed to the House of Hanover, not to the Catholic 'pretender' in exile, and wished to bind Scotland to such a settlement. Prudence persuaded Scots leaders to enter Union, which at least gave their people licit access for the first time to England's possessions and trading posts over-seas.

Sentiment ensured that few of the many Scots who backed the abortive Jacobite rebellion of 1715 suffered for their commitment. But by 1745, advantages from Union seemed plain to many more. Charles Edward led a minority of Gaelic-speaking Highlanders (the great Camp-bell clan, amongst others, fought against him), allied with disaffected Episcopalian elements in the Lowlands. English-speaking, Presbyterian Scotland triumphed at Culloden in 1746, though it was convenient to attribute the brutalities against Gaels which followed to the 'English' leadership of the Hanoverian army. The outcome was richly noted by Johnson and Boswell on their tour of the Highlands in 1773.

The feudal powers of clan chiefs were taken away. Tartan and weapons were (ineffectually) forbidden to Gaels unless they served in the king's Highland regiments. For a time, many clan chiefs tried to har-monize their traditional position as fathers of their clans, conceived as families, with the need to make money. Finding a cash crop in kelp (sea-weed yielding potash, used in bleaching cloth) they resisted for some decades the drive to emigrate among their followers – who were often spurred to do so by raised rents. Meanwhile, many Highlanders washed up in the cotton mills of Glasgow or the richly cultivated fields of Lothian rather than the wastes of Canada.

However, going to Canada might be no bad thing. A Scot with views in that direction, Samuel Veitch, had revived, immediately after the 1707 union, the term '*British* Empire' first used by a Welshman in the sixteenth century, and for the same reason – it meant that Celts were in on the act. England's richest colony was Jamaica: Scots soon supplied a disproportion-ate number of planters in, and governors of, that prime sugar-producing island. Glasgow, rose to greatness by trading in Virginian tobacco. From the 1720s, Scots secured a remarkable quantity of patronage at the disposal of the East India Company. Money from trade in India, together with for-tunes amassed by soldiers in the EIC service, helped to transform the physical appearance of Scotland, with stately homes and 'improved' fields. Scots – Highlanders – dominated the fur trade of Canada after Wolfe's conquest and made an indelible mark on its vast area.

After 1707 Scotland remained an independent country, as much as Denmark, say, is independent in the present European Community. In return for delivering Scottish votes at Westminster, the managers of the country and their allies were allowed a free hand. Plenty of Scots sat for English parliamentary seats: no Englishman became a Scottish MP. Many Scots, including the Murray who became Lord Mansfield, did well as law-yers in England. But Scotland retained its own law, closer to continental models than to the English one. First the Campbell Dukes of Argyll, then, from the 1770s, Henry Dundas, a Lothian lawyer of lairdly stock, 'managed' Scotland masterfully. Though Dundas was nicknamed 'King Harry the Ninth' he was more like the president-for-life of a comfortably corrupt republic: first among equals with his fellow Edinburgh lawyers; a commoner (till he got a peerage himself as Viscount Melville) with no need to defer to the progressive aristocrats who went along with his way of doing things. It was a great convenience to him that the electoral base in Scotland – some 3,000 – was even smaller and more open to bribery than in most parts of England.

Scottish society gravitated towards the middle. Great hereditary landowners – Campbells in the Highlands, Gordons in the north-east, Scotts in the Borders, for instance – retained enormous territorial influence buttressed by the 'clannishness' which characterized Lowland as well as Highland society. But in return for loyalty, they often gave it, furthering the 'improvement' of their domains and assisting the careers of fellow-countrymen.

In Edinburgh where parliament still served as a law court, landed magnates had less to do with setting the social tone than did the legal profession. The Lords of Session, judges who took non-hereditary titles on appointment, formed Scotland's supreme court in criminal causes. Fourteen in number, they were presided over in the Court of Session by a fifteenth, the Lord President. These were men of learning, and some of them made important intellectual contributions: Hailes, Kames, Monboddo, for instance (*alias* Dalrymple, Home and Burnet).

So did many ministers of the established Church of Scotland. Aristocrats and lairds retained rights of patronage in many parishes. But ideally the Presbyterian minister was installed with the favour of his congregation. Regional synods held some sway, but the Church's governing body was the annual General Assembly in Edinburgh, with a Moderator appointed, or re-appointed, annually. Calvinist bigotry was far from dead, as the young Robert Burns found growing up in Ayrshire. But the generally diffused 'Puritanism' of the 'grave livers' (Wordsworth's phrase) in the Kirk of Scotland now quite commonly consorted with intellectual open-mindedness. Dr William Robertson, a pioneering historian with an international reputation, served both as Moderator of the Church and as Principal of Edinburgh University. The 'moderate' element dominant in the Church in the later eighteenth century was socially conservative (deferential to patrons) but could be intellectually innovative.

The Edinburgh which Johnson visited for the first time in 1773 had long been possessed by the spirit of 'improvement'. It was physically a very strange city: basically, two rows of immensely tall houses facing each other across the spine of the volcanic rock which ran from the Castle down to Holyrood Palace. Aristocrats lived in flats in these tenements above and below commoners – not merchants and clerks merely but also plebeian dregs. The English were astonished by this. It wouldn't do. James Craig's plan for a 'New Town' across the festering swamp of the Nor'Loch was approved in 1765. Slowly it rose, till in the new century, the vastly expanded Edinburgh middle class was installed in a handsome pattern of regular 'Georgian' stone streets, crescents and 'circuses'. But the social *apartheid* which this entailed, with the prosperous settled in the New Town and the Old becoming one of Europe's worst slums, did not prevail in the day of David Hume (though he was an early New Town resident).

Gravitating towards the middle, alumni of the University (often from modest backgrounds) could mingle in all kinds of clubs and debating societies with 'improving' aristocrats and famous intellectuals. There seems to have been a sense of co-operative mission infusing this great centre of 'enlightenment', giving scope for 'genius' large and small. Beside the towering achievements of Hume in philosophy, Adam Smith in economics, Adam Ferguson in sociology, we should set those of lesser figures such as George Wallace. In 1760, Wallace produced a *System of the*

Principles of the Law of Scotland which attacked the legal basis of the slavery from which so many of his compatriots profited in the New World. Plagiarized by the French *Encyclopédie,* his arguments attained comprehensive influence. As for encyclopedias, the Scots were not backward: 'Britannica' was launched by obscure young men in Edinburgh in 1771.

'North *Britain'* : surprising numbers of Scots accepted that term. This helps to explain why some historians (and not only English ones) have assumed that Enlightenment followed Union as effect from cause. Their view may be simplistically stated thus: after centuries of poverty-stricken barbarism, the Reformation brought Scotland a new basis for violence – religious bigotry. Whether mouthing biblical texts or hunting down those who did so sword in hand, the Scots were helplessly immersed in internecine fighting until first the Union, then Culloden, brought peace. Striving to 'emulate' their English fellow-citizens, the Scots civilized themselves very quickly. Result: instant Enlightenment.

Dr Johnson believed something like that: Walter Scott after him produced a more sympathetic account on the same broad lines. But the 'North British' view of Scottish Enlightenment now seems extremely suspect.

Take the case which favours it most – 'agricultural improvement'. Certainly the creation by John Cockburn MP of a famous 'model' village on his property at Ormiston in Lothian was inspired by the desire to drag Scotland up to the level of southern England. (See TV4, 'Scotland and the Enlightenment'.)

The zeal for improvement of the countryside which flavoured so much high talk in Edinburgh did have an anglophile tone. But advanced English methods in agriculture had come, in the seventeenth century, from Holland. Through Calvinist religion and the similarity of the Dutch 'Roman' law to Scottish law, independent contact between Scotland and the Netherlands was incessant long before the Union. The opportunities of Empire depended on Union and largely helped to supply cash for 'improvement'. It does not follow from this that England was the necessary source of new ideas.

Some Jacobite landlords were keen improvers. Those devoted to the Stewarts had their own links with the Continent – with France, where the exiled family sojourned, and with Italy. While the influence of such English thinkers as Newton and Locke, and of English literature of all kinds, was powerful in the 'Scottish Enlightenment', this could easily have happened without Union. David Hume, cannot be explained as leaping fully formed from the Union like Minerva from the brow of Zeus.

Scotland had four universities to England's two. Boys entered them before what we would now consider 'sixth form' age. Buildings were not fine as at Oxford and Cambridge. But the breadth of the Scottish curriculum was such that it attracted away from Oxbridge not only religious Dissenters, who were debarred from English universities, but even, by the end of the eighteenth century, such English aristocrats as the future Prime Ministers Melbourne, Palmerston, and Russell.

The Scottish curriculum, like the English, featured the study of Latin heavily. But it combined, rather momentously, two further features: an acute commitment to discussing all subjects to and from first principles (i.e. a strong 'philosophical' bias) and a strong 'improving' bias toward the practical, which favoured the development of natural and social science. The two emphases can be seen together in Adam Smith's great *Wealth of Nations* (1776), the work of a man who had made his first reputation as a moral philosopher, but now proceeded to set economics on a systematic 'scientific' basis.

Smith had lectured at the University of Glasgow. That institution, and Aberdeen's colleges, provided centres of Enlightenment to rival Edinburgh. Thomas Reid, professor first in Aberdeen, then in Glasgow, produced the subtlest riposte to the dangerously anti-Christian views of David Hume, and his philosophy had vast international influence.

John Millar, author of *The Origin of Distinction of Ranks* (1771) was a long-serving Glasgow professor. Together with Adam Smith, his one-time teacher, he crystallized an immensely influential conception: human society, it was thought, had progressed in sequence through four 'stages'. First people had lived by hunting, then by 'pasturage' (keeping cattle), then by settled agriculture. Finally, commerce became dominant, with the middle classes in the driving seat. Scotland had entered the 'commercial' phase. Belief, as with Smith and Millar, in a conception of 'progress' related easily to the remarkable innovations of Scottish businessmen, helped by scientists and technologists.

The great chemist, Joseph Black, moved from Glasgow to Edinburgh in 1766. Like his friend, the pioneering geologist James Hutton, he had been a medical student. In this area, Scotland's pre–Union connections with Holland were decisive. The inspiration of the Edinburgh 'medical school' undoubtedly came from Leyden. Between 1705 and 1807, nine chairs associated with medicine were founded at Edinburgh University. (Glasgow acquired ten between 1713 and 1818.) By the late eighteenth century, Scotland was supplying the world with doctors. Of students enrolled under James Gregory, Professor of Physic at Edinburgh, between 1785 and 1790, an average of well under half came from Scotland, almost exactly matched by numbers from England and Ireland: the remainder came from America and Europe (Chitnis, 1986, p.35). The practical need for doctors provided an academic basis for wide-ranging scientific enquiry which in turn had practical results. Black continued to work as a doctor while teaching chemistry and acting as an industrial consultant, advising textile manufacturers on bleaching processes, brewers on beer, sugar refiners, tar makers, and so on. One of his earlier associates, a Glasgow instrument maker named Watt, owed something to Black's science when he perfected his world-transforming steam engine. As for Hutton, the author of the *Theory of the Earth* (1795) employed his geological skills on the cutting of the Forth–Clyde Canal, opened in 1790 to link the North Sea with the Atlantic.

The strong practical emphasis of the great figures (and small ones) of Scottish Enlightenment has been linked with the relatively democratic character of education in Scotland. The touching notion that the country's universities were crammed with the sons of ploughmen and stonemasons, 'lads o'pairts', released into light and fame by devoted dominies in village schools, does not bear sceptical examination. But it retains imaginative force, if only because a ploughman, Robert Burns, showed what intellectual stuff the Scottish rural proletariat was made of.

Scottish Calvinism (not least thanks to Burns) has had a very bad press: as prudish, life-denying, bigoted, and hypocritical. Hume reacted profoundly against it. Yet the dominance of a disputacious creed which emphasized the need for literacy (so that the Bible could be endlessly jawed over) was probably the most important precondition of Scottish Enlightenment. Presbyteranism laid down that every parish should have a school open to all. Calvinism is a pre-eminently logical creed, and its hard line with superstition and ceremony clears the way for cold, clear thought about nature and society. Furthermore, Calvinism can be seen as a bridge between Hume and the philosophers of medieval Scotland, from Duns Scotus (*c*.1266–1308), through to John Mair (or 'Major') who taught John Knox theology at St Andrews. Alexander Broadie points out that by Hume's day Scotland 'had acquired a rich philosophical tradition, and it is past belief that in the absence of that tradition the philosophy of the Scottish Enlightenment could have been written' (Broadie, 1990, p.3).

Though Scottish Presbyterianism eschewed vain and frivolous things like pictures on church walls and profane stage plays, the achievements of Robert Adam in architecture were not merely utilitarian. Scottish painting, by the latter part of the eighteenth century, produced what has been called its 'Golden Age', with outstanding portraitists, Allan Ramsay and Raeburn, whose informal warmth conveys the benevolent good feeling towards which Enlightenment Edinburgh aspired. No Scot excelled in musical composition of the kind we now call 'classical', but native traditions of folk-song (including Gaelic song) and fiddle playing were strongly developed.

Did Enlightenment, as Scots practised it, stunt 'literature'? Dedication to dry, systematic thought might seem likely to inhibit creative expression. It is sometimes suggested that the polished English prose style cultivated by Hume and others was inimical to the maintenance of Scottish tradition in the vernacular; that a gulf opened up between head (English) and heart (Scots or Gaelic).

Yet the century of Enlightenment saw a revival in published Scottish literature which carried forward into the early nineteenth century heyday of Walter Scott. Many important collections and editions of old poems and songs in Scots appeared. The fame of James Thomson, author of *The Seasons* (1730) – a long poem acclaimed throughout Europe which eventually inspired a choral work by Haydn – might be discounted because he emigrated to London. But before his early death Robert Fergusson wrote in Edinburgh the most vivid poetry in Scots to appear for nearly two centuries, and it made a profound impression on Robert Burns.

Both anglicizing and nationalistic tendencies flourished not merely within the one Scottish intellectual community, but within its individual members. Hume earnestly tried to rid his English prose of 'Scotticisms', yet sneered at 'barbarians who live on the banks of the Thames' and was active for a time (though he did cool off) in encouraging James Macpherson in his 'translation' of 'epic' poetry from Gaelic.

Macpherson attended Aberdeen University in the 1750s. Professor Thomas Blackwell there was an enthusiast for the epic Greek poetry of Homer. His contention was that Homer was so powerful because he wrote directly from experience of a violent society. Unfortunately, great art, as Blackwell had to conclude, was self-defeating. Poetry helped to civilize savage peoples: civilized people couldn't produce great poetry.

This dilemma was at the heart of the Scottish Enlightenment. Its great thinkers tended to yearn for the nobler attitudes and values of the past which 'improvements' were designed to erase: see, for instance, the *Essay on the History of Civil Society* (1767) by Adam Ferguson. As his editor Duncan Forbes remarks, Ferguson 'is typical of the Scottish enlightenment in his emphasis on sympathy, humanity, fellow-feeling, social solidarity ...' (Forbes, 1966, p.xxvi). But modern commerce and statecraft tend to destroy solidarity, along with the heroic virtues: men became self-centred and partisan. People, in fact, don't become more 'civilized' with the progress of civil society. Amongst the Iroquois Indians of North America, for instance, 'the titles of *magistrate* and *subject*, or *noble* and *mean*, are as little known as those of *rich* and *poor* ... While the community acts with an appearance of order, there is no sense of disparity in the breast of any of its members' (Forbes, 1966, p.84).

Dangerous stuff. Such views help to explain why Ferguson, too, encouraged Macpherson. This young man rose on a tide of sentimental interest, after Culloden, in the culture of the Gaels. Out of old manuscripts and texts transcribed from current Gaelic singing he assembled materials for an 'epic', *Fingal* (1762), which conquered Europe completely. Instead of the ponderous measures (couplets, etc.) of fashionable English verse, he offered incantatory prose. The blind bard Ossian was supposed to have composed this epic in the third century AD after the mighty Fenian warriors of whom he sang had gone down into death, like the heroes of Culloden Moor. The plangent, elegiac tone connected specifically with widespread sense of loss among Macpherson's fellow Gaels, but more generally with fears in intellectual circles, not only in Scotland but in Rousseau's France and throughout Europe, that luxury and over-improvement were destroying essential human virtues:

> Often have I fought and often won in battles of the spear. But blind, and tearful, and forlorn, I now walk with little men. O Fingal, with thy race of battle I now behold thee not. The wild roes feed upon the green tomb of the mighty King of Morvern. (Macpherson, 1971, p.48)

Jefferson loved this. Goethe loved this. Napoleon loved it. The major British 'romantic' poets, from Burns and Blake onwards, were all deeply affected by Ossian. However, Macpherson did not bring adequate reinforcement to the egos of quasi-nationalist Scottish professors because spoilsports, mostly English, objected that Macpherson wasn't *really* 'translating' *ancient* epic.

So if Burns hadn't surfaced, with the publication of a volume of poems in Kilmarnock in 1786, someone would have had to invent him. There was nothing inauthentic about Burns. He could write polished couplets when he chose, could also perform in certain fiendishly tricky metres peculiar to the tradition of writing in Scots, and had a touching way with 'pastoral' song. He was well-read, knew how Reid had answered Hume, and carried his plebeian person into aristocratic *salons* and 'enlightened' clubs with sturdy dignity. He was something the English didn't have, and the English also loved and admired him.

How could Scotland's flourishing commercial civilization be 'decadent', if it produced a man like this? And now that he had given the vernacular language such memorable new life in literature, surely the old Scotland of heartfelt sentiment, true solidarity and heroic gallantry must (somehow) be destined to live forever?

3.2 References

Broadie, A. (1990) *The Tradition of Scottish Philosophy*, Polygon (Edinburgh University Press), Edinburgh.

Chitnis, A.C. (1986) *The Scottish Enlightenment and Early Victorian Society*, Croom Helm, London.

Forbes, D. (ed.) (1966) Adam Ferguson's *An Essay on the History of Civil Society* (1767), Edinburgh University Press, Edinburgh.

Galt, J. (n.d.) *Annals of the Parish*, Nelson Classics, London.

Lucas, P.G. (trans.) (1953) Kant's *Prolegomena to Any Future Metaphysics that will be Able to Present Itself as a Science*, Manchester University Press, Manchester.

Macpherson, J. (1971) *Poems of Ossian* (facsimile reprint), James Thin, Edinburgh.

Smout, T.C. (1972) *A History of the Scottish People 1560–1830*, Fontana, London.

Stevenson, D. (1988) *The Origins of Freemasonry: Scotland's Century 1590–1710*, Cambridge University Press, Cambridge.

3.3 Further Reading

Daiches D., Jones P., and Jones J. (1986) *A Hotbed of Genius: The Scottish Enlightenment, 1730–90*, Edinburgh University Press, Edinburgh. (A well-illustrated collection of very readable essays on Hume, Adam Smith, Black and Hutton.)

Hook, A. (ed.) (1987) *History of Scottish Literature*, vol. 2, Aberdeen University Press, Aberdeen. (This particular volume, covering the period 1600–1800, contains much of interest.)

Lenman, B. (1981) *Integration, Enlightenment, and Industrialization: Scotland 1746–1832*, Edward Arnold, London. (An incisive and readable short study.)

Macmillan, D. (1986) *Painting in Scotland: the Golden Age*, Phaidon, Oxford. (This contains much that is of relevance and interest for this period.)

Smout, T.C. (1972). (See 'References' above for full details. A lively introduction to social and economic trends.)

Stafford, F. (1988) *The Sublime Savage: James Macpherson and the Poems of Ossian*, Edinburgh University Press, Edinburgh. (Although a scholarly monograph, this is not tough going; it opens up important vistas on both Lowland and Gaelic Scots societies.)

Index